This book provides the first comprehensive overview of the economic development of Singapore, throughout the twentieth century easily Southeast Asia's leading commercial and financial centre. From the late nineteenth century Singapore's development was based on a strategic location at the crossroads of Asia, a free trade economy and a dynamic entrepreneurial tradition. Dr Huff argues that the rapid urbanization experienced by Singapore is most convincingly seen as that of a staple port heavily dependent on tin, rubber and petroleum exports. He shows how these staple trades drew large inflows of immigrant workers from south China and India. An overwhelmingly immigrant population which contrasted with a predominantly Malay hinterland made Singapore unique among the staple ports and helped to keep it politically separate from Malaysia – ultimately as a city state.

Initial twentieth-century economic success was linked to a group of legendary Chinese entrepreneurs, but after 1965 independent Singapore looked to multinational enterprise to deliver economic growth. Nonetheless, exports of manufactures accounted for only part of Singapore's expansion, and by the 1980s the Republic was a major international financial centre and leading world exporter of commercial services. Throughout this study, Dr Huff assesses the interaction of government policy and market forces, and places the transformation of Singapore's economy in the context of development theory. Growth in Singapore is viewed in its Southeast Asian regional setting, and recent rapid economic development compared with other of East Asia's 'four dragons'.

The economic growth of Singapore

The economic growth of Singapore

Trade and development in the twentieth century

W. G. Huff

Department of Economics, University of Glasgow

CAMBRIDGE
UNIVERSITY PRESS

Published by the Press Syndicate of the University of Cambridge
The Pitt Building, Trumpington Street, Cambridge, CB2 1RP
40 West 20th Street, New York, NY 10011-4211, USA
10 Stamford Road, Oakleigh, Melbourne 3166, Australia

First published 1994

Reprinted 1995

First paperback edition published 1997

Printed in Great Britain at the University Press, Cambridge

A catalogue record for this book is available from the British Library

Library of Congress cataloguing in publication data
Huff, W. G.
  The economic growth of Singapore: trade and development in the
twentieth century / W.G. Huff.
      p.   cm.
  Includes bibliographical references and index.
  ISBN 0 521 37037 X
  1. Singapore – Economic conditions.   2. Singapore - Economic Policy.
3. Singapore – Commerce.   4. Singapore – Strategic aspects.
5. Singapore – Emigration and immigration – Economic aspects.
I. Title.
HC445.8.H84   1994
338.95957′009′04 – dc20   93-3977   CIP

ISBN 0 521 37037 X hardback
ISBN 0 521 62944 6 paperback

UP

Contents

Part Three: Staple port and rapid growth, 1947–1990

Figures

Tables

1. Text

Preface and acknowledgements

'The history of Singapore', it has been remarked, 'is written mainly in statistics.'[1] Fortunately, these were remarkably reliable by the 1880s, partly because of a strong administrative tradition, and partly because a free port and low taxes gave little incentive wilfully to deceive.[2] But statistics relating to the pre-World War II period can sometimes appear confusing, and attention is drawn to the geographical definitions and figures 1.1 and 1.2. In 1928 the Under-Secretary of State for the Colonies, W. G. A. Ormsby Gore, found that:

I am rather baffled in attempting to get at the real trade figures of the (1) Straits Settlements (2) Federated Malay States (3) Unfederated Malay States. They seem to do so much importing and exporting through each other that I find it difficult to get the real imports and real exports of the different component parts of Malaya. Have you any print – say a Trade Customs Report or Reports – which would help me to unravel what produces what and how much. If so can you send the file or print down please?[3]

In the judgement of Wong Lin Ken, Singapore's 'pre-war statistics are something of a nightmare. A minor statistical bureau would be required to rearrange the statistical data' to study the port's trade.[4] That task, it is hoped, has been substantially accomplished in what follows. Singapore's statistics after 1960 are more accessible and often more detailed than those before that date; but for a full consideration of Singapore's commerce, they are seriously marred by the omission of any reference after 1962 to trade with Indonesia.

As a rule, in this study original or historical spellings relating to Southeast Asia, and for Chinese names and placenames, Wade-Giles spellings, have been retained.

The principal sources used have been official reports and records. The

[1] Richard Winstedt, *Malaya and its history* 7th edn (London, 1966), p. 60.
[2] 'Report of the trade statistics committee', *SSLCP 1927*, p.C228.
[3] PRO CO/273/550 W. Ormsby Gore to W. D. Ellis, 2 Feb. 1928, with reference to 'Trade statistics committee', *SSLCP 1927*.
[4] Wong Lin Ken, 'Singapore: its growth as an entrepot port, 1819–1941', *JSEAS* 9, 1 (1978), p. 50.

main libraries and record offices at which this material was consulted were the National University of Singapore Library, Institute of South East Asian Studies Library, Singapore, University of Malaya Library, National Museum of Singapore, Archives and Oral History Department, Singapore, Port of Singapore Authority, Public Record Office, London, School of Oriental and African Studies, British Library of Political and Economic Science, Foreign and Commonwealth Office Library, National Library of Scotland, Library of Congress and New York Public Library. Thanks are due to librarians at all these institutions.

A great many individuals helped with the study. People who granted me interviews included Andrew Gilmour, Hashim Abu Shamah, R. Jumab-hoy, George Abraham, T. W. Ong, Tan Ee Leong, Tan Yeok Seong, Yap Pheng Geck, Yeo Tiam Siew, Teo Kim Yam, Ong Siong Kai and Goh Keng Swee. I received generous assistance from J. T. M. van Laanen and W. L. Korthals Altes of the Koninklijk Instituut voor de Tropen, Mary Yeo at the Port of Singapore Authority, Kok Yit Hoe at the Economic Development Board, Ian Brown, K. G. Tregonning and David Piachaud. Much of the study was originally written at the London School of Economics, where F. J. Fisher, H. Myint and P. T. Bauer had a strong interest in economic development from an historical viewpoint. Professor Fisher in particular contributed many helpful comments and ideas. The manuscript also benefited from discussion with A. I. MacBean, D. T. Nguyen, P. N. Snowden and R. Rothschild as colleagues at the University of Lancaster. At the University of Durham, R. Morley's stimulating approach to problems of economic development was of considerable assistance. J. H. Drabble offered many useful and detailed comments and Anne Booth gave helpful suggestions on the post-World War II sections of this study. R. B. DuBoff, J. B. K. Hunter and J. M. Gullick read the entire manuscript; it greatly benefited from their numerous helpful criticisms, corrections and observations. I owe a particular debt of gratitude to R. B. DuBoff, who read some chapters more than once, and whose advice and help greatly facilitated the completion of this book. I am grateful to J. C. B. Chau for many stimulating discussions. G. W. Carrickfergus was a constant source of wisdom, encouragement and good sense. In 1989 I had the benefit of a Visiting Fellowship at the Institute of South East Asian Studies, Singapore. Work being undertaken by a number of people in conjunction with the Economic History of Southeast Asia project at the Australian National University, directed by Anthony Reid, encouraged this book's comparative approach to Singapore's economic development. A. Markworthy and G. Maclean at The Ballantine Institute, Glasgow, were unstinting in their editorial work on the finished manuscript. Richard Fisher at Cambridge University Press saw the book through press. Maria

Coughlin prepared the index. I owe a deep debt of gratitude to my parents, who unfailingly helped in many ways with this book. I owe my greatest debt of gratitude to G. Cronje, who read and worked extensively and repeatedly on the entire manuscript.

Grants from the Canada Council, Central Research Fund (University of London) and the University of Lancaster helped to finance research. I am grateful for a grant from the Nuffield Foundation which allowed a trip to Singapore at a crucial stage of research. Preparation of the tabular material for publication was furthered by grants from the University of Glasgow Publications Committee and Department of Political Economy.

Abbreviations and conventions

Abbreviations

BIES	*Bulletin of Indonesian Economic Studies*
BRGA	*Bulletin of the Rubber Growers' Association*, London
CO	Colonial Office
CPF	Central Provident Fund, Singapore
Directory	*Singapore and Straits Directory* and (from 1922) *Singapore and Malayan Directory*; from 1949 *Straits Times Directory of Singapore and Malaya* (or *Malaysia*); from 1984 *Times Business Directory of Singapore*
EDB	Economic Development Board, Singapore
EDCC	*Economic Development and Cultural Change*
FCP	*Proceedings of the Federal Council of the Federated Malay States*
FMS	Federated Malay States
GATT	General Agreement on Tariffs and Trade
ISC	Imperial Shipping Committee
JMBRAS	*Journal of the Malayan [Malaysian] Branch of the Royal Asiatic Society*
JSEAH	*Journal of Southeast Asian History*
JSEAS	*Journal of Southeast Asian Studies*
MAJ	*Malayan Agricultural Journal*
MER	*Malayan Economic Review*
MRCA	*Monthly Review of Chinese Affairs*
PAP	People's Action Party
PP	British Parliamentary Papers
PRO	Public Record Office
SHB	Singapore Harbour Board
SLA	Legislative Assembly of Singapore
SS	Straits Settlements
SSAR	*Annual Departmental Reports of the Straits Settlements*
SSLCP	*Proceedings of the Legislative Council of the Straits Settlements*

SSTC 1933–34	*Report of the Commission to enquire into and report on the trade of the Colony, 1933–1934*
UMS	Unfederated Malay States

Conventions

/	annual average – e.g. 1957/59
–	inclusive dates – e.g. 1957–1959 or 1957–59
n.a.	not available (i.e. not published)
n.l.	not listed in the published statistics
$	Straits Settlements dollar or Singapore dollar, unless otherwise specified – e.g. US$

Between 1906 and 1966 one Straits Settlements (Malayan) dollar was equivalent in value to 2*s*.4*d*. Hence £1 equalled $8·57, and $60 equalled £7. In 1927 one Straits dollar equalled United States $0·5678.

One ton equals 2,240 lb.

Unless otherwise stated, all monetary figures are in nominal terms.

Geographical definitions

Straits Settlements (*SS*) – the island of Singapore, the island of Penang (with Province Wellesley on the mainland opposite), Malacca and including (at various times) the other small territories of the Dindings, Labuan, Christmas Island and the Cocos or Keeling Islands. For administrative purposes, Christmas Island and the Cocos Islands were included in the Settlement of Singapore. The Straits Settlements became a crown colony in 1867 and was often referred to as the Colony. Inter-port refers to Singapore's trade with the other SS.

Singapore – World War II and the Japanese occupation ended the Straits Settlements as a political entity. After the War, Singapore alone was reconstituted as a crown colony. The island existed as the Colony of Singapore until 1959, when it gained a large measure of political independence. Between 1959 and 1963 Singapore was the State of Singapore. In 1963 Singapore joined the Federation of Malaya in the formation of Malaysia, but in 1965 separated to become the fully independent Republic of Singapore. This study refers to Singapore as 'the town' until the turn of the century, and afterwards either as 'the city' or, beginning in 1965, as 'the Republic'. However, Singapore did not acquire city status until 1951.

Federated Malay States (*FMS*) – Perak, Selangor, Negri Sembilan and Pahang. These states came under British protection between 1874 and 1888, and in 1895 were joined in an administrative federation.

Unfederated Malay States (*UMS*) – Kedah, Perlis, Kelantan, Trengganu (Terengganu) and Johore (Johor). In 1909 Siam ceded to Britain its suzerainty over the four northern States, leading to the appointment of a British Adviser in Kedah, Perlis and Kelantan, and a British Agent (British Adviser with normal powers from 1918) in Trengganu. Johore, which had a close but informal relationship with the SS from the mid-nineteenth century, accepted a British 'General Adviser' in 1910 and conceded to him the normal powers (advice to be sought and acted upon) in 1914.

British Malaya – the SS, FMS and UMS. There was no formal entity of British Malaya, but before World War II the expression was a common way to refer to these areas under British control. Others have used the term Malaya for what is here referred to as British Malaya.

Mainland Malaya and Malay Peninsula – geographical descriptions used here to include the FMS and UMS. In some other usage, the Malay Peninsula may refer to the mainland plus Penang.

Malaya – British Malaya except Singapore. In 1946 this became the Malayan Union, and from 1948 to 1963 the Federation of Malaya.

Malaysia and Federation of Malaysia – formed in 1963 by the Federation of Malaya, Singapore, Sarawak and North Borneo (Sabah). In 1965 Singapore separated from the Federation of Malaysia to become an independent state. The remaining parts of the former Federation constitute what is now known as Malaysia.

Netherlands India and Indonesia – the Indonesian archipelago is the largest island complex in the world, and most of this – Netherlands India, also known as the Dutch East Indies or the Netherlands Indies – was under Dutch rule until World War II. Afterwards it is referred to as Indonesia. In 1950 Indonesia was unified as a republic, following the final end of Dutch rule throughout the archipelago and collapse of the United States of Indonesia. Java (Jawa) and Madura are distinguished from the other islands, known collectively as the Outer Provinces. Important areas to Singapore included Sumatra (Sumatera), Borneo (Kalimantan), and to a lesser extent the Celebes (Sulawesi) and the Moluccas (Maluku).

British Borneo – Sarawak, North Borneo (Sabah) and Brunei, all on the northern part of the island of Borneo. These areas were placed under British protection in 1888. Sarawak and North Borneo joined the Federation of Malaysia in 1963, but Brunei remained a British protectorate.

The Region – a shorthand term for the surrounding area with which Singapore traded, including Malaya, Netherlands India (Indonesia), British Borneo, Siam (Thailand) and, to a lesser extent, Burma and Indo-China. The last was mainly the southern area of Indo-China centred on Saigon, which became South Vietnam in 1954.

The Nanyang – what is now regarded as Southeast Asia, i.e. the region (above) plus the Philippines.

The West – North America, Britain, Continental Europe and Japan.

Introduction

Singapore is an economic development success story. With three million people, the island ranked in 1990 as the world's eighteenth largest exporter of merchandise, and thirteenth in commercial service exports; merchandise exports were three times those of the whole of India.[1] Singapore's population was one quarter of 1 % of China's, but its GNP 9·5 %. By the 1990s few commercial decisions relating to Southeast Asia could be taken without reference to Singapore; almost any multinational enterprise, whether in manufacturing or services, planning to expand outside North America, Western Europe or Japan would naturally consider it as a location.

Economic development in Singapore is not new. Rapid late nineteenth century growth had produced a large, modern city on the island by 1900. In 1939, and even more in 1959, when British colonial rule effectively ended, Singapore was a metropolis. Throughout the twentieth century, it has flourished as easily Southeast Asia's most important commercial, transportation and communications centre, and from at least World War I onwards played a global economic role. During the 1950s Singapore already had high per capita income than almost anywhere else in Asia. Post-independence economic development in Singapore therefore began from a strong foundation and with very substantial advantages.

The present book takes this longer-term view of Singapore's economic growth. It concentrates on economic development[2] during the first four decades of the twentieth century, but also links the pre- and post-World War II periods. The book's focus on the pre-World War II decades fills something of a gap: relatively little has been written on this earlier phase of economic development, although a substantial literature exists on the post-war years, especially those after 1959. Perhaps all too often, however, the literature leaves the impression that economic development is a recent phenomenon in Singapore which – somehow – has arisen from unlikely circumstances and altogether departs from earlier patterns. The book

---

[1] GATT, *International trade 1990/91*. Two vols. (Geneva, 1990), 2, pp.3, 4.
[2] Throughout the book the terms 'growth' and 'development' are used interchangeably. In Singapore the former implied the latter.

attempts to make Singapore's post-1959 economic development more explicable by considering it in the light of previous growth.

It is hoped that an examination of Singapore's long-term growth also has something to contribute to the study of development economics. That subject, when not pronounced dead, is often said to be undergoing crisis. If so, perhaps a leading reason is what W. A. Lewis pointed out as 'one of the weaknesses of our subject, namely the widening gap between Economics and Economic History in Development Economics. If our subject is lowering its sights, this may be because the demise of Economic History in economics departments has brought us a generation of economists with no historical background'.[3] Economic development is, after all, about change over time, and economic history alone can provide the empirical analysis to study this growth process.[4] Since 1960 growth in less developed countries has been extremely rapid by any standards and, as J. G. Williamson remarked, 'we would understand this experience far better if more development economists would engage in serious comparative economic history'.[5] The present book attempts to establish such a comparative historical framework for Singapore.

Yet the factors which lead to economic development are never obvious except *ex post*. At best, economic history can be no more than 'prediction written backwards',[6] in the sense of identifying initial conditions and relevant circumstances which, together with departures from past programmes and practices, made highly likely an observed outcome. After World War II and in 1959, Singapore's large accumulated physical infrastructure, substantial human capital, experience of considerable, if not extensive, industrialization, high per capita income and effective government, were clearly conducive to continued economic growth. Much the same was true by 1900. Throughout the twentieth century, Singapore exemplifies the 'first law of development': 'To those who have shall be given'.[7]

From this long-term perspective, Singapore's fundamental advantages – favourable 'initial conditions' in that term's broad sense – are apparent. Consideration of these advantages also permits identification of some of the main themes of Singapore's twentieth-century economic development.

[3] W. Arthur Lewis, 'The state of development theory', *American Economic Review* 74, 1 (1984), p.7.
[4] Attention has been drawn to economic history's empirical role by Nicholas Stern, 'The economics of development: a survey', *Economic Journal* 99 (1989), pp.622, 673.
[5] Jeffrey G. Williamson, 'Comments on "Reflections on development"' in Gustav Ranis and T. Paul Schultz, eds. *The state of development economics* (Oxford, 1988), p.30.
[6] Cf. Alfred Marshall, *Principles of economics* 9th [variorum] edn (London, 1961), I, p.773.
[7] The 'law' was suggested by A. K. Cairncross and strongly endorsed by R. Nurkse. Ragnar Nurkse, *Patterns of trade and development* (Stockholm, 1959), p.17.

Great ports like Singapore are seldom, if ever, accidents of history. London, New York, Rotterdam, Shanghai and Hong Kong all developed on a basis of unchallenged locational advantages in linking productive regions with world shipping routes, and this was also true of Singapore. Nor, recalling Hong Kong, was Singapore unique in its heritage of a free trade policy, instituted to derive maximum benefit from geographical advantage.[8]

The peopling of Singapore, however, was surely unique. In Singapore, British colonialism and Chinese economic expansion into the Nanyang (i.e. Southeast Asia) met to produce a cosmopolitan society almost wholly lacking in the indigenous population of the Malayan hinterland. Singapore's human resource 'endowment' of immigrants, together with a geographical location which drew people to Singapore by providing an obvious means to realize their material ambitions, combined to encourage the openness and very rapid adaptability to changes in the world economy which are such marked features of Singapore's economic development. During the twentieth century Chinese comprised three-quarters of Singapore's population, and as an overwhelmingly immigrant society it naturally reflected the culture of south China. But in a city so pragmatic, outward-looking and oriented towards economic gain, one development economist overstates his position in describing Singapore as among Asia's 'isolated, tradition-bound peasant societies' until after World War II.[9]

The economic development of Singapore, where the annual value of commerce always far exceeded the combined incomes of its inhabitants, provides an extreme example of trade as an 'engine of growth'. Over the twentieth century, trade, to adapt D. H. Robertson's formulation, allowed Singapore's inhabitants to become fifteen times as numerous and probably about fifteen times as wealthy.[10] Singapore's is a story of how a dual economy, which emerged before World War II, ended in the post-war period. But just as economic dualism developed under the particular conditions of rapid British Malayan growth which led to mass immigration from distant rural areas in China and India, so Singapore required the peculiar conditions of city statehood to transform itself into a single economy.

In Singapore's economic development since 1900, the state stands out for the sharply contrasting roles it played. Before World War II the colonial administration restricted itself to the maintenance of peace, stability and

---

[8] For discussion of institutional heritage and initial conditions as promoting subsequent economic development, see Gustav Ranis, 'The role of institutions in transitional growth: the East Asian newly industrializing countries', *World Development* 17, 9 (1989), pp.1443–53.

[9] Dwight H. Perkins, *China: Asia's next economic giant?* (Seattle, 1986), p.84.

[10] D. H. Robertson, 'The future of international trade', *Economic Journal* 48 (1938), p.5.

an atmosphere conducive to future progress; but after 1959 government was pivotal in promoting development. The commitment of the political leadership to economic development was total, and featured strong, if selective, intervention. In an era of development theory which has turned its back on economic planning, Singapore is prominent as a country where planning succeeded.

Throughout this study, Singapore's economic development is analysed primarily as the result of long-term flows in the international economy rather than its short-term fluctuations. But the latter must be borne in mind: for economic development as a response to long-term change had as its corollary openness to short-term fluctuations, and just as the first shaped Singapore's history, so the second imposed an external pattern of war, booms and slumps. Yet only World War II stands out as a turning point. After Singapore's foundation in 1819, fundamental to economic development were the 12 decades of unbroken peace for the island until World War II, the only war from which Singapore did not benefit economically. Politically, World War II made practically inevitable Singapore's early attainment of independence from British colonial rule. However, Singapore during World War II is a subject on its own and, except in the longer-term effects of war, not integral to a study of Singapore's economic development. Consequently, the Japanese occupation of 1941 to 1945 is not covered, nor, with few exceptions, are the years immediately before or after the occupation, due to the lack of statistics.

The book is structured in three parts. The first begins with a framework of analysis and interpretation of Singapore's economic development between 1870 and 1990. It is argued that from the late nineteenth century, as trade increasingly consisted of a narrow range of commodities, Singapore's economic development was that of a staple port. Accordingly, chapter 2, which examines Singapore's development before 1900, pays particular attention to the impact of tin as its first staple. The book's second part analyses Singapore's economic development as a staple port between 1900 and 1939. Rather than adopting a chronological approach, as would have been logical had the main influence on Singapore's development been short-term fluctuations, separate chapters are devoted to the pattern of trade; shipping and the growth of the port; immigration and population; the staples of rubber and petroleum; industrial development and Chinese banking; and Singapore's distribution of imported manufactures. Post-World War II growth is the subject of the study's third part. Two chapters deal, respectively, with the years 1947–59 as a resurgence of the staple port, and 1960–90 as a successful departure from it.

Part One

Themes and beginnings

1   Patterns in the economic development of Singapore, 1870–1990

The basis for the economic development of Singapore was – and for most of its history has remained – geography. That comparative advantage can derive from 'natural resource endowment and geographical position' was well known to Classical economists.[1] Geography can be thought of as a natural resource like, for example, mineral deposits in the sense that both are 'superior' land. The 'natural resource' of Singapore – an island of just 225 square miles – was location. As Alfred Marshall emphasized, geography is fundamental to any reckoning of a nation's wealth: the Thames, though a free gift of nature, 'has added more to the wealth of England than all its canals, and perhaps even than all its railroads'.[2] Yet few areas – even Hong Kong – can have benefited as much as Singapore from the gift of geography.[3]

The present chapter examines the inflows of people and capital attracted by Singapore's geographical endowment and the human organization which built on it. Together, these themes allow an understanding of Singapore's development in a context of international and comparative economic growth since the settlement began in 1819.

I

'It has been my good fortune', Stamford Raffles recognized when founding Singapore, 'to establish this station in a position combining every possible

[1] D. P. O'Brien, *The Classical economists* (Oxford, 1975), p.181.
[2] Marshall, *Principles of economics* I, p.59.
[3] By contrast, the literature typically draws attention to Singapore's lack of natural resources. For example, J. K. Galbraith finds Singapore and Hong Kong 'uniquely devoid' of natural resources; D. Morawetz points to 'a poor natural-resource endowment'; while J. S. Hogendorn emphasizes that in regard to natural resources, Singapore has 'none at all', which he suspects helped development through unleashing work effort. John Kenneth Galbraith, *The nature of mass poverty* (Cambridge, MA, 1979), p.4; David Morawetz, 'Employment implications of industrialisation in developing countries', *Economic Journal* 84 (1974), p.509; Jan S. Hogendorn, *Economic development* (New York, 1987), pp.487–88.

advantage, geographical and local'.[4] There were three such advantages. First, the island lay at the southernmost extension of continental Asia, and from its vantage point at the tip of the Malay Peninsula and the narrow southern entrance to the Straits of Malacca controlled one of two gateways (the other being the Sunda Straits) between the Indian Ocean and China Sea (figure 1.1). Second, Singapore was 'in the very seat of the Malayan empire'[5] and a natural point for regional and international transport routes to converge. Finally, Singapore possessed a natural harbour 'in every way superior',[6] making it easy to provide ample port facilities at minimal cost.

Together with Raffles' free port policy, which quickly became an article of faith in the town, Singapore's resource endowment offered three logical possibilities for development, namely as a port of call, an entrepot for the Malayan region and an entrepot for the China trade. In the first two respects, Singapore proved an immediate and unqualified success. But repeated attempts by Singapore merchants to develop an entrepot trade with China met with frustration and set-back.

Singapore developed instead as an entrepot for the Malayan region. As late as 1870 this was a small trade based on the export of a variety of tropical produce and a return flow of imports, especially British cotton piece goods and opium. In 1871 Singapore Municipality remained a modest settlement of perhaps 65,000 inhabitants, a town which 'extends in very few points more than a mile from the beach'.[7] Yet the settlement stood poised on the brink of changes which would revolutionize it.

Two developments in the international economy were responsible for this revolution: the inauguration of the Suez Canal in 1869, which opened 'at one stroke'[8] the Eastern trade to steamships, and the rapid increase in world demand for the primary products which the Malayan region could produce. Steamships needed to stay close to the shore to obtain coal. In the Malayan region, the consequence was to channel these vessels principally through the Straits of Malacca rather than the Sunda Straits, since using the latter would necessitate a longer voyage across the Indian Ocean to and from Colombo (figure 1.1). As steamships were increasingly drawn through the Straits of Malacca, Singapore became the chief port of call in the region and 'the gate of the East'.[9]

[4] Lady Raffles, *Memoir of the life and public services of Sir Thomas Stamford Raffles* (London, 1830), p.378.   [5] Ibid. p.376.
[6] Sir T. S. Raffles, 'The founding of Singapore', *JMBRAS* 42, 1 (1969), p.74.
[7] John Cameron, *Our tropical possessions in Malayan India* (Kuala Lumpur, 1965), p.73.
[8] Max E. Fletcher, 'The Suez Canal and world shipping, 1869-1914', *Journal of Economic History* 18, 4 (1958), p.558, and see pp.557, 559.
[9] Address of Sir William Matthews, President, *Minutes of the proceedings of the Institution of Civil Engineers* 171, 1 (1907-1908), p.27.

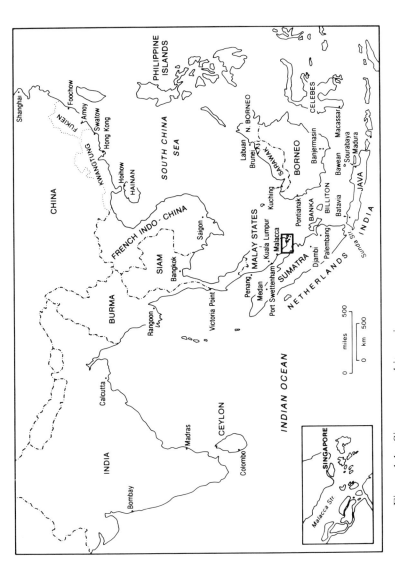

Figure 1.1 Singapore and its region

Figure 1.2   British Malaya, 1931

Abundant ocean-going shipping worked in conjunction with increased exports from the Malayan region to promote Singapore's development. The ready availability of shipping helped to draw regional exports to the port, and this growth of trade at Singapore attracted even more vessels by making it likely that they could obtain at least some cargo with little additional difficulty or expense while stopping to bunker.[10] A large supply of shipping gave Singapore lower freight rates than competing ports until 1897, when rates began to be fixed by shipping conferences based in the metropolitan countries.

[10] *Trade and shipping of South-East Asia* (PP 1900, LXXXVII), p.112.

In the Malay Peninsula, Singapore's hinterland (figure 1.2) extended along the west coast as far north as Kuala Lumpur and encompassed the entire east coast. Transport serving the Peninsula, which is divided by a series of parallel mountain ranges with peaks in the central range rising to 7,000 feet, ran north-south to Singapore. In 1911 Port Swettenham near Kuala Lumpur was created by the British authorities in the Federated Malay States as a rival to Singapore, but became primarily a feeder to it. Port Swettenham found competition with Singapore difficult because of the latter's position on world shipping routes, and because, until 1934, shipping conferences, anxious to minimize ports of call, levied a surcharge on all homewards cargo, except rubber, from Port Swettenham.[11] Penang, 376 miles from Singapore at the north end of the Straits of Malacca, and like Singapore politically part of the Colony of the Straits Settlements, was British Malaya's other main ocean-going port, and conducted most of the remaining trade of the Peninsula.[12] The pull of these two Straits Settlements ports became – and in the case of Singapore has remained – a source of discontent to peninsular interests.[13]

For Singapore, Netherlands India (the Netherlands Indies or Dutch East Indies, subsequently Indonesia), on the other side of the island's surrounding seas, was as important a hinterland as the Malay Peninsula. From the end of the nineteenth century the area of Singapore's Netherlands Indian hinterland shrank significantly, but the port remained 'the natural collecting and distributing centre for a considerable area of … the Malayan Archipelago, including Borneo and central Sumatra', where the output of tropical commodities expanded enormously.[14]

In Singapore the combined roles of an entrepot for the Malayan region and port of call ignited a commercial explosion which few contemporary observers could possibly have imagined. Between 1871/73 and 1900/02 Singapore's trade (imports + exports) increased more than sixfold from an annual average of $67 million to $431 million.[15] A second phase of growth began after 1910, and by 1925/27 trade had expanded a further fourfold to reach a pre-World War II apex of $1,832 million. These are current-dollar figures, but they indicate rapid real growth for Singapore's

---

[11] ISC, *Report on Port Swettenham, Federated Malay States* (PP 1930–31, XIV), pp.8–10; D. F. Allen, *Report on the major ports of Malaya* (Kuala Lumpur, 1951), pp.34–37.

[12] ISC, *Report on Port Swettenham*, pp.8–9; ISC, *Report on the harbour of Singapore* (PP 1928–29, VII), pp.7–10; E. H. G. Dobby, *Monsoon Asia* (London, 1961), p.201.

[13] PRO CO 273/580/92044, Andrew Caldecott, Acting Chief Secretary to Government, FMS, 'Remarks on the report of the Straits Settlements customs duties committee', 7 March 1932; Allen, *Report on major ports*, p.34.

[14] *SSTC 1933–34*. Five vols. (Singapore, 1934), I, p.48.

[15] As indicated in the Abbreviations and conventions, references in this study are to Straits or Singapore dollars.

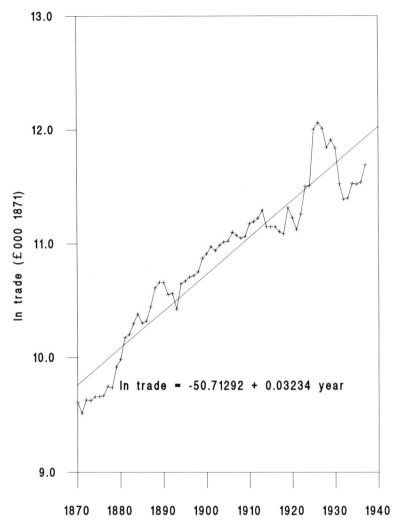

Figure 1.3   Singapore trade (imports + exports) real growth,
1870–1937

trade sector – and thus for its highly trade-dependent economy as a whole.
(National income data are not available for pre-1939 years.) Figure 1.3
shows that real trade growth averaged 3·3% between 1870 and 1937,
representing a doubling in volume every 22 years.

Fortunately, the pre-war trade returns for Singapore appear to be
reliable. They are complete except for the omission of trade with Malaya

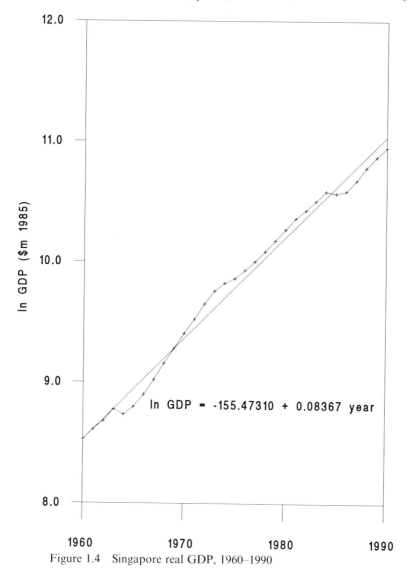

Figure 1.4   Singapore real GDP, 1960–1990

after 1927, when statistically British Malaya began to be regarded as a single unit. However, other official statistics showing trade are available through 1932, and the subsequent lack of data can largely be overcome by estimates. An important advantage of the trade statistics is their exclusion of goods transhipped on through bills of lading. Consequently, the official data are a good guide to the merchandising activity in Singapore, since goods merely handled there in transhipment do not appear as trade. During the twentieth century transhipment at Singapore grew substantially, increasing the demand for port facilities and adding to income and employment. But to avoid drawing regional attention to dependence on Singapore, comprehensive figures for this movement of cargo have seldom been published.

In the post-World War II period this apprehension over the publication of data led to serious omissions from the trade statistics. However, the compilation of national income accounts began from the 1960s. Between 1960 and 1990 Singapore's economy expanded at substantially above its apparent long-term historical rate. Over these three decades the real growth of Gross Domestic Product, shown in figure 1.4, averaged 8·7% annually.

II

Staple theory focuses on surplus natural resources, where the term staple denotes a raw material or resource-intensive good central to the exports of a region.[16] Until the 1960s the growth in Singapore's trade depended largely on three staple exports from the Malayan region, and the city's economic development is best analysed as that of a staple port. During the 1880s and 1890s the rapid increase in tin production in the Malay Peninsula in response to Western demand brought Singapore its first staple. A second phase of trade growth stemmed from the establishment of the rubber industry in Malaya and Netherlands India and from the increase in petroleum exports from Netherlands India, both resulting from the development of motorized transport in the advanced countries. By the end of the 1920s rubber and petroleum completed Singapore's transition to staple port.

The economic development of Singapore as a staple port fits a general pattern. One of the principal features of the nineteenth century was that regions with surplus natural resources and, sometimes, surplus labour, in relation to demand in the domestic economy, experienced a very rapid expansion in the production of primary commodities for export, largely to

---

[16] For discussion on staples, 'vent for surplus' trade and the role of natural resources in the economic development of primary commodity exporting regions, see Richard E. Caves, '"Vent for surplus" models of trade and growth' in Robert E. Baldwin, et al., *Trade, growth and the balance of payments* (Chicago, 1965), pp.95–115, and 'Export-led growth and the new economic history' in Jagdish N. Bhagwati, et al., eds. *Trade, balance of payments and growth* (Amsterdam, 1971), pp.403–42; P. J. Drake, 'Natural resources versus foreign borrowing in economic development', *Economic Journal* 82 (1972), pp.951–62.

industrial countries. It is only to be expected that international trade which served as an engine of growth and created, through the export of primary commodities, an outlet or 'vent' for the surpluses would lead to the development of port cites to service the new trade. But just as the international economic specialization which lay behind staple trade created relatively few major flows of commodities, so the ports that grew as part of that specialization were similarly few.

Nineteenth-century major staple ports included Rangoon and Colombo in Asia; Saõ Paulo and Buenos Aires in Latin America; New Orleans in North America and Accra and Lagos in Africa. Many were old towns; all achieved their modern status as 'great cities' essentially or entirely on the basis of trade with a staple producing hinterland. Dependence on staple trade gives them a common history. Lillian Knowles observed that 'Practically all history in new countries is economic history';[17] the same is true of staple ports. The best approach to their history is through the staples themselves and the linkages arising from the staples which led to economic development in other spheres.[18] Staples dominated the ports' exports and became the basis of their economies.

Favourable geography was a necessary condition for the development of staple ports. Their location afforded optimal, or near optimal, physical access to the exporting region, the transport system of which was linked through the port to a network of ocean communications.[19] Use of the port as a communications centre where goods being exported changed their means of transport and thereby received physical handling brought the expansion of facilities to deal with a greater volume of goods and shipping. But transport installations were not always sited at the staple port itself. For example, Saõ Paulo is separated from its port of Santos by 45 miles and a 793-metre coastal range and 'Traditionally ... has used Santos only as a stevedore'.[20] All rail communications from the interior converged on Saõ Paulo, and a single railway line, mainly consisting of a cableroad down

[17] L. C. A. Knowles, *The economic development of the British overseas empire* (London, 1924), p.viii.
[18] On the concept of linkages and their importance in staple theory, see Albert O. Hirschman, *The strategy of economic development* (New Haven, 1958), pp.29–75, 'A generalized linkage approach to development, with special reference to staples', *EDCC* 25 supplement (1977), pp.67–98, and 'Linkages' in John Eatwell, Murray Milgate and Peter Newman, eds. *The new Palgrave: economic development* (London, 1989), pp.210–21; Melville H. Watkins, 'A staple theory of economic growth', *Canadian Journal of Economics and Political Science* 29, 2 (1963), pp.144–46.
[19] Rhoads Murphey, 'New capitals of Asia', *EDCC* 5, 3 (1957), pp.216–19; Douglass C. North, 'Location theory and regional economic growth', *Journal of Political Economy* 63, 3 (1955), p.251.
[20] Richard M. Morse, 'Saõ Paulo in the nineteenth century', *Inter-American Economic Affairs* 5, 3 (1951), p.3.

the steep mountain range, connected Saõ Paulo to Santos.[21] African geography has given particular scope for the growth of inland centres for staple trade such as Kampala[22] which relied on the railway for transport to the port of Mombasa.[23]

However, favourable geography was not a sufficient condition for staple port development. While geography determined the use of certain points for stevedorage, economic considerations gave the great staple ports their distinguishing characteristics. There were five main, related, characteristics: the performance of entrepreneurial, investment, management and mercantile functions connected with production of the staple; the provision of financial services; processing of the staple commodity; marketing services including the role of the port as the region's main market for the staple; and the close involvement of business interests in the port with hinterland production.

Together the five constitute a veritable check list of staple port characteristics. The first four – the economic functions of the staple port – made it a commercial centre where decisions were taken and power exercised; their combined effect gave rise to the fifth characteristic, close involvement with the hinterland. The requirements of producing, processing and marketing the staple, and the need for a base near the hinterland but with links to metropolitan centres, drew those in the staple port into performing these functions. The result was the characteristic tendency for business interests in the staple port to become intertwined with the interests of hinterland producers. In contrast to the staple port, the international entrepot generally has only weak links with producers because of its great variety of trade and the distance at which this is conducted. London was the extreme example of an international entrepot, having the world as a hinterland for its huge nineteenth-century entrepot trade. Although furnishing credit for the expansion of primary production, the City could hardly reach out and organize it.[24]

Development as a staple port was largely responsible for changing Singapore from an autonomous trading post in 1870 to an economy closely involved with hinterland production. The activities of Singapore merchants were vital to 'opening up' the Malay Peninsula where 'in 1867 the interior was still almost unknown and even the coasts not completely surveyed'.[25]

[21] W. G. McCreery and M. L. Bynum, *The coffee industry in Brazil* (Washington, DC: US Department of Commerce, 1930), p.32.
[22] Thomas Hodgkin, *Nationalism in colonial Africa* (London, 1956), pp.64–65.
[23] ISC, *Report on the control and working of Mombasa (Kilindini) harbour Kenya colony* (PP 1926, XII), pp.8, 17–18.
[24] Cf. Sir John Clapham, *An economic history of modern Britain.* Three vols. (Cambridge, 1951), III, pp.3–4.
[25] C. M. Turnbull, *The Straits Settlements, 1826–67* (London, 1972), p.314, and see p.313.

In Netherlands India, economic relationships between Singapore Chinese and local traders which had built up around a late nineteenth-century trade in tropical produce were strengthened when rubber became Singapore's main import from the Dutch colony.

The economic functions assumed by the staple port sometimes depended on the advent of foreigners attracted by an emerging staple trade and anxious to control it. In the 1860s European merchants and millers who came to Rangoon helped to transform Burma into a rice economy and made the port its centre.[26] Often, however, foreign firms already in a port responded to opportunities for staple trade and developed this commerce. In Singapore, adaptation by established merchant houses predominated, and the history of the city's European mercantile community from entrepot to staple port therefore has a remarkable continuity. A comparatively small group of European merchants remained dominant until the 1960s, when staples were replaced as the main force in the Singapore economy.

The argument is that Singapore should be thought of as a staple port rather than an international entrepot, as its trade came to depend on a few commodities; and that this resulted in a new set of economic relationships between port and hinterland. A hinterland is an elastic concept, and is subject to competition from other ports and changes in transport. Nevertheless, the hinterland of staple ports usually fell largely or wholly within the same sovereignty. Although a port such as Lagos was administratively separate from the bulk of its hinterland, the whole of Nigeria was under British rule.[27] Singapore, however, had a politically fragmented hinterland, and one which, owing to the importance of the Dutch colony of Netherlands India for the port, lay mainly outside British control. Insofar as Singapore performed mercantile, processing, financial and marketing functions, it did so for all parts of its hinterland. But the performance of investment and management functions was largely confined to the Malay Peninsula.

Comparisons of staple ports show that the four economic functions listed above (entrepreneurial/managerial, financial, processing, and marketing) varied in importance, and some, principally in connection with production of the staple, may have been absent, since the needs of the staple and therefore the opportunities available to the staple port differed. Of key importance was the nature and the substitutability of factor requirements in staple production. These technological considerations governed ease of entry to the staple industry, its range of producers and

---

[26] Cheng Siok-Hwa, *The rice industry of Burma, 1852–1940* (Kuala Lumpur, 1968), pp.9–12, 77.

[27] *Report of the commission on the marketing of West African cocoa* (PP 1938, IX), p.79; ISC, *Report on the harbours of Nigeria* (PP 1928–29, VII), pp.7–11.

their mode of production, and thus firms and individuals with whom merchants and traders in the staple port dealt and linkages which arose from factor inputs and services coming via the port. Because factor requirements might vary over time, so might the impact of the staple on the port. Tin had much greater spread effects for Singapore during the late nineteenth century when mining was highly labour-intensive than in the twentieth century when, with the progressive exhaustion of easily-won deposits, the industry entered a second phase characterized by capital-intensive, technologically-based means of extraction.

Mining often has this two-phase history. Since the second requires comparatively little labour and may assume enclave aspects due to its reliance on international companies and lack of linkages with the local economy, hinterland agricultural production is generally more important than mining for the staple port. But agriculture may divide into 'polar cases' of estate and peasant production.[28] The range of staple port functions connected with production is greatest when substitutability of factor requirements allows an 'ideal case' in which estate and peasant production can flourish side by side. Rubber's impact on Singapore was particularly great because as the boom spread, it spread swiftly and to small- and medium-size growers as well as estate producers. Together they drew on a full range of staple port functions.

All staple ports provide financial services. In the British Empire, the most important contribution of these services was to open channels to the London money market for both short-term credit and long-term finance. Short-term credit, required mainly for trade, came principally through the branches of a few European banks, usually with London head offices, which operated in a number of countries. Singapore's three main European banks had been established prior to the expansion of staple production, so that there was no difficulty in financing staple exports; while in Rangoon, European banks arrived on the heels of the merchants and millers.[29] In the Empire, institution of the sterling exchange standard made the currency of a colony freely convertible at a fixed rate of exchange with sterling. For Singapore, this standard was adopted in 1906 when the Straits Settlements dollar was pegged at 2s.4d. (a parity which remained until 1967) and was backed throughout by 100% to 110% sterling reserves.

The Straits Settlements adopted the sterling exchange standard, it was

---

[28] R. E. Baldwin, 'Patterns of development in newly settled regions', *Manchester School of Economic and Social Studies* 24, 2 (1956), pp.161–79. In this study, the term 'peasant' is used to mean a small farmer, either a smallholder or tenant, as distinct from an agricultural labourer or landowner with 100 acres or more. This last constituted an estate. The peasant economy in the region around Singapore consisted very largely of smallholders.

[29] Cheng, *Rice industry*, pp.9, 82; U Tun Wai, *Burma's currency and credit* (Bombay, 1962), p.23.

later observed, 'to link their currency with that of the United Kingdom where debts were payable and from whence capital might be expected'.[30] Once a colony's currency had been tied to sterling, its banks could invest surplus funds in London without significant risk of exchange loss and the colonial banking system was 'based on the London Money Market in exactly the same way as is the banking system of England and Wales'.[31] Because of the European banks' orientation towards financing export trade, also typical of other Empire staple ports, a particularly important and distinctive developmental feature of Singapore was the emergence of a substantial local banking sector. Singapore Chinese began deposit banks, and several, reversing the European pattern, set up international branches with the head office in the staple port.

The institutional gap for the provision of long-term finance left by the adherence of British banks to a policy of short-term, strictly commercial lending was partially filled by the managing agency system. Managing agencies emerged in India during the latter half of the nineteenth century and were applied to a variety of undertakings.[32] But in staple ports the system's main use was for European estate agriculture, which required overseas finance because of the high investment costs of establishing estates and then a period of up to seven years before the first generation of plants came into bearing. In Colombo, the agency house system evolved from the late nineteenth century when the development of Ceylon's tea, and to some extent rubber, estates required capital from London. The result was 'the modern agency house, with its commercial system in Ceylon and in London, its flotation at either end of plantation companies, and its function of providing a wide range of services over all the stages of growing and processing as well as of insuring, shipping and selling the plantation product'.[33] From the turn of the century Singapore merchant houses transformed themselves into agency houses, and in that capacity were central to the establishment of a large European rubber estate sector and assumed a major commercial role in it.

The first European estates in Malaya, begun without agency house involvement, were analogous to those in Brazil where early Paulista planters 'prided themselves on self-sufficiency',[34] and 'financed their

---

[30] Frank H. H. King, *Money in British East Asia* (London, Colonial Office, research studies no.19, 1957), p.89.
[31] W. T. Newlyn, 'The colonial empire' in R. S. Sayers, ed. *Banking in the British Commonwealth* (London, 1952), p.440, and see pp.441, 423.
[32] Radhe Shyam Rungta, *The rise of business corporations in India, 1851–1900* (Cambridge, 1970), pp.221–25, 248.
[33] Kathleen M. Stahl, *The metropolitan organization of British colonial trade* (London, 1951), p.133, and see pp.127, 171.
[34] Warren Dean, *The industrialization of Saõ Paulo, 1880–1945* (Austin, 1969), p.4.

ventures independently, using city middlemen, or *commissarios*, as mere selling agents'.[35] But as an expanding coffee economy gave rise to a much greater range of services – those of the staple port – so the functions of the *commissario* 'developed until he became the city agent of the *fazendeiro* for every possible kind of service'.[36] As well as marketing the coffee, *commissarios* extended credit to planters, held mortgages against the *fazendas* and traded in them. By 1890 'the ascendancy of the urban middleman in agricultural Brazil' appears clear.[37] It was reflected in 'the shift of power from the rural "big house", or *casa grande*, of the planter class to the town house, or *sobrado*, of the urban bourgeoisie'.[38] Similarly, during the inter-war years almost all European rubber estates in Malaya, whether or not started by the agency houses, ended up under their management.

Because peasant export production does not require large capital inflows, it offers the staple port a narrower potential range of functions than does estate production. Nevertheless, port merchants still find themselves drawn into the hinterland. Expansion of peasant exports in West Africa compelled European firms, previously confined to the coast, to move into the hinterland to collect crops and finance trade, frequently through Levantine and African buyers. By 1938 in the Gold Coast, 13 European firms, which normally purchased and exported 98% of the cocoa crop, maintained 'some 130 buying stations with European agents, and a much larger number of stations operated by Africans'.[39] In Malaya, Singapore agency houses also established branches and buying stations, which they used in purchasing much of smallholder rubber output from local Chinese dealers.

Singapore's main contribution to Netherlands Indian rubber production was commercial. Chinese traders and rubber millers in Singapore built up a complementary relationship with Netherlands Indian dealers. The typical arrangement was an interlinked transaction. Interlinkage existed because outport dealers who marketed primary commodities through Singapore also obtained consumer goods and credit as part of the same exchange. The credit from Singapore Chinese, usually in the form of goods, worked its way through a network of traders in Netherlands India ultimately to finance growers. Singapore's role as a centre for such interlinked

[35] Morse, 'Saõ Paulo in the nineteenth century', p.22.
[36] McCreery and Bynum, *Coffee industry*, p.37, and see p.38.
[37] Morse, 'Saõ Paulo in the nineteenth century', p.31.
[38] Gilberto Freyre, referred to in Richard M. Morse, 'Latin American cities: aspects of function and structure', *Comparative Studies in Society and History* 4, 4 (1962), p.481.
[39] *Report of the commission on the marketing of West African cocoa*, p.29, and see pp.9–10, 26–31, 129–30; W. K. Hancock, *Survey of British Commonwealth affairs, 1918–1939* II, 2 (London, 1942), pp.204–15.

transactions, also known as quasi-credit contracts, reflected the fragmentation of hinterland export trade among a large number of outport dealers and the absence of well-developed hinterland markets for consumer goods and credit.[40] The marketing and financial functions associated with interlinked transactions and performed by numerous Singapore Chinese traders, each with some degree of monopoly power and specialized knowledge of hinterland requirements and risks, made the staple port especially hard to by-pass. Through the system of advances from Singapore traders, outport dealers became tied to their source of credit in the staple port, as well as reliant on the staple port's traders to market primary commodities and supply small quantities of consumer goods in varying mixes.

The import and distribution of a return flow of goods destined for hinterland producers constituted a significant part of the staple port's mercantile function. Typically, both the port and its hinterland had a high marginal propensity to import which, since demand generated by staple exports quickly leaked out as imports, reduced the value of the foreign trade multiplier and limited the stimulus to domestic production. The corollary, however, was to expand the size and importance of the port's mercantile community. Furthermore, there was not one import trade but three: foodstuffs, consumer manufactures and producer goods. The import of foodstuffs was generally in the hands of local, non-European traders, as in Singapore where the Chinese controlled commerce in rice, dried fish and sugar. Manufactured imports had a more complex pattern. Initially, they came almost entirely through foreign firms, of which the most prominent in Empire ports were British merchant houses. Many houses had first been primarily interested in the distribution of manufactured imports, although also exporting produce.[41] But as a trade in staples developed, it often replaced imports as the European merchant's main activity.[42] This was partly because of the size of the staple trade and the frequent involvement of European merchants in production, although it was also because of growing competition, particularly in distributing non-durable consumer goods, from local, non-European, and in the case of Singapore also Japanese, importers.

---

[40] Jean-Philippe Platteau and Anita Abraham, 'An inquiry into quasi-credit contracts: the role of reciprocal credit and interlinked deals in small-scale fishing communities', *Journal of Development Studies* 23, 4 (1987), pp.461–90; Clive Bell, 'Credit markets and interlinked transactions' in H. Chenery and T. N. Srinivasan, eds. *Handbook of development economics* I (Amsterdam, 1988), pp.797–823.

[41] Robertson, 'Future of international trade', p.13.

[42] Cf. Robert Greenhill, 'Merchants and the Latin American trades' in D. C. M. Platt, ed. *Business imperialism, 1840–1930* (London, 1977), pp.163–64, 172; Peter Kilby, *Industrialization in an open economy: Nigeria 1945–1966* (London, 1969), pp.61–63.

If the processing of staples lay within the orbit of the producing area, it frequently centred on the port as the cheapest location.[43] The growth of Singapore as a staple port brought major processing industries. By 1900 Singapore boasted the world's largest and most technically advanced tin smelting enterprise. During the inter-war period Singapore became the region's – and so the world's – main centre for remilling smallholder rubber. Similarly, Rangoon had a large rice milling industry, and Buenos Aires became an important centre for meat packing. In New Orleans, although cotton came in the form of gin bales, it was recompressed at the port before transfer to ocean-going vessels. Even when processing took place in the hinterland, it often led to the manufacture of engineering goods in the port. Ceylon's need for plantation machinery supported a flourishing engineering industry in Colombo.[44] Similarly, Singapore firms made and installed rubber factories for Malayan estates and fabricated tin dredges, and in the 1970s they began to manufacture oil exploration equipment.

The market for the commodity was in the staple port, where the expansion of hinterland staple production made possible the introduction of specialized marketing facilities on a scale sufficiently large to take advantage of the considerable economies of scale associated not just with port and storage facilities but also trading and financial services.[45] Hinterland producers looked to the port as the focus of a characteristically complex network of dealers, commission agents, brokers and exporters, who purchased and assembled the commodity for shipment abroad. The staple port linked the hinterland marketing network to metropolitan centres and might rival them as an international market. Singapore established itself as the world's greatest market for rubber and tin. Other staple ports also became major international markets. Buenos Aires was a leading grain market, New Orleans was a world cotton market, while Rangoon had a similar status for rice. An important futures market developed in these cities,[46] as in Singapore for rubber. However, in contrast to Singapore, the markets in other staple ports did not always compete

[43] R. G. Hawtrey, *The economic problem* (London, 1926), p.99; Charlotte Leubuscher, *The processing of colonial raw materials: a study in location* (London, 1951), pp.169–70; Edgar M. Hoover, *The location of economic activity* (New York, 1948), pp.38–40.

[44] O. H. Spate, 'Beginnings of industrialisation in Burma', *Economic Geography* 17, 2 (1941), pp.79, 82, 83; Robert J. Alexander, *An introduction to Argentina* (London, 1969), p.32; H. S. Ferns, *The Argentine Republic, 1516–1971* (Newton Abbot, 1973), pp.95, 97–98, 109–11; Harold D. Woodman, *King cotton and his retainers* (Lexington, 1968), p.273; K. Dharmasena, *The port of Colombo, 1860–1939* (Colombo, 1980), pp.107, 114.

[45] R. E. Baldwin, 'Export technology and development from a subsistence level', *Economic Journal* 73 (1963), p.83.

[46] Vernon C. Fowke, *The national policy and the wheat economy* (Toronto, 1957), p.179; Graham L. Rees, *Britain's commodity markets* (London, 1972), p.100; Woodman, *King cotton*, pp.289–94; Cheng, *Rice industry*, pp.74–76, 64–69.

successfully with those in metropolitan countries. Thus, in the later 1930s most Ceylon tea was still auctioned in London.[47]

III

In many of its demographic features Singapore resembled other staple ports. The explosion of trade experienced by all led to rapid city growth.[48] This was particularly true of Latin America. Buenos Aires, for example, had population growth averaging 5% per annum between 1869 and 1914 to become a city of 1·5 million, while São Paulo grew at 6·3% from 1873 to 1920, to reach 600,000 persons.[49] The pace tended to be slower in Southeast Asia; Rangoon expanded at three-fifths Buenos Aires' rate over a similar period, and at 2·5% annually from 1872–1931.[50] Similarly, Singapore Municipality grew at 3% per annum between 1881 and 1936. Nevertheless, growth rates were sufficient to double Singapore's population (to 193,000) in the 20 years leading up to 1901 and to make it a metropolis of over half a million by World War II.

'Vent for surplus' theory presupposes surpluses of both natural resources and labour. But often in nineteenth-century staple-producing regions, only natural resources were surplus, and consequent inflows of labour had a major impact on staple ports. The rapid population growth often observed in staple ports depended on such inward movement, and in the majority, as in Singapore, this took the form of immigration from abroad rather than migration from the hinterland. The commercial opportunities of the city have generally proved more attractive to immigrant than to either migrant or indigenous groups. For example, in Argentina the 1914 census showed that

about three-tenths [of the total population of 7·9 million] were of foreign birth ... In the group of males over 20 years of age the foreign-born were 52 per cent and in the federal capital, for each native Argentinian over 20 years of age, there were almost three foreign-born of like age; 72 per cent of the business heads and 75 per cent of the owners of business houses were of foreign birth.[51]

[47] Rees, *Britain's commodity markets*, pp.209–12; Stahl, *Metropolitan organization*, pp.167, 172.

[48] The analysis of urbanization here and elsewhere in this book focuses on city growth rather than the pace of urbanization – i.e. the share of total population of a region or country living in urban areas. See Allen C. Kelley, 'Economic consequences of population change in the third world', *Journal of Economic Literature* 26, 4 (1988), pp.1691–92.

[49] Richard M. Morse, 'Trends and patterns of Latin American urbanization, 1750–1920', *Comparative Studies in Society and History* 16, 4 (1974), p.435.

[50] O. H. K. Spate and L. W. Trueblood, 'Rangoon: a study in urban geography', *Geographical Review* 32, 1 (1942), p.60.

[51] Alejandro E. Bunge and Carlos Garcia Mata, 'Argentina' in Walter F. Willcox, ed. *International migrations vol. II interpretations* (New York, 1931), p.151.

Even so, the reliance on immigration was extreme in Singapore: it was one of 'the world's greatest assemblages of people' brought together through immigration.[52] Only in the inter-war years did large numbers of immigrants begin to stay and have children to add to the native-born.

Due to population movement to staple ports, occupational structure typically reflected at least as much the inflow of labour as employment opportunities in the international trade which helped to attract new workers. In Singapore, as elsewhere, newcomers were not generally employed in the international economy, but had to be absorbed into a supporting local economy. Within this latter, the need for self-created jobs gave rise to the phenomenon which, although recently discovered as the informal sector, is neither new nor confined to the staple port.[53] Aspects of the labour market in the staple port now recognized as common in developing countries were immigration or migration in response to expected wage differentials, together with the emergence of noncompeting groups and a bifurcation into superior and inferior job categories.[54] In Singapore, this labour market segmentation was especially pronounced because of a chronic over-supply of labour and the city's extraordinary ethnic diversity, which extended to several Chinese ethnic groups. But in the present context, the relevant point is that these local-economy features arose from trade in staples as the mainspring of economic growth.

Yet among staple ports Singapore was unique in differing from its hinterland both demographically and politically, and in the extremity of these differences. 'Modern Rangoon', it could be averred even of that predominantly Indian city, 'is the commercial, cultural and political capital of Burma'.[55] Singapore performed no more than the first of these functions for either Malaya or Netherlands India. An international creation for purposes of trade, Singapore remains almost wholly commercial. Hong Kong is similar in this respect, but has neither Singapore's staple port origins, nor, since it is overwhelmingly Cantonese like its hinterland, Singapore's demographic singularity.

The demographic peculiarity of Singapore arose from its extreme dependence on immigration, and from the pronounced ethnic distinctiveness of these immigrants from the indigenous hinterland population with

---

[52] Galbraith, *Nature of mass poverty*, p.79

[53] Cf. T. G. McGee, *The Southeast Asian city* (London, 1976), pp.57–59; Hodgkin, *Nationalism in colonial Africa*, pp.75–77; R. H. Tawney, *Land and labour in China* (White Plains, NY, 1966), pp.119–21.

[54] Lewis, 'State of development theory', p.6; Arnold C. Harberger, 'Comment on Lewis' in Gerald M. Meier and Dudley Seers, eds. *Pioneers in development* (New York, 1984), p.145; John R. Harris and Michael P. Todaro, 'Migration, unemployment and development: a two-sector analysis', *American Economic Review* 60, 1 (1970), p.129.

[55] John L. Christian, *Burma* (London, 1945), p.71.

which they did not assimilate. The combined effect was to make a difference in degree into a difference in kind.[56] Like other Asian and African staple ports, Singapore had a small European community. But it drew more extensively than any port on the other two main sources of nineteenth-century immigration – China and India – owing to a position half-way between them on the main world shipping route and to the lack of Malay migration from the surrounding hinterland. In Singapore the presence of three Asian 'races' – the term sanctioned by usage[57] – and a remarkable ethnic diversity within the Chinese, Indian and Malay communities made the city 'probably the most cosmopolitan in the world'.[58]

Above all, however, Singapore grew as a Chinese city under British rule. In 1879 a Victorian traveller found Singapore had 'the air of a Chinese town with a foreign settlement'.[59] Development as a staple port greatly increased this Chinese presence. Most Chinese immigrants were drawn by the staple industries and passed quickly through Singapore, but others stayed longer or, increasingly, settled. In 1936 more than three-quarters of the inhabitants of Singapore Municipality were Chinese. Singapore contained the world's biggest concentration of overseas Chinese, had become 'the most important city so far as the economy of overseas Chinese is concerned' and was the largest Chinese publishing centre in Southeast Asia.[60]

Immigration made Singapore a city foreign to its hinterland and this relationship did not change. As a funnel for Chinese immigration, Singapore helped to alter the stock of population in the surrounding region, but the flow of immigrants was not sufficient to make the racial composition of the hinterland resemble that of the city. Nor did the city come to resemble its hinterland. Singapore's large Chinese population made this possibility unlikely, and the absence of an urban melting pot precluded it. 'Little racial mixture', it was remarked in 1940, 'takes place today. No inter-racial conflicts arise socially or in competition for jobs. The races maintain their individual integrity and customs by tacit agreement without proselyting'.[61]

---

[56] In the case of Singapore, it is useful to distinguish newcomers from the surrounding hinterland and newcomers from distant countries. The former are described as migrants, the latter as immigrants.

[57] C. A. Vlieland, *British Malaya: a report on the 1931 census* (London, 1932), p.73.

[58] J. Alexis Shriver, *Pineapple-canning industry of the world* (Washington, DC: US Department of Commerce, 1915), p.19.

[59] Isabella L. Bird, *The golden chersonese and the way thither* (Kuala Lumpur, 1967), p.115.

[60] Chen Chun-Po, 'Chinese overseas', *Chinese Year Book, 1936–37* (Shanghai, 1936), p.210, and see Alan J. A. Elliott, *Chinese spirit-medium cults in Singapore* (London, 1955), p.17.

[61] E. H. G. Dobby, 'Singapore: town and country', *Geographical Review* 30, 1 (1940), p.104, and see Elliott, *Chinese spirit-medium cults*, p.16.

A nineteenth-century English diplomat considered that 'at Singapore there is no apathetic population indigenous to the soil to be nursed, but one composed of the two most industrious and enterprising races in the world'[62] – the British and the Chinese. During the twentieth century in Singapore there has been a diminution in the role of the former, but the importance of the latter has increased. Singapore remains a Chinese city alien to the surrounding 'Malay world'.

IV

Just as Singapore was not linked racially to any of its hinterland, neither was the port politically a part of it. The island had only tenuous political connections with most of what was known as British Malaya to denote the group of territories under British sovereignty centred on the Malay Peninsula. These included the Straits Settlements, Federated Malay States and Unfederated Malay States. Together with Penang and Malacca, Singapore was governed as the Colony of the Straits Settlements, while the Malay Peninsula (except Malacca and Province Wellesley) was divided into the four Federated Malay States (FMS) of Selangor, Perak, Negri Sembilan and Pahang and five Unfederated Malay States (UMS) (figure 1.2). In consequence of the Federation Agreement of 1895, the Governor of the Straits Settlements became High Commissioner of the FMS over a Resident-General (after 1909 called Chief Secretary) in Kuala Lumpur. But from the start there was 'a strong tendency for ... [the Resident-General] to become in practice the head of a separate administration which ran on its own lines with only meagre consultation with Singapore'.[63] The Unfederated Malay States of Kedah, Perlis, Kelantan and Trengganu in the north, which passed from Siamese to British suzerainty in 1909, and the southern state of Johore had separate administrations and fiscal autonomy. Their British advisers were subordinate to the High Commissioner in Singapore, but he intervened little in State affairs.[64] Singapore was unlike many staple ports in that rapid urbanization was not reinforced by population being attracted to the city in connection with an administrative and political role for a large territory.

The difference in economic function between the staple port and its hinterland makes almost inevitable some conflict arising from the opposed interests of buyer and seller. Thus, in speaking of New Orleans, Louisiana

---

[62] Laurence Oliphant, *Elgin's mission to China and Japan*. Two vols. (Hong Kong, 1970), I, p.39.

[63] Rupert Emerson, *Malaysia: a study in direct and indirect rule* (Kuala Lumpur, 1964), p.146.   [64] Ibid. pp.355–56; Winstedt, *Malaya*, pp.88–95.

planters referred to 'the system of robbery of our commission houses'.[65] Yet in the case of Singapore and the Malay Peninsula relatively little such friction existed. There was a 'definite clash of commercial interests between the Straits Settlements and the Malay States',[66] but this involved more than tension between producer and middleman: it arose because their political interests were often different. Some form of economic/political union might have been fashioned between the Straits Settlements, dominated by Singapore, and the 'patchwork of "political experiments"'[67] in the Malay Peninsula. But Malayan union, first mooted by colonial officials in 1910, ultimately foundered. In the Malay states, the British authorities, the Malay rulers and the entire commercial sector feared the subordination of their interests to those of Singapore and the influence of its Chinese community.[68] More important for Singapore, economic union would have required forfeiture of the status of a free port and exclusion from the most important part of its hinterland in terms of the value of trade – Netherlands India, with which, under Dutch control, political unification was clearly out of the question.

The political fragmentation of its hinterland required that Singapore remain a free port, independent of Malayan involvement and international in outlook, to protect existing economic interests. Even in the 1930s slump influential business opinion in Singapore did not break with the past and deny the 'fundamental faith, free trade'.[69] In 1932 the Straits Settlements Customs Duties Committee, after drawing attention to the Colony's chiefly extra-Malayan commerce, concluded flatly that a Malayan customs union to include the Straits Settlements was 'undesirable in any circumstances that can reasonably be foreseen'. The 'prime consideration is the maintenance of the policy of free trade and free ports'.[70] The Straits Settlements Trade Commission agreed.[71]

These Singapore attitudes were well known. 'The findings of the Customs Duties Committee', observed the Acting Chief Secretary in the FMS,

have come to me as a disappointment but as no surprise ... I could not see how the Settlements of Singapore and Penang would reconcile entry into such a Union with

[65] George D. Green, *Finance and economic development in the old south* (Stanford, 1972), p.28, and see p.114.
[66] R. H. Bruce Lockhart, *Return to Malaya* (London, 1936), p.93.
[67] PRO CO 273/580, H. C. Eckhardt and W. E. Pepys, 'Remarks on the report of the Straits Settlements customs duties committee', 12 March 1932.
[68] *Report of Brigadier-General, Sir Samuel Wilson, Permanent Under-Secretary of State for the Colonies on his visit to Malaya, 1932* (PP 1932–33, X), pp.3–4, 6–14, 19–20, 24, 32–35; Emerson, *Malaysia*, ch. VII, passim; Winstedt, *Malaya*, p.91.
[69] Roland Braddell, *The lights of Singapore* (London, 1934), p.100.
[70] 'Customs duties committee', *SSLCP 1932*, pp.C155, C162.
[71] *SSTC 1933–34* I, pp.52, 162.

their essential present interests ... They are still ports of Malaysian and not merely Malayan significance, and to deprive them of their 'freedom' at this stage would certainly hasten their decline; unless very large free trade zones were possible, which they are unfortunately not; because the entrepot trade has ramifications far outside the dock limits.[72]

Two other FMS government officials recognized 'it to be only natural that the business interests of Singapore look to the 50 million people of the Netherlands East Indies rather than to the $4\frac{1}{2}$ m of this Peninsula'.[73]

It should thus be clear why Singapore's economic development before World War II will be dealt with primarily as that of a staple port. Equally apparent is that Singapore had attributes which other staple ports lacked. Singapore was in the centre of an especially rich area of primary production, and its role as a port of call provided an exceptionally large supply of shipping. Additional attributes – ones which set Singapore apart from other staple ports – increasingly emerged in the process of attaining staple port status. As developments in the world economy offered opportunities to exploit Singapore's locational advantages and those in the city responded, commercial ties, which spread over both sides of the Straits of Malacca to reach into much of Netherlands India and beyond, were strengthened. Within the region Singapore had a larger non-Malayan than Malayan trade. At the same time, mainly because of British Malayan economic development and Singapore's situation on the main sea route from China, the city grew into a Chinese metropolis, although the hinterland stayed predominantly Malay.

V

The legacies of economic, demographic and political separation from its hinterland were fundamental to Singapore's post-World War II development. Features which made Singapore unique before World War II kept it so afterwards. The incompatibility of an international, Chinese port and a primary producing, Malay hinterland defeated British administrators. They consequently omitted Singapore – but not the other Straits Settlements of Penang and Malacca – from a Malayan Union and then from the Federation of Malaya, both in 1948 and when Malaya obtained independence in 1957. In the Federation, the combined Chinese and Indian population – the so-called immigrant races – were as numerous as the

---

[72] PRO CO 273/580, Caldecott, 'Remarks on the Report of the Straits Settlements customs duties committee'.

[73] Ibid. Eckhardt and Pepys, 'Remarks on the Report of the Straits Settlements customs duties committee'.

Malays. However, since the Federation had substantially more Malays than Chinese, constitutional recognition could safely be given to the Malays' 'special position' as an 'indigenous' population.[74]

As part of the political process of winding up British Malaya, the Colony of Singapore became the internally self-governing State of Singapore in 1959. But the 1959 elections for Singapore's new government did not lead to a final political settlement. Many would have agreed with a former member of the Malayan Civil Service that 'Singapore is politically an accidental creation and not in any real sense a "country" (being geographically and economically part of Malaya)'.[75] More important, this was the position of the People's Action Party (PAP), formed in 1954 and winners of the 1959 election. According to their leader, Lee Kuan Yew, 'nobody in his senses believes that Singapore alone in isolation can be independent'.[76] For the PAP – since 1959 the sole party to govern Singapore – the merger of Singapore and Malaya was 'a historical necessity'.[77] Nevertheless, the PAP was equally emphatic that 'no sane government would want to destroy the foundations on which our economy now rests … The free port status of Singapore must not be attacked or modified save for the most compelling reasons'.[78]

In an attempt to overcome historical differences, in September 1963 a Federation of Malaysia was fashioned to comprise Malaya and Singapore together with Sarawak and Sabah – these last two the former British Borneo except for Brunei. Singapore's Chinese population, by then over 76% of the island's 1·8 million people, had posed a problem from the point of view of union with the Malay Peninsula. However, when the population of Sarawak and Sabah was added to that of the Malay Peninsula, a non-Chinese numerical dominance prevailed, even with the inclusion of Singapore in the new state of Malaysia. That new state was a compromise involving a recognition of Singapore's special economic position, the predominance of Chinese in its population and their economic role. In exchange, the island was under-represented politically in Malaysia – an

---

[74] See for example Sir Harold Macmichael, *Report on a mission to Malaya* (London, 1946); *Malayan Union and Singapore, statement of policy on future constitution* (PP 1945–46, XIX); 'Report of the Singapore constitutional conference held in London in March and April 1957', *SLA* (sessional paper no. misc. 2 of 1957); F. G. Carnell, 'British policy in Malaya', *Political Quarterly* 23, 3 (1952), pp.270–77; G. L. Peet, *Political questions of Malaya* (Cambridge, 1949), pp.17–19.

[75] Victor Purcell, *The Chinese in Southeast Asia* 2nd edn (London, 1965), p.349.

[76] *SLA Debates* 13, 1 (1960), cols.58–59; see also Lee's speech, 'Merger and the stakes involved' in Lee Kuan Yew, *The battle for merger* (Singapore, 1961), pp.5–6.

[77] S. Rajaratnam, 'Towards a Malayan nation' in PAP, *The tasks ahead: PAP's five year plan*, part 1 (Singapore, 1959), p.12.

[78] Goh Keng Swee, 'Our economic policy' in PAP, *The tasks ahead: PAP's five year plan*, part 1, pp.26–27.

enfranchisement for Singapore on a quasi-racial rather than a strictly numerical basis.[79]

The government of Indonesia (the now-independent Netherlands India) responded to the formal constitution of Malaysia by declaring a policy of Confrontation (economic boycott and political opposition extending to violent incidents) against the new state, and especially Singapore. Confrontation was motivated in part by the fear of the Javanese who dominated Indonesia's government that the Outer Provinces of Indonesia might break away to join Malaysia[80] (where, because of Singapore, so many of their economic interests centred). Linked to this was anti-Chinese feeling and the further fear, reflecting a 'traditional Javanese contempt for Malays', that Chinese, though outnumbered, would dominate Malaysia.[81] A side effect of Confrontation (but significant for this study) was that from late 1963 Singapore ceased publication of statistics for trade with Indonesia: 'In the economic war which is now being waged ... this kind of information constitutes valuable economic intelligence'.[82]

Yet for the indigenous, elected leaders of the Federation of Malaysia and Singapore, the problems of over a century of divergent development proved as intractable as they had to British civil servants. Within two years, in August 1965, Malaysia and Singapore were divorced amid the glare of world publicity. In Singapore, the radio announcement of separation 'was greeted by the firing of crackers in Chinatown'.[83] Singapore immediately became the independent Republic of Singapore; subsequent negotiations for a Malaysian common market to include Singapore failed. Indonesian Confrontation ended in June 1966, but statistics for trade with Indonesia remained 'a jealously guarded secret'.[84] However, after Confrontation, Indonesia almost certainly remained easily Singapore's main source of primary commodity exports.

VI

During the first half of the 1960s, Singapore's Gross Domestic Product (GDP) grew rapidly, despite a reversal in 1964 owing to the effects of Confrontation (figure 1.4). A further acceleration of economic growth in the later 1960s almost coincided with political independence and reflected

[79] For details of the compromise see John Gullick, *Malaysia* (London, 1981), pp.107–8; see also Lennox A. Mills, *Southeast Asia* (Minneapolis, MN, 1964), pp.44–60.
[80] Gullick, *Malaysia*, p.110.
[81] Jan M. Pluvier, *Confrontations: a study in Indonesian politics* (Kuala Lumpur, 1965), p.71, and see pp.65–72.
[82] *SLA Debates* 22, 1 (14 Dec. 1963), col.555, Goh Keng Swee.
[83] Goh Keng Swee, *Decade of achievement* (budget speech, 1970) (Singapore, 1970), p.9.
[84] C. M. Turnbull, *A history of Singapore, 1819–1975* (Kuala Lumpur, 1977), p.329. Throughout, references are to the 1977 edition.

it. From 1966 to 1980 GDP (at 1985 market prices) increased fourfold, growing at an annual average of 10·3%. Despite a recession in 1985 and early 1986, GDP nearly doubled during the 1980s, with an annual growth rate of 7·2%. Typically, investment in gross fixed capital formation amounted to a third to two-fifths of GDP. In 1990 Singapore's Gross National Product (GNP) per capita reached US$11,160, the nineteenth highest in the world, ahead of Ireland and Spain and 69% of the United Kingdom figure.[85] Measured in 1985 international dollars, 1990 real per capita GDP in Singapore was $10,965; the island's per capita GDP was 17·5% of the United States level in 1960 and reached 59·6% of United States GDP in 1990.[86]

The economic success of Singapore – remarkable, though not a 'miracle' as sometimes suggested[87] – is explicable on two counts. One is that Singapore started from a high base. The other is the favourable international economic forces on which Singapore capitalized.

Before World War II Singapore had already experienced very considerable economic development. At the beginning of the 1950s it was 'the most important communications centre in the Far East', not just for shipping but as 'a focal point for airlines, telecommunications and distribution of mail'.[88] Singapore, as in the inter-war period, was 'the biggest market in the world' for natural rubber,[89] internationally important as a specialized futures market for tin,[90] and a major world oil distribution centre. There existed a reservoir of human capital: the city had

[85] World Bank, *World development report 1992* (Oxford, 1992), p.219. If Kuwait and the United Arab Emirates are included, Singapore was twenty-first. Not all these gains in output accrued to 'indigenous' Singaporeans. To indicate this, the concept of indigenous GDP was developed. In 1985/90 indigenous GDP was 69·5% of Singapore's GDP. Singapore, *Yearbook of statistics 1991* (Singapore, 1992), pp.80, 83.

[86] Robert Summers and Alan Heston, 'The Penn world table (mark 5): an expanded set of international comparisons, 1950–1988', *Quarterly Journal of Economics* 106, 2 (1991) and new computer diskette supplement mark 5·5 (15 June 1993). On the United Nations Human Development Index, Singapore in 1990 ranked 15 places below its ranking in terms of GDP. The lower ranking mainly reflected low mean years of schooling for the island's population as a whole, explicable largely as a result of pre-1950 adult immigration from China, where little formal education was available. United Nations, *Human development report 1992* (New York, 1992), p.127.

[87] For example, Lawrence B. Krause observed that 'the phrase "economic miracle" is well deserved' in 'Hong Kong and Singapore: twins or kissing cousins?', *EDCC* 36, 3 supplement (1988), p.s46. See also 'Prime Minister Lee Kuan Yew – who made the miracle happen, transforming a backwater seaport into a high-tech financial trade centre – is stepping aside' in '25 years after its birth, Singapore is in transition', *Philadelphia Inquirer*, 24 Nov. 1990.

[88] Colony of Singapore, 'Communications', *Annual report 1950* (Singapore, 1950), p.140. See also E. J. Meyer, 'Why Singapore will succeed in industry', *Singapore Trade* (Jan. 1962), p.6.

[89] State of Singapore, 'Commerce', *Annual report 1961* (Singapore, 1963), p.117.

[90] J. W. F. Rowe, *Primary commodities and international trade* (Cambridge, 1965), p.47.

'an entrepreneur class which is both extensive in numbers and high in quality',[91] and substantial industry, not least as a centre for ship repair with the skilled labour force this implied. A tradition of strong and stable government had been established: Singapore 'inherited an administration which worked',[92] and built on it. The provision of social services reflected the island's economic growth: after rapid expansion beginning in 1953, in the early 1960s they were probably the best in Southeast Asia.[93] Infant mortality, after sharp inter-war declines, fell even more precipitately, by over 50% between 1947 and 1957 to 41·4 per thousand – above, but in reach of, developed countries.[94] By contrast, in 1958, infant mortality in Jakarta was 170·6, more than four times the level in Singapore.[95]

Quantitative evidence confirms this impression of rising living standards. In 1956 the first estimates of national income for Singapore showed that per capita income 'has been increasing fairly steadily and rapidly since 1948' and was very much greater than almost anywhere else in Asia.[96] Per capita income was probably over a third of that in the United Kingdom.[97]

[91] Goh Keng Swee, 'Entrepreneurship in a plural economy', *MER* 3, 1 (1958), p.1.

[92] Lee Kuan Yew, *Social revolution in Singapore* (speech to the British Labour Party conference, 1967) (Singapore, 1967), p.2.

[93] Frederic Benham, *Economic survey of Singapore 1957* (Singapore, 1957), p.21; Singapore, Economic Planning Unit, Prime Minister's Office, *First development plan 1961–1964: review of progress for the three years ending 31st December 1963* (Singapore, 1964), p.25.

[94] P. Arumainathan, *Report on the census of population 1970 Singapore* (Singapore, 1973), I, pp.33–34.

[95] Widjojo Nitisastro, *Population trends in Indonesia* (Ithaca, 1970), p.141.

[96] Frederic Benham, *The national income of Singapore 1956* (London, 1959), pp.1–2. See also Benham, *Economic survey*, pp.27–28; Ronald Ma, 'Review of Benham', *MER* 5, 1 (1960), pp.77–78; Frederic Benham, 'Western enterprise in Indonesia and Malaya', *MER* 2, 2 (1957), pp.44, 50. It was estimated that in 1956 per capita income was $1,200 in Singapore and $2,750 in the United Kingdom. For an estimate similar to that reached by Benham, but for 1957, see Amy Wong, *National income estimates of Singapore* (Singapore: Economic Research Centre, University of Singapore, 1968), tables 2a and 2b. However, the income differential was probably greater than these figures suggest. In 1960 Singapore's per capita GDP was 35·4% of that in the United Kingdom. It is also clear that by the 1960s Singapore had the highest per capita income in Asia after Japan and Hong Kong. United Nations, *Yearbook of national account statistics 1971* (New York: United Nations, 1973), II, pp.302, 488. For United Kingdom population figures, see B. R. Mitchell and H. G. Jones, *Second abstract of British historical statistics* (London, 1971), p.5, and for Singapore figures, see Singapore, Department of Statistics, *Economic and social statistics, 1960–1982* (Singapore, 1983), p.7. It was estimated that in Singapore in 1960 domestically-earned income accruing to non-nationals was about 4%. Lee Soo Ann, *Economic growth and the public sector in Malaya and Singapore, 1948–1960* (Singapore, 1974), p.13. H. T. Oshima drew attention to Singapore's past history and pre-World War II growth in explaining subsequent high growth. But in contrast to other estimates, Oshima put Singapore's per capita GNP growth during the 1950s at only 1·3% per annum. Harry T. Oshima, 'East Asia's high growth', *Singapore Economic Review* 31, 2 (1986), pp.4, 9, 11.

[97] The point needs emphasis, since the gap between LDCs and developed countries is generally very much greater than this. See, for example, Gerald M. Meier, *Leading issues in economic development* 5th edn (New York, 1989), p.77.

Prosperity had spread, so that Singapore was 'almost certainly the only place in Asia where there is a really substantial middle class'. In the mid-1950s the island had 30 people per private car and British Malaya 70. No other country in Asia had under 120.[98]

Despite this favourable picture, Singapore had two potentially serious economic difficulties. One was low voluntary personal saving and so a lack of capital formation needed for development; the other, a legacy of 'surplus labour' resulting in underemployment and a newer phenomenon of unemployment.[99] The last reflected rapid natural population increase but also, after China's 1949 revolution, an end to the pre-World War II 'safety valve' of immigrants returning to that country if sufficiently remunerative employment could not be found in Singapore.

The description by the later 1980s of Singapore as in such dire circumstances as to constitute a 'basket case' economy when the island obtained independence in 1959[100] is unwarranted. Assessments like this may reflect in part an historical interpretation encouraged by independent Singapore's very real achievements: these are apt to promote a feeling that in the past the economy must have been undeveloped. In part, it is explained by the ascendency of the PAP which, although gaining power in 1959 by means of a colonial government-sponsored election, acquired additional political legitimacy if its advent could be seen as a revolution.[101] The party and government, identical in Singapore, therefore encouraged such an interpretation. There was in Singapore an analogy with the 1952 Free Officers coup in Egypt where

As with so many other 'revolutions' the official mythology has it that before the revolution there was nothing; everything began with the revolution. As so often, for Egypt this is patently untrue. Industrialization in Egypt dates back to the inter-war period.[102]

So too, Singapore experienced significant inter-war industrialization, and during the 1950s further staple port development added to this industrial base.

The second strand of the explanation for Singapore's economic success relates to a highly favourable world economic environment – good access

---

[98] T. H. Silcock, *The Commonwealth economy in Southeast Asia* (Durham, NC, 1959), pp.43, 158.

[99] Benham, *Economic survey*, pp.15, 29, 31.

[100] Lim Chong Yah and associates, *Policy options for the Singapore economy* (Singapore, 1988), p.xi.

[101] The PAP's adoption of crisp all-white trousers and shirts as a 'uniform' and lightning flash symbol are examples of revolutionary imagery; compare also the title of Lee's speech, *Social revolution*.

[102] Bent Hansen, 'Egypt decolonized', *Journal of Economic History* 45, 3 (1985), p.716.

to the United States market to which the Singaporean economy has been closely tied through most of the twentieth century, coupled with Singapore's undoubted ability to exploit these opportunities. Initially, Singapore also had some luck in the timing of opportunity. In 1966, just when it was needed, a new flow in the world economy quickly began to gain strength: the investment made by multinational enterprises (MNEs) in search of low-cost locations for the manufacture – or, often, assembly – of goods with low value-added per worker for export to the West. From the start, a high proportion of the exports which multinationals began to manufacture in Singapore were electronics goods destined for the United States, which made special tariff provision for offshore assembly.[103]

By the 1970s, when manufacturing became the economy's leading sector, Singapore could no longer be described as a staple port. During the Malaysian experiment, and for a year afterwards until late 1966, Singapore had only the briefest phase of protected import-substitution industrialization, the usual next step in an attempt to transform staple ports: policies of import substitution were tried, for example, in Accra, Rangoon and Buenos Aires.[104] Singapore, by contrast, moved to export-oriented industrialization from the end of 1966 as a deliberate policy to grow away from the staple port economy.[105]

Thus once again for Singapore trade afforded an engine of growth – this time in the opportunity to export manufactured goods to the West. Singapore stood out as one of the most successful less-developed country

---

[103] G. K. Helleiner, 'Manufactured exports from less-developed countries and multinational firms', *Economic Journal* 83 (1973), pp.28–31; Michael Sharpston, 'International subcontracting', *Oxford Economic Papers* 27, 1 (1975), pp.95–97. In 1959 Puerto Rico was the sole less developed country example of industrialization through manufacturing for export, and could be regarded as a special case; by 1967 a number of countries had embarked on this path. H. W. Arndt, *Economic development: the history of an idea* (Chicago, 1987), p.84.

[104] The date at which a city ceases to be a staple port obviously varies, and depends on linkages created by the staple, the discovery of new staples and emergence of alternative sources of demand. For example, it has been argued that as early as 1900 Saõ Paulo's urban economy began to grow in response to agricultural production other than coffee exports, and at the same time that immigrant industrialists took the leading role in import-substituting industrialization which arose. Mauricio A. Font, *Coffee, contention and change in the making of modern Brazil* (Oxford, 1990). By contrast, between 1900 and 1930 Singapore's hinterland increasingly specialized in staple production and no hinterland engine of growth appeared to supplant staples; indeed, an alternative engine was still absent in the 1950s.

[105] Quantitative restrictions were the intended instrument to promote Singapore's industrialization as part of Malaysia, but because of the separation from Malaysia and failure to form a common market, the Singapore government had applied import restrictions on only 88 of 230 commodities proposed. Singapore, *Annual report of the Trade Division of the Ministry of Finance 1965* (Singapore, 1968), pp.11–12; Ng Kait Chong, *A comparative evaluation of the industrialisation of Hong Kong, Taiwan, South Korea and Singapore* (Singapore, Ministry of Finance, 1970), p.23.

economies in taking advantage of this new production function available through trade.[106] Export-oriented manufacturing enabled Singapore simultaneously to make rapid advances in GDP, and quickly to provide employment and reallocate workers from less productive occupations. The share of manufacturing in GDP rose from 16·3 % in 1966 to 22·5 % by 1973 and reached 23·9 % in 1980; while the labour-intensive character of manufacturing was reflected in a fivefold increase in employment in this sector from 1966 to 1980.

After 1980 the relative importance of manufacturing slightly declined, but the swift pace of change was maintained in the electronics industry. Individual production processes in an industry like electronics, requiring cheap labour but relatively little fixed capital, can be regarded as 'footloose' owing to a considerable flexibility of location and the capacity for either swift expansion or contraction.[107] In Singapore during the 1980s the former possibility prevailed, and the electronics industry kept up its rapid growth. Between 1980 and 1990 exports of office machines and telecommunications equipment grew at an annual average rate of 22 %. In 1990 Singapore ranked as the world's fifth largest exporter of these goods, with 6·5 % of world exports.[108] The introduction of products new to international trade was particularly important: from almost a standing start a few years earlier, Singapore was by the later 1980s the world's largest exporter of Winchester disk drives.[109]

There is no shortage of 'explanations' for Singapore's dynamic entrepreneurial achievements. These include Confucian values, the unique qualities of Chinese businessmen and sheer destiny.[110] In fact, independent Singapore turned decisively away from its Chinese entrepreneurial class, to achieve export-oriented growth almost entirely through foreign multinationals. By the mid-1970s foreign firms accounted for over four-fifths of manufactured exports, and intra-firm trade was a high proportion of these exports. Singapore, even in 1986, was industrially 'still predominantly a manufacturing production base. Products are designed overseas, and then

[106] James Riedel, 'Trade as the engine of growth in developing countries, revisited', *Economic Journal* 94 (1984), p.61; W. Arthur Lewis, 'The slowing down of the engine of growth', *American Economic Review* 70, 4 (1980), pp.555–56, 559–60.
[107] Richard E. Caves and Ronald W. Jones, *World trade and payments* 4th edn (Boston, 1985), pp.150–53.   [108] GATT, *International trade 1990/91* 2, p.57.
[109] 'Singapore's economic policy: vision for the 1990s', speech by B. G. (Res) Lee Hsien Loong at the Commonwealth Institute, London, 30 Jan. 1986, p.25; Singapore, Economic Development Board, *Singapore electronics manufacturers' directory 1990/91* (Singapore, 1990), p.26.
[110] E. S. Mason, et al., *The economic and social modernization of the Republic of Korea* (Cambridge, MA, 1980), p.285; Perkins, *China*, pp.13, 24; Paul R. Krugman, 'Developing countries in the world economy', *Daedalus* 118, 1 (1989), p.191–92.

only produced in Singapore factories on our production lines'.[111] In 1990, of 'the top 20 % of key positions in our society ... non-Singaporeans would comprise at least 40 % of the key decision makers ... At the moment we are using borrowed brain power, that of the multinationals'.[112] As a substitute for the market in organizing international exchange, multinational enterprises are 'islands of conscious power in an ocean of unconscious cooperation';[113] an island of conscious cooperation best described Singapore's place in MNE production. Singapore took in its entirety the MNE 'package' of capital, technology, entrepreneurship, management and marketing.[114]

What needs explanation is not Singaporean entrepreneurship, but how the island was able to attract MNEs, and accept and cater for a very high foreign presence. Development through multinationals as a substitute for local entrepreneurship required no more than what historically Singapore had always done – to respond to changes in the international economy and the resulting requirements of foreigners. A willingness to accept foreign enterprise from the late 1960s continued a long tradition of adaptability. Singapore's strong locational advantages, successful economic development during the staple port phase and a virtually unbroken history as a free port all pointed to the likelihood of a continued responsiveness to the world economy. There was acceptance of MNEs as well as compromise and cooperation with them. As Lee Kuan Yew observed, Singapore 'had no xenophobic hangover from colonialism'.[115]

During the late 1960s and 1970s South Korea, Taiwan and Hong Kong achieved growth rates comparable to Singapore's. By the mid-1970s common terminology bracketed together these four East Asian Newly Industrialized Countries (NICs) in phrases like the 'baby tigers', 'four dragons' or 'gang of four'. All four illustrate the achievement of economic development through competitively priced labour, access to the United States market and manufacturing for export. Yet in other, equally important respects, Singapore's development experience fits uncomfort-

[111] 'Singapore's economic policy', Lee, speech, p.7. A similar point was made for an earlier date by Lim Chong Yah, *Economic development in Singapore* (Singapore, 1980), pp.132, 142.

[112] Interview with Lee Kuan Yew in 'Singapore needs 10 more years to become a more mature society', *Straits Times Weekly*, 5 May 1990.

[113] Stephen H. Hymer, 'The efficiency (contradictions) of multinational corporations', *American Economic Review* 60, 2 (1970), p.441.

[114] A member of the Singapore National Trade Union Council observed of LDC attitudes towards MNEs that it seemed 'the response is all or none. In Singapore our attitude has been almost total acceptance'. T. H. Elliott, 'Multinationals in developing countries', *Spectrum* (published by SEATO) 2, 1 (1973), p.44.

[115] Lee Kuan Yew, 'Extrapolating from the Singapore experience', speech to the World Congress of the International Chamber of Commerce, Orlando, Florida, 5 Oct. 1978 (Singapore, 1978), p.13.

ably in this group, and indeed with many less developed countries (LDCs). Singapore's lack of an agricultural sector allowed more rapid GDP growth rates than would otherwise have been possible, since agriculture can grow at an annual rate of no more than about 3 %. Nor, unlike South Korea and Taiwan, was major agricultural reorganization needed for economic development.

A comparison sometimes suggested between Singapore and Canton, Bombay or Calcutta[116] is also hard to sustain. Political independence effectively delinked Singapore's labour market from its traditional hinterland to allow a close regulation of population flows, in contrast to the rest of Asia and even Hong Kong, where between 1945 and 1955 massive labour inflows caused population increase of about 400 %, with continued rapid population growth into the mid-1960s.[117] Singapore did not have the difficulty which confronts even medium-sized LDCs of workers being drawn to urban areas from the countryside faster than industrial jobs can be created. Instead, the problem was how to prevent wages from rapidly being bid up above internationally competitive levels in a country undergoing rapid industrialization and at full employment.

In Singapore, full employment could be reached relatively quickly. The resulting increase in income enlarged the savings and tax bases. In consequence, the Singapore government could address the problem of low domestic capital formation. Through a combination of public savings and a retirement fund operated on the provident fund principle, in which government collects and invests workers' savings, to be paid back to them on retirement, Singapore achieved savings of over 40 % of GDP in the 1980s – the highest savings ratio in the world.[118] Savings accumulating under Singapore's provident fund could be borrowed by the government at low interest rates, which allowed an extensive infrastructure to be easily and cheaply financed. Infrastructural development, government control of the labour market as well as of savings, planning effected through efficient government and reliance on foreign multinationals attracted by low-cost but highly productive labour, became hallmarks of the Singapore model of economic development from 1967.

The Singapore model carries the lesson – perhaps in its most emphatic form – that an extensive role for the government can be combined with free trade, and that laissez-faire (absence of government intervention) and laissez-passer (free trade) are distinct concepts. Because of a small,

[116] Stern, 'Economics of development', p.601.
[117] Edward Szczepanik, *The economic growth of Hong Kong* (London, 1958), pp.25–28, 153–54; Steven C. Chow and Gustav F. Papanek, 'Laissez-faire, growth and equity – Hong Kong', *Economic Journal* 91 (1981), p.466.
[118] World Bank, *World development report 1990* (Oxford, 1990), pp.194–95. Other high savers were South Korea (38 %) and Hong Kong (33 %).

extremely open economy, Singapore planners lacked the scope to use tariffs and target industries to shift comparative advantage towards manufacturing, as in South Korea and Taiwan.[119] Interventionism in Singapore aimed to adapt the domestic economy to the requirements of the international economy. Although interventionism could therefore be regarded as selective, there was total government control of those parts of the domestic economy crucial to international competitiveness.

The PAP, led by Lee Kuan Yew as Prime Minister until 1991, came to hold practically all seats in Parliament. The party's dominance was greater than even this might suggest. The direction of Singapore was orchestrated from the top of the PAP; a handful of its leaders called the shots.

VII

After 1978 international services became a leading sector in Singapore's export economy and, along with staple port activities and manufacturing, its third distinct growth component. As had been true of Singapore's growth since the 1870s, this post-1978 phase of its economic development was a response to new developments in the world economy. In 1990 the value of Singapore's commercial services exports was 86 % of Switzerland's and equal to 1·8 % of world exports of services.[120]

Like manufacturing, new opportunities for service-based growth dated from the later 1960s – just when they were needed in Singapore. Beginning in the 1970s, transport and communications services which can be traded (i.e. sold to non-residents) gained an increasing share in Singapore's economy. By the end of the 1980s Singapore was the world's busiest port in terms of shipping tonnage (the equivalent of one-half of world registered tonnage passed through each year) and was a world air traffic centre. Singapore's Changi Airport had 'the widest network of direct city links in the Asia-Pacific region'.[121] Related to this was the large industry which Singapore established in tourism and as a convention centre; by 1990, five million visitors arrived annually.[122]

Financial and business services, however, were the most important aspect of services sector diversification, and grew to become easily the largest single component in the Republic's services-dominated economy. After 1968 the emergence of Singapore as an international financial centre derived from the greater tradeability of these services and their consequent

---

[119] Larry E. Westphal, 'Industrial policy in an export-propelled economy: lessons from South Korean experience', *Journal of Economic Perspectives* 4, 3 (1990), pp.41–59; Robert Wade, 'Dirigisme Taiwan-style', *Institute of Development Studies Bulletin* 15, 2 (1984), pp.65–70.   [120] GATT, *International trade 1990/91* 2, p.4.
[121] Singapore, Ministry of Trade and Industry, *Economic survey of Singapore 1990* (Singapore, 1991), p.99.   [122] Singapore, *Yearbook of statistics 1991*, p.207.

internationalization, made possible by communications and transport revolutions. For example, in 1959 only seven United States banks operated abroad and these had less than 100 branch offices; by 1985 over 150 American banks did so, with over 1,000 branches.[123] Many of these banks, along with European and Japanese banks, opened in Singapore. By the mid-1980s the city had 116 foreign banks and 55 merchant banks,[124] and was one of the world's leading foreign exchange dealing centres.

Growth as an international service centre gave a high degree of continuity to Singapore's economic development. For the island, comparative advantage in the provision of international services derived from location, as it had previously for the staple port.[125] Singapore also depended on human capital and infrastructure, which could be built up as a result of earlier staple port and manufacturing development. Together with political stability, open and honest markets – both for financial services and a continued large commodity trade – remained a fundamental attraction of Singapore for foreigners.

The growing dependence of Singapore on services caused its economy sharply to diverge from the Asian NICs of South Korea and Taiwan, where the trend from the later 1970s was from light to heavy industry and towards the development of an indigenous technological capacity, difficult for a small economy like Singapore's.[126] During the 1980s Hong Kong's economy also reflected the new internationalization of services, but much of its services-oriented growth was a direct result of more goods being shipped through the port to China.[127] Moreover, Hong Kong Chinese organized extensive manufacturing in China. Singapore's lack of land and labour suggested the benefits of a similar expansion into Malaysia and Indonesia, or beyond – by the 1990s, a move referred to on the island as the need to develop an 'external economy'.[128] But opportunities for this expansion to be carried out by Singaporeans were limited by Singapore's

---

[123] Ingo Walter, *Global competition in financial services* (Washington, DC, 1988), p.10.

[124] Monetary Authority of Singapore, *Annual report 1990/91* (Singapore, 1991), p.81; Dimitri Germidis and Charles-Albert Michalet, *International banks and financial markets in developing countries* (Paris: OECD, 1984), pp.30, 77.

[125] H. W. Arndt, 'Comparative advantage in trade in financial services', *Banca Nazionale del Lavoro Quarterly Review* 164 (1988), pp.72–73.

[126] Tibor Scitovsky, 'Economic development in Taiwan and South Korea: 1965–81', *Food Research Institute Studies* 19, 3 (1985), pp.256–59; Rudiger Dornbusch and Yung Chul Park, 'Korean growth policy', *Brookings Papers on Economic Activity* no. 2 (1987), pp.439–43.

[127] See *Hang Seng Economic Monthly* (Hang Seng Bank, Hong Kong): 'Towards a service economy' (Sept. 1988); 'The revival in re-export trade' (June 1988); 'Economic growth – quantity versus quality' (Oct. 1988); 'The expansion of the service sector and its macroeconomic impact' (Feb. 1990).

[128] 'S[enior] M[inister] [Lee Kuan Yew]: Way to take Singapore Inc. abroad', *Straits Times Weekly*, 9 Jan. 1993; 'Going global: who dares, win', *Straits Times Weekly*, 16 Jan. 1993.

lack of industrialization on the basis of indigenous entrepreneurial resources.

As a model for LDCs, the international services aspect of Singapore's development has limited applicability. Few LDCs have Singapore's locational advantages in linking regional and global markets, and the number of cities needed to fill this role is, by its nature, small. Political considerations and arguments for the protection of the domestic market are likely to be stronger in most countries than in Singapore. For example, local politics has worked against Bahrain's attempt to copy the services-led development in Singapore.[129] Efforts in Mauritius to emulate Singapore's services development are hindered by the absence of a substantial regional market in Africa to link to the global one, as Singapore does for Southeast Asia, and a less advantageous position in connecting financial markets in different time zones.[130]

VIII

By the 1990s Singapore appeared increasingly an anomaly – a product of world economic development but a special case within it. Just as the post-1965 Singapore model of economic development cannot be applied in any wholesale way, so too Singapore had to find its own way towards development. When asked whether, in 1965, Singapore's leadership had 'a model in mind', Lee Kuan Yew replied,

No, we borrowed in an eclectic fashion, elements of what Hong Kong was doing, what Switzerland was doing, what Israel was doing, and we improvised. I also went down to Malta to see how they ran the dry docks.[131]

During its post-World War II development, Singapore acquired many features which made it like history's best-known city states, especially those of twelfth- to fifteenth-century Italy.[132] Similarities included the fundamental importance of location, the large role of trade (Singapore's ratio of trade to GDP, normally between 3·5 and 4, was the world's highest) and a stable currency. All three promoted a role as a financial

---

[129] Elias T. Ghantus, 'The financial centre and its future' in Jeffrey B. Nugent and Theodore H. Thomas, *Bahrain and the Gulf* (London, 1985), pp.132–40; 'Bahrain banks see few hopes met', *Financial Times*, 7 June 1988; 'Banks in Bahrain debt dispute', *Financial Times*, 27 June 1988.

[130] Richard C. Kearney, 'Mauritius and the NIC model redux: or, how many cases make a model?', *Journal of Developing Areas* 24, 2 (1990), p.208.

[131] Geoffrey Stern, 'The Geoffrey Stern interview: Lee Kuan Yew', *LSE Magazine* 2, 4 (Winter 1990/91), p.24.

[132] The following comparison draws on Ursula K. Hicks, 'The finance of the city state', *MER* 5, 2 (1960), pp.1–9; see also John Hicks, *A theory of economic history* (London, 1969), pp.42–59; Pang Eng Fong and Linda Lim, 'Political economy of a city state', *Singapore Business Yearbook 1982* (Singapore, 1982), pp.7–33.

centre, which had also been important to Venice and Florence. Politically, city states have tended to be run by an oligarchy or a single party: smallness conduces to a monopoly of power, and this is encouraged by the prosperity of inhabitants and their recognition of the economy's need for political stability.

But Singapore lacked the city state's usual high degree of loyalty from its citizens – 'a Singaporean identity'. By contrast, Athens and Venice are examples where 'closely packed, polyglot, ethnically diverse' populations developed a nationalism.[133] Also missing in Singapore were domestically-inspired, high-grade manufactures and a liberal immigration policy. However, Singapore's easy access for MNEs and their foreign personnel could be thought of as the modern equivalent to skilled, or entre-preneurially-motivated, immigrants. And the attractiveness of government jobs for the most talented Singaporeans offered an analogy with classical Athens, where 'trade and industry was almost entirely in the hands of... immigrants, while the Athenians proper worked in the public services'.[134] Like almost all successful city states, Singapore developed a strong public sector after 1959; 'Of the great Italian city states Genoa was exceptional in having an ideology of pure private enterprise', and this proved a weakness.[135] In common with other city states, Singapore's survival required well-disposed neighbours; a much higher income than elsewhere in the region was likely to stir up envy for which Chinese ethnicity was an easy focus. The danger was apparent, since 'Irrespective of political system, Asian societies have made little if any progress in race relations'.[136]

The continuity in Singapore's economic development, reliance on departures in the world economy and adaptability to them have been this chapter's themes. Almost everything in Singapore's pre-World War II development encouraged it to seek solutions in the international economy rather than through a nation state. Much the same was true after World War II. By the 1960s, in contrast to almost all other LDCs, for Singapore the abandonment of free trade would have required precisely the 'difficult and painful adjustment' which the Asian Development Bank considered necessary if Asian countries were to adopt Singapore's policies and discard protectionist import-substitution strategies.[137]

---

[133] Edmund Leach, 'Buddhism in the post-colonial order in Burma and Ceylon', *Daedalus* 102, 1 (1973), p.32. On the government's desire 'to develop a Singapore identity', see 'Government proposes 5 shared values', *Straits Times Weekly*, 12 Jan. 1991.

[134] Hicks, 'Finance of the city state', p.5.   [135] Ibid.

[136] Robert A. Scalapino, *The politics of development: perspectives on twentieth-century Asia* (Cambridge, MA, 1989), p.122. See also 'Chinese–Malay relations turn sour in Singapore', *New York Times*, 13 May 1990; 'PM: Malays should get out of their psychological "trap"', *Singapore Bulletin* (Aug. 1987), p.6.

[137] Asian Development Bank, *Southeast Asia's economy in the 1970s* (London, 1971), p.232. The author was Helen Hughes.

Singapore has alternatively been regarded as unlucky in a PAP leadership unable to agree terms with Malaysia between 1963 and 1965, or almost singularly fortunate in being led by men able to chart so successful a course in the world economy after 1965. But there is danger in leaning too far towards either view. Each supposes that 'great' men are at liberty to shape the course of events. Surely, the weight of history constrains such freedom of choice. In promoting economic development, Singapore's post-1965 native actors and the policies they initiated were remarkably successful. But both men and policies are best understood first as products and reflexions of Singapore's twentieth-century economic growth.

2   Singapore in the late nineteenth century

Singapore was brought into existence to grasp the opportunities of trade, and its economic development has remained intimately bound up with trade expansion. For 1870 to 1939, Singapore's trade is shown in broad outline by figures 2.1 and 2.2 and appendix tables A.1 and A.2. Table 2.1 gives export growth rates derived from a constant pound sterling series and indicates annual average growth of 3·4% between 1870 and 1937.[1] Over these seven decades, three growth phases can be identified. The first, lasting until 1900, was one of a high, sustained increase in exports. In a second phase between 1900 and 1909, both the value and volume of exports remained relatively stable. The final phase, dominated by rubber, stood apart from Singapore's earlier experience in the magnitude of increase in export value and the sharp short-term fluctuations. There were further large increases in export volume.

Data for 1870–1900 suggest apparently contradictory movements in the value and volume of exports from the late 1880s. Export growth, when expressed in constant pounds sterling, slowed considerably between 1889 and 1900 (table 2.1). However, this slowing in export growth reflected a 36% fall in the (silver-based) Straits dollar against the British pound sterling. Figures for the volume of exports give a better indication of Singapore's late nineteenth-century trade expansion. Volume growth concentrated in the decade beginning in 1886, when tin exports quadrupled from 8,100 tons to 32,900 tons and exports of tropical produce increased from 142,500 tons to 252,300 tons. Over the slightly longer period 1886–1897 rice exports grew from 123,900 tons to 332,400 tons.

By 1900 Singapore could therefore look back on a period of rapid growth. Some account must be taken of this experience: because of it, 1900 is a logical point to begin this study, for by then Singapore had acquired both its first staple and many of its characteristic features. Facilities built up because of earlier trade growth allowed the shift to rubber and

---

[1] The Sauerbeck–Statist overall price index was chosen as probably the best available deflator, but affords only a rough approximation. In particular, for Singapore's exports it does not take adequate account of rubber.

Table 2.1 *Real annual average growth rates of Singapore merchandise exports, 1870–1937 (constant £, 1871 = 100)*

	%		%
1870–1937	3.4	1900–1929	3.4
1870–1900	5.0	1900–1909	1.9
1870–1889	6.5	1909–1929	4.7
1889–1900	2.5	1922–1929	9.0
1900–1937	2.4	1929–1937	−2.1

Notes:
1   Singapore exports were converted to pounds sterling by using exchange rates in Chiang and deflated with the Sauerbeck–Statist overall price index. Growth rates are calculated by fitting a least–squares linear regression trend line to the logarithmic annual values for the relevant period.
Sources: Appendix table A.1; Chiang, *Straits Settlements trade*, pp.178-79; Mitchell and Deane, *Abstract of British historical statistics*, pp.474-75.

petroleum to be accomplished without difficulty. They make twentieth-century development as a staple port a story not of economic revolution but one of adaptation through the expansion of existing services. Similarly, there was substantial continuity in Singapore's late twentieth-century transition from staple port to a more diversified, international service centre and to export-oriented manufacturing.

By the close of the nineteenth century existing European merchant houses had greatly expanded to handle the growth in exports to the West, while the concomitant increase in regional trade had multiplied both the number of Chinese firms and their wealth. The once-leisurely European business system had been revolutionized after the establishment in 1871 of direct telegraphic communication with Europe. Singapore had also acquired new port facilities. Until the mid-nineteenth century shipping anchored in the roads, and cargo was transferred by lighter, mainly to and from the Singapore River. However, steamships required wharves, especially for coaling, and by 1885, 6,600 feet of wharfage and four dry docks had been built in Keppel Harbour.

Although the founding of institutions such as banks and associations of merchants often did not coincide with late nineteenth-century export growth, most reflected its influence. The three main British banks were already in Singapore by 1877, while the (European) Singapore Chamber of Commerce, begun in 1837, saw its membership rise from 20 in 1890 to 47 in 1897, followed by a further substantial increase from 1910 to 1915.[2] In

[2] The Chamber's early story is told in Chiang Hai Ding, *A history of Straits Settlements foreign trade, 1870–1915* (Singapore, 1978), pp.221–31.

$000,000

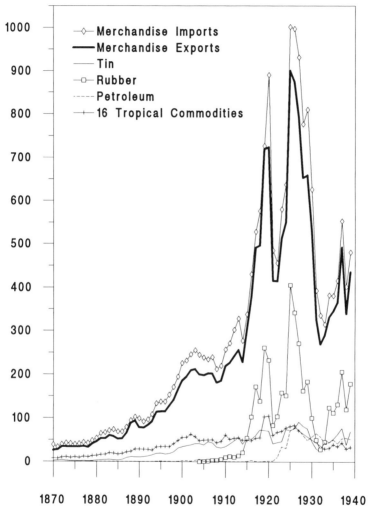

Figure 2.1   Singapore merchandise imports and exports and main commodity exports, 1870–1939

1906 the Singapore Chinese Chamber of Commerce was established and soon afterwards the Chinese Produce Exchange; Singapore's earlier export-led growth no doubt encouraged the formation of both. This was certainly true of the contemporaneous development of the first local Chinese deposit banks.

Tons 000

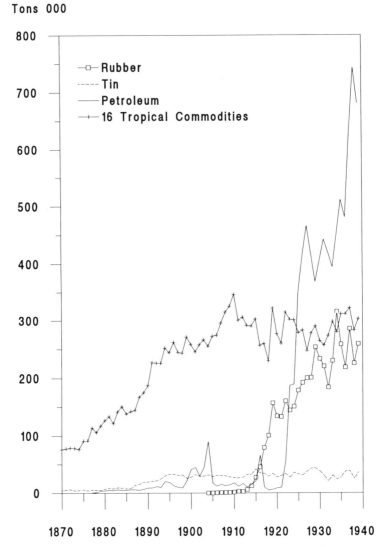

Figure 2.2   Singapore volume of main primary commodity exports, 1870–1939

In the two decades after 1880 Chinese immigration reached unprecedented levels. This period marked the transition to large-scale immigration which in the twentieth century was to continue to fuel Singapore's rapid population growth, and to warrant on St. John's Island at the port's southern approaches the world's largest quarantine station after Ellis Island, New York.[3]

The physical appearance of Singapore was transformed after 1870,[4] and the city acquired a number of the features it would still have in 1939 (figure 2.3) and retain until the 1970s. Modern Singapore was a very late nineteenth century creation. Although begun as a coastal settlement, from the 1870s the principal thrust of Singapore's development was inland, more or less following the lines of the Singapore and Rochore Rivers and in a grid-iron pattern. At the turn of the century the European business district (known as the Central Business District) and government precinct centring on Empress Place, which were immediately adjacent to and on either side of the Singapore River, where Raffles had originally located them, were well-established and had some of their major buildings. By 1925, reflecting the prosperity brought by rubber, the erection of large, new premises for European agency houses, shipping companies and banks had 'quite changed the architectural aspect of the business quarter'.[5] The Municipal Offices (later called City Hall) – which served as the venue for the Japanese surrender in 1945 and, after independence, the focal point for official Singapore occasions – were not completed until 1929. It was only in 1937 that work began on the Supreme Court, another imposing building in a style dubbed, perhaps unkindly, 'Calcutta Corinthian'.[6] Otherwise, Singapore was a city of shophouses, and mixed land use predominated. This Asian Singapore pressed against the relatively small European government and business zones, and once away from the latter the visitor was quickly lost in a teeming town of open shop fronts, bazaars, hawkers and rickshaw pullers. Only in the 1970s were these Asian areas demolished and the population re-housed on large estates throughout the island.

In 1900, as in 1959 before government re-housing on estates, practically all Singapore's inhabitants lived in readily distinguishable racial and, in the case of the Chinese pang (dialect) groups, ethnic areas. During the latter part of the nineteenth century the European population had retreated to the suburbs and central Singapore came to be dominated by two increasingly densely populated Chinatowns on either side of the Singapore River. By the early years of the twentieth century some wealthy Chinese

[3] G. W. A. Trimmer, 'The port of Singapore', *Singapore: a handbook of information presented by the Rotary Club and municipal commissioners of the town of Singapore* (Singapore, 1933), p.17.

[4] Turnbull, *History of Singapore*, p.113. This also applied to other tropical cities: see W. Arthur Lewis, 'The export stimulus' in W. Arthur Lewis, ed. *Tropical development 1880–1913* (London, 1970), p.34.

[5] Allister Macmillan, *Seaports of the Far East* 2nd edn (London, 1925), p.428.

[6] Rhoads Murphey, 'Colonialism in Asia and the role of port cities', *East Lakes Geographer* 5 (1969), p.46.

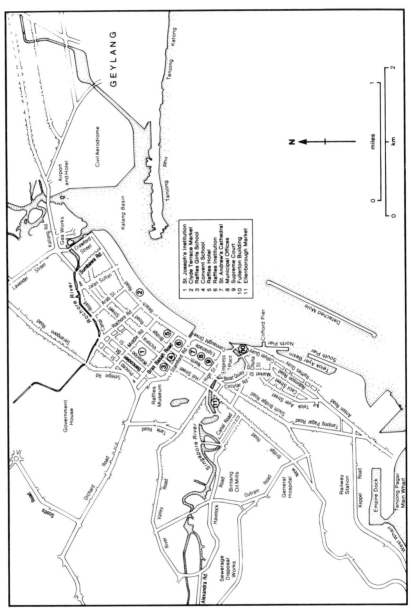

Figure 2.3 Central Singapore, 1939

merchants had built palatial residences outside Singapore and, like their inter-war successors, helped to change the face of the city through generous donations for schools and hospitals. But the great mass of Singapore's population, in part owing to its immigrant character, continued to cluster around the central core of settlement.[7] The development of a tramway system from 1882 did relatively little to promote suburbanization; in 1918 a European official could state, 'I have no recollection of having been in any town of similar size in any part of the world before where residential suburbs have been so limited as they are in Singapore'.[8] The city really began to spread only in the inter-war period with the widespread adoption of the motor car, greater use of bus transport and a growing Asian middle class, all now so apparent in Singapore.

I

In the late nineteenth century Singapore's exports increased in response to demand in the West for tin and tropical produce from Malaya and Netherlands India. Singapore was responsible for neither the discovery of these commodities, which had long been principal constituents of the region's trade,[9] nor for the growth of demand for them; but as these trades expanded, the port found itself at the centre of a rapidly emerging pattern of regional economic specialization.

The role Singapore played in this process was fundamental to its economic development as well as to that of the region of Southeast Asia served by the town. Singapore's trade was largely bilateral in the sense that increased exports brought return imports of roughly equivalent value, while merchants in the town – often of the same firm – handled both exports and imports. This trade linked the region to the West and different parts of the region to each other.

In Singapore the effect of bilateral trade and the port's linking function was to give rise to three main commercial flows: exports to the West; a regional exchange of food, largely rice, dried fish and sugar; and a return flow of manufactured goods from the West. There was a rapid acceleration in total trade, since exports to the West had multiplier effects, leading to an increase in trade exceeding their own value. The exports drew to Singapore

[7] Arnold Wright and H. A. Cartwright, *Twentieth century impressions of British Malaya* (London, 1908), pp.600–1, 631–39; Song Ong Siang, *One hundred years' history of the Chinese in Singapore* (London, 1923), pp.332–33.

[8] *Proceedings and report of the commission to inquire into the cause of the present housing difficulties in Singapore*. Two vols. (Singapore, 1918), II, p.C13.

[9] Sinnappah Arasaratnam, *Pre-modern commerce and society in southern Asia* (Kuala Lumpur, 1972), pp.7, 16–18.

Table 2.2 *Singapore imports by country and region, 1871/73 and 1897/99* (*annual averages*)

	1871/73		1897/99	
	$000	%	$000	%
Southeast Asia	**18,397**	**43.1**	**105,001**	**52.6**
Malay Peninsula	2,562	6.0	31,215	15.6
Inter–Port	4,801	11.2	6,380	3.2
Netherlands India	6,485	15.2	32,779	16.4
Siam	1,930	4.5	16,034	8.0
Indo–China	593	1.4	7,462	3.8
British Borneo	447	1.0	3,364	1.7
Burma	1,130	2.7	7,030	3.5
Philippine Islands and Sulu Archipelago	448	1.1	737	0.4
Europe, North America and Japan	**11,698**	**27.4**	**39,868**	**19.9**
United Kingdom	10,079	23.6	24,399	12.2
Europe	1,587	3.7	9,451	4.7
United States	18	0.1	774	0.4
Canada	0	0.0	4	0.0
Japan	13	0.0	5,240	2.6
Rest of world	**12,593**	**29.5**	**54,836**	**27.5**
Hong Kong	4,195	9.8	18,058	9.1
China	858	2.0	4,642	2.3
British India	5,829	13.7	29,135	14.6
Ceylon	45	0.1	549	0.3
Australia	178	0.4	1,425	0.7
Others	1,489	3.5	1,028	0.5
Total	**42,688**	**100.0**	**199,705**	**100.0**

Notes:
1   The figures include treasure of bullion and specie.
2   Labuan did not become part of the Straits Settlements until 1906 but is included with Penang and Malacca under Inter–Port to make the figures more comparable with later periods.
3   For 1871/73 figures for Burma are for 1872 and 1873 only.
4   For 1897/99 the Malay Peninsula includes Johore, Kedah, Perak, Selangor, Sungei Ujong, Kelantan, Pahang and Trengganu. Siam includes Siam Proper, Siam West Coast, Patani and Singora.
5   Columns may not add to totals due to rounding.
Sources: SS, *Blue books*, 1871–1873, 1899.

imports of both manufactures and food for re-shipment to producers exporting to the West, while the inflow of food created another return flow of manufactures and food sent from Singapore for food cultivators.

In Malaya and Netherlands India, Singapore promoted the export expansion on which development was based by giving hinterland producers access to new markets in the West. In Siam, Burma and Indo-China, Singapore stimulated export expansion by giving producers greater access to the expanding regional market for food. In both cases, Singapore enabled producers to obtain the consumer goods necessary for economic specialization. As a link for trade flows arising in the international and regional economies, Singapore helped to transform the surrounding countries and was itself transformed in the process.

The geographical distribution of Singapore's trade, set out in tables 2.2 and 2.3 for 1871/73 and 1897/99, shows the process of late nineteenth-century trade expansion.[10] Growth was set in motion by the rapid increase in imports from Malaya and Netherlands India which, mediated through Singapore, became its exports to the West. During the period, Singapore's imports from Malaya and Netherlands India (including inter-port trade with the other Straits Settlements) and exports to the West both rose over fivefold, somewhat faster than Singapore's trade (imports + exports) as a whole.

By 1897/99, while the Malay Peninsula and Netherlands India each provided the same share (16%) of Singapore's imports, their composition (table 2.4) was quite different. Imports from Netherlands India remained a wide selection of tropical produce, with none accounting for over 13% of the total from the Dutch colony. Tropical produce from Netherlands India came largely from Sumatra and Borneo. As a result, in 1894, 65% of Outer Province exports went to Singapore. Rapid Outer Province export expansion, fostered by the Dutch colonial government's new, late nineteenth-century policy of Liberalism (a freeing of the market and emphasis on private enterprise) caused the share of exports sent to Singapore from the whole of Netherlands India (Java and Madura plus the Outer Provinces) to rise from 8·6% in 1871/73 to 20·7% in 1897/99.[11]

But Singapore had only two principal imports from the Malay Peninsula. One was gambier and pepper, which were nearly always grown together because of complementary economies of production, although meeting different demands in the West, where gambier was a brown dye and

---

[10] For 1895–1899 statistics of Singapore's imports and exports by commodity by country, see 'Report on the trade of the Straits Settlements', *SSAR 1899*, pp.213–34.
[11] Netherlands India, Central Bureau of Statistics, Concept Publicatie C. K. S. (Mededeeling no. 162), 'Het Handelsverkeer met Singapore, 1825–1937' (unpublished typescript, 1938), pp.4, 6, 8, 10.

Table 2.3 *Singapore exports by country and region, 1871/73 and 1897/99* (*annual averages*)

	1871/73		1897/99	
	$000	%	$000	%
Southeast Asia	**18,033**	**48.0**	**82,176**	**49.0**
Malay Peninsula	1,681	4.5	17,041	10.2
Inter–Port	3,908	10.4	6,121	3.7
Netherlands India	7,723	20.5	34,525	20.6
Siam	2,446	6.5	14,093	8.4
Indo–China	1,009	2.7	3,084	1.8
British Borneo	517	1.4	2,588	1.5
Burma	476	1.3	3,284	2.0
Philippine Islands and Sulu Archipelago	273	0.7	1,440	0.8
Europe, North America and Japan	**11,585**	**30.8**	**63,759**	**38.1**
United Kingdom	7,655	20.4	22,031	13.2
Europe	586	1.6	21,010	12.5
United States	3,325	8.8	18,283	10.9
Canada	0	0.0	12	0.0
Japan	20	0.0	2,424	1.5
Rest of world	**7,974**	**21.2**	**21,638**	**12.9**
Hong Kong	3,596	9.6	10,963	6.5
China	1,148	3.0	4,018	2.4
British India	787	2.1	4,132	2.5
Ceylon	29	0.1	377	0.2
Australia	91	0.2	1,325	0.8
Others	2,322	6.2	823	0.5
Total	**37,592**	**100.0**	**167,572**	**100.0**

Notes and sources: as for table 2.2.

tanning agent.[12] Tin, however, was by far the main import. Between 1874/77 and 1896/99 Malayan tin production increased more than sixfold and from less than one-fifth to over a half of world output in response to the growing demand for tin plate in the West, especially the United States. This demand came from two product innovations: barrels for transporting petroleum and, more important, canned foods.[13] By 1899 tin accounted for nearly a fifth of the value of Singapore's exports, and the port had become the world's main tin exporter.

[12] James C. Jackson, *Planters and speculators: Chinese and European agricultural enterprise in Malaya, 1786–1921* (Kuala Lumpur, 1968), pp.6, 9–10, 24–25; Captain S. W. Kirby, 'Johore in 1926', *Geographical Journal* 71, 3 (1928), p.245.
[13] W. E. Minchinton, *The British tinplate industry* (London, 1957), pp.25–28, 254–58, 261.

Table 2.4 Singapore imports from the Malay Peninsula and Netherlands India, 1897/99 (annual averages)

Malay Peninsula	$000	%	Netherlands India	$000	%
Tin ore and tin	19,392	62.1	Arecanuts	579	1.8
Gambier	3,721	11.9	Borneo rubber	1,283	3.9
Pepper (black, white, long)	2,520	8.1	Coffee	1,857	5.7
Others	5,582	17.9	Copra	3,700	11.3
			Gambier	1,712	5.2
			Gums (benjamin, copal, dammar)	865	2.6
			Gutta percha	4,359	13.3
			Pepper (black, white, long)	1,335	4.1
			Rattans	3,093	9.4
			Sago (flour, raw)	716	2.2
			Sugar	2,439	7.4
			Tin ore and tin	706	2.2
			Tobacco	532	1.6
			Others	9,604	29.3
Total	31,215	100.0	Total	32,779	100.0

Notes:
1 Singapore's imports from Penang and Malacca were $1,522,000 of tin ore and tin, $146,000 of gambier and $132,000 of pepper.
2 Columns may not add to totals due to rounding.
Sources: SS, Blue books, 1897–1899; 'Trade of the Straits Settlements', SSAR 1899.

Between 1871/73 and 1897/99 the increase in Singapore's exports to the West was accompanied by a striking change in their direction. At the beginning of the period Britain was the main outlet, taking two-thirds of exports, but by 1897/99 combined exports to Europe and the United States were almost double those to Britain. Part of the explanation was that Continental and American demand for the region's products expanded more rapidly than British. However, the shift in exports also reflected the relative decline of London as an entrepot in the late nineteenth century, and the establishment of the Straits Homeward Conference as a cartel controlling international shipping services to the United Kingdom and Europe. The Conference facilitated direct shipment to Continental ports through better connections with Singapore. It also had the effect of encouraging direct exports from Singapore to the United States by-passing the London entrepot, since the cartel raised freight rates to the United Kingdom and Europe relative to those to America until the formation of the New York Freights Conference in 1905.[14] The return flow of manufactured imports from the West – with cotton piece goods the largest single item – continued to come mainly from Britain.

A high proportion of Singapore's imports of food and manufactures were redistributed from the port to become its exports to the region. The food required by workers in the Malayan and Netherlands Indian export industries derived chiefly from Siam, Burma and Indo-China. The three countries furnished almost all Singapore's imports of rice and dried fish (table 2.5). Siam was the main source of rice, and Singapore a major outlet for Siam's rice; it took 20% in 1870/74, 50% in 1880/84 and 36% in 1900/04 of exports which grew sixfold during this period.[15]

The dominant feature of Singapore's exports of food and manufactures to the region was the size of the Netherlands Indian market, which was twice that of the Malay Peninsula (excluding inter-port trade). Singapore was as important to the Outer Provinces – where its Netherlands Indian market concentrated – as they were to it. In 1894 Singapore provided 49% of Outer Province imports, while in 1897/99 Netherlands India as a whole received nearly a third of its imports through Singapore, only slightly less than from the Netherlands.[16]

---

[14] S. B. Saul, *Studies in British overseas trade, 1870–1914* (Liverpool, 1960), p.59; *Commission on the ... Straits Homeward Conference* (Singapore, 1902), pp.5–10; A. Stuart, 'Report on shipping freight conferences operating in the Straits Settlements', *SSLCP 1908*, pp.C96, C101.

[15] James C. Ingram, 'Thailand's rice trade and the allocation of resources' in C. D. Cowan, ed. *The economic development of South-East Asia* (London, 1964), p.107.

[16] Netherlands India, 'Het Handelsverkeer met Singapore, 1825–1937', pp.7, 10; Netherlands India, Central Bureau of Statistics, Concept Publicatie C. K. S. (Mededeeling no. 163), 'Handelsbetrekkingen met Nederland, 1825–1937' (unpublished typescript, 1938), p.13.

Table 2.5 *Singapore imports of rice and dried and salted fish, 1897/99* (*annual averages*)

	Rice		Dried and salted fish	
	$000	%	$000	%
Siam	11,113	51.5	1,449	26.8
Burma	6,138	28.4	14	0.2
Indo–China	3,186	14.8	2,352	43.5
Others	1,152	5.3	1,597	29.5
Total	**21,589**	**100.0**	**5,412**	**100.0**

Sources: as for table 2.4.

Examination of the main goods Singapore re-shipped to the region (table 2.6) indicates how trade grew through successive rounds of import and re-shipment. Rice, comprising 13% of the value of Singapore's exports in 1897/99, and second only to tin, went chiefly to Netherlands India and Malaya, which took four-fifths of the port's rice exports. While Malaya bought some cotton piece goods, the port's main markets were in Netherlands India, and in Siam where Singapore Chinese traders paid for rice partly with piece goods.[17] Dried fish was required chiefly in Netherlands India, but Burma provided a significant market, since Chinese merchants in Rangoon traded fish for rice. Sugar imports, very largely from Java, were used partly in Singapore, which manufactured confectionery for export. But most sugar was sold to the region, including the Outer Provinces.

A further feature of the structure of Singapore's trade was the importance of China (including Hong Kong) and India (tables 2.2 and 2.3). Trade with both areas was essentially an extension of the regional economy. Imports from China were principally food and simple manufactures to meet the demand created by Chinese workers in Malayan and Netherlands Indian export industries. Similarly, India provided a range of goods required by Indian workers, while gunnies from Bombay mills were sent via Singapore to Indo-Chinese and Siamese rice exporters and to Javanese sugar exporters. However, specie accounted for about half of imports from India and opium another quarter. The opium was used by Chinese labourers throughout the region as well as in Singapore, where

[17] C. W. Darbishire, 'Commerce and currency' in Walter Makepeace, Gilbert E. Brooke and Roland St. J. Braddell, eds. *One hundred years of Singapore*. Two vols. (London, 1921), II, p.41.

Table 2.6 *Singapore exports to the region, 1897/99 (annual averages)*

	Malay Peninsula and Straits Settlements		Netherlands India		Siam		Burma		Indo–China		Others		Total	
	$000	%	$000	%	$000	%	$000	%	$000	%	$000	%	$000	%
Rice	7,052	37.2	8,017	42.2	5	0.0	3	0.0	1	0.0	3,900	20.6	18,978	100.0
Cotton piece goods	667	9.6	2,755	39.8	2,508	36.2	105	1.5	102	1.5	789	11.4	6,926	100.0
Dried and salted fish	287	5.5	3,602	69.1	2	0.0	966	18.5	19	0.4	337	6.5	5,213	100.0
Sugar	391	22.4	230	13.2	448	25.7	68	3.9	0	0.0	607	34.8	1,744	100.0
Gunnies	124	5.1	412	16.8	586	24.0	1	0.0	1,094	44.7	230	9.4	2,447	100.0
Opium	1,515	22.6	1,512	22.5	1,020	15.2	0	0.0	27	0.4	2,643	39.3	6,717	100.0

Sources: as for table 2.4.

60% of coal coolies were said to be smokers.[18] Opium, rice and sugar accounted for a considerable proportion of exports to China, which otherwise consisted largely of tropical produce, also the main exports to India.

II

The significance for Singapore of the tin industry's late nineteenth-century organization was the port's role in the provision of the two main factor requirements: labour and circulating capital. Malaya's rich alluvial tin deposits could be exploited by simple open cast mining which allowed the industry to be developed by small-scale Chinese enterprises numbering well over a thousand towards the end of the century. In 1903 it required 224,000 men to produce 51,000 tons of tin because of the industry's extensive nature and its dependence on manual labour to excavate large quantities of the overburden of alluvial soil and then repeatedly to wash the tin-bearing gravel in the extraction of tinstone.[19]

Chinese immigration via Singapore furnished the great bulk of the constantly changing mining labour force. The tin industry was the chief influence on immigration, and the two were closely correlated. The number of Chinese immigrants landed annually at Singapore rose from 10,000 in 1877 to 101,000 in 1887, corresponding with an increase in Malayan tin production from 3,000 tons in 1877 to 24,000 tons in 1887. In the first part of the 1890s another burst of expansion began, which culminated in 1895, when immigration and tin production simultaneously peaked at 150,000 persons and 50,000 tons respectively, before both declined somewhat at the end of the century.[20] Singapore's Chinese population, however transient, reflected this immigration, and between 1881 and 1901 more than doubled, to reach 142,000 persons. By the end of the century, three-quarters of the town's inhabitants were Chinese.[21]

The tin industry's other main factor requirement was for the circulating capital – at least four-fifths of production costs – needed to maintain the

[18] *Commission to enquire into the use of opium in the Straits Settlements and the Federated Malay States.* Three vols. (PP 1909, LXI), I, p.12.

[19] Henry Louis, 'The production of tin', *Mining Journal, Railway and Commercial Gazette* 69 (10 June 1899), p.676; C. G. Wardford Lock, *Economic mining* (London, 1895), pp.624–25; *Reports on the Federated Malay States for 1903* (PP 1905, LIV), pp.6–7; Wong Lin Ken, *The Malayan tin industry to 1914* (Tucson, 1965), pp.63, 85.

[20] *Reports on the Federated Malay States for 1901* (PP 1902, LXVI), p.24; A. M. Pountney, *Federated Malay States: review of census operations and results, 1911* (London, 1911), p.64. For the immigration figures see *Report of the commissioners appointed to enquire into the state of labour in the Straits Settlements and protected native states, 1890* (Singapore, 1891), appx. E, p.1; 'Report of the protector of Chinese', *SSAR 1899*, p.306.

[21] SS, *Blue book 1881*, p.P12, and see tables 5.4 and 5.5 below.

mining labour force.[22] Singapore Chinese traders, who supplied much of this circulating capital, typically did so through a goods-credit-marketing interlinked transaction.[23] The goods (food and manufactures) required by the mine owner were advanced on credit and the debt liquidated by the return shipment of tin produced; these transactions were interlinked, because they depended on one another and were simultaneously, not separately, negotiated and agreed.

This goods-credit-marketing arrangement conducted through Singapore is best described as book-keeping barter.[24] The transaction was barter in the sense that goods were supplied in exchange for a promise of the future provision of primary commodities such as tin, which were used to repay or to reduce the debt created by the initial advance of goods. A book-keeping element entered because it was necessary to keep track of the balances between the two parties over successive transactions. A monetary standard based on one or other of the various metallic monies which circulated in the region could provide a numeraire to express debits and credits. However, metallic money was typically unimportant, if used at all, in settlement. Such arrangements were prevalent in Singapore's late nineteenth- (and, indeed, twentieth-) century trade and will be referred to in this study simply as barter rather than book-keeping barter.

In the tin industry this barter system was mutually convenient to miners and merchants as a means of credit in a pioneer economy.[25] Debts could

[22] Yip Yat Hoong, *The development of the tin mining industry of Malaya* (Kuala Lumpur, 1969), pp.86, 90, 119; C. G. Wardford Lock, *Mining in Malaya for gold and tin* (London, 1907), p.173; Drake, 'Natural resources', pp.954–55. Circulating capital refers to capital, mainly in the form of raw materials and wages to maintain the labour force, consumed in the process of mining. It contrasts with fixed capital such as machinery or permanent improvements. The concepts of circulating and fixed capital were developed by J. S. Mill, *Principles of political economy* (London, 1909), book 1, chapters 5 and 6. For a discussion of the classical idea of circulating capital, see Walter Eltis, *The classical theory of economic growth* (London, 1984), pp.75, 76, 167–68, 224–25.

[23] On the concept of interlinked transactions, see Pranab K. Bardhan, 'Interlocking factor markets and agrarian development: a review of issues', *Oxford Economic Papers* 32, 1 (1980), pp.82–98; Pan A. Yotopoulos and Sagrario L. Floro, 'Income distribution, transaction costs and market fragmentation in informal credit markets', *Cambridge Journal of Economics* 16, 3 (1992), pp.303–26.

[24] On barter, see W. G. Huff, 'Bookkeeping barter, money, credit and Singapore's international rice trade, 1870–1939', *Explorations in Economic History* 26, 2 (1989) and 'Editor's note' 27, 3 (1990). In addition to the discussion of regional monetary arrangements in the above article, see King, *Money*, pp.1–11; Lee Sheng-Yi, *Monetary and banking development of Malaysia and Singapore* (Singapore, 1974), p.7; P. J. Drake, 'Southeast Asian monies and the problem of a common measure, with particular reference to the nineteenth century', *Australian Economic History Review* 31, 1 (1991), pp.90–96.

[25] This and the next paragraph are based on Martin Lister, *Mining laws and customs in the Malay Peninsula* (Singapore, 1889), pp.5–11, 17–19; Patrick Doyle, *Tin mining in Larut* (London, 1879), pp.9–11; J. C. Pasqual, 'Chinese tin mining in Selangor', *Selangor Journal* 4 (1895), p.100; Wong, *Malayan tin industry*, pp.60, 64, 154.

run over long periods and credit had an important role for Singapore traders and for those in the hinterland. Barter offered both a form of insurance against a cessation of business. For miners, barter might be the only way to obtain necessary goods, for the purchase of which they lacked either cash or an alternative source of credit. For Singapore Chinese traders, there was a preference for advancing in goods rather than in cash. Advancing in goods had four advantages. First, it helped to overcome chronic late nineteenth-century shortages of cash in the region and even in Singapore. When sufficient cash was unavailable, barter allowed the adoption of a single monetary standard as a unit of account. Second, Singapore Chinese traders could obtain many of the goods on credit from European merchants. Third, some profit could be realized from the supply of goods. Finally, because goods were less fungible than cash, barter arrangements helped to ensure that the loan would be used to prospect for tin. Typically, goods were supplied through a mines advancer whose knowledge of a mining district and ability to collect loans minimized a Singapore trader's risk.

The framework of property rights and contracts which, under British rule, developed with the mining industry were important to its expansion, since this legal underpinning largely ensured a supply of credit even when the miner failed to discover enough tin to cover the advances. The system of advancing to miners which emerged in effect provided a substitute for the collateral which miners lacked. Once having received an advance, a miner remained bound to his advancer wherever he went, so long as the advancer continued to make credit available. Once tin had been found in sufficient quantities, the advancer could exercise his right to buy it at below market prices. But an advancer who ceased credit could not legally recover his advances, and forfeited the right to buy tin subsequently discovered by a miner. Trust and social sanction in the Chinese community, backed up by legally enforceable contracts but also by abundant, and relatively easily found, surface tin deposits, combined to promote a smooth working of these credit arrangements.

The stimulus of the tin industry to Singapore's commercial development was considerable. Singapore Chinese traders made profits from providing credit and financial services as well as goods. Thus, it was observed that in the tin industry 'advances bear a very enhanced rate over cash purchases',[26] a margin which included the Chinese traders' profit, administration costs and a risk premium. Chinese in Singapore may also have realized at least some element of monopoly profit due to superior knowledge of, and contacts in, a specific tin-producing region. By 1889/91 Singapore exported

---

[26] Lister, *Mining laws*, p.8.

an annual average of 19,900 tons of tin, which suggests that its mercantile community was providing goods and credit in the form of barter, with its substantial profits, for as many as 87,000 miners in the Malay States.[27]

The barter system also had significance for Singapore because British administrators considered its credit structure essential to the tin industry. To protect this credit structure, the export of tin ore from the Malay Peninsula was prohibited to discourage its theft and sale for cash to an emerging class of tin ore dealers. The prohibition protected Chinese smelters in the Malay states from outside competition. As a result, all tin ore was smelted at or near the mines and reached Chinese merchants in the Straits ports in the form of slag metal. There it was sold to European merchants, probably partly as payment for credit which had been extended in the form of goods. These merchants further refined the metal before exporting it.[28]

In non-ferrous metallurgy, ore has almost invariably moved to fuel, since this is the main raw material in the smelting process. Chinese smelting near the mines had economic advantages while transport costs remained high and as long as charcoal was locally available as fuel. However, it had two increasingly serious drawbacks as a British Malayan transport network developed and charcoal became more scarce: a smelting technique which recovered only about 60% of tin from ore 75% pure, and the need for European merchants further to refine the metal. Both drawbacks could be overcome by reverberatory furnace smelting, but early attempts to do this in the Malay states failed because of the high cost of importing the necessary coal.

So long as political constraints demanded that smelting be confined to British Malaya, Singapore had two great locational advantages which reconciled this protectionism with technical efficiency. First, Singapore was a major port and coaling station, which made it easy to import fuel from the cheapest world sources. Second, Singapore offered an excellent site for the smelting industry on the island of Pulau Brani in the harbour half a mile from the main wharves. Coal could be brought by barge from the main store at the port or discharged directly from ships; while the

[27] On the basis of 1903 figures, it took 4·4 mine workers a year to produce one ton of tin. *Reports on the FMS, 1903*, pp.6–7; FMS, *Report on the administration of the mines department and on the mining industry 1905* (Kuala Lumpur, 1906), p.5.
[28] Discussion of tin smelting is based on Walter Makepeace, 'The machinery of commerce' in Makepeace, et al., eds. *One hundred years* II, pp.219–25; Lock, *Mining in Malaya*, pp.116–17; John McKillop and Thomas Flower Ellis, 'Tin smelting at Pulau Brani, Singapore', *Proceedings of the Institution of Civil Engineers* 125, 3 (1896), pp.145–49, 161; Thomas Flower Ellis, 'A brief account of the Malay tin industry', *Proceedings of the Chemical and Metallurgical Society of South Africa* 2 (1897), pp.10–12; Wong, *Malayan tin industry*, pp.156, 160–66; K. G. Tregonning, *Straits tin* (Singapore, 1962), pp.13–18, 21; Yip, *Development of tin mining*, pp.106–8.

island had sufficient storage space to allow fuel to be purchased in quantity when prices were low.

James Sword and Herman Muhlinghaus, who worked for different Singapore agency houses, recognized these advantages, but before they could begin smelting by reverberatory furnace in Singapore, two problems had to be solved. The first was to gain permission to export ore from the Malay states. Having obtained this, the second was to find ore to buy. Sword and Muhlinghaus had been granted a monopoly on the export of ore from Selangor which led them initially to set up a reverberatory furnace in Perak, as the largest tin-producing state and one from which ore could not be exported. But with the failure of this project, and following the renewal of the Selangor monopoly, in 1890 Sword's and Mulinghaus' enterprise, now called the Straits Trading Company (STC), opened its head office in Singapore, near the company's reverberatory furnaces on Pulau Brani. Subsequently, prohibitive duties on the export of tin ore outside the Straits Settlements except to the United Kingdom protected tin smelting at Singapore. The duties were imposed, not on infant industry grounds, but because of official British determination to keep tin supplies entirely under Empire control. That was successfully done, despite repeated attempts by United States interests to smelt Malayan tin either in America or in the Straits Settlements.[29]

The STC met the problem of purchasing ore by developing an alternative to the Chinese barter system. The company established a credit structure using cash rather than goods. The effect was to reduce interlinkage to only a credit-marketing one. Buying stations were set up by the STC throughout the principal mining districts. The cash payments and advances made by these stations competed effectively with the barter system, since with cash miners and tin ore dealers could obtain goods at lower shop prices,[30] either from local Chinese shops or from Singapore. Moreover, the STC usually offered substantially higher prices than its Chinese rivals because of more efficient smelting and a superior assay method. The STC was not interested in buying tin ore through mines advancers, as the company could obtain ore more cheaply through paying cash. Nor did the company wish to advance goods in competition with mines advancers, since it found cash more convenient, and was a smelter, not a merchant. Access to Singapore's

[29] Wong, *Malayan tin industry*, pp.229–30; S. B. Saul, 'The economic significance of "constructive imperialism"', *Journal of Economic History* 18, 2 (1957), pp.184–87; PRO CO 273/508/Y21011, CO minute, 30 April 1920, and see CO 273/501/Gov.48674, letter from Sir Laurence Guillemard, Governor SS to Rt. Hon. Viscount Milner, Secretary of State, CO, 25 Aug. 1920; CO 273/512/B of T 138, letter from the Board of Trade to Under Secretary of State, CO, 1 Jan. 1921.

[30] *Further papers relating to the Malay States. Reports for 1890* (Annual report by the British resident of Perak) (PP 1892, LVI), p.10.

European banks allowed the STC easily to obtain cash and secure credit at lower interest rates than Chinese ore buyers. Furthermore, as the STC increasingly gained a monopsony position in Malaya, default risk due to advancing in cash rather than goods lessened. It became harder for Chinese miners to take the company's cash for use outside the tin industry, while continuing to mine for tin by dealing with independent Chinese mines advancers.

In the 1890s the STC, with no European competitors, rapidly expanded at the expense of Chinese smelters in the Malay states. By 1898/99 the company produced an annual average of 25,100 tons of tin, nearly two-thirds of Malayan, and one-third of world, output. Nor did a dominant position and shelter behind export duties breed inefficiency: the STC 'attained a greater degree of scientific and technical perfection than can probably be claimed for any other tin-smelting establishment'.[31]

The attenuation of the barter system altered – and probably reduced – the tin industry's commercial impact on Singapore. By the end of the century the expansionary effects on the Chinese mercantile community arising from the profitability of the barter system had lessened. Nevertheless, supplies for tin miners had to be obtained directly or indirectly through Straits ports, and by the late 1890s the shift in tin production to the southern Malay states meant that Singapore merchants and traders may have supplied up to 100,000 mine workers in Selangor, Negri Sembilan and Pahang.[32]

The development of smelting in Singapore concentrated tin marketing there, and put Singapore's role in financing the tin industry in the hands of European institutions. Initially, the STC borrowed from the Chartered Bank of India, Australia and China to pay cash for tin ore. The company soon established a policy whereby it offset cash purchases of ore by simultaneously selling the metal content to exporters for delivery when the tin had been smelted. Consequently, tin-exporting European merchant houses, which borrowed from their own British bankers, were financing purchases of ore and its smelting.[33] However, advances to Chinese ore dealers and miners were still financed by the STC, under a system described in chapter 3.

The STC was the outstanding example in colonial Singapore – and one of the few instances in pre-World War II Southeast Asia – of the investment of expatriate European mercantile capital in industry. When

---

[31] Henry Louis, *Metallurgy of tin* (New York, 1911), p.117, and see p.130; FMS, *Manual of statistics relating to the Federated Malay States, 1920* (Kuala Lumpur, 1920), p.217.
[32] *Reports on the FMS, 1903*, pp.6–7.
[33] Makepeace, 'Machinery of commerce', p.221; Tregonning, *Straits tin*, pp.11–12; Wong, *Malayan tin industry*, p.165.

the partnership of Muhlinghaus and Sword went public in 1887, finance was raised through members of the European agency house, Gilfillan Wood & Co. But 'the handsome profits' realized by the STC and its obvious strength[34] soon attracted widespread support from Singapore's European business community: the '1901–1906 Share Register List, a book of 466 pages, had listed as shareholders nearly all the names of the local business leaders'.[35]

III

Late nineteenth-century exports of tropical produce had at least as great an expansionary effect on Singapore as those of tin, exceeding them in value as well as in volume (appendix tables A.1 and A.2). The produce trade spread even more widely than tin through Singapore's mercantile community. It relied entirely on a complementary relationship between Chinese importers and European exporters, while the variety of produce imports and geographical diversity of their source involved a large number of Singapore Chinese firms in the collection of produce from the port's hinterland. The produce and tin trades shared a common structure of European merchant houses and Chinese rice firms. Produce contributed as much, and probably more, than tin to the development of merchant houses and rice firms, because of the high value of produce exports and because hinterland production depended on small producers who required imports of rice and consumer goods in exchange for exports.

For produce, Singapore developed as 'the largest and most representative market in this part of the world' and through its merchants 'finances the majority of the ventures in the surrounding countries'.[36] The links between Singapore and its hinterland were those established by the Chinese, as 'The European merchant does nothing to introduce the imports of produce, nor does he have any share in the distribution of the imports of manufactured goods'.[37] Throughout the Outer Provinces, local Chinese dominated trade. Singapore Chinese were in a strong position to deal with these traders: in much of this commerce they had advantages over their Javanese counterparts of closer blood ties with local Chinese and

[34] Louis, 'Production of tin', p.707, and see Louis, *Metallurgy*, pp.128–29.
[35] Tregonning, *Straits tin*, p.26, and see pp.15–16; Makepeace, 'Machinery of commerce', p.226. [36] *Commission on the Straits Homeward Conference, 1902*, p.13.
[37] Song, *One hundred years' history*, p.382. Song quoted J. M. Allinson, a former member of the Straits Settlements Legislative Council, writing from Manchester in 1906; *SSTC 1933–34* II, p.85; Tan Tek Soon, 'Chinese local trade', *Straits Chinese Magazine* 6, 23 (1902), pp.93–95.

in Singapore a better location and regional shipping network than
Batavia.[38]

Finance from Singapore Chinese was through a goods-credit-marketing
interlinkage – or barter system – like that described for tin. In trade with
the Outer Provinces, copra, for example, was bartered for rice and other
goods.[39] For this regional trade, barter mediated through Singapore
helped to reduce uncertainty over the value and acceptability of money
arising from the lack of a single monetary standard, since Netherlands
India had a gold, rather than the more common silver, standard. Singapore
Chinese secured a hold over the Netherlands Indian produce trade by
financing it, and the same was true of the Malayan gambier and pepper
industry, chiefly in Johore, with perhaps 30,000 cultivators. There the
credit system had two stages. Initially, a so-called kangchu, backed by
several Singapore gambier and pepper firms, secured land and attracted
cultivators by supplying them with all their needs for the 18 months before
the first crop. Then the kangchu, while retaining opium, gambling and
other profitable monopolies, distributed among his Singapore creditors the
cultivators' debts and their produce. In this second stage, until the
cultivator could pay his debt (if ever) he was bound to a Singapore trader,
who 'supplies him with rice, groceries and money for further planting, all
at stipulated prices, and receives his produce in exchange, with deductions
for weight according to a defined scale, and at prices regulated by his guild
(the Gambier and Pepper Society), about 30% below the actual market
value'.[40]

Late nineteenth-century expansion gave rise to several large Chinese
produce firms. Some of the largest traders were also shipowners, for the
two activities were at this time closely related. Trade expansion appears to
have led to an increase in the number of firms and resulted in greater
specialization among them. By 1900, in addition to Singapore's many
gambier and pepper firms, there were others which specialized in the copra,
sago, rattan and gutta percha trades.[41]

Unlike Chinese firms, European exporters of produce were comparatively few and often long-established. They linked Singapore's produce

[38] G. C. Allen and Audrey G. Donnithorne, *Western enterprise in Indonesia and Malaya*
(London, 1954), pp.216–18; M. G. de Boer and J. C. Westermann, *Een Halve Eeuw
Paketvaart, 1891–1941* (Amsterdam, 1941), pp.38, 53–58, 224.

[39] *Commission on the Straits Homeward Conference, 1902*, evidence, pp.29, 28, 19, 89–90.

[40] Tan, 'Chinese local trade', pp.91–92, and see A. E. Coope, 'The kangchu system in
Johore', *JMBRAS* 14, 3 (1936), pp.249, 251, 261; Jackson, *Planters*, pp.16–22, 36–45;
Song, *One hundred years' history*, pp.36–37; C. M. Turnbull, 'The Johore gambier and
pepper trade in the mid-nineteenth century', *Journal of the South Seas Society* 15, 1 (1959),
p.46.

[41] *Directory 1899*, pp.158F–158I; *SSTC 1933–34* II, pp.99, 102; Song, *One hundred years'
history*, pp.160, 173, 350–52, 382.

trade to Western markets just as the Chinese did to hinterland sources. European exporters bought the produce through Chinese brokers, and a large market centred on Boat Quay along the Singapore River (figure 2.3).[42] Most of the big European exporters were also agents for shipping lines and/or merchant charterers, in which capacities they bargained to handle the exports of other European firms.[43]

IV

In the late nineteenth century the regional transport network acquired its modern components. Local shipping services organized by interests in Europe and a shipping line started by Europeans and Chinese in Singapore were added to Singapore's many Chinese shipowners. Further, development of the Malayan railway system began, in the wake of the tin industry's need for efficient transport in the Malay states. In comparison to other staple ports, the regional transport network which focused on Singapore was unusual because of the maritime nature of Singapore's hinterland, Singapore's own status as an island and the fact that until 1923 Singapore could be reached directly only by sea. As a result, regional transport established in conjunction with exports to the West relied heavily on local shipping services. Much of the developmental impact of this transport network accrued to Singapore, since local shipping was largely based on the port. Moreover, because shipping lines, unlike railways, required relatively small amounts of capital to establish, especially with the frequent use of second-hand shipping tonnage,[44] they could easily be owned by Singaporeans, with consequent substantial spread effects for Singapore's economy.

Local shipping had long proved an attractive investment outlet for Chinese capital. In 1885 a new arrival in Singapore found 'The harbour was pretty well filled with a fleet of small steamships', belonging to various Chinese in the town.[45] Among the most important late nineteenth-century Chinese lines were the Bun Hin (Green Funnel) of Khoo Tiong Poh with some 15 steamers, and Wee Bin & Co., which had a fleet of 20 vessels. As well as shipowners, Wee Bin & Co. were also traders, sago manufacturers and merchant bankers, and had several branches in Netherlands India.[46]

[42] *SSTC 1933–34* I, p.42, II, pp.85–86, 93–94, 98, 362, 376; Chiang Hai Ding, 'Sino-British mercantile relations in Singapore's entrepot trade 1870–1915' in Jerome Ch'en and Nicholas Tarling, eds. *Studies in the social history of China and South-East Asia* (London, 1970), p.257.
[43] *SSTC 1933–34* II, pp.99, 80; Chiang, *History of Straits Settlements trade*, p.47.
[44] *SSTC 1933–34* IV, p.255.   [45] Ibid. II, p.99.
[46] Ibid. II, pp.74–75, 93, 98, 99, IV, p.255; *Directory 1899*, pp.154–55, 158H; 'The shipping commission', *SSLCP 1899*, p.C182; Song, *One hundred years' history*, pp.114, 119,

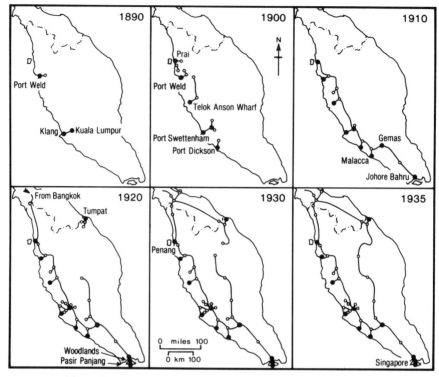

Figure 2.4   Malayan railway system, 1890–1935

From 1880 Chinese shipping lines were joined by three new companies representing interests in Europe: Alfred Holt & Company's Ocean Steamship Co. (the Blue Funnel Line), Norddeutscher Lloyd and the Koninklijke Paketvaart Maatschappij.[47] All three companies were attracted to the Netherlands Indian carrying trade because of the bulkiness of its produce. They established fleets which, by obtaining transhipment cargo, could act as feeder services to specific companies operating main line vessels.

By contrast, there was little incentive for ocean-going firms concerned with finding profitable transhipment cargoes to invest in the transhipment of tin and tin ore from the Malayan west coast to Singapore. While

143–44, 164, 173, 176, 201, 218, 350–53; Wright and Cartwright, *Twentieth century impressions*, pp.177, 180–81.

[47] A. Jackson and C. E. Wurtzburg, *The history of Mansfield & Company, part I, 1868–1924* (Singapore, 1952), pp.1–6; Francis E. Hyde, *Blue Funnel: a history of Alfred Holt and Company of Liverpool from 1865 to 1914* (Liverpool, 1956), pp.51–53, 83–86, 93–98, 158; Francis E. Hyde, 'British shipping companies in East and South-East Asia' in Cowan, ed. *Economic development*, pp.37–39.

smelting centred in the Malay states, tin, even insofar as it was transhipped at Singapore, was an unremunerative cargo for ocean-going vessels. They carried tin at low rates, or sometimes even free, because its compactness and easy stowage made it a good ballast.[48] The shift in smelting to Singapore, which coincided with a rapid expansion of Malayan production, greatly increased the demand for local shipping to the port. But because it was essentially a demand for the carriage of tin ore to be smelted and not transhipped at Singapore, this business also held little attraction for ocean-going firms, and was left to local interests.

The foundation of the Straits Steamship Company (SSC) was a direct and immediate response from Singapore to new opportunities in the west coast trade for the carriage of tin ore, and also of immigrant workers and a return flow of imports. Formation of the shipping company depended on the entrepreneurship of local Europeans and Chinese as well as chiefly on their investment, although Holts was also involved. The SSC was established in 1890, when the Straits Trading Company began its Singapore smelting operations in earnest, and 'both new Companies grew together'.[49] All tin ore which the STC smelted in Singapore was carried by the SSC, and for the shipping company the backward and forward linkages set up by the tin industry were the basis of its business: in 1900 its six vessels, including two new ones, were almost wholly confined to routes along the west coast of the Peninsula.[50]

The Malayan railway (figure 2.4) complemented the network of local shipping. Between 1885 and 1895 railways took the form of short, east–west lines which connected each of the main tin-mining districts with its coastal port: Port Weld (1885), Klang (1888), Port Dickson (1891) and Telok Anson (1895). Local shipping linked these ports to Singapore and Penang. Even before the turn of the century, however, the railway system, following the major valleys, began to turn north–south, and so towards Singapore. By 1903 the north-south pattern was well-established, although it was only because of the influence of rubber that the railway finally reached Singapore.[51]

The experience of British Malaya supports economic development theories of unbalanced growth and leading-sector linkage effects as

[48] *Report of the royal commission on shipping rings*. Five vols. (PP 1909, XLVII and XLVIII), IV, pp.1–2, 3, 179, 275; *Commission on the Straits Homeward Conference, 1902*, evidence, p.2.   [49] Tregonning, *Straits tin*, p.18.
[50] K. G. Tregonning, *Home port Singapore: A history of the Straits Steamship Company Limited, 1890–1965* (Singapore, 1967), pp.16–39; 'The story of the Straits Steamship Co.', *British Malaya* (May 1927), pp.19–20; Jackson and Wurtzburg, *Mansfield & Co.*, p.3.
[51] C. A. Fisher, 'The railway geography of British Malaya', *Scottish Geographical Magazine* 64, 3 (1948), pp.124–28; *Reports on the FMS, 1901*, p.3, *1903*, p.22; Federated Malay States Railways, *Fifty years of railways in Malaya, 1885–1935* (Kuala Lumpur, 1935), p.7.

opposed to a 'big push' stressing simultaneous creation of a large number of industries and facilities in a balanced development effort.[52] Development began with rapid growth in one sector – mining – and this led to response in others – transport, processing and trade. The result was to shift the whole west coast Malayan economy onto a higher development plane, with Singapore as its communications, commercial and financial centre. A fundamental difference between the usual assumption of a closed economy made in a big push model and circumstances in British Malaya was the latter's extreme openness to international trade. The high degree of British Malayan economic specialization resulting from this openness to trade and consequent unbalanced growth, persisted into the 1960s; Malaya's was a 'lopsided pattern of development'.[53] The particular role of Singapore in this pattern, established in the late nineteenth century, was as a service centre.

Late nineteenth-century developments shaped the way that those in Singapore viewed the hinterland. From 1874 the extension of British rule over the four tin mining states, which led to the establishment of the Federated Malay States, and Singapore's new economic and political interest in them, might have presaged British Malayan political unification. However, Singapore began as an international fair and late nineteenth-century trade expansion based on the simultaneous growth of imports from Netherlands India and Malaya perpetuated the idea of a fair. The increase in Singapore's trade with Netherlands India kept this commerce larger than trade with Malaya. In consequence, the sympathies of the town's residents remained strongly in favour of free port status.

Singapore's history in the twentieth century was to be similar. In British Malaya, the rubber industry underscored the case for political union by promoting British rule in the Unfederated Malay States and emphasizing geographical unity through the development of a common staple and the railway system. But in Singapore, the rapid growth after 1910 of trade with Netherlands India ensured that those in the city retained wide economic interests, difficult to accommodate within any British Malayan or Malaysian political grouping.

---

[52] For a discussion of these theories, see P. N. Rosenstein-Rodan, 'Problems of industrialisation in eastern and south-eastern Europe', *Economic Journal* 53 (1943), pp.202–11 and 'Notes on the theory of the "big push"' in Howard S. Ellis, ed. *Economic development for Latin America* (London, 1961), pp.57–73; Hirschman, *Strategy of economic development*, pp.29–75 and 'Generalized linkage approach to development'.

[53] Nurkse, *Patterns of trade and development*, p.18; see also Ragnar Nurkse, 'International investment to-day in the light of nineteenth-century experience', *Economic Journal* 64 (1954), p.753.

Part Two

Development as a staple port, 1900–1939

3   Trade, finance and development

Singapore developed in response to changes occurring outside it and independent of its existence. The point was made in chapter 2 that the chief factors underlying this development were a growing world demand for the primary products of Malaya and Netherlands India and the shipping links available to Singapore by virtue of its strategic position on the primary world east–west shipping route. These factors were equally important during the first four decades of the twentieth century.

Since trade as an engine of growth depended on rubber and petroleum after 1900, this study now turns to an examination of their expansion and role in Singapore's economic development. The focus cannot be exclusively on these two commodities, however. The traditional trades of tin, tropical produce and rice, although no longer the dynamic elements in growth, were important to it, for as well as continuing to demand infrastructural services and providing a fund of experience on which Singapore could draw, their still high volume and value made growth a matter of building on an existing foundation of trade rather than of having to start anew.

The present chapter analyses why trade centred on Singapore, how it was financed and what its principal development implications were. Sections I and II consider the course of Singapore's trade and the main volume, value and development features of primary commodity exports to the West. The third section looks at the geographical distribution of Singapore's primary commodity imports re-exported to the West, and changes in the source of these imports as Singapore became a staple port. Finance for primary commodity exports is considered in a fourth section. Because hinterland rubber and petroleum production did not simply reproduce earlier developmental patterns, and because these patterns also changed for tin, Singapore's trade became much more complex in its organization. The next four sections of the chapter discuss how trade was organized and some of the implications of differences in organization for Singapore's economic development. A final section draws attention to perceptions in Singapore of its economic interests consequent on the port's patterns of trade.

I

After 1900 Singapore's trade, shown by figures 2.1 and 2.2 and appendix tables A.1 and A.2, was a story of the relative stability in the volume of tin and tropical produce exported, a decline in rice exports during the inter-war period and very rapid expansion in the volume of rubber and petroleum. Tin exports fluctuated around the 32,000 tons attained in 1901; changes mainly reflected the effects of international tin restriction schemes in the 1920s (the Bandoeng scheme) and again beginning in 1934 (the First International Tin Agreement). Exports of tropical produce, shown by appendix table A.2, grew from an average of 252,000 tons in 1900/01 to 336,000 tons in 1909/10, but moved around an average of 286,000 tons during the next three decades, when world prices for these commodities remained stable or, more often, declined.

After 1910, however, the composition of tropical produce exports changed considerably (tables 3.1 and 3.2). Demand for some commodities contracted markedly, for example rattans because cane furniture became less popular.[1] Similarly, exports of gutta percha, required chiefly as an insulator for submarine and underground cables, declined due to the greater use of the wireless.[2] In other instances, hinterland output fell as producers shifted into rubber, especially in Malaya, where gambier and pepper cultivation virtually disappeared and large areas of tapioca land were abandoned.[3] Decreases in produce coming to Singapore were largely made good by increased exports of copra and coconut oil, the former used as vegetable oil in the West and the latter as cooking oil in Asia.[4] By 1938/39 copra alone accounted for two-fifths of the volume and nearly a quarter of the value of Singapore's produce exports.

Rice was less stable than Singapore's other traditional trades. A World War I boom in exports arising from a shortage of shipping in the region and need to charter rice boats, which Singapore Chinese were quick to exploit, was immediately followed by a rice crisis from 1918 to 1921 when drought and poor harvests in producing countries drastically curtailed supplies. The control over rice sales which British Malayan governments assumed to protect local consumers[5] cost Singapore most of its rice trade,

---

[1] *SSTC 1933–34* I, p.44, IV, pp.137, 150, II, p.371.

[2] Ibid. I, p.44, IV, p.193, II, p.542; *Report by the Right Honourable W. G. A. Ormsby Gore, M. P. (Parliamentary Under-Secretary of State for the Colonies) on his visit to Malaya, Ceylon and Java during the year 1928* (PP 1928–29, V), p.60.

[3] *SSTC 1933–34* I, pp.43, 44, 46, IV, pp.85, 137, II, p.359; Kirby, 'Johore in 1926', p.244; J. N. Milsum, 'Pepper in Malaya', *MAJ* 18, 6 (1930), p.275; Jackson, *Planters*, pp.49–50.

[4] *SSTC 1933–34* I, p.43, III, pp.3, 420, 421, IV, pp.150, 407.

[5] 'Report on the Straits Settlements', *SSAR 1919*, pp.51–54, 57–58; *SSLCP 1919*, pp.B75, B183; 'Address by the Governor to members of the Legislative Council', *SSLCP 1920*,

Table 3.1 *Singapore volume of exports of ten important tropical commodities, 1900/01–1938/39 (tons, annual averages)*

	Arecanuts	Copra	Coconut oil	Gambier	Gums (ben-jamin, copal, dammar)	Gutta percha and gutta inferior (jelutong)	Pepper (black, white, long)	Rattans	Sago (flour, pearl)	Tapioca (flake, flour, pearl)	Total
1900/01	24,688	28,978	5,628	43,534	8,525	12,505	11,945	33,469	39,469	27,724	236,465
1909/10	39,857	66,622	6,988	29,504	13,282	25,150	21,811	25,914	64,237	24,163	317,528
1912/13	41,102	63,857	4,970	22,622	14,727	14,295	16,252	27,250	56,378	17,642	279,095
1917/18	33,847	56,712	8,723	11,142	9,324	6,750	22,297	18,063	35,535	17,543	219,936
1925/26	33,560	102,112	6,223	5,314	10,613	8,688	14,269	17,386	46,486	16,720	261,371
1929	37,134	117,851	n.a.	4,189	11,702	8,184	12,716	15,058	46,605	14,717	268,156
1933/34	29,404	122,179	10,552	4,013	9,595	5,504	17,589	11,224	61,671	12,573	284,304
1938/39	42,760	116,331	21,765	4,031	11,187	8,132	11,063	8,111	60,623	4,158	288,161

Notes:
1 Excludes exports to the Straits Settlements, 1929 and to Malaya, 1933/34 and 1938/39.
Sources: SS, *Return of imports and exports*, 1900–1927; *SSTC 1933-34* IV, pp.467–78; Malaya, *Foreign imports and exports*, 1933-1937; Malaya, *Foreign trade of Malaya*, 1938-1939.

Table 3.2 *Singapore value of exports of ten important tropical commodities, 1900/01–1938/39 ($000, annual averages)*

	Arecanuts	Copra	Coconut oil	Gambier	Gums (ben- jamin, copal, dammar)	Gutta percha and gutta inferior (jelutong)	Pepper (black, white, long)	Rattans	Sago (flour, pearl)	Tapioca (flake, flour, pearl)	Total
1900/01	2,335	3,582	1,340	6,955	1,948	15,492	6,512	6,592	2,316	3,012	50,085
1909/10	3,356	10,616	1,899	5,625	2,524	7,350	5,859	3,863	3,633	2,316	47,041
1912/13	4,402	12,646	1,722	3,827	3,084	5,292	6,676	4,340	3,710	2,048	47,747
1917/18	4,458	7,649	3,045	3,442	2,080	4,161	12,835	3,668	2,620	3,214	47,171
1925/26	9,926	20,894	2,355	1,986	3,471	7,303	11,210	4,733	5,077	2,112	69,066
1929	n.a.										
1933/34	2,765	7,502	1,109	515	1,591	1,931	8,215	1,723	2,547	1,068	28,965
1938/39	5,234	7,616	2,692	833	1,726	4,304	2,229	1,482	3,800	390	30,305

Notes:
1 Excludes exports to Malaya, 1933/34 and 1938/39.
2 Rows may not add to totals due to rounding.
Sources: as for table 3.1.

but by 1925/27 exports exceeded pre-war levels. In the 1930s, although rice exports declined substantially, due mainly to measures to promote food self-sufficiency in Netherlands India, the fall in Singapore's exports was less than suggested by appendix tables A.1 and A.2, which exclude shipments to Malaya after 1932.

From 1910 the change in the international economy which profoundly influenced Singapore's whole history was the great new demand for rubber; the growing need for petroleum further modified the course of development. World demand for rubber and petroleum resulted from product innovations in which Singapore played no part: the development of motorized transport. The automobile industry needed rubber for various components such as gaskets and tubing, but by far the main use for the commodity was in the manufacture of tyres. Between 1913 and the slump of the 1930s, the United States annually imported a half to three-quarters of world rubber production. Its automotive industry took three-quarters of these imports.[6] The market for petroleum was more varied than for rubber, but the enormous growth in Singapore's petroleum exports arose primarily from the spread of the motor car to the Far East and Australasia and the conversion of the world's mercantile marine to predominantly oil-fired ships.

A feature of Singapore's exports was the tendency for their growth to be out of phase with that of world trade in primary products as a whole. The expansion of tin and tropical produce had preceded the great increase in world primary exports between 1896 and 1913. Now the expansion of rubber and petroleum came at a time when world trade in primary products was once more sluggish.[7] Singapore's emergence as a staple port, begun with tin, was completed by rubber and petroleum. Rubber, the widespread planting of which started only at the beginning of this century, and petroleum, 'the twentieth century boom commodity',[8] provided late but spectacular opportunities for staple port development. From 1909 to 1929 Singapore's exports expressed in constant pounds sterling grew at an annual average rate of 4·7%, well above the 1870–1937 rate of 3·4% annually (table 2.1).

In response to the growing demand for rubber, the swift increase in its

pp.C175–C177 and *1921*, pp.C282–83; *Report of the commissions on the present state of trade depression and the extension of credit facilities* (Singapore, 1921), appx.1, p.19.
[6] William Woodruff, 'Growth of the rubber industry of Great Britain and the United States', *Journal of Economic History* 15, 4 (1955), pp.382–85; T. R. McHale, 'Changing technology and shifts in supply and demand for rubber: an analytical history', *MER* 9, 2 (1964), pp.31, 41. World rubber trade and absorption statistics are from Sir Andrew McFadyean, *The history of rubber regulation, 1934–1943* (London, 1944), pp.226–39.
[7] Folke Hilgerdt, *Industrialization and foreign trade* (Geneva: League of Nations, 1945), p.157.   [8] Nurkse, *Patterns of trade and development*, p.20.

cultivation in Malaya and Netherlands India put Singapore at the centre of one of history's greatest commodity booms; indeed, 'No other branch of agriculture has ever developed so rapidly'.[9] Because of the *Hevea* (rubber) tree's five- to seven-year maturation period, Singapore did not begin to export large quantities of rubber until World War I, but when earlier plantings came into bearing the port became the world's largest exporter. By 1919 Singapore exported 157,000 tons of rubber, accounting for two-fifths of world exports. During the 1920s the port began to receive large amounts of rubber from Netherlands India and by 1929 exported 254,000 tons, nearly a third of the world total, as well as handling a considerable volume of transhipment rubber, so that about 40% of world rubber exports still passed through the British port. In the 1930s rubber exports continued to increase, reaching an inter-war peak of 316,000 tons in 1934 prior to the International Rubber Regulation Scheme, agreed among producing countries to restrict output.

Rubber was linked to pineapples and palm oil, which, although relatively unimportant in export value, added substantially to the volume of exports, as appendix table A.2 shows. Both commodities were sent mainly to Britain, where British Malayan pineapples achieved a virtual monopoly as 'the poor man's dish'[10] and accounted for about one-quarter of all British imports of tinned fruit. Palm oil met some of the West's growing demand for vegetable oils.

Singapore Chinese grew pineapples between rubber saplings while waiting for these to mature: income from sales of the fruit greatly reduced the capital outlay needed to bring a rubber estate into bearing, and until the 1930s pineapple cultivation existed almost solely 'as a means to the end of inauguration of rubber plantations'.[11] The use of pineapples for estate development on Singapore island explains the increase in exports of the fruit ahead of rubber. By 1907 canned pineapple exports reached 27,000 tons and until World War I remained greater than rubber exports. During the 1920s the rapid opening of Chinese rubber estates in Johore caused pineapple exports to double to 55,000 tons; Singapore became the world's largest exporter of tinned pineapples after Hawaii.[12]

In the 1930s canned pineapple exports rose, initially because low rubber

[9] P. T. Bauer, *The rubber industry: a study in competition and monopoly* (London, 1948), p.25.
[10] D. H. Grist, 'The Malayan pineapple industry', *MAJ* 18, 4 (1930), p.189, and see *SSLCP 1934*, p.B9; 'Report on the pineapple conference', *SSLCP 1931*, p.C220.
[11] 'Pineapple conference', *SSLCP 1931*, p.C225, and see W. G. Huff, 'Sharecroppers, risk, management, and Chinese estate rubber development in inter-war British Malaya', *EDCC* 40, 4 (1992), pp.743–73.
[12] C. E. Courtenay, 'Malayan pineapples: part 1. Pre-war and post-war conditions', *British Malaya* (July 1952), p.30.

prices kept pineapples already inter-planted with *Hevea* in cultivation longer than normally. But from 1934 Singapore Chinese took the lead in growing the fruit on a permanent basis, and started large pineapple estates in Johore.[13] By 1939 Singapore's pineapple exports amounted to 74,000 tons.

Unlike pineapples, the development of oil palm estates in Malaya represented, not the spread of rubber, but an attempt to diversify by some European agency houses which had a leading role in the rubber industry. The provision in Singapore of bulk shipment facilities for palm oil facilitated the industry's expansion by greatly reducing its costs, and exports quadrupled from 9,000 tons in 1933 to 36,000 tons by 1939.

Petroleum was a twentieth-century addition to trade insofar as the two new products of motor spirit and fuel oil rather than the older one of kerosene brought petroleum exports to prominence in Singapore. In the inter-war period, distribution installations on islands near the western entrance to Singapore harbour formed 'a major world centre for the petroleum industry'[14] and transformed export volume at the port (figure 2.2). While as late as 1921 petroleum exports stood at only 10,000 tons, five years later they were 415,000 tons and by 1938 had increased to 743,000 tons.

The dominating position in Singapore's exports of rubber, tin and petroleum is shown by table 3.3. In 1915/17 the three comprised two-fifths by value of Singapore's exports; the proportion rose to nearly three-fifths in 1925/27, due to further rapid increases in rubber exports and the sudden growth of the petroleum trade. The actual importance of the three staples was even greater, since, due to Singapore's political independence from its hinterland, export statistics included the return flow of food and manufactured goods re-shipped from Singapore to the surrounding region, largely for sale to the producers of staple exports.

The impact on Singapore of the three staples is only broadly indicated by their respective contributions to exports. Despite tin's comparative stability, its economic role declined absolutely, while petroleum had a much less dramatic effect on the economy than on the statistics. The importance of rubber to the economy exceeded even its statistical prominence. Immigration moved largely in response to the rubber industry, and a greater inflow of immigrants was reflected in the growth of Singapore, where population doubled between 1911 and 1936. Rubber led to the expansion of shipping, railway and port facilities. Moreover, it was associated with several other major developmental features in the

---

[13] *SSTC 1933–34* I, p.200, II, pp.793, 802; A. W. King, 'Plantation and agriculture in Malaya, with notes on the trade of Singapore', *Geographical Journal* 93, 2 (1939), p.142; D. H. Grist, *Malayan agricultural statistics 1939* (Kuala Lumpur, 1940), table 49.

[14] King, 'Plantation and agriculture', p.146.

Table 3.3 Singapore exports of five major commodities, 1900/02–1937/39* (annual averages)

	Tin	Rubber	Petroleum	Rice	Cotton piece goods**	Total merchandise exports
(a) Tons						
1900/02	29,491	n.l.	38,192	321,006	2,833	
1911/13	28,784	3,752	12,675	371,178	2,697	
1915/17	36,724	50,492	32,252	610,159	2,990	
1925/27	33,950	190,704	410,694	379,510	78,653	
1933/35	27,487	268,307	453,166	123,054	44,961	
1937/39	32,993	256,974	683,903	137,311	26,299	
(b) $000						
1900/02	36,664	n.l.	2,021	22,778	8,793	196,625
1911/13	48,376	12,222	606	33,403	8,626	241,579
1915/17	55,746	109,844	1,753	48,802	11,717	391,220
1925/27	80,274	339,842	74,481	49,638	21,226	855,408
1933/35	49,755	93,958	45,948	7,155	4,512	284,950
1937/39	62,100	168,483	53,844	9,003	3,328	390,790
(c) % of total merchandise exports						
1900/02	18.6	n.l.	1.0	11.6	4.5	35.7
1911/13	20.0	5.1	0.3	13.8	3.6	42.8
1915/17	14.2	28.1	0.4	12.5	3.0	58.2
1925/27	9.4	39.7	8.7	5.8	2.5	66.1
1933/35	17.5	33.0	16.1	2.5	1.6	70.7
1937/39	15.9	43.1	13.8	2.3	0.9	76.0

*   Excludes exports to Malaya, 1933–39.
** Pieces 000 and, from 1925/27, yards 000.

Sources: SS, *Return of imports and exports*, 1900–1927; Malaya, *Foreign imports and exports*, 1933–1935; Malaya, *Foreign trade of Malaya*, 1937–1939.

European business community, principally the widespread adoption of the managing agency system and the establishment of oil palm estates.

Rubber had a much greater effect on the Chinese than the European mercantile community. A complex of rubber-pineapple interests, including estates, the milling of Netherlands Indian smallholder rubber and pineapple cultivation and canning, became easily the most conspicuous source of Singapore Chinese wealth, and provided a springboard for industrialization and the growth of local Chinese deposit banking. After 1910 major administrative and economic changes affecting Singapore's Chinese business community included the abolition of monopoly rights – so-called farms – to collect taxes on the sale of opium, which had formerly yielded Chinese syndicates substantial profits with little financial outlay or risk;[15] new technological requirements and greater capital intensity in tin mining and local shipping which began to make these once predominantly Chinese activities into European-dominated industries; and the stagnation of the tropical produce and rice trades. All these would have diminished the Chinese presence in Singapore's economy; it was the advent of rubber which offset such changes and fuelled an expansion of Chinese economic interests.

II

As in the late nineteenth century, movements in the value of Singapore's trade did not correspond to those in its volume. For value, growth in response to the international economy yielded the pattern of fluctuations shown by figure 2.1: a boom during World War I; the immediate post-war buying euphoria and world-wide inflation; collapse into depression from mid-1920 to 1922; a sharp upswing to the mid-1920s; and the slump in the early 1930s, succeeded by only partial recovery with a mini-boom in 1937. Imports and exports followed a closely similar course. The consistent margin of imports over exports represented imports retained for consumption in Singapore itself and items, chiefly coal and fuel oil bunkers, supplied to ships calling at Singapore, which were not deemed to be exports.

There are no estimates for Singapore's balance of payments. However, the inclusion in the official trade statistics of supplies for ships would have reduced somewhat the deficit on the trade account if the balance of payments had been compiled. Net exports of services related to trade, shipping and finance would probably at the least have made good much of the remaining current account deficit.

[15] W. G. Huff, 'Capital markets, sharecropping and contestability: Singapore Chinese in the inter-war British Malayan estate rubber and pineapple industries' in Gareth Austin and Kaoru Sugihara, eds. *Local suppliers of credit in the third world* (London, 1993), pp.291–92.

Commodity exports to the West were the main determinant of trade fluctuations. Most other exports were manufactures and food brought to Singapore for re-shipment to producers of primary commodities, and so fluctuated in response to Singapore's exports to the West. Similarly, imports reflected the export curve: a large proportion of imports were in fact primary commodities for re-export to the West, and most of the remainder were generated in the first instance through purchasing power arising from exports. The value of merchandise imports tended to lead rather than lag behind merchandise exports, principally because virtually all Singapore's exports to the West appeared first as imports, received services in the city and then were re-shipped.

While tin and to a lesser extent other major exports shared a similar chronological pattern to that of rubber, the last created the main contours of trade value, although never exceeding half of total merchandise exports (figure 2.1). Rubber did this because of its importance in Singapore's exports to the West and the large return flows of goods generated by rubber exports. The commodity's extreme fluctuations in value reflected high price inelasticities of supply and demand – even more so than for tin, since the supply of rubber was harder to curtail in a slump and more difficult to expand in the early stages of a boom. Demand for both rubber and tin was inelastic, because they provided a small but unsubstitutable proportion of the materials used in the production of automobiles and of tinned food, which remained the principal use for tin.[16]

From 1915 to the 1930s slump two-thirds to four-fifths of rubber was sent to the United States. Tin increased this dependence on the United States economy: over the period 1915 to 1939 usually between a half and two-thirds of tin exports went to America.[17] Because of rubber and tin, Singapore's exports shifted decisively towards the United States (table 3.4); in 1925/27 exports there were nearly two and a half times those to Europe and Britain, respectively the port's two largest markets for tropical produce. Manufactured imports did not mirror the realignment of Singapore's export markets in the West, and still came primarily from Britain and Europe (table 3.5). Petroleum shipments to Japan and Australia mainly explained the increased exports to those countries.

Because of the high export dependence on the United States and the demand and supply conditions for rubber, instability in the American

[16] League of Nations, *Economic stability in the post-war world* (Geneva, 1945), pp.77–81; Minchinton, *Tinplate industry*, pp.162–63; Bauer, *Rubber*, pp.28–30, 40; J. K. Eastham, 'Rationalisation in the tin industry', *Review of Economic Studies* 4, 1 (1937), p.13.

[17] SS, *Return of imports and exports* (Singapore), annual series, 1900–1920; *SSTC 1933–34* IV, pp.476, 479; Malaya, *The foreign trade of Malaya* (Singapore), annual series, *1935*, pp.155, 158, *1939*, pp.116, 119.

Table 3.4 *Singapore exports by country and region, 1911/13 and 1925/27*
(*annual averages*)

	1911/13		1925/27	
	$000	%	$000	%
Southeast Asia	**123,111**	**47.8**	**304,543**	**35.1**
Malay Peninsula	41,702	16.2	108,517	12.5
Inter–Port	16,783	6.5	40,114	4.6
Netherlands India	39,358	15.3	102,041	11.8
Siam	9,666	3.8	22,405	2.6
Indo–China	2,323	0.9	9,463	1.1
British Borneo	6,182	2.4	14,102	1.6
Burma	5,467	2.1	5,900	0.7
Philippine Islands and Sulu Archipelago	1,630	0.6	2,000	0.2
Europe, North America and Japan	**105,916**	**41.1**	**470,440**	**54.2**
United Kingdom	35,925	13.9	49,208	5.7
Europe	33,372	13.0	75,460	8.7
United States	31,188	12.1	316,768	36.5
Canada	638	0.2	2,378	0.3
Japan	4,793	1.9	26,626	3.0
Rest of world	**28,597**	**11.1**	**93,295**	**10.7**
Hong Kong	8,137	3.2	6,826	0.8
China	3,240	1.2	7,959	0.9
British India	11,553	4.5	14,399	1.6
Ceylon	1,919	0.7	4,152	0.5
Australia	1,501	0.6	30,619	3.5
Others	2,246	0.9	29,339	3.4
Total	**257,624**	**100.0**	**868,278**	**100.0**

Notes:
1   The figures include treasure of bullion and specie.
2   Inter–Port includes Penang, Malacca, Labuan, Dindings and Christmas Island.
3   For 1925/27 the sub-totals for imports added to $1,006,856,260 (the correct total),
    but the figures for individual countries added to $996,856,260. The discrepancy is
    probably explained by clerical or printing error.
4   Columns may not add to totals due to rounding.
Sources:'Trade of the Straits Settlements', *SSAR*, 1911–1913, 1925–1927; SS, *Return of imports and exports*, 1911–1913, 1925–1927.

economy had a powerful impact on Singapore. Initially, the link with the United States enabled Singapore to avoid the World War I contraction experienced by colonies normally dependent on exports to Europe,[18] and,

[18] Thomas B. Birnberg and Stephen A. Resnick, *Colonial development* (New Haven, 1975), pp.215, 220–24.

Table 3.5 *Singapore imports by country and region, 1911/13 and 1925/27 (annual averages)*

	1911/13		1925/27	
	$000	%	$000	%
Southeast Asia	**182,584**	**57.3**	**694,775**	**69.7**
Malay Peninsula	55,541	17.5	182,910	18.4
Inter-Port	9,024	2.8	20,627	2.1
Netherlands India	56,577	17.8	344,747	34.6.
Siam	30,329	9.5	72,565	7.3
Indo-China	11,560	3.6	20,196	2.0
British Borneo	5,431	1.7	40,087	4.0
Burma	12,430	3.9	12,336	1.2
Philippine Islands and Sulu Archipelago	1,692	0.5	1,306	0.1
Europe, North America and Japan	**65,382**	**20.5**	**184,419**	**18.5**
United Kingdom	34,656	10.9	89,396	9.0
Europe	16,183	5.1	35,860	3.6
United States	4,825	1.5	30,824	3.1
Canada	104	0.0	2,328	0.2
Japan	9,614	3.0	26,011	2.6
Rest of world	**70,572**	**22.2**	**117,662**	**11.8**
Hong Kong	25,909	8.1	27,180	2.7
China	8,395	2.6	32,233	3.2
British India	19,934	6.3	30,821	3.1
Ceylon	621	0.2	798	0.1
Australia	10,781	3.4	13,481	1.4
Others	4,932	1.6	13,151	1.3
Total	**318,538**	**100.0**	**996,856**	**100.0**

Notes and sources: as for table 3.4.

moreover, to join in the wartime boom in the United States economy. The expansion of American automobile production sustained high rubber prices until May 1918, when the United States imposed quotas and price restriction on rubber as a consequence of entry into the European war.[19] At the beginning of the 1920s, however, recession in the United States automobile industry precipitated a collapse in the price of rubber, leading to the Stevenson scheme in 1922. This restricted rubber output only in British colonies, but the curtailment, combined with renewed expansion of United States demand, was sufficient to raise rubber prices dramatically

---

[19]   W. Bartley, 'Singapore and the great war' in Makepeace, et al., eds. *One hundred years* I, pp.415–16.

until 1925. In response, smallholder planting in Netherlands India – under Dutch control and outside the scheme – spread rapidly, and since much of the eventual output was exported through Singapore, greatly increased its volume of rubber exports. But after 1925 the growth in Netherlands Indian production contributed to a continuous slide in the value of rubber, while the abandonment of the Stevenson scheme in 1928 allowed a large increase in Malayan exports which further depressed prices. In 1929 the average value per ton of Singapore's rubber exports was a third of that in 1925.

During the slump at the beginning of the 1930s, the fall in world rubber absorption was wholly the result of the decrease in the manufacture of tyres and tubes in the United States. Consequent price falls were exacerbated by the 1920s' addition to productive capacity in Netherlands India.[20] In 1932 the average value per ton of Singapore's rubber exports was a fifth of the 1929 level and a fifteenth of that in 1925, a much sharper drop than for any other major primary commodity.[21] After 1932 prices recovered somewhat, and in 1934 Singapore's rubber exports reached an inter-war peak in volume. The implementation in June that year of the International Rubber Regulation Scheme encouraged further improvement in prices by restricting supply. Higher prices benefited Singapore, where trading margins had been squeezed in the 1930s slump, but restrictions imposed by the Netherlands Indian government in conjunction with the Regulation Scheme caused the port to lose most of the milling of, and a substantial amount of imports of, rubber from the Dutch colony.

III

Growth as a staple port substantially modified Singapore's pattern of imports from Asia: the city became more dependent on imports from its immediate hinterland of Malaya, Netherlands India and British Borneo, and within this region Netherlands India stood out as Singapore's main source of exports to the West. Tables 3.4 and 3.5 show that in contrast to the late nineteenth century, and even 1911/13, by 1925/27 imports from the hinterland of Malaya, Netherlands India and British Borneo comprised the majority of total trade. The three countries accounted for 59% of imports, while Singapore's exports to the West (almost all of which first came as imports from the three countries) grew to become 54% of the port's total exports. Conversely, imports from elsewhere in Southeast Asia, mostly of food, and imports of manufactures from the West declined as proportions of total trade. Similarly, the share of China (including Hong Kong) and India in Singapore's trade fell.

[20] Bauer, *Rubber*, pp.26–28.   [21] Cf. League of Nations, *Economic stability*, p.85.

After 1913 rubber, tin and petroleum made Singapore more than ever an outlet for exports from Netherlands India rather than Malaya. Imports from Malaya consisted almost entirely of rubber and tin (table 3.6). In both 1917 and 1920 imports from Malaya were much larger than those from Netherlands India, because initially Singapore's rubber came chiefly from the Peninsula, while tropical produce (for Netherlands India the main constituent of 'others' in table 3.6) still comprised the bulk of imports from the Dutch colony. However, by 1925 Netherlands India was the main source of Singapore's three staples of rubber, tin and petroleum, as well as of tropical produce. Only tapioca came primarily from Malaya, although it was also a major supplier of arecanuts and copra. As a result, in 1925/27 imports from Netherlands India far exceeded those from Malaya (table 3.5). Furthermore, imports from Malaya included inter-port trade, a proportion of which originated in Netherlands India, reaching Singapore mainly through reshipment from Penang. Between 1928 and 1933, after which the relevant statistics cease to be available, the value of Singapore's imports from the Malay Peninsula was less than half those from Netherlands India.[22] However, after 1933 government intervention in the Dutch colony greatly reduced exports of tin and rubber, if not tropical produce, through Singapore.

Although Singapore's primacy as a port for Malaya is well known, its importance as a port for Netherlands India is often less appreciated. Singapore was 'the great entrepot for the Outer Provinces'.[23] Between 1894 and 1925/27 the value of exports sent by the Outer Provinces to Singapore grew over twelvefold. In 1925/27, 37% of Outer Province exports went to Singapore,[24] while commodities from Netherlands India, re-shipped through Singapore, made up more than a quarter of the exports of British Malaya. This fact casts some doubt on claims that export production in British Malaya was greater than in any British colony or self-governing dominion, and that its per capita exports exceeded those of any country in the world.[25] Additionally, during the inter-war period British Borneo emerged as an important source of rubber and several items of produce, including gum copal, pepper and sago.

Such was the international importance of production in the Outer Provinces that Singapore's status as a world centre for exports of rubber, tin and petroleum was largely supported by this output. Furthermore, Netherlands Indian smallholder rubber gave the Singapore market a

---

[22] 'Trade of the Straits Settlements', *SSAR*, 1928–1933; *SSTC 1933–34* IV, p.497.

[23] Jan O. M. Broek, *Economic development of the Netherlands Indies* (New York, 1942), p.143.

[24] Netherlands India, 'Het Handelsverkeer met Singapore, 1825–1937', p.10.

[25] For a contemporary statement of these claims, see *Ormsby Gore visit, 1928*, p.21.

Table 3.6 *Singapore imports from Malaya and Netherlands India, 1913–1929*

	1913		1917		1920		1925		1929	
	$000	%	$000	%	$000	%	$000	%	$000	%
(a) *Malaya*										
Rubber	11,452	18.7	116,952	65.7	142,005	61.4	161,512	73.5	n.a.	
Tin ore and tin	41,699	68.0	41,399	23.2	52,920	22.9	26,310	12.0		
Others	8,145	13.3	19,747	11.1	36,338	15.7	31,885	14.5		
Total	**61,296**	**100.0**	**178,098**	**100.0**	**231,262**	**100.0**	**219,707**	**100.0**	**153,091**	
(b) *Netherlands India*										
Rubber	409	0.6	12,246	12.8	29,069	19.3	185,382	50.4	59,776	24.5
Tin ore and tin	3,855	6.4	9,739	10.2	15,755	10.5	40,268	10.9	40,191	16.5
Petroleum	1,544	2.6	2,425	2.5	4,915	3.3	57,437	15.6	61,840	25.4
Others	54,679	90.4	71,169	74.5	100,648	66.9	85,131	23.1	81,808	33.6
Total	**60,487**	**100.0**	**95,579**	**100.0**	**150,386**	**100.0**	**368,217**	**100.0**	**243,616**	**100.0**

Notes:
1 Figures for total imports include treasure.
2 For 1929 the figure is for the Malay Peninsula only. In 1933 total imports from the Malay Peninsula were $54,828,000 and from Netherlands India $96,751,000.
3 Columns may not add to totals due to rounding.

Sources: SS, *Return of imports and exports, 1913–1920; SSTC 1933–34* IV, pp.485, 492, 494, 497; 'Trade of the Straits Settlements', *SSAR 1925*, pp.558–60; 'Foreign trade of Malaya', *SSAR 1929*, pp.778–79.

valuable variety; these were grades which 'consumers (chiefly American) ... require for mixing with the tougher standard qualities'.[26] Similarly, the very pure Netherlands Indian tin ore made it easier to smelt the high purity Straits product which was particularly suitable for tin plate manufacture.[27]

In the inter-war years Singapore was a world market for several produce trades. Again, it was mainly Netherlands Indian output which was sold through the port. Singapore was 'an extremely important market for copra',[28] 'probably the most important centre in the world for the rattan or cane industry',[29] 'the world's market for gutta percha',[30] and 'ranks with the biggest markets in the world for arecanuts'.[31] Netherlands Indian pepper went principally to Singapore as the main pepper distribution centre in the East.[32] The city was 'a particularly important market' for black pepper which 'has always been known as Singapore pepper'.[33]

IV

Finance for Singapore's exports to the West other than petroleum came very largely through the European banks. All were branches of metropolitan banks, and while among staple ports Singapore was notable for its variety of foreign banks, the main overseas banks were the three British institutions already in the town by the late nineteenth century, namely, the Chartered Bank of India, Australia and China, the Mercantile Bank of India and the Hongkong and Shanghai Banking Corporation.[34]

The European banks were no longer, as in the late nineteenth century, strictly 'exchange banks' in the sense of concentrating almost exclusively on trade and associated foreign exchange business,[35] but finance for exports was their principal function. The manager of the Mercantile Bank pointed out, 'We finance the exports of the Colony as a matter of course; that is what we are here for. We never refuse to buy a bill against exports of produce unless it is with people unfit to be traded with'.[36] Although the

---

[26] Department of Agriculture, Industry and Commerce, Netherlands Indies, 'Native rubber cultivation in the Netherlands East Indies', *BRGA* 13, 11 (1931), p.487.
[27] *SSTC 1933–34* III, pp.325–26.   [28] Ibid. I, p.43.
[29] *British Malaya: trade and commerce* (Malay States Information Agency, London, 1924), p.40.
[30] *British Malaya: Malayan trade facts and figures* (Malayan Information Agency, London, 1929), p.33.   [31] Ibid. p.27.
[32] Netherlands Indies, *1930 handbook of the Netherlands East-Indies* (Buitenzorg, Java, 1930), p.335; *SSTC 1933–34* II, pp.409, 412; Milsum, 'Pepper in Malaya', p.275.
[33] *SSTC 1933–34* II, p.87.
[34] Newlyn, 'Colonial empire', pp.445–46; Makepeace, 'Machinery of commerce', pp.176–80; Wright and Cartwright, *Twentieth century impressions*, pp.141–46; Allen and Donnithorne, *Western enterprise*, p.203; Lee, *Monetary and banking development* (1974), pp.65–70, 77.   [35] King, *Money*, p.51.
[36] *Commissions on trade depression 1921*, appx. 1, p.167, and see pp.169, 170, 172.

European banks also functioned as ordinary domestic banks, 'Overdrafts are more acceptable if they carry exchange business with them'.[37] A number of brokers, organized as the Singapore Exchange Brokers Association, helped merchants to obtain competitive rates when dealing with the banks.[38]

For exports, finance from the European banks frequently involved a system of trust receipts against goods stored in godowns (warehouses). Since the European banks did not usually own godowns, and Singapore, unlike most ports, did not have public warehouses, small dealers without warehouse facilities lacked direct access to European bank finance. They depended on European merchants to store their produce and make advances against it. Advances were 80% of the market value of the produce, which was stored and held 'on trust' by the merchant for 15 days to two months. At any time during this period the dealer could close the sale at the price then current. European merchants were in turn financed by the European banks. The property in the stored produce vested in the bank, and the term 'trust receipts' referred to the fact that the European merchants held the produce in trust for the bank.[39]

Although Singapore's European banks efficiently met the needs of export trade and helped to lay the basis for subsequent financial development, they did relatively little to push financial sector growth beyond its early stages. Two observations on financial development in Singapore emphasize the point. First, the European banks had not been responsible for the early development of trade, nor did they subsequently make Singapore an independent financial centre. Finance from the banks was mainly in response to demand in Singapore itself, and dependent on primary commodity exports traded through the city. As was observed, 'if the volume of trade were to drift away from Singapore and go somewhere else, then the financing and exchange arrangements would go somewhere else too'.[40]

Second, Singapore's pre-World War II capital market remained weak and fragmented. There was as yet no local stock exchange, and the banking system was the only significant European institutional source of finance. The ability of larger European businesses to borrow on the London capital market and comparative lack of European interest in manufacturing industry in Singapore gave European banks no strong reason to depart from a policy of finance 'against stocks only' and 'not for capital

[37] *SSTC 1933–34* III, p.425, and see III, pp.424, 429, 241–43, 249–51, I, pp.222–23.
[38] Ibid. I, p.222.
[39] Ibid. I, pp.223, 41, II, pp.356, 525, 527, III, p.424; British Military Administration, Singapore, *The entrepot trade of Singapore* (Singapore, 1945), pp.16–18.
[40] *SSTC 1933–34* III, p.246, and see II, pp.331–32.

expenditure'. In explaining this, the manager of the Chartered Bank went on to comment that 'The question of financing industry has never really arisen in Singapore'.[41]

By the inter-war period a few of the most important Chinese businessmen could borrow from European banks to finance exports and stocks in progress, for example in rubber milling, but for all Asian entrepreneurs, the poor Singapore market for long-term institutional finance was a constraint. The development of a local Chinese banking system, discussed in chapter 7, helped to overcome this, as did the planting of pineapples to finance rubber estate development. Nevertheless, Asian entrepreneurs could not borrow in London, and for them secure long-term finance was difficult to obtain.

So long as Singapore's capital market was segmented and Asian entrepreneurs borrowed mainly from Chinese banks or from a large informal sector including Chettiar moneylenders and rotating credit and savings associations (chit funds), the monetary arrangements in the Straits Settlements, together with rubber's dominance in the economy and its extreme price instability, created a major source of uncertainty. Under the currency board system and sterling exchange standard in the Straits Settlements, the adverse movements in the current account of the balance of payments which almost certainly followed any substantial fall in rubber prices did not have to lead to a large contraction in the money supply.[42] But in practice this occurred, since the colonial government avoided deficit spending and insofar as possible European banks appear not to have borrowed from their metropolitan headquarters. Appendix table A.9 shows the sharp fluctuations British Malaya experienced in base money supply, M0. During the inter-war period these were closely correlated with, although lagging somewhat behind, the main fluctuations in the value of rubber exports. Money supply fell from an inter-war peak of $183 million on 4 March 1920 to $102 million by the end of the year but recovered to $163 million by June 1926. In December 1931 the monetary base was less than two-thirds of its level two years previously. Taking the figures for each December, over the inter-war period as a whole the monetary base had a coefficient of variation of 31·3%, indicating the large movements in British Malayan money supply.

European banks were protected from Singapore's liquidity crises consequent on sharp contractions in the money supply, since for them London, where their head offices were located, effectively acted as a central

[41] Ibid. III, pp.422–23, and see IV, p.419; *Commissions on trade depression 1921*, appx. 1, pp.174–75.
[42] Alan Walters, 'Currency boards' in John Eatwell, Murray Milgate and Peter Newman, eds, *The new Palgrave: money* (London, 1989), pp.109–14.

banker.[43] But these liquidity crises had a severe effect on the Chinese business community and anyone dependent on the informal financial sector. Chinese banks, unlike European, did not have direct access to an external wholesale credit market, and Singapore had no central bank to serve as a lender of last resort.

In the following chapters reference will be made to the serious consequences of inter-war economic downturns for the Chinese business community. Unlike the European agency houses and banks, which survived the 1930s slump without undue difficulty, several of the largest Chinese businesses were forced into amalgamation or liquidation, while bankruptcies among smaller Chinese firms multiplied. Distress increased further down the social scale, and was particularly acute among poorer Chinese, as indicated in chapter 5.

V

The remainder of this chapter looks at the organization of Singapore's trade, which divided along five lines. First, there was an entirely European-dominated sector for exports, considered in this section. A second category, dealt with in section VI, was the produce exchange trade. It involved tropical produce and smallholder rubber, and was characterized by one or more interlinkages between Singapore and its hinterland, effected through the city's Chinese. A third category, the subject of section VII, was a regional exchange of food, primarily rice. Finally, there existed two categories of manufactured imports distributed from Singapore, examined together in section VIII. They consisted of the 'old' trade in textiles and simple manufactures and a 'new' one in consumer durables and producer goods.

The most important change in Singapore's twentieth-century trade organization was the emergence of an entirely European-dominated sector, which stemmed from the growing role of European enterprise in hinterland production and in the processing of hinterland staples. This sector in Singapore's trade first arose when tin smelting became a European industry, as discussed in chapter 2, and from World War I grew rapidly as the production of estate rubber, tin and petroleum developed mainly under the control of European enterprise. The commercial links between Singapore and the hinterland varied according to the commodity produced; but all parts of Singapore's entirely European-dominated trade sector had in common that European merchants in the city could deal

---

[43] Ida Greaves, *Colonial monetary conditions* (London, Colonial Office, research studies no.10, 1953), p.26.

directly with European hinterland enterprises, eliminating Singapore Chinese traders; that large units of production in the hinterland provided merchant services for themselves and without reference to Singapore as the enterprise grew and trade became more specialized; and that finance for production had to be raised in the West because of the time it took for investment to come on stream, or the scale and capital intensity of European undertakings.

Nevertheless, the differences within Singapore's entirely European-dominated trade sector were substantial. Agency houses were the main Singapore buyers of estate rubber, although increasingly purchases were made up-country, which limited the merchandising function performed in Singapore, while purchases on long-term contracts reduced this even further. The STC, practically the sole buyer of tin ore in Singapore, brought ore to the city for smelting, and sold the tin to European merchants for export. Petroleum had even less impact on the mercantile community than tin, since the international oil companies used Singapore only as a distribution point, and not as a market. Thus, one main consequence for Singapore's trade of the growth of European hinterland production was that it created fewer linkages for the city in terms of mercantile and financial functions than Singapore's nineteenth-century trade in tin and tropical produce had done.

The other main consequence for Singapore's trade of European hinterland production was to reduce the multiplier effects of primary commodity exports to the West by making trade less bilateral than in the late nineteenth century; neither Singapore's exports of petroleum nor a substantial new source of tin coming from Netherlands India gave rise to a significant return flow of imports to Singapore for reshipment to primary producing areas. Although rubber, like tropical produce and Malayan tin, did create such a flow, these commodities no longer generated an increase in trade exceeding their own value. Previously, primary exports had provided the purchasing power for, and been stimulated by, imports of consumer goods and food, while the 'barter effect' associated with the goods-credit-marketing interlinkage described in chapter 2 had channelled both sides of the trade through Singapore. Now, reflecting the expansion of relatively capital-intensive European production in the hinterland, a higher proportion of profits arising from exports went to capital rather than labour. These profits were largely repatriated to metropolitan owners rather than being spent on imported goods to the extent that peasant cultivators did. Insofar as exports through Singapore continued to create a demand for imports, there was a smaller return flow of goods through the port because of the absence of the barter effect in trade with European producers. The absence of barter allowed the growth of direct trade

Table 3.7 *Singapore primary exports, manufactured imports and food imports, 1900/02–1935/37 (annual averages)*

	Primary exports	Manufactured imports		Food imports		Total manufactures and food	
	$m	$m	% of primary exports	$m	% of primary exports	$m	% of primary exports
1900/02	96.7	53.4	55.2	38.1	39.3	91.5	94.5
1911/13	117.8	68.3	58.0	57.7	49.0	126.1	107.1
1925/27	580.9	199.7	34.4	97.1	16.7	294.0	50.6
1935/37	313.7	115.3	36.8	32.1	10.2	147.4	47.0

Notes:
1   Primary exports are rubber, tin, petroleum, 16 important tropical commodities, canned pineapples and palm oil.
2   Food imports are rice, dried and salted fish and sugar.
3   Manufactured imports were calculated as follows. The trade returns divide trade into three classes:
    class I 'animals, food, drink and tobacco';
    class II 'raw materials and articles mainly manufactured'; and
    class III 'articles wholly or mainly manufactured'.
    Manufactured imports are class III imports but including cigarettes and cigars and excluding coke. From 1925/27 they include these imports, but also exclude petroleum (liquid fuel, motor spirit, kerosene, lubricating oils, paraffin wax, and other sorts of petroleum), tin and opium, which began to be included in class III.
4   The figures for 1935/37 exclude trade with Malaya.
5   Percentages are derived from unrounded data.
Sources:SS, *Return of imports and exports*, 1900–1927; Malaya, *Foreign imports and exports*, 1935–1937.

(especially in the case of Netherlands India) which bypassed Singapore. Therefore, Singapore's earlier role in promoting export expansion and as a catalyst for economic development in the region increasingly operated through giving producers access to export markets rather than providing them with imports.

Table 3.7 indicates the alteration in the pattern of Singapore's trade growth in response to the changes in hinterland production. In contrast to the nineteenth century, exports to the West led to a much slower growth in total trade because they did less to generate Singapore's other two main commercial flows: imports of manufactures from the West and a regional exchange of food with its own return trades in manufactures and food. During the chief period of export expansion between 1911/13 and 1925/27, Singapore's primary exports to the West increased fivefold to $580·9 million. Imports of food and manufactures grew at half that rate, to $294 million, although to some extent in the case of manufactures this reflected import-substituting industrial development in Singapore. In 1911/13 the value of manufactured imports and food imports together exceeded the value of Singapore's primary exports; by 1925/27 the value of manufactures and food had fallen to half the value of primary exports, while in the 1930s these imports as a proportion of primary exports further declined under the pressure of trade restrictions.

VI

The produce exchange trade was typical of the late nineteenth century when small Asian producers were almost entirely responsible for output; it persisted for tropical produce and, as considered in chapter 6, grew considerably through the addition of smallholder rubber from Netherlands India and British Borneo. The trade was characterized by interlinkages both between Singapore Chinese and regional traders and within Singapore's mercantile community. The regional interlinkages were an important part of the explanation of why the city drew together such a large part of Southeast Asia's trade. In Singapore's dealings with the region, a goods-credit-marketing interlinkage which constituted the system of book-keeping barter predominated. Barter was organized around finance from Singapore Chinese through advances – more often in kind than in cash – against the delivery of commodities. Shipment of these commodities by outport dealers to Singapore liquidated debt to Singapore Chinese, and prompted further outflows of goods from the port on credit. However, outport dealers generally incurred new debt before their existing debt had been entirely cleared, so that in practice debt owed to Singapore Chinese was never wholly liquidated. The goods sent on credit to outport traders allowed them, in turn, again to extend credit to producers. Rice and the traditional imports, especially textiles and cigarettes, largely comprised the goods advanced, and were in effect the currency of the produce exchange trade.

Describing the produce exchange trade in 1932, the Customs Duties Committee drew attention to its barter component: 'The trade of the Colony is still largely a matter of barter. Produce arrives from all parts of the Archipelago and payment therefor is frequently made, not in cash, but in a return shipment of various articles required by the original sender'.[44] Two years later the Straits Settlements Trade Commission analysed this goods interlinkage, the accompanying credit linkage and the book-keeping

[44] 'Customs duties committee', *SSLCP 1932*, p.C162, and see p.C158; *SSTC 1933–34* II, p.508.

element in the barter. By the inter-war years this last relied on the Straits dollar as a unit of account and, when necessary, as a medium of exchange:

the produce pays for the manufactures, and the machinery of collection is closely interlocked with that of distribution ... The trade is essentially one of exchange; it is 'barter with prices fixed' and accounts as a rule are settled by drafts on Singapore, though sometimes actual goods are exchanged (e.g. rice for native rubber) ... The trade is financed from Singapore and advances to outport middlemen secure for Singapore dealers a lien on the produce collected from the actual growers.[45]

The role of Singapore in interlinked transactions derived partly from geography. A central location in the Malayan region meant that for much of its trade shipping had to pass by or near Singapore. Thus, specialized ships could bring rice from the main exporting countries as far as Singapore where bulk was broken, and the 224lb gunny bags of rice which had arrived from the producing countries distributed, along with manufactured goods, by small vessels to the Archipelago's many minor undeveloped ports from which produce was collected.[46]

This hub-and-spoke arrangement in regional trade, a development encouraged by the shipping conference system discussed in chapter 4, helped to keep transport costs via Singapore competitive through the use of specialized shipping and provision of cargo both to and from outports. The arrangement also lowered costs for outport traders, since regular shipping through the use of small vessels reduced the need to accumulate produce or hold inventories with associated loss of interest, danger of spoilage and risk of price fluctuations. At Singapore these intra-regional shipping arrangements were supported by the constant availability of ocean-going shipping. The intermeshed transport networks ensured that primary commodities could be dispatched virtually when sold, and also a continuous replenishment of manufactured goods from the West. The volume of trade at Singapore made possible by this transport system encouraged, and was encouraged by, the development of specialized handling and grading facilities, and conferred economies in performing these functions.

Although a necessary condition, geography does not provide a sufficient explanation of why the produce exchange trade centred on Singapore. By the late nineteenth century, the numerous small steamships in Southeast Asia made direct intra-regional commerce feasible; or shipment could have continued via Singapore, but with transhipment only. For rice – the largest regional trade conducted through Singapore – the port never had

[45] *SSTC 1933–34* I, p.41.
[46] Ibid. I, p.98, II, pp.634, 849, 862, 865, 867, IV, pp.244–49; J. S. Furnivall, *Netherlands India* (Cambridge, 1939), p.206; Huff, 'Bookkeeping barter', pp.169–70.

an important milling industry or stockholding function, roles which would have tended to keep trade focused on Singapore.[47] Similarly, much of the primary commodity export trade transacted at Singapore could have by-passed the port or relied only on transhipment there. On grounds of shipping freight costs alone, transhipment via Singapore was cheaper than export to Singapore and re-export from the port on a new bill of lading.[48]

Explanation of why the produce exchange trade centred on Singapore involves an additional set of considerations. Although building on locational advantage, these emerge as the more important, and derived from Singapore's ability to finance the interlinked transactions charac-teristic of the produce exchange trade. Outer Province exports of produce and rubber were very largely in Chinese hands and, as a contemporary observer emphasized, the financial dependence of these traders on their Chinese counterparts in Singapore was fundamental in understanding the port's predominance as a market for Outer Province exports:

the importance [of Singapore]...must be sought in [its] importance as a world centre of trade in South-East Asia, and, maybe even to a greater extent, in the peculiar nature of Chinese trade at Singapore which more or less directly finances a great part of the commerce and industry of the Netherlands Indies.[49]

Remarking on Netherlands Indian dependence on finance from Singapore, the Straits Settlements Trade Commission instanced 'the control exercised over sago factories in the Archipelago: they are given advances of cash and provisions and are in return bound to sell their produce to the Singapore creditor. A similar financial hold assisted in preserving Singapore's share in the Macassar rattan trade even after more convenient channels had been established'.[50] In the decades after 1900, more distant areas of the Archipelago – notably the Celebes and the Moluccas or so-called 'Great East trade' – had slipped out of Singapore's orbit; indeed, that the trade of these areas had stayed within Singapore's orbit for so long was due to a reliance on finance from Singapore Chinese.[51]

Singapore's advantages in financing the produce exchange trade can be grouped under two broad headings: commodity price and transaction costs. Both advantages arose from the incompleteness or absence of markets in the region served by Singapore traders, who provided a

---

[47] Singapore's rice milling industry disappeared during the 1920s. See table 7.2.
[48] *SSTC 1933–34* I, pp.46–48, 93–94, II, p.99, III, p.71, IV, pp.247, 255.
[49] W. J. Cator, *The economic position of the Chinese in the Netherlands Indies* (Oxford, 1936), p.136, and see pp.72, 175–76, 245; Tan Ee Leong, 'Dr. Lee Kong Chian (1893–1967)', *Annual of the China Society of Singapore* (1964–1967), p.7.
[50] *SSTC 1933–34* I, p.41.
[51] Allen and Donnithorne, *Western enterprise*, pp.217–18; de Boer and Westermann, *Een Halve Eeuw Paketvaart*, p.224; *SSTC 1933–34* I, pp.43–45, 47, IV, pp.85, 137, 138, 142.

substitute for this lack of well-developed markets. Because interlinked transactions unite potentially separate markets, the price at which finance can be offered becomes a 'composite price' or a 'package deal'. For example, in a goods-credit-marketing interlinkage, finance at an apparently zero rate of interest, often found in Singapore's trade, has no meaning without a knowledge of prices charged for the goods and paid for the commodities.[52] Because Singapore was better able to combine financial, commodity and goods markets than any other port in the region, it was also in a position to offer the best prices and so extend the lowest-cost finance. Thus, the credit in Singapore available through European banks and merchant houses via the system of trust receipts – although essential in a region with poorly developed formal financial markets – only partially explained Singapore's finance of regional trade.

Singapore offered the highest commodity prices in the region, partly due to 'subsidies' for some merchant houses arising from the shipping conference system, as discussed in chapter 4. Furthermore, the port had the region's cheapest and widest selection of manufactured goods: 'The producer finds in Singapore an extremely efficient and favourable market. There are no restrictions: a man can get the best price for his goods and take in return anything that his own market requires'.[53] Although traders in Rangoon and Bangkok had comparatively well-developed financial facilities and could have bartered rice, they lacked Singapore's opportunities for trade in tropical produce and Western manufactures, in part because of the location of these ports in 'steamer backwaters'.[54]

The fragmented markets in Netherlands India and British Borneo which gave rise to interlinkages also created a potential for high transaction costs. The potential arose because this commerce required dealers in a port like Singapore to conduct business with a large number of outport traders, to handle often small quantities of goods, and to possess specialized knowledge of the outport traders and their markets. Through being able to hold down transaction costs, and to provide at a low cost the services required by outport traders, Singapore's 'numerous and illiterate class of [Chinese] traders'[55] engaged in the produce exchange trade constituted a critical mass which contributed decisively to the port's locational and shipping advantages. Contemporaries recognized the fundamental role played by Chinese in the produce exchange trade: 'The principal agent of this vital, valuable and complex organization is the Chinese dealer'.[56]

[52] Platteau and Abraham, 'Inquiry into quasi-credit contracts', p.471; Kaushik Basu, *The less developed economy* (Oxford, 1984), pp.162–63.   [53] *SSTC 1933–34* I, p.41.
[54] Spate and Trueblood, 'Rangoon', p.73; James M. Andrews, *Siam, second rural economic survey* (Bangkok, 1935), pp.391–92.   [55] Song, *One hundred years' history*, p.382.
[56] 'Customs duties committee', *SSLCP 1932*, p.C158, and see *Report of the Harbour Boards' Committee appointed by the government of the Straits Settlements* (Singapore, 1926), p.112.

Good market information and a climate of trust were basic to book-keeping barter.[57] In these respects, the ties of kinship and blood with outport traders put Singapore Chinese at an advantage over their counterparts in Java.[58] Similarly, Singapore Chinese had this edge over other Asians in the city. Indian merchants handled the export of arecanuts to India – the most important export to the subcontinent – but relied on Chinese to bring the produce to Singapore. A 'Bombay merchant' considered the replacement of Chinese impossible in the arecanut trade 'because it is very troublesome to collect in small lots and we would have to advance money to the sellers up-country'.[59]

Unlike produce and rubber imports from Netherlands India and British Borneo, barter did not predominate in Singapore's rice imports, and by World War I was in decline. Nevertheless, it could be remarked in 1921

what a hold Singapore still has on the Bangkok trade. In spite of many attempts to do a direct trade between Europe and Bangkok, these have generally proved unsuccessful. The Singapore dealer has an agent or a branch in Bangkok to ship rice to Singapore in exchange for piece goods, and this interchange of commodities is still considerable.[60]

In trade with Burma, 'rice and dried fish ... form the two sides of the barter and are handled by the same Chinese firms: dried fish (salted in Saigon or Siam and re-dried, sorted and cleaned in Singapore) is exported to Rangoon and rice is imported in exchange'.[61]

Barter was probably often advantageous for outport traders, especially in Netherlands India, or at least no great hardship, but it was Singapore Chinese who appear to have been the more anxious to perpetuate the arrangement. Two considerations – risk and volume – explain the Singapore Chinese preference for barter. Examination of these reveals how, in important economic ways, it was barter which cemented the social ties Singapore Chinese had with outport traders.

A Singapore Chinese dealer trading with outports had risks of default and of cessation of the supply of primary commodities; barter substantially reduced both. By extending credit, Singapore Chinese traders obtained a lien on primary commodities. This served as a substitute for the collateral which outport traders lacked. The addition of barter to the credit-

[57] C. A. E. Goodhart, *Money, information and uncertainty* (London, 1975), pp.7–8.
[58] Chiang, *Straits Settlements trade*, pp.51–53; J. J. van Klaveren, *The Dutch colonial system in the East Indies* (Rotterdam, 1953), p.174; Cator, *Economic position of the Chinese*, pp.72, 175–76, 245.
[59] *SSTC 1933–34* II, p.673, and see pp.670–72, 675, V, p.34; R. Jumabhoy, *Multiracial Singapore* (Singapore, 1970), pp.36–39, 52–53.
[60] Darbishire, 'Commerce and currency', p.41.
[61] *SSTC 1933–34* I, p.46, and see I, p.216, II, pp.651, 859, 860.

marketing interlinkage substantially lessened risk for a Singapore Chinese trader by adding a further tying dimension to the lien already secured on primary commodities. Barter provided this tie-in because, so long as markets in the Archipelago were poorly developed, it substantially increased an outport trader's cost of defaulting or otherwise ending his relationship with a Singapore financier. The outport trader would have to find not just another source of credit and outlet for commodities; he would also have to establish an alternative supply of goods. In practice, barter relationships seem often to have persisted over long periods and default not to have been a problem. Probably at least in part this was because a defaulter would have found difficulty in forming new links with any individual within the closely-knit Singapore Chinese trading community.

The second consideration – volume – helped to explain barter, because a two-way trade allowed Singapore Chinese traders to spread transaction costs over both imports and exports. The Singapore manager of the KPM shipping line emphasized this aspect of the system from the point of view of the Singapore financier:

it has always been the idea to make money both ways. He makes money on the rice he sends down as well as on the produce he brings up. The margin of profit would be too small if one of these [trades] went.[62]

The Straits Settlements Trade Commission cited his evidence as authoritative, adding piece goods and cigarettes to rice as items sent by the Singapore dealer.[63] The need for two-way profits suggests that the margins realized by Singapore Chinese traders in the produce exchange trade were not high. The possibility of entry to the trade and contestable, if not competitive, markets helped to keep margins low.

For dealers in extra-Malayan markets, an attractive feature of trade with Singapore was the ability of its Chinese dealers to break bulk and meet diverse needs, in the form of small, mixed cargoes. A Chinese trader might principally send piece goods and rice, but with these he probably packed a variety of other articles such as oilcloth, shoes and lamps.[64] If Singapore was to maintain this trade, access to low-cost manufactures was essential. As a representative of Guthrie & Co. was quick to agree in a discussion of Singapore's trade which used copra as an example: 'Barter implies a quid pro quo and if you lose the quid you don't get the quo. If the local dealer has not got anything to send there he will not get the copra back.'[65]

Until 1911 Singapore Chinese traders in tropical produce 'had to

[62] Ibid. II, p.889.   [63] Ibid. I, p.51, and see II, p.858.
[64] Ibid. I, p.51, and see I, p.19, II, pp.335–43; 'Report on quotas', *SSAR 1934*, pp.41–42.
[65] *SSTC 1933–34* II, p.331, and see II, p.332.

content themselves every morning with meeting and consulting each other in the five-foot ways and by-lanes of the business quarter'.[66] That year the trade acquired a more formal market structure with the establishment of the Chinese Produce Exchange at 3, Change Alley in the centre of Singapore just off Raffles Place (figure 2.3). The stated purpose of the Exchange was to facilitate business between European merchants – strong supporters of its foundation – and Chinese firms. But the Exchange must also have contributed to trade and interchange of market information among the Chinese, including details of the creditworthiness of outport traders. In the 1930s the Exchange had a membership of about 100 firms, while individual members were mostly storekeepers of European merchant houses.[67]

Within Singapore, the produce exchange trade typically depended on a credit-marketing interlinkage and complementary relationship between the European merchant houses and the city's Chinese – and often among Chinese themselves, who specialized in different aspects of trade. European merchants were involved in both the import and export sides of the produce exchange trade. They financed the distribution of manufactured goods through 60- to 90-day trade credits and the collection of produce through the system of advances and holding commodities on trust described in section IV above. However, in Singapore, Chinese firms which dealt with European merchants often specialized either in selling produce to the Europeans or in buying manufactures from them, so that a goods interlinkage was absent and accounts were settled in cash.

The distributive system in Singapore for manufactured imports from the West might widen through several stages as goods were re-sold in successively smaller quantities. There was no clear-cut division of stages. Even the term 'dealer' was imprecise. A Singapore (Chinese or Indian) dealer might assume any of five different roles in distributing manufactured goods obtained from a European importer. He might be an exporter to the hinterland; a merchant selling to other Singapore dealers, themselves re-sellers; a wholesaler supplying local retailers; or even a retailer himself. The fifth possibility was selling to hinterland traders who journeyed to Singapore.[68]

In the produce exchange trade, 'The reticulation of dealers and sub-dealers, commission agents and brokers ... is too elaborate and various for concise description',[69] and in addition to the variety of dealers indicated, specialization among Chinese firms made other major contributions to this

[66] *Singapore Free Press*, 20 April 1911, and see *Straits Times*, 13 April 1911; *SSTC 1933–34* II, p.637.
[67] *SSTC 1933–34* II, pp.636–37, 640; R. N. Walling, *Singapura sorrows* (Singapore, 1931), pp.114–15.   [68] *SSTC 1933–34* II, p.509, I, pp.51–52.   [69] Ibid. I, p.41.

Table 3.8 *Singapore rice exports by destination, 1900/02–1937/39 (annual averages)*

	Total tons	Malaya Tons	Malaya %	Netherlands India Tons	Netherlands India %	Others Tons	Others %
1900/02	321,006	117,104	36.5	162,306	50.6	41,596	12.9
1911/13	371,178	163,827	44.1	151,738	40.9	55,613	15.0
1925/27	379,510	138,449	36.5	166,264	43.8	74,797	19.7
1937/39	181,350	44,039	24.3	93,551	51.6	43,760	24.1

Notes:

1 Until 1927 rice (as distinct from padi) was a single category in the trade returns. Bran, consisting almost entirely of rice bran, was a separate category under the classification 'feeding stuffs for animals'. In 1937/39 rice includes cargo, parboiled, cleaned (white) and broken, clean.

2 For 1925/27 recorded trade statistics for Singapore divide exports into those to Malaya and those to foreign countries. The figure used for exports to Netherlands India is the one given in Mansvelt for that country's imports from Singapore. Others are the difference between Singapore's exports to foreign countries and the figure from Mansvelt. For 1937/39 a similar procedure was followed to divide a recorded figure for Singapore's exports to non-Malayan destinations into exports to Netherlands India and to Others.

3 For 1937/39 retained imports, total exports, and exports to Malaya are estimated. Based on earlier trade (1925/27 retained imports) and population statistics (1931 census), yearly average per capita rice consumption in Singapore was estimated as 656.617 lbs. Multiplication of this figure and Singapore's estimated population of 651,486 persons in mid-1937 showed retained imports of 190,972 tons. An estimate of Singapore's exports to Malaya was derived by subtracting from the recorded figure for rice imports of 372,322 tons (imports from Malaya being negligible) recorded exports to non-Malayan destinations of 137,311 tons and the estimate for retained imports. This gave exports to Malaya of 44,039 tons. That estimate was added to the recorded figure for non-Malayan exports to produce an estimate for total exports of 181,350 tons. The possibly somewhat high figure for per capita consumption is partly explained by a population structure bias towards working-age males; the use of rice in the manufacture of food, some of which was exported; and a proportion of 'cargo brokens' used in Singapore for animal feed.

4 Others are mainly British Borneo and Ceylon.

Sources: SS, *Return of imports and exports, 1900–1927*; Malaya, *Foreign imports and exports, 1933–1937*; Malaya, *Foreign trade of Malaya, 1938–1939*; Mansvelt, *Rice prices*, pp.71–72.

Table 3.9 *Singapore dried and salted fish trade, 1900/02–1937/39 (annual averages)*

	Exports		Retained Imports		Imports		
	tons	as % of imports	tons	as % of imports	tons	($000)	%
1900/02	40,313	92.6	3,231	7.4	43,544	(6,549)	100.0
1911/13	47,879	80.1	11,929	19.9	59,808	(9,922)	100.0
1925/27	62,237	97.3	1,731	2.7	63,968	(15,851)	100.0
1937/39	50,698				48,093	(6,739)	

Notes:
1 For 1937/39 the recorded trade statistics exclude trade with Malaya. In 1925/27 this accounted for (by volume) 17.6% of imports and 7.9% of exports. Thus, for 1937/39 imports and exports are probably understated by about 18% and 8% respectively, and no figure is given for retained imports.

Sources: SS, *Return of imports and exports*, 1900–1927; Malaya, *Foreign imports and exports*, 1933–1937; Malaya, *Foreign trade of Malaya*, 1938–1939.

Table 3.10 *Singapore sugar trade, 1900/02–1937/39 (annual averages)*

	Exports		Retained imports		Imports		
	tons	as % of imports	tons	as % of imports	tons	($000)	%
1900/02	23,865	59.2	16,475	40.8	40,340	(4,786)	100.0
1911/13	57,702	67.7	27,518	32.3	85,220	(9,481)	100.0
1925/27	48,742	54.2	41,113	45.8	89,855	(12,447)	100.0
1937/39					73,992	(5,449)	

Notes:
1 For 1937/39 the recorded trade statistics exclude trade with Malaya. Singapore imported almost no sugar from Malaya, but this was its main export market by the mid-twenties. In 1925/27 Singapore sent (by volume) 64.2% of its sugar exports to Malaya. For 1937/39 the recorded figure for exports (12,385 tons) is therefore not comparable with earlier periods and is omitted from the table. An approximate estimate of retained imports is not possible because of sugar's extensive use by Singapore industries.

Sources: as for table 3.9.

structure. Thus, Chinese firms importing produce for sale to Europeans might sell through a commission agent. For example, in the 1930s virtually all copra sales were handled by two such men, one of whom – Ong Hup Keng – earned the title of the 'Copra King'.[70] Chinese brokers appear to have been found mainly in the rubber trade, as discussed in chapter 6.

Just as the Chinese gave access to the hinterland for the produce exchange trade, so the Europeans ensured a market for anything the Chinese could collect by linking Singapore to London. The latter was 'a Central market to which the Western nations sent their orders for Straits Produce', giving these either to the London offices of Straits firms or to Mincing Lane brokers and dealers. During the day offers and counter-offers flashed between London and the Continent, while in the afternoon New York joined the market. By the end of the day those in London were 'in a position to select the best bids and cable them out to the East for reply to reach London the following day'. Although sold through London, the produce was shipped direct from Singapore to the buyer.[71]

During the inter-war period Chinese firms began to replace some of the functions of European merchants in the produce trade. European exporters usually sorted, graded and bulked the produce. But Chinese firms started to do this during the inter-war years as trades became more standardized, and so began to provide an important component of the value added, or Singapore 'uplift', in these trades. With the development of business on an f.o.b. basis, it became common for Chinese firms to load copra and pepper onto ships for European exporters who never saw the commodities. The essence of the system, explained the manager of Ban Hock Hin, was 'Quality, weight and everything guaranteed'.[72]

In the produce trade, European merchants had three main advantages which prevented Chinese firms from exporting directly. One was better access to finance, the second a commission on freight costs which European merchants obtained through holding shipping agencies, as discussed in chapter 4. Third, and perhaps most important, European merchants had market connections, and probably an office, in London. Even so, Chinese overcame these barriers in exporting rubber, a subject explored in chapter 6, and from the 1960s did so in the produce trade as well.

VII

Trade in the foodstuffs of rice, dried fish and sugar stayed large mainly because of re-exports rather than consumption in Singapore (tables 3.8, 3.9

[70] Ibid. II, p.642, and see II, pp.640, 86.
[71] Ibid. IV, p.243, and see II, pp.832–83, 836.
[72] Ibid. II, p.636, and see II, pp.637, 640–42, 524.

and 3.10). Although during the century demand in Singapore became an increasingly important reason for imports of rice and sugar, not until 1937/39 was as much as half of the rice coming to the port retained there.

Rice accounted for most of Singapore's imports from Siam, Burma and Indo-China (table 3.5). Singapore remained a major outlet for Siamese rice, particularly the 'garden' variety favoured by consumers in the Outer Provinces as 'Singapore rice'.[73] Along with Penang, Singapore's importance to Burma's exports was sufficient to lead Rangoon traders to market a grade known as Straits Quality.[74] Siam normally relied on Singapore as a market for a third to two-fifths of its rice.[75] In 1925/27, mainly reflecting rice exports, the port of Singapore handled two-fifths of all the Kingdom's total exports. By 1937/39 rice made up a much smaller proportion of Siam's total exports to Singapore. But the British port still handled almost one third of total Siamese exports, because of the growth of shipments of tin ore and rubber from the Kingdom to Singapore. These additions to trade made Siam, like British Borneo (rubber and some petroleum), a peripheral part of Singapore's hinterland for staples.[76]

The rice trade was the most prominent branch of commerce which in Singapore was exclusive to Chinese firms. Accordingly, a substantial part of the credit to finance rice shipments to outports in the produce exchange trade came from Chinese sources, although no doubt some of the credit derived from European finance made available for other components of the produce exchange trade. Chinese firms could trade in, and finance, commerce in rice, because it required little capital compared to that needed for many primary commodity exports. Capital requirements were low, since the risk of holding stocks was limited by the comparative price stability of rice, and its high liquidity or 'moneyness', which arose from the commodity's role in regional barter relationships.

A substantial group of Singapore firms were the rice trade's market makers in buying from importers and re-selling to distributors. They might share purchases to spread risk, a practice facilitated by the organization of these dealers – some 18 firms in the early 1930s – into the Singapore Rice Traders' Association. Shipments generally arrived by the boatload, and as

---

[73] Ibid. II, p.859, and see II, p.390.
[74] Burma, *Interim report of the committee appointed to enquire into the rice and paddy trade* (Rangoon, 1931), pp.7, 65.
[75] Although by 1937/39, when 47% of Siamese rice exports went to Singapore, about half was merely transhipped there. Cf. Ingram, 'Thailand's rice trade', p.107, and see *SSTC 1933–34* II, p.44.
[76] *The foreign trade and navigation of the Kingdom of Siam years 2468 (1925–26) and 2469 (1926–27)* (Bangkok, 1927), pp.77–80, 87, 96, 158; *Foreign trade of Siam 1938–39*, pp.105–11, 118–20, 195; Kenneth P. Landon, *The Chinese in Thailand* (New York, 1941), p.137.

one of the Association's members explained: 'we form our own little parties and tender for the rice'.[77] No doubt the Association was also useful in any disputes with importers, by 1902 themselves organized into the Siam Traders' Association and Rangoon Traders' Association; a third association subsequently established was probably for rice from Indo-China.[78]

The export of foodstuffs from Singapore was often closely bound up with the interlinkages in regional trade which derived from tropical produce and smallholder rubber. In the late nineteenth and early twentieth century, the basis of Singapore's regional entrepot role in rice had been credit provided through a goods-credit-marketing interlinkage, together with the scarcity of cash, uncertainty over a regional monetary standard and the money qualities possessed by rice itself. During the twentieth century, however, credit became the principal explanation for Singapore's role in the region's rice trade.[79]

Singapore could be by-passed when, as in much of Malaya's trade, finance through a barter relationship was no longer required because of the growing importance of the entirely European-dominated sector and rapidly developing Peninsular commercial facilities. Between 1911/13 and 1937/39 Singapore's rice exports to Malaya (table 3.8) declined continuously to about a quarter of their pre-war volume, while the Peninsula's own direct imports, with at most transhipment via the Straits Settlements, grew rapidly. Peninsular traders imported 4,700 tons of rice directly in 1921, but this rose to 79,300 tons in 1926, 175,100 tons in 1934 and 245,100 tons by 1939.[80]

By contrast, in Singapore's commerce with Netherlands India the distribution of rice stayed 'one of the most important branches of that trade, rice providing one side of a large part of the barter'.[81] As a result, after 1913 Singapore's rice exports to Netherlands India held up much better than those to Malaya. The rice crisis of 1919 to 1921 almost totally halted exports to Netherlands India, but Singapore quickly regained most of its former markets there, and between 1911/13 and 1925/27 rice shipments to the Dutch colony increased (table 3.8).

During the 1930s Singapore's rice exports to Netherlands India fell by substantially less than that country's imports of rice overall, which more than halved, mainly due to a policy of food self-sufficiency in response to

[77] *SSTC 1933–34* II, p.636, and see II, pp.651–52.
[78] Tan, 'Chinese local trade', pp.94–95; Wright and Cartwright, *Twentieth century impressions*, p.726; *SSTC 1933–34* II, p.634.   [79] Huff, 'Bookkeeping barter'.
[80] Malaya, *Foreign imports and exports* (Singapore), annual series, 1921–1934; Malaya, *Foreign trade of Malaya 1939*, and see *SSTC 1933–34* II, p.636, III, p.364, IV, p.37.
[81] *SSTC 1933–34* I, p.47, and see IV, p.252.

the 1930s slump. In 1925/27 Singapore was already Netherlands India's main source of rice; by 1937/39 the share of the British port had increased further, and its traders supplied 36% of total imports by volume.[82] The need for finance made it difficult for Outer Province traders to purchase Java rice even when officially encouraged to do so: 'Rice from Singapore is sold on credit, from Java for hard cash against documents'.[83]

Dried fish, though not of great value, was a steady trade of considerable bulk (table 3.9), as well as an item which Singapore Chinese traders could offer in barter with their counterparts in Rangoon, appropriately known as Straits rice merchants.[84] The trade illustrated how commerce via Singapore drew together the Southeast Asian region it served and, in the city itself, how different aspects of this regional trade were mutually reinforcing. Bangkok and Saigon were the main sources of the fish which was re-dried, prepared and graded in Singapore.[85] Exports went primarily to Netherlands India, especially Java. The latter, in turn, provided almost all Singapore's imports of sugar. After 1900 sugar imports increased substantially (table 3.10). By World War I, when Java began to import rice direct from the producing countries rather than via Singapore,[86] ships which brought sugar from Java to Singapore began to carry dried fish, instead of rice, as the principal return cargo to the Dutch island. However, the fish sent to Java was not usually bartered for sugar.[87]

For sugar, unlike rice and dried fish, retained imports always accounted for a substantial proportion of Singapore's sugar imports, and contributed to major industries on the island, including pineapple canning and biscuit manufacture. Sugar came from Java already refined. But so-called sugar refineries in Singapore, numbering 18 before World War I and 15 in 1926 (table 7.2), made the Javanese product into sugar candy and re-boiled the liquid left from this process into what was called Singapore brown sugar.[88] Between 1925/27 and 1937/39 the decline in sugar imports was probably caused mainly by a loss in re-exports to the FMS because sugar from Java did not receive Imperial Preference given British empire goods, and by a collapse in sugar candy exports to China owing to increased tariffs. At the

[82] Ibid. I, p.51, II, p.890; W. M. F. Mansvelt, *Rice prices* (re-edited and continued by P. Creutzberg as Vol.4 *Changing economy in Indonesia*) (The Hague, 1978), pp.17–23, 68–72; J. van Gelderen, *The recent development of economic foreign policy in the Netherlands East Indies* (London, 1939), pp.28–29; Howard W. Dick, 'Interisland trade, economic integration, and the emergence of the national economy' in Anne Booth, W. J. O'Malley and Anna Weidmann, eds. *Indonesian economic history in the Dutch colonial era* (New Haven, 1990), p.304.   [83] *SSTC 1933–34* V, p.57.

[84] Ibid. I, p.46; Burma, *Report of the rice export-trade enquiry committee* (Rangoon, 1937), p.15; Christian, *Burma*, p.72.   [85] *SSTC 1933–34* II, pp.859–60, 651, I, pp.46, 216.

[86] *Annual statement of the sea-borne trade and navigation of Burma 1913–1914* (Rangoon, 1914), p.195.   [87] *SSTC 1933–34* I, pp.46, 98, 216, II, pp.859–60, 891, IV, p.252.

[88] Ibid. II, pp.650, 811, 860, 891, V, p.129; 'Pineapple conference', *SSLCP 1931*, p.C225.

end of the 1930s just five refineries operated in Singapore.[89] Like most of Singapore's trades conducted by the Chinese, commerce in sugar gave rise to its own organization, the Singapore Sugar Merchants' Association formed in 1911 with a membership of 30 to 40 firms including refineries.[90]

The trades in foodstuffs created in Singapore their own worlds of Chinese commerce. Prior to World War I rice traders – men like Chua Chu Yong, Sim Kheng Hoo and Tan Jiak Ngoh – were among the most wealthy and influential members of Singapore Chinese society.[91] More important, before the War the rice trade was fundamental to the prosperity of Singapore's Chinese community in that most Chinese commerce depended on the collection of hinterland commodities, which largely involved the exchange of rice. The centre of Chinese commerce was Boat Quay where, as subsequently, rice godowns concentrated,[92] and the adjacent Circular Road, a principal location of shops dealing in cotton piece goods – the barter trade's other main component (figure 2.3). Not until the inter-war period did Singapore's Chinese mercantile elite, in estate rubber, the cultivation and canning of pineapples, manufacturing industry and banking, establish major economic interests substantially independent of the rice trade. But just as prior to World War I the rice trade had supported one Chinese mercantile elite, so in the inter-war decades it served to promote the succeeding mercantile elite by helping to draw to Singapore the Netherlands Indian smallholder rubber from which a significant proportion of new wealth derived.

VIII

Like food, manufactured goods distributed from Singapore had three main markets, namely domestic, Malayan and extra-Malayan (table 3.11). Exports kept the trade in manufactured goods large, and depended more on the extra-Malayan than on the Malayan market. During the inter-war period Singapore's domestic market, measured in terms of retained imports, was substantially larger than indicated by table 3.11, although probably still accounting for no more than about half of total imports.[93]

[89] *SSTC 1933–34* II, pp.649, 860, 869, 890–91, I, p.146; Andrew Gilmour, *My role in the rehabilitation of Singapore: 1946–1953* (Singapore, 1973), p.3; Malaya, *Foreign imports and exports 1937.*   [90] *SSTC 1933–34* II, pp. 649–50.

[91] 'Report of the commissioners to enquire into the state of traffic on the Singapore River', *SSLCP 1899*, p.C197; *Directory 1902*, pp.174B–174E; C. F. Yong, 'A preliminary study of Chinese leadership in Singapore', *JSEAH* 9, 2 (1968), pp.274–75.

[92] *Chinese commercial directory of Singapore, Penang, Malacca, Kuala Lumpur, Batu Pahat, Muar* (Singapore, 1932), section L; *SSTC 1933–34* II, p.636, and see II, pp.634, 651; Yap Pheng Geck, *Scholar, banker, gentleman soldier: the reminiscences of Dr. Yap Pheng Geck* (Singapore, 1982), p.97.

[93] Since manufactured exports and re-exports cannot be distinguished in the statistics, for the inter-war period the term 'manufactured exports' is used to refer to both, although re-

Table 3.11 *Singapore trade in manufactures, 1900/02–1935/37 (annual averages)*

	Manufactured imports retained in Singapore (imports less exports)		Manufactured exports to Malaya		Manufactured exports outside Malaya		Total manufactured imports	
	$000	%	$000	%	$000	%	$000	%
1900/02	22,212	41.6	31,194 [a]	58.4 [a]	a	a	53,406	100.0
1911/13	33,063	48.4	15,755	23.0	19,526	28.6	68,344	100.0
1925/27	68,220	34.2	63,723	31.9	67,777	33.9	199,720	100.0
1935/37	86,918 [b]	75.4 [b]	b	b	28,407	24.6	115,325	100.0

Notes:

[a] Includes Manufactured exports to Malaya and Manufactured exports outside Malaya.

[b] Includes Manufactured imports retained in Singapore and Manufactured exports to Malaya.

Sources: SS, *Return of imports and exports*, 1900–1927; Malaya, *Foreign imports and exports*, 1935–1937.

In Singapore, imports of manufactured materials and machinery were essential to industrialization, and were a major aspect of inter-war economic development, together with additions to the mercantile structure associated with the distribution of imports, considered in chapter 9. But the principal contributions of imported manufactures to development were more general – they provided incentives to regional export production and the means to transform Singapore into a thoroughly modern international service centre with good roads, telecommunications, port facilities and water, gas and electricity supplies.

Compared to the late nineteenth century, the importance of the Malayan market for manufactured goods increased considerably, reflecting both rapid Peninsular development brought about by rubber and Singapore's continued dominance in the supply of manufactured goods to the Peninsula (table 3.12). Kuala Lumpur developed to only a limited extent as an import centre and towns in the UMS hardly at all. The inauguration of direct rail services to the Malay states in 1923 facilitated distribution of imports there from Singapore. In the new trades, the island had an advantage because of

exports remained considerably the larger. As Singapore began to industrialize, the statistics calculated for retained imports become misleading, since these are the residual of manufactured imports less manufactured exports, and the latter included domestically-produced manufactures. After 1910 a primary import-substitution phase in Singapore gained pace, and manufactured exports increased more rapidly than the imported manufactures required as inputs for this production. As a result, between 1911/13 and 1925/27, table 3.11 understates the growth in the value of Singapore's retained imports relative to exports to the region.

its own large demand: a substantial Singapore market for the 'new' imports of consumer durables and producer goods served to build up groups of merchants dealing in these items and to keep their transaction costs comparatively low, helping to forestall the emergence of rival importers in the Malay Peninsula.

Singapore's role as the distribution centre for Malaya appeared to be threatened in 1932 by the adoption of Imperial Preference in the Malay Peninsula, and in June 1934 by the introduction of a British Malayan quota system on all cotton and rayon piece goods from outside the British Empire. Both measures were aimed at Japanese goods. However, Imperial Preference proved unimportant to Singapore's exports of manufactures to Malaya, and the quotas for piece goods had relatively little effect.[94] By driving up prices, they reduced demand somewhat, while higher prices encouraged Peninsular merchants to try to obtain supplies of piece goods more cheaply by importing themselves. Between 1933/34 and 1937/38, in the FMS direct imports of cotton and rayon piece goods increased from an

[94] The effect of Imperial Preference on Singapore's trade is further discussed in chapter 9.

Table 3.12 *British Malaya imports of manufactures, 1925/26 and 1935/37* (*annual averages*)

	Total	Singapore	Penang and Malacca	FMS	UMS
	$000	%	%	%	%
1925/26	291,170	70.4	20.5	9.0	0.1
1935/37	167,171	69.0	18.8	11.7	0.5

Notes:
1 Data were not published for 1927.
2 Imports to Malacca were negligible as were those to Labuan, Christmas Island and the Dindings. The last three territories are included in the figure for Penang and Malacca for 1925/26, but together with the Cocos Islands are omitted for 1935/37.
3 Manufactures imported into Malaya may have been transhipped at Singapore.
4 Rows may not add to totals due to rounding.
Sources: SS, *Return of imports and exports*, 1925–1926; British Malaya, *Return of imports and exports*, 1925–1926; Malaya, *Foreign imports and exports*, 1935–1937.

annual average of 3·4 million to 8·4 million yards, and in the UMS from 82,000 to 252,000 yards. But the total value of these increases amounted to no more than about $1 million. For most of the period after May 1934, piece goods exports to Malaya were relatively unhindered by quotas, because Singapore was allowed to establish a system of bonded re-export depots which functioned as free trade zones.[95] The main, longer-term impact on Singapore of British Malayan trade restriction was to emphasize both the uncertainties of continued separation from the Peninsula and, paradoxically, the danger to the port's extra-Malayan trade of any economic union, since this might involve it in a restrictive Malayan regime.

Singapore's larger extra-Malayan than Malayan market for manu- factures strengthened the city's already predominantly international orientation. In exports to Netherlands India – the bulk of the extra- Malayan market – rice was the single most important item, but manu- factured goods made a bigger contribution even than food as a whole (table 3.13). Because of Singapore's large combined exports of manu- factures and foodstuffs to Netherlands India, the Dutch colony remained a more important market for Singapore than Malaya for most of the period between 1900 and 1933 (although not in 1911/13 and 1925/27, as table 3.5 shows).

[95] Sources used for this paragraph are *SSTC 1933–34* I, pp.19–20, 53–54; *SSLCP 1934*, pp.B86–B95; 'Report on the working and effects of quotas on cotton and artificial silk piece goods', *SSAR 1934*, pp.39–43, and Reports for *1935* I, p.481, *1936* I, pp.460, 467, *1937* I, pp.641–42, 647, *1938* I, pp.325, 331–32, 336–38; Malaya, *Foreign imports and exports*, 1933–1937; Malaya, *Foreign trade of Malaya*, 1932–1939; Emerson, *Malaysia*, pp.369–71.

Table 3.13 *Straits Settlements exports to Netherlands India, 1925/27* (*annual averages*)

	$	%
Principal manufactures		
Textiles	17,101	15.0
Holloware	435	0.4
Crockery and porcelain	963	0.9
Cigarettes	6,839	6.0
Galvanized iron	724	0.6
Sewing machines and parts	619	0.5
All other machinery	398	0.4
Bicycles	421	0.4
Motor cars	573	0.5
Tyres and tubes	731	0.6
Principal food		
Rice	26,915	23.7
Dried and salted fish	11,609	10.2
Condensed milk	1,594	1.4
Onions and garlic	1,288	1.1
Coconut oil	1,720	1.5
Petroleum	10,112	8.9
Others	31,709	27.9
Total SS exports	**113,751**	**100.0**
of which exports from Singapore	102,041	

Notes:
1   Petroleum includes kerosene, motor spirit and liquid fuel.
2   Total SS exports and exports from Singapore include treasure of bullion and specie.
Sources: SS, *Return of imports and exports*, 1925–1927.

The point has been made that Singapore served a particular part of the Netherlands Indian market which concentrated in Sumatra and Borneo. Consequently, unlike Malaya, Netherlands India as a whole did not rely heavily on Singapore. Even the Outer Provinces, although using Singapore as an outlet for exports, turned increasingly to Batavia for imports. By 1925/27, 22% of Outer Province imports by value came from Singapore but 30% from Java and Madura; while in 1935/37 these shares were 10% and 45% respectively, mainly as a result of trade restriction.[96] The Netherlands Indian Crisis Import Ordinance of 1933, once in force, 'was

[96] Netherlands India, 'Het Handelsverkeer met Singapore, 1825–1937', p.10; Broek, *Economic development of the Netherlands Indies*, pp.112–16, 124–25; J. H. Boeke, *Economics and economic policy of dual societies* (Haarlem, 1953), pp.269–73.

Table 3.14 *Netherlands India manfactured imports from Singapore, 1925/27 and 1935/37 (annual averages)*

	1925/27		1935/37	
	f.000	%	f.000	%
Cotton textiles	14,748	24.3	593	5.7
Other textiles	6,931	11.4	1,555	15.0
Apparel	4,025	6.6	459	4.4
Cigarettes and cigars	9,847	16.3	580	5.6
Paper and paperware	841	1.4	568	5.5
Cement	55	0.1	26	0.2
Steel and iron	3,675	6.1	440	4.2
Tin plate	976	1.6	227	2.2
Machinery	1,842	3.0	1,171	11.3
Bicycles	317	0.5	112	1.1
Motor cars	868	1.4	128	1.2
Tyres and tubes	708	1.2	115	1.1
Others	15,788	26.1	4,411	42.5
Total	**60,621**	**100.0**	**10,385**	**100.0**

Notes:
1 Cotton textiles include sarongs.
2 Total imports from Singapore were f.122,513,000 in 1925/27 and f.31,381,000 in 1935/37. But the fall in the value of Netherlands Indian imports from Singapore, if expressed in terms of Straits dollars, was considerably less. Between 1925/27 and 1935/37 the guilder appreciated by about a third against the Straits dollar. (van Laanen, *Money and Banking*, table 8).
3 The series 'Survey of values of import of the principal articles . . .' on which this table is mainly based did not begin until 1926. There are a few slight discrepancies between figures taken from the detailed trade returns for 1925 and the survey table for 1926. Figures for Other textiles are from the detailed returns and include wool, silk, rayon and others, yarns, rope and cordage and in 1925/27 bags, but in 1935/37 gunnies. In comparison to the classification 'Textiles' in Singapore's trade statistics, coverage in the Netherlands Indian statistics is less complete.
Sources: 'Jaaroverzicht van den In-en Uitvoer van Nederlandsch-Indie', *Mededeelingen van het Centraal Kantoor voor de Statistiek*, 1925-1927, 1935-1937.

regarded as a splendid enabling act which permitted the taking of all kinds of measures'.[97] Many of them hurt Singapore's trade because, as discussed in chapter 9, it had developed as an entrepot for Japanese manufactures which were a target of restrictive measures. Table 3.14 shows the sharp reduction in Netherlands Indian imports from Singapore and the very severe effect on the textile trade. In the 1930s it was Netherlands Indian, not Malayan, trade restrictions which principally affected Singapore.

The extra-Malayan market's other main constituents were Siam and British Borneo. Siam was the more important, but, like Netherlands India,

[97] Boeke, *Economics of dual societies*, p.270.

Table 3.15 Singapore manufactured imports, 1900/02–1935/37 (annual averages)

	1900/02		1911/13		1925/27		1935/37	
	Volume	$000	Volume	$000	Volume	$000	Volume	$000
Cotton piece goods	3,641,000 pieces	11,230	3,942,000 pieces	13,969	124,183,000 yards	32,128	100,508,000 yards	13,199
Other cotton goods	–	7,547	–	9,271	–	17,501	–	4,841
Non-cotton textiles	–	10,307	–	8,040	–	20,401	–	10,575
Apparel	n.l.	3,831	–	4,329	–	7,702	–	4,701
Holloware	–	–	–	481	3,297 tons	1,836	2,745 tons	822
Crockery and porcelain	–	1,217	–	1,401	1,236,861 packages	1,953	–	656
Cigarettes	n.l.	–	–	4,173	13,118 tons	19,254	9,584 tons	10,117
Cutlery and hardware	–	1,803	–	2,302	–	5,141	–	2,841
Paper and paperware	–	1,559	–	1,807	–	3,905	–	3,630
Cement	74,792 casks	403	311,610 casks	1,313	105,374 tons	2,871	161,243 tons	2,029
Steel	4,829 tons	489	8,619 tons	618	16,918 tons	1,342	34,758 tons	2,670
Galvanized iron	2,060 tons	333	3,371 tons	458	11,014 tons	2,456	9,236 tons	1,163
Tin plate	59,746 boxes	547	101,765 boxes	735	13,630 tons	2,876	19,531 tons	3,464
Machinery	–	1,166	–	1,972	–	6,980	–	4,889
Electrical goods and apparatus (except machinery)	–	565	–	422	–	2,833	–	3,346
Bicycles	–	63	–	277	12,647	579	20,361	348
Motor cars	n.l.	–	–	1,586	6,829	10,761	6,804	7,628
Tyres and tubes	n.l.	–	n.l.	–	–	5,661	–	1,862

Notes:

1   Non-cotton textiles include woollen goods, silk and silk manufactures and manufactures of other textile materials.

2   Apparel includes boots and shoes, haberdashery and millinery, hosiery, outer garments, underwear and other apparel. In the 1900/02 and 1911/13 trade statistics, boots and shoes were not classified as apparel and have been added to that classification. For 1935/37, but not earlier periods, apparel includes buttons, studs, pins and buckles, etc.

3   Holloware consists of cooking and household utensils. For 1911/13 it includes only cooking utensils.

4   For 1900/02 Crockery and porcelain is classified as earthenware in the trade statistics and for 1911/13 as the two classifications earthenware and crockery and porcelain.

5   Cutlery and hardware includes hardware and cutlery, tools, implements and instruments, clocks and watches and photographic materials. For 1925/27 and 1935/37 it corresponds to the trade statistics classification of cutlery, hardware, implements and instruments.

6   For 1900/02 and 1911/13 Paper and paperware includes the three classifications: paper and paperware, stationary, and playing cards. Subsequently it became a single classification.

7   Galvanized iron includes corrugated and sheet.

8   In 1900/02 and 1911/13 Steel was simply classified as steel. From 1925/27 it includes steel, bars, rods, angles, shapes and sections; steel plates and sheets; steel girders, beams, joints and pillars; and steel rails.

9   For 1900/02 and 1911/13 Electrical goods and apparatus (except machinery) includes only telegraph and telephone materials. The trade statistics did not show other electrical goods and apparatus.

10   Until 1937 Bicycles were listed as cycles. For 1900/02 accessories are included. For 1911/13 the value is for 1913 only, since in 1911 and 1912 bicycles were included with motor cars.

11   Motor cars include passenger and commercial. For 1911 and 1912 the value includes the whole of the classification cycles, motor cars and accessories. In 1937 second-hand motor cars were shown separately but are included in the figure given.

Sources: SS, *Return of imports and exports,* 1900–1927; Malaya, *Foreign imports and exports,* 1935–1937.

Table 3.16 *Singapore manufactured and textile imports, 1900/02–1935/37 (annual averages)*

	Manufactured imports $000	Textile imports $000	Textiles as a % of manufactured imports
1900/02	53,406	29,084	54.5
1911/13	68,344	31,280	45.8
1925/27	199,720	70,030	35.1
1935/37	115,325	28,615	24.8

Notes:
1   Textiles include cotton yarn and manufactures, woollen goods, silk and silk manufactures and manufactures of other textile materials. For 1900/02 and 1911/13 the figures include all items in the trade statistics classification 'C.(A) – Textiles' but excluding apparel.
2   For 1935/37 textile imports from Malaya are excluded but were negligible.
Sources:as for table 3.15.

relied on Singapore more as a market for exports than a source of imports. In the inter-war period textile exports from Singapore to Siam declined markedly as their use in barter for rice lessened. Nevertheless, in 1911/14 and in 1925/27 the Kingdom obtained one-seventh, and in 1937/39 nearly one-sixth, of all its imports from Singapore.[98] British Borneo was comparatively unimportant to Singapore, although looking to the city as a principal market for its commodity exports and as a major source of imports. In 1925/27 British Borneo took less than 2% of Singapore's total exports and provided 4% of Singapore's imports, of which the chief component was rubber (tables 3.4 and 3.5).

Table 3.15 indicates the great change in the composition of Singapore's manufactured imports over the first four decades of the century; there was a relative decline in textiles and shift towards manufactured materials and new, durable consumer goods. Until World War I, by value about a half of all manufactures were textiles (table 3.16), of which cotton piece goods made up approximately two-fifths, other cotton goods, mainly sarongs, a further third and non-cotton textiles, including silk piece goods, the remainder. Between 1911/13 and 1925/27 textiles, although increasing little in volume, doubled in value. However, by the latter period they

[98] Siam, *Foreign trade of Siam* (*Bangkok*), *1910–11 and 1912–13*, p.84, *1912–13 and 1913–14*, p.118, *1925–26 and 1926–27*, p.158, *1938–39*, pp.195, 338. As late as 1925/27, 20% of the piece goods Siam imported came from Singapore. But in the 1930s, as Siam increasingly began to buy Japanese piece goods directly, the proportion obtained through Singapore fell to 13% in 1936/39. For statistics of cotton piece goods, see *Foreign trade of Siam*. They consisted of 'prints and chintzes', 'white shirting', 'grey shirting', 'turkey red cloth' and 'all other piece goods'.

accounted for only just over a third, and in 1935/37 a quarter, of the value of manufactured imports. To some extent, this decline was explained by swifter growth in other traditional trades, especially cigarettes, which in the inter-war period became, after cotton piece goods, Singapore's most valuable manufactured import. After 1925/27, however, a more important factor in the declining share of textiles was sharper price falls for these goods than for other manufactures.[99]

But until the 1930s the principal reason for the relative decline in the importance of textiles in Singapore's manufactured imports was the rise of the new trades. Imports of producer goods such as cement, galvanized iron and tin plate expanded rapidly until 1925/27 and, generally, continued to increase in the 1930s. More remarkable, if lacking the buoyancy of manufactured materials in the 1930s, was the inter-war growth in consumer durables. Many were product innovations, notably motor cars, tyres and tubes and a variety of electrical goods, including refrigerators, radios and telephones.

Changes in the composition of Singapore's imports of manufactured goods reflected growing differences in the levels of structural trans-formation and economic development, not just between Singapore and its hinterland but also between different parts of the hinterland. Consequently, Singapore's trade composition mirrored, not simply an urban–rural dualism, but more a tripartite division; this broadly corresponded to the domestic, Malayan and extra-Malayan markets. Table 3.17 indicates this threefold division and the reliance of the new and the old trades on substantially different markets. Before World War I, when textiles had accounted for nearly half of Singapore's retained imports, there was no very significant distinction between the types of manufactures retained in the city and those exported. By 1925/27 the proportion of textiles in manufactured imports retained in Singapore was not much over a quarter, although textiles still accounted for more than two-fifths of manufactured exports from the port. By contrast, a half to two-thirds of most producer goods and consumer durables imported by Singapore were retained there. Most of the new trades reflected the tastes of a growing urban middle class among whom the use of automobiles and electrical appliances had become commonplace, and were contingent on Singapore's infrastructure.

The Malay Peninsula formed a subsidiary outlet for the new trades; from 1911/13 to 1925/27 and (judged on the basis of incomplete statistics) probably 1935/37, demand for producer goods and consumer durables was the main factor behind the rapid growth of Singapore's Malayan

---

[99] For unit value indices of manufactured imports between 1924 and 1939, see Malaya, *Average prices, declared trade values, exchange, currency and cost of living* (Singapore), annual series, 1930, 1935, 1939.

Table 3.17 *Distribution of manufactured imports, 1925/27 (annual averages)*

	Retained imports (imports less exports)		Exports to Malaya		Exports outside Malaya		Total imports	
	$000	%	$000	%	$000	%	$000	%
Textiles	24,822	35.5	15,925	22.7	29,283	41.8	70,030	100.0
Apparel	346	4.5	3,436	44.6	3,920	50.9	7,702	100.0
Holloware	755	41.1	452	24.6	629	34.3	1,836	100.0
Crockery and porcelain	233	11.9	764	39.1	956	49.0	1,953	100.0
Cigarettes	2,801	14.6	7,132	37.0	9,321	48.4	19,254	100.0
Cutlery and hardware	380	7.4	3,697	71.9	1,064	20.7	5,141	100.0
Paper and paperware	2,439	62.5	960	24.6	506	12.9	3,905	100.0
Cement	1,696	59.1	1,001	34.9	174	6.0	2,871	100.0
Steel	913	68.0	307	22.9	122	9.1	1,342	100.0
Galvanized iron	801	32.6	694	28.3	961	39.1	2,456	100.0
Tin plate	1,588	55.2	849	29.5	439	15.3	2,876	100.0
Machinery	3,178	45.5	2,403	34.4	1,399	20.1	6,980	100.0
Electrical goods and apparatus (except machinery)	1,675	59.1	775	27.4	383	13.5	2,833	100.0
Bicycles	(−6)		213	36.4	372	63.6	579	(100.0)
Motor cars	4,696	43.7	5,092	47.3	973	9.0	10,761	100.0
Tyres & tubes	(−179)		3,835	72.7	1,443	27.3	5,099	(100.0)

Notes:

1 Retained imports are imports less exports. However, the export statistics reflect value added in Singapore and local manufacture. A problem of interpretation therefore arises when, as discussed below, there was substantial value added in Singapore or, more important, local manufacture. For these trades Singapore's own market was larger than the figures for retained imports indicate, and manufactured re-exports were less than suggested.

2 For textiles demand in the town was somewhat greater than indicated, because value was added to imports of plain cotton piece goods by the dyeing and printing industry. To a limited extent the manufacture in Singapore of apparel for export affects the statistics for that trade.

3 Because of the manufacture of cigarettes in Singapore, demand in the town was considerably higher than the figure for retained imports suggests and correspondingly re-exports were less.

4 The bicycle–assembly industry in Singapore was large enough to give a false impression of re-exports and make retained imports appear as a negative figure.

5 For motor cars Malaya's importance is overstated and that of Singapore understated because of Ford's assembly plant in the town. Motor car exports to foreign countries mainly reflect the fact that Ford in Canada used Singapore as a centre to distribute automobiles to Netherlands India and Siam. (Boulter, *Economic conditions, 1931*, p.38).

6 For tyres and tubes retained imports appear as a negative figure due to local manufacture, mainly by Tan Kah Kee & Co.

7 The high proportion of cutlery and hardware re-exported to Malaya was primarily because this category had a large component of agricultural implements.

8 Re-exports of galvanized iron to foreign markets principally reflect its widespread use as a roofing material in the region.

Sources: SS, *Return of imports and exports*, 1925–1927.

market. The European enterprise which spread in Malaya differed sharply in its production structure from Malayan peasant and small-scale producers in using more capital and requiring a managerial and administrative class. As a result, European enterprise did less than these producers to expand the demand for traditional consumer goods via Singapore, but absorbed a much larger component of imported capital goods. At the same time, European enterprise encouraged the growth of a Peninsular middle class which considerably increased in importance during the inter-war period. However, European-controlled production in Malaya, and the new imports, which closely paralleled its development and were largely sustained by it, accounted for a high proportion of Singapore's manufactured exports to Malaya and involved comparatively few merchants. For the most part, they were the European merchant and agency houses already established in Singapore in the late nineteenth century; the appearance of the entirely European-dominated trade sector and new imports did not give rise to a major new mercantile structure.

The Netherlands Indian market became the main outlet for the traditional trades because it continued primarily to involve the supply of goods required by peasant producers. Neither the international oil companies operating in the Dutch colony nor its tin mines, largely under government control, took any significant return flow of imports from Singapore. Nor did these enterprises do much to foster the growth of a middle class in the Outer Provinces where Singapore's Netherlands Indian hinterland lay. Traders in Netherlands India, as well as Siam and British Borneo, who traditionally had obtained textiles and other non-durable consumer goods via Singapore, by the mid-1920s occasionally also took a bicycle or perhaps a manual or treadle sewing machine, but not much else.

IX

After 1900 the organization of trade along the five lines indicated – the produce exchange trade, an entirely European-dominated sector for exports, the two categories of old and new imports, and commerce in food – helps to explain some of the most prominent aspects of Singapore's economic development and, by implication, the religious regard paid to the maintenance of a free port which necessitated political independence. The produce exchange trade remained large through the addition of small-holder rubber, and both produce and rubber came almost wholly from Netherlands India. The trade was especially important in accounting for much of the distribution of rice and simple manufactures from Singapore. Their distribution, like the collection of produce, required substantial physical facilities and an extensive mercantile and financial structure in

Singapore. Together, the collection of produce and export of rice and simple manufactures were fundamental to the size and strength of Singapore's Chinese mercantile community.

The produce exchange trade's dependence on Netherlands India, the extensive linkages and spread effects for Singapore arising from this trade and the need for a free port to assure the availability of competitively-priced manufactures and so attract primary commodity exports, all throw light on the weight which interests in Singapore continued to attach to international rather than Malayan status. In rejecting closer association with the Peninsula, the Customs Duties Committee emphasized that

The prosperity of Singapore and Penang, greatly though the tin and rubber of Malaya have aided their development, is still based on the exchange trade with neighbouring countries in general tropical produce ... This produce exchange trade is then an industry in itself. It is in fact a primary industry of the Colony and gives employment in one form and another to a large part of the population.[100]

[100] 'Customs duties committee', *SSLCP 1932*, p.C158.

4   Ocean-going shipping, the port and regional transport

By World War I Singapore was the seventh busiest port in the world in terms of shipping tonnage handled; in the 1920s over 50 different lines stopped there.[1] Ocean-going shipping was neither organized from Singapore nor built up with it in mind. But merchants in the city could draw on passing international shipping traffic to lift exports, with the result that Singapore had a readily available supply of tonnage. Within this framework of economic growth dependent on a largely exogenously determined flow of world shipping, three questions specific to Singapore arise: the effect of the introduction of the shipping conference system; the provision of adequate port facilities; and the need to develop regional transport. After examining the pattern of ocean-going shipping in section I of this chapter, each of these issues is considered respectively in sections II to IV.

I

Three streams of outward-bound shipping from the West converged on Singapore – one using the Suez Canal, a second taking the Cape route and joining the Suez stream in the area of the Indian subcontinent, and a third beginning in the Indian area. Beyond Singapore shipping fanned out, partly to termini in Siam, Indo-China, British Borneo and Netherlands India, and partly as a main stream to Far Eastern ports. In returning and now sailing 'homewards' in the direction of the United Kingdom, these streams of shipping again came together at Singapore.[2]

Ocean-going shipping and Singapore's trade were not closely correlated: the port's world position and lack of sufficient cargo either outward or homeward to make it profitable as a terminus meant that 'Singapore is a port of call for a large number of ships which take little part in the trade of

---

[1] Chiang, *History of Straits Settlements trade*, p.39; 'Report on the Straits Settlements', *SSAR 1923*, p.335, *1929*, p.506.

[2] ISC, *British shipping in the orient* (London, 1939), pp.5–9.

Singapore'.[3] The most common arrangement was that ocean-going liners, which dominated the Singapore carrying trade, picked up or deposited small amounts of cargo *en passant*. Ordinarily, liners called twice at Singapore during a voyage, 'once on the outward lap to discharge and again on the inward one to load'.[4]

In the inter-war period rubber and petroleum created two important exceptions to this general picture. Rubber was carried mainly by eight shipping lines on a 'round the world' route which started from the Atlantic coast of the United States and went westward by the Panama and Suez Canals. Although this 'round the world' service brought few goods to Singapore, rubber provided a large cargo for its 'homeward leg' to New York.[5] Petroleum distribution gave rise to the principal use of Singapore as a terminal port by ocean-going shipping.[6]

Shipping statistics for Singapore were divided into vessels of under 50 tons net register (75 tons from 1931) and those of 50 (or 75) tons net register and over. This division did not clearly distinguish between ocean-going and local shipping, defined as vessels confined wholly to regional waters bounded by Burma, Siam and Netherlands India. Instead, the collection of shipping statistics was determined by licensing requirements: masters of smaller ships needed only a local steam vessel's ticket, but masters of larger ships required a ticket of the British merchant marine.[7] The very large number of ships under 50 (or 75) tons traded almost entirely to small, nearby ports. However, many local shipping services also operated with vessels of 50 (or 75) tons and over. For vessels over 50 (or 75) tons, ocean-going shipping dominated the statistics for tonnage. Although ocean-going vessels were also the main determinant of the number of ships, here local shipping exerted a substantial influence, and during the 1920s perhaps even the principal one with rapid growth in the local fleet. After 1930 the new limit of 75 tons excluded up to a third of local vessels from the statistics.

The total net registered tonnage of merchant vessels cleared at Singapore divides into four periods (appendix table A.6). Since tonnage statistics reflect mainly ocean-going shipping, these periods corresponded primarily to growth phases in the world economy rather than to phases in Singapore's own growth. The first period to 1913 was one of continuous expansion, as shipping tonnage rose from 5·4 million tons in 1900 to reach 9·2 million tons. A second period during World War I was the only time when ocean-

[3] Ibid. p.22.
[4] Allen, *Report on major ports*, p.9, and see *SSTC 1933–34* I, pp.112, 116.
[5] ISC, *British shipping*, pp.9, 87; *SSTC 1933–34* II, p.894, IV, p.505; E. G. Holt, *Marketing of crude rubber* (Washington, DC: US Department of Commerce, 1927), p.186.
[6] *SSTC 1933–34* I, pp.116, 189, II, p.909.   [7] Tregonning, *Home port*, pp.79–80.

going shipping moved in the opposite direction to Singapore's trade. The availability of shipping contracted sharply, especially after 1916, because vessels (mostly ocean-going) were requisitioned for wartime usage; by 1918 total tonnage had fallen to three-fifths of its 1913 level. After the War shipping services were quickly re-established, and a third period of rapid growth began in the 1920s. Reflecting an over-expansion of world capacity, tonnage reached 16·5 million tons by 1929. The fourth period during the 1930s was one of stagnation, although the mini-boom in the world economy took shipping tonnage to an inter-war peak of 17·1 million tons in 1937.

During World War I the shipping links available to Singapore as a port able to look to the Pacific Ocean as well as to Europe and the Atlantic allowed it to circumvent the wartime shortage of tonnage for exports which affected many British colonies,[8] and so to participate in the boom in the United States economy. As late as 1913 shipments of rubber and tin went predominantly to London, an entrepot for both commodities,[9] and at the beginning of World War I an embargo was imposed, compelling exporters to send all rubber through Britain. But when the embargo was relaxed in 1915, Singapore merchants could send rubber and tin direct to the United States, using Pacific routes and relying partly on Japanese and American tonnage.[10]

For Singapore the contraction of ocean-going shipping during World War I created two problems. First, it seriously curtailed two exports of high bulk: copra and canned pineapples. For a time the Chinese industry of pineapple canning 'ceased to exist, and practically all the factories were closed down'.[11] Second, the lack of tonnage led to a considerable congestion of produce in Singapore. By early 1917 this congestion, which did not yet include rubber, had brought about an acute shortage of warehouse accommodation, causing many residential dwellings to be turned into godowns.[12]

The tonnage of shipping handled by Singapore increased primarily because ships became larger (appendix table A.6). Between 1900 and 1930 the number of ships over 50 tons doubled, but their total tonnage more

---

[8] Birnberg and Resnick, *Colonial development*, pp.220–22.
[9] *Annual statement of the trade of the United Kingdom with foreign countries and British possessions* (PP 1913, LXII, PP 1914, LXXXIV).
[10] H. Price, 'Growth of the rubber trade' in Makepeace, et al., eds. *One hundred years* II, p.86; 'Rubber supplement', *Straits Budget*, 6 Oct. 1916, p.4; 'Report on the Straits Settlements', *SSAR 1917*, p.121; J. H. Drabble, *Rubber in Malaya, 1876–1922* (Kuala Lumpur, 1973), p.125.
[12] 'Report on the Straits Settlements', *SSAR 1916*, pp.13–14, *1918*, p.163, *1919*, p.25; *Proceedings and report of the commission to inquire into housing* (1918) I, p.A22, II, pp.B146–B147.

Table 4.1 *Merchant vessels of 50 tons net register and over entering Singapore, 1904/05–1928/29 (annual averages)*

Countries from which arrived	1904/05				1912/13				1928/29			
	Vessels	%	Tons 000	%	Vessels	%	Tons 000	%	Vessels	%	Tons 000	%
Southeast Asia	**3,718**	**69.8**	**2,206**	**35.2**	**4,245**	**70.3**	**2,992**	**35.5**	**7,238**	**74.3**	**5,697**	**37.6**
Malay Peninsula	736	13.8	189	3.0	747	12.4	252	3.0	1,841	18.9	461	3.0
Penang	253	4.8	204	3.3	305	5.0	233	2.8	303	3.1	229	1.5
Malacca	279	5.2	37	0.5	350	5.8	63	0.7	580	6.0	154	1.0
Netherlands India	1,768	33.2	897	14.3	1,998	33.1	1,407	16.7	3,292	33.8	3,258	21.5
Siam	394	7.4	299	4.8	454	7.5	359	4.3	710	7.3	645	4.3
Indo-China	83	1.6	105	1.7	139	2.3	203	2.4	126	1.3	281	1.9
British Borneo	17	0.3	13	0.2	114	1.9	78	0.9	245	2.5	321	2.1
Burma	114	2.1	295	4.7	82	1.4	244	2.9	64	0.6	147	1.0
Philippines	74	1.4	167	2.7	56	0.9	153	1.8	77	0.8	201	1.3
Europe, United States and Japan	**692**	**13.0**	**1,964**	**31.3**	**935**	**15.5**	**3,224**	**38.2**	**1,494**	**15.4**	**6,478**	**42.8**
United Kingdom	196	3.7	510	8.1	235	3.9	862	10.2	259	2.7	1,178	7.8
Europe	213	4.0	618	9.9	312	5.2	1,027	12.2	523	5.4	2,220	14.7
United States	70	1.3	182	2.9	49	0.8	174	2.0	136	1.4	497	3.3
Japan	213	4.0	654	10.4	339	5.6	1,161	13.8	576	5.9	2,583	17.0
Rest of world	**916**	**17.2**	**2,099**	**33.5**	**854**	**14.2**	**2,214**	**26.3**	**1,005**	**10.3**	**2,963**	**19.6**
Hong Kong	220	4.2	562	9.0	202	3.4	591	7.0	136	1.4	302	2.0
China	244	4.6	452	7.2	205	3.4	446	5.3	199	2.0	405	2.7
British India	229	4.3	554	8.8	322	5.3	928	11.0	375	3.8	1,214	8.0
Australia	55	1.0	102	1.6	71	1.2	155	1.9	104	1.1	296	2.0
Others	168	3.1	429	6.9	54	0.9	94	1.1	191	2.0	746	4.9
Total	**5,326**	**100.0**	**6,269**	**100.0**	**6,034**	**100.0**	**8,430**	**100.0**	**9,737**	**100.0**	**15,138**	**100.0**

Sources: 'Marine Department', *SSAR*, 1904–1929.

than trebled. After 1930 this trend continued, although the new limit of 75 tons makes comparison with earlier years impossible. The greater size of individual vessels led to the need for more fuel, water and other supplies, but not for additional wharf facilities so long as ships anchored in the roads. The demand for additional wharfage became pressing only when vessels began to be drawn to the wharves, a development discussed below.

Statistics for arrivals and departures of vessels of 50 tons and over (tables 4.1 and 4.2) indicate the nature of shipping activity at Singapore. Liner traffic to and from the industrialized countries and local shipping engaged in regional distribution met at Singapore; together the two flows increasingly dominated shipping at the port. By 1928/29 the movement of ships between Singapore and the United Kingdom, Europe, the United States and Japan made up over two-fifths of shipping tonnage, although less than one-sixth of ships. Southeast Asian arrivals and departures comprised nearly two-fifths of tonnage and three-quarters of ships. However, these proportions overstate shipping wholly confined to the region because they include liner traffic which originated outside the region but had a terminus there, usually in Netherlands India, Siam or Indo-China. This traffic appeared under regional totals when leaving Singapore for a terminus in the region and again when calling at the port on the return voyage. Even so, the flow of regional shipping was a fairly close reflection of Singapore's trade. Netherlands India had the greatest share of shipping traffic and tonnage, followed by British Malaya and Siam. Although the last country was relatively unimportant to Singapore, in 1925/27 and 1937/39 at Bangkok half of all ships and almost two-fifths of shipping tonnage came from Singapore, while a like proportion cleared for it.[13]

Because of the essentially shuttle pattern of local as well as ocean-going shipping, arrival and departure statistics by port of origin and destination were not significantly different. One exception was the United Kingdom, for which arrivals considerably outweighed departures. The imbalance probably reflected Britain's much greater importance as a source of manufactured imports than as a market for primary exports, so that not all vessels from the United Kingdom which called at Singapore on their outward journey had reason to do so on their homeward leg. A feature of shipping patterns was the paucity of direct services between Singapore and the United States, partly because there were few direct connections with the American west coast, despite its relative nearness.[14]

Statistics for the nationality of vessels (table 4.3) emphasize Singapore's linkages to the world at large rather than just to Britain. The British

[13] *Foreign trade of Siam 1925–26 and 1926–27*, pp.162–63, *1938–39*, pp.200–1.
[14] *SSTC 1933–34* IV, p.253, II p.893.

Table 4.2 *Merchant vessels of 50 tons net register and over clearing from Singapore, 1904/05–1928/29 (annual averages)*

Countries to which departed	1904/05				1912/13				1928/29			
	Vessels	%	Tons 000	%	Vessels	%	Tons 000	%	Vessels	%	Tons 000	%
Southeast Asia	**3,800**	**71.7**	**2,176**	**34.7**	**4,267**	**70.9**	**2,912**	**34.6**	**7,408**	**76.1**	**5,970**	**39.4**
Malay Peninsula	675	12.7	187	3.0	767	12.7	252	3.0	2,022	20.8	855	5.7
Penang	239	4.5	169	2.7	287	4.8	225	2.7	345	3.6	316	2.1
Malacca	342	6.5	40	0.6	312	5.2	54	0.6	572	5.9	128	0.8
Netherlands India	1,871	35.3	1,039	16.6	1,988	33.0	1,331	15.8	3,282	33.7	3,101	20.5
Siam	449	8.5	348	5.5	489	8.1	403	4.8	751	7.7	658	4.3
Indo–China	74	1.4	118	1.9	164	2.7	199	2.4	117	1.2	339	2.2
British Borneo	23	0.4	18	0.3	105	1.8	79	0.9	227	2.3	297	2.0
Burma	62	1.2	135	2.2	92	1.5	243	2.9	49	0.5	97	0.6
Philippines	65	1.2	122	1.9	63	1.1	126	1.5	43	0.4	179	1.2
Europe, United States and Japan	**693**	**13.1**	**2,059**	**32.8**	**1,035**	**17.2**	**3,612**	**42.9**	**1,437**	**14.7**	**6,486**	**42.9**
United Kingdom	53	1.0	177	2.8	74	1.2	297	3.5	117	1.2	606	4.0
Europe	251	4.7	703	11.2	400	6.7	1,387	16.5	546	5.6	2,654	17.6
United States	57	1.1	181	2.9	67	1.1	249	3.0	172	1.7	714	4.7
Japan	332	6.3	998	15.9	494	8.2	1,679	19.9	602	6.2	2,512	16.6
Rest of world	**806**	**15.2**	**2,044**	**32.5**	**719**	**11.9**	**1,896**	**22.5**	**892**	**9.2**	**2,682**	**17.7**
Hong Kong	163	3.1	352	5.6	62	1.0	149	1.8	118	1.2	352	2.3
China	226	4.3	516	8.2	147	2.4	420	5.0	146	1.5	369	2.4
British India	340	6.4	851	13.5	358	6.0	1,017	12.1	298	3.1	948	6.3
Australia	60	1.1	117	1.9	68	1.1	147	1.7	124	1.3	404	2.7
Others	17	0.3	207	3.3	84	1.4	163	1.9	206	2.1	609	4.0
Total	**5,299**	**100.0**	**6,279**	**100.0**	**6,021**	**100.0**	**8,420**	**100.0**	**9,737**	**100.0**	**15,138**	**100.0**

Notes:
1   For 1905 the figure in the *SSAR* for the total number of vessels should read 5,268.
2   Columns may not add to totals due to rounding.
Sources: as for table 4.1.

Table 4.3 *Nationality of merchant vessels of 50 tons net register and over, 1900/01–1928/29, and 75 tons net register and over, 1938/39, clearing from Singapore (%, annual averages)*

	1900/01	1912/13	1919/20	1928/29	1938/39
(a) *Vessels*					
United Kingdom	51.7	47.4	49.6	51.3	36.8
Netherlands	23.9	25.9	23.4	27.8	33.6
Japan	1.7	4.4	12.2	5.1	6.8
Germany	10.4	8.7	0.2	2.1	2.3
France	2.7	2.5	3.5	2.2	2.9
Norway	2.4	3.7	1.1	5.6	8.8
United States	0.2	0.0	2.6	0.7	0.5
Siam	0.2	2.0	3.3	1.9	1.4
British Borneo	0.2	1.3	1.4	1.2	1.3
Others	6.6	4.1	2.7	2.1	5.6
Total number	**4,787**	**6,021**	**5,694**	**9,737**	**6,465**
(b) *Tons*					
United Kingdom	52.8	50.1	46.4	41.1	35.4
Netherlands	7.3	12.4	13.8	22.3	25.0
Japan	5.3	10.5	22.4	13.0	12.3
Germany	16.5	11.9	0.0	5.4	4.8
France	4.7	4.1	4.5	6.5	5.7
Norway	2.3	2.1	0.8	4.1	6.8
United States	0.3	0.0	5.2	2.1	0.9
Siam	0.1	0.8	1.4	0.6	0.4
British Borneo	0.0	0.6	0.6	0.5	0.3
Others	10.7	7.5	4.9	4.4	8.4
Total tons	**5,144**	**8,420**	**7,793**	**15,138**	**15,720**

Notes:
1   For 1900/01 the figure for Norway includes Sweden.
2   For 1900/01 the figure for British Borneo is for Sarawak only.
3   Columns may not sum to totals due to rounding.
Sources:'Marine Department', *SSAR*, 1900–1929, SS, *Blue books*, 1938–1939.

merchant marine made only a modest contribution to the growth of shipping using Singapore: while at the turn of the century British shipping accounted for over half of vessels and tonnage, by 1938/39 these proportions were little more than a third. Over the four decades the growing importance of Dutch shipping, chiefly at the expense of British, represented the success of the late nineteenth-century decision by the Netherlands government to develop both local and ocean-going services as an instrument of policy.[15] The figures for Japanese and American shipping

[15]   Ibid. IV, pp.12–13, 36; ISC, *British shipping*, pp.24–25, 56; Dick, 'Interisland trade', pp.301–2.

for 1919/20 indicate the wartime role of these countries, but subsequently neither held their gains. German shipping interests never recovered from World War I, when the local services of Norddeutscher Lloyd were liquidated as enemy property. During the inter-war period vessels under the British flag enjoyed a virtual monopoly in the coasting trade of British Malaya, because of the disappearance of the German lines and an agreement between the two principal (British and Dutch) shipping companies to limit competition. Without this monopoly, in the inter-war period the British share in shipping as a whole would have declined even further.[16]

II

The establishment of the shipping conference system by metropolitan shipowners based in Britain, Europe and, to a lesser extent, the United States affected Singapore in two main ways. One was its impact on the city's European mercantile structure. The other involved a much wider question: the relationship between Singapore's resource endowment of location and its economic development. These two aspects of the conference system are discussed in turn.

The purpose of a shipping conference was (and is) to set and maintain rates of freight on a particular trade route. It sought to bind shippers, often by loyalty or deferred rebates, to the exclusive use of conference vessels, to discourage independent competitors and entrants by rate wars or other means, and to suppress internal competition among conference members. The successful 'conference' among shipowners functioned as a collective monopoly.

Because in the late nineteenth century homeward shipping much greater than Singapore's needs already called regularly at the port, its shippers did not attach much weight to the usual advantages of a conference – regularity of service and certainty of price. Singapore's location on the main world east–west shipping route, together with the late nineteenth-century excess of tonnage homewards, meant that numerous ships with space available stopped at the port to bunker and, already there, could take on cargo at low marginal cost, amounting to no more than selling and cargo handling expenses. Large shippers in Singapore were 'almost in a position to dictate ... terms to the steamship lines';[17] in 1896 freight rates from Singapore to London fell to less than those charged by coasting steamer from London to Liverpool.[18]

---

[16] ISC, *British shipping*, pp.22, 50, 105.   [17] *RC on shipping rings, 1909* I, p.15.
[18] Ibid. IV, p.180.

Tramp shipping was readily available and responsive to any increase in liner freight rates at Singapore. Tramps offered a good substitute for liners, since much of the port's cargo was suitable for chartering, something which certain of the merchant houses, and also the specialist produce firms, constantly did. In Singapore's open freight market, charterers bargained with other exporters to sell unwanted shipping space and load ships.[19] Although most shipowners employed one or other of the large merchant houses as shipping agents, these agency contracts were not of much value so long as Singapore had a competitive freight market. Fees which merchant houses received for acting as shipping agents tended to be competed away in bidding against each other to attract cargo from non-agent Singapore merchants. In 1879 a Straits Outward Conference came into existence without occasioning much comment in Singapore, but mercantile opposition there soon destroyed the initial two attempts by shipowners in the 1880s and 1890s to form a conference for homewards cargo.

The Straits Homeward Conference was established in 1897 only by the exceptional means of a 'secret' rebate. Among the world's ports, this was unique to Singapore.[20] The 'secret' rebate was the payment made by the shipowners to a group of merchant houses to buy their agreement to a conference system; it was additional to a 10% deferred rebate allowed all Singapore shippers adhering to the Conference. The agreement incorporating the 'secret' rebate – a non-standard commercial contract – resulted in quasi-vertical integration between shipowners and shippers.[21] Five merchant houses were crucial to the establishment of the Conference and shared in the 'secret' rebate – hereafter described as the Conference merchants. They handled a substantial proportion of Singapore's exports to the West, although exactly how much remains unclear, as no evidence on this was given until 1907. The Conference merchants were the four British houses of Boustead & Co. (founded 1827), Adamson, Gilfillan & Co. (1867), Paterson, Simons & Co. (c. 1828) and the Borneo Co. (1857), together with the German house of Behn, Meyer & Co. (1840).

After the formation of the Straits Homeward Conference, its spokesmen acknowledged a 35% rise in freight rates, although owing to earlier fluctuations opponents could easily produce much higher figures. However, taking 35% as the rise, the Conference shipowners had to surrender as the 'secret' rebate about a fifth of the increase in revenue obtained from

---

[19] *Commission on the Straits Homeward Conference, 1902*, pp.1–2, 9, evidence, pp.48–49, 86, 101; *SSTC 1933–34* II, pp.80, 99–100, IV, p.82.

[20] *RC on shipping rings, 1909* I, p.80.

[21] On quasi-integration and non-standard commercial contracts, see Steve Davies, 'Vertical integration' in Roger Clarke and Tony McGuinness, *The economics of the firm* (Oxford, 1987), p.85.

raising freight rates above the competitive level. By 1907 the Singapore merchant houses party to the agreement with the shipowners controlled about 60% of exports of produce, but received as the 'secret' rebate 5% of the value of *all* freight loaded in Singapore. The merchant houses divided this payment among themselves, and for some it represented as much as 20% of their total expenditure on freight.[22] This mercantile share of revenue from the Conference probably outweighed even short-term profits potentially available in the open freight market; over the longer term, the payment had the decided attraction of being riskless.[23]

The Straits Homeward Conference almost immediately became a monopoly seller of shipping services from Singapore to Britain and Europe. Moreover, from 1905 the monopoly was extended over all homeward services with the formation of the New York Freights Conference (later the Straits-New York Conference) for liner traffic from Singapore to the east coast of the United States. The New York Conference involved the same merchant houses and many of the same shipowners as the Straits Homeward Conference; the 'secret' rebate was again the price for mercantile participation. The two conferences – commonly referred to together as the Conference – controlled all liner traffic homewards from Singapore and effectively eliminated competition from tramps. Although a large number of tramp ships still called at Singapore, for example when bringing coal, they were not engaged to carry homewards cargoes and usually left the port empty. By the inter-war period several other shipping conferences existed at Singapore, but were much less important than the two homewards conferences: they carried relatively little cargo and sometimes were only loosely organized.

In contrast to the shipowners' monopoly, the five Conference merchants strengthened their position more slowly and never fully attained a monopsony. Yet even during the first decade of the century, the effect of the conference system on Singapore's European mercantile structure was permanently to alter it. The sum repaid by the Conference to all merchants as the 10% deferred rebate on shipping freight expenditure during the year in practice represented for many merchants their profits for that period.[24] The impact on the mercantile structure of the 'secret' rebate, giving its recipients as much as a further 20% rebate on freight expenditure, was therefore dramatic. All Singapore European merchant houses faced the same demand curve in exporting tropical produce to world markets. The

[22] *Straits Times*, 3 June 1911.
[23] PRO CO 273/368/Y35305, C. McArthur to Sir Arthur Young, 8 Nov. 1910; *RC on shipping rings, 1909* IV, p.179.
[24] PRO CO 273/379/A15738, Sir John Anderson, Governor, SS to Under-Secretary of State, CO, 12 May 1911.

advantage gained by merchant houses receiving the 'secret' rebate was that this acted as a subsidy and substantially lowered their marginal costs. With lower costs, the merchant houses were able to pay a premium for produce in Singapore and still re-sell it abroad for less than unsubsidized merchants could.[25] The recipients of the 'secret' rebate fully realized this advantage of a subsidy so long as in expanding their own business the cost of buying additional produce remained constant. Conference merchants also had to maintain internal discipline to prevent price competition in the sale of shipping space, and avoid non-price competition. These conditions appear to have been met in the crucial pre-World War I period. Non-Conference merchants, in 1907 some 48 firms with about 40% of exports to the West, were too numerous and too small to combine against the Conference. In Singapore, recognition of the impact of the 'secret' rebate was immediate: if merchants 'from the Conference earn a return of freight of 5%, that is *not* given to others, they will do the business while the others must go to the wall'.[26]

By 1911 exports of tropical produce from Singapore concentrated in the hands of Conference merchants at the expense of their competitors excluded from the 'secret' rebate and without shipping agencies for major lines. Some of these firms had successfully switched to the rubber industry, notably Guthrie & Co. (1821). Others were less fortunate, particularly the specialist produce firms, hitherto a feature of Singapore's European mercantile structure, which ceased to be able to compete effectively. Several of these firms closed down or were forced into merger by Conference merchants, including Wm. McKerrow & Co., Stiven & Co., Puttfarcken & Co. and Brauss & Co.[27] Apparently in pre-Conference days 'McKerrow's thought nothing of shipping 2,000 tons of one commodity at one time',[28] and even subsequently the firm's size probably explained receipt of a small share of the 'secret' rebate in the last two years of its existence.[29]

At the end of 1911 a public outcry in Singapore against the conference system resulted in the termination of the 'secret' rebate, as discussed below. Nevertheless, the conference system remained a fundamental determinant of Singapore's European mercantile structure until the 1960s. In pre-independence Singapore, the same European merchant and agency houses constantly reappear because of their dominance in export trade

[25] Darbishire, 'Commerce and currency', p.44.
[26] PRO CO 273/256/Gov.14113, 'Eastern Shipping Conference', Report by John Anderson, partner in Guthrie & Co., Singapore, 13 April 1900; *SSLCP 1905*, p.B109.
[27] *SSTC 1933–34* II, pp.62, 79–85, 99–105, IV, p.82; Makepeace, 'Machinery of commerce' II, pp.186–87, 217–18.   [28] *SSTC 1933–34* II, p.99.
[29] *RC on shipping rings, 1909* IV, p.20.

associated originally with receipt of the 'secret' rebate and with holding homeward shipping agencies for conference lines. These houses included the five main recipients of the 'secret' rebate, except for the German house of Behn, Meyer, which was liquidated as an enemy company during World War I.[30]

The protest in Singapore afforded the shipowners an opportunity to terminate the 'secret' rebate and in effect to recontract on much more favourable terms with the merchant houses. The shipowners were now able to keep the revenue which had been paid as the 'secret' rebate and achieve quasi-integration with a select group of Singapore merchants through an agency system. So long as a shipping monopoly existed at Singapore, a shipping agency was a valuable privilege. Once established, the Conference found that it could buy the support of the city's merchant houses through the ability of member lines to grant these agencies.[31]

After 1911 the conference system shaped Singapore's European mercantile structure in two ways. One was that possession of shipping agencies helped to determine the mercantile structure, since merchant houses with these agencies obtained on their own exports, and on any export cargo handled for rival firms, a commission on freight from shipping lines. These merchant houses probably also received at least a small fixed fee for agency work. By the inter-war period it was apparent that Singapore merchant houses with a shipping agency were bidding up prices paid in the city for export commodities. These merchant houses could pay prices for produce as high as, or even higher than, the price in London, because, with commission on freight for cargo thus obtained, a profit could still be made on the overall transaction. For example, copra was usually, and pepper sometimes, bought for more in Singapore than in London.[32] In competing to buy exports in Singapore, a merchant lacking this 'subsidy' from shipping connections could not pay the same high prices.

The scope of 'the steamer-agent-cum-merchant' to work on a 'finer margin' in the export trade than competitors without shipping connections varied, but was chiefly determined by the number and importance of shipping agencies held and the bulkiness of export commodities relative to their weight and value.[33] A high bulk to weight ratio implied a higher

[30] Makepeace, 'Machinery of commerce' II, p.188; Bartley, 'Singapore and the great war' I, pp.420, 423.
[31] Cf. Davies, 'Vertical integration', pp.93–94. As part of a settlement with the Straits Settlements government which ended the 'secret' rebate, the Conference also agreed to some alteration of the deferred rebate system. However, this proved insignificant. *SSLCP 1910*, pp.B159–B162; *Straits Budget*, 22 Dec. 1910; Darbishire, 'Commerce and currency', pp.43–44.
[32] *SSTC 1933–34* II, pp.340, 363, 376, 834–36, IV, pp.82, 94, V, p.49, I, pp.42, 91–92.
[33] Ibid. II, p.80, and see II, pp.62, 79, IV, p.82.

freight rate, and therefore more commission, for a given tonnage of a commodity shipped; while a high bulk to value ratio allowed merchants to pay relatively more for the commodity in Singapore, because commission on freight became a larger proportion of the commodity's price. After the Conference's establishment as an effective cartel, a merchant with a shipping agency had a clear incentive to support the maintenance of high freight rates because commissions were a proportion of these. During the inter-war period commission on freight became more important to overall profitability in Singapore's produce trade. The change occurred as produce exports shifted more towards commodities with high freight rates due to their bulkiness in relation to weight, notably copra, pepper and sago; and as, after the mid-1920s, declining produce prices squeezed trading margins.

The second main effect of the conference system on Singapore's mercantile structure was that it restricted the entry of new firms to the export trade.[34] Quasi-vertical integration created a major entry barrier when all shipowners and merchant houses were integrated. Potential European entrants to Singapore's export trade now needed to be able to secure the promise of a shipping agency on the commencement of business. The only alternatives were to be shipowners themselves or to have good enough contacts with Chinese suppliers to obtain sufficient cargo for chartering, and the finance to withstand possible adverse price fluctuations on cargo being accumulated for shipment. It was unlikely that a shipper who chartered would have gained any but very short-term competitive advantage. During the inter-war period the Conference was flexible in meeting such challenges, and, for example, responded to lower freights, which a firm of Singapore rubber dealers obtained through chartering, by temporarily cutting rates for all loyal shippers.[35]

In the export of tropical produce from Singapore, the advantage of holding shipping agencies or being shipowners proved decisive. By the 1930s, apart from some specialized export trades like rattans, Singapore firms without a shipping agency found 'produce business absolutely impossible. One by one our produce firms have succumbed and produce now remains in the hands of a few steamship agents scrambling to fill their ships.'[36] As the President of the Straits Settlements Trade Commission observed, 'Since the Conference the result has been that the produce business has passed into the hands of those merchants who are also steamer agents. Is that not a natural development?'[37]

In the export of produce the 'half a dozen firms, who have a practical monopoly'[38] included the British houses of Boustead & Co., Paterson,

[34] Davies, 'Vertical integration', pp.99–102.   [35] *SSTC 1933–34* I, pp.86–87.
[36] *Singapore Free Press*, 17 May 1930.   [37] *SSTC 1933–34* II, p.80.
[38] Ibid. II, p.104.

Simons & Co., Adamson, Gilfillan & Co. and McAlister & Co., which made up the powerful Produce Sub-Committee of the Singapore Chamber of Commerce. The first three had received the 'secret' rebate, while as early as World War I McAlister had obtained, apparently through a previous connection, the shipping agency for a line in both homeward conferences. Also prominent as a produce exporter was the East Asiatic Co., a Danish house, which differed from other European merchants in being ship-owners.[39]

The development of the rubber industry created no serious problem for the shipowners in maintaining Singapore as a Conference port. Conference merchant houses evolved into managing agency houses and became large rubber shippers. It seems likely that this evolution reflected the houses' strong commercial position as a result of receiving the 'secret' rebate and the possession of shipping agencies. Relatively few other European merchants became agency houses and so also large rubber shippers, but one was Guthrie & Co., previously an implacable opponent of the Conference. The fewness of these houses facilitated quasi-integration between them and the Conference shipowners through the distribution of shipping agencies, in part made available with the demise of Behn, Meyer.[40]

There was only one big European house exporting from Singapore which did not hold homeward shipping agencies for Conference lines. But that house, Adamson, Gilfillan, had agencies for shipping lines in other conferences operating in Singapore and through the placement of homeward cargo gained cargo for itself as a quid pro quo.[41] In Singapore the 'very close connection between the Conferences and the comparatively small number of firms which export the greater part of the produce [including rubber], and their position as agents for Conference lines as well as exporters' ruled out the possibility of a shippers' association to counter the conference system.[42] Through the conference system, the major European merchant houses gained monopoly advantages over potential Chinese competitors in exporting to the West, and this worked against the possibility of European merchants combining with Chinese exporters to charter ships.

The second aspect of the establishment of the conference system to be considered is its effect on Singapore's economic development. During the first decade of the century this became an issue which led to widespread protest against the Conference and made it a hotly debated question in

[39] Ibid. IV, pp.47, 137–39, II, pp.82–83, 97–98, 363, 834–35, V, p.49, I, pp.91–92; *Directory 1911*, p.180, *1916*, p.158; SS, *Blue book 1929*, section 32.
[40] *Directory 1911*, p.136.   [41] *SSTC 1933–34* I, pp.42, 79, II, pp.363, 376.
[42] Ibid. I, p.76.

Singapore. Clearly, the advantage certain merchants gained from the Conference would always have led to protest from their competitors, but the Conference became an overriding issue in Singapore because it threatened the port's competitive position by imposing freight rate parity.

The policy of rate parity, an example of basing-point pricing often used by cartels to suppress competition among members arising from geographical factors,[43] was designed 'to equalise costs to all shippers not only in one area but as far as practicable in adjacent areas exporting similar products'.[44] By introducing a uniform tariff for different areas, the Conference eradicated freight rate differentials which Singapore shippers had enjoyed over rival ports because of Singapore's more favourable geographical position. Additionally, uniform tariffs nullified Singapore's policy of not levying port dues. Shippers in Singapore now paid freight rates which reflected homewards transport costs from other ports in the region less well situated and imposing port dues. The uniform tariffs were from so-called basis ports, which in the Straits of Malacca were designated as Singapore and Penang.

Furthermore, there was a second way in which the Conference raised relative freight rates at Singapore. It developed a system of through bills of lading, and, partly to attract cargo from outports – ports not on the itinerary of its ships – to the basis ports, set a somewhat lower rate for homewards transhipment cargo on these through bills than the costs of local and ocean-going freight on separate bills of lading. By lowering the cost of direct export for outport merchants, the arrangement gave them some encouragement to export direct to the West, with only transhipment at Singapore, goods formerly consigned to its merchants for shipment and sale abroad.[45]

The conference system challenged, virtually for the first time, the Singapore ideology of freedom of trade and a free port which exploited the port's geographical location. In the 1900s the threat to Singapore's economic future, and so to the livelihood of all its inhabitants, appeared particularly serious. The value of exports was stagnant, and, according to the estimates of a Straits Settlements government official, the effect of the Conference was annually to divert as much as 100,000 tons of cargo from the port.[46]

[43] Cf. Steven T. Call and William L. Holahan, *Microeconomics* 2nd edn (Belmont, CA, 1983), pp.317–18; F. M. Scherer and David Ross, *Industrial market structure and economic performance* 3rd edn (Dallas, 1990), pp.502–6.

[44] *SSTC 1933–34* I, p.82, and see I, p.83, IV, p.39; *RC on shipping rings, 1909* IV, Q.17233.

[45] *Commission on the Straits Homeward Conference, 1902*, pp.4–5; *RC on shipping rings, 1909* I, p.67; *SSTC 1933–34* I, pp.83, 93–94.

[46] Stuart, 'Report on shipping freight conferences', *SSLCP 1908*, p.C100; *RC on shipping rings, 1909* I, p.68.

Protest against the Conference gathered force in Singapore and, following the inconclusive report of the 1909 Royal Commission on Shipping Rings, led early in 1910 to a large public meeting. A petition demanding legislation against shipping conferences was signed by 700 persons, including 92 European firms, 140 European professional men, 329 Chinese and Chinese firms and 119 Indian and Mohammadan firms.[47] By October, legislation which the Governor of the Straits Settlements called 'an instrument of war ... absolutely necessary in the interests of this Colony' had been passed against the Conference as the Freight and Steamship Ordinance, 1910, to take effect on 1 January 1911.[48] It was remarkable as 'the first attempt [anywhere] to break a Shipping Conference by legislation', and with the exception of the Conference merchants enjoyed near unanimous support in Singapore.[49]

Singapore opposition to the Conference crumbled in the face of the shipowners' threat to boycott the port when the legislation took effect. The Straits Settlements government made no move to intervene in the market by chartering against the Conference, while merchants opposing the Conference found it impossible to combine against it by chartering, probably as a result of the large number of these firms. In London the Colonial Office decided against supporting the Governor. Early in 1911 at a meeting in London with the Governor, the shipowners were able to negotiate repeal of the legislation in exchange for the abolition of the 'secret' rebate. In Singapore 'the settlement was regarded as a Conference victory and received with great dissatisfaction'.[50] But protest against the Conference disappeared almost magically, and although the conference system was questioned in the 1930s, it never again became a major issue. The proximate cause of this was rubber. By 1911 Singapore's exports had again begun to expand under the stimulus of rubber, and all eyes in the city had turned from the issue of the Conference to 'the scramble for rubber profits'.[51]

In the longer term, probably the main reason for a general acceptance of the conference system in Singapore was that it could no longer be seen as a serious obstacle to economic development.[52] The advantages Singapore derived from its resource endowment of geography encompassed much more than relative ocean freight rates between competing ports, which had been affected by the Conference. Although during the first decade of the century the Conference system had probably cost Singapore some trade, chiefly with more distant outports like Macassar, the port would almost

---

[47] 'Petition of merchants, etc. ... regarding shipping conferences', *SSLCP 1910*, pp. C115–C116; *SSLCP 1910*, p.B38; *SSTC 1933–34* I, pp.74–75.
[48] *SSLCP 1910*, p.B100.   [49] *The Times*, 25 Nov. 1910.
[50] *SSTC 1933–34* I, p.75.   [51] Ibid. IV, p.80.   [52] Ibid. I, pp.79–80, 94.

certainly have suffered this loss in any case as a result of the very considerable world expansion of ocean-going shipping.[53] Similarly, through bills of lading, once a source of protest, came to be seen as an inevitable development.

After 1910 Singapore retained a large hinterland because of its several advantages as a market (see chapter 3). Further, the city's merchants who received rebate and agency payments from shipping companies helped to draw produce to Singapore because these payments were used to bid up produce prices. Finally, despite the introduction of freight rate parity, Singapore still offered lower overall transport costs than any rival port due to the mutually-reinforcing advantages of a large supply of ocean-going shipping, cheap and quick port services, and the regional transport networks focused on the port (discussed below). Freight attracted to Singapore because of low transport costs increased the value of shipping agencies to merchants holding them. This completed the 'virtuous' circle through which produce was drawn to Singapore by allowing the city's merchants competing for freight to pay higher prices for commodities than in other regional ports.

In other respects, too, the Conference promoted Singapore's long-term economic development. Overriding the divergences created by rate parity was the fact that the interests of the shipowners organizing the Conference and those of Singapore's inhabitants coincided: both were anxious to preserve existing world shipping routes and to keep the number of regional ports served by ocean-going shipping to a minimum. Conference sailing restrictions, and even more, its determination of shipping routes had this effect. Ocean-going shipping was also focused on the port by the Conference use of basing-point pricing and absorption in through bills of lading of some of the freight costs from outports to Singapore.

Among shipowners, the prohibition of price competition tended to promote the use of service as a competitive weapon.[54] During the inter-war years much of this service concentrated on Singapore. The ready supply and extreme regularity of Conference tonnage at Singapore, an almost certain availability of space, and a wide choice of final destinations made shipping services from the port cheap and advantageous for regional traders. The early shipment of cargo which could be obtained at Singapore facilitated a rapid turnover of capital and minimized storage costs. Under

---

[53] *Commission on the Straits Homeward Conference, 1902*, pp.4–5; *RC on shipping rings, 1909* I, pp.67–68.

[54] For general discussion of this tendency, see Scherer and Ross, *Industrial market structure*, p.506; George W. Douglas and James C. Miller, 'Quality competition, industry equilibrium, and efficiency in a price-constrained airline market', *American Economic Review* 64, 4 (1974), pp.657–69.

the Conference, the abundance of shipping – fundamental to Singapore's economic development – was maintained.

III

A second, basic issue for Singapore was that to attract ocean-going vessels passing through the Straits of Malacca, efficient and cheap port facilities had to be made available. Liner traffic required above all quick dispatch. The cost arising from delay at a port of call such as Singapore which, moreover, offered individual vessels relatively small amounts of cargo, could eventually have driven shipping elsewhere. Uncompetitive port charges might have had a similar effect.

In Singapore, however, the provision of port facilities (figure 4.1) posed no problem; 'one of the finest natural Harbours in the world'[55] enabled ocean-going vessels to be accommodated easily and cheaply in both roads and wharves. Before World War II ocean-going tonnage which came to Singapore divided in roughly equal proportions between use of these two facilities. On the whole, manufactured goods were discharged at the wharves to avoid the risk of transferring varied, often difficult, cargoes in the roads and the expense of additional handling and of lighter transport to godowns. Produce (including rubber until the mid-1920s) was handled in the roads: it reached Singapore by local shipping, was taken by lighter to the private godowns along the Singapore River in the centre of the city for collection and sorting, and was then lightered back to the roads for export. Thus, on their outward voyage vessels generally came to the wharves, but homeward anchored in the roads, although perhaps then going to the wharves for transhipment cargo. Local shipping used the inner roads and did not normally come to the wharves except to collect or deposit goods transhipped on through bills of lading, in the inter-war period a service almost wholly confined to the two European companies, the Straits Steamship Co. and the Koninklijke Paketvaart Mij.[56]

At Singapore the pattern of ocean-going shipping and cargo handling favoured quick dispatch, because it had the advantage that vessels usually discharged and loaded on different calls and usually required wharf facilities only to discharge. The rapid turnover thus created meant that even at times of temporarily excess demand, vessels faced a relatively short wait to berth. Moreover, if the wharves were congested, service in the roads offered a safety valve for vessels requiring immediate clearance.

[55] 'Singapore harbour improvements', *SSLCP 1902*, p.C44.
[56] *SSTC 1933–34* I, p.112; G. W. A. Trimmer, 'Singapore port problems', *Straits Budget*, 17 Oct. 1929; *Harbour Boards' Committee* (1926), pp.17–18, 25–27; Allen, *Report on major ports*, pp.9–14.

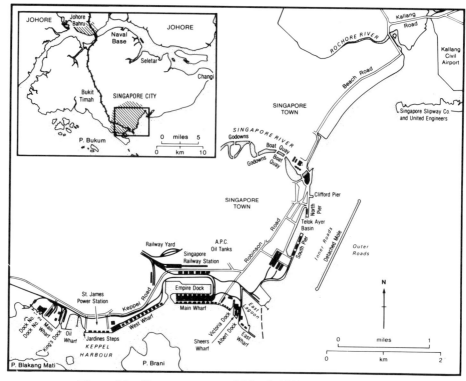

Figure 4.1   Singapore port and Island, 1950

The outer roads, situated in the extensive bay around which Singapore developed and to the east of the city, provided 'a fine natural open anchorage suitable for ocean-going vessels of deep draught'.[57] Ships could be serviced there immediately. A large fleet of privately-owned, mostly Chinese, lighters and twakows (cargo boats usually with an open hold) gave ships quick dispatch because of an elastic supply, which reflected willingness to work additional hours. Further, lighters could work on both sides of vessels, although from the inter-war period this was also a feature of cargo handling at the wharves. Competition among lightermen, 'who work on fine margins',[58] kept costs in the roads low; mealtime hours were disregarded as 'coolies snatch their meals at odd times and there is continuity of work without extra rates'.[59] Lighterage was probably, as it remained after World War II, organized on a profit-sharing basis between owners and crew. However, the latter received a basic wage which meant

[57] ISC, *Harbour of Singapore*, p.7.
[58] *Harbour Boards' Committee* (1926), p.39, and see pp.40, 107.   [59] Ibid. p.43.

that they did not have the risk of too much variance in income.[60] Such a contractual arrangement would help to account for the high work effort of lightermen.

Lighterage was the only charge which ships using the roads encountered. Local interests argued that any port dues would constitute a tax on shipping which might 'turn a nicely balanced scale against us'; in 1912 even light dues were abolished.[61] The roads could be maintained as a free facility because they required little capital expenditure, receiving neither dredging nor mooring and buoying services. The main items of expenditure were the regular dredging of the Singapore River, provision of some landing facilities and the construction from 1907 of a mile-long detached mole. The protection it gave lighters, twakows and local shipping in the inner roads was especially valuable for the up to 50 days of rough seas during the north-east monsoon period between December and mid-March. The mole proved popular with small, local steamers, although less so with lighters and twakows, which, it had been hoped, instead of crowding into the Singapore River, would lie in the shelter of the breakwater and make greater use than they did of the associated landing facilities at Telok Ayer.[62]

At the beginning of the twentieth century government intervened decisively in the domestic economy to ensure the adequate provision of infrastructure. When serious congestion developed at the port owing to the failure of the Tanjong Pagar Dock Company to extend and modernize existing wooden wharves, both the Colonial Office and public opinion in Singapore strongly supported expropriation of the company.[63] This action was taken in 1905, and the price settled by arbitration the next year. The size of the settlement created an outcry which led to a public meeting, at the time said to be the largest ever held in Singapore, and demands to cancel construction of the mole to safeguard the Colony's financial position. However, the government continued with the work as the contract had already been let.[64]

After this decision, the provision of port facilities was never again a major issue in Singapore. A port trust set up by the government, and known from 1913 as the Singapore Harbour Board, oversaw the

---

[60] 'Our lighters move cargo quickly', *Singapore Trade* (Jan. 1961), pp.46–48.
[61] *SSTC 1933–34* I, p.105, and see I, p.106, II, pp.38–39, IV, pp.55, 258.
[62] 'Singapore harbour improvements', *SSLCP 1902*, pp.C43–C64; 'Telok Ayer Basin battle ended', *Straits Budget*, 29 Sept. 1932; *SSTC 1933–34* I, pp.101–6.
[63] 'Correspondence regarding the position and requirements of the Tanjong Pagar Dock Company, Limited', *SSLCP 1905*, p.C12, and see *SSLCP 1901*, p.B120; *SSLCP 1902*, pp.B53, B77, B84, B93; *SSLCP 1905*, pp.B4, B11–B12, B16–B17, B21–B23, B24.
[64] *SSTC 1933–34* I, p.126; Bernard Nunn, 'Some account of our governors and civil service' in Makepeace, et al., eds. *One hundred years* I, pp.134–35; *SSLCP 1907*, pp.B13–B26.

construction between 1908 and 1917 of modern facilities which made Singapore 'second to no port out East'.[65] Singapore had a superb natural site for wharves in Keppel Harbour beginning about a mile and a half south-south-west of the city centre. There the island's coastline ran westwards in a virtually straight line for nearly three miles, the Mt. Faber Ridge extended in close parallel to the shore, affording an abrupt coastal profile, and outlying islands formed a practically landlocked harbour.[66] The initial phase of wharf development from 1908 comprised the construction of a lagoon dock – the Empire Dock – which provided 3,522 feet of wharfage dredged to 30 feet. With the completion of this dock in 1914, wharfage was easily and cheaply obtained simply by building the main line of wharves along the north shore of Keppel Harbour. Concrete structures replaced the old wooden ones, and the new wharves were deepened to 33 feet. By 1917 Singapore had 9,822 feet of wharfage, nearly 8,000 feet of which was new and offered ships over 30 feet of water.[67]

In conjunction with the new facilities, quick dispatch at the wharves was facilitated by an abundant supply of casual labour available in Singapore which made it easy to call on a reserve of manpower at times of exceptional demand. Furthermore, the large labour supply enabled quick handling of cargo even without mechanization, which was substantially absent until after World War II. In Singapore, unlike most ports, the Harbour Board had the exclusive right to supply labour, nearly all of which was obtained through three private contractors. This arrangement did not, as sometimes alleged, make labour expensive through limiting competition. In 1926 the Harbour Boards' Committee concluded that rates charged by labour contractors 'compare very properly with those paid to them in 1914, after making allowance for the all round rise in wages of labour in the interval, and we have no evidence to show that the 1914 rates were unreasonable'.[68]

Nor was there much cause for complaint about wharf tariffs: these were among the lowest in the East. To some extent tariffs were low because Singapore's dry docks, also under Harbour Board control (as discussed in chapter 8), realized a large surplus between 1915 and 1925 which could be used to offset losses at the wharves during this period. But the main reason for low tariffs was that the site available had allowed wharfage to be built at minimal expense and because the extensive construction of wharves and

[65] Singapore Harbour Board, *A short history of the port of Singapore* (Singapore, 1922), p.5.
[66] Dobby, 'Singapore: town and country', p.101; Trimmer, 'Port of Singapore', p.17.
[67] Tanjong Pagar Dock Company, Singapore, *Report on proposed re-construction of wharves, and extension of dock accommodation*, by Coode, Son & Matthews and Mr. J. R. Nicholson, 15 Oct. 1904, pp.7–16, 20; 'Singapore harbour and dock works', *Engineering*, 29 Nov. 1918, pp.603–4, 13 Dec. 1918, pp.666–70; Singapore Harbour Board, *Report and accounts for the half-year ending 30th June, 1917* (Singapore, 1917), p.8.
[68] *Harbour Boards' Committee* (1926), p.41, and see p.34; *SSTC 1933–34* I, pp.119–20.

Table 4.4 *Cargo dealt with by the Singapore Harbour Board, 1906/07–1938/39 (annual averages)*

	Tons inward				Tons outward				Grand total
	Fuel oil	Coal	General cargo	Total	Fuel oil	Coal	General cargo	Total	
1906/07		576,200	712,803	1,289,003		582,432	497,603	1,080,035	2,369,037
1912/13		611,820	886,558	1,498,378		610,452	467,274	1,077,726	2,576,103
1920/21		442,464	939,858	1,382,322		445,482	564,506	1,009,987	2,392,309
1922/23		360,569	748,354	1,108,923		392,571	498,681	891,252	2,000,175
1925/26	145	308,144	1,161,656	1,469,945	18,917	347,154	741,848	1,107,918	2,577,863
1929/30	113,366	341,330	1,386,500	1,841,195	107,727	344,824	937,590	1,390,140	3,231,334
1934/35	64,991	191,517	1,036,435	1,292,943	64,379	214,149	1,067,084	1,345,611	2,638,553
1938/39	123,309	246,484	1,368,843	1,738,635	107,150	238,797	1,212,084	1,558,030	3,296,665

Notes:

1 For 1906/07 figures are for calendar years. All other figures are for the years ended 30 June, for example those for 1912/13 are the annual average for the period 1 July 1911 to 30 June 1913.

2 For 1925/26 fuel oil inward is for 1926 only. Fuel oil statistics vary in different reports. All statistics are from the 1947 report.

3 General cargo includes transhipment cargo.

4 Rows may not add to totals due to rounding.

Sources: SHB, *Report and accounts for the half-year ending 30th June, 1917*; SHB, *Report and accounts for the year ended 30th June, 1929*; SHB, *Report and accounts for the period 1st April, 1946, to 30th June, 1947.*

Table 4.5 *Merchant vessels clearing from Singapore and vessels berthing at Singapore Harbour Board wharves, 1906/07–1938/39 (000 tons, annual averages)*

	All merchant vessels	Vessels berthing at SHB wharves	% berthing at SHB wharves
1906/07	7,270	4,621	63.6
1912/13	8,972	5,396	60.1
1920/21	9,618	5,026	52.3
1922/23	10,458	5,624	53.8
1925/26	13,250	7,572	57.1
1929/30	16,533	10,003	60.5
1934/35	15,638	9,410	60.2
1938/39	16,412	9,775	59.6

Notes:
1   Figures for merchant vessels clearing from Singapore are for calendar years, but for vessels berthing at the wharves are for the years ended 30 June. Both sets of figures are for net registered tonnage.
Sources: 'Marine Department', *SSAR*, 1906–1939; SHB, *Report and Accounts*, 1917, 1929, 1947.

docks was unnecessary. In 1933 three-fifths of the capital of the Harbour Board was accounted for by the 1905 expropriation settlement. Without such a large settlement, wharf tariffs could have been even lower.[69]

The expanding demand for port facilities associated with rubber did not immediately put pressure on available wharf capacity: there was a sharp decline in the earlier demand for wharfage which had arisen from the Singapore Harbour Board's provision of coal bunkers. At first, the decline was mainly because the sale of bunkers was lost to the roads, where vessels could bunker cheaply ex-ship, but latterly it was due also to the growing proportion of oil-fired ships which came to the port. Between 1912/13 and 1922/23 the volume of coal handled at the wharves, previously accounting for about half of all cargo there, fell by nearly two-fifths (table 4.4). Owing primarily to the collapse of the Harbour Board's bunkering trade, although also because of the depression of the early 1920s, the proportion of shipping tonnage calling at Singapore which came to the wharves decreased from 60% in 1912/13 to 54% in 1922/23, and the tonnage of vessels berthed remained virtually static (table 4.5).

By the inter-war period Singapore was in the fortunate position of having built infrastructure ahead of demand. It could cope easily when considerable new demands for port facilities arose. These partly reflected Singapore's role as a transhipment depot for the East, but rubber was

[69] *SSTC 1933–34* I, pp.122–27; *Harbour Boards' Committee* (1926), pp.4–9.

primarily responsible for the expansion in demand. Between 1912/13 and 1938/39 total inward and outward general cargo almost doubled to reach 2.6 million tons and comprised four-fifths of all cargo at the wharves (table 4.4). Rubber contributed to this growth in three ways. First, a shift from the roads to the wharves of practically all rubber exported from Singapore, in 1938/39 averaging 242,000 tons, added substantially to outward general cargo. The shift began during the later 1920s when the owners of Chinese factories remilling Netherlands Indian wet rubber found that an intermediate stage of lighter transport in the roads could be avoided if lorries were used to take the milled rubber directly to the wharves for export. By the 1930s the centre for rubber storage had moved near the wharves, and all ships loading rubber had to go there. Second, the transhipment of rubber on through bills of lading, by 1938/39 an average of 128,000 tons, added to both inward and outward general cargo. Third, purchasing power generated by the rubber industry led to a rapid expansion of imports from the West which formed the largest component of inward general cargo and chiefly explained its growth until 1929/30.[70]

The increase in total general cargo drew shipping back to the wharves – by 1929/30 60% of tonnage coming to Singapore again called there – (table 4.5) – and helped to preserve a bunkering trade for the Harbour Board, since it was normally most economical for vessels to bunker when loading cargo. However, the new demand for fuel oil bunkers created much less need for wharf facilities than coal had done. Discharging colliers took up wharfage. Furthermore, coal required storage space along the wharves and was carried to ships in baskets by coolies. In contrast, oil bunkering, described in chapter 8, was capital-intensive, used a central store and was quickly accomplished.

By the later 1920s the growth in shipping tonnage at the wharves, combined with a rise in the average tonnage (table 4.6), and therefore the greater length, of these vessels brought about the full utilization of wharfage. To prevent serious delays arising, plans for wharf development were made and, after postponement owing to the 1930s slump, carried out from 1934 to 1937. Westward extension of the existing line of deep-water wharves increased wharfage by a quarter to 12,224 feet, over three-fifths of which offered a minimum depth of 33 feet. The development maintained Singapore's status as a first class port,[71] and gave it facilities which, after

---

[70] Singapore Harbour Board, *Report by G. W. A. Trimmer, chairman, on his proposal to extend the facilities of the wharf department* (Singapore, 1927), pp.15, 21, 22; *Harbour Boards' Committee* (1926), pp.5, 20–22; Trimmer, 'Singapore port problems'; *SSTC 1933–34* I, pp.112–13, II, pp.863, 896–97, IV pp.61–62.

[71] Allen, *Report on major ports*, pp.10, 4; *Straits Times*, 2 Feb. 1935; Singapore Harbour Board, *The port of Singapore* (Singapore, 1949), n.p.

Table 4.6 *Vessels berthing at Singapore Harbour Board wharves, 1906/07–1938/39 (annual averages)*

	No. of vessels	Net registered tonnage 000 tons	Average net registered tonnage tons
1906/07	2,447	4,621	1,888
1912/13	2,684	5,396	2,010
1920/21	2,398	5,026	2,096
1922/23	2,305	5,624	2,440
1925/26	2,753	7,572	2,750
1929/30	3,590	10,003	2,786
1934/35	3,102	9,410	3,034
1938/39	3,176	9,775	3,078

Notes:
1   Figures are for the years ended 30 June.
Sources: SHB, *Report and Accounts*, 1917, 1929, 1947.

further improvements and additions, independent Singapore inherited in 1959.

IV

The third issue for Singapore was that to capitalize on the flow of ocean-going vessels, the city needed a regional transport system to link hinterland with world markets. The regional transport network which had been established in the late nineteenth century drew rubber to Singapore and promoted the development of that industry. In the twentieth century this system rapidly expanded. Singapore residents found that outsiders were increasingly willing to invest in regional transport, and that this focused on the port. As the growth in trade resulting from rubber led to the expansion of this regional network, both the port's nodality and linkages arising from transport were strengthened.

Because Singapore was an island and had its largest trade with Netherlands India, regional transport relied above all on local shipping. Table 4.7 indicates the broad trends in the growth of local shipping by showing the movement of vessels of 50 tons net register and over between Singapore and ports in Malaya and Netherlands India. After a relatively static period from 1904/05 to 1912/13, local shipping increased between 1912/13 and 1928/29 under the stimulus of new demand for transport consequent on trade expansion. During this period the number and tonnage of ships trading between Singapore and Malaya approximately doubled, and shipping between the British port and Netherlands India,

Table 4.7 *Merchant vessels of 50 tons net register and over entering and clearing from Singapore, 1904/05–1928/29 (annual averages)*

	1904/05		1912/13		1928/29	
	No.	Tons 000	No.	Tons 000	No.	Tons 000
(a) *Arrivals*						
Malay Peninsula	736	189	747	252	1,841	461
Penang and Malacca	532	241	655	296	883	383
Netherlands India	1,768	897	1,998	1,407	3,292	3,258
Total	**3,036**	**1,327**	**3,400**	**1,955**	**6,016**	**4,102**
(b) *Departures*						
Malay Peninsula	675	187	767	252	2,022	855
Penang and Malacca	581	209	599	279	917	444
Netherlands India	1,871	1,039	1,988	1,331	3,282	3,101
Total	**3,127**	**1,435**	**3,354**	**1,862**	**6,221**	**4,400**

Sources: 'Marine Department', *SSAR*, 1904–1929.

although partly reflecting the growth of ocean-going services, similarly increased. Comparable statistics are not available for the 1930s, but that decade was, if anything, one of contraction for local shipping.

By 1900 the salient features of local shipping were well established. The transition to steam had been completed and two new interest groups had emerged. One comprised a large metropolitan presence because companies in Europe had invested in local fleets. The other was a Singapore Anglo-Chinese enterprise, the Straits Steamship Co. (SSC). Together European companies and the SSC had brought about the relative, if not the absolute, decline in the traditional, purely Chinese interest in local shipping.

In the twentieth century three interrelated developments altered the configuration of local shipping. First, the metropolitan presence became predominantly British rather than European. Second, in the inter-war period the vigorous expansion of this British interest was at the expense of Chinese local shipping, which now declined absolutely. Third, the dominance in local shipping of two metropolitan companies fostered cartels which became as prominent as the conference system for ocean-going services.

The first of these three developments, the increased British involvement in local shipping, was set in motion by World War I, when German firms were liquidated. Alfred Holt & Co. was instrumental in replacing the services of the German shipping line, Norddeutscher Lloyd, through an agreement by which the Liverpool firm provided new ships for the SSC to expand its operations and in exchange acquired the ownership of just under a third of that company. Since Holts thereby became by far the largest shareholder in the hitherto primarily Singapore company and gained equity outweighing that of the Straits Chinese, local shipping took on a much greater metropolitan flavour as well as a British one.[72]

With the expulsion of the Germans, British ascendancy became relatively easy. After 1914 the Koninklijke Paketvaart Mij. (KPM) was the only European line other than the SSC to operate local shipping at Singapore. During the inter-war period the Dutch company had to continue to base a number of ships on Singapore and treat it 'more like a head port'[73] because so much of the trade with Sumatra and Borneo centred there. Nevertheless, the KPM, although growing rapidly, restricted the expansion of its tonnage at Singapore, partly because of keenness to promote Dutch commercial interests and partly owing to agreement reached with the SSC.[74] That agreement, discussed below, freed the SSC to concentrate its full competitive efforts on rival Chinese firms, still numerous in regional waters.

The second development, the inter-war rise of the SSC and concomitant decline in Chinese shipping, reflected the strength of metropolitan compared to local organization and the impact of rubber on Singapore's economy. In the inter-war decades rubber, as the main expansionary force in the region's trade, also provided the principal stimulus to the growth of local shipping. At the same time, however, rubber substantially increased the risk attached to local shipping, as to the entire British Malayan economy, by contributing to economic instability through violent price fluctuations. There were two main reasons why the SSC could take advantage of the long-term investment opportunities rubber created. One was that the company's metropolitan base allowed good access to capital markets, and at the same time enabled the SSC to shift a significant part of the risk of economic downturn onto shareholders. The other was that substantial accumulated reserves made the SSC relatively immune to short-term fluctuations. By contrast, Chinese shipping lines, typically owned by one or a few individuals, lacked the backing of an established financial structure. These men found it hard to withstand cash flow problems created by an economic downturn, particularly as they were often involved in other enterprises under similar financial pressure at a time of stringency for the whole Chinese business community.

Between 1922 and 1934 the SSC either absorbed entirely or took control of seven Chinese shipping lines, all but one in the wake of the depression

[72] Tregonning, *Home port*, pp.45–48; Jackson and Wurtzburg, *Mansfield & Co.*, p.7; *SSTC 1933–34* II, pp.63–64, 872, IV, p.2.   [73] *SSTC 1933–34* II, p.891.
[74] Ibid. I, pp.80, 97.

at the beginning of the 1920s or in the 1930s slump. The main acquisition in the earlier period was the large, Penang-based Eastern Shipping Company, a long-established Chinese family business. Its purchase had the support of Holts. Immediately prior to the formal take-over, the link with Liverpool was strengthened when Mansfield & Company, controlled and principally owned by Holts, became managers of the SSC. Policy decisions involving the SSC, if not its day-to-day running, thus shifted more towards Britain, as had the company's equity, both through the holdings of Holts and, it may reasonably be supposed, through a tendency for the early European shareholders to return home. In the 1930s the SSC's greatest gain was in obtaining the management and substantial equity in the Ho Hong Steamship Company, giving it control of a large fleet of ships and important new routes. The take-over became possible when the conglomerate, built up by Lim Peng Siang and his brother, was forced into financial re-organization after the Ho Hong Bank and other enterprises ran into difficulty during the 1930s slump.[75]

In 1934 the SSC, having expanded its fleet fourfold since 1914, had 55 of the 81 local steamers based on Singapore. The services of the SSC covered 78 ports throughout the region.[76] Expansion was accompanied by the extensive modernization of the SSC's fleet and so of local shipping at Singapore. The SSC adopted a policy of commissioning new vessels designed to meet regional needs, for 'the trades in Malaya are so specialised that there are generally speaking few ships in the world which are suitable and economic units for those trades'.[77] But the SSC did not commission any ships from Singapore dockyards; as a rule the company constructed 75-tonners at its Sungei Nyok shipbuilding yard near Penang, ordered larger vessels from the Taikoo Dockyard in Hong Kong, and had the largest built in the United Kingdom.[78]

The SSC's investment was primarily in response to opportunities arising from the carriage of passengers and the rubber industry: twentieth-century experience largely repeated with rubber, and so considerably extended, the nineteenth-century transport linkages associated with the tin industry. Between 1903 and 1911 the SSC introduced six new ships to develop services for first-class passengers and to make the most of the region's large

[75] Tregonning, *Home port*, pp.51–68, 124–31, 143, 150–51; *SSTC 1933–34* I, pp.96–98, II, pp.63, 847, 871–72, IV, pp.261–64, V, p.61; Jackson and Wurtzburg, *Mansfield & Co.*, p.8; A. McLellan, *The history of Mansfield & Company, part II, 1920–1953* (Singapore, 1953), pp.4–7; 'Story of the Straits Steamship Co.', pp.20–21; Victor Sim, *Biographies of prominent Chinese in Singapore* (Singapore, 1950), p.34.

[76] *SSTC 1933–34* I, p.96, IV, p.250; Tregonning, *Home port*, pp.43, 69, map between pp.162 and 163.

[77] C. E. Wurtzburg, 'Singapore Straits Steamship Company Ltd.', *British Malaya* (Nov. 1946), p.115.   [78] *SSTC 1933–34* II, pp.872–73; Tregonning, *Home port*, pp.71–85.

traffic in deck passengers. In the inter-war years rubber was the major reason for the introduction of new ships. The 75-tonners were general purpose vessels although relying substantially on cargoes of rubber, while larger, so-called 'biscuit-tin ships ... were designed with a square appearance to enable them to carry the absolute maximum quantity of cased rubber with the absolute minimum amount of loss of space'.[79] Equally specialized were three 75-tonners built in the 1930s to transport palm oil.[80]

The third development in local shipping, the emergence of cartels, stemmed both from the pre-eminence of the SSC and the KPM and from their control by metropolitan interests, whose involvement in ocean-going conferences led easily to a desire similarly to restrict competition in regional waters. As part of negotiations also involving Holts and members of the Java Homeward Conference who were large shareholders in the KPM, the SSC and KPM in 1924 reached comprehensive agreement dividing local shipping routes and setting freight rates. Possible competition between the SSC and another company from Britain was forestalled by the 1925 Victoria Point Agreement: this divided among major British companies spheres of operation for coastal shipping between Aden and Japan and gave the SSC the Straits sphere, stretching from Victoria Point, Burma to Bangkok. In 1934, with a few minor exceptions, the handful of Chinese shipping companies which operated from Singapore mostly did so on the basis of routes and freight rates agreed with the SSC, the KPM, or both. The SSC made extensive use of the deferred rebate system to back up cartel arrangements, but without creating significant local dissatisfaction.[81]

After 1900 the extension of the railway and roads in British Malaya strengthened the role of Singapore as the Peninsula's main link with world markets. Railway development in British Malaya (figure 2.4) illustrates how transport established as the result of a linkage arising from one staple, tin, promoted the growth of a second, rubber. Rubber trees were grown near the railway to obtain cheap transport, and in turn this new demand for transport brought the swift expansion of the rail network throughout the Peninsula. In 1923, when the railway reached its logical southern terminus in Singapore with the opening of the Johore causeway, the port gained direct rail access to most of Malaya.

Like the railway, the roads built on the north–south character of British Malayan transport, with Singapore as their focal point. By the end of the

---

[79] Tregonning, *Home port*, p.145, and see pp.34–36, 53, 149–50, ch.4, passim; 'Chinese migration statistics', *MRCA* 9 (May 1931), pp.34–35; 'Story of the Straits Steamship Co.', pp.20–21.   [80] Tregonning, *Home port*, pp.83–84, 144.
[81] *SSTC 1933–34* I, pp.96–99, II, pp.27, 63–64, V, pp.61, 64–65; Tregonning, *Home port*, pp.59–61, 254.

1920s a west coast trunk road ran the length of the Peninsula to Singapore, and 'a magnificent road system'[82] existed. The rail and road networks could scarcely have been better designed to give maximum advantage to Singapore's trade, but they owed almost nothing to organization or investment by the Straits Settlements government or commercial interests. The FMS undertook the railway, and Singapore benefited from a system 'constructed and maintained by a foreign Government';[83] the same was largely true of the roads.

During the 1930s local shipping lost some business to alternative transport systems. This must have hurt Singapore, as shipping constituted its main stake in the British Malayan transport network. Local shipping suffered from the growing competition of road services on short hauls and, even more, because similar competition affected the railway. The latter had previously carried exports to the nearest port for onward shipment by coastal steamer. Now, in response to competition from road transport, the railway attempted, with some success, to channel Malayan exports along its main line.[84] Although changing local transport patterns cannot be established reliably, owing to the lack of data for freight traffic by sea and by road, the volume of cargo which came to Singapore is unlikely to have altered much because of shifts in its mode of transport. Whatever changes occurred in the usage of transport systems, all three converged on Singapore.

[82] *SSTC 1933–34* IV, p.250, and see *1931 census*, p.10.   [83] *SSTC 1933–34* I, p.136.

[84] Ibid. I, pp.136–37; Tregonning, *Home port*, pp.142–43, 236. Railway policy and diversion of cargo may be traced in Federated Malay States Railways, *Annual report 1930*, published as a supplement to *FMS government gazette*, 11 Sept. 1931 and from 1932 published as *Railways report* in Kuala Lumpur. See *1930*, p.60, *1932*, p.70, *1934*, p.16, *1937*, pp.19, 22, *1939*, pp.16, 18, 24.

5 Immigration, population and employment

Immigration to British Malaya vividly illustrates that 'There have been, in fact, in the past century three mother countries of the British Empire, i.e. the United Kingdom, India and China'.[1] Chief among the immigrants drawn to British Malaya were the southern Chinese. The relationship of Singapore to British Malayan immigration was threefold. First, immigrants produced and consumed commodities in which Singapore traded. Malaya's staple industries were almost entirely developed with immigrant labour, and their impact on Singapore is a central concern of this study. Second, a substantial part of immigration was through Singapore. It served as the main entry and exit point for Chinese immigrants. Flows of immigration, and the shipping and labour market services consequent on them, are discussed in section I of this chapter. Third, immigration largely provided Singapore with its population, the growth and characteristics of which are considered in sections II and III.

Singapore's demographic growth was the result rather than the cause of its expanding economic functions and generated a labour supply greater than these functions required. Between 1881 and 1901 Singapore Municipality's population increased at an average annual rate of 3·6%, high by historical demographic standards. By the beginning of the century Singapore already had an abundance of labour. Yet in each of the decades 1901 to 1921, the Municipality grew at 3·0% annually, and from 1921 to 1931 at 2·4%. Growth rates of these magnitudes ensured a highly elastic supply of labour, especially as population expansion was largely through the inflow of able-bodied male immigrants who needed employment. And when business boomed, even more immigrants came. As contemporary observers emphasized, Singapore was near 'two unlimited sources of supply for cheap labour, namely India and China'.[2]

Mass immigration helped to shape the structure of employment and labour markets in Singapore – the subject of section IV. A proportion of workers in Singapore became 'surplus' labour in the sense that they added

[1] Knowles, *Economic development of the empire*, p.viii.
[2] Rotary Club of Singapore, *Singapore as an industrial centre* (Singapore, 1931), p.2.

150

little or nothing to total output. Surplus labour was accommodated very largely by absorption into casualized occupations in the supporting local economy rather than by employment in the port's international economy. Singapore's labour surplus condition allows it to be described as a dual economy.

I

As in the late nineteenth century, Singapore received large inflows of labour primarily because of export production in Malaya rather than in the port's hinterland as a whole or due to economic development in the city itself. Singapore's immigration history cannot be separated from Malaya's, but is only a partial reflection of it. First, while most Chinese immigrants entered British Malaya through Singapore, nearly all Indian immigrants landed at Penang or (from 1923) Port Swettenham. Second, immigration data are ambiguous: a number of Indian immigrants found their way down the Peninsula to Singapore; while for Chinese, the available statistics (appendix tables A.7 and A.8) show immigrants examined, but not necessarily landed, at the port. Normally, about four-fifths of Chinese immigrants appear to have landed in Singapore; most of the remainder went to Penang, with smaller flows to Netherlands India, Burma and India.[3] There are no figures which separate Chinese immigrants landing in Singapore and continuing to Malaya from those remaining in the city. However, the latter constituted a significant proportion of the total: in 1931 Singapore Municipality contained one-fifth of British Malaya's Chinese population.[4]

Income differentials between large parts of south-eastern China and the Nanyang (Southeast Asia), and consequent immigration there, were long established.[5] Most Chinese immigrants coming to Singapore had two related objectives. First, they wanted to better their occupations. Almost invariably, this meant 'realizing their ambition either of building up a business abroad or of saving enough to start one at home'.[6] Second, they hoped to remit money to China, discussed below. Throughout the emigrant areas of south-eastern China, whole villages relied on remittances from abroad, and otherwise were not economically viable.[7] Often, the only future both for young, aspiring Chinese and for their relations remaining

---

[3] 'Secretary for Chinese Affairs', *SSAR*, 1900–1915; 'Statistical Office', *SSAR*, 1923–1928; 'Chinese migration statistics', *MRCA* (May 1931), pp.33–37.

[4] *1931 census*, pp.36, 117.

[5] For example, see George Thompson Hare, *Federated Malay States, census of population, 1901* (Kuala Lumpur, 1902), p.50.

[6] Chen Ta, *Emigrant communities in south China*, (London, 1939), p.71, and see pp.60–64, 69–72.

[7] Ibid. pp.59–60, 68–85, and see Freedman, *Chinese family and marriage in Singapore*, pp.16–17.

in China appeared to be in the Nanyang. An individual's emigration from China probably reflected a household decision which was subject to calculation of the difference between the family member's expected income at home and various possible destinations in the Nanyang.[8] Clearly, this income differential was influenced by factors like floods, bad harvests or political violence in China. However, at least for immigration to British Malaya, by far the most important consideration appears to have been the likelihood of employment and wage levels there.[9]

During the pre-World War II period, adjustment to changes in the British Malayan demand for labour came principally through net immigration rather than wages. Although quantity adjustment led to large labour outflows through Singapore, prior to World War II, as considered below and in section IV, net immigration was negative only during the early 1930s. Both the distances and transport costs from Singapore to south China substantially slowed adjustment to changes in the British Malayan labour market. By contrast, almost all migrants to Hong Kong came from the adjacent Chinese countryside, to which return was cheap and easy.[10] Travel costs, compensation for the often high psychological costs of immigration and the need for immigrants to earn enough in British Malaya to be able to remit home[11] helped to make labour in Singapore expensive by Asian standards, a problem which persisted into the 1960s.

It seems unlikely that most Chinese who went to Singapore did so in the hope of joining a high wage, modern (as opposed to, in China, a traditional, rural) sector, a process sometimes described in the economic development literature.[12] Singapore's international economy, in which the modern sector concentrated, was too small for this hope to seem realistic. Moreover, for several ethnic groups the reality of Singapore's segmented labour market, discussed below, sharply restricted the range of highly remunerative job possibilities. Although it was recognized at the time in China that to make 'money, especially big money, one should become a merchant – if possible in the Nanyang',[13] in this, of course, most failed

---

[8] Cf. T. R. Gottschang, 'Economic change, disasters, and migration: the historical case of Manchuria', *EDCC* 35, 3 (1987), pp.480–81.

[9] For example, see Ta Chen, *Chinese migrations with special reference to labor conditions* (Washington, DC: US Department of Labor, Bureau of Labor Statistics, miscellaneous series no. 340, 1923), p.11; Chen, *Emigrant communities*, pp.59–64.

[10] Hong Kong, *Report of the commission to enquire into the causes and effects of the present trade depression in Hong Kong, 1934–1935* (Hong Kong: Government Printers, 1935), pp.9, 16; *FMS census, 1901*, p.48.   [11] *1921 census*, p.22.

[12] William E. Cole and Richard D. Sanders, 'Internal migration and urban employment in the third world', *American Economic Review* 75, 3 (1985), pp.481–94, and Michael P. Todaro, 'Internal migration and urban unemployment: comment' and Cole and Sanders, 'Reply', *American Economic Review* 76, 3 (1986), pp.566–72.

[13] Chen, *Emigrant communities*, p.69.

and, worse, in times of depression had to leave British Malaya without the savings they had hoped to accumulate. Prospective Chinese immigrants must have known all this: they came because, the chance of becoming a Nanyang merchant apart, they still could anticipate doing sufficiently well in a Singapore Chinese world of commerce and industry, whether in the local or international economy, to cover their transport and psychic costs, remit home and accumulate at least modest savings.

The volume and timing of Chinese immigration at Singapore was determined principally by conditions in the rubber and, to a diminishing extent, the tin industry in Malaya. As well as being the main determinants of overall economic conditions in British Malaya and a good proxy for those elsewhere in Singapore's hinterland, the staple industries exerted a major direct influence on immigration because of their reliance on immigrant labour and importance in total employment. By 1931, with the spread of European mines, tin mining occupied only 4% of the working population in British Malaya, 79,000 persons, but rubber cultivation engaged probably a third of all workers, or about 650,000 persons.[14] In the rubber industry, short-term fluctuations in employment tended to be positively correlated with rubber prices at an interval of about a year. High prices encouraged the recruitment of more labour for the clearing and planting of additional land, on estates a task usually done by Chinese, as well as for routine field work. However, employment fluctuations tended to be negatively correlated with export volume, since the maturation of rubber trees planted at times of high prices increased the supply of rubber and depressed prices, which reduced the demand for labour.

Statistics for Chinese immigration are summarized in table 5.1. At the turn of the century immigration was already high. The annual average of a gross inflow of 202,000 immigrants in 1900/03 was not substantially exceeded until 1911/13, when the figure reached 254,000, after 'the tide of immigration had set in with increased force owing to the increased demand for Chinese labour on rubber estates'.[15] Prior to World War I over four-fifths of all Chinese immigrants were men.

From 1914 to 1924 immigration remained well below earlier levels for a variety of reasons, including wartime disruption and the depression at the beginning of the 1920s.[16] After 1925 immigration stayed high through 1930, following movements in rubber prices with a lag of about a year.[17] During the peak years 1926/29 no fewer than 324,000 Chinese immigrants arrived annually in Singapore. Men still predominated, but during the

---

[14] *1931 census*, p.99; M. V. Del Tufo, *Malaya, a report on the 1947 census of population* (London, 1949), p.104.   [15] *FMS census, 1911*, p.18, and see p.64.

[16] J. E. Nathan, *The census of British Malaya, 1921* (London, 1921), pp.20–22, 24, 33.

[17] 'Protector of Chinese', *SSAR 1926*, p.43, *1927*, p.65.

Table 5.1 *Composition of Chinese immigrants examined at Singapore, 1900/03–1934/38 (annual averages)*

	Total	Men %	Women %	Children %
1900/03	201,801	88.8	6.4	4.8
1911/13	254,159	82.6	9.1	8.3
1921/23	160,983	73.0	14.3	12.7
1926/29	324,181	69.7	16.2	14.1
1934/38	147,101	45.4	36.1	18.5

Notes:
1   Children were defined as under 12 English years of age.
Sources: Appendix tables A.7 and A.8.

1920s the immigration of women and children increased markedly as more families came to British Malaya, a trend to which political turmoil in China gave a fillip.[18]

The 1930s collapse in staple export prices reversed the flow of population from China: between 1931 and 1933 half a million more Chinese deck passengers left British Malaya than immigrants arrived there. In August 1930 quotas on immigration were introduced and subsequently incorporated into the Straits Settlements Aliens Ordinance of 1933. The legislation had the intention, privately expressed by the government but publicly denied, of limiting only Chinese immigration.[19] Although in 1934/38 immigration recovered to average 147,000 persons, women and children now constituted more than half of the total. Women, exempt from quota restrictions until May 1938, came for the first time in large numbers to British Malaya in search of employment, a development reflected in the findings of the 1947 census which revealed a much wider range of female occupations than previous censuses.[20]

Several shipping lines carried Chinese to Singapore from the four emigration ports of Hong Kong, Amoy, Swatow and Hoihow (figure 1.1), charging individual fares of about ten Hong Kong dollars from that port and 15 dollars from the smaller ports. Scheduled services carrying immigrants were mainly organized by European shipping companies which were based outside Singapore and employed only agents there.

[18] Colony of Singapore, *Master plan, reports of study groups and working parties* (Singapore, 1955), p.14, and see *1921 census*, pp.48–49, 56, 96; *1947 census*, p.64.
[19] PRO CO 273/569/82001, H. R. Cowell, minute 18 May 1932, and see this CO file, passim; *SSLCP 1932*, pp.B141–B154; Victor Purcell, *The Chinese in Malaya* (Kuala Lumpur, 1967), p.204.
[20] W. L. Blythe, *Methods and conditions of employment of Chinese labour in the Federated Malay States* (Kuala Lumpur, 1938), p.3; *1947 census*, pp.33, 109.

Mansfield & Company were the agents for the most important of these lines, the China Navigation Company. The one Singapore shipping line bringing Chinese immigrants was the Ho Hong Steamship Company, which operated a fortnightly service between Amoy and Rangoon and had three ocean-going steamers on this route. Additionally, as many as eight chartered ships, organized principally by Hong Kong and Swatow Chinese, transported immigrants to Singapore. The Ho Hong line and Chinese charterers carried rice from Rangoon to China, thus largely overcoming the problem of unused capacity on the return journey from the Nanyang which arose from the usual excess of immigrants over emigrants. The practice gave Singapore the advantage of a regular supply of rice on which its traders could draw as circumstances required.

Ships transporting immigrants to Singapore became vital to its economy: they brought much of the city's supply of Chinese foodstuffs and provisions. These could be carried in relatively small quantities by immigrant vessels at little additional cost. Because Singapore depended on immigrant shipping for the regular conveyance of Chinese foodstuffs, especially fresh vegetables, the Straits Settlements government was careful during the 1930s slump not to set monthly immigration quotas too low and to divide these among shipping lines so as to avoid any dislocation of the links with China.[21]

The flow of immigrants through Singapore required no elaborate machinery on its part. Broadly speaking, immigrants came through either personal recruitment or a system of lodging houses.[22] The former, which accounted for a considerable volume of immigration, used Singapore as no more than a transit point, since the recruiter sent to China by an employer in Malaya 'would pay all expenses from village to port and from port to Malaya and with his assistants shepherd the flock to the place of employment'.[23]

The immigrant lodging house system, which depended on a chain of

---

[21] Details of shipping arrangements and immigrant fares can be found in PRO files CO 273/566/72141; CO 273/572/82051; CO 273/577/92001/12; Planters' Association of Malaya, General Labour Committee (British Malaya), *Report of special committee on Chinese labour* (Kuala Lumpur, 1922), pp.28, 32; *SSTC 1933–34* I, p.98, II, pp.767–75, 847–48, 856, IV, pp.244–45.

[22] *Report of the commissioners appointed to enquire into labour, 1890*, pp.10–11, 24, 29, 31; *SSLCP 1891*, pp.B7–B11; *Report of the commission to enquire into the conditions of indentured labour in the Federated Malay States* by C. W. C. Parr (Federal Council Paper no. 11 of 1910), p.10; Planters' Association, *Report of special committee on Chinese labour*, p.6; 'Recruitment of labourers by permit under section 12A of the Aliens Ordinance', *MRCA* 55 (March 1935), pp.31–36; PRO CO 273/613/50037; 'Methods of supply of Chinese labour to rubber estates in Malaya', *MRCA* 80 (April 1937), pp.39–49.

[23] W. L. Blythe, 'Historical sketch of Chinese labourers in Malaya', *JMBRAS* 20, 1 (1947), pp.98–99.

Table 5.2 *Singapore number of Chinese native passenger lodging houses registered, 1900–1934*

1900	46	1929	80
1913	44	1930	75
1920	43	1931	63
1926	47	1932	56
1927	55	1933	48
1928	69	1934	51

Sources: 'Secretary for Chinese affairs', *SSAR*, 1900–1934.

linked establishments transmitting labour from China to British Malaya, required of Singapore a greater role in handling the flow of immigration. In Singapore the lodging houses were no more than Chinese houses of the ordinary street type. They normally numbered around 50 but rose to 80 in 1929 (table 5.2).[24] The houses were licensed by the government to contain perhaps as many as 150 men. A British Consul in China justified the lodging house system as necessary because:

The passengers themselves and especially passengers of the type that the Straits Authorities wish to encourage are for the most part ignorant peasants from the interior who have never seen a ship and who are bewildered by a town even of the size of Swatow. They are without capital and would be quite incapable of finding their [own] way to the South Seas ... A large proportion are given credit by the Lodging Houses for all their travelling and other expenses including the steamer ticket.[25]

Nevertheless, a substantial and growing number of immigrants paid their own passage, and this became usual after the enactment of the Aliens Ordinance.

However immigration was financed, the Singapore lodging house keeper was important in the chain of labour supply. As an agent for a labour recruiter or lodging house in China, immigrants were consigned to him and then either passed on to up-country lodging houses or hired by labour contractors. The Singapore keeper also played a part in financing immigration. When passengers being paid for through the lodging house system arrived in Singapore, the keeper might assume their debts by remitting to his counterpart in China a sum to cover the latter's expenses and profit margin. Alternatively, self-financed immigrants awaiting additional funds from relatives or friends might obtain credit from the

[24] 'Secretary for Chinese Affairs', *SSAR*, 1900–1934.
[25] PRO CO 273/613/50037, R. S. Pratt, British Consul, Swatow to Sir Alexander M. G. Cadogan, His Majesty's Ambassador, Peking, 20 Dec. 1935.

Table 5.3 *Malay arrivals in British Malaya from Netherlands India and departures to Netherlands India from British Malaya, 1923/24–1936/39 (annual averages)*

	Arrivals	Departures	Excess or deficit
1923/24	49,739	49,423	316
1926/29	70,753	67,334	3,419
1930/33	39,826	40,455	-629
1936/39	41,900	38,208	3,692

Sources: 'Statistical Office', *SSAR*, 1923–1929.

Singapore keeper. Furthermore, Singapore lodging houses functioned as a market for labour when they were used by contractors for local or Malayan employers as a place to recruit workers.

Singapore was the principal port of entry for Indonesian migrants from Netherlands India, who originated mainly in Java and Sumatra. Available statistics (table 5.3) include all Malays arriving from Netherlands India and departing to it. Reference to the gross flow shows that the movement was much smaller than Chinese immigration; the net flow suggests that the statistics included a large number of ordinary travellers, or pilgrims to Mecca for whom Singapore remained a main port of departure. Labour recruited in Netherlands India was chiefly Javanese indentured labour for European rubber estates, notably in Johore. Although some European firms in Singapore acted as agents for labour recruited by their offices in Java, the flow of these workers was never very large, and the indenture system was finally abolished in 1932.[26] Rather, 'the vast majority of the Malayan races who migrate to British Malaya come as permanent settlers, bringing their women folk with them and planting up their own small holdings'.[27] There is nothing to suggest that any institution developed in Singapore to handle this inflow of settlers.

II

In 1901 Singapore Municipality was still a relatively small city of 193,000 persons. Within 35 years its population had risen to 490,000 (table 5.4). By World War II the city was certainly well past the half million mark.

[26] *Report of the commission to enquire into indentured labour in the FMS*, pp.1–2; 'Department of Statistics', *SSAR 1930*, p.105.

[27] *1921 census*, p.99, and see p.20; *1931 census*, p.71.

Table 5.4 *Population of Singapore, 1871–1939*

	Singapore Municipality 000 persons	Singapore Island 000 persons	Municipal as % of Island
1871	n.a.	94.3	-
1881	95.3	132.1	72.1
1891	153.0	175.0	87.4
1901	193.1	229.9	84.0
1911	259.6	303.3	85.6
1921	350.4	418.4	83.7
1931	445.7	557.4	80.0
1936	490.2	603.2	81.3
1939	n.a.	727.6	-

Sources: *Census of Singapore 1871* in SS, *Blue book 1871*, p.P10; *Census of Singapore 1881* in SS, *Blue book 1881*, p.P12; *SS census 1891*, pp.51–52; *SS census 1901*, pp.28–30; *SS census 1911*, pp.13–16; *1921 census*,p.155; *1931 census*, pp.120–21; *1947 census*, pp.45, 135, 158–59, 588; Colony of Singapore, *Annual report on the registration of births and deaths, 1940–1947*, p.12.

Table 5.5 *Singapore Municipality population by race, 1901–1936*

	Total 000 persons	Chinese %	Indians %	Malays %	Europeans %	Others %
1901	193.1	73.5	8.1	13.6	1.4	3.4
1911	259.6	74.7	9.4	10.8	1.9	3.2
1921	350.4	78.0	7.9	9.8	1.5	2.8
1931	445.7	76.4	9.3	9.7	1.5	3.1
1936	490.2	76.3	9.7	9.2	1.7	3.1

Sources: as for table 5.4.

Although its boundaries remained virtually unchanged,[28] Singapore Municipality continued to hold some four-fifths of the island's population; the following discussion refers to the Municipal population unless otherwise indicated.

Although Singapore's population grew over two and a half times, its racial composition changed little (table 5.5). The Chinese and Indian proportions rose slightly to account for over three-quarters and almost one-tenth of the population respectively. These gains were at the expense of the Malays whose share of the population fell to under one-tenth.

Inward movement was largely responsible for population increase.

[28] *1921 census*, p.38; *Master plan, study groups*, p.18; F. J. Hallifax, 'Municipal government' in Makepeace, et al., eds. *One hundred years* I, p.339.

However, little is known about its character and timing in the absence of statistics for immigrants and migrants settling in Singapore or for population movements within British Malaya. Furthermore, although fertility became an increasingly important source of population growth, its contribution cannot be reliably estimated. The registration of births remained substantially incomplete until the 1920s, and even with fuller registration it is unknown how many of those born in Singapore survived and stayed there to add to population at the next census.[29]

It is apparent, though, that Singapore gained population in broadly similar proportions to towns in the FMS and Penang. In 1931 the racial composition of urban areas in Malaya was nearly two-thirds Chinese, one-fifth Indian and one-eighth Malay. Immigrants dominated the towns, since the Malays were interested in neither distributive work nor physical employment, and apart from this, urban life had little to offer them. The 1931 census found only 11 % of Malays in urban areas. British Malayan towns were disproportionately Chinese: in 1931 British Malaya had almost three Chinese for every Indian, and one out of every two Chinese lived in towns, while less than one in three Indians did so.[30]

Singapore differed from other British Malayan towns in having such a high proportion of Chinese. The reason for this was partly Singapore's attractiveness to Chinese as British Malaya's main urban centre and its established Chinese character, which offered the chance for commercial advancement; a large casual labour market with attendant job possibilities; and the lure of extensive Chinatowns with bright lights, street markets, bustle, brothels and opera. However, the explanation was also partly fortuitous: just as Penang had a more conspicuous Indian element because that port received immigrants from the subcontinent,[31] so Singapore had a greater Chinese one because it was the centre for immigration from China.[32]

Like other urban areas, Singapore's population was numerically more stable than that of the surrounding countryside. While both urban and rural areas gained population in a boom, the towns did not shed it nearly so rapidly in a slump. Three aspects of urban development applied with greater force to Singapore than to other urban areas, and further account for its Chinese character. One was the city's attraction for Chinese female

---

[29] *1931 census*, pp.105–14.
[30] Ibid. pp.48–49, 1, 36; *1921 census*, p.93; C. A. Vlieland, 'The population of the Malay peninsula', *Geographical Review* 24, 1 (1934), pp.75–76. In the 1921 and 1931 censuses '"urban" population ... means population resident in towns of over a thousand inhabitants, and "rural" means all population enumerated outside these towns'. *1931 census*, p.44. In this chapter, the terms 'urban areas' and 'towns' follow this definition, and are used interchangeably.
[31] *1921 census*, p.44.   [32] Cf. *1931 census*, p.2; *1947 census*, p.84.

immigrants and relatively high proportion of inhabitants organized in families, which gave it a more settled population than rural areas.[33] Second, whenever business was slack, unemployed Chinese labourers came to Singapore from rural areas of Malaya in search of work or hoping to return to China.[34] Third, Chinese, unlike Indian, workers generally did not have any right to repatriation and, if unable to finance the return journey to China after being thrown out of employment in Malaya, tended to congregate in Singapore, doing whatever jobs were available.[35]

Published figures for remittances from the Nanyang are, unavoidably, speculative, but it is clear that their value was considerable, and that Singapore Chinese accounted for a substantial share of the total.[36] Even in 1947 two-fifths of Chinese in Singapore remitted money.[37] The immigrant remittance business gave rise to its own financial sector in the city. Remittance services largely dealt with money sent from Singapore itself, and were characterized by numerous small units specialized according to specific areas in China. In the early 1920s there were about 250 shops acting as remittance agents,[38] and although during the inter-war period local Chinese banks handled some remittances, the 1947 *Social survey* found the bulk were still 'made through a great number of small shops'.[39] As well as converting money into Chinese currency and transmitting it, remittance shops also dispatched the sender's letter, wrote one for those who were illiterate and arranged for a reply which served as a receipt. A nominal fee was charged by the shops; their profits came from lending money while waiting for the remittances to accumulate and perhaps through exchange rate speculation or by converting the money into commodities for sale in China.[40]

During the inter-war period a trend began, so evident after World War II, towards a more balanced and settled Chinese, if not Indian, community. This, in turn, became an important factor in Singapore's growth as a

[33] Vlieland, 'Population', p.75; Colony of Singapore, *Annual report on the registration of births and deaths for the years 1940–47* by E. J. Phillips (Singapore, 1948), p.12.

[34] *1921 census*, pp. 24, 38, 88; *Commissions on trade depression 1921*, appx. 1, p.32; *1931 census*, pp.82, 85.

[35] *SSLCP 1930*, pp.B54, B129–B131; PRO CO 273/569/82004, Memorandum 'A survey of labour conditions in British Malaya generally' by W. J. K. Stark, Acting Controller of Labour, Malaya, 20 April 1931, p.13.

[36] C. F. Remer, *Foreign investments in China* (New York, 1933), pp.183–87; Chen Chun-Po, 'Chinese overseas', *Chinese Year Book, 1935–36*, p.443.

[37] Singapore Department of Social Welfare, *A social survey of Singapore ... December 1947* (Singapore, 1948), pp.108–21.

[38] Song, *One hundred years' history*, pp.67–68.

[39] Singapore Department of Social Welfare, *Social survey, 1947*, p.111; see also Allen and Donnithorne, *Western enterprise*, p.206; Tan Ee Leong, 'The Chinese banks incorporated in Singapore and the Federation of Malaya' in T. H. Silcock, ed. *Readings in Malayan economics* (Singapore, 1961), p.469.

[40] Chen, *Emigrant communities*, pp.79–80; Remer, *Foreign investments*, p.183.

Chinese city. The increasing number of Chinese female immigrants coming
to British Malaya exercised a disproportionate influence on Singapore's
Chinese community, since they were much more likely to settle in the city
than unaccompanied males.[41] In 1901 Singapore Municipality had 3,574
Chinese males for every 1,000 Chinese females, but by 1931 the ratio
had fallen to 1,703.[42] The higher proportion of Chinese females led to a
greater number of births; between 1931 and 1940, 217,000 Chinese were
born on the island compared to 123,000 during the previous decade and
59,000 during 1911–1920. The increase in births promoted a more normal
age structure, and, moreover, the trend to permanent settlement.[43] In 1931
two-thirds of the Chinese inhabiting Singapore island had been born
outside British Malaya, but in 1947 the latter was the birthplace of three-
fifths of the island's Chinese (table 5.6).

The Indian community in Singapore Municipality remained 'male
pioneer' in character. Indeed, as the Indian population grew, its sex
structure became more unbalanced, from 3,727 males per 1,000 females in
1901 to 5,369 males in 1931. Throughout British Malaya, Indian
immigration had a transient character partly because 'The return to their
native country is easier, quicker and less expensive for the Indians than the
Chinese'.[44] In Singapore, however, the sex ratio for Indians was more
unbalanced than in rural areas. Indian women found little urban
employment, and generally stayed at home when their husbands immi-
grated to cities, but women often accompanied their husbands to work on
plantations.[45] Singapore's Indian businessmen usually left their families in
India, and did spells of work 'interspersed by leave at regular intervals in
the same manner as Europeans'.[46]

The structure of Singapore Municipality's Malay community bears out
the description of Indonesian migrants as married couples and as
permanent settlers. In 1901 the Malay population was already fairly evenly
balanced with 1,267 males for every 1,000 females; while in 1931, despite
substantial migration from Netherlands India and a significant inflow
from Malaya, mainly Johore,[47] the ratio had improved to 1,181 males.
Because of its more even male–female balance, the Malay population had

[41] *1921 census*, pp.48–49; *1931 census*, pp.52, 56–58, 70; *1947 census*, pp.45, 59–60, 76.
[42] Figures for distribution by sex and age group are from J. R. Innes, *Report on the census of
the Straits Settlements, 1901* (Singapore, 1901), pp.30, 57–58; H. Marriott, *Census report
of the Straits Settlements, 1911* (Singapore, 1911), pp.13–15; *1921 census*, pp.155, 203, 206,
209; *1931 census*, pp.120–21; *1947 census*, pp.158–59, 178–93.
[43] *1947 census*, pp.84–85; Singapore Department of Social Welfare, *Social survey, 1947*,
pp.113–14.   [44] *1921 census*, p.98, and see p.93; *1931 census*, pp.53, 70–71.
[45] *1931 census*, pp.57–58, 101; *1947 census*, pp.79, 115; *1921 census*, pp.122, 58.
[46] Singapore Department of Social Welfare, *Social survey, 1947*, p.123, and see p.53;
Jumabhoy, *Multiracial Singapore*, pp.52, 53.
[47] *1921 census*, pp.42, 73; *1931 census*, pp.71–72.

Table 5.6 *Singapore Island population born in British Malaya, 1911–1947*

	000 persons born in British Malaya	% of Island population
(a) *Chinese*		*% of Island Chinese*
1911	43.9	19.7
1921	79.7	25.1
1931	150.1	35.6
1947	437.2	59.9
(b) *Indians*		*% of Island Indians*
1911	4.6	16.4
1921	5.5	17.1
1931	9.0	17.7
1947	25.0	36.3
(c) *Malays*		*% of Island Malays*
1911	n.a.	
1921	40.1	68.5
1931	52.2	73.4
1947	94.9	82.0

Notes:
1   For 1911 and 1921 the figures for Chinese may not be strictly comparable, since for 1911 they are for 'Straits–born' and probably include Chinese born in Burma, Siam and Netherlands India. (*1921 census*, p.95).
Sources: *1921 census*, pp.95, 97, 224; *1931 census*, pp.69–70, 219, 222, 225; *1947 census*, pp.84–85, 310–33.

a higher birth rate than the Chinese or Indian; the Malay share of population declined relative to the immigrant races because it was supported far less by inward movement.

III

The composition of Singapore's three Asian communities reflected the diverse sources of their origin. Chinese immigrants came from south-eastern China (figure 1.1), where 'there is a diversity of language, allegiance, mode of life, and characteristics generally similar to that found among representatives of different European nations'.[48]

Singapore Chinese were divided into the *pang* or dialect groups shown by table 5.7. Hokkien is the dialect pronunciation for Fukien, but the

[48] Vlieland, 'Population', p.67.

Table 5.7 *Singapore Chinese dialect groups, 1921–1931*

	1921		1931	
	000 persons	%	000 persons	%
Hokkien	109.5	40.1	133.5	39.2
Cantonese	76.4	27.9	90.6	26.6
Teochew	44.7	16.4	63.4	18.6
Hainanese	12.7	4.6	17.1	5.0
Hakka (Khek)	11.6	4.2	14.7	4.3
Others	18.5	6.8	21.3	6.3
Total	273.4	100.0	340.6	100.0

Sources: *1921 census*, p.187; *1931 census*, p.181.

overseas Chinese known as Hokkiens came only from the area around the port of Amoy in that province. In the context of this study, it is particularly significant that inter-intelligible dialects were spoken by Hokkiens and Teochews, the latter originating from that part of Kwangtung province near the port of Swatow and adjacent to the Fukien border. The Hokkien and Teochew dominated Chinese commercial life; reference to a Chinese businessman in Singapore usually meant a member of one of these two groups, especially the Hokkien.

The other Chinese groups, speaking dialects understood by no group in Singapore but themselves, were the Cantonese from Kwangtung province; the Hainanese from the island of Hainan off Kwangtung; and the Hakka from the provinces of Kwangtung and Fukien. 'Others' were mainly the Hokchia and Hokchew, who were from northern Fukien including the area around the port of Foochow, and spoke dialects resembling each other but distinct from those of the larger groups.[49]

The Chinese were also divided into the Chinese- and the English-educated, forming 'two solid and distinctive classes'[50] which persisted into the 1990s.[51] However, the much greater inter-war numerical strength of the Chinese- over the English-educated is not always appreciated. In 1921 only a fifth, and in 1931 a quarter, of Chinese born in British Malaya had a knowledge of English.[52] The so-called 'Straits Chinese' – those born in

---

[49] Freedman, *Chinese family*, pp.12–15.
[50] C. F. Yong, 'A preliminary study of Chinese leadership in Singapore, 1900–1941', *JSEAH* 9, 2 (1968), p.283.
[51] This split and dissatisfaction among the Chinese-educated was emphasized as an important factor in the 1991 General Election. 'More attention for Chinese silent majority, says Mr. Lee [Kuan Yew]', *Straits Times Weekly*, 28 Sept. 1991; 'The Chinese-educated just want their place in the sun', *Straits Times Weekly*, 12 Oct. 1991.
[52] *1921 census*, pp.327, 335; *1931 census*, pp.354, 369.

British Malaya – cannot be identified as comprising the English-educated, as was sometimes done.[53]

However, the increased number of Chinese with some English education reflected the growth in English-language schools. On one level the spread of English education soon created an over-supply of clerks in Singapore;[54] at the top it gave rise to a Chinese professional and political elite, whose members were often the products of English or Scottish universities.[55] The Straits Settlements government favoured education in English, but the Chinese business community strongly supported the development of Chinese-language education. Many more Chinese passed through the Chinese than the English education system, and the large body of Chinese-educated thus produced was inevitably oriented towards the culture of China, as was the intention.

Before World War II the Chinese, despite these various divisions, managed to remain remarkably united among themselves. A small minority of Chinese, amounting to fewer than 8,000 in the inter-war period, were Christians and a handful were Mohammadan, but otherwise Singapore Chinese shared a system of beliefs organized around domestic devotion and ritual of which ancestor worship was one aspect.[56] Moreover, Chinese society was effectively bound together by a complex of cross-cutting voluntary associations based on like origin in China (district, 'county' or province), clan (common surname) and similar interests or experience in Singapore.

The two chief organizations providing leadership in the Chinese community were the Singapore Chinese Chamber of Commerce (SCCC) begun in 1906 and the Straits Chinese British Association (SCBA) founded in 1900. The former was the pre-eminent representative of the Chinese business community, and, with places on its working committee strictly allocated between the five main *pang* groups, to a large extent represented Chinese society as a whole. The influence and prestige of the SCBA, which 'united the elite of the Straits-born',[57] derived from the political voice given its leaders by the British authorities. The consequent ability of SCBA leaders to serve as a bridge between government and Chinese businessmen and, partly owing to this role, their participation in Chinese business

[53] Singapore Department of Social Welfare, *Social survey, 1947*, pp.59–60, 120–21; *1931 census*, p.67.
[54] 'Report of the Committee to consider the problem of destitution among various sections of the community', *SSLCP 1923*, pp.C237–C238; *SSLCP 1929*, p.B144.
[55] Examples are well known and given in Yong, 'Preliminary study of Chinese leadership', pp.262–66, and see Straits Chinese British Association, *Golden jubilee souvenir* (Singapore, 1950).
[56] *1921 census*, pp.102, 215; *1931 census*, p.203; Freedman, *Chinese family*, pp. 43–44.
[57] Yong, 'Preliminary study of Chinese leadership', p.263.

Table 5.8 *Singapore Indians by ethnic origin and religion, 1931*

	Ethnic origin			Religion	
	000 persons	%		000 persons	%
Tamils	31.0	74.9	Hindus	24.1	58.2
Punjabi, etc.	4.3	10.4	Muhammadans	11.7	28.3
Malayalam	2.5	6.0	Sikhs	2.7	6.5
Others	3.6	8.7	Christians	2.5	6.0
			Others	0.4	1.0
Total	**41.4**	**100.0**	Total	**41.4**	**100.0**

Sources: *1931 census*, pp.193, 208.

ventures, had two important implications for Singapore's economic development. One was that it helped to unite the parallel elites of the SCCC and SCBA, and so all Singapore Chinese.[58] The other was that it encouraged the growth of a tradition of government-business co-operation in Singapore: this was not a phenomenon of post-independence economic development.

The Indians showed much less tendency than the Chinese to co-operate among themselves. They were divided by ethnic origin and so language, and particularly by religion (table 5.8). The Singapore Indian Association was not formed until 1923, and even then the great mass of Indians, who were Tamil labourers, remained unorganized, since the Association consisted of the professional and business classes and favoured northern Indians: most Indians in the professions and business did not wish to be associated with the Tamil labourers. In 1923 the Indian Merchants' Association was also begun, but almost all its 35 members were Bombay firms and exporters; neither other exporters nor the textile importers joined 'as they were unwilling to pay subscriptions unless there were immediate results'.[59] In Singapore no truly representative body of Indian merchants emerged until 1935 with the formation of the Indian Chamber of Commerce, although the Chettiars remained aloof even from this.[60]

[58] Ibid. pp.262–85.
[59] Jumabhoy, *Multiracial Singapore*, p.58, and see pp.55–56, 89–90; R. B. Krishnan, *Indians in Malaya* (Singapore, 1936), pp.26–31; Sinnappah Arasaratnam, *Indians in Malaysia and Singapore* (Bombay, 1970), pp.83–88; Singapore Indian Chamber of Commerce, *A brief history of the Singapore Indian Chamber of Commerce* (Singapore, 1984), pp.1–8. There is a discrepancy between the sources as to whether the Indian Merchants' Association was founded in 1923 or 1924.
[60] Jumabhoy, *Multiracial Singapore*, pp.66–68, 90; 'Indian Chamber of Commerce: first annual meeting', *Malaya Tribune*, 17 Sept. 1935; Indian Chamber of Commerce, Singapore, *Memorandum and articles of association* (Sept. 1937); Indian Chamber of

Table 5.9 *Singapore Malay population by ethnic group, 1921–1931*

	1921		1931	
	000 persons	%	000 persons	%
Malays	19.9	58.4	23.5	54.2
Javanese	8.8	25.8	11.3	26.0
Boyanese	4.5	13.2	7.0	16.1
Others	0.9	2.6	1.6	3.7
Total	**34.1**	**100.0**	**43.4**	**100.0**

Sources: 1921 census, pp.180–81, 74–76; 1931 census, p.169.

While in commerce as in social organization the Chinese combined pragmatic accommodation with an undoubted toughness, Singapore Indians lacked these qualities. The memoirs of a leading Indian merchant of the period reflect on Indian commercial failure relative to the Chinese. The Chinese firms were exclusively Chinese, and 'Each and everyone from a manager to a labourer put in his best effort to make the maximum money'. By contrast, 'Indian business mentality generally is selfish', and so unsuited to the co-operation found among the Chinese; 'Every Indian firm had of necessity one head Chinese coolie's "kepala"' to supervise the firm's day-to-day operation.[61] (The kepala occupied a position somewhere between a foreman and a labour contractor.)

Migration from Netherlands India gave Singapore a diverse Malay population (table 5.9) – by far the most heterogeneous of any urban area in British Malaya. There was, however, relatively little impediment in Singapore to cultural assimilation into the dominant Malayan Malay community, even for single men, since all Malays professed the Mohammadan religion, and all, except the Boyanese, spoke a common language.[62]

Most Malay migrants found themselves in Singapore for economic reasons, which was expressed by the Boyanese saying that 'if you want to make money and buy clothes, go to Singapore'.[63] Nevertheless, in the Malay community economic motivation was far weaker than for other races: 'Singapore Malays...attached great importance to easy and graceful living'.[64] Malays found it impossible to compete with Chinese and Indians economically, and most were driven to the outskirts of the city

Commerce, Singapore, *Report of the year*, 1936–1940, especially *1936*, p.49, *1938*, p.13, *1940*, p.12.   [61] Jumabhoy, *Multiracial Singapore*, pp.51–53.

[62] Vlieland, 'Population', p.65; Singapore Department of Social Welfare, *Social survey*, *1947*, p.126.

[63] Jacob Vredenbregt, 'Bawean migrations', *Bijdragen Tot de Taal – Land -, en Volkenkunde* 120, 1 (1964), p.128.

[64] Judith Djamour, *Malay kinship and marriage in Singapore* (London, 1959), p.10.

itself, or beyond, by rising property values.[65] In the inter-war years the
resentment that this created among Malays found articulation in a new
group of English-educated Malay leaders, and in the Malay press,
exemplified by the 1939 comment that

The free port of Singapore, for example, which the British government has taken
such pains to secure against attack, is in substance neither British nor Malay. Who
is it that has derived most of the wealth of the city? None other than the land and
house-owning Chinese, Arabs and Jews.[66]

The European community included a cross-section of the various
nations which traded with Singapore, but was mostly British. Britons fell
broadly into two groups: government and commercial. The presence of
both increased from the late nineteenth century as these functions
expanded in Singapore, and European numbers grew even faster, since by
the inter-war period it became common for European wives to accompany
their husbands.[67] The growth in trade in particular required more
personnel: 'You will find, in the early [18]70s, one or two Europeans in a
firm, in the [18]80s there are four or five, and nowadays [1918] it is nothing
uncommon to get six or a dozen European assistants'.[68] The far higher
remuneration of businessmen than government officials enabled the former
to set the pace in terms of lavish life-style and extravagant expenditure,
helping to make Singapore a 'place of high living and low thinking';[69] the
'government house crowd' remained well ahead in terms of social
snobbery. Although making a career in Singapore, or at any rate British
Malaya, virtually all Britons had in common the intention of returning
home to retire; generally they survived to do so, as Singapore was 'the
healthiest city East of Suez'.[70]

English was the language of expatriate business, of an educated section
of all three Asian populations, and the only feasible language for
administration, as the Japanese military rulers discovered.[71] However, the
large majority of Singapore's inhabitants knew no English, and even for
the Chinese to learn Mandarin or a second dialect generally proved
impracticable. The relatively easily acquired bazaar Malay was therefore
adopted as a crude lingua franca. Most people, and practically all
businessmen, knew at least a few words of 'pidgin Malay'.[72]

[65] *SSLCP 1927*, pp.B24, B25, B30.
[66] *Straits Times*, 8 Aug. 1939, translated from an editorial in *Mujlis*. See also W. R. Roff, *The origins of Malay nationalism* (Kuala Lumpur, 1967), pp.180–95.
[67] *1931 census*, p.73, and see Lockhart, *Return to Malaya*, pp.84–85.
[68] *Proceedings and report of the commission to inquire into housing* (1918) II, p.B186.
[69] Manicasothy Saravanamutu, *The sara saga* (Penang, 1970), p.54.
[70] Walling, *Singapura*, p.79.   [71] Turnbull, *History of Singapore*, p.207.
[72] Vlieland, 'Population', p.67; *1921 census*, p.77.

As part of the Colony of the Straits Settlements, the government of Singapore differed little in form from that of other Crown Colonies, and 'a country of sojourners [where] ... The instinct of loyalty to a mother land has been confined to the Malays, the Eurasians, and a growing body of Straits-born Chinese'[73] made administration easy. A society of expatriates tends to limit serious political discussion, and even more so in one of people 'whose intelligence, sentiments and energies are almost exclusively absorbed in the pursuit of the material interests of private life'.[74] In a settlement so largely transient, so split along racial (not class) lines and so commercially minded, the maxim of divide and rule hardly needed to be applied.

The Colony was ruled by the British colonial service, which was said to embody 'the virtues of bureaucracy'.[75] The Legislative Council had a minority of unofficial (i.e. non-civil service) members. Under a formula adopted in 1924, their numbers were increased so that two were elected by the (European) Chambers of Commerce of Singapore and Penang, and 11 more appointed by the Governor to represent other European interests and those of the Asian communities. It was, in effect, 'a government run by and for those who have won through to power and wealth, and devil take the hindermost'.[76] One result of Singapore's political arrangements was that 'The government had no roots in the life of the people of the country'.[77]

In the Straits Settlements, government was clearly subordinate to the forces of the market and designed to give them free play. Singapore was lightly taxed through various easily-administered indirect taxes, which offered 'tax handles'. The largest single source of revenue came from the monopoly sale of opium to the Chinese.[78] The burden of taxation was thus effectively shifted onto the poor, which suited the wealthier classes in Singapore and an economy dependent on trade rather than on industrial production for a domestic market. Government conceived of its role as primarily to enforce law and order and to secure property rights. Almost without exception, government intervened in the economy with great hesitation, and only after it was apparent that the market would not respond, as, for example, in the 1905 government organization of good

---

[73] 'Report of the select committee to consider the constitution of the Legislative Council of the Straits Settlements', *SSLCP 1921*, p.C30.

[74] *SSLCP 1930*, p.B153. The speaker was Tan Cheng Lock.

[75] 'Constitution of the Legislative Council', *SSLCP 1921*, p.C31.

[76] Emerson, *Malaysia*, p.306.

[77] 'Why Singapore fell', *The Times*, 18 Feb. 1942, and see Roland Braddell, 'Reconstruction of Malaya', *British Malaya* (Aug. 1944), pp. 42–44.

[78] Emerson, *Malaysia*, pp.303–5; Lennox A. Mills, *British rule in eastern Asia* (London, 1942), pp.80–82.

port facilities. The role of government therefore finds little space in a discussion of Singapore's pre-World War II economic development.

IV

Employment in Singapore changed remarkably little, even if the 1947 census is taken into account to provide an historical depth otherwise lacking because of the absence of statistics before 1921 (appendix table A.10). Unfortunately, the figures for 1921 and 1931 suffer from being taken in abnormal, depression years, and from the high proportion of workers unclassified by industry.[79] Because 1931 is the only year with figures for the Municipality separate from the island as a whole, changes in employment structure are analysed by comparing island statistics, which differed from those of the Municipality mainly in having a larger agricultural sector.

Rapid labour force growth and the absence of widespread industrialization inevitably produced a predominantly service population in Singapore. In 1931 three-quarters of those in the Municipality provided services. A fifth were in manufacturing and construction, and one-twentieth in agriculture. Service employment split roughly equally into three groups: commerce and finance, transport, and other, mainly personal, services.

Between 1921 and 1947, apart from agriculture's relative decline, the principal changes in employment were three. One was the fall in rickshaw pullers, although their number remained very high in view of the growing availability of motorized transport. Trolley buses were introduced in 1926 to replace a tramway system 'almost derelict and entirely incapable of carrying the traffic',[80] and by 1927 seven-seater 'mosquito' buses numbered over 450. Motor car ownership increased rapidly with accompanying problems of traffic congestion, which made 'the streets of Singapore ... reminiscent of London during an omnibus strike'.[81]

Second, by 1931 the emergence of a substantial professional class was apparent. Its growth was thought in 1947 to have been overestimated,[82] but inter-war expansion of the professions was probably still considerable,[83] and a reflection as well as a cause of economic development.

The third change was the sharp increase in public administration and defence recorded in 1947, although this was substantially overstated. It reflected greater direct employment by public authorities after the War and

---

[79] *1931 census*, pp.95–99; *1947 census*, pp.102–3.
[80] R. J. Farrer, 'The Municipality in my time' in *One hundred years of progress, centenary number of the Singapore Free Press*, 8 Oct. 1935, and see Colony of Singapore, *Report of the commission of inquiry into the public passenger transport system of Singapore* (Singapore, 1956), pp.7–11.   [81] *1931 census*, p.10.   [82] *1947 census*, pp.103, 104.
[83] Cf. Turnbull, *History of Singapore*, pp.120–21, 154.

the fact that the 1931 census excluded from public administration and defence labour employed by outside contractors, while the 1947 census did not always do so.[84]

A major reason why Singapore attracted a large inflow of labour was that much employment was casual with a high involuntary turnover, increasing the probability of finding a job, or, more accurately, a succession of jobs. The largest single outlet for casual labour was the port itself; the Singapore Harbour Board hired most of its daily average of 9,000 workers on a casual basis.[85] Manufacturing industry in Singapore also relied substantially on unskilled labour hired daily; while in the building trades most labour was recruited locally for a particular job.[86] Whatever the industry, almost all casual labour was hired through a system of contractors, sub-contractors and kepalas.[87] The arrangement freed employers from the need to deal with labour and afforded a way to manage labour, which would otherwise have proved difficult with a heterogeneous and transient work force.

For those in Singapore outside wage employment, statistics for earnings are fragmentary, while even for workers receiving wages, the varying terms of employment make meaningful comparison of levels of remuneration difficult. The bulk of workers were paid by the day or on piece rates, which together with the casual element in employment make it hard to know whether a worker regularly obtained a full week's work. Furthermore, employers frequently provided food and housing for workers, which constituted substantial in-kind remuneration.[88] Although available evidence points to an upward trend in real wages over the four decades after 1900,[89] during the inter-war years rises in nominal wages of 60% or more, but also large falls, and sharp changes in retail prices make real wage fluctuations impossible to establish on the basis of the material considered in this study. The importance of rice in every meal, low rice prices and the commodity's ready availability in Singapore contributed to much higher real wages in the city than would otherwise have obtained.[90]

---

[84] *Master plan, study groups*, p.51; *1947 census*, pp.100, 105, 45; R. P. Bingham, *Report of the Labour Department 1946* (Singapore, 1947), p.6; *1931 census*, pp.37, 85.

[85] *Proceedings and report of the commission to inquire into housing* (1918) II, pp.B63–B64; *Harbour Boards' Committee* (1926), p.41; *SSTC 1933–34* II, pp.42–43, I, p.119; *Master plan, study groups*, p.51.

[86] *Master plan, study groups*, pp.49, 81–82; *SSTC 1933–34* II, p.791.

[87] *Master plan, study groups*, p.81.

[88] Bingham, *Report 1946*, pp.8, 26; S. S. Awbery and F. W. Dalley, *Labour and trade union organisation in the Federation of Malaya and Singapore* (London, 1948), p.6.

[89] *Harbour Boards' Committee* (1926), pp.41–42; Blythe, *Methods and conditions of employment of Chinese labour*, pp.27–50.

[90] Bingham, *Report 1946*, pp.17, 25; Awbery and Dalley, *Labour and trade union organisation*, pp.5, 17.

Effectively, the minimum male wage in British Malaya was set by the basic wage paid to Indian male rubber estate workers. Although this wage fluctuated very considerably in response to changes in the price of rubber, in 1929 a statutory minimum daily wage excluding in-kind benefits for Indian men working on rubber estates was set at $0·50 (1s 2d).[91] This was close to the 1s a day for which W. A. Lewis argued that in the late nineteenth century there existed 'an unlimited supply of Indians and Chinese willing to travel to the ends of the earth to work on plantations'.[92]

In Singapore, wages, although again subject to substantial variance influenced by rubber prices, were not always too much above the minimum estate wage. Contemporary data showed that Singapore wages (exclusive of in-kind benefits) were $0·60–$0·90 a day.[93] For example, wages in pineapple canning, rubber processing and sago factories were within this range, but here, as even more with the $20–$30 a month earned by the city's domestic servants, the weighting appropriate to in-kind benefits confuses comparison of occupational wages.[94]

It is clear, however, that wages for industrial labour in Singapore were well above those paid to most workers in the city.[95] To some extent, this reflected higher rates of pay obtaining in what could be regarded as a modern, European sector. For example, in the late 1930s average pay in the Bata shoe factory was $1·36 per day, but in a neighbouring Chinese factory only $0·70. More important, however, the shortage of skilled labour in Singapore[96] gave rise to significant wage differentials, and industrial undertakings required the highest proportion of skilled workers. In the late 1930s Chinese men working in Singapore engineering factories earned $45 a month and foundry workers $40–$50 a month.[97]

Comparison of United Kingdom and Singapore wages suggests a relatively small wage gap between the two areas, and one which was significantly less in relation to industrial countries than the wage levels on which Singapore's post-1966 export-oriented industrialization was based. In 1938 the average weekly earnings of United Kingdom manual workers

[91] US Department of Labor, 'Labour in Malaya' in P. P. Pillai, ed. *Labour in South East Asia* (New Delhi, 1947), p.152; *Labour conditions in Ceylon, Mauritius and Malaya. Report by Major G. St. Orde Browne* (PP 1943, IX), p.97. In 1913 Indian male estate wages were $0·30. Estate wages fell substantially in the 1930s slump. Bauer, *Rubber*, pp.222–44.
[92] W. Arthur Lewis, 'The diffusion of development' in Thomas Wilson and Andrew S. Skinner, eds. *The market and the state* (London, 1976), p.142.
[93] SS, *Blue book 1929*, section 23, p.2; Rotary Club, *Singapore as an industrial centre*, p.16.
[94] *Labour conditions in Ceylon, Mauritius and Malaya*, pp.104–6; US Department of Labor, 'Labour in Malaya', p.152.
[95] US Department of Labor, 'Labour in Malaya', p.151.
[96] *SSLCP 1919*, p.B159; *SSLCP 1931*, p.B131.
[97] *Labour conditions in Ceylon, Mauritius and Malaya*, pp.106–7.

in manufacturing was 69s for a 47·7-hour week.[98] Wages in Singapore of $1 a day, or $6 a week – not unusual in manufacturing,[99] and excluding any in-kind benefits – were equivalent to 14s, or about one-fifth of the United Kingdom level. The Singapore engineering wage of $45 a month, about 22s a week, was over a third of the UK manufacturing level, and more than a quarter of average earnings of adult male workers in 1938 in the highly-paid, new United Kingdom industries of motor vehicle and aircraft manufacture.[100] Along with the lack of labour skills, the costs of immigration to Singapore, both in terms of transport and psychic strain, requiring wage compensation, kept the city a relatively high-wage centre during the inter-war period, as discussed in chapter 7.

Employment in Singapore divided broadly into the international economy, in which approximately one-quarter of the labour force was engaged, and a supporting local economy which employed the remainder. The international economy consisted mainly of activities providing internationally-traded services, and employment concentrated in commerce and finance and in water transport, including wharves and warehouses. Additionally, the international economy had a significant manufacturing component. The local economy consisted of agriculture, local retailing and transport, the majority of those in the professions, entertainment and much of manufacturing industry.

A dual economy emerged in Singapore because successful economic development drew workers in search of employment faster than new 'modern' sector jobs absorbed immigrant labour.[101] The result was to create surplus labour and, identified with this, the 'traditional' sector of Singapore's dual economy. A small part of the surplus labour from which this dualism in Singapore arose lodged in its international economy. But surplus labour was largely absorbed through employment in Singapore's local economy. To some extent this was reflected in a tendency to overmanning: 'Many operations which in European countries are performed by one man (or one woman) in Singapore require two or more. As

---

[98] Mitchell and Jones, *Second abstract of British historical statistics*, p.148.
[99] US Department of Labor, 'Labour in Malaya', p.151. In 1938 wages of industrial labour ranged between $0·80 and $1·20 per day for men.
[100] Derek H. Aldcroft, *The inter-war economy: Britain, 1919–1939* (London, 1970), p.358.
[101] For discussion of dual economies, see W. Arthur Lewis, 'Economic development with unlimited supplies of labour', *Manchester School of Economic and Social Studies* 22, 2 (1954), pp.139–91; Gustav Ranis and John C. H. Fei, 'A theory of economic development', *American Economic Review* 51, 4 (1961), pp.533–65; Gustav Ranis, 'Analytics of development: dualism' in Chenery and Srinivasan, eds. *Handbook of development economics* I, pp.74–92. Lewis makes particular reference to the development of a dual economy in countries with heavy immigration. W. Arthur Lewis, 'The dual economy revisited', *Manchester School of Economic and Social Studies* 47, 3 (1979), p.219.

a small example, in England a delivery van has one man in it, the driver, in Singapore such a van requires a driver, a clerk, and two men to carry the articles for delivery'.[102]

The bulk of surplus labour concentrated in three groups: hawkers, rickshaw pullers and domestic servants. In 1931 these occupations engaged some 53,000 persons and accounted for 27% of Singapore Municipality's labour force, as high a proportion as the international economy (appendix table A.10). Some workers in these three occupations could be said to be surplus labour: output levels would probably have remained unchanged if their labour had been withdrawn.[103]

Mass immigration greatly expanded hawking, rickshaw pulling and domestic service, since many immigrants drawn to Singapore were compelled on arrival to take whatever employment was available, and in the absence of demand for their labour elsewhere such personal service occupations were the main ones on offer. They had two features which enabled them to accommodate large numbers of newly-arrived immigrants. One was that the amount of employment in these occupations was not fixed but capable of considerable extension; people could obtain a footing in them so long as the price of their labour was sufficiently low. The second was that services of this kind could provide employment for people without capital or skills and in need of housing. An official committee 'clearly established that a good number of immigrants take to hawking as a means of livelihood immediately on arrival in Singapore'.[104] The tendency to do so was considerably influenced by an immigrant's connections in Singapore and opportunities for job search: 'If on arrival they are accommodated in a relative's house, as a rule they serve an apprenticeship or become coolies. Failing that, they are compelled by circumstances to hawk'.[105] Hawkers could begin with as little capital as $1 to $10, perhaps obtained from a shopkeeper or moneylender, and find accommodation in coolie houses.[106]

In 1931 about a tenth of Singapore's Municipal workforce, or some 20,500 persons, were hawkers and the number on the island as a whole was 22,700. At this time, the findings of a government committee suggested the existence of substantial surplus labour in this occupation. The committee recommended that on the island only 12,000 hawkers be licensed. But this

---

[102] Bingham, *Report 1946*, p.28.
[103] For a discussion of this interpretation of 'disguised unemployment', in which the marginal product of a man, but not a man-hour, is zero, see Lewis, 'Economic development with unlimited supplies of labour', pp.139–42 and 'Reflections on unlimited labour' in Luis Eugenio di Marco, ed. *International economics and development* (New York, 1972), pp.76–82; A. K. Sen, *Choice of techniques* 3rd edn (Oxford,1972), pp.3–5.
[104] 'Report of the committee to investigate the hawker question in Singapore', *SSLCP 1932*, p.C15, and see pp.C69, C82.   [105] Ibid. p.C79.
[106] Ibid. pp.C50, C76, C23, C59, C66–C69, C79, C107; *Proceedings and report of the commission to inquire into housing* (1918) II, pp.C75, C83, B10.

implied reduction in hawker numbers on Singapore island by almost half occasioned a reservation from two Committee members 'that the limit of 12,000 hawkers is grossly in excess of all possible needs of the population'. They considered even 7,000 hawkers to be excessive.[107]

Like hawkers, rickshaw pullers, who engaged in 'The deadliest occupation in the East, the most degrading for human beings to pursue',[108] showed the need of immigrant labour for capital. Most pullers did not own their vehicles, which cost some $300 to put on the street, but rented them for between $0·15 and $0·25 for a half day and slightly more at night. Typically, a puller shared a house with up to 175 men. These houses concentrated in certain parts of central Singapore, for example in the neighbourhood of Bencoolen Street and Waterloo Street. There, in 1918, each man paid a headman who rented the house about $0·60 a month for lodging and a further $1 a month for a rickshaw kept inside the house and $0·20 if kept outside in the yard.

A puller might hope to accumulate sufficient capital, or gain enough creditworthiness, to borrow money to buy his own rickshaw, which then could be rented at least part of the time to others. But until this was achieved, if ever, the absence of any wage component in a puller's earnings and so his assumption of all income risk fomented a common feeling of discontent among rickshaw men which lay behind their frequent and bitter strikes.[109]

In 1931 Singapore Municipality had over 10,000 rickshaw pullers, and a surplus of labour in the occupation was apparent. The Governor observed that the Municipalities 'licence fewer rickshaws each year, but difficulty always occurs in finding suitable occupation for the pullers displaced. As things are, owing to motor competition, pullers find it difficult to earn a livelihood'.[110]

Just as hawking and rickshaw pulling created outlets for immigrant labour through self-employment, domestic service (in 1931 employing

[107] 'Hawker question', *SSLCP 1932*, pp.C15, C17. Indeed, the Committee itself recognized that a limit of 12,000 hawkers was excessive, but set this to minimize hardship. The figure of 7,000 hawkers consisted of 5,000 in the Municipality and 2,000 in the rest of the island.

[108] Song, *One hundred years' history*, p.484. The quotation is from a *Straits Times* editorial in 1911.

[109] 'Rickshaw strike in Singapore', *MRCA* 54 (Feb. 1935), pp.29–31; 'Labour affairs, Singapore rickshaw pullers', *MRCA* 98 (Oct. 1938), pp.23–26 and 99 (Nov. 1938), pp.27–28; 'Societies legislation in the Straits Settlements', *MRCA* 27 (Nov. 1932), pp.26–28; *Proceedings and report of the commission to inquire into housing* (1918) II, pp.B72, B89–B91, B152–B153, C11–C12, C16, C17; Song, *One hundred years' history*, pp.294–95, 328; Walling, *Singapura*, pp.103–4; N. I. Low, *Chinese jetsam on a tropic shore* (Singapore, 1974), p.73; James Francis Warren, *Rickshaw coolie* (Singapore, 1986), pp.24, 40–48, 58; Turnbull, *History of Singapore*, p.114.

[110] PRO CO 273/569/82001, Sir Cecil Clementi to Rt. Hon. Sir Philip Cunliffe Lister, Colonial Secretary, 11 Dec. 1931. See also Warren, *Rickshaw coolie*, pp.66, 76–77.

21,800 people, two-thirds of whom were male[111]) did so through a willingness of Singapore's growing middle class to take on servants so long as their wages remained low. Domestic service 'was a popular form of employment with newly arrived immigrant labour [and]...the high standard of living in the Colony amongst certain sections of the community has made it possible for large numbers of these persons to be so employed'.[112] Although domestic service might meet the need for housing, it rarely solved the almost universal problem of overcrowding among immigrants, since 'boys' quarters' in private houses, usually no more than adequate for their intended occupants, generally also sheltered one or more friends.[113]

Emigration provided some relief to the pressure of abundant labour, although it was always a lagged and imperfect response to poor trade conditions. Nevertheless, emigration prevented the development of much open unemployment. In the 1930s slump, however, emigration alone could not avert a serious glut of labour and some open unemployment. Three factors contributed to this. First, many Singapore residents in wage employment lost their jobs or were made part-time to spread available work. Second, Singapore experienced an 'invasion of unemployed persons from other parts of the Peninsula, no doubt hoping to find work in this wonderful city or, if they cannot get work, perhaps to get away by sea'.[114] A third, and crucial, consideration was that many Chinese wishing to return to China could not do so because of their straitened circumstances;[115] although as the 1930s slump worsened the government, fearing social unrest, extended free repatriation to unemployed as well as to decrepit and destitute Chinese labourers.[116]

These three factors gave Singapore all the symptoms of a seriously overcrowded labour market, and after 1929 led to an influx into the three service occupations examined above, especially hawking. By 1932 it was said that 'the "out-of-work" [had] taken to hawking in considerable numbers as the only means of earning even a small pittance'.[117] These hawkers 'sometimes with goods that would hardly cover a small handkerchief'[118] were among the most obvious signs of widespread distress caused by the 1930s slump among the poorer classes.

[111] *1931 census*, p.247.   [112] *Master plan, study groups*, p.50, and see p.54.
[113] *Proceedings and report of the commission to inquire into housing* (1918) II, pp.B16–B17.
[114] *SSLCP 1930*, p.B130.
[115] For example, see 'Conditions of male labour in rubber factories', *MRCA* 24 (Aug. 1932), pp.30–32.
[116] *SSLCP 1930*, p.B131; Bauer, *Rubber*, p.229; J. N. Parmer, *Colonial labor policy and administration* (Locust Valley, NY, 1960), pp.241–42.
[117] 'Hawker question', *SSLCP 1932*, p.C12, and see pp.C23, C26–C27, C31, C40–C41, C43, C73, C89, C105, C108–C109.   [118] Ibid. p.C59, and see p.C116.

As in other staple ports, immigration in response to Singapore's economic development was accompanied by a marked division of employment along racial and ethnic lines. Because of a very heterogeneous population, this division of labour was particularly complex in Singapore. Two factors were essential to the continuance of this labour market segmentation characterized by several non-competing groups. One was a sense of group cohesion: employees and employers alike supported maintenance in the workplace of Singapore's sharp racial, ethnic and language cleavages. Most immigrants and migrants lacked job experience and skills appropriate to Singapore, and tended to be pushed into certain jobs according to their racial and ethnic affiliation.[119] A group might originally specialize in an occupation because its time of arrival coincided with that occupation's expansion. Subsequently, new arrivals expected, and were expected, to seek jobs associated with their particular group. The presence of their fellows in these jobs made it natural to do so, and continuous labour force turnover through immigration and migration perpetuated the process and provided its rationale.

The other important factor in continued market segmentation was different supply prices of labour in areas of emigration, since this was essential to preserving income differentials in Singapore. These in turn reinforced the determination of a dominant group to exclude others, to avoid wages being bid down. After an occupation and its racial and ethnic composition was established, that employment attracted to Singapore more recruits from the groups already concentrated in it, and tended to gain its own momentum through their arrival in increased numbers. Like other employments, occupations absorbing marginal, poorly paid labour grew primarily as the preserve of specific groups; more of their numbers only further swelled these occupations and eroded remuneration levels. So long as these groups' supply price of labour remained less than that of others, they found their role in Singapore largely confined to the provision of marginal labour. This was particularly true of rickshaw pulling and domestic service; hawking was a more universal overspill occupation, although divided along racial and ethnic lines according to the type of hawking and its likely return.[120]

The 1931 census gives statistics for employment by race in Singapore,[121]

[119] Cf. J. D. Vaughan, *The manners and customs of the Chinese of the Straits Settlements* (Singapore, 1879), pp.15–16; Lee Poh Ping, *Chinese society in nineteenth century Singapore* (Kuala Lumpur, 1978), pp.38–40; B. W. Hodder, 'Racial groupings in Singapore', *Malayan Journal of Tropical Geography* 1 (1953), pp.27, 33, 34; U. A. Aziz, 'The interdependent development of agriculture and other industries', *MER* 4, 1 (1959), p.28.

[120] Cf. 'Hawker question', *SSLCP 1932*, pp.C26–C28 and Warren, *Rickshaw coolie*, pp.36, 38.   [121] *1931 census*, pp.252–79.

but not by ethnic group which would be the more revealing distinction. Indian employment displayed the divergence which underlay the social chasm in that community. A disproportionate share of Indians, mostly Tamils, were general and dock labourers, or filled menial jobs such as messengers and peons. Their presence in these largely casual jobs was reflected in the inability of the census to place nearly two-fifths of Indian workers in any specific occupation. A relatively small but significant number of Indians were to be found in comparatively higher status occupations in commerce and finance and in public administration. In commerce Indians offered the only counterweight to Chinese at the level of the bazaar, principally in the import and distribution of textiles; while the main moneylenders in Singapore were Chettiars and Sikhs, the latter often combining this with work as gatekeepers or watchmen.[122] The Indians' prominence in government occupations, as shown by the census, was because Sikhs, often former soldiers, formed the majority of the lower ranks of the police force.[123] However, the census classification of employment by occupation rather than industry considerably understated government employment of Indians, mostly in the lower echelons.[124]

Both Malay and European employment was more specialized than Indian. In 1931 a fifth of Malays were in agriculture and over two-fifths in transport and communications, mostly as drivers. The latter tendency was most apparent among the Boyanese who had once comprised the bulk of the town's grooms and coachmen, and were said to regard learning to operate a motor car as their first task in Singapore.[125] The remaining two-fifths of Malays were scattered throughout the economy, although there was some concentration in government and as electricians and mechanics. The latter was in part owing to a preference for lighter or 'cleaner' work,[126] but probably also because these occupations were expanding and created new opportunities for employment at a time when Malays were joining the labour force in increasing numbers.

European employment clustered in three categories – government, commerce and the professions – and otherwise was little represented.[127]

Chinese dominated the main employment categories, apart from government, where they were excluded from the upper ranks by the colour bar and shunned the lower ones. But to point out this Chinese

---

[122] Ibid. pp.85–86; *SSLCP 1929*, p.B104; Goh Keng Swee, *Urban incomes and housing: a report on the social survey of Singapore, 1953–54* (Singapore, 1956), pp.18, 96; Walling, *Singapura*, pp.83–89.   [123] *1921 census*, p.106; *1931 census*, pp.86, 90.
[124] *1921 census*, p.122; *1931 census*, pp.37, 85; *1947 census*, p.81; Bingham, *Report 1946*, pp.4, 6, 8.
[125] *1921 census*, p.75; Vredenbregt, 'Bawean migrations', p.131; *1931 census*, p.49.
[126] Bingham, *Report 1946*, p.4.   [127] Cf. Emerson, *Malaysia*, p.270.

predominance tells only a fraction of the story, because of the marked ethnic divisions in Chinese employment.

The Hokkien, who 'are of an urban habit and have a genius for trade and shopkeeping',[128] dominated Chinese commerce, including the rubber trade and banking.[129] Hokkien were also the most prosperous hawkers in Singapore.[130]

The Teochew achieved their greatest commercial presence in the trades in tropical produce, piece goods, rice and other foodstuffs.[131] 'Practically the whole of the trade between China and Singapore in fruit and vegetables is in the hands of a syndicate of Teochew' with headquarters near Ellenborough Market. Their shops employed Teochew hawkers on a commission basis to retail these goods throughout the city, as did Teochew stall holders in Ellenborough Market who controlled the distribution of fresh fish.[132]

Cantonese, reflecting what was considered to be a mechanical proclivity, supplied the bulk of artisans in Singapore;[133] while, at least until the late 1930s, most Cantonese women who joined the labour force became either domestic servants or prostitutes. In 1921 'practically all the Chinese prostitutes are Cantonese'.[134]

Most rickshaw pullers in Singapore came from poor areas of China and were the Hokchew and, especially, Hokchia, so that in 1931 Singapore Municipality contained well over half of all Hokchia in British Malaya.[135] Furthermore, 'The Hokchia and Hokchew dialects control most of the night stalls in Singapore ... Their customers are mostly rickshaw pullers'.[136]

Like the Hokchew and Hokchia, the Hainanese emigrated from a poor part of China. They occupied only the margins of Singapore's economy, and among them political radicalism flourished. Although Hainanese managed to establish themselves to some extent in shopkeeping and particularly the coffee shop trade, the majority 'engaged in domestic service, nine out of ten servants in European establishments belonging to this tribe'.[137] The employment of seamen on oil tankers based in Singapore illustrates the ethnic division of labour among the Chinese: 'As a rule the

[128] *1947 census*, p.76, and see *1921 census*, p.79; *1931 census*, p.80.
[129] Goh, *Urban incomes*, p.19; Lee, *Chinese society*, pp.100–6; Tan Tek Soon, 'Chinese emigration', *Straits Chinese Magazine* 6 (1903), pp.44–45.
[130] 'Hawker question', *SSLCP 1932*, pp.C25–C26.
[131] Goh, *Urban incomes*, p.19; Lee, *Chinese society*, pp.100–6.
[132] 'Hawker question', *SSLCP 1932*, p.C26.
[133] Bingham, *Report 1946*, p.3; Hodder, 'Racial groupings', p.34.
[134] *1921 census*, p.80.
[135] *1931 census*, p.82; *1921 census*, p.84. For fuller information on the territorial and dialect divisions of rickshaw pullers coming from in and around Foochow, see Warren, *Rickshaw coolie*, pp.33–37.   [136] 'Hawker question', *SSLCP 1932*, p.C27.
[137] *1931 census*, p.81, and see *1921 census*, p.83; *1947 census*, p.76.

deck hands on steamers making up a crew in Singapore are Hokchews, the firemen, greasers, carpenters, etc., are Cantonese, and the stewards' staffs Hainanese'.[138]

Hakka had more varied employment than other groups, probably because they came from scattered areas in China and often spoke a second dialect. However, Hakka ran most pawnshops and Chinese drugstores.[139]

Until well after World War II a segmented labour market persisted in Singapore, with consequent large income differentials. The Malays had been pushed to the fringes of the economy and the city, but even among the economically dominant Asian race – the Chinese – income differentials were substantial. In 1953–54 a survey found that 'The Hokkien are the best off, followed by the Hakka and the Teochew. The Cantonese are fourth, while the Hainanese come a very bad last'.[140] Like labour market segmentation, economic dualism was a legacy which Singapore carried forward into the 1950s. Both were to disappear under the pressure of rapid 1960s and 1970s economic growth.

[138] 'Unrest among unemployed Chinese seamen', *MRCA* 23 (July 1932), p.22.
[139] Goh, *Urban incomes*, p.19; Hodder, 'Racial groupings', p.36; *1947 census*, p.75.
[140] Goh, *Urban incomes*, p.18, and see p.19.

6   Rubber: boom and spread of a twentieth-century staple

It has been shown that the growth of Singapore's traditional primary exports to the West represented a response by regional producers to Western demand; that entrepreneurial and service functions performed in Singapore facilitated this response; that these functions were an important part of Singapore's development; and that they created opportunities for further development. What set rubber apart from the traditional primary exports to the West was the extent of these effects on Singapore. In rubber exports, Singapore found an engine of growth which operated more powerfully than its predecessors and made possible the emergence of a much more diversified and developed economy.

There were four reasons for the sweeping impact that rubber had on Singapore. First, as observed in chapter 3, it increased the value of Singapore's exports considerably more than any other commodity. Second, the bulkiness of rubber led to an expansion of transport, handling and port facilities, discussed in chapter 4. Third, for most of the period the rubber industry, in providing the main stimulus to immigration to British Malaya, also promoted Singapore's own rapid population growth, considered in chapter 5.

The fourth reason, taken up in this chapter, was that the economics of rubber production left entry to the industry open to all types of producers, because the same commodity could be produced competitively with very different factor combinations, and because most of the processing could wait until the coagulated latex reached a central mill. Since a variety of hinterland producers could grow rubber but had different production and marketing requirements, the range of functions performed in Singapore expanded accordingly, and both Europeans and Chinese in the city were drawn into the industry.

Four main types of producers contributed to the rubber boom in Singapore. Three were to be found in Malaya – European estates, Chinese and Indian estates and Asian smallholdings. The fourth type of producers were Netherlands Indian native smallholders, principally in Sumatra and Borneo. Sections I and II of this chapter trace Singapore's contribution to the emergence of British Malaya's European estate rubber and oil palm industries. The third section analyses how the city's Chinese entrepreneurs acquired substantial estate holdings. Singapore's part in the establishment of smallholder production is dealt with in the fourth section, while the fifth and sixth sections focus on the city's role as a rubber market.

I

In Singapore the managing agency house system developed with European estate rubber. Although this arrangement, locally known as the agency house system, built largely on an existing mercantile structure, it resulted in what became the principal form of European enterprise in Singapore until the 1960s. An agency system can develop in two ways. First, a firm can decentralize a part of its business by appointing a local agent, and from the late nineteenth century, international shipping lines and many United Kingdom manufacturers wishing to distribute from Singapore did this. In Singapore, European firms which handled this agency business were still referred to as merchant houses.

The second way an agency system can develop is through the promotion of a new company which sells shares and appoints as its managing agent an agency house. In Singapore this approach was utilized to establish British Malayan rubber estates, and created the agency house system.[1] Because in Singapore the two paths by which an agency system can emerge were strongly mutually reinforcing, a small group of dominant European merchant/agency houses was formed. The group increased somewhat in number, but its core membership changed little between the turn of the century and World War II.

The main obstacle to establishing estate rubber was an exceptionally long investment period. Because *Hevea* requires about six years to mature, there is a corresponding need for finance and assumption of risk by investors. For land planted only with *Hevea*, as was typical on European estates, investment of roughly $600 (£70) an acre was necessary to bring a rubber estate into bearing. The bulk of expenditure was on labour and supervision costs in planting and, more important, upkeep of the unproductive estate while the trees matured.[2]

The swift increase in European estate acreage to 646,000 acres by 1913 (table 6.1) was financed chiefly from London. Finance on the scale needed

[1] The present study follows British Malayan convention. Reference to an agency house indicates a managerial/secretarial connection with a rubber company.
[2] David M. Figart, *The plantation rubber industry in the middle east* (Washington, DC: US Department of Commerce, 1925), pp.13, 47–53, 87–90; R. Soliva, *An economic view of rubber planting* (Singapore, 1931), p.37.

Table 6.1 *British Malaya area planted in rubber, 1900–1939 (000 acres)*

	European estates	Chinese estates	(Total Asian estates)	Small-holdings	Total
1900	2				2
1904	28				28
1907	168			2	170
1911	494			256	750
1913	646			428	1,074
1918	1,050			836	1,886
1921	1,077		(291)	858	2,226
1932	1,398	348	(479)	1,276	3,153
1939	1,573	342	(527)	1,328	3,428

Notes:
1 Figures include mature and immature acreage and exclude Brunei.
2 All smallholdings may be assumed to be Asian–owned.
3 Before 1921 Asian estates are included in the figures for smallholdings.
4 For 1921 the figure for Asian estates is a rough one, based partly on an estimate which Figart made but regarded as 'guesswork'. Chinese estates are included in Total Asian estates.
5 Almost all Asian estate acreage other than Chinese was owned by Indians or Japanese and was evenly divided between them.
Sources: Figart, *Plantation rubber*, pp.273–77; Drabble, *Rubber*, pp.215–18; Grist, *Malayan agricultural statistics, 1932*, tables 1, 2, *1939*, tables 7, 8; Grist, *Ownership of rubber estates*, pp.2, 3; Malaya, *Rubber statistics handbook, 1940*, pp.15–16.

for such a rapid expansion was unavailable in British Malaya: Singapore was the main centre for finance in British Malaya, but had no local stock exchange, and European banks in the city, reflecting British practice, would not finance rubber estate development, either European or Chinese, or even advance to cultivators against crops. As the Singapore manager of the Mercantile Bank explained 'No one cares to lock-up money for such a long time and before the rubber attains maturity anything might happen'.[3] Divergent property rights prevented Dutch banks in Singapore like the Netherlands Trading Society from lending long-term to rubber estates, as they did in Netherlands India. Under the British legal system, banks making these loans 'could not get enough protection by law' to ensure their rights as, in effect, partners in estate enterprises.[4]

In Singapore, Europeans responded to the problem of financing estate rubber development by transforming merchant houses into managing agency houses, and using the latter to float rubber companies on the London stock market. Through these activities, Singapore houses had a

[3] *Commissions on trade depression 1921*, appx. 1, p.166, and see pp.169–70 for similar evidence from the manager of the Hongkong and Shanghai Bank.
[4] Ibid., appx. 1, p.174, and see the Commissions' *Report*, pp.15–16.

pioneering role in the development of Malayan estate rubber.[5] Three considerations largely account for this. First, Singapore merchant houses were already in British Malaya when rubber began to be grown. Second, existing business relationships in supplying and financing proprietary planters often helped merchant houses to assume the agency house functions of entrepreneur, in floating a rubber company around an estate (or beginning a new estate), and of financier, in injecting some capital to prepare the company for flotation. Third, and most important, large merchant houses had the advantage of a well-known position in Eastern trade: overseas investors were attracted to a rubber company by the reputation of its sponsor, and by a belief that agency house management of the company would safeguard their investment.[6] Limited liability and public status for rubber companies meant that overseas shareholders bore most of the financial risk of rubber estate development, as well as the uncertainty associated with a new and unknown industry. At the same time, partners in the merchant houses limited their own risk exposure, since the firm's transformation into an agency house typically involved the assumption of limited liability.[7]

In 1899 few managing agencies were held in Singapore, and only Guthrie & Co. – perhaps in part anxious to make up for its loss of the shipping agency for a Conference line – had substantial interests in managing rubber companies.[8] During the first decade of the century, however, the managing agency house system spread rapidly in Singapore because of rubber. The 1911 *Directory* gives details for over 400 rubber estates in British Malaya, including a number of proprietary estates and some planted partly in other crops like coconuts, coffee or sugar. Singapore managing agents and/or secretaries could be identified for 116 of these estates, more than one quarter of the total. In the large majority of cases, it would appear that the Singapore firm was the managing agent, and with

[5] For discussion of the issues, see Richard T. Stillson, 'The financing of Malayan rubber, 1905–1923', *Economic History Review* 2nd ser. 24, 4 (1971), pp.591–95 and the comment by J. H. Drabble and P. J. Drake, 'More on the financing of Malayan rubber, 1905–1923', *Economic History Review* 2nd ser. 27, 1 (1974), pp.110, 113–16, 119.

[6] Lewis, *Growth and fluctuations*, p.188. Agency houses were an important manifestation of what has been called the free-standing company. Its main purpose was to link British investors with investment opportunities abroad. Mira Wilkins, 'The free-standing company, 1870–1914: an important type of British foreign direct investment', *Economic History Review* 2nd ser. 41, 2 (1988).

[7] J. H. Drabble and P. J. Drake, 'The British agency houses in Malaysia', *JSEAS* 12, 2 (1981), pp.307–9. On the agency house system, see also Allen and Donnithorne, *Western enterprise*, pp.52–53, 57, 112–13; Drabble, *Rubber*, pp.21–22, 63–65, 78–86, 128–29, 229; J. J. Puthucheary, *Ownership and control in the Malayan economy* (Singapore, 1960), pp.37–40, 43–44.

[8] *Directory 1899*, pp.103–56, 396–413; see also the similar, but in the case of rubber companies incorrect, analysis in Chiang, 'Sino-British mercantile relations', pp.254–55.

a few exceptions performed this function for rubber estates incorporated as limited liability companies. The principal managing agents in Singapore and the number of their estates were Boustead & Co. (7); Barlow & Co. (13); Behn, Meyer & Co. (6); Sandilands, Buttery & Co. (2); Paterson, Simons & Co. (9); East Asiatic Co. (4); Borneo Co. (1); F. W. Barker & Co. (15); and Guthrie & Co. (24). Additionally, H. L. Coglan & Co., chartered surveyors in London, had agencies for 11 estates, but disappeared from Singapore during World War I; Evatt & Co. were secretaries for five estates; while no other Singapore firm performed agency and/or secretarial functions for more than four estates.[9]

After the turn of the century Singapore agency houses displayed a distinctive development pattern: established merchant houses and those with homeward shipping agencies predominated. By contrast, agency houses elsewhere in British Malaya did not grow out of earlier mercantile involvement there, but either started business with the rubber industry or, more often, came from other countries in Asia, notably Ceylon, where they already managed estates. Bousteads, Behn, Meyer, Paterson, Simons and the Borneo Company were in Singapore by the mid-nineteenth century, and from 1897 were leading Conference merchants. Although without a homeward shipping agency and excluded from the 'secret' rebate, Guthries was among Singapore's oldest and biggest merchant houses. Barlow & Co., deriving from a firm begun in 1877, was a large distributor of manufactured imports and the agent for a Conference shipping line. Sandilands, Buttery & Co. came to Singapore only at the end of the century, but it was present in Penang from the 1830s, and in 1911 held agencies there for major homeward shipping lines and six rubber companies. An important newcomer was the East Asiatic Company, well-established in Bangkok and, as shipowners, a member of the Straits Homeward Conference, which opened a branch in Singapore in 1903.

The only large Singapore agency house without antecedents previous to the rubber industry was F. W. Barker & Co. It was founded in about 1902 when F. W. Barker set up as an accountant and estate agent, having left the merchant house, Gilfillan, Wood & Co. (perhaps partly explaining the latter's late start as an agency house under the name of Adamson, Gilfillan & Co.)[10] The experience of F. W. Barker & Co. shows that new or small firms could become successful in the rubber industry, but it may be

---

[9] *Directory 1911*, pp.606–64, 128–215, and see *1916*.

[10] See above, chapters 2, 3, 4; Makepeace, 'Machinery of commerce', pp.183–84; *Directory 1903*, p.133, *1911*, pp.135, 152, 266–67; *Trade of the British empire and foreign competition. Despatch from Mr. Chamberlain to the governors of colonies and the High Commissioner of Cyprus and the replies thereto* (PP 1897, LX), p.313; Allen and Donnithorne, *Western enterprise*, pp.55–56, 275.

questioned why Barker was the sole example. In part, this was because in seriously hurting or driving out of business many of Singapore's produce firms, the conference system and 'secret' rebate had more or less eliminated a likely group of potential competitors as agency houses for rubber companies.

Furthermore, new entrants faced substantial entry barriers which various forms of quasi-vertical integration constituted. One barrier arose from this integration between merchant houses and shipping lines after the establishment of the conference system. Another entry barrier, considered in chapter 9, was due to integration between merchant houses and overseas manufacturers which granted exclusive distribution rights. A third entry barrier related to yet a further instance of quasi-vertical integration, which had the effect of restricting competition: integration between the merchant, as an agency house, and the rubber company for which it had an exclusive right to procure supplies. For overseas manufacturers, this prerogative of an agency house made the grant of exclusive distribution rights to the house more attractive. Merchants could expect profits above the competitive level to result from any of the forms of quasi-vertical integration.

Agency houses put a works manager (still often called a planter) in charge of a rubber estate and provided a full range of technical and administrative services. Insofar as the management function of an agency house involved the administration and technical supervision of a rubber estate, a nearby base was desirable.[11] By 1911 the need to perform these functions caused several Singapore agency houses to establish branches in Kuala Lumpur. Over the next decade Singapore agency houses multiplied their branches in the Peninsula as European estate acreage increased to some 1.1 million acres by 1921 (table 6.1). During the inter-war period there was a very marked tendency for the detailed administration and supervision of estates to devolve to the local branch of an agency house. By the 1930s estates in Johore and east coast states of Malaya were the main ones for which the *Directories* still listed the agency as in Singapore. The fact that largely routine administrative and supervisory work was undertaken elsewhere was of course of some consequence, and contributed significantly to Kuala Lumpur's growth. But Singapore benefited from the expansion of other commercial services connected with estate management, discussed below; just one agency house actually moved its head office from the city.

---

[11] The next two paragraphs draw on *Directory 1900, 1902, 1911, 1912, 1916, 1917, 1921*; *Harrisons & Crosfield: one hundred years*, p.41; *SSTC 1933–34* II, p.726; R. H. Benis, 'Reminiscences of the old firm' (Barker & Co.) (unpublished typescript, 10 Nov. 1953); 'Planting companies and estates' section in *Directory 1931*, pp.350–504, *1939*, pp.747–898; Drabble and Drake, 'More on financing', p.114; Soliva, *Economic view*, pp.10–11.

Together with the entry barriers noted above, the distance of Singapore from the locus of European estate production probably explains why only two of the several important agency houses which opened first in Malaya subsequently came to the city. Sime Darby & Co., begun in Malacca in 1902, appeared in the *Directories* with a Singapore office just over a decade later, while the large eastern agency house of Harrisons & Crosfield Ltd., having acquired the share capital of Barker & Co. (formerly F. W. Barker & Co.) in 1917, started up in Singapore as Harrisons, Barker & Co. in 1922. Sime Darby and Harrisons, Barker were significant additions to the European mercantile establishment in Singapore, but did not change its underlying structure and orientation towards export and shipping. They joined an already dominant group of European houses and during the inter-war period, under the influence of the European estate rubber industry, that group became more unified and powerful, and its interests increasingly focused on export and shipping.

Since different aspects of the agency system were complementary and exerted a mutual attraction, they tended to concentrate in the hands of the same Singapore houses. For Malayan estate rubber, an agency house

usually held some shares in each of the various plantation companies under its management. In descending order of involvement, an agency house could be owner, majority shareholder, minority shareholder, contract manager, or secretary to any given rubber producing company ... Any managerial/secretarial connection with a rubber company ... brought lucrative selling and supplying agencies to the agency house.[12]

In its commercial role, the agency house sold the product of an estate, procured its supplies and arranged for shipping and insurance, all on a commission basis. Therefore, possession of agencies for the distribution of estate supplies and for shipping and insurance had greater value for an agency house which also managed estate companies: it could successfully integrate import and export activities and receive two further commissions 'by shipping the rubber on the line it represents and insuring it with the insurance company it represents'.[13] Houses managing estates were at an advantage over other merchants in competing for shipping and insurance agencies: shippers and insurers sought as agents an agency house with rubber companies owing to the business it could offer through controlling the export of estate output. Although not Conference merchants at the time of the 'secret' rebate, the importance of Guthries and of Harrisons, Barker as agency houses clearly assisted in their subsequent acquisition of homeward shipping agencies in Singapore.

During the inter-war period the correspondence between the two types

[12] Drabble and Drake, 'British agency houses', p.309.
[13] Stahl, *Metropolitan organization*, p.105, and see Puthucheary, *Ownership*, pp.51–53.

of agency in Singapore became almost exact. Eight of the city's main agency houses in the rubber industry had homeward shipping agencies for Conference lines, if not in Singapore then in Penang or Kuala Lumpur: Guthries, Bousteads, Harrisons, Barker, Sime Darby, Paterson, Simons, Adamson Gilfillan (as Harper Gilfillan & Co.), Barlows and Sandilands Buttery. Of the other main Singapore agency houses, the East Asiatic Co. owned ships; the Borneo Co. held numerous shipping agencies in Kuching, Sarawak and Bangkok; Francis Peek & Co. were important shipping agents in Medan as was the Anglo-Siam Corporation in Bangkok.[14]

The extreme price fluctuations in rubber also made an important contribution to the inter-war strengthening of the agency system and thereby to European export and shipping interests in Singapore. Slumps in rubber prices tended to create financial difficulty for independent estates while emphasizing the capital resources and borrowing power of the agency houses.[15] Although many estates had initially been independent of agency houses, by 1932 few remained.

In assessing how important the management of European estates was to Singapore agency houses, the organization of the estate sector of the rubber industry is significant. Of the 1·4 million European estate acres in 1932, roughly 400,000 acres were owned by some 12 large companies and the remaining 1 million acres by around 600 to 800 small companies with an average area of about 1,200 to 1,500 acres each. A few of the very biggest companies, like Dunlop Rubber Plantations, were their own managers; the remainder of the big companies, with about 200,000 acres among them, were under agency house management, as were the large majority of the small companies.

The degree of agency house control over the small companies varied, but was generally greatest when the agents were 'large firms which are at the same time doing business in Import and Export, Insurance and Shipping', and/or strongly represented on the boards of the companies which they managed.[16] Estate management had become a major source of business, indeed 'often ... a dominant aspect of the agency houses' activities'.[17] In this regard, the large number of small rubber companies, coupled with the tendency for companies managed by the same agency house to invest in

[14] *Directory 1927, 1930, 1931, 1934, 1935, 1939* including 'Classified business directory' section; SS, *Blue books 1925, 1929, 1934,* section 32; *SSTC 1933–34* IV, p.47, II, p.104.
[15] Drabble and Drake, 'British agency houses', pp.309–10.
[16] Soliva, *Economic view,* p.10, and see pp.9, 11, 82, 88; D. H. Grist, *Nationality of ownership and nature of constitution of rubber estates in Malaya* (Kuala Lumpur, 1933), pp.3–5; Bauer, *Rubber,* pp.8–10; Figart, *Plantation rubber,* p.95.
[17] Drabble and Drake, 'British agency houses', p.309, and see Sir Eric Macfadyen, 'Managing agents in the eastern plantation industry', *Tropical Agriculture* 31 (1954), p.270.

each other which 'served to multiply directorships and secretarial and agency fees',[18] made European estate rubber substantially more important for its managing agents than might otherwise have been the case.

From the point of view of European rubber companies, the managing agency system was a convenient way to obtain supplies and technical advice. It also offered forms of insurance against both firm-specific risk and industry-wide risk, which was considerable, due to rubber's extreme price fluctuations. However, the agents' exclusive right to procure supplies under the agency contract was a significant monopolistic element, which might be further strengthened by the agency house's strong representation on the rubber company's board of directors. As a result, for rubber companies, the agency system was 'generally rather expensive, as agents derive fair profits from their "Estates Department"' and at least until the 1930s slump 'could be supported easily by Estates'.[19] For Singapore agency houses, this profitability, together with an established business centred on the rubber industry, may well have encouraged caution towards investment in the manufacturing sector and tempered the need to compete in the distribution of manufactured imports, as discussed in chapters 7 and 9.

II

Yet some agency houses diversified into the allied plantation crop of oil palm, which laid the basis for an important Malayan export crop after World War II. In factor requirements, oil palm was sharply differentiated from rubber only by the need for large-scale processing immediately after harvesting. But this did imply substantial investment in processing facilities, which made oil palm exclusively an estate crop in Malaya until the 1960s, and caused the industry's initial development to depend on the agency houses. However, despite early government promotional efforts, agency houses showed little interest in oil palm until rubber's inter-war price uncertainty increased the attractiveness of an alternative estate crop.

Singapore had two principal roles in the development of the oil palm industry in Malaya. One was that it afforded a convenient base from which to initiate operations in the hinterland, and by 1939 the neighbouring state of Johore accounted for 37,000 acres of the 76,000 Peninsular acres under oil palm.[20] Guthries was the main agency house in Singapore responsible

---

[18] Bauer, *Rubber*, p.11.
[19] Soliva, *Economic view*, p.10; see also J. H. Drabble, *Malayan rubber: the interwar years* (London, 1991), pp.57, 82.
[20] B. Bunting, C. D. V. Georgi and J. N. Milsum, *The oil palm in Malaya* (Malayan planting manual no. 1) (Kuala Lumpur, 1934), pp.1–5, 244–52, 261–63; *Malayan agricultural statistics* by D. H. Grist (Kuala Lumpur), annual series, 1931–1939, *1939*, tables 32–33, 97.

for this expansion and, from 1924, having created large estates in Johore and Negri Sembilan through a combination of company flotation and investment of their own profits, by 1942 managed almost 20,000 acres in Malaya planted in oil palm. The Singapore office of Guthries must have been useful in obtaining land for new plantations and as a conduit for capital from London. When the estates were established, however, the agency for these oil palm companies was in Kuala Lumpur.[21]

Marketing was Singapore's other, and more important, role in the oil palm industry. The commercial viability of the industry required bulk shipment which, in comparison to transport in barrels, reduced the all-in cost of production by almost a third. There were two ways in which Singapore interests contributed to the provision of the necessary marketing facilities. First, between 1933 and 1938 the Straits Steamship Company constructed three 750-ton vessels for the bulk carriage of palm oil, and to promote their use acquired the Malayan Water Transport Company in Selangor which took palm oil to Port Swettenham for onward shipment to Singapore.[22]

The second contribution dated from 1933 when the Singapore Harbour Board arranged to lease a bulk palm oil installation to Guthries and erected it adjacent to the West Wharf. The Harbour Board built four – and by 1939 six – 500-ton tanks together with a modern pumping and steam-heating plant. Guthries founded and managed the Malayan Palm Oil Bulking Company which organized the reception of oil and its dispatch by ocean-going steamers. By 1938/39 the 35,000 tons of oil Singapore exported annually accounted for three-fifths of British Malayan exports, while a substantial proportion of the remainder was probably transhipped at the port. Thus, in providing for bulk shipment, those in Singapore ensured that the port became – as it has remained – a centre for the export of palm oil from the Malay Peninsula.[23]

[21] 'Guthrie & Company, Limited', *BRGA* 13, 1 (1931), pp.6–7; *Centenary Singapore Free Press*, section 2, p.22; *Directory 1931*, pp.355–68, *1939*, pp.753, 758, 761, 804; Stahl, *Metropolitan organization*, pp.84, 88; Allen and Donnithorne, *Western enterprise*, pp.54–55, 143; Sjovald Cunyngham-Brown, *The traders* (London, 1971), pp.251–53, 258, 320.

[22] Bunting, et al. *Oil palm*, pp.215–22, 247–48; C. D. V. Georgi, 'The Selangor bulk oil installation plant', *MAJ* 21, 11 (1933), p.565; *SSTC 1933–34* II, p.13; Tregonning, *Home port*, pp.83–84, 143–44.

[23] 'Review of the affairs of the Colony of the SS', *SSLCP 1932*, p.C364; *SSTC 1933–34* IV, p.60; Department of Agriculture, SS and FMS, 'Packing and transport of palm oil', *MAJ* 21, 4 (1933), p.174; Trimmer, 'Port of Singapore', p.25; Malaya, *Foreign trade of Malaya 1939*, p.114.

III

A feature of estate agriculture as it developed in Asia was the paucity of local Asian compared with European ownership. Singapore was an exception: a number of its Chinese entrepreneurs acquired considerable rubber estate holdings. In 1932 they owned virtually all of the 13,000 Chinese-owned estate acres on Singapore island and the 145,000 acres in Johore, which together constituted over two-fifths of Chinese-owned, and one-ninth of European-owned, estate acreage in British Malaya (table 6.1). Ownership was widely diffused. Furthermore, unlike the public limited company ownership of European estates, in 1932 77% of Chinese estate acreage on Singapore island and 92% in Johore was owned by individuals or unincorporated partnerships. In 1932 there were 323 Chinese-owned estates in Johore of between 100 and 1,000 acres, and 28 estates over 1,000 acres.[24] Profits from Chinese estates very largely went to Singaporeans.

The city's Chinese developed rubber estates largely in conjunction with pineapples.[25] When rubber was first being established on Singapore island, Chinese often planted the *Hevea* seeds among an existing crop, generally pineapples or gambier, and kept it in cultivation until the rubber trees had matured. In bringing uncultivated land under rubber on Singapore island, pineapples became a temporary – or 'catch' – crop among the maturing rubber trees, and during the 1920s this practice spread: in 1932 the bulk of Chinese rubber estate acreage in Johore had been or was being developed with a catch crop of pineapples.

For Chinese entrepreneurs a catch crop of pineapples overcame the need for heavy capital investment in rubber estate development: the plants began to yield fruit within 18 months, producing a cash flow to help meet outgoings, and, not having received fertilizer or other capital expenditure, could be abandoned without much loss when the rubber trees were mature. There was no sacrifice in terms of rubber density, since the grown trees would require the inter-row space occupied by the pineapples. With this catch crop and somewhat less elaborate fixed capital expenditure than was usual for Europeans, it cost roughly $150 per acre to develop a Chinese estate, or about a quarter of the investment per acre necessary for European estates.[26] Finance on this scale was within the reach of Singapore Chinese entrepreneurs, who probably depended mainly on borrowing from the expanding local Chinese banking system (see chapter 7), as well as on the reinvestment of profits from their own business ventures.

---

[24] Grist, *Ownership of rubber estates*, pp.3–6, 17–26.
[25] Chinese estate development with pineapples is discussed fully in Huff, 'Sharecroppers, risk, management' and 'Capital markets, sharecropping'.
[26] Figart, *Plantation rubber*, pp.87–90; Drabble, *Rubber*, p.100.

Singapore Chinese entrepreneurs developing estates in Johore usually favoured a sharecropping arrangement for the duration of the development period. Sharecropping substituted for the London stock market which European rubber companies used to obtain finance and to shift risk when starting estates, and through this substitution Singapore Chinese entrepreneurs overcame, at least in part, their lack of access to the London capital market because of being unknown there. On pineapple-rubber estates, a 'mixed' or share-wage contract was typical.[27] It stipulated that the sharecropper would cultivate pineapples and be responsible for planting, weeding and tending the rubber trees until mature; sharecroppers commonly received a share of 50% of the net revenue from the sale of the pineapples and fixed payments, or wages, of $1 per acre per month. This wage component was substantial: entrepreneurs paid $2·50 per acre per month for workers on a pure wage contract, including the cost of their supervision by a labour contractor who employed the men. Labour requirements appear to have been similar whether a share-wage or pure wage contract was used.

Since the pineapple plants did not yield fruit for 18 months, during this period sharecroppers received no income from the sale of fruit but only the wage component of the share-wage contract. Thus entrepreneurs were in effect borrowing from their workforce against the promise of an equity share in eventual yields of the pineapple plants. For the first 18 months, sharecroppers had to rely for their subsistence on the wage payments, supplemented by cultivation of their own plots and keeping livestock. Subsequently they bore, through their equity stake in the pineapple crops, part of the risk of estate development, while the entrepreneur gained a corresponding reduction in risk. This risk-shifting afforded the entrepreneur protection against the danger that revenue from the pineapple crop would be insufficient to cover the wages of his labourers and, at the same time, that he would be able to borrow only at high interest rates, if at all, and be unable to pay his workforce. Unpaid labourers would have left, causing the disintegration of the entrepreneur's estate, with a consequent loss of both past investment and future capital revenue. Under the share-wage contract, sharecroppers could expect, at mean pineapple prices in the later 1920s, a substantially higher income than workers on a pure wage contract. Over the six years of development of a rubber estate, at these late 1920s' prices, sharecroppers' lending of their labour time yielded an implicit interest rate of 20%.[28]

For Singapore Chinese entrepreneurs, a share-wage contract was an

---

[27] D. H. Grist, 'Cultivation of pineapples', *MAJ* 18, 5 (1930), p.245; 'Pineapple conference', *SSLCP 1931*, p.C222.

[28] For discussion of these implicit interest rates, see Huff, 'Sharecroppers, risk, management'.

effective management device in replacing the good contract enforceability and resident supervision of workers by a labour contractor available under a pure wage contract. A number of aspects of the share-wage contract worked together to provide this alternative. An equity share in the pineapple crops gave workers an incentive to self-supervision, while the possibility of high pineapple prices with consequent equity gains was a reason to remain on an estate throughout the development period. In fact, sharecroppers, after lending to an entrepreneur, were effectively tied to an estate for six years of development if they were to earn a positive return on their investment. A further tying device was an $8 per acre 'bonus' payment for cleaning the land of pineapple plants when the rubber trees were ready for tapping.

The importance of the system of pineapple-rubber estate development described was considerable. Indeed, the 1932 estate ownership figures probably understate the rubber land opened by Singapore Chinese, since 'not infrequently rubber plantations established [with pineapples]... changed hands at very profitable figures once they came into tapping'.[29] Ownership of rubber estates, and in some instances capital gains from the sale to Europeans of rubber estates established with pineapples, contributed to the creation of major Chinese entrepreneurial figures in Singapore, men like Lim Nee Soon known as the 'Pineapple King', and others discussed in chapter 7.[30] Although the 1930s slump led to a ban on the further alienation of land for planting rubber, Singapore Chinese were able to finance estates already being developed through revenue from the pineapple crops. There is no evidence during the slump of any significant Singapore Chinese loss of rubber land due to the financial risks of estate development.

Like cultivation, pineapple canning or packing was a Chinese activity. In the inter-war years a few big pineapple packers, also usually using the fruit to develop rubber estates, accounted for much of the industry's output. However, the desire for diversification rather than gains from vertical integration appears to have been the reason why the same entrepreneurs both grew and packed pineapples. Even when Chinese entrepreneurs engaged in both rubber estate development and pineapple canning, no firm link existed between the activities. Although in the 1930s slump a number of big Chinese packers failed, it was said that they 'failed through their speculations outside the pineapple industry entirely'.[31]

During the inter-war period the need for proximity to the raw fruit drew most canning factories to Johore, although a handful of large ones remained in Singapore and could stay open the year round owing to the

[29] 'Pineapple conference', *SSLCP 1931*, p.C219, and see p.C225.
[30] Song, *One hundred years' history*, pp.516–17.   [31] *SSTC 1933–34* II, p.813.

island's role as a collecting centre for the limited quantities of pineapples available between harvests. Reflecting the labour-intensive nature of pine-apple canning, these Singapore factories were significant as a source of employment. In 1936 the island's four canning factories employed over 1,000 men during the peak harvest months, but no more than about half that number at slack times of the year.[32]

Just as rubber led to pineapples, so the latter created in Singapore's many Chinese sawmills an important linkage of its own. A high proportion of sawmills' output was low grade or waste products for which the hinterland offered no real market. In Singapore, the export of pineapples gave rise to a large demand for low grades of wood to make packing cases. For the sawmills, 'demand like that of the pineapple canneries is a godsend',[33] and together with an urban sale of sawdust and woodchips was a major reason why sawmills were located mainly in Singapore rather than near the source of a raw material subject to great weight loss in processing.

Despite the Chinese dominance in growing and canning pineapples, export of the fruit was largely in the hands of a few European merchant houses, notably Paterson, Simons, Adamson Gilfillan, McAlisters and the East Asiatic Company. These firms were also largely responsible for the export of tropical produce from Singapore, and in the case of pineapples their principal advantage was similar: control of, or access to, a homeward shipping agency. Even those few Chinese packers with production large enough to sell in the quantities generally required by London buyers were at a disadvantage in exporting. As exporters, the European houses could earn commission on freight – particularly important for a bulky, low-value item like pineapples – and insurance commission. Nevertheless, during the inter-war years two large Chinese packers exported at least part of their output to London through an agent there. Through integration as packers and exporters, these two Chinese exporters countered to some extent the freight and insurance commission advantages of the merchant houses by selling direct to their London agents, and because these agents again sold direct to British buyers rather than through brokers.[34]

[32] On the canning industry, see Huff, 'Capital markets, sharecropping'; Shriver, *Pineapple-canning industry*, pp.19–24; 'Pineapple conference', *SSLCP 1931*, pp.C223–C226, C231; *SSTC 1933–34* I, pp.199–200, II, pp.788–92, 798, 800, 805, 808–9, III, p.455, IV, pp.232, 234, V, p.128; 'Labour unrest in Singapore: pineapple canning factories', *MRCA* 73 (Sept. 1936), pp.9–12; Grist, 'Cultivation of pineapples', p.245. For the number of factories in Singapore, see below, table 7.2.

[33] *SSTC 1933–34* IV, p.185, and see I, pp.186–87, II, pp.534, 624–25.

[34] Ibid. III, pp.454, 457, II, p.791, V, pp.128–30, IV, p.232; 'Pineapple conference', *SSLCP 1931*, pp.C225–C232, C245; *Directory 1940*, p.314.

IV

In British Malaya the rapid spread of smallholder rubber acreage (table 6.1) was the first demonstration in the region of how quickly smallholders responded to price and acted as their own entrepreneurs in entering the rubber industry. The initial stimulus to smallholder cultivation was the high rubber prices in 1909 and 1910. By 1922 British Malayan smallholders, mainly Malays and Chinese but including some Indians, had planted almost as much rubber acreage as on European estates.

Singapore, however, did little to provide factors of production to smallholders with less than 15 acres, as they needed only seeds and simple agricultural implements: rubber could be interplanted with an existing crop or family labour used to clear land. For so-called medium holdings of between 15–20 and just under 100 acres, the reliance on outside factors of production was greater. Those who began medium holdings were generally small Chinese entrepreneurs such as storekeepers, contractors or tin miners who became absentee owners. Medium-holders in the vicinity of Singapore may have made their money in the city or received finance from traders there. Further, immigration through Singapore helped to supply the Chinese labour employed on medium holdings.[35]

In Netherlands India, estimating the acreage cultivated by smallholders, practically all Indonesians, is largely a matter of guesswork. But between 1922, when the Stevenson scheme to restrict rubber output in British-controlled areas was adopted, and 1929, acreage probably increased about sixfold to reach approximately 1·8 million acres, of which some 550,000 acres were mature. This rapid expansion of smallholder acreage was important for Singapore because most of it was in the Outer Provinces: by 1929 natives had planted rubber trees all over Sumatra and near the coasts of Borneo.[36]

Singapore did not do much to channel factors of production to Indonesian smallholders for, like their counterparts in Malaya working a few acres, they could use their own labour and required little capital to grow rubber. But Singapore made two very important contributions to the development of smallholder production in Sumatra and Borneo. One resulted from the port's role as a centre for Indonesian pilgrims and their tendency to find plantation work on Singapore island or the Peninsula to

[35] Figart, *Plantation rubber*, pp.89–90; Bauer, *Rubber*, pp.3–6; Drabble, *Rubber*, pp.69–77, 100. There is some difference between authorities in the definition of small and medium holdings. The latter are sometimes defined as holdings of 25 acres or more and 'true' smallholdings as below 25 acres. Drabble, *Malayan rubber*, p.1.
[36] Figart, *Plantation rubber*, pp.278–81; Soliva, *Economic view*, pp.51–57; Bauer, *Rubber*, pp.3–5, 28–29, 342–43.

pay for the journey to Mecca: 'This close contact with Malaya has been the primary cause of the emergence of native rubber cultivation; hadjis became acquainted there with rubber cultivation and subsequently introduced it into their native regions'.[37] Given the knowledge of how to grow rubber, the chief need of smallholders was trade facilities which put them in touch with the world market; these Singapore largely provided.

V

By the time Netherlands Indian rubber came to Singapore in very large quantities, the city had, with Malayan output, become the world's leading primary rubber market.[38] Yet the marketing of Malayan rubber rapidly reached a stage where the commodity was bought and sold in the Singapore market but never physically passed through it, except possibly in transhipment. By contrast, Netherlands Indian rubber came to constitute the main demand for physical handling, since until the later 1930s the bulk of this rubber sold through Singapore continued to be sent there for processing and re-export. More important, Netherlands Indian rubber, unlike Malayan, often involved a number of intermediaries and, in the Singapore Chinese who handled this trade, added a whole new sector to Singapore's business community.[39]

Attempts to establish a Singapore rubber market before World War I met with stiff resistance from London, which remained dominant as a rubber market even after 1911, when the Rubber Association was formed under the auspices of the Singapore Chamber of Commerce, 'with the main idea of having local auctions'.[40] During World War I, however, just as substantial amounts of rubber from Malaya began to reach Singapore, it became the easiest place in which to sell, owing to the wartime cessation of the London auction and the shift to direct export to the United States. Singapore's weekly auction grew rapidly in importance. By 1916 over half of the rubber exported from the port passed through the auction, and in

---

[37] J. Vredenbregt, 'The Haddj', *Bijdragen Tot de Taal, – Land -, en Volkenkunde* 118, 1 (1962), p.118, and see T. A. Tengwall, 'History of rubber cultivation and research in the Netherlands Indies' in Pieter Honig and Frans Verdoorn, eds. *Science and scientists in the Netherlands Indies* (New York, 1945), p.350.

[38] London and New York were the main markets in manufacturing countries, and along with Singapore the principal world rubber markets. Singapore ranked with London as the leading market for the reception and distribution of rubber, but behind London and New York as a price-making market. Holt, *Marketing*, pp.5, 117.

[39] For a more detailed discussion of the development of the Singapore rubber market than this chapter contains, see W. G. Huff, 'The development of the rubber market in pre-World War II Singapore', *JSEAS* 24, 2 (1993).

[40] Price, 'Rubber trade', p.87, and see p.85.

Table 6.2 *Singapore rubber imports, 1906–1939*

	Malaya		Netherlands India		Others		Total	
	tons	%	tons	%	tons	%	tons	%
1906	331	98.2	6	1.8	0	0.0	337	100.0
1910	1,430	98.2	24	1.7	2	0.1	1,456	100.0
1913	4,947	93.2	184	3.5	178	3.3	5,309	100.0
1915	23,916	89.9	2,104	7.9	593	2.2	26,613	100.0
1917	61,799	87.6	6,801	9.6	1,943	2.8	70,543	100.0
1918	94,798	81.1	19,094	16.3	3,081	2.6	116,973	100.0
1920	90,586	77.9	21,579	18.5	4,153	3.6	116,318	100.0
1923	74,735	54.0	56,839	41.0	6,969	5.0	138,543	100.0
1925	69,141	32.0	131,859	61.0	15,087	7.0	216,087	100.0
1927	71,166	29.7	148,798	62.1	19,685	8.2	239,649	100.0
1929	n.a.		127,943		n.a.		n.a.	
1933	114,555	49.7	96,435 (133,025)	41.9	19,362	8.4	230,352	100.0
1934	131,951	41.8	157,192	49.7	26,847	8.5	315,990	100.0
1937	107,010	37.4	133,146	46.6	45,777	16.0	285,933	100.0
1939	107,984	41.6	90,101	34.8	61,153	23.6	259,238	100.0

Notes:
1   For 1906–32 recorded trade statistics are available. Imports came as both wet and dry rubber, but these are not differentiated in the statistics. Nor was wet rubber expressed in dry weight which was about 20% to 30% less. In consequence, there is substantial over-statement in the relative importance of trade with Netherlands India from the mid–1920s, when it began to account for the bulk of wet rubber imported. In dry weight total imports from Netherlands India were approximately 25% less than the figures shown, assuming that wet rubber had a moisture content of 30% (see below note 3) and comprised 85% of imports from Dutch colony. In 1933 85.5% of British Malayan imports from Netherlands India were recorded as wet rubber.
2   For 1933 the figure in brackets of 133,025 tons for imports from Netherlands India is a recorded trade statistic. It does not show wet rubber in dry weight and is comparable to pre–1933 statistics shown for imports from Netherlands India.
3   For 1933–39 the figures are estimated and are expressed in terms of dry weight. The estimates were made as follows. For Singapore the recorded trade statistics show all exports but do not show all imports, because they exclude imports from the Malay states and the other Straits Settlements (together Malaya). Therefore total imports are assumed to be equal to recoded exports. This assumption is considered reasonably accurate, although imports are overstated insofar as exports included rubber produced on Singapore island and understated insofar as rubber goods were manufactured in the town. Yearly estimates are also subject to inaccuracy owing to variations in stocks held in the town. Imports from Malaya are the difference between Singapore's recorded exports and recorded imports. For 1933 only, the figure for Singapore's imports in terms of dry weight had to be estimated. The estimate was obtained by using the recorded statistic for dry rubber imports and adding to this 69.53% of the recorded statistic for wet rubber imports. That percentage was the dry rubber content in wet rubber imported by British Malaya as a whole in 1933. From 1933 the recorded statistics available for imports by origin are for imports to British Malaya as a whole and are in dry weight. Singapore's imports from Netherlands India are estimated to be 95.8% of British Malayan imports from

1918 the 51,200 tons brought for auction amounted to nearly one quarter of world exports.[41]

Thus a leading merchant could declare that Singapore would remain 'pre-eminently the rubber market of the world';[42] and to almost anyone living in Singapore, two sets of consequences must have been evident. One stemmed from Singapore's sudden acquisition of handling, storage and grading functions for rubber from Malaya. In 1918 Malayan rubber comprised four-fifths of rubber imports coming to Singapore (table 6.2), while in that year Singapore imported for re-export some four-fifths of the rubber produced in Malaya (table 6.3).

The other set of consequences was the impact on the mercantile community. Japanese, and to a lesser degree Americans and other Europeans, 'flocked to the city owing to its having almost involuntarily become during the War a great mart and repository for rubber'.[43] Three large American rubber manufacturing companies – so-called manufacturers' buyers – set up their own organizations in Singapore to purchase the raw material: the United States Rubber Company, Firestone and Goodyear.[44] A number of small firms specializing as rubber traders or brokers, run by Americans, Britons or other Europeans, also appeared in Singapore.

Initially, Singapore received most of the rubber from Malaya, because it was of an unknown quality, and so had, at the least, to be unpacked for

[41] Ibid. pp.84–88; 'S', 'A planting pioneer', *BRGA* 10, 9 (1928), p.581. For figures of sales at the auction, see Singapore Chamber of Commerce, *Report*, 1912–1939, and on the formation of the Rubber Association, see *Report 1911*, pp.34–35, *1912*, pp.33–36; Rees, *Britain's commodity markets*, pp.269–70.

[42] Darbishire, 'Commerce and currency', pp.54–55. The main sources for the history of rubber marketing and milling in Singapore on which the following draws are *SSTC 1933–34* I, p.45, II, pp.347–56, 410, 422–25, 639, 718–28, 746–55, 794–97, III, pp.141, 187, IV, pp.135, 136, 233–34; Hugh M. Devitt, 'The Singapore rubber market', *BRGA* 1, 1 (1919), pp.18–22; Price, 'Rubber trade', p.88; Singapore Chamber of Commerce, *Report 1926*, p.14; Walling, *Singapura*, pp.111, 115.

[43] *Report of the commissions appointed by the Governor of the Straits Settlements and High Commissioner of the Federated Malay States to enquire into certain matters relating to the public service*. Two vols. (Singapore, 1919), I, p.189, and see *1921 census*, p.71.

[44] Glen D. Babcock, *History of the United States Rubber Company* (Muncie, IN, 1966), pp.83, 177–78; Macmillan, *Seaports*, p.458; *Singapore dollar directory 1919* (Singapore, 1919), section III, pp.36, 38, 68.

the Dutch colony. This was the proportion of total Straits Settlements imports from Netherlands India which Singapore took during the period 1930–33. Imports from 'Others' are the difference between the estimate for total imports and the sum of imports from Malaya and Netherlands India. These imports came mostly from Siam and British Borneo, although there were also small trades with Indo–China and Burma.

Sources: SS, *Return of imports and exports*, 1906–1927; *SSTC 1933–34* IV, p.492; Malaya, *Foreign imports and exports*, 1933–1937; Malaya, *Foreign trade of Malaya*, 1938–1939.

sampling and sale – a principal reason for the auction. The consequent scope for intermediaries to arrange for rubber to be brought to Singapore and to trade in the commodity largely explained the appearance of specialized firms in the city.[45] However, the physical presence of rubber traded soon became unnecessary: most Malayan rubber sold in Singapore could be exported direct from the producing areas.

After 1918 Singapore's rubber imports from Malaya hardly increased in volume (table 6.2). The growing need for physical services accompanying the great expansion of Peninsular production chiefly affected employment in Malaya rather than Singapore, because direct export of rubber from Malaya increasingly replaced export through Singapore (table 6.3). Although Malayan rubber continued to be sold through Singapore, and perhaps transhipped there, by 1923 the city exported just two-fifths of Malayan rubber; in 1926 the proportion had declined to a third; and by 1938/39 was little more than a quarter. During the inter-war years rubber from Malaya which came to Singapore averaged around 100,000 tons annually (table 6.2). Most of it consisted of better quality estate rubber and smallholder output sent – mainly from Johore and the east coast of Malaya – to Singapore as the nearest economic point for collection and export.

Three developments in the marketing of Malayan rubber, largely instigated in Singapore itself, made possible direct shipment from Malaya. In Singapore the agency houses were chiefly associated with these developments and were the main beneficiaries from them. First, the Singapore Chamber of Commerce, the leading members of which were the agency houses, organized the introduction of standard qualities comparable to London standards to facilitate the sale of rubber.[46]

Second, Singapore was instrumental in the production of these standard qualities. Rubber milling factories on Malayan estates were often fitted out either by the agency houses[47] or by Singapore engineering firms, while agency house management of many estates facilitated the rapid transmission of a knowledge of standard qualities. Smallholder rubber of qualities ready to be graded into standard types by European buyers was processed, either at Chinese factories established throughout the Malay states or by smallholders who had their own rubber mangles. Through a process of passing wet rubber between hand-operated rollers, mangles wrung out about 30% of the water content of coagulated latex and allowed smallholders to make sheet needing only treatment at Chinese smoke-

[45] *SSTC 1933–34* II, p.719; *Directory 1921*, pp.134–254; and cf. J. E. Nathan, 'Changes in the flow of trade', *Manchester Guardian Commercial*, special section on British Malaya, 19 Feb. 1925.   [46] Devitt, 'Singapore rubber market', p.18.
[47] *Directory 1916*, p.138.

Table 6.3 *Distribution of exports of rubber produced in Malaya, 1918–1938/39*

	Singapore		FMS, UMS and Malacca with transhipment at Singapore		Malaya (Penang, Malacca, FMS and UMS)		Total	
	tons	%	tons	%	tons	%	tons	%
1918	94,798	83.2	10,690	9.4	8,434	7.4	113,922	100.0
1923	74,735	41.7	32,557	18.2	71,739	40.1	179,031	100.0
1926	89,587	32.3	79,607	28.7	107,937	39.0	277,131	100.0
1938/39	103,539	27.5	127,946	34.0	144,901	38.5	376,386	100.0

Notes:

1 Exports from Singapore were estimated as follows. For 1918–26 they are assumed to be equal to recorded imports from the Malay Peninsula and the Straits Settlements. These figures may include some rubber produced outside Malaya owing to re-shipment from Penang. For 1938/39 (an annual average) exports from Singapore are estimated to be the difference between the port's recorded exports and recorded imports (see table 6.2, note 3).

2 The figures for rubber transhipped at Singapore are recorded statistics. The 1938/39 figure includes transhipment from Penang, but this was negligible.

3 Exports from Malaya are recorded exports from Penang, Malacca, the FMS and UMS less (i) the recorded imports of these areas from foreign countries, i.e. everywhere except the FMS, UMS and Straits Settlements, (ii) in the case of Penang and Malacca, inter-port exports to the Straits Settlements and exports to the Malay states, (iii) transhipment at Singapore as shown in the third column of the table. The figure for 1918 includes Penang and Malacca only, but this comprised the bulk of transhipped rubber: exports without re-shipment from, or transhipment at, Singapore from Port Swettenham – the Malay states port which handled ocean-going shipping – were not significant. For 1918 the exclusion of inter-port exports is particularly important, as most exports from Penang and Malacca still went to Singapore. Inter-port exports from the two ports were 28,425 tons and all other exports 9,103 tons. In 1938/39 Penang handled an annual average of 46,121 tons of transhipped rubber from the Malay states and Straits Settlements, virtually all from the former. Exports from Port Swettenham but including transhipped rubber from other FMS ports averaged 46,129 tons in 1938/39. A high proportion of rubber exported from Port Swettenham was transhipped at Singapore.

4 Total exports are estimated to be the sum of the first three columns. These figures should almost equal net exports from British Malaya less production on Singapore island, and this is the case (cf. McFadyean, *History of rubber regulation*, pp.226–29).

Sources: SS, *Return of imports and exports*, 1918, 1923, 1926; Malaya, *Foreign imports and exports*, 1923, 1926; Malaya, *Foreign trade of Malaya*, 1938, 1939; Grist, *Malayan agricultural statistics*, 1938, 1939.

houses. The manufacture of rubber mangles became a Singapore activity. At first it was largely in the hands of European firms like United Engineers. But in the 1930s these linkage effects spread, and a large Chinese industry also emerged, in response to developments in Netherlands India discussed below, and in Victoria Street and Lavender Street 'numbers of small shops opened as manufacturers of rubber mangles'.[48]

The third development was the move to up-country buying in the producing areas of Malaya. The agency houses were the principal firms in Singapore which began up-country buying: 'all ... houses are represented up-country',[49] and usually in every important centre. By the 1930s almost all rubber buying was done in Malayan towns rather than in Singapore.[50]

Agency houses were entitled (by the agency contract) to arrange the shipment and sale of rubber from estates which they managed. Export through branches of the agency house in important Malayan towns or through smaller up-country buying stations afforded a cheaper way to handle this rubber than bringing it to Singapore for export.[51] In addition, these up-country buying facilities were probably also a cheaper way to purchase rubber from independent estates and to buy smallholder rubber (the latter outside the control of any agency house and known as 'free' rubber) than if agency houses had to negotiate with an independent class of European dealers and pay their dealing charges and transport costs to Singapore. If a branch or a buying station could obtain any rubber for export which the office in Singapore could not, the agency house was in a position to realize a commission as shippers of this rubber, and if the house had insurance agencies, also a commission for insuring the rubber shipment.

Access to finance and the ability to accept the risk of carrying stocks gave the agency houses which moved into up-country buying an advantage over smaller, rival firms. Stockholding could be substantial under the 'trust rubber' system which, after its introduction in 1921, quickly took hold owing to competition among European buyers. Under this system, Chinese dealers or commission agents were advanced on delivery of rubber 80 % or more of the current market price and allowed to sell this rubber, held in trust by European buyers, within any of the next 30 days at the then ruling price. In the 1920s, before the general adoption of a clause entitling buyers to force the sale of trust rubber if the commodity's value fell below the advance, 'many of the European firms [in Singapore] ... lost big sums of money'.[52] But even subsequently, under the trust rubber system European buyers risked loss from sharp price fluctuations and still had to finance up-

---

[48] *SSTC 1933–34* III, p.140, and see I, p.146.   [49] Ibid. II, p.750.   [50] Ibid.
[51] For a transaction-costs explanation of the development of up-country buying, see Huff, 'Development of the rubber market'.   [52] *SSTC 1933–34* II, p.352.

country buying. Considerable stocks of trust rubber frequently accumulated, both because European buyers were normally willing to extend the
30-day selling period and because Chinese were quick to use the
opportunity for European credit and speculate on world rubber prices.

Thus, from the early 1920s the agency houses, through the move to up-
country buying, largely internalized the specialization accompanying the
expansion of Malayan output. There was consequently little scope for
firms like those which at first had come to the offices of Singapore's big
buyers offering rubber. Specialized rubber buyers bore the brunt of the
shift to up-country trading, and were driven to the fringes of the rubber
trade, or out of business. By 1930 the *Directory* shows only ten specialized
European rubber merchants in Singapore, and most were small. In 1939
the majority of the specialized rubber firms listed in the 1930 *Directory*,
including some of the most prominent, had disappeared, and although
others had become rubber merchants the total number of firms had fallen
to eight.[53] The role of Singapore's rubber brokers had also diminished:
they were represented by a group of seven European firms, of which just
three were the same in 1930 and 1939.[54]

During the inter-war period the main function still undertaken in
Singapore for Malayan rubber was to link the British Malayan and world
market; a rubber market established in Penang in 1919 never really
challenged Singapore's supremacy.[55] Twentieth-century additions to the
British Malayan telegraphic network, already centred on Singapore as a
result of the tin industry,[56] and the introduction of the telephone, allowed
agency houses in Singapore to keep in constant touch with buying
throughout British Malaya. The communications network, together with
competition among buyers for free rubber, made British Malaya into a
single, efficient market for rubber.[57] Thus, Singapore agency houses with
an office in Kuala Lumpur used this both to purchase rubber there and, by
relying on the telephone and representatives in a few of the bigger towns,

[53] *Directory 1930*, pp.1161, 127, *1931*, pp.274, 24, *1939*, pp.309–10, 295, 399.
[54] *Directory 1930*, p.1148, *1939*, p.285, and see *1931*, p.261.
[55] See, for example, Heah Joo Seang, 'Foreword' in Rubber Trade Association of Penang,
     *Souvenir number in commemoration of the thirty-second anniversary of the Rubber Trade
     Association of Penang and the official opening of the new premises, 1951* (Penang, 1951),
     p.10.
[56] Ellis, 'Brief account of the Malay tin industry', p.11, and see T. A. Melville, 'The post
     office and its history' in Makepeace, et al., eds. *One hundred years* II, pp.150–53.
[57] Bauer, *Rubber*, p.59. The same was true in the 1950s, when the British Malayan marketing
     network was little changed from the inter-war period. The 1954 Mudie Committee argued
     that rubber marketing in Malaya was efficient, judged both on the small difference between
     prices paid to smallholders in Malaya and Singapore f.o.b. prices, and on extensive
     competition in marketing which kept charges for services low. Federation of Malaya,
     Report of the mission of enquiry into the rubber industry of Malaya (Kuala Lumpur, 1954),
     pp.42–47.

to buy from dealers over much of Selangor and Negri Sembilan.[58] Up-country Chinese dealers could get official price quotations from Singapore three times a day through a Reuters service, but many relied on Singapore brokers for advice of market fluctuations. Some of these brokers were Chinese: an example was Change Alley Rubber Communication Office, which advertised as 'Rubber Brokers & Market Reporters', while around the corner on Raffles Quay, Wee Thong Poh & Co. operated as 'Rubber and Share Brokers'.[59]

Most overseas buyers telegraphed orders specifying quantities with price limits to Singapore, which at least 20 Singapore dealers received every morning. The most important group of these dealers was European, and among them only three firms specialized as rubber traders; the rest were departments of Singapore's merchant and agency houses. Other dealers included some Japanese firms, notably Mitsui Bussan Kaisha, and a large number of Chinese; but the latter, like Chinese brokers, were mainly interested in the Netherlands Indian trade, discussed below. Guided by overseas orders but trading mainly as principals, European dealers telegraphed instructions to their up-country buyers, but by the late afternoon, if unable to obtain the desired rubber, attempted to buy in Singapore itself, possibly through brokers. Some of the larger Singapore dealers also had agents or representatives in New York who sold on their own account or on a commission basis and kept the Singapore office advised of market conditions in the United States.[60]

Few representatives of foreign buyers set up in Singapore: in 1933 only the three American manufacturers established there by 1918 and a French manufacturer operated in the rubber market, but 'do not deal, they merely buy on instructions or on orders'.[61] If a manufacturers' buyer purchased rubber from a dealer, the chances were that this was an agency house; while if he turned to a producer, the latter was probably represented by an estate selling agent and therefore an agency house.

In the inter-war period, other than rubber from Johore and the east coast of Malaya, the main kinds of Malayan rubber coming to Singapore were estate off-grades and scrap. These arrived from a large part of Malaya because of the need for specialized physical handling and marketing facilities, and relied on a European business structure distinct from the agency houses. Estate off-grades, about 10% of total estate output or at most around 25,000 tons per year, were selected and packed in Singapore; while scrap, only a small proportion of the lower grades, also required remilling, which was most economical in Singapore, owing to ease in collecting large amounts of the rubber and the opportunity to mix it with

[58] SSTC 1933–34 II, p.750.   [59] Directory 1931 pp.27, 160.
[60] Holt, Marketing, p.190.   [61] SSTC 1933–34 II, p.354.

imports from Netherlands India. These trades – still involving inspection by purchasers – became the mainstay of the Singapore auction, where in the years after 1920 the 14,300 to 39,000 tons of rubber offered annually became of little interest to Singapore's 'big buyers'.[62] Instead, it was specialized, non-agency house firms like Bruce Petrie Ltd.[63] and Anglo-French & Bendixsens,[64] along with Chinese millers looking for scrap, which mainly bought at the auction.

Although the auction, like its European habitués, became largely relegated to filling a specialized niche in the rubber trade, auction sales remained important in the price-discovery function performed by the Singapore market for all of British Malaya:

the up-country people know exactly what is paid in the auction and if anybody goes into that auction and puts up the price it affects almost the whole of Malaya at once. They watch very closely the Singapore prices which are cabled up.[65]

For Malayan rubber, Singapore provided 'effective and cheap facilities ... probably unexampled elsewhere in the East to producers to market their output'.[66] As a result, employment and physical infrastructure associated with Malayan rubber marketing were much more evident in the Malay states than in the city itself. Although the general prosperity and expansion of the rubber industry which resulted from efficient marketing was reflected in various aspects of the Singapore economy, these effects were largely indirect. The principal impact on Singapore's business structure of the trade in Malayan rubber was to bolster the agency houses and further strengthen their export and shipping orientation.

VI

From 1918 Netherlands Indian rubber was a major trade for Singapore, and in most inter-war years after 1923 it made the largest single contribution to rubber imports (table 6.2). Although smallholder output from Malaya had given a start to the rubber milling industry in Singapore, imports from Netherlands India were very largely responsible for sustaining and developing it. Until the later 1930s native output imported from Netherlands India consisted almost entirely of wet rubber, which came to Singapore as slabs coagulated 'in any shape or form' and in which 'everything is mixed, even old boots'.[67] In 1929 wet rubber imports from the Outer Provinces comprised 105,000 tons of Singapore's total rubber

[62] Ibid. II, p.719.   [63] Ibid. II, p.724.
[64] Ibid. II, pp.746–47, 753, 754; *Directory 1930*, pp.8, 16, *1936*, pp.350–51, 501, *1939*, pp.381–82, 555.   [65] *SSTC 1933–34* II, p.354.   [66] Ibid. IV, p.136.
[67] Ibid. II, p.794.

imports of 128,000 tons from the Dutch colony.[68] Until 1933 the volume of rubber imports from Netherlands India was somewhat overstated because the trade statistics did not show wet rubber as the dry weight to which full processing reduced it (table 6.2).[69] However, in 1925/27, 46% of Singapore's rubber imports by value were from Netherlands India; that country's contribution to volume (in terms of dry weight) was probably greater than this, because Netherlands Indian rubber usually sold for less than Malayan.

About two-thirds of Netherlands Indian wet rubber exports were from the four ports of Djambi, Bandjermasin, Palambang and Pontianik, but the rest came from up to 41 other ports. In dealing with such a fragmented market, Singapore Chinese employed a system of barter trade like that used for tropical produce. The rubber, probably already having passed through three or four hands in Netherlands India, almost invariably reached Singapore through a Chinese outport dealer in Netherlands India. Singapore Chinese controlled this commerce because as part of the barter system they financed the trade by advancing goods, mostly rice and simple manufactures, against future deliveries of rubber. The 'dealers have to send their rubber to Singapore owing to the credit before the rubber is sent along [to Singapore]'.[70] In Netherlands India large-scale investment directed from the Netherlands was initially favoured as the solution to breaking this hold which Singapore Chinese had on the rubber trade:

In 1926 the Dutch actually started a powerful company [Nederlandsche Rubber Unie] with a capital of Fl.7,000,000 to do the milling business in the Dutch East Indies ... They established four factories at the mouths of the rivers in Sumatra and Dutch Borneo, but owing to this [barter trade] competition in Singapore they were not able to carry on and actually closed down two years ago [in 1931].[71]

Dealers importing native rubber from Netherlands India might also be millers. More often, however, the two appear to have been distinct, and the dealer usually did not retain ownership of the rubber and finance the miller but sold to him or to another dealer. This trade created a daily market for Netherlands Indian rubber at Boat Quay; among its participants would have been many, if not all, of the 59 rubber merchants listed in the *Chinese*

[68] Data for exports of wet slab rubber from Netherlands India are from Netherlands India, 'Jaaroverzicht van den In-en Uitvoer van Nederlandsch-Indie, deel II Buitengewesten', *Mededeelingen van het Centraal Kantoor voor de Statistiek* (Batavia), annual series, 1926–1933.

[69] In addition to the table, on the moisture content of wet rubber see Soliva, *Economic view*, p.132; Tengwall, 'History of rubber cultivation', p.351. Between 1922 and 1928 Singapore's imports from Netherlands India may have been somewhat overstated because the Stevenson scheme created an incentive to smuggle rubber from Malaya to Sumatra for re-export to Singapore and Penang. Drabble, *Malayan rubber*, p.328.

[70] *SSTC 1933–34* II, p.794.

[71] Ibid. The Dutch rubber syndicate is described in Holt, *Marketing*, pp.89–90.

commercial directory in 1932.[72] Europeans, dealers or possibly millers using the market, generally went through a Chinese, either a broker or their own storekeeper.

Imports from Netherlands India made Singapore the largest milling centre in British Malaya, and probably the world. Sumatra and Borneo almost entirely lacked the local milling facilities prevalent in Malaya, and it was because Netherlands Indian smallholders did not own rubber mangles that they made wet slab. As this would deteriorate on a long voyage, it had to be remilled into blanket rubber near the producing areas. By 1917 Singapore already had ten rubber mills but the next year, with the first large imports from Netherlands India, the number jumped to 25. In 1925 there were said to be 20 mills in Singapore working on Netherlands Indian rubber alone, and before the 1930s slump as many as 790 power-operated milling machines may have been employed in Singapore's remilling industry. In 1933, when it was reliably estimated that 80% of the rubber milled in Singapore came from Netherlands India, there were 24 mills with 582 machines.[73]

A few large Chinese entrepreneurs controlled the great bulk of milling capacity. However, not all survived the 1930s slump, and the 1933 figures, which are comprehensive, indicate a considerable change in ownership, if not in the predominance of a handful of millers: five Chinese operated a total of 14 mills with 469 machines, while seven other Chinese controlled 85 machines. The three European mills had only 28 machines between them.[74]

Rubber milling was typically labour-intensive, and employment at the industry's peak just before the slump of the 1930s may have been as high as 5,000 persons.[75] However, some large rubber mills or factories had elaborate machinery and layout in which water supply and independent power sources were major considerations. In these factories, investment might exceed $500,000, and 'the most expensive one in Singapore cost the owner over $800,000'.[76] Value added by the mills was represented by milling charges, which in 1933 were $12·50 per ton, about 12% of the average value of a ton of wet rubber imported that year.[77] Finance and marketing services performed in Singapore no doubt accounted for a

[72] *Chinese commercial directory* (1932), section D.   [73] *SSTC 1933–34* II, p.794.

[74] Nathan, 'Changes in the flow of trade', p.24; Department of Agriculture, Netherlands Indies, 'Native rubber cultivation', p.487; *SSTC 1933–34* IV, pp.233–34, and see below, table 7.2.

[75] The 1947 census enumerated 5,240 persons in rubber milling, packing, etc., and employment is likely to have been about the same on the eve of the 1930s slump. *1947 census*, p.475. In the early 1930s Singapore rubber mills alone employed about 6.1 persons per machine, or a total of some 3,500 persons for the 582 machines in Singapore. 'Labour Department', *SSAR 1931*, p.237, *1933*, p.209.   [76] *SSTC 1933–34* II, p.795.

[77] Ibid. V, p.46; Malaya, *Foreign imports and exports 1933*, p.406.

higher percentage of value added, although at times of low rubber prices Singapore traders accepted much-reduced margins.[78]

Until the later 1920s the bulk of Netherlands Indian rubber was sold to overseas buyers by European dealers, and so was marketed internationally in the same way as rubber from Malaya. In some instances, the European dealers purchased wet rubber, possibly to mix with scrap from Malaya, and paid a Chinese miller to process it. More often, European dealers, usually through a Chinese broker, bought the milled rubber from the miller or a Chinese dealer.

From the mid-1920s, however, this complementary relationship in Singapore between European dealers and Chinese millers began to break down as the latter started to export Netherlands Indian rubber themselves. By the early 1930s the few important Chinese millers were also major rubber shippers. They accounted for a large proportion, although not the majority, of Singapore's rubber exports to New York,[79] and probably exported more Netherlands Indian rubber than Europeans in Singapore. But large Chinese millers often had substantial estate holdings in Malaya and may also have been exporting that rubber.

Chinese appear to have sold rubber exports through agents in London or New York, generally with the price having been agreed before export, although in the late 1930s Lee Rubber Company set up a selling office in New York.[80] There is no evidence that Chinese dealers as distinct from the millers had any substantial role in the sale of rubber abroad. It is clear, however, that Chinese millers, after starting to use lorries to transport rubber directly from their mills to the wharves for export (see chapter 4), reduced costs sufficiently through this vertical integration successfully to export rubber in competition with the European agency houses. In this way they added a distinctive Chinese sector to Singapore's international rubber market. There may also have been advantages for Chinese rubber growers of vertical integration into exporting, but this remains unclear.

From mid-1934 Singapore's rubber trade with the hinterland entered a new phase following on the introduction of the International Rubber Regulation Scheme. Singapore was adversely affected by the reduction in the volume of rubber from Malaya and Netherlands India brought about by the Scheme; however, it raised rubber prices, which helped to restore the margins of Singapore traders eroded in the 1930s slump. The Scheme also led to an increase in Singapore's rubber imports from countries other than

---

[78] Cf. W. Collier and Suhud Tjakra Werdaja, 'Smallholder rubber production and marketing', *BIES* 8, 2 (1972), pp.70–82; Bauer, *Rubber*, pp.71–73.

[79] *SSTC 1933–34* II, p.896, and see II, p.721; Nathan, 'Changes in the flow of trade', p.24.

[80] Singapore, Archives and Oral History Department, *Pioneers of Singapore* (Singapore, 1984), interview with Lee Seng Gee, B000040/08, pp.12, 63; interview with Goh Tjoei Koh, B000082/11, pp.62, 68.

Malaya and Netherlands India (table 6.2). These imports came principally from Siam and reflected a rapid expansion of rubber cultivation there in the late 1920s in response to the high prices which resulted from the Stevenson scheme. Consequently, Siam was able to negotiate a liberal allowance under the 1934 Regulation Scheme.[81]

But for Singapore the main outcomes of regulation were that imports from Netherlands India changed almost entirely from wet to dry rubber which led to a loss of milling in Singapore, and that increasingly Netherlands India exported rubber direct to overseas markets.[82] In implementing International Rubber Regulation, the Dutch authorities tried to restrict the production of smallholders by taxing their exports. The authorities also took this as an opportunity to reduce exports through Singapore by prohibitively taxing wet rubber exports. Both Netherlands Indian smallholders and Singapore Chinese millers quickly responded to the tax – the former by obtaining mangles through Singapore to make sheet, the latter by re-locating in Netherlands India to export direct from there. In 1934, 43% of total rubber exports from Netherlands India went to Singapore and 21% directly to the United States, but by 1939 these proportions were almost exactly reversed: 25% of exports went to Singapore and 45% to the United States. If Singapore had held the 43% share of 1934, over the five-year period 1935 to 1939 its total rubber imports from Netherlands India would have been about 225,000 tons greater than they actually were. Even so, in 1938/39 Netherlands India still sent an annual average of 85,200 tons of rubber to Singapore,[83] much of it drawn at least in part by the need for treatment in Singapore's smokehouses.

After World War II the handling, milling and re-export of Indonesian rubber returned to Singapore. During the 1950s, and again at a crucial juncture for Singapore's economy in the later 1960s, rubber from Indonesia was of considerable importance, as discussed in chapters 10 and 11.

[81] Laurence D. Stifel, 'The growth of the rubber economy of southern Thailand', *JSEAS* 4, 1 (1973), pp.118–19, 130.

[82] The story may be traced in Malaya, *Foreign imports and exports*, 1933–1937; Malaya, *Foreign trade of Malaya*, 1938–1939; 'Report on the workings of the rubber regulation scheme in the islands of Singapore and Penang', *SSAR 1935* II, pp.417–27, *1936* I, pp.903, 908, *1937* I, pp.925, 933–36, 938, *1938* I, pp.375–76; *Straits Times*, 26 Feb. 1935; *SSTC 1933–34* V, pp.46–47; J. H. Boeke, *The structure of the Netherlands Indian economy* (New York, 1942), pp.116–18; Cecile G. H. Rothe, 'Commodity control in Netherlands India' in W. L. Holland, ed. *Commodity control in the Pacific area* (London, 1935), pp.302–6.

[83] Netherlands India, Central Bureau of Statistics, *Statistical pocket book of Indonesia 1941* (Batavia, 1941), p.80.

7   Rubber, industrialization and the development of Chinese banking

Singapore was in no way an industrial city. Unlike Bombay or Shanghai, with industries serving large hinterland markets, it did not develop as a major manufacturing centre for Malaya, and certainly not for Netherlands India. At the end of the 1930s, first-stage import substitution, involving a replacement of non-durable consumer goods, remained incomplete. Nevertheless, in the inter-war period Singapore acquired a substantial amount of industry. As the present chapter shows, rubber largely formed the basis for this industrialization.

Primary commodity exports often directly create opportunities for industry, in addition to making an indirect contribution to industrialization through increasing local and hinterland incomes and thus stimulating import substitution. The direct contribution of rubber involved all three possible paths to industrialization. First, rubber milling became by far Singapore's largest primary commodity processing industry. Second, rubber had important backward linkages in the development of import-substituting industries which made capital equipment for the commodity's production. Third, manufacturing for export emerged, since rubber's availability as a raw material led to the export of rubber goods outside Singapore's hinterland. The pattern and timing of industrialization is examined in this chapter's first section.

At the same time, rubber encouraged the development of domestic (i.e. Singapore-based) manufacturing by promoting the emergence of entrepreneurs and by putting profits in their hands. In Singapore, Europeans showed relatively little interest in investing in manufacturing, and the agency houses almost none. This opportunity mainly attracted the city's Chinese. Their extensive participation in the rubber industry therefore had particular significance for Singapore's economic development; most of the large Chinese trader/entrepreneurs whom the rubber industry brought to prominence moved into domestic manufacturing. These men and the industries they began are the subject of section II. Moreover, the same entrepreneurs, as discussed in the chapter's final section, were instrumental in the establishment of local Chinese deposit banking.

I

Singapore's manufacturing sector, already of some importance by 1910, became much more prominent under the influence of rubber during the inter-war period. Although the slump of the 1930s checked vigorous growth, in 1934 the Straits Settlements Trade Commission could draw attention to 'the remarkable industrial progress achieved by the Colony in recent years'.[1]

The pace and extent of industrialization, however, cannot easily be gauged from the existing industry statistics, which suffer from incompleteness and lack of comparability. One set (table 7.1) derives from the figures first available in the inter-war censuses for employment by industry. These show that some 16% of Singapore's labour force was in the manufacturing sector, and that between 1921 and 1931 employment in it increased by nearly 15% (appendix table A.10). It is doubtful whether this fully reflects Singapore's industrial expansion during the 1920s. Although both 1921 and 1931 were depression years, the latter was the more severe. Furthermore, in 1931 the size of the manufacturing sector may have been understated, because most of the large number of workers left unclassified by the census were unskilled, and this type of labourer was widely employed in Singapore industry. The 1931 census also clearly under-recorded some industries. For example, tin smelting had more than the 13 workers recorded by the census. Other industries, such as rubber milling, went entirely unrecorded.

The other main set of statistics derives from an annual return of industrial establishments (table 7.2). There is, however, no information about the size of establishments and, moreover, many were omitted.[2] In 1932 an attempt to compile a census of manufacturing industries was abandoned, because manufacturers were unwilling to disclose information.[3]

Two further features which make Singapore's industrialization hard to pin down were the lack of any obvious industrial zone and the existence of numerous small industries. Industry was located either around the Kallang River Basin or in the vicinity of Alexandra Road, broadly defined as the Singapore River Basin (figure 2.3). But even in these areas industry was scattered, while 'On practically any main road in Singapore you like to look at you will find a factory'.[4] In 1929 there was one manufacturing enterprise in Singapore with more than 4,000 employees, another with nearly 2,000 and over 25 employing between 100 and 500 persons each.[5] However, most factories were smaller than this, 'ranging in size down to

---

[1] *SSTC 1933–34* I, p.145.   [2] Rotary Club, *Singapore as an industrial centre*, p.21.
[3] *SSTC 1933–34* I, p.146.
[4] Ibid. II, p.213, and see II, pp.195, 206, 210, 212, 217, IV, pp.107, 108, 267; *Master plan, study groups*, p.50.   [5] 'Labour Department', *SSAR 1929*, p.204.

Table 7.1 *Singapore Island manufacturing employment, 1921 and 1931*

	1921		1931	
	persons	%	persons	%
Woodworking; furniture and basketware manufacture	10,805	32.5	12,463	32.6
Food, drink and tobacco manufacture	2,947	8.8	2,704	7.1
Clothing manufacture	4,428	13.3	4,148	10.9
Footware manufacture	1,652	5.0	1,933	5.1
Rubber goods manufacture	n.l.		2,455	6.4
Manufacture of metals, machines, implements, conveyances, jewellery and watches	10,118	30.4	11,363	29.7
Other	3,343	10.0	3,151	8.2
Total	**33,293**	**100.0**	**38,217**	**100.0**

Sources: Appendix table A.10.

the common Chinese shophouses, where a few workmen live and work together in the same premises'.[6] Small enterprises were often carried on cheek by jowl with other activities in the city and practically indistinguishable from them to the passer-by. A number of industries were sited just beyond the boundaries of the Municipality, usually to avoid its rates or regulations, especially those governing offensive trades.[7] Statistics in this chapter therefore relate to the island as a whole.

Power sources were not a serious impediment to the dispersal of industry in Singapore. Steam power was never very important in Singapore's industrial development, and by 1906 the public supply of electricity had been introduced. In 1907 the Municipality sold 128,000 kWh; this had increased to 2 million in 1919 and 9 million in 1927. The next year the St. James' Power Station opened, making electricity available anywhere within the municipal limits and to most of the rest of the island. By 1931 electricity consumption had risen to 27 million kWh and to 51 million in 1939. Electricity tariffs were considered reasonable, and bulk consumers with a 24-hour load received special rates. Even so, a number of factories relied on their own power sources, usually an oil engine.[8]

[6] *SSTC 1933–34* I, p.145.
[7] Ibid. II, pp.94, 178, 195–96, 206–7, 217, IV, pp.99, 100.
[8] 'Singapore municipality', *Singapore: handbook*, p.34; Rotary Club, *Singapore as an industrial centre*, p.20; *SSTC 1933–34* I, pp.132, 147; International Bank for Reconstruction and Development (hereafter IBRD), *The economic development of Malaya* (Singapore, 1955), p.271.

Table 7.2 *Singapore Island industrial establishments, 1900–1939*

	1900	1910	1913	1918	1923	1926	1929	1934	1939
Manufactures by steam power or oil engine									
Bread, biscuits and bakeries	15	15	24	27	29	23	19	5	6
Ice	4	4	5	4	5	5	1	3	3
Aerated water	3	2	6	6	9	11	10	8	8
Coconut oil	3	4	3	3	3	4	3	2	2
Ground nut oil	–	–	–	1	–	–	–	–	–
Pineapples	4	13	12	6	7	7	5	4	3
Gas	1	1	1	1	1	1	3	2	1
Manufactures by manual labour									
Copra	14	14	14	14	–	–	–	–	–
Coconut oil	2	2	2	2	1	8	3	4	4
Ground nut oil	–	–	–	4	2	2	0	4	2
Sugar refining	-	18	21	17	14	15	9	3	5
Pineapples	23	–	–	–	–	–	–	–	–
Sago (in suburbs)	16	10	7	4	7	5	4	4	5
Kachang oil	1	–	–	–	–	–	–	–	–
Soap (in town)	10	8	8	20	13	11	10	6	4
Melting tallow	39	37	35	33	40	29	21	23	16
Blachan (prawn sauce)	36	9	10	7	11	11	10	7	3
Aerated water	6	14	7	8	–	–	–	–	–
Dye-houses	33	27	26	16	9	7	9	7	6
Atap (palm thatch) depot	30	22	22	27	25	29	31	35	30
Tanneries	21	16	18	17	18	13	9	4	4
Lime	13	13	13	13	–	–	–	–	–
Charcoal kilns	–	10	12	12	5	8	14	10	48
Brick kilns	18	10	11	9	19	16	8	3	7
Potteries	10	9	9	14	11	8	3	5	7
Mills by steam power									
Sawmills	16	20	22	22	19	23	19	11	13
Rice–cleaning	9	6	4	2	1	1	–	–	–
Works									
Carpenters' shops	–	322	275	215	449	548	420	328	405
Tin smelting	1	1	1	1	1	1	1	1	1
Rubber factories	–	–	1	25	22	26	38	33	24
Engineers, iron and brass foundries	7	10	8	10	11	20	18	17	25
Smithies	–	189	174	155	156	189	154	95	87
Patent slip and dock	1	1	1	1	1	1	1	3	7
Graving docks	5	5	7	7	5	–	–	–	–
Shipbuilding yards	1	1	2	2	2	2	2	2	3

Notes:
1 Not listed for years with –.
2 Until 1934 most bread and biscuit factories do not appear to have used steam power, although classified in that category. In 1934, 20, and in 1939, 24, bakeries were listed as manufacturers by manual labour.
Sources:SS, *Blue books*, 1900–1939, section X or 22.

The available statistics nonetheless offer a clear picture of the lines along which industry developed. One type of industry – processing – is largely described in chapters 3, 5 and 8. Tin smelting alone owed its location in Singapore to tariff protection; otherwise, the island's natural advantages were decisive in attracting primary commodity processing. When processing needed to be near the source of raw material production because of weight loss or the cost of shipping the unprocessed commodity any distance, Singapore had an advantage in attracting these industries. Its role as a collection and distribution centre created economies associated with bulking and with being a place where commodities changed modes of transport.

By the inter-war years processing industries associated with the traditional trades – rice, sugar, sago and groundnuts – had stagnated or, more often, were actually in decline, with the exception of the production of coconut oil (table 7.2). But this lack of growth was more than made up for by new industries arising from the development of rubber: pineapple canning, the sawmilling thus drawn to Singapore and, above all, rubber milling. In 1929 more than a dozen of the 25 or so enterprises employing between 100 and 500 persons were rubber mills. The employment in rubber milling – among the omissions of the 1931 census – of upwards of 5,000 persons was a major addition to the industrial sector.

The second broad type of development was import-substituting industry, which emerged in Singapore's free trade regime. Tariff protection for Singapore in its single most important hinterland market – Netherlands India – was not possible because the Dutch colony had customs arrangements quite separate from Singapore's. Until the mid-1930s, however, the Netherlands Indian tariff structure did not discriminate unduly against Signapore, since tariffs in the Dutch colony consisted of purely revenue duties, equally applicable to all countries.[9] In British Malaya, a customs union to include Singapore had been a possibility since 1910, and in the early 1930s was actively pressed for by the Governor, Sir Cecil Clementi.[10] The concept complemented a more ambitious scheme which he had – that Singapore should become 'a great centre for manufacture'.[11] In 1931 Clementi declared that 'it is high time we aimed at a greater measure of self-sufficiency than we possess at present', and advocated a sweeping policy of import substitution to extend to textile mills, a tin plate factory and even a local steel industry. The Colonial Office reacted to the proposal with annoyance and some alarm; it was unwilling to encourage any

[9] *SSTC 1933–34* I, p.148.   [10] *SSLCP 1932*, pp.B100–B102.
[11] *Straits Times*, 11 Jan. 1932.

industries in colonies which might compete with those in the United Kingdom.[12]

Nor did businessmen in Singapore support a British Malayan tariff, apart from the Singapore Manufacturers' Association, formed in 1932 and consisting of 16 firms, and some European merchants mainly interested in protective duties for imports from Britain, on which their business largely depended. The Singapore business community as a whole, reflecting the tradition of free trade, strongly opposed British Malayan protective duties to assist industrial development, in this instance principally because of the danger of disruption to the port's closely-linked trades of distributing manufactured imports to the region and exporting primary commodities. In any case, industrialization fostered by means of a tariff was unlikely to be very extensive, owing to the smallness of the British Malayan market. In 1931 the population of British Malaya was 4·36 million, of which Singapore's 567,000 inhabitants constituted easily the main concentration of purchasing power.[13]

Import-substituting industry which developed in Singapore may be divided into two categories: industries which arose specifically as a result of the rubber industry and industries which emerged with the general expansion of the Singapore and hinterland markets. Most industries in the latter category found their markets in Singapore itself and Malaya; Singapore developed only limited import-substituting industry to serve Netherlands India.

An important group of industries, although to some extent traditional, and so not all strictly import-substituting – woodworking and furniture making, and clothing manufacture – were very closely tied to consumer markets, and were major activities in Singapore before the growth of the rubber industry. Exports to Malaya, where the same industries developed, were not significant. In 1931 the two industries comprised over two-fifths of those employed in Singapore's manufacturing sector (table 7.1). The typical unit of production was small, hence Singapore's numerous carpenter shops, a prominent feature of table 7.2, and the 86 tailors listed in the *Chinese commercial directory* of 1932. In the inter-war period some clothing began to be manufactured for export.[14]

The majority of Singapore's import-substituting industries, although not strictly tied to the consumer market, were advantageously carried on in close proximity to it, typically due to the high weight to cost ratio of

[12] PRO CO 273/582/92080, file on Singapore manufacturers' exhibition, passim. Clementi's speech was reported in the *Straits Times*, 2 Sept. 1931.
[13] *SSTC 1933–34* I, pp.147–52, 163, 145, II, pp.275, 286–87.
[14] *Chinese commercial directory* (1932), section X; 'Manufacture of furniture', *Singapore: handbook*, p.68; *SSTC 1933–34* I, p.146, II, p.271.

products. These industries included the manufacture of bricks and tiles, cement products, earthenware, iron pans, pipes, metal bedsteads, inks, oxygen, acetylene and other gases, patent medicine, aerated water, biscuits, sugar candy and other foodstuffs. There were also several tanneries and soap and candle manufacturers in Singapore.[15] A number of these activities developed with Singapore's late nineteenth-century growth, but the establishment of several others, as described below, awaited the stimulus of rubber. Most relied at least partly on a Malayan market; even in Penang and Kuala Lumpur there was remarkably little industrialization.

Cigarettes had a large local and regional market, but their manufacture in Singapore was not sufficiently protected by transport costs to make this more than a marginal industry. There were several Chinese cigarette factories. However, a modern plant opened by British American Tobacco in 1930 with 1,200 employees was soon closed. BAT's request for a slight preference on the duty on imported loose tobacco had been refused by the Secretary of State for the Colonies because 'the development of local manufactures in the Colonies ... is undesirable except where the industry can be regarded as natural to the dependency concerned'. The Straits Settlements Trade Commission – no proponent of protectionism – observed that the conversion of imported tobacco into cigarettes was 'about as "natural" to Singapore as to Bristol or Liverpool'.[16] In 1932 two new brewing companies in Singapore began to supply much of the beer consumed in British Malaya, and a firm making toothpaste and motor car polish was established, but these were the principal additions to the industrial sector, which suggests that during the early 1930s the shift in the net barter terms of trade against primary commodities did little to promote industrialization.[17]

Assembly industries set up in British Malaya to overcome the cost of transporting the finished item there were usually sited in Singapore, owing to its large urban market and good distribution facilities. There was a sizeable industry in bicycle assembly. In 1926 Ford established an automobile assembly plant with a capacity of 100 cars a month, although the refusal by the Singapore Municipal Commissioners to give General Motors a licence for a factory site because it bordered on a residential area led that company to locate in Batavia's port of Tanjong Priok.[18]

The most striking omission from the list of import-substituting industries in Singapore is a local textile industry, which only began to appear in the 1950s. Because of the port's big distributive trade in cotton textiles, their manufacture was the principal opportunity to develop large import-

[15] *SSTC 1933–34* I, p.146.   [16] Ibid. I, p.161, and see I, p.146, III, pp.316–17.
[17] Ibid. I, p.146; Ian M. D. Little, *Economic development* (New York, 1982), pp.70–71.
[18] *SSTC 1933–34* I, pp.146, 50, II, p.192, IV, p.108.

substituting industry, especially for the Netherlands Indian market, which had no discriminatory tariffs against Singapore, nor a local textile industry. The failure to manufacture textiles in Singapore illustrates why, in the absence of a protective tariff, import-substituting industry in the city remained relatively undeveloped.

Two possible reasons for Singapore's lack of a textile industry may be suggested. One was the absence of entrepreneurial initiative, possibly because of an 'entrepot mentality', leading to concentration on the foreign trade sector at the expense of investment in domestic manufacturing. For Europeans the argument has some force, but for the Chinese it is unconvincing. Chinese willingly invested in industry, and industrialists like those discussed in the next section could have begun to manufacture textiles. The technology of setting up weaving mills was well known and easily within the capabilities of Singapore Chinese enterprise, while established Chinese entrepreneurs could obtain capital.[19]

The second possibility – the lack of substantial economic grounds for beginning a textile industry – is the more likely reason that one did not develop in Singapore. In textile manufacture, labour costs are a major consideration. Data on wage levels for the industrial labour force – preponderantly male Chinese – are scattered, but it is clear that wages were high by Asian standards. By the inter-war period competition in textiles, especially in the cheaper ranges Singapore might have hoped to make, came increasingly from Japan, India, Hong Kong and China. In comparison to Japan, Singapore did not have particularly low wages, and taking productivity into account certainly not low unit labour costs, while its wages were substantially higher than in India, Hong Kong or China. As the Straits Settlements Trade Commission pointed out, immigrants came to Singapore from these countries because of the prospect of higher wages.[20] Uncompetitive wages caused a sharp decline in the number of Singapore's dye houses (table 7.2), which coloured and printed imports of plain cotton piece goods.[21] High wages were probably the most important reason why the basic textile industries failed to develop in Singapore.

By the inter-war years, however, there was already some reliance on cheap female labour in Singapore industry. This afforded women – then virtually all Chinese – one of their main opportunities for employment outside of domestic service and enabled Singapore to move towards internationally competitive wage levels. In the 1931 census, women

[19] Rotary Club, *Singapore as an industrial centre*, p.20, and see L. Cresson, 'Industrial Singapore', *Singapore: handbook*, p.59.

[20] *SSTC 1933–34* I, p.149, and see I, pp.150, 119, III p.271, V, p.72.

[21] For the size of the dyeing industry, in addition to table 7.2, compare imports and exports of plain, dyed and printed cotton piece goods in SS, *Return of imports and exports*, 1900–1927, and see *SSTC 1933–34* I, pp.53, 54, 146.

accounted for about 2,400 workers in the manufacturing sector, just over one-twentieth of its employment. Children aged 11 to 14 were a significant, but unknown, addition to this female component of the industrial workforce, mainly because mothers usually took their offspring with them to the factory. Most female employment was as casual labour on a piecework basis, and wages varied from $0·22 to about $0·50 for an 8·5 to 9·5 hour day. In Singapore a daily rate of $0·22 was not a living wage, but rather a family income supplement. Although in a few industries the practice of employing women considerably reduced average wage costs, females were not in the labour force in sufficient numbers to make Singapore a low wage centre.[22] In Shanghai, by contrast, women and children constituted two-thirds of the about 250,000 factory workers.[23]

Singapore industries which made capital goods for rubber production exported largely to Malaya. For example, one small industrial concern fabricated aluminium coagulating tanks, cups, buckets and latex guides; another made canvas bags for packing rubber, advertised as giving 'Durability – Hundred Times Over'.[24]

Engineering was, however, by far the most important import-substituting industry in Singapore arising from linkages created by hinterland rubber production. In 1931 the census category which encompassed the manufacture of metals and machines included more than a quarter of those in Singapore's industrial sector (table 7.1). It is not possible to attribute this employment to specific industries, but, apart from some 1,200 persons in motor car and cycle repair, a high proportion was in engineering work relating to the port, as discussed in the next chapter, or to the tin and rubber industries. During the inter-war period the number of 'engineers, iron and brass foundries' in Singapore more than doubled to reach 25 in 1939 (table 7.2). Most of these were small, Chinese works, like those making rubber mangles referred to in chapter 6. But the largest engineering enterprises were European. Of these, United Engineers was the firm noted above as employing almost 2,000 workers in 1929; it was also important in the tin industry, as discussed in chapter 8. The company had its origins in two partnerships formed by Britons who had come to Singapore in the late nineteenth century. Both ventures had grown into well-established firms before merging in 1912; by 1932 United Engineers, with headquarters in River Valley Road, had five branches in Malaya, and operated in Burma and Siam.[25]

[22] 'Employment of women and children in Singapore', *MRCA* 24 (Aug. 1932), pp.22–26; Bingham, *Report 1946*, p.38.
[23] Fang Fu-an, 'Shanghai labour', *Chinese Economic Journal* 7, 2 (1930), pp.854, 857.
[24] *SSTC 1933–34* I, p.145, II, pp.814–17; *Manufacturers' exhibition*, pp.117–21, 126, 127.
[25] Makepeace, 'Machinery of commerce', pp.199–200, 214–15; *Manufacturers' exhibition*, p.111.

The rubber industry contributed to the growth of this engineering sector in Singapore mainly through the need for processing equipment in the form of rubber factories. The demand was considerable, since factories were to be found on practically all of British Malaya's several thousand estates and there were numerous Chinese mills treating smallholder rubber. Proximity to the hinterland promoted the growth of a mechanical engineering sector in Singapore because it permitted easier collaboration between makers and users of equipment and encouraged local adaptation and development.[26] It was principally on this basis that by the inter-war years United Engineers had become a large manufacturer of sheeting machines, rubber mangles, scrap washers and smokehouses; supplied and erected plant for lighting, power and water schemes; and built turnkey rubber factories. In the 1930s it was said that 'many of the principal estates throughout the rubber growing area are equipped with U. E. machinery, housed in U. E. structures'.[27]

The third type of industrial development in Singapore was manufacturing for export. For any country this is a difficult step, and in inter-war Singapore there was no particular reason to expect the export-oriented industry which emerged. One possible basis for such industrialization is low wage costs which, as noted above, Singapore did not have. Nor did Singapore derive any marked advantage from its ready access to raw materials, which is typically the other possible basis for success in manufacturing for world markets. Singapore's two raw materials were tin and rubber. The principal use of tin was for tin plate, but this consisted chiefly of steel. The need to import steel – Malayan coal was unsuitable for its manufacture – and the absence of a substantial domestic market for tin plate made this industry uneconomic in Singapore. Rubber offered a more realistic possibility for industrialization, although not a spectacular one. Manufacturers in other countries could use rubber at not much greater cost than in Singapore, since in manufacture it was not a high weight-losing raw material, and this minimized the importance of transport costs.

Nevertheless, the two major export industries which developed in Singapore made rubber goods. Both benefited from an important advantage of Singapore in manufacturing for export: its location, which kept distribution costs low by offering good access to world markets.[28] This was important primarily for rubber products which did not weigh much. In exporting heavier or bulkier rubber manufactures like tyres, transport costs tended to offset more purely distributional advantages. The

---

[26] Similarly, the economic development literature suggests that these advantages of proximity make mechanical engineering a sector worth promoting in developing countries: Little, *Economic development*, pp.181, 242–43.   [27] *Manufacturers' exhibition*, p.111.

[28] Cf. *SSTC 1933–34* I, p.147.

production of these goods in Singapore had to rely chiefly on the market available in British Malaya.

One industry which developed was the Singapore Rubber Works, a Dutch enterprise which came to Singapore in 1898 and soon started to manufacture rubber products. The firm found that the production of tyres and tubes was unprofitable and made mostly technical rubber goods such as plugs, valves, hoses and belting for use in engineering industries. British Malaya took only about a fifth of the output of the firm. It exported to India, China, Africa, Netherlands India, the Philippines and Siam, and there was 'hardly a railway company in the East that is not equipped with Singapore-made Westinghouse brake fittings and other rubber equipment'[29] made by the Singapore Rubber Works. In 1929 the firm, which had a number of European managerial, supervisory and technical personnel, employed over 300 workers. Its activities were indicative of Singapore's locational advantage in distributing to the global market, which contributed to post-1966 export-oriented industrialization.

The other industry developed mainly around the manufacture of rubber shoes. The enterprise began in 1921 with fewer than 50 workers, but grew rapidly until by 1929 it was the one Singapore firm which had over 4,000 employees. Built by the Singapore Chinese entrepreneur, Tan Kah Kee, this enterprise is discussed in the next section.

II

This section seeks to explain the relative lack of European investment in Singapore's manufacturing sector and, by contrast, the close association between the city's industrialization and its Chinese entrepreneurs. As a European representative of the Singapore Manufacturers' Association pointed out, 'It is to the Chinese merchants of the City that Singapore is largely indebted for its industrial development'.[30] Chinese with a substantial stake in the rubber industry were the most prominent in this industrialization process.

For Singapore's Chinese entrepreneurs, profits from the rubber-pineapple complex, described in chapters 3 and 6, provided a large new source of finance for industrial expansion, and, probably more important, enabled these men to establish their creditworthiness and launch industries with borrowed capital. The rubber-pineapple complex opened these possibilities because, as discussed in the previous chapter, the viability of

---

[29] 'Rubber manufactures', *Singapore: handbook*, p.62, and see p.98; *SSTC 1933–34* II, pp.288, 291–93, 300; *Manufacturers' exhibition*, pp.81–89; Macmillan, *Seaports*, p.454; *Directory 1939*, p.519; Allen and Donnithorne, *Western enterprise*, p.261.

[30] Cresson, 'Industrial Singapore', p.59.

small production units facilitated Chinese entry; because of the several opportunities in the complex for profits; and, furthermore, because the complex was expanding. For most Europeans the rubber boom ended with the depression at the beginning of the 1920s and implementation of the Stevenson scheme. By contrast, Chinese participation in the rubber industry came principally with the upsurge in Netherlands Indian production consequent on that scheme, and the 1920s spread of estate cultivation in Johore. For Singapore Chinese, these opportunities extended the rubber boom until 1930. Thus, during the 1920s, just as there was the greatest scope to invest in manufacturing industry because of the rise in incomes created by rubber, so too were there the largest profits within the Chinese community which could be mobilized for investment.

A substantial proportion of these profits concentrated in a few hands, and created the fortunes of men who became the city's leading industrialists and Chinese bankers. Concentration was promoted by the fact that often the same Chinese entrepreneurs were prominent in several aspects of the rubber-pineapple complex, considerably helped by its complementary activities, for instance between pineapples and estate ownership and between rubber trade and milling. There are examples of Chinese who were successful in the Malayan planting boom before World War I, and were then able to build on this success by expanding their Malayan interests and moving into Netherlands Indian rubber. But often Chinese rubber entrepreneurs acquired their wealth only in the inter-war period. In Singapore Chinese society, those most successful in the rubber-pineapple complex became not just leaders but legendary, almost mythical figures.

Five such men – prominent Singapore Chinese rubber magnates – were Tan Kah Kee, Lim Nee Soon, Tan Ean Kiam, Tan Lark Sye and Lee Kong Chian. Tan Kah Kee's career was the most significant and spectacular. He employed, before they branched out on their own, Tan Ean Kiam, Tan Lark Sye and Lee Kong Chian, all born in or not far from his home village near Amoy, Fukien province. After Tan Kah Kee took control of his father's declining rice trading and milling businesses in 1904, he almost immediately began to build his commercial empire by extending his operations to pineapple planting and canning and rubber. As early as 1907 Tan purchased 180,000 rubber seeds to plant on his pineapple holdings; subsequently, he bought large tracts of land to cultivate pineapples and rubber. During World War I Tan must have profited from the boom in rubber exports but, more important, he seized the opportunity which the wartime dislocation of shipping created in the rice trade. He began his own shipping line to carry rice from the producing countries for distribution in Asia, and, when the pineapple industry was suffering from a shortage of shipping, could use his own vessels to export canned pineapples. By 1918

Tan had cash assets of $1·4 million from shipping profits and from compensation for two of his vessels sunk in the Mediterranean.

Tan ploughed this cash back into his rubber-pineapple interests, which expanded rapidly after the War. In the early 1920s Tan Kah Kee & Co. operated four rubber mills in Singapore and was the island's largest miller. Among Singapore Chinese, Tan took the lead in exporting rubber to the West, and as early as 1925 was 'well-known in Mincing Lane and on the New York Rubber Exchange'.[31] In the 1930s his company controlled two large rubber mills in Singapore, another ten mills in Malaya, four of 17 British Malayan pineapple canneries accounting for about 40% of total output, and had acquired more than 10,000 acres of rubber estates.[32]

Of the other rubber magnates mentioned, Lim Nee Soon, a Teochew born in Singapore in 1879, was most nearly Tan's contemporary, and also became a pioneer Chinese pineapple and rubber planter. By 1911 he had founded Lim Nee Soon & Co. and engaged in business as a planter, estate consultant and contractor, miner, the owner of rubber and pineapple factories, merchant and general commission agent. During World War I Lim's rubber estates and factories made him a millionaire. In 1921 the firm, of which Lim was sole proprietor, owned seven rubber estates and by 1931, 14.[33]

The fortunes of the other three rubber magnates – Tan Kah Kee's erstwhile employees – were amassed primarily in the inter-war years. In 1899 Tan Ean Kiam, aged 18, came to Singapore with his father. By 1909 Tan had established the Joo Guan Co., and 'As his business flourished he invested in rubber estates and factories, and within ten years he had become a man of great wealth'. But Tan's major success came in 1922 when he organized the milling firm of Bing Seng & Co. and purchased large stocks of rubber. With the introduction of the Stevenson scheme and recovery of rubber prices, 'Tan's foresight brought him a huge fortune'.[34] In 1933 Bing Seng & Co. operated two rubber mills with 57 of the 582 machines in Singapore.

Tan Lark Sye (born in 1896) came to Singapore and found work accounting and weighing in a rubber factory. In 1923, with his elder

[31] Nathan, 'Changes in the flow of trade', p.24.

[32] Sim, *Biographies*, p.i; Song, *One hundred years' history*, p.430; Macmillan, *Seaports*, p.451; Drabble, *Rubber*, p.41; C. F. Yong, 'Emergence of Chinese community leaders in Singapore, 1890–1941', *Journal of the South Seas Society* 30, 1 and 2 (1975), pp.8–9; Yong, 'Preliminary study of Chinese leadership', p.273; *Directory 1921*, pp.242–43, *1931*, p.147; 'Pineapple conference', *SSLCP 1931*, p.C224; *SSTC 1933–34* II, pp.301, 311, 788, IV, p.234.

[33] Song, *One hundred years' history*, pp.516–17; *Directory 1921*, p.199, *1927*, p.280, *1931*, p.84; Yong, 'Preliminary study of Chinese leadership', p.276; Yong, 'Chinese community leaders', p.10.   [34] Sim, *Biographies*, p.75, and see *SSTC 1933–34* IV, p.234.

brother and the help of a loan from a local Chinese bank, he established Aik Hoe & Co. to deal in and mill rubber. The firm rapidly became successful, in 1933 operating three mills with 90 machines in Singapore. By the end of the decade Aik Hoe, with numerous branches, was said to be the largest rubber milling business in Southeast Asia, and the biggest rubber exporter in British Malaya.[35]

The collapse of Tan Kah Kee's empire, discussed below, made Lee Kong Chian (born in 1893) 'the leading rubber magnate of the 1930s'.[36] Lee was trained in civil engineering at the National University of Communications in China, and fluent both in English and Chinese. His recruitment by Tan Kah Kee in 1916 represented the union of Western knowledge and traditional Chinese business acumen; four years later, after he had been promoted to the position of Tan's manager, Lee's marriage to Tan's eldest daughter illustrated the Singapore Chinese dictum that although you cannot choose a son, you can choose a son-in-law to try to ensure the success of the family business.

Although still closely connected with Tan, Lee set up on his own in 1927 by establishing a rubber smokehouse business in Muar, later named Lee Rubber Co. This became a limited liability company in 1931, with two of Lee's close friends – one a fellow villager – each taking a sizeable number of shares. A key aspect of Lee's rise was his dealings with European banks on behalf of Tan Kah Kee. Because Lee had the confidence of European bankers, he was useful to Chinese bankers in dealing with their European counterparts. Lee's own financial position was strengthened by the willingness of Europeans to lend to him, which made the Chinese banks also anxious to do so.[37] Lee could certainly borrow from the Chinese Commercial Bank, of which he was a director, and later from the Oversea-Chinese Banking Corporation, which he was instrumental in forming in 1932. Lee's borrowing power and his own liquidity meant that, at a time of knock-down asset prices during the 1930s, he could fashion his empire from other, failing Chinese businesses, notably those of Tan Kah Kee. In 1933 Lee Rubber Co. operated 245 machines in Singapore's rubber mills, over two-fifths of the total. All these machines were rented, from, among others, Tan Kah Kee and Lim Nee Soon. In the same year Lee Pineapple Co. operated three factories in Johore, more than any other canner. Lee was chairman of the Singapore Pineapple Packers Agency, a trade association which leased and kept idle three of Tan Kah Kee's factories.

[35] Sim, *Biographies*, pp.2, 10; *SSTC 1933–34* IV, p.234; Yong, 'Preliminary study of Chinese leadership', p.276; Ilsa Sharp, 'Tax and the tycoon', *Singapore Trade and Industry* (Nov. 1972), p.18; *Straits Times*, 12 Sept. 1972; *New Nation*, 15 Sept. 1972.

[36] Dick Wilson, *Solid as a rock: the first forty years of the Oversea-Chinese Banking Corporation* (Singapore, 1972), p.40.

[37] Oral History, *Pioneers*, interview with Tan Ee Leong, A000003/21, pp.104, 139.

During the 1930s Lee earned the title of the 'Rubber and Pineapple King of Singapore and Malaya'. He owned thousands of acres of rubber and pineapple plantations and was a leader in establishing pineapples as a permanent crop, in 1934 controlling 8,000 of a total of 12,000 acres under permanent cultivation. In the course of the decade Lee extended his operations throughout Malaya, and to Netherlands India and southern Siam.[38]

In the inter-war period, it was of considerable importance for Singapore's economic development that large profits from rubber were accruing to the Chinese: the interest of that community in domestic industry was in sharp contrast to the hesitancy with which Europeans in Singapore viewed investment in manufacturing. European immigration consisted very largely of employees in big firms, not individual entrepreneurs, and European profits were realized principally by corporations and not by individuals. These were circumstances unlikely to produce much European investment in local industry. There were, however, some notable examples of European investment in domestic manufacturing, apart from that by multinationals which on the whole remained uninterested in import-substituting industry prior to World War II. In addition to United Engineers, European firms included Fraser & Neave (aerated water); Archipelago Brewery Co.; Malayan Breweries; Alexandra Brickworks; Diamond Metal Products (bedsteads, mattresses and flashlight batteries); and the Straits Manufacturing Co. (toothpaste and motor car polish). In most instances these enterprises seem to have been started as partnerships by men already resident in Singapore.[39]

There was a conspicuous lack of agency house investment in Singapore industry. In part, the explanation was that much of the capital under agency house management belonged to shareholders in Britain and the remittance of profits to them was automatic. Overseas shareholders were better able to diversify their own portfolios than if agency houses tried to achieve this for them. Consequently, shareholders had little reason to press for agency house diversification. And investment elsewhere by shareholders may have been more attractive than putting additional funds into British Malaya; significant diversification there through portfolio investment was in any case impossible, since rubber companies offered the primary opportunity for such investment.

Nevertheless, the agency houses had control of substantial profits from

---

[38] Tan, 'Lee Kong Chian', p.3; Sim, *Biographies*, p.5; *SSTC 1933–34* I, p.200, II, p.788, IV, p.234; *Directory 1939*, p.426; Sharp, 'Tax', p.18.
[39] Makepeace, 'Machinery of commerce', pp.194–95; *Manufacturers' exhibition*, passim; *Directory 1939*, passim; *SSTC 1933–34* I, p.146, II, pp.281, 286, 287, 923–30, IV, p.270, V, pp.73–77.

trade and, perhaps more significant, usually had a shareholding in the rubber companies they managed. Some of these profits could have been invested in domestic industry. For example, after World War I 'Guthrie time and again toyed with the idea of undertaking local manufacturing activities, especially rubber goods, but did not act'.[40] Possibly those controlling Singapore agency houses considered many industrial investments too small or uncertain, felt that these projects did not really complement their interests in the rubber industry and conflicted with those in the import of manufactured goods, or decided that they lacked technical expertise and experience in the industrial sector. Agency houses were typically limited liability companies and their partners, like rubber company shareholders, had good access to the London stock market. They could probably use this access more successfully than investment in British Malayan industry to diversify away from the high risk of plantation agriculture. It must have seemed hard for agency houses to find affirmative answers to why they should invest in local manufacturing.

Like Europeans, most Chinese rubber entrepreneurs in Singapore came from outside British Malaya, but in other respects their circumstances were very different. The Chinese were entrepreneurs in their own right, and not the representatives of overseas corporations; therefore none of their profits would be repatriated automatically, but only as the result of an active decision. If Singapore Chinese had made that decision, the obvious place to repatriate their capital would have been China. But in the inter-war period conditions in China could hardly have appeared favourable for investment. Much of the country was in a state of endemic civil war. Furthermore, the rapaciousness of petty officialdom in China was a major deterrent to the would-be Nanyang entrepreneur, as indicated by a Singapore Chinese-language newspaper editorial:

Sin Chew Jit Poh of 6·6·33 points out that 'Extortion and squeeze' by local minor officials in China are responsible for the hesitation on the part of the Overseas Chinese to return to China and warns the Chinese government that if it wants to encourage Overseas Chinese to return and invest in home industries, severe punishment must be meted out to those minor officials who try to bully and extort from Overseas Chinese on their arrival in China.[41]

Investment in the treaty ports would largely have overcome these objections to investing in China. But Chinese investment in treaty ports

[40] Drabble and Drake, 'British agency houses', p.311, and see p.326.
[41] 'Editorials from local Chinese newspapers', MRCA 34 (June 1933), p.67, and see Michael R. Godley, The mandarin-capitalists from Nanyang: overseas Chinese enterprise in the modernization of China, 1893–1911 (Cambridge, 1981), pp.108–9, 112; Yen Ching-Hwang, 'The overseas Chinese and late Ch'ing economic modernization', Modern Asian Studies 16, 2 (1982), pp.231–32; Singapore Chinese Chamber of Commerce, Fifty-eight years of enterprise (Singapore, 1964), p.79.

appears to have been dominated by the usual Chinese pattern of personal relationships, and therefore each treaty port tended to draw its business-men from a fairly narrow local area.[42] Since most Singapore Chinese rubber entrepreneurs came from Fukien, and Amoy was the treaty port with which they had the closest personal connections, this was where they might have invested in manufacturing. To a limited extent these entre-preneurs did invest, but Amoy did not develop very significantly as an industrial centre and offered few opportunities for investment.[43] Singapore Chinese entrepreneurs were required by their position of social leadership to give money to good causes in China.[44] Otherwise, however, these men acted very much like the capitalists of W. A. Lewis, who save and invest in capitalist enterprise.[45] With few exceptions, this investment was in Singapore or Malaya. In a sense, Singapore could be viewed economically as a treaty port. For Chinese making their residence there, it served much the same economic function as the treaty ports did for Chinese who remained in China. But for Singapore Chinese it did this much more advantageously than any of China's treaty ports.

Decisions by Singapore Chinese entrepreneurs to invest in manu-facturing industry were at least in part an attempt to diversify, and reflected a lack of opportunities for diversification outside British Malaya. These decisions also suggest that manufacturing was profitable when compared with further investment in the rubber-pineapple complex or in trade. The relative profitability of industrial investment must have reflected the impact of the rubber industry, which created new opportunities for investment in domestic manufacturing. Equally, however, there is little reason to think that in the absence of Chinese entrepreneurs these opportunities would generally have amounted to anything more than missed chances. The difference which Chinese entrepreneurs made to economic development in Singapore was substantial. Their involvement in manufacturing promoted a more diversified economy. It also captured for British Malaya a greater share of the benefits of trade through raising the foreign trade multiplier, since the proceeds of primary exports circulated through more rounds of spending in the local economy before leaking out as demand for imports. Perhaps more important, it was very largely

[42] Cf. Parks M. Coble, *The Shanghai capitalists and the nationalist government, 1927–1937* (Cambridge, MA, 1980), pp.23–25.

[43] Chen, *Emigrant communities*, pp.202–12; 'Overseas Chinese remittances to China', *Far Eastern Economic Review*, 17 March 1948, pp.253–54.

[44] Cf. Lin Yu, 'The Chinese overseas', *Chinese Year Book* 1937, pp.1257–58; Yong, 'Emergence of Chinese community leaders', pp.4–11, 14; C. F. Yong, 'Leadership and power in the Chinese community of Singapore during the 1930s', *JSEAS* 8, 2 (1977), pp.196–99, 204–6.

[45] Lewis, 'Economic development with unlimited supplies of labour', pp.155–60.

Singapore's Chinese entrepreneurs who first demonstrated that the port could make a substantial part of its living by industrial production.

Most of the manufacturing enterprises begun by Chinese rubber entrepreneurs had certain important features in common. One is that this group relied largely on their ability as entrepreneurs rather than on any managerial or technical experience. To some extent, the need for technical expertise was met by hiring European engineers.[46] It was also true that the manufacturing enterprises of rubber entrepreneurs tended to be more capital-intensive than most other Chinese industry, possibly because interests in the rubber-pineapple complex gave greater access to finance, considered below. In capital intensity, these Chinese enterprises were close to, or the equal of, European-owned industries. For both Chinese and European firms, however, Singapore's large pool of casual labour discouraged the use of capital. Yet perhaps the most striking feature of Chinese investment was the tendency to diversify into a number of industries. No doubt diversification stemmed from a desire to spread risk, but probably as important an explanation was the shallowness of the market. Whatever the combination of reasons, the result was the Chinese industrial conglomerate.

The forerunners of the great Chinese industrial conglomerates which became prominent in Singapore during the inter-war years were already evident in the late nineteenth century.[47] A decisive move in the development of the Chinese conglomerate came in 1904 with the foundation of the Ho Hong group by Lim Peng Siang and his brother Peng Mau, who had both emigrated to Singapore from Fukien. The Lim brothers began their business with coconut oil mills and rice mills, and within five years had started a shipping line. As for Tan Kah Kee, World War I proved of great advantage to Ho Hong, providing an opportunity for the firm to expand its rice trade and shipping interests as well as to take control of German-owned oil mills which had been its main rival. Thus the early development of the Chinese industrial conglomerate did not necessarily depend on rubber. During the inter-war period other industrial enterprises run by Ho Hong included a soap factory, saw mills and a cement works, although by 1921 they also included rubber estates.[48]

But rubber was primarily responsible for the development of Chinese

---

[46] F. B. Ritchie, 'The early days of ship surveying in Singapore and of Ritchie & Bisset, 1866–1928' (unpublished typescript, 1952), p.16; Macmillan, *Seaports*, pp.442, 451.

[47] Cf. Turnbull, *History of Singapore*, p.94; Yong, 'Preliminary study of Chinese leadership', pp.276–77.

[48] Sim, *Biographies*, p.34; *Manufacturers' exhibition*, pp.140–41, 143; Song, *One hundred years' history*, pp.116–17, 349; Macmillan, *Seaports*, pp.441–42, 448, 450; *Directory 1912*, p.165, *1916*, pp.141–42, *1921*, pp.183–84, *1922*, pp.207, 209, *1931*, pp.66–68, *1939*, pp.444–45.

industrial conglomerates. Among their founders, the figure of Tan Kah Kee looms largest. He began to invest in manufacturing industry in the early 1920s; by 1928 Ormsby Gore could marvel at 'One of the most remarkable enterprises in Asia, if not in the world ... where rubber shoes in vast quantities, and now even motor tyres, are being manufactured under Chinese management and with Chinese labour'.[49] Tan's factory could, for example, make 6,000 bicycle tyres a day. Tan Kah Kee & Co., owned entirely by Tan, also manufactured sweets, medicines, felt hats, bricks, tiles, soap and biscuits – the last catering for a range from 'the most discriminating buyers to the coolie class'.[50] Furthermore, there was an engineering works, a tannery and a printing works which produced labels and advertising material. Tan also owned the Chinese language newspaper, *Nanyang Siang Pau*, which he had started in 1923. His chain of factories producing manufactured goods covered some ten acres, and was said to represent a capital investment of over $8 million.

By far the most important of Tan's industrial activities was the manufacture of canvas shoes with rubber soles, which he had taken up seriously in 1923. The shoes were mass produced in a modern plant with a capacity of 20,000 pairs a day – some 7 million pairs a year. The production of shoes occupied 75% of the floor space in the main factory complex. The 80 branches of Tan's firm throughout Southeast Asia and in China and India indicate the extent to which export markets for shoes had been developed. Moreover, considerable market penetration is reflected in a comment reportedly made by a south Fukien rice grower: 'We farmers must thank Mr. Tan Kah Kee for supplying us with rubber shoes which are cheap and suitable for rainy weather'.[51] Tan has been called the 'Henry Ford of Malaya', but this is to mistake his role: it was not innovation in the sense of developing new production processes, but implantation of well-established ones in an industrially underdeveloped area.

The 1930s slump sealed the fate of Tan's empire.[52] It caught him heavily over-extended financially and drastically reduced rubber and pineapple profits as a source of liquidity. Simultaneously, there was a fall in demand for manufactured goods, the erection of tariff barriers, and, above all,

---

[49] *Ormsby Gore visit, 1928*, pp.13, 145.

[50] *Manufacturers' exhibition*, p.71. The sources used for the discussion of Tan's industrial activities are ibid. pp.68–69, 71; *SSTC 1933–34* I, p.145, II, pp.301, 306, IV, pp.124–25; 'Rubber manufactures', pp.62, 99; *Straits Times, Singapore Manufacturers' Exhibition Supplement*, 2–9 Jan. 1932; *Directory 1921*, pp.242–43, *1922*, pp.284n–284o, *1931*, p.147.

[51] Chen, *Emigrant communities*, p.103.

[52] The following is based on 'Closure of factories of Tan Kah Kee & Co. Ltd., in Singapore', *MRCA* 42 (Feb. 1934), pp.19–20 and 43 (March 1934), pp.16–17; 'Tan Kah Kee's affairs', *MRCA* 44 (April 1934), pp.56–57; 'Cheng Kung Po and Tan Kah Kee', *MRCA* 50 (Oct. 1934), pp.16–19; *SSTC 1933–34* I, p.145, 147–50, 156, 161–62, II, pp.301–13, IV, pp.124–27, V, p.9; PRO CO 273/583/92101 Cunliffe-Lister to Clementi, 2 Jan. 1933.

currency depreciation which greatly favoured Tan's foreign competitors. Manufacturers in both Hong Kong and Japan were now able to sell rubber shoes in Singapore for less than it cost Tan to produce them. They could do this because both the Japanese and Hong Kong currencies depreciated sharply against the Straits dollar (which for Tan had the great disadvantage of being linked to sterling); and because in neither country was currency depreciation offset by an increase in labour and overhead costs, which together accounted for nearly half of the total manufacturing costs of rubber shoes. Although there had never been much advantage for Tan in the fact that the raw material – rubber – was available in British Malaya, he had hitherto been able to keep his wage costs competitive because two-thirds of his factory employees were women.

British Malaya took no more than about a quarter of the output of Tan's shoe factory. In the Asian markets outside British Malaya on which Tan depended, notably China and Netherlands India, he faced the same Japanese and Hong Kong competition as was able to undersell him in Singapore. Furthermore, in most of these countries tariffs were raised, greatly restricting foreign imports. Tan tried to turn to British Empire markets and must have hoped to benefit from Imperial Preference. It was, however, of limited value because India, Australia and South Africa granted no preference to rubber manufactures from Singapore, and preference in Canada was partly offset by an exchange dumping duty levied on goods imported from the Straits Settlements. But the United Kingdom gave preference to rubber shoes from Singapore, and exports to Britain rose from 49,000 pairs in 1932 to just over 1 million in 1933. That increase was, however, insufficient to compensate for Tan's loss of sales in other markets. His factory had to produce 1·3 million pairs of shoes a year before any profit could be made. In the slump of the 1930s it became impossible to push enough shoes onto the world market, already glutted with cheap footwear, for Tan to stay in business.

In 1931 the British banks, departing from their practice of lending short term and not financing industrial undertakings, had given Tan massive financial assistance. Although perhaps reassured by the possibilities of his empire as collateral, either as a going concern or in liquidation, they must also, possibly under colonial government pressure, have intended to support Singapore's local Chinese banks. Those banks were in deep trouble because of loans extended to Tan and because of the fall of the Hong Kong against the Straits dollar. Tan's company was converted into a limited liability one, in which he held 95% of the shares and his brother the remainder; debentures were issued to the British banks as security. The management of the company was reorganized, and a committee of bank representatives set up to determine its financial policy. On 31 July 1931 the first English balance sheet of the company showed liabilities of almost \$11 million, \$10 million of which were mortgages and bank overdrafts. The principal assets of land, buildings, factories and estates were valued at nearly \$4 million and plant and machinery at \$3 million. Stock in trade amounted to \$4·7 million. Virtually from the outset Tan Kah Kee & Co. was unable to meet the 3% interest on the \$7·5 million overdraft that the British banks had extended. The balance sheet on 31 March 1931 showed a debit on profit and loss account of \$1·3 million, but by 30 June 1933 this had increased to \$3·1 million. In early 1934 the company went into voluntary liquidation.

The value of Tan's land, buildings, plant and machinery of \$7 million (over £800,000) shows how large his enterprise was in comparison to most European businesses in British Malaya: the capitalization of the bulk of sterling rubber companies was about £100,000 to £200,000.[53] The strong impression one gains of Tan's enterprise is that it was remarkable for a high ratio of debt to equity capital. During the 1920s high borrowing allowed Tan rapidly to expand his manufacturing activities. It also permitted him personally to dispense substantial philanthropy, notably in China, distinguishing only casually, if at all, between business profits and loans in his dispensation.[54] Tan's success as an entrepreneur depended above all on being able to raise finance through an ability to create confidence, engendered by his leading role in the rubber-pineapple complex. It was not until 1931 that, as a Chinese banker recalled, 'The local banks found that collectively, they had lent him too much'.[55]

It is of more than passing interest – and significant for Singapore's post-World War II history – that Tan himself was not ruined. Insofar as his rubber and pineapple assets in liquidation were acquired by his son-in-law, Lee Kong Chian, they stayed in the family, while in the later 1930s Tan, freed from business worries and possessing a known record of philanthropy, became undisputed leader of the Nanyang Chinese. Long an advocate of communism, Tan was excluded from Singapore in 1950 by the British colonial authorities and settled in Fukien, where he was made an official of the Chinese Communist Party.[56]

Not all rubber entrepreneurs moved into manufacturing, but, like Tan, those who did showed a similar tendency to diversify, although they were more conservative in their choice of investments, looking to import-

---

[53] Bauer, *Rubber*, pp.9–10.
[54] Cf. Tan Kah Kee, *My autobiography* (text in Chinese) (Singapore, 1946), pp.17–18; Oral History, *Pioneers*, interview with Tan Ee Leong, A000003/21, p.163.
[55] Yap, *Scholar, banker*, p.31.
[56] 'Depression and the southseas Chinese', *MRCA* 32 (April 1933), pp.60–61; Yong, 'Emergence of Chinese community leaders', pp.5–6; Yong, 'Singapore Chinese leadership', p.205; Turnbull, *History of Singapore*, p.245.

substituting and processing industries. The former were aimed largely at the British Malayan market and usually derived considerable natural protection from the high transport cost of imports. Thus, Tan Ean Kiam established biscuit and sawmill as well as insurance and realty companies; all became 'well-known institutions in Singapore'.[57]

The collapse of Tan Kah Kee must have affected the subsequent course of Singapore Chinese investments. As Tan's protégé, Lee Kong Chian was probably considerably influenced by his business failure. It almost certainly strengthened Lee's conclusion that 'I do not consider Singapore suitable for manufacture of finished goods except certain classes of semi-finished articles such as sawing-timber, rubber-milling and pineapple-canning and some other products for local use'.[58] Exemplifying this strategy, Lee went on to found Lee Sawmills, Lee Biscuits, Lee Printing and Lee Produce Company.[59]

The rubber industry also provided early opportunities for other entrepreneurs who subsequently developed large manufacturing interests. Among the most prominent was Lee Kim Soo. He began business in Singapore in 1914 as an estate supply merchant and general commission agent. After the War he turned to manufacturing, and in 1922 opened a match factory in Singapore. By the 1930s Lee operated several factories on the island. These included a concrete works, tyre works, a nail factory and potteries which produced earthenware, agricultural pipes and latex cups. Lee also made steel and rattan furniture. From his head office in High Street he conducted a merchant business, and, as a sideline to concrete goods and building materials, entered house and property construction. Lee's factories employed a total labour force of about 1,000.[60]

Chinese industrial expansion was certainly financed in part through profit plough-back. Since many of the Chinese industrial entrepreneurs at the very early stages of their careers had interests in the rubber-pineapple complex, it is likely that this provided a proportion of the profits reinvested. But Chinese entrepreneurs like those described expanded their industrial conglomerates too fast to be consistent with a reliance on retained profits alone. Like Tan Kah Kee, most must also have borrowed to finance industrial expansion. The problem of the emergent business man anywhere is to become creditworthy; as the Singapore saying had it, 'In Chinese business, if you can win people's trust and amass your first $10,000

[57] Sim, *Biographies*, p.75.   [58] *SSTC 1933–34* IV, p.233.
[59] Sim, *Biographies*, p.5; Wilson, *Solid as a rock*, p.40; *Straits Times directory of Singapore and Malaya 1949* (Singapore, 1949), p.59.
[60] *SSTC 1933–34* I, pp.145, 68, II, pp.729–34, IV, p.225, V, pp.40–43; *Manufacturers' exhibition*, pp.95, 97; Cresson, 'Industrial Singapore', pp.60, 102; *Directory 1931*, p.82, *1934*, p.379, *1939*, pp.461–62, *1949*, p.59.

[£1,167], you should be on the road to prosperity'.[61] The rubber-pineapple complex, by providing Singapore's entrepreneurs with profits, gave them a credit rating which allowed rapid expansion. Chinese industrialists could have borrowed from friends or moneylenders. But in regard to the latter, Chettiar loans, for example, were at interest rates of 24% to 36% and few prospective industrial investments could have appeared profitable at these levels. Industrialists are much more likely to have turned mainly to local Chinese banks, discussed below.

That Singapore Chinese did not embark on even more manufacturing projects reflected above all the restricted scope for investment in import-substituting industry and a realistic assessment of cost constraints, especially wage levels, in manufacturing for export. In inter-war Singapore these considerations, as well as the concentration of profits in European rather than Chinese hands, meant that the frontiers of industrialization could not be pushed too far. After 1929 world economic conditions pulled these frontiers back towards earlier stages of an industrialization process.

III

The development of Chinese deposit banking relates mainly to three, predominantly Hokkien banks: the Chinese Commercial Bank (1912), the Ho Hong Bank (1917) and the Oversea-Chinese Bank (1919). In 1932 they amalgamated to form Singapore's dominant Chinese bank, the Oversea-Chinese Banking Corporation (OCBC). At the end of the 1930s it was the largest Chinese-owned bank outside China with nearly three-quarters of the assets of all Chinese banks incorporated in the Straits Settlements and 18 branches throughout Southeast Asia and in China.[62]

The assets of Singapore's Chinese banks were no doubt small compared to those of the European banks. Furthermore, the ability of Chinese banks to lend was seriously constrained by the ever-present danger of severe contractions in the money supply caused by sharp falls in rubber prices, as noted in chapter 3. At such times of liquidity crisis, the Chinese banks were highly exposed to risk due to the absence of either a central bank in Singapore to act as a lender of last resort or access to an external wholesale credit market, except possibly through the city's European banks.

Nevertheless, the development of Chinese banking was of fundamental importance to Singapore's economic development, since so few Chinese used the European banks. In 1896 less than 50 Chinese traders had European bank accounts; although a decade later the number had risen,

[61] Yap, *Scholar, banker*, p.38.
[62] *Directory 1939*, p.492; Brock K. Short, 'Indigenous banking in an early period of development: the Straits Settlements, 1914–1940', *MER* 16, 1 (1971), p.71; Chen, 'Chinese overseas', *Chinese Year Book 1936–37*, p.220.

the banks were 'not intimately in touch with the Chinese traders themselves, or with their methods of doing business'.[63] Even in the inter-war period 'the European banks had an air about them which intimidated many local people [and] ... would not accept small accounts'.[64] Because the Chinese banks could overcome these difficulties by transacting business on a close personal basis and in dialect, they promoted Singapore's economic development by providing a more efficient means of mobilizing Chinese savings for productive investment and integrating credit and capital markets.

It was the establishment of the Chinese Commercial Bank which 'did much to popularize the current account system among the Chinese merchants and shopkeepers'.[65] In adopting limited liability trading, this bank made another major contribution to financial modernization, as, for the same reason, did the Ho Hong Bank and the Eastern United Assurance Corporation. This last was begun in 1913 and operated in close association with the two banks. The three companies, with paid-up capitals totalling $5 million 'marked a new era in the commercial life of the Singapore Chinese'.[66] The Oversea-Chinese Bank also worked in conjunction with an insurance company, the Overseas Assurance Corporation, founded in 1920, a year after the bank. Overseas Assurance and Eastern United Assurance were Singapore's main Chinese insurance companies and dealt in fire, marine, workmen's compensation and motor car insurance. Evidence from the chairman of the OCBC suggested that by 1934 Chinese merchants, insurance companies and estates made widespread use of Chinese banking facilities and all, especially estates, kept large sums on current account, on which generous interest was paid.[67] In the later 1930s the OCBC went a step further in the institutional mobilization of Chinese savings when it set up a savings branch to cater for 'the working people'.[68]

Evidence of the part played by the Straits Settlements Chinese banks in financial development is the strong long-run increase in their estimated liabilities (effectively deposit liabilities), which rose from $3·3 million in 1914 to an annual average of $40·4 million in 1925/27 and $55·5 million by 1937/39. Chinese banks appear frequently to have made unsecured (or minimally secured) loans, often in the form of overdrafts and without any very specific time limit. It seems probable that at least part of such loans financed investment by Chinese entrepreneurs in manufacturing industry

[63] Song, *One hundred years' history*, p.383. Song was quoting J. M. Allinson.
[64] Yap, *Scholar, banker*, p.36, and see pp.28, 37–38.   [65] Tan, 'Chinese banks', p.460.
[66] Song, *One hundred years' history*, p.474. The history of Chinese insurance companies may be traced in ibid. pp.493–94, 152, 322–23, 446; W. Allan Eley, 'Insurance', *Singapore: handbook*, pp.70–71; *Directory 1916* pp.101–2, *1921*, pp.129, 131, *1931*, pp.29–30, 44, 66–67, 110–11, *1939*, pp.299–300, 383, 422, 492, 534.
[67] *SSTC 1933–34* III, p.416, IV, pp.412, 414.   [68] Wilson, *Solid as a rock*, p.49.

and estate development as well as trade. The incentive to use Chinese bank loans for industrial investment was that even when Chinese entrepreneurs could borrow from European banks, the credit extended was in the form of short-term, self-liquidating loans against stocks in progress, while money-lenders offered at best a costly source of finance, and one which was insecure in the long term.

The scope for Chinese bank intermediation to promote economic development was less in Singapore than would have been true in a more modern economy. In addition to the considerable risk exposure of Chinese banks, at the times when this was greatest the liquidity demands of banks' depositors were likely to be especially volatile. Between June 1920 and January 1921 total deposits in Singapore's five local Chinese banks fell by a third; similar contraction occurred in the six months from December 1931. These considerations probably encouraged Chinese bankers towards a conservative reserve ratio policy. As a rule, Chinese banks kept 50% of their current account money liquid, and maintained large reserves as currency and deposits with the British banks. In the inter-war period the two sets of banks remained complementary because of this deposit-reserve practice and the fact that the Chinese banks developed a constituency which their British counterparts were largely unable to reach. This relationship did not fully give way to a competitive one until after Singapore's independence.[69]

Rubber and the industrial conglomerates were fundamental to the development of Chinese banking, which depended on successful Chinese businessmen as founders and organizers.[70] The first Chinese bank, the Kwong Yik Bank (1903), had a large gambier planter as its principal promoter and managing director; the second, the Sze Hai Tong Bank (1906), had a produce merchant as its leading shareholder. But the Kwong Yik Bank failed in 1913, while the Sze Hai Tong Bank never became very significant. Two other, comparatively unimportant, banks were the Ban Hin Lee Bank (effectively 1918), closely connected with Chop Ban Hin Lee and its rice trade, and the Lee Wah Bank which specialized in remittance

---

[69] *SSTC 1933–34* III, pp.415–17, IV, p.414. The reference to half of current account money kept liquid is in III, p.416. For analysis of the balance sheets of Chinese banks and high proportion of liquid assets, either cash or deposits with other banks, to deposit liabilities, see Short, 'Indigenous banking', pp.59–63, 71–74. See also Tan, 'Chinese banks', pp.459–61; Yap, *Scholar, banker*, pp.37–38.

[70] Sources for the following discussion are Tan, 'Chinese banks', pp.458–69; Sim, *Biographies*, pp.34, 75; Tan, 'Lee Kong Chian', pp.9–10; Yap, *Scholar, banker*, pp.26–39; *Directory 1931*, pp.29–30, 66–67, 111, *1939*, pp.492–93; Allen and Donnithorne, *Western enterprise*, p.206; Lee, *Monetary and banking development* (1974), p.75; S. Y. Lee, 'The development of commercial banking in Singapore and the states of Malaya', *MER* 11, 1 (1966), pp.87, 88, 90; K. G. Tregonning, 'Tan Cheng Lock: a Malayan nationalist', *JSEAS* 10, 1 (1979), pp.25, 43, 46.

business. Given the need for mercantile sponsorship, a major drawback of all these banks was that their promoters had a base in either a declining or a small sector of the economy. By 1910 this limitation could be overcome only by sponsors associated with the rubber-pineapple complex and the Chinese industrial conglomerate.

The essence of deposit banking is confidence. Above all, what the participation of entrepreneurs in the rubber-pineapple complex and, to a lesser extent, manufacturing industry did for banking development was to give the Hokkien banks a status which instilled that confidence in a wider Chinese public and allowed it to feel safe in lending its money to the banks. To be sure, deposits from the banks' sponsors and directors may often have been substantial. But this could have served only to increase the banks' reputation and therefore public confidence. It was the latter which during the inter-war years transformed Singapore's Chinese banks into something much more than financial syndicates with a restricted membership – a sort of super chit fund extension of the so-called millionaires' club, the Ee Ho Hean, frequented by the city's Chinese business elite and effectively run by its rubber magnates. The success of the Hokkien banks in spreading the banking habit by attracting a broadly-based clientele allowed the chairman of the OCBC to observe in 1933 that 'Most of our customers are Chinese merchants who have only of recent years learnt to make use of banking facilities'.[71]

The evidence of the personal links between those involved in the rubber-pineapple complex and Chinese industrial conglomerates and the successful development of local deposit banking is strong. However, in tracing these links, one major omission from the entrepreneurs already discussed was Tan Kah Kee, whose involvement with banks was as a borrower. Another key figure, who had little direct involvement with rubber, was Lim Peng Siang of the Ho Hong conglomerate. 'Having early realized the close relationship between banking and shipping with trade', he was a prime mover in organizing the Chinese Commercial Bank and the Ho Hong Bank.[72]

But both banks depended heavily on rubber. Lim Nee Soon was vice-chairman of the Chinese Commercial Bank, and Lee Kong Chian served on its board of directors and later as vice-chairman. Both, as already noted, were rubber magnates. The first chairman of the bank's board of directors and one of its founders, Lee Choon Guan, had large rubber interests. So did another founder, Tan Chay Yan, who was a pioneer planter. Another man in the rubber business, See Boh Ih, was a director and managing director of the Chinese Commercial Bank.

---

[71] *SSTC 1933–34* IV, p.414, and see III, p.416.   [72] Tan, 'Chinese banks', pp.460–61.

The Ho Hong Bank was largely an offshoot of the Ho Hong conglomerate. Like the Chinese Commercial Bank, however, it was supported by Lee Choon Guan. Important rubber estate owners closely involved with the bank included Tan Cheng Lock, Chee Swee Cheng and Lee Choon Seng. Tan and Chee were among its first directors, while they and Lee were later associated with the OCBC.

Rubber also played a conspicuous role in the founding of the Oversea-Chinese Bank. Its founders included two rubber magnates, Lim Nee Soon and Tan Ean Kiam. Lim became the bank's second chairman – when also vice-chairman of the Chinese Commercial Bank – while at the beginning of the 1930s Tan, by then 'almost the idol of the Hokkien community'[73] served as the Oversea-Chinese Bank's managing director.

In the 1930s slump all three Hokkien banks encountered financial difficulty which led to the merger forming the OCBC in 1932. One of the four architects of merger, Yap Twee, managing director of the Chinese Commercial Bank and proprietor of a successful hardware business, was an ally of Tan Kah Kee; the other three had extensive rubber interests. They were Chee Swee Cheng, owner of rubber estates including 5,000 acres in Borneo and founder of the Atlas Ice Company, who was the OCBC's first chairman; Tan Ean Kiam, who emerged as sole managing director soon after the bank's formation; and Lee Kong Chian, who became the OCBC's second chairman in 1938. At that time Lee Choon Seng was elected vice-chairman of the bank. Thus, in 1939 rubber entrepreneurs filled the bank's top three positions. Another Chinese bank, the United Chinese Bank (formed in 1935) had as its two chief architects former senior officers in the Oversea-Chinese Bank and Ho Hong Bank. But like other banks, the United Chinese Bank depended on the backing of prominent merchants.

Along with that backing, the other main requirement for the establishment of Chinese banks in Singapore was a body of men more highly educated than most Chinese entrepreneurs of the period and able to work in English, to see to the administrative and legal side of banking and to serve as a bridge to the European banks and colonial administration. Such skills were not, however, easy to find.[74] The Straits Settlements government never had any real interest in promoting higher education in Singapore – a medical college was begun, in 1905, but no university; Raffles College, the forerunner of the post-World War II University of Malaya, opened only in 1928. The Chinese business elite concentrated on furthering education in Chinese, often in China. In the inter-war years Tan Kah Kee was the founder and financier of Amoy University and Chip Bee schools

---

[73] Yap, *Scholar, banker*, p.34.
[74] Tan, 'Chinese banks', pp.462, 465; Yap, *Scholar, banker*, p.35.

and college in Fukien, while Tan Lark Sye was instrumental in the foundation in 1956 of the Chinese-language Nanyang University in Singapore.

Nor was there any great demand for Chinese with a high standard of English education. In British Malaya the colour bar restricted Chinese to the bottom rungs of the civil service. The preference of Tan Kah Kee and Tan Lark Sye for Chinese education was in keeping with the attitude of most Singapore Chinese businessmen. Among them – traditionalists of a kind who dressed in the standard black, baggy trousers and saw in these the virtue of reversibility when one side began to wear out – there was a generally scornful attitude towards a nascent English-educated Chinese middle class of businessmen who, when seen going to lunch in their Western-style business suits, were disparagingly referred to as 'clerks'.[75]

In these circumstances, Chinese banking was a developmental feature of some importance in Singapore, not just as an institutional evolution but in its encouragement of an English-educated Chinese professional and administrative class. Chinese banks became an important source of business employment for secondary and university graduates educated in English, in which all accounts were kept. The banks appear in several instances to have obtained legal services from Chinese law firms or law firms with Chinese partners, like Aitken & Ong Siang and Chan & Eber.[76] In the longer term the remunerative job opportunities which Chinese banking helped to create for those able to acquire a good education in English must have made such education appear attractive for young Singapore Chinese.

It was, of course, a body of English-educated Chinese professionals, more than Chinese entrepreneurs like those described in this chapter, who inherited modern Singapore. Among such men, Lee Kuan Yew, a Cambridge-educated lawyer, and Goh Keng Swee, an LSE Ph.D. in economics, were the supreme examples, but subsequently their places were taken by Lee Hsien Loong, educated at Cambridge and Harvard, and Goh Chok Tong, trained in Singapore in English and then at Williams College in the United States. This group, which did not look to China, was instrumental in the decision to pursue economic development through bringing Western multinationals to Singapore and in providing these corporations with local employees, services and political stability. In independent Singapore, education in English, reflecting a combination of government decisions and individual preference due to higher expected remuneration, became well-established.

[75] Tan Ee Leong, 7 Aug. 1972, interview with the author. Other interviews with the author confirmed this sharp division: Tan Yeok Seong, 13 Aug. 1972; Yeo Tiam Siew, 8 Sept. 1972.   [76] Yap, *Scholar, banker*, pp.32, 36.

8 Petroleum and tin: the twentieth-century boom commodity and a staple in decline

To enjoy one mineral boom in little more than half a century – as Singapore did with tin – might be described as fortunate; to benefit from two – as happened from World War I onwards when the region around Singapore became a large petroleum producer – can only be described as uncommonly lucky. The growth of the port's petroleum trade was spectacular, and in the mid-1930s caused a traveller returning after 25 years to think 'the numerous islands with which the entrance to Singapore is studded ... an indication of the new Singapore. Where formerly all had been greenness were now great patches of hard yellow soil disfigured by huge oil tanks'.[1] Yet prior to World War II petroleum created few major linkages, while some important linkages associated with tin production weakened. The two commodities contrasted with rubber's strong linkage effects, and serve as a reminder that staples may differ greatly in their spread effects over time.

During the inter-war period petroleum in many ways remained an enclave industry. Physically it did not enter Singapore except for the island's own use, and since the product was not owned by Singapore residents, there was no petroleum market in Singapore. Petroleum imports and exports relied on a new set of entrepreneurs, the international oil companies, which did not need the assistance of Singapore firms as managers or to raise capital. The oil companies controlling the industry at Singapore used it as a place where, on the islands near the western entrance to the harbour (figure 4.1), petroleum produced in Netherlands India and British Borneo could be collected, blended and distributed. In contrast to Singapore's importance as a merchant and financier in other commerce, for petroleum its principal trade functions were handling, storage and shipment, with consequent low value added and limited employment. Petroleum exercised its greatest effect on economic development through volume, and the commodity's chief linkage was a large demand for ship repair facilities.

---

[1] Lockhart, *Return to Malaya*, p.77.

Like petroleum, the hinterland production of tin increasingly depended on direct foreign investment which was not mediated through Singapore. Furthermore, the tin smelting industry – once a local enterprise – was increasingly owned by capitalists living abroad. As with petroleum, tin smelting provided little opportunity for learning by, and technology transfer to, Singaporeans. Nevertheless, the marketing of tin remained a local activity, and one of international significance. More important for Singapore, tin mining, like the extraction of petroleum, had a key linkage for the city's engineering industry.[2]

The present chapter first discusses Singapore's trade in petroleum. A second section deals with the provision of dry dock facilities associated with trade in petroleum. The chapter's last section traces the changing relationship between Singapore and hinterland tin production.

I

The petroleum trade consisted of three main products, namely kerosene, liquid fuel (fuel oil) and motor spirit (petrol, gasoline). Other minor petroleum products such as lubricants are not considered here, nor included in the statistics presented.[3] At the beginning of the century the main constituent of the petroleum trade was kerosene (table 8.1), used primarily as an illuminant by the poorer sections of the population. After World War I, despite the spread of electric lighting,[4] Singapore's kerosene exports increased rapidly as trade extended to more markets. But the phenomenal expansion in petroleum exports during the inter-war period resulted almost entirely from the new products of liquid fuel and motor spirit. Liquid fuel was required chiefly for the bunkering of oil-fired ships and to a lesser extent to run industrial machinery, while motor spirit was needed for automobiles. In 1911/13 imports of liquid fuel averaged 36,000 tons and those of motor spirit were negligible; by 1937/39 Singapore imported an annual average of 602,000 tons of liquid fuel and 411,000 tons of motor spirit. Exports were considerably less than this, however, because much of the liquid fuel was sold to ships in Singapore as oil bunkers.

The story of Singapore's petroleum trade was – and remained – the use which multinational oil companies found for the port in their world-wide operations.[5] Apart from some kerosene imported from the west coast of

---

[2] For discussion of the employment and linkage effects of natural resource-based industries, see Michael Roemer, 'Resource-based industrialization in the developing countries', *Journal of Development Economics* 6 (1979), pp.185–88.

[3] *SSTC 1933–34* I, p.189, III, pp.304, 305, V, p.105.

[4] Ibid. IV, p.384, III, p.304; 'The petroleum industry', *Singapore: handbook*, p.64.

[5] Detailed information in the following account is taken from *SSTC 1933–34* I, p.189, III, pp.295–300, IV, pp.376, 381, V, p.100; 'The mineral oil trade' in Makepeace, et al., eds. *One hundred years* II, pp.97–100; Royal Dutch Petroleum Company, *Diamond jubilee*

Table 8.1 *Singapore petroleum imports, 1900/02–1937/39 (annual averages)*

	Total	Kerosene	Liquid fuel	Motor spirit
	tons	%	%	%
1900/02	59,700	65.0	35.0	n.l.
1911/13	50,082	26.6	71.7	1.7
1925/27	657,624	13.8	51.6	34.6
1937/39	1,139,042	11.0	52.9	36.1

Notes:
1   Import values would give a different picture but are not shown because volume was the important aspect of the petroleum trade. In 1937/39, the value of petroleum imports was:

	$000	%
Kerosene	12,565	17.8
Liquid fuel	17,509	24.8
Motor spirit	40,510	57.4
Total	70,584	100.0

2   In the inter-war period a great excess of petroleum imports over exports was largely accounted for by oil bunkers supplied to ships at Singapore. Oil bunkers provided at the wharves are shown by table 4.4, but there was also a large trade in the roads. For 1922 to 1939 oil fuel supplied to steamers engaged in foreign trade at Singapore and Penang is shown in Malaya, *Foreign trade of Malaya* 1933, p.99, *1939*, p.121. In 1929/30 oil bunkers furnished at the two ports reached a peak of 304,165 tons, probably mostly accounted for by Singapore which was the main bunkering station in British Malaya.
3   For 1937/39 imports from British Malaya are excluded but were negligible.
Sources: SS, *Return of imports and exports*, 1900–1927; Malaya, *Foreign trade of Malaya*, 1937–1939.

the United States, petroleum distribution in and via Singapore was by 1939 in the hands of two subsidiaries serving three oil majors: the Asiatic Petroleum Company, established by Royal Dutch Shell, and the Standard-Vacuum Oil Company associated with Standard Oil of New Jersey and Standard Oil of New York. The story began in 1891 when M. Samuel & Co. of London decided to use Singapore to import kerosene in bulk from Russia for distribution in Asia, and engaged the agency house of Syme & Co. to establish and manage a petroleum tank depot – the first of its kind in the East. Since the municipal government refused to allow bulk storage in the town, Syme & Co. established facilities on the island of Pulau Bukum (or Bukom) in Singapore harbour (figure 4.1) to receive and distribute

book, 1890–1950 (The Hague, 1950), pp.15–16, 124, 169–72; Allen and Donnithorne, *Western enterprise*, pp.175–78; Furnivall, *Netherlands India*, p.328; 'Edward Boustead & Company', *BRGA* 13, 4 (1931), pp.171–72; Compton Mackenzie, *Realms of silver: one hundred years of banking in the East* (London, 1954) p.214; Broek, *Netherlands Indies*, pp.32, 44, 101.

petroleum. In 1897 M. Samuel & Co. formed the nucleus for the new Shell Transport and Trading Co. which started up production in Borneo; the Singapore storage depot became part of this enterprise.

One of Shell's principal rivals in the region was the Royal Dutch Company, given a royal charter in 1890 to produce oil in Netherlands India. It also established storage facilities just off Singapore, on the Dutch island of Pulau Samboe. In 1903 the British and Dutch companies set up the Asiatic Petroleum Co. as a joint marketing company in London for distribution in the East, and in 1907 merged to form Royal Dutch Shell. The new organization began two holding companies, the N. V. de Bataafsche Petroleum Maatschappij, for oil exploration and production, and the Anglo-Saxon Petroleum Company for transport. In Singapore the latter company was initially represented jointly by Syme & Co. and Hoogland & Co. (formerly the agents for Royal Dutch), but in 1908 the agency disappeared when the Asiatic Petroleum Co. opened a local office. This became the head office in the East of the Asiatic Petroleum Co. and took control of the Anglo-Saxon Petroleum Co. which managed Royal Dutch Shell's fleet in Eastern waters. Although no longer requiring the services of Singapore agency houses, Royal Dutch Shell drew initially on the pool of management they had created. The first Singapore representative of the Asiatic Petroleum Co. had been a partner in Boustead & Co. and his assistant (and later successor) had been employed by Syme & Co.

Standard Oil of New York (Socony) and Standard Oil of New Jersey were the other great oil companies in the region. In 1898 Socony opened a Singapore office as part of its network throughout the East to distribute kerosene, while in 1912, after several unsuccessful attempts, Standard Oil of New Jersey gained a foothold in the production of oil in Netherlands India through a subsidiary, the Nederlandsche Koloniale Petroleum Mij. (NKPM). The Singapore office of Socony handled distribution for the NKPM and developed another of the small islands in Singapore harbour, Pulau Sebarok, for storage. In 1931, when Standard Oil of New York merged with another American company, the Vacuum Oil Company, which distributed lubricants in Singapore, the firm was named the Socony-Vacuum Corporation. In 1934 it became the Standard-Vacuum Company, following the merger of the NKPM and the branches of the Socony-Vacuum Corporation (later Socony-Mobil and then Mobil) in the Orient, Australasia and South Africa.

Oil companies were drawn to Singapore by its geographical advantages – both local and international – and freedom from regulation. Offshore islands afforded a deep water anchorage adjacent to Singapore harbour, so that use could easily be made of its facilities, while at the same time

Table 8.2 *Petroleum imports to the Straits Settlements, 1925/27 and British Malaya, 1937/39 (annual averages)*

	Total	Netherlands India		Sarawak	Others
		Sumatra %	Borneo %	%	%
	tons				
1925/27	711,055	33.6	40.3	19.6	6.5
1937/39	1,303,043	71.3	7.5	15.3	5.9

Notes:
1   Others were mainly kerosene from the United States in 1925/27 and liquid fuel and motor spirit from Iran in 1937/39.
Sources: SS, *Return of imports and exports*, 1925–1927; Malaya, *Foreign imports and exports 1939.*

allowing safe storage of large quantities of petroleum. Oil was not refined in Singapore, but collected from several refineries in the region and blended.[6] During the inter-war period this location on world and regional shipping routes enabled petroleum companies to keep distribution costs low by using a single store to serve distinct markets with different product mixes.[7] The same was true in Singapore's post-World War II growth as an oil port.

From the outset in Singapore, local and government opinion alike appears to have favoured few if any restrictions or taxes on the oil companies. Certain safety measures were framed for Singapore's own protection,[8] but the government apparently considered that the siting of oil depots on islands separated from Singapore itself provided a margin of safety which obviated their substantive regulation. The Asiatic Petroleum Co. was said to find Singapore a very suitable base 'owing to there being so few restrictions on oil tankers at this Port'.[9]

Table 8.2 shows petroleum imported by the Straits Settlements in 1925/27 and by British Malaya in 1937/39; both sets of statistics indicate fairly accurately the pattern of Singapore's imports, as the port was the only large petroleum depot in British Malaya. The lion's share of petroleum came from Netherlands India, chiefly Sumatra and to a lesser extent Borneo, while Sarawak furnished most of the remainder of imports. The Asiatic Petroleum Co. was responsible for the bulk of the port's imports

[6] *SSTC 1933–34* I, p.189, IV, p.382, V, p.100.
[7] Ibid. III, pp.295–97, IV, pp.377, 381–83.
[8] There were various committees appointed and bills passed to deal with this. See, for example, *SSLCP 1908*, pp.B85–B86; 'Report of the committee to consider what amendments, if any, should be made to the existing rules and by-laws under ordinance no. 109 (petroleum)', *SSLCP 1926*, pp.C69–C73; *SSTC 1933–34* IV, p.383.
[9] *SSTC 1933–34* V, p.125, and cf. IV, p.258.

and received petroleum from all Singapore's main sources of supply. By 1933 the Company's principal storage and distribution centre at Pulau Bukum had 27 tanks of between 1,000 tons and 12,000 tons each and a total capacity of 130,000 tons. It also had large godowns and storage yards for petroleum packed in tins, cases, barrels and drums. Standard-Vacuum Oil was supplied from the main refinery of the NKPM in Palembang, Sumatra but also received some kerosene from the United States.[10]

In the inter-war years the Asiatic Petroleum Co. accounted for most of the international distribution of petroleum from Singapore. It used small, specially constructed coastal tankers in the region, and large tankers for bulk shipments elsewhere.[11] Table 8.3 reflects Singapore's extensive markets for petroleum exports, and shows clearly the importance of bulk shipments to Japan and Australia.

The sale of oil bunkers developed by the Asiatic Petroleum Co. made Singapore a pioneer in their provision and helped to attract the new oil-burning vessels there, promoting a continued role as a main port of call. During World War I the Company had gained experience in the bunkering trade through supplying Allied vessels, and subsequently rapidly expanded its oil installations. By 1921 the port had a 'large oil-bunkering business ... chiefly due to the far-seeing enterprise of the "Shell" Company's directors in providing facilities for the berthage of large ocean-going vessels at Pulau Bukum and Pulau Samboe, and for the supply of fuel oil in bulk from tank lighter to steamers discharging cargo in the roads'. These facilities at Singapore stimulated, as well as being a response to, the adoption of oil-fired ships for world trade, and made the port the largest British station for the storage and sale of oil bunkers in the East.[12]

In 1926 Singapore's convenience for oil-fired ships was further increased when the Asiatic Petroleum Co. began to supply oil bunkers at the wharves. The Company erected storage tanks and a central pumping station at the north end of the wharves on land leased to it by the Singapore Harbour Board (figure 4.1). Pipelines connected the tanks with most of the wharves, allowing the simultaneous transfer of fuel and cargo.[13] In 1921 one-fifth of vessels berthed at the wharves were oil burners; by 1930 the proportion had risen to nearly a half and by 1939/40 to two-thirds. However, the volume of fuel oil supplied at the wharves, having reached 123,400 tons in 1930, then stagnated.[14]

[10] Ibid. IV, pp.376, 381, III, p.295, I, p.189, V, p.99.
[11] Ibid. I, pp.189, 191, III, pp.300–2, II, p.909, IV, pp.381–83.
[12] 'Mineral oil trade', p.100. By contrast, oil bunkering facilities developed later in Australia. See Kevin Burley, *British shipping and Australia, 1920–1939* (London, 1968), p.95.
[13] *SSTC 1933–34* I, p.113, IV, p.61; Trimmer, 'Port of Singapore', p.25.
[14] *SSTC 1933–34* IV, p.68; Singapore Harbour Board, *Report and accounts for the period 1st April 1946 to 30th June 1947* (Singapore, 1947), pp.8, 11.

Table 8.3 *Petroleum exports from the Straits Settlements, 1925/27 and British Malaya, 1937/39 (annual averages)*

	Total tons	Japan %	Australia %	New Zealand %	Malay Peninsula %	Netherlands India %	Siam %	Egypt %	Others %
1925/27	381,137	1.6	25.4	4.1	16.8	12.3	6.1	7.0	26.7
1937/39	702,477	16.1	26.3	5.3	–	6.8	7.2	9.0	29.3

Notes:

1 The figures for 1925/27 exclude inter-port trade. In 1925/27, 24.6% of the volume of Singapore's petroleum exports went to Malaya.

2 Others were mainly 'Other British Possessions' in 1925/27 and British India, Ceylon and South Africa in 1937/39.

3 Figures are not available for 1938 and 1939 for New Zealand for liquid fuel and for Egypt for kerosene. In both instances the trades were negligible.

Sources: SS, *Return of imports and exports, 1925–1927*; Malaya, *Foreign imports and exports 1937*; Malaya, *Foreign trade of Malaya 1939*.

By the 1930s Singapore had lost much of its advantage as an early leader in the provision of oil bunkers: other ports had obtained good bunkering facilities, and the trade in bunkers had become competitive because ships could go further without re-fuelling. In contrast to the experience of Singapore in the 1980s, the port's distribution of petroleum did not make oil bunkers cheap, as might be expected. If anything, prices were higher than in Hong Kong and Colombo.[15]

In 1931 the NKPM shifted most of the international distribution of petroleum which had been undertaken from Pulau Sebarok to the nearby Dutch island of Pulau Bintang. The Company's decision may have been connected with the merger between Standard Oil of New York and the Vacuum Oil Co. that year. The Singapore representative of Socony-Vacuum suggested that the NKPM had moved 'to give them the advantage of eliminating one additional country and customs control'.[16] Apart from packed kerosene sent to Siam on vessels of the British India Steam Navigation Co., after 1931 Pulau Sebarok became almost exclusively a centre for distribution to British Malaya, where Standard-Vacuum Oil maintained several local depots.[17]

The export of petroleum did not give rise to a merchant class in Singapore, nor make it an international petroleum market. The Straits Settlements Trade Commission observed that 'Singapore is not a market for the oil, there are no middleman's or dealer's profits involved and oil is merely distributed from here for the sake of convenience'.[18] The Commission emphasized that this had 'a most misleading effect upon our statistics'[19] because 'Singapore is a distributing rather than a marketing centre'. It drew particular attention to the favourable trade balance with Japan created by petrol sent there, which 'does not represent trade in the sense that exports of rubber or tin to Japan or imports of piece goods from Japan in fact do. Such petrol comes from what is virtually a bonded store'.[20]

The handling and packaging of petroleum required only a limited amount of labour. In 1929 Standard Oil of New York employed as few as 100 workers, almost all Indian, while the Asiatic Petroleum Co. had about 1,000 employees, approximately half Chinese and half Malay.[21] One reason for Asiatic Petroleum's larger workforce was the development of related industry on Pulau Bukum. The Company erected a modern emulsion manufacturing plant on the island to produce Colas, an asphalt substance for surfacing roads, while by the beginning of the 1930s its tin-

---

[15] *SSTC 1933–34* II, p.49, III, pp.298, 303, IV, p.61.   [16] Ibid. III, p.297.
[17] Ibid. III, pp.296–97, 301–2, I, p.189, IV, pp.376–77, 379.   [18] Ibid. I, p.189.
[19] Ibid. I, p.190.   [20] Ibid. I, p.230.
[21] 'Labour department', *SSAR 1929*, p.204.

making factory there manufactured and filled some 2·5 million tins annually.[22]

Singapore had limited control over the operations of the oil companies. Company policy was made outside Singapore and decisions taken without reference to its welfare. The oil companies' senior employees in Singapore were representatives who simply carried out corporate policy.[23] By contrast, the Singapore managers of agency houses enjoyed a much freer hand in management, while Chinese entrepreneurs were their own masters. The NKPM's move to Pulau Bintang showed the lack of influence by those in Singapore over decisions taken by the oil companies. As the Straits Settlements Trade Commission pointed out, 'It might at any future date suit the Asiatic Petroleum Company to distribute direct from the oil fields ... or to establish another depot, as the Nederlandsche Koloniale Petroleum Maatschappij have done'.[24] During the inter-war period, unlike the period after 1959, there was no question of government intervention through tax concessions, infrastructure provision or joint ventures to try to increase the role of oil companies in Singapore or linkages arising from the petroleum trade.

II

The important linkage of dry dock facilities which oil tankers created at Singapore is normally associated with a terminal port, where the longer stay of vessels affords the most economic place to obtain repairs.[25] During the inter-war period this linkage depended very largely on the operations of the Asiatic Petroleum Co. The Standard-Vacuum Oil Co. did not base a fleet of oil tankers on Singapore and kept no marine superintendents there to supervise repairs. Its vessels usually docked at Sourabaya, Java, although a successful tender might bring them to Singapore.[26]

As early as the first decade of the century, oil tankers provided most ship repair work carried out in Singapore. Over the next two decades this linkage strengthened, and in the 1930s oil tankers formed 'the backbone of the repair business'[27] at Singapore, and as such were 'the mainstay of the dock'.[28] The port was not a centre for shipbuilding, and, apart from oil tankers, ocean-going shipping afforded little but minor and chance custom

[22] *Manufacturers' exhibition*, pp.37–38; 'Petroleum industry', p.64.
[23] Cf. *SSTC 1933–34* III, pp.297, 299.   [24] Ibid. I, pp.189–90.
[25] For a similar reason, a terminal port is also the most economic place to change crews. As a result, oil tankers together with local shipping based on Singapore also had linkages in the development of a labour force of seamen in Singapore. This is not discussed for reasons of space.   [26] *SSTC 1933–34* I, p.189, II, pp.295–96, IV, pp.381–82.
[27] Ibid. I, p.116.   [28] Ibid. II, p.909.

for the docks: 'most other steamers pass Singapore in the course of their scheduled voyages to other ports and cannot conveniently stop for lengthy repairs'.[29]

In largely supporting the dry docks, tanker repair contributed to Singapore's economic development in two important respects. One was to add substantially to Singapore's attractiveness as a port. Superior dry dock facilities encouraged Singapore's use by ocean-going shipping, which in transit would not normally stop for repairs, but needed to be sure of their availability. A major port like Singapore had to provide some dry dock facilities, which were also necessary for local shipping.[30] As it happened, because Singapore was a petroleum distribution centre, the Singapore Harbour Board could maintain extensive, modern dry docks.

Second, the dry docks helped Singapore to develop a major engineering industry. The docks were judged 'one of the most modern ship-repairing establishments in the East' by an 'expert and highly critical' witness: 'I do not think there is a place in the world in which you can get work as solid or as sound or as good a job as you can get in Singapore'.[31]

The dry docks employed a substantial but unknown number of workers and, more important, had a significant developmental feature in the growth of a skilled labour force in Singapore. Although initially skilled dock labour was mainly recruited from elsewhere, principally Hong Kong, by 1933 most of the younger men employed as fitters, turners, blacksmiths, electricians, moulders, patternmakers and coppersmiths had served their apprenticeships in Singapore, and about 100 apprentices, mostly Chinese, were being trained.[32]

Among major British ports, Singapore was unusual in that the Harbour Board administered dry dock as well as wharf facilities.[33] This arose because, with the expropriation of the Tanjong Pagar Dock Co. in 1905, the Harbour Board acquired four dry docks (figure 4.1). These comprised two separate dockyards. One was located at the western entrance to the harbour and consisted of the No. 1 Dock and No. 2 Dock, which had extreme lengths of 396 feet 6 inches and 463 feet respectively. These docks had been obtained by the Tanjong Pagar Dock Co., when it took over a rival company in 1899. The other was at the eastern entrance to the harbour, where the Tanjong Pagar Dock Co. had established the Victoria Dock and the Albert Dock, with extreme lengths of 484 feet 9 inches and 496 feet 7 inches respectively. In addition, by 1913 the Harbour Board had constructed in the western yard a fifth dry dock, the King's Dock of 879

[29] Ibid. I, p.116, and see II, pp.784, 909, III, p.284, V, pp.68–69.
[30] Ibid. I, p.125, II, pp.904, 911–13, IV, p.63.   [31] Ibid. I, p.115, and see V, p.71.
[32] Ibid. I, p.119, II, p.908, III, pp.274, 275.   [33] Allen, *Report on major ports*, p.150.

feet, which, because it was required by the Admiralty and built to its specifications, was not commercially viable.[34]

The Singapore Naval Base was established on the north side of the island, about 35 miles by sea from the port (figure 4.1). Here, in 1928 the Admiralty installed a floating dock of 857 feet brought from England, and in 1938 finally completed a large graving dock. These facilities were sometimes available for commercial use. Moreover, by providing established port facilities and a site for shipbuilding and repair industry, they constituted an important legacy for Singapore's post-independence economic development.[35]

After the 1905 expropriation of the Tanjong Pagar Dock Co., the likelihood of a continued demand for oil tanker repair led to the reconstruction and modernization between 1908 and 1910 of the workshops serving the No. 1 and No. 2 Docks in the western dockyard.[36] Reorganization of the western yard took place in conjunction with the construction of the King's Dock. The important new western dockyard was therefore ready just in time to benefit from an increased demand for ship repairs arising from World War I. Furthermore, although upon completion of the King's Dock, the Singapore Harbour Board had planned to close the Victoria and Albert Docks, 'the War broke out and kept them in full employment until about 1930'[37] (compare table 8.4). Initially, this was because of the diversion of ship repairing from Europe, but subsequently because the cost of shipbuilding stayed high, so increasing the number of older ships kept in service by large repair outlays. Dockyard profits from the war-induced boom enabled the Harbour Board to accumulate a substantial surplus, especially in 1920 and 1921, from the reconditioning of German-interned ships, and helped to ensure the Board's financial viability during the inter-war period. It was this surplus which, as mentioned in chapter 4, allowed the Harbour Board between 1915 and 1925 to subsidize losses at the wharves before custom there increased under the impact of rubber.

By the time the demand for ship repair arising from World War I began to subside, the upsurge in the petroleum trade multiplied the number of oil

---

[34] *SSTC 1933–34* I, pp.115–16, II, p.907, IV, pp.62–63, V, pp.3, 122. For full details of the measurements of dry dock accommodation in 1934, see I, p.115.

[35] Ibid. II, p.50, IV, p.259; ISC, *Harbour of Singapore*, p.18; *1931 census*, pp.85, 37; W. David McIntyre, *The rise and fall of the Singapore naval base, 1919–1942* (London, 1979), pp.86, 114, 135.

[36] The following discussion is based on *SSTC 1933–34* I, pp.115–16, 122, 124–27, 149–50, 189, II, pp.50–51, 904–7, 909, III, pp.299–301, IV, pp.62–64, 255–59, V, pp.3, 4, 66–71, 100, 116–17, 122–27; *Harbour Boards' Committee* (1926), pp.6–9, 48, 74, 109, 111–12, 115; Singapore Harbour Board, *Report and accounts for the year ended 30th June 1929* (Singapore, 1929), p.3, *1947*, p.6; Allen, *Report on major ports*, pp.4–5, 9, 87–89.

[37] *SSTC 1933–34* II, p.907.

Table 8.4 Gross tonnage of vessels at Singapore Harbour Board dry docks, 1912/13–1938/39 (annual averages)

From 1920 year ended 30 June	Victoria and Albert Docks	No.1 and No.2 Docks	King's Dock	Gross tonnage of vessels docked
1912/13	1,043,984	650,529	127,897	370,610
1917/18	1,239,761	754,915	1,759,606	579,088
1920/21	1,479,373	982,072	1,459,705	733,043
1925/26	1,232,456	914,329	2,036,390	810,272
1929/30	1,088,786	615,593	1,586,521	863,471
1933/34	599,915	511,663	1,075,037	677,838
1936/37	335,497	405,196	769,034	630,433
1938/39	567,736	550,285	1,148,649	733,595

Notes:
1 The first three columns show the gross tonnage of vessels docked, based on daily tonnage in the docks. This was calculated by taking the gross tonnage of vessel times the number of days it remained in a dock and adding the daily totals together for the year. The fourth column shows the gross tonnage of vessels which came to the docks during the year. For example, in 1929/30 this amounted to 863,471 tons of shipping or 5.2% of the 16,533,000 net registered tons of merchant vessels clearing from Singapore.
2 The King's Dock was opened for use on 26 August 1913.
Sources: SHB, Report and accounts 1929, p.5, 1947, p.9.

tankers based on Singapore. In this, Singapore was fortunate that tankers 'are always expensive in upkeep'[38] and 'require reconstructing after 12 years, and again when 20 to 22 years old'.[39] Although in the early 1920s the Asiatic Petroleum Co. briefly took repair work elsewhere as a protest against high charges in Singapore, it returned when these were reduced. In 1926 a local representative of the Company estimated that it furnished 80% of work at the western dockyard. During 1925/26 the annual average gross tonnage of vessels docked in the western yard was 914,000 tons at No. 1 and No. 2 Docks and 2,036,000 tons at the King's Dock, together over two-thirds of the total at the Harbour Board's dry docks (table 8.4). Until 1930 most oil tankers of the Asiatic Petroleum Co. docked at Singapore. It had a substantial cost advantage in being their terminal port, as well as competitive repair charges. Although when returning to Singapore in ballast tankers could have docked elsewhere, such a practice would have lost revenue by keeping vessels out of service longer than necessary. Tanker repair was most economically done at a terminal port, because it could be carried out at the same time as routine maintenance work and re-crewing, and because use of the terminal port's repair facilities ensured that tankers did not have to go out of their way to obtain repairs. The Asiatic Petroleum Co. stationed all eight of its marine superintendents in Singapore; the need to send superintendents to other ports if repairs had to be supervised further helped to keep the work in Singapore.

In the 1930s slump demand for ship repair contracted sharply, and dry dock gross revenue fell from an annual average of $4·3 million in 1929/30 to $1·8 million by 1933/34. Figures for the gross tonnage of vessels at the dry docks (table 8.4) probably understate the actual fall in demand for repairs, since the Harbour Board, even when not actually working on a ship, often found that the most convenient arrangement was to keep it in the dry docks rather than at the wharf. By 1931, as a temporary measure, the workshops in the eastern yard had been virtually closed, except for docking and painting, and operations centralized in the western yard used by oil tankers. But a substantial proportion of tanker business was also lost, owing partly to less frequent repair of ships and partly to competition from other dockyards.

Competition increased because Hong Kong benefited from the devaluation of its currency against the Straits dollar, and because with a fall in freight rates it became relatively less expensive for tankers to lose custom when going out of their way to dock. By 1933 many Asiatic Petroleum Co. tankers were repaired outside Singapore. The Company had moved two marine superintendents to Hong Kong and one each to Sourabaya and

[38] Ibid. V, p.122.   [39] Ibid. V, p.124.

Batavia. Nevertheless, in 1933 the Asiatic Petroleum Co. still had 32 ships repaired in Singapore. For the rest of the 1930s, business at the dry docks (cf. table 8.4) remained depressed, although recovering considerably in 1938/39 when, probably with increased repair of oil tankers, dry dock gross revenue reached an annual average of $3·2 million.

Singapore was a terminal port for local shipping, but this did not prove so great an advantage in obtaining repair work on these vessels as it did for oil tankers. The Chinese lines based on Singapore were virtually forced to patronize its dry dock and repair facilities, but in the inter-war period this shipping declined. The two European lines which dominated local shipping, the Straits Steamship Company (SSC) and Koninklijke Paket-vaart Mij. (KPM), set up their own dock facilities elsewhere. The SSC could use its Sungei Nyok dockyard near Penang, and took ships there from Singapore for bottom work. In addition, the Company sometimes sent big jobs to Hong Kong. However, SSC vessels based on Singapore usually had their normal overhauls at its dockyards, and the Company's ships trading to Bangkok always docked at the British port. After failing to negotiate reduced charges with the Singapore Harbour Board, the KPM established its own repair shops at Tanjong Priok (Batavia), where, from 1923, it took most work. Even so, in 1925 Singapore repaired a quarter of the KPM's fleet. This amounted to work on 50 ships, since KPM vessels docked for repair twice in a year. The policy of the KPM was to repair ships operating from Singapore at the port if they would otherwise have been out of service for too long. This generated sufficient work for the KPM to maintain a technical staff in Singapore to supervise repairs.[40]

Local shipping did not sustain a significant shipbuilding industry in Singapore, although between 1880 and 1900 Singapore had several small shipbuilding yards, both Chinese and European, which constructed many of the small craft employed in regional trade.[41] Subsequently, however, most of this industry was lost: shipbuilding became increasingly cen-tralized, notably in Hong Kong, with the growing use in regional trade of large launches and small steamers able to come from distant yards. In the inter-war years the development of Sungei Nyok by the SSC for the construction of its 75-tonners made this the centre for shipbuilding in British Malaya.

For the Singapore Harbour Board shipbuilding was 'really a side line

---

[40] Ibid. I, p.122, II, pp.864, 887, 905, 906, III, pp.284–85, IV, p.256, V, pp.68–69, 100, 122–26; *Harbour Boards' Committee* (1926), p.113; Tregonning, *Home port*, pp.81, 87.

[41] The discussion is based on *SSTC 1933–34* I, pp.116–17, 146, II, pp.53, 173, 872–73, 903, 904, III, p.276, IV, pp.255–56, 258, 259, V, pp.121–22; Ritchie, typescript, p.6; *Harbour Boards' Committee* (1926), pp.48, 109, 110, 111, 113–14; *Manufacturers' exhibition*, p.115; Walter Makepeace, 'The port of Singapore' in Makepeace et al., eds. *One hundred years* I, p.579; Tregonning, *Home port*, pp.73, 75, 81–85.

taken up to give work in slack times'.[42] The Board constructed tugs, launches, ferry boats and occasionally a small steamer, but was never equipped for building vessels of any size and had no slipway, the most economical way to build a ship. Of the port's five private slipways, three were owned by the Singapore Slipway and Engineering Company and two by United Engineers. As well as building small ships, these companies actively competed with the Harbour Board for repair work which did not necessitate dry docking. Although for repairs the Harbour Board enjoyed a competitive edge over both companies, in shipbuilding United Engineers had the advantage. It constructed small craft for the Asiatic Petroleum Co.

The post-1970 growth of Singapore as a centre for the construction of oil rigs was based on the development during the inter-war years of dry dock facilities and a skilled labour force. But the establishment of this construction industry could not have been predicted before World War II, because it also depended on the availability of low-cost labour. In comparison to other centres, especially Hong Kong, Singapore labour was expensive in the inter-war period.[43]

III

During the twentieth century tin illustrates how, for a port, a staple may become less influential absolutely as well as relatively. In Singapore, the need for services associated with the late nineteenth-century tin industry diminished after 1900, and few new service demands or linkages arose. There were three reasons for this. The first was the emergence of smelting by reverberatory furnace in Penang where, in 1901, the Straits Trading Company (STC) opened and then rapidly expanded a works, followed in 1907 by a Chinese enterprise which was taken over by British interests to become the Eastern Smelting Company.[44] Most of the ore smelted in Penang – by 1909/10 as much as in Singapore – came from the Malay Peninsula, especially Perak and northern Selangor. In consequence, Singapore's imports of tin-in-ore from Malaya remained near, or fell substantially below, earlier levels (table 8.5).

The second reason was that by the inter-war period Singapore, as table 8.5 also shows, began to receive a large proportion of its tin ore from outside Malaya, especially from Netherlands India. For this extra-Malayan hinterland, the city, as discussed below, provided mainly handling, processing and exporting services, in contrast to the greater range of services required by Malaya. However, in the twentieth century

---

[42] *Harbour Boards' Committee* (1926), p.111.

[43] See, for example, *SSTC 1933–34* I, p.119.

[44] Wong, *Malayan tin industry*, p.229; Louis, *Metallurgy*, pp.117, 118.

Table 8.5 *Singapore estimated imports of tin-in-ore, 1901/02–1939 (annual averages)*

	Malaya		Netherlands India		Indo-China		Others		Total	
	tons	%	tons	%	tons	%	tons	%	tons	%
1901/02	23,730	92.8	1,747	6.8	n.a		88	0.4	25,565	100.0
1909/10	18,162	77.5	3,072	13.1			2,211	9.4	23,445	100.0
1912/13	20,574	73.4	2,685	9.6			4,772	17.0	28,031	100.0
1916/17	21,183	68.3	5,505	17.8			4,320	13.9	31,008	100.0
1919/20	18,364	71.7	5,768	22.5			1,495	5.8	25,627	100.0
1922/23	8,449	33.2	15,704	61.7			1,283	5.1	25,436	100.0
1928/29	18,951	44.0	22,037	51.2	580	1.3	1,487	3.5	43,054	100.0
1931/32	11,292	44.6	11,565	45.7	1,266	5.0	1,191	4.7	25,312	100.0
1935/36	29,225	89.2	41	0.1	2,018	6.2	1,472	4.5	32,755	100.0
1939	25,844	71.7	8,081	22.4	1,632	4.5	487	1.4	36,044	100.0

Notes:

1 The average tin content of ore imports was assumed to be 75%. The assumption, made by Fermor, resulted in 'reasonably close' agreement between his estimate for Straits Settlements imports of tin-in-ore and exports of tin. (Fermor, *Mining industry*, pp.79–80; see also Yip, *Development of tin mining*, pp.164, 269, 279.)

2 For 1921–27 figures are available for Singapore's imports of tin ore (SS, *Return of imports and exports*, 1921–1927 [quarterly and half-yearly returns]). For 1928–39 imports of tin-in-ore are estimated by assuming these were equivalent to Singapore's exports of tin. This gives a fairly accurate picture of imports with the possible exception of the slump years 1931 and 1932 when substantial stocks of smelted tin were accumulated in Singapore. (SSTC *1933–34* III, p.322, IV, p.388; Fermor, *Mining industry*, p.80.)

3 The trade returns for 1923–27 (quarterly and half-yearly) give Singapore's imports from Malaya (the Malay Peninsula and Straits Settlements), while the remainder of imports are shown only as imports from foreign countries. The sources of these imports were estimated by assuming that all Straits Settlements imports of tin ore (available in SS, *Return of imports and exports* [yearly returns]) from Netherlands India and Indo-China went to Singapore. Imports from these two countries plus those from Malaya were subtracted from total imports to obtain the figure for 'Others'. This is slightly greater than actual Straits Settlements imports of ore from these sources (mainly South Africa), exceeding them by an annual average of 824 tons for the years 1923–27.

4 No figures are available for Singapore's imports by direction for 1921–22 and for 1928–39. Imports for these years are estimated. It was assumed that Singapore took all tin ore which the Straits Settlements or British Malaya imported from Netherlands India, Indo-China and from all other extra-Malayan sources, except Siam and Burma. Imports from the last two countries were assumed to go to Penang. The difference between total imports of tin ore (estimated for 1928–39) and the estimate of Singapore's imports from extra-Malayan sources was taken to represent imports from Malaya. The assumed division of the Straits Settlements extra-Malayan hinterland is very near the actual pattern of imports. A check on the method of estimation for 1922 and 1928–39 by applying it to 1923–27 showed a close approximation to the recorded figures.

5 Others are mainly Australia until 1919/20, South Africa from 1912/13 and Japan in the inter-war period.

6 In 1939 the outbreak of World War II caused Netherlands Indian tin ore again to be smelted in Singapore.

7 Rows may not add to totals due to rounding.

Sources: SS, *Return of imports and exports*, 1921–1927; Fermor, *Mining industry*, pp.79–80; Malaya, *Foreign imports and exports*, 1928–1939; Malaya, *Foreign trade of Malaya*, 1938–1939.

the requirements of the Malayan industry for services in Singapore also decreased with the development of new mining techniques, and these changes constituted the third and most important reason for tin's declining impact on the city.

During the twentieth century the Malayan tin industry entered a second, capital-intensive phase associated with a shift from Chinese to European mining. In 1913, 225,000 men produced 51,000 tons of tin, but by 1937 an output of 75,000 tons required just 88,000 men; over the same period in the FMS mechanical horsepower employed in the industry increased from about 25,800 to 283,700. The introduction of the tin dredge to exploit previously unprofitable or inaccessible deposits was largely responsible for this increase in horsepower and, as dredging was a European monopoly, also for the growth in the European share of production from 26 % in 1913 to 68 % in 1937.[45]

By 1929, because of the tin industry's reduced labour force, the demand it generated for consumer goods had fallen off dramatically. Even if Singapore had been the sole supplier of these goods for miners in its widest possible Malayan hinterland of Selangor, Negri Sembilan and Pahang, this would have amounted to no more than 39,000 men, less than two-fifths of the mining labour force in the three states in the later 1890s.[46] Evidence on the rise in per capita purchasing power does not suggest an increase sufficient to offset the decline in the size of the labour force.[47]

The main requirements of European mining were for capital, both in the sense of finance and of physical equipment, and while the latter created a significant new role for Singapore, the former did not. The establishment of a European industry depended largely on international flows of finance which made little use of either Singapore entrepreneurs or intermediaries. Insofar as the European industry also depended on a core of skilled expatriate mining personnel, these men were recruited directly, particularly in Cornwall, and used Singapore, if at all, only as a port of entry.[48] Moreover, the impact on Singapore of the immigration of unskilled Chinese mining labourers lessened with the growth of the European industry. As well as becoming smaller, the mining labour force progressively became less purely Chinese, with greater employment by the

[45] Lewis Leigh Fermor, *Report upon the mining industry of Malaya* (Kuala Lumpur, 1939), pp.63–67, 74; FMS, *Mines Department report 1925*, p.19, *1937*, p.28, *1939*, pp.36–38.

[46] Fermor, *Mining industry*, p.67.

[47] Figures for wage rates in the late nineteenth century and at the end of the 1930s respectively are given in Wong, *Malayan tin industry*, pp.99–100, 175, 206 and Blythe, *Methods and conditions of employment of Chinese labour*, pp.31–38.

[48] Fermor, *Mining industry*, pp.24–25; Wong, *Malayan tin industry*, pp.145–53, 211–16; Stahl, *Metropolitan organization*, pp.114–17; Allen and Donnithorne, *Western enterprise*, pp.156–58; John Rowe, *Cornwall in the age of industrial revolution* (Liverpool, 1953), p.326.

dredging companies of Indian and Malay workers. During the inter-war period the tin industry also increasingly relied on recruitment in Malaya rather than direct Chinese immigration for its labour force.[49]

Once established, European mining companies required management, agency and secretarial services, but, unlike rubber companies, these were mostly furnished by a new set of specialist firms which found a location near the producing areas a more convenient base than Singapore and never opened offices in the city. Although several of the existing Singapore agency houses became agents and/or secretaries for mining companies, almost all this business was handled through branches in the FMS or Penang; agency services furnished from Singapore were principally for a relatively few mining companies in the minor tin producing states of Pahang, Johore and Trengganu, for which the city was the obvious communications centre.[50]

The other capital requirement, for producer goods, gave rise to a major linkage in Singapore through the demand for engineering equipment and services. The engineering industry, already established in Singapore in connection with shipbuilding and repair, and later estate rubber, was thus further stimulated by changes in hinterland mining. In the production of mining equipment, Singapore benefited from the specialized nature of goods required, from local knowledge and ability to provide service facilities, and from high transport costs of importing machinery. The needs of Malayan tin mining became the basis for a considerable manufacturing industry developed by United Engineers, the principal Singapore engineering firm which expanded to supply and equip mines in Malaya. Activity centred on the company's Singapore works, where there was a large machine and boiler shop, an iron foundry and a modern steel foundry, the only one in British Malaya, which was able to make castings of up to ten tons. By 1932 United Engineers had built 12 important tin dredges in Singapore, as well as redesigning and reconstructing a number of dredges built abroad. It also built gravel pumps and was a large manufacturer of stout-riveted steel pipes used to convey gravel and silt-laden water.[51]

[49] Blythe, *Methods and conditions of employment of Chinese labour*, pp.13, 15, 19, 1–2; Wong, *Malayan tin industry*, pp.219–20, 65–66; FMS, *Mines Department report 1937*, p.26.
[50] *Directory*, various issues, 1922–1939; Allen and Donnithorne, *Western enterprise*, p.157; Stahl, *Metropolitan organization*, pp.115–16; Yip, *Development of tin mining*, pp.181–84; Puthucheary, *Ownership*, pp.89–92; Puey Ungphakorn, 'The economics of tin control' (unpublished Ph.D. thesis, University of London, 1949), pp.197–203; *Sixty years of tin mining: a history of the Pahang Consolidated Company, 1906–1966* (London, 1966), pp.16, 23.
[51] *Singapore Manufacturers' Exhibition*, pp.111–15; United Engineers, *Progress* (n.d.), pp.4–5; SSTC 1933–34 I, p.145; *Singapore: handbook*, pp.69, 94; *Directory 1939*, pp.541–43.

Netherlands Indian mines, mainly on the nearby islands of Banka and Billiton, provided over half of the tin ore Singapore smelted between 1922 and 1932, after which the Dutch government decided to smelt Netherlands Indian ore in the Netherlands. However, even when Netherlands India was Singapore's main source of ore, the mines, because they were under government control, did not demand financial, managerial or administrative services from Singapore, and, furthermore, gave rise to no more than a tiny return flow of imports. Consumer goods for the mines might have been supplied through Singapore if Chinese there had purchased the ore through barter, as they did in the case of Netherlands Indian smallholder rubber and produce; but the STC bought ore for cash from the islands through its local agency, and this allowed Netherlands Indian mines to import the supplies required for their large labour force via merchants in the Dutch colony rather than Singapore.[52] In both 1925 and 1929 Singapore received over $40,000 worth of tin ore from Netherlands India, very largely from Banka and Billiton, but between those dates its exports to the two islands, including goods exchanged for pepper and copra, averaged less than $6,000 yearly.[53]

In the twentieth century tin marketing required no important new services in Singapore, and business concentrated in the hands of the STC and a small number of European exporters, chiefly the established agency houses. The STC was almost the sole Singapore purchaser of tin ore, and through its agents in the mining districts either dealt directly with European mines on a contractual basis or with Chinese mines, usually through the intermediary of a Chinese tin ore dealer. Consistent with a policy of only smelting and not dealing in tin, the STC operated with two objectives in mind. One was to secure a steady supply of ore for its furnaces. The company encouraged this regular flow by adopting a system similar to that found in rubber and tropical produce (see chapter 3), under which it advanced 80% of the price of the tin-in-ore on delivery but allowed the miner or ore dealer to sell at the current price on any of the next 28 days. The STC had to arrange finance for these advances, either from its own funds or through Singapore's British banks, causing the company's chairman to complain that the STC was forced to underwrite the speculation of Malayan Chinese ore dealers on the world tin market.[54]

The STC had as its other objective to shift the risk associated with tin's price fluctuations. This was achieved by selling to European exporters the

[52] *SSTC 1933–34* I, p.154, III, p.329; Tregonning, *Straits tin*, p.39; J. van den Broek, 'The Netherlands Indies as a producer of tin', *Bulletin of the Colonial Institute of Amsterdam* 3, 1 (1939), pp.62–66; Furnivall, *Netherlands India*, p.327; Ungphakorn, thesis, pp.183, 185–86, 199; Cator, *Economic position of the Chinese*, pp.180–81, 192–93, 205.
[53] *SSTC 1933–34* IV, pp.246, 485, 494.   [54] *Straits Budget*, 20 Jan. 1922.

tin content of the ore as soon as it was purchased from miners or dealers, but specifying delivery of the smelted metal in two months. The STC therefore acted, insofar as possible, as a broker, bringing together miners and European exporters. In effect, the Company smelted the exporters' tin on a fixed price basis.

Singapore agency houses which exported tin regularly received telegraph orders from the West specifying either quantity and price, or quantity with price 'at market'. They might fill these orders either from tin already bought on their own account or as an agent on commission. However, large stocks of tin were not usually held in Singapore.[55]

The STC's technologically advanced and capital-intensive Singapore smelting works, which attracted ores not only from Netherlands India but also from Indo-China and elsewhere, helped Singapore to remain a tin smelter of world importance;[56] but the company's very technical efficiency made smelting of much less significance to Singapore itself. In this century the STC took on three main features associated with an enclave industry: low employment, absence of linkages, and drain of profits. First, at the end of 1929 just 367 men were employed at Pulau Brani, and even at the end of 1933, after the Penang works were temporarily closed during the 1930s slump in favour of Singapore, employment increased only to 455 men. The labour force, more or less evenly divided among Chinese, Indian and Malay, was obtained in Singapore. Engineers and managers were recruited in Britain, however,[57] probably minimizing the transfer of skills to local workers.

Second, after the turn of the century, the Pulau Brani works, physically separated from Singapore, did not generate significant new spread effects. Coal and subsequently fuel oil, the main raw materials used to smelt ore,[58] could largely be accommodated by facilities built up for the works in the nineteenth century. The same was true of local shipping, since the need to transport ore to the smelting works did not expand significantly.

Third, the STC made large and regular profits because of its technical efficiency, a fixed profit margin above smelting and handling costs, and the

[55] *SSTC 1933–34* I, p.154, III, pp.322–24, 328, IV, pp.388–89; *Straits Budget*, 27 Dec. 1918, 20 Jan. 1922; Sir Ewen Fergusson, 'Singapore and tin: a unique system of purchasing ore', *Malaya* (March 1955), pp.39, 49; *RC on shipping rings, 1909* IV, pp.1, 4; Tregonning, *Straits tin*, pp.40–43, 76–78; Eastham, 'Rationalisation in the tin industry', pp.15–16.
[56] *SSTC 1933–34* I, p.154, III, pp.324, 328, 329, IV, p.389; Straits Trading Company, *Straits refined tin* (Singapore, 1924); *RC on shipping rings, 1909* IV, p.6; Charles Robequain, *The economic development of French Indo-China* (London, 1944), pp.259, 261. The STC was the largest tin smelting company in the world. W. R. Jones, *Tinfields of the world* (London, 1925), p.30.
[57] 'Labour Department', *SSAR 1929*, p.204, *1933*, p.209; *SSTC 1933–34* III, p.323, IV, p.389; *Straits Times*, 8 Nov. 1937; Tregonning, *Straits tin*, pp.44, 49–50.
[58] *SSTC 1933–34* III, p.324, IV, p.389; *Straits Times*, 9 Nov. 1937.

richness of Malayan ore as well as the high purity of its metal,[59] but only a small proportion of these profits found their way back into the Singapore economy. In this century ownership of the STC was transferred abroad as the original, European shareholders either returned home or died, bequeathing their shares to relatives at home. By 1921 at least 56 % of the shares in the STC were held in Britain, and the majority of the large dividends it paid must have drained abroad.

Non-resident shareholders were unlikely to re-invest in Singapore (and in the absence of a local stock market would have found difficulty in doing so); while the STC itself showed no particular Singapore loyalty apart from modernizing the Pulau Brani works. The company concentrated new investment on its second, Penang, site, until capacity there expanded to rival the Singapore works. In 1927 the STC started to repay share capital, which suggests that it felt there was no opportunity for further profitable investment of shareholders' earnings. By 1930 the STC's paid up capital had been reduced from $9 million to $900,000. In 1937 the company began a policy of using its substantial cash reserves to diversify its holdings. However, in British Malaya the STC diversified no further than into the established European sectors of mining and plantations; while insofar as the company initiated industrial investment, it did so by opening a new smelter at Litherland near Liverpool.[60] The effect was to emphasize the new status of the STC: once a Singaporean enterprise, it was now a multinational owned primarily in Britain but with large production interests in the less developed area of British Malaya.

Throughout the twentieth century petroleum was even more obviously under the control of multinational enterprise than tin smelting. The relationship of Singapore as the 'host country' to multinational enterprises in both the tin and petroleum industries, which took decisions on a global basis, was unusual in the city's pre-World War II development. However, it became common in Singapore's post-1966 economic growth.

[59] *Straits Budget*, 6 Oct. 1916; Louis, *Metallurgy*, pp.128–29; Michael Greenberg, 'Malaya – Britain's dollar arsenal', *Amerasia* 5, 4 (1941), p.147; Ong Theng Hong, 'The Straits Trading Company, 1887–1937' (unpublished B.A. Honours academic exercise, University of Malaya, Singapore, 1958), appx. E for profit and dividend figures.

[60] *Straits Budget*, 20 Jan. 1922; *Straits Times*, 26 Nov. 1934, 8 Nov. 1937, 9 Nov. 1937; Makepeace, 'Machinery of commerce', p.226; Tregonning, *Straits tin*, pp.44, 50–55, 66–67; Tregonning, *Home port*, p.141; Eastham, 'Rationalisation in the tin industry', p.27.

9   The distribution of manufactured imports

So far, the argument of this book has been that Singapore and its hinterland grew as part of the same process of export-led growth, and that specialization in a few export staples shaped Singapore's economic development. For those in the hinterland and port alike, this specialization raised incomes, and so generated demand for imports of food and manufactured goods. Since the region obtained a high proportion of manufactured goods through the port, Singapore's import of manufactures was large, as discussed in chapter 3.

The present chapter examines the mercantile structure in Singapore associated with its distribution of manufactured imports to city and hinterland. Section I considers the organization of Singapore's import and distribution of manufactured goods until World War II. During the inter-war period agency house dominance in this distributive sector was challenged both in the 'new' trade in producer goods and consumer durables, as examined in section II, and in the 'old' trade in textiles and non-durable consumer goods, the subject of section III. As a result, the distribution of imported manufactured goods contributed powerfully to the increasingly cosmopolitan structure of Singapore's mercantile community which post-World War II economic development would continue to require.

I

The sources of Singapore's imports of manufactures and its own mercantile structure were closely related, and will be discussed together. Although statistics for imports from the West (table 9.1) contain some non-manufactured items, the figures approximately correspond to the origin of manufactured imports. Before World War I the sources of manufactured imports and the mercantile structure associated with these goods were straightforward: imports came from the same countries in the West to which Singapore sent primary exports, and the same European merchant

Table 9.1 *Singapore imports from the West, 1900/02–1937/39 (annual averages)*

	Total	United Kingdom	Europe	United States	Canada	Japan
	$000	%	%	%	%	%
1900/02	49,111	55.0	27.0	3.1	0.0	14.9
1911/13	65,382	53.0	24.7	7.4	0.2	14.7
1925/27	184,419	48.5	19.4	16.7	1.3	14.1
1929	172,817	49.3	23.0	14.0	1.1	12.6
1932/34	81,837	46.4	16.1	6.4	1.6	29.5
1937/39	112,238	48.5	20.7	10.6	4.0	16.2

Sources: 'Trade of the Straits Settlements' and 'Foreign trade of Malaya', *SSAR*, 1900–1934; Malaya, *Foreign imports and exports 1937*; Malaya, *Foreign trade of Malaya*, 1938–1939.

houses in the city engaged in both import and export trades.[1] Britain supplied over a half of manufactures and Continental Europe another quarter.

The distribution of imported manufactures was a major interest for all European merchant houses, and too competitive for them to restrict themselves to purchases from their home country. Most of the largest houses were British, but they imported Continental manufactures, while the German house, Behn, Meyer, had a London office. Other houses with strong German connections included Brinkmann & Co., Katz Brothers and Huttenbach Bros. & Co.; the first had its head offices in both Manchester and Bradford under the name of Hitlermann Brothers, while the other two maintained branches in London. Cotton piece goods were the greatest single element in imports from Britain, which supplied Singapore with three-quarters of these goods prior to World War I.[2]

For the distribution of imported manufactures in the so-called bazaar trade, which consisted very largely of non-durable consumer goods, European merchant houses relied almost entirely on a complementary relationship with Chinese dealers in Singapore. In distributing cotton piece goods, merchant houses maintained the close contact with the bazaar necessary through 'one or more Chinese salesman besides a foreign salesman. These men canvass the trade almost daily, visiting the large

[1] The term 'merchant house' refers to a European or Japanese firm distributing a range of manufactured imports. Merchant houses included, but were by no means exclusively, European agency houses, as defined in chapter 6.
[2] *Directory 1911*, pp.135–37, 142–43, 165–66, 169–70; *Trade of the British empire* (1897), p.276.

dealers and the bazaar owners ... and receive orders from samples'.[3] In bazaar trade, the extension of liberal credit was a key factor in the competition among European merchant houses to obtain the custom of Chinese dealers.[4] A few Chinese firms imported direct from the West and held agencies for manufacturers there; but despite some suggestion to the contrary,[5] neither of these activities was of much consequence.

European merchant houses no longer dominated the import trade in the inter-war period to the extent that they had before World War I, due to competition from Japanese and from Singapore Chinese and Indian importers, discussed in section III. But manufactures as a whole still came mainly through European houses. They conducted a general import trade and had London offices or associated firms. All of the most important merchant houses were British; the closure of German firms due to World War I had eliminated the main competition from other European merchants, although to some extent it re-emerged in the inter-war period with the growth of Continental houses. British merchant houses generally took upon themselves the market risk, ordering on their own account and paying cash against documents in London.[6]

An agency system in the form of manufacturers' agencies was a prominent feature of the import trade. The larger merchant houses invariably held a number of manufacturers' agencies, and this was the usual form of representation for the more important proprietary articles. In Singapore, the essential feature of a manufacturer's agency was that a merchant house typically gained the exclusive right or franchise to distribute the manufacturer's products and in return agreed to promote them. There was, in particular, 'a wide representation of important United Kingdom manufacturers by sole agents in Malaya'.[7] For merchant houses the advantages of holding manufacturers' agencies were often consider-

---

[3] Ralph M. Odell, *Cotton goods in the Straits Settlements* (Washington, DC: US Department of Commerce, 1916), p.45, and see p.49.

[4] *Trade of the British empire* (1897), p.277; *Reports on British trade in British West Africa, Straits Settlements, British Guiana and Bermuda* (PP 1913, LXVIII), p.43; Odell, *Cotton goods*, pp.45–46; *SSTC 1933–34* I, p.50.

[5] Chiang, 'Sino-British mercantile relations', p.258.

[6] Sources for this and the following paragraph are *SSTC 1933–34* I, p.50, II, pp.280, 329, 339, 342, 497, 504, III, pp.378, 414; *1921 census*, p.117; L. B. Beale, *A review of the trade of British Malaya in 1928* (London, 1929), pp.10–12, 63; R. Boulter, *Economic conditions in British Malaya to 28th February 1931* (London, 1931), pp.14–16; A. Hartland, *Economic conditions in British Malaya to 20th December 1934* (London, 1935), p.6; *Malayan trade facts*, p.50; Allen and Donnithorne, *Western enterprise*, pp.237–40; Puthucheary, *Ownership*, pp.70–80.

[7] *SSTC 1933–34* I, p.50; see also Boulter, *Economic conditions, 1931*, pp.14–17. However, as a counterpart to exclusive franchises, exclusive dealing arrangements, explicitly preventing a merchant from handling the products of competing manufacturers, appear to have been unusual.

able. Agencies helped to limit competition, and, since product differentiation associated with brand preferences was of great importance in a wide range of goods, probably allowed above normal profits in these lines.

The agency system of exclusive distribution rights for recognized brands had significant anti-competitive effects.[8] It restricted the opportunity for Asian or new European merchant houses to enter the import trade with Britain, Europe or the United States, since sole agencies for well-known manufacturers and popular brands tended to gravitate to Singapore's established houses. Moreover, on the whole the British merchant houses with numerous and important manufacturers' agencies for imported goods also dominated the export trade. There were various reasons for this. First, exporting generated profits which could be used in the import trade. Second, an established reputation and dominant position in the export trade helped to attract major import agencies. Third, agencies might directly relate to export activities, particularly the exclusive right of merchants, as agency houses, to obtain supplies for rubber companies under their management. For example, Guthries' agencies included Francis Shaw & Co. (plantation rubber machinery, etc.), The Tyneside Engineering Co. (copra and rubber dryers) and 'Kris' Rubber Chests.[9] Thus, in important respects mercantile concentration in the export trade tended to carry through into the import trade and the process to become cumulative. During the inter-war period no new British or Continental merchants managed to establish themselves as large houses in the general import trade.

A striking aspect of the agency system was the lack of participation in it by local Asian (that is Chinese or Indian) firms. The *Directories*, although possibly incomplete, show that even in 1939 there were remarkably few agencies for manufacturers in Britain, the Continent or the United States held by Singapore Chinese firms and almost none by Indian firms.[10]

It is apparent why British, Continental and American manufacturers which chose representation by the agency system almost always decided to appoint European merchant houses in preference to local Asian firms. A European house had an office in Europe with which the manufacturer could deal, usually enjoyed an established reputation, was financially strong and normally could provide distribution through a large organization with a number of branches in the region. Asian firms could not offer the same advantages, being smaller, largely untested and, at least to manufacturers, probably almost unknown. So long as manufacturers

[8] For a general discussion of exclusive dealer franchises, see Scherer and Ross, *Market structure*, pp.558–64.   [9] *Directory 1927*, p.188.
[10] *Directory 1925*, pp.115–247, 257–285F, *1927*, pp.128–272, 283–288FF, *1939*, pp.1–278, 377–553.

generally used sole agents, that system worked against Asian importers. In denying them access to almost all the popular brands and in making impossible direct trade with most British, Continental and American manufacturers, an agency system ruled out competition on an equal footing with European merchant houses in manufactured goods from these countries.[11]

A further reason for British, Continental and American manufacturers to use sole agents, especially relevant in a geographically extensive but often shallow market, was that distribution through a single merchant kept transaction costs of dealing with distributors low. Perhaps more important was that in a market where an agency system predominated, there was greater reason to use it. By granting a sole agency, a manufacturer created an incentive to push his product line, since the merchant with the agency stood to benefit from sales efforts to promote the product. Merchants with sole agencies allocated advertisements in trade directories and local newspapers to the manufacturer's product.[12] By contrast, a manufacturer could expect little help in the Singapore market if he did not appoint a sole agent, and sought distribution through several merchants. Thus, for cotton goods, potential American exporters were advised that:

it might be wise to work with only one [Singapore] firm because the question of brands is highly important, and with the keen rivalry which exists in the market one firm would hardly be disposed to take up a line or brand of cotton goods and push its sale aggressively if the same brand was being offered to competitors.[13]

Probably above all, however, a manufacturer's gain in awarding his agency to a Singapore merchant house was access to and knowledge of the local and regional market. This usually implied branch offices, and in Singapore often depended on contact with a number of Chinese dealers and an ability to assess the risk of trading with them. The matter was often complicated because 'The obscure form of partnership in which the Chinese ... prefer to trade, renders it a difficult matter to ascertain their financial standing'.[14] European houses had extensive local knowledge of risk assessment: Paterson, Simons, for example, held 'tremendous dossiers of the history of every Chinese firm'.[15] Such information was largely firm-specific, and could not be quickly or easily duplicated by a newcomer in Singapore.

---

[11] However, as discussed in section III, by the late 1920s agencies for some United Kingdom manufacturers, especially of piece goods, were of little value.

[12] There were, however, some complaints about the laxness of agents. Boulter, *Economic conditions, 1931*, p.16.

[13] Odell, *Cotton goods*, p.49, and see *SSTC 1933–34* III, pp.67, 70, IV, pp.305–6, V, pp.75–76.

[14] Boulter, *Economic conditions, 1931*, p.15, and see Beale, *Review of trade, 1928*, pp.12–13.

[15] *SSTC 1933–34* III, p.109.

II

During the inter-war period established merchant houses were successfully challenged by the large number of firms formed to handle the new trades.[16] This considerably broadened the mercantile structure, and gave it a much more modern as well as an international look. It is hard to imagine that inter-war Singapore would have developed as a centre for distributing new imports if this marketing had depended solely on the European merchant houses. New firms, by opening in Singapore, perpetuated its position as an import centre.

Replacement of the agency system of representation – either by special-ized organizations or departments set up by merchant houses or manu-facturers – may be expected when this economizes on transaction costs.[17] Such replacement becomes more likely the bigger the sales, the more complex the product, the greater the investment in specialized distribution and services, and the higher the rents in the form of supranormal profits for a distributor arising from brand name advantages. But a transaction costs framework also suggests why merchant houses without specialized distribution facilities often continued to handle the new imports. Imports were generally distributed by merchant houses so long as sales volume was small. Since this remained the case for many products, merchant house distribution of new imports was, in aggregate, substantial. During the inter-war period manufactured materials and non-electrical machinery came primarily through European merchant houses, in part reflecting the absence of particular distributive requirements and of rents from brand name advantages.

It was, however, probably often inevitable that the merchant houses would lose the distribution of new trades. In Singapore, increased distributive business for a product – or its apparent growth potential – and a recognized brand name appear to have been particularly important reasons for manufacturers to open a local sales branch. These con-siderations proved especially relevant for multinational enterprises. Branch offices were prominent in the import of tyres: Firestone, Dunlop and Pirelli

[16] The growth of the new trades may be traced in *SSTC 1933–34* I, pp.50, 202, II, pp.572, 582, III, p.445, IV, p.417; *Directory 1927, 1939*; Beale, *Review of trade, 1928*, p.81; Boulter, *Economic conditions, 1931*, pp.13–16, 35; Hartland, *Economic conditions, 1934*, pp.6–7, 31; R. B. Willmot, *Report on economic and commercial conditions in Malaya to 5th March 1939* (London, 1939), p.86; Cunyngham-Brown, *Traders*, p.247; Drabble and Drake, 'British agency houses', pp.310–11; Eric Jennings, *Wheels of progress: 75 years of Cycle and Carriage* (Singapore, 1975), pp.30–35.

[17] For an application of these ideas of R. H. Coase on the theory of the firm, see Stephen Nicholas, 'Agency contracts, institutional modes and the transition to foreign direct investment by British manufacturing multinationals before 1939', *Journal of Economic History* 43, 3 (1983), pp.675–86.

all opened in Singapore. Other multinationals which came to the city included Kodak (photographic materials), Singer (sewing machines) and ICI (chemicals).

For electrical goods and machinery, six firms represented the majority of manufacturers exporting to Singapore and divided the bulk of the market. The six included two United Kingdom manufacturers (General Electric and Standard Telephones and Cables); three engineering companies, also major contractors (United Engineers, Huttenbachs Ltd. and John Morey & Co.); and a merchant house (the Borneo Co.). In the distribution of electrical goods and machinery, the arrival of manufacturers and the advantages of being contractors left little room for merchant houses. Both manufacturers and contractors were in a strong position to offer the technical knowledge and after-sales service needed to distribute electrical goods and machinery.

On the whole, the import and distribution of motor cars gave rise to specialized firms from the start. By 1927 a conspicuous sector had grown up around their import. Of the ten Singapore firms importing motor cars, only Guthries was a merchant house. The others, all located along Orchard Road and forming the backbone of the Motor Traders' Association, dealt almost exclusively in motor cars and accessories. Most held several agencies for the import of motor cars, although the business of one was as the representative of the Ford Motor Co. That company subsequently established a Singapore office for wholesale distribution, while Fiat also opened a local office.

The new trades contributed to Singapore's development by making the city's mercantile community more international in composition, and in this regard imports from the United States contributed most. For many of the new, unlike the old, trades, United States' manufacturers were 'extremely active and well represented'.[18] American multinationals tended to favour opening their own sales branches in Singapore; additionally, in the interwar period some merchants and manufacturers' agents specialized in importing United States goods. The United States was Britain's main competitor in the new trades, notably domestic electrical appliances, radios, photographic material, galvanized iron and, above all, motor cars, tyres and accessories. The growth of the new trades largely accounts for the rise in the United States' share of Singapore's imports, which reached 17% in 1925/27. Similarly, the marked fall in imports from America in the 1930s concentrated in the new trades, due mainly to a sharp decline in demand for consumer durables (table 9.1).

Colonial rule was an important reason for Britain's prominence in the

---

[18] Beale, *Review of trade, 1928*, p.40, and see pp.10, 12.

new trades and helps to explain why the United Kingdom retained a share in Singapore's import trade greater than in world manufactured exports as a whole. A considerable part of Singapore's demand in the new trades came from government and municipal authorities, including those controlling public utilities, who gave preference to British goods, and 'thus a large volume of trade … is more or less reserved for the British manufacturer. Under these circumstances it is difficult in many lines to ascertain how far he is holding his own in competition in the open market'.[19] Apart from some goods produced in British Malaya, official supplies came through the Crown Agents, and did not involve Singapore merchants.[20]

In terms of employment, the new trades did not have a major impact on Singapore's economic development. Their distinguishing feature was simple distributive arrangements. The new imports involved little, if any, barter. In most cases, importers were able to deal with consumers or retailers. For estates and tin mines, supplies 'pass direct from the importer to large consumers', although small enterprises were supplied through dealers.[21] Similarly, machinery and tin plate were sold direct to the consumer and building materials to the contractor. Motor car importers for British Malaya concentrated in Singapore. They were retailers in the city and distributed to Malaya through a system of sub-agents.

III

The old trades possessed two prominent features, both of which, by the inter-war period, had already contributed significantly to the economic development of Singapore. One was their large Chinese mercantile structure, the second that profits were widely diffused, with a major proportion of the whole accruing to local Asian traders.

To describe distribution in the old trades is really to describe the bazaar trade. Here, during the inter-war period European merchant houses continued to rely on a complementary relationship with Asian, principally Chinese, dealers.[22] In the piece goods trade, British merchant houses enjoyed a particularly close relationship with the Chinese (mostly Teochew) dealers located in Circular Road, who were organized as the Singapore Piece Goods Traders' Guild with about 30 members in 1929.

[19] Boulter, *Economic conditions, 1931*, p.17, and see Beale, *Review of trade, 1928*, p.29.
[20] *SSTC 1933–34* I, pp.219–21; Boulter, *Economic conditions, 1931*, p.17; Hartland, *Economic conditions, 1934*, pp.4–5; Sir Laurence Guillemard, *Trivial fond records* (London, 1937), p.100; Mills, *British rule*, p.135.
[21] Boulter, *Economic conditions, 1931*, p.14.
[22] *SSTC 1933–34* I, pp.50, 51, III, pp.85–86; Song, *One hundred years' history*, p.382; Nathan, 'Changes in the flow of trade'; Beale, *Review of trade, 1928*, p.63.

The association listed as an objective the trade in British piece goods, which was the mainstay of its members' business.[23]

In the bazaar trade, European merchant houses still usually sold goods on credit during the inter-war period; but with the attenuation of German competition they were able to adopt a more cautious approach towards granting credit.[24] The main flow of credit came from London: goods purchased in Britain could be more easily and cheaply financed there than in Singapore, and no local arrangements like the 'Hundi' system familiar in India and Netherlands India developed to enable European merchants to discount local Asian dealers' acceptances at banks. In the cotton piece goods trade, credit from European merchants was for 60 to 90 days, the latter being usual for Circular Road dealers. In turn, Singapore dealers, financed by European houses, themselves extended credit, but generally for a shorter period.

In the old trades, the basis for the challenge to European merchant houses was largely associated with increased imports from Japan, since Europeans handled few goods from that country. Between 1929 and 1932/34 imports from Japan more than doubled to reach 30% of Singapore's total imports from the West (table 9.1), and therefore for almost a third of manufactured imports. The volume of Japanese goods handled by Singapore traders and merchants importing those manufactures increased much more than reference to the value figure in table 9.1 suggests, since the prices of manufactures fell sharply between 1929 and 1934. Where brand names had created preferences which constituted an entry barrier to the bazaar trade, Japan effectively countered this by using price as a weapon: 'revolutionary changes in the price of manufactured goods' explained Japan's higher share in Singapore's imports.[25] Cotton and rayon piece goods and cotton sarongs were the most important Japanese items imported, although between 1932 and 1934 these goods fell from over a half to one-third of total British Malayan imports from Japan. By 1934 Japan had a major share of the market in a wide range of manufactures.[26] It appeared that Japan would gain 'a practical monopoly

[23] *SSTC 1933–34* II, pp.332, 343, 505, 509–12, IV, p.216; Beale, *Review of trade, 1928*, pp.10, 63–64; Boulter, *Economic conditions, 1931*, p.14; Charles Gamba, 'Chinese associations in Singapore', *JMBRAS* 39, 2 (1966), p.136.

[24] Discussion of credit here and subsequently in connection with Japanese merchants is based on *SSTC 1933–34* I, pp.50, 60, II, pp.508, 512, 782–83, III, pp.105, 112, 116–17, 425–26; *Commissions on trade depression 1921*, appx. 1, p.39; Beale, *Review of trade, 1928*, pp.63–64; Jumabhoy, *Multiracial Singapore*, p.51; Victor Purcell, *The memoirs of a Malayan official* (London, 1965), pp.208–11.

[25] *SSTC 1933–34* I, pp.62–63, and see I, pp.58–59; W. Arthur Lewis, *Economic survey, 1919–1939* (London, 1949), pp.118–23; William W. Lockwood, *The economic development of Japan* expanded edn (Princeton, 1968), pp.65–69.

[26] *SSTC 1933–34* I, pp.64–70; Malaya, *Foreign imports and exports 1934*.

of the bazaar trade', and that Singapore, through which virtually all imports from Japan entered British Malaya, would be increasingly transfigured into a distribution centre for Japanese goods.[27]

In Singapore, Britain was 'the principal sufferer'[28] from Japanese competition, because of the large quantity of British manufactures which had been sold in the bazaar. There was an abrupt fall in Britain's share in British Malayan imports of cotton piece goods, from over a half in 1925/29 to one-quarter in 1932 and 18% by 1934; while the Japanese proportion rose from one-fifth in 1925/29 to nearly three-fifths in 1932, stood at over two-thirds by 1933 and continued to grow in early 1934. Over the period the total volume of imports was almost unchanged. There was therefore a large absolute rise in Japanese imports for the bazaar.

The decision taken by the United Kingdom in 1932 to establish Imperial Preference had little effect on Singapore's imports of cotton piece goods or other traditional manufactures: the proportion of these coming from Britain continued to decline and the share from Japan to increase. There were three main reasons for this. First, Singapore remained outside Imperial Preference. The Straits Settlements, led as always by Singapore, was not forced to adopt Imperial Preference, because of the strong opposition to any administrative interference with the free port.[29] Second, while governments in the FMS and, in a more haphazard fashion, the UMS, implemented Imperial Preference, this system did not discriminate sufficiently against goods from Japan to have much effect on Japanese competition. Singapore lost some exports, mainly to the FMS and in cotton piece goods, owing to administrative regulations which Kuala Lumpur deemed necessary for Imperial Preference, but the port continued to sell large quantities of Japanese manufactures to the Malay Peninsula.

The third reason – more important than the second – was Singapore's large distributive trade in Japanese goods to extra-Malayan markets, especially Sumatra and Siam.[30] One reason for Singapore's bigger exports of Japanese goods to Netherlands India than to Malaya was that Japanese merchants from Singapore had established a presence in the Dutch colony. For example, commercial connections through Singapore-based Japanese firms largely explained why in Palembang, Sumatra, three-fifths of goods from Japan came through the British port and only two-fifths through Java.[31]

[27] *SSTC 1933–34* I, p.60, and see pp.59, 61, 63.   [28] Ibid. I, p.61.

[29] *SSLCP 1932*, pp.B100–B101; 'Customs duties committee', *SSLCP 1932*, pp.C159, C162–C163; *Malay Mail*, 24 June 1933; Emerson, *Malaysia*, pp.363–68.

[30] *SSTC 1933–34* I, pp.55–63, II, pp.780, 781, IV, p.229.

[31] 'The development of Japanese trade with Sumatra and the activities of Singapore Japanese merchants', *MRCA* 30 (Feb. 1933), and see 'Japanese in the Straits Settlements', *MRCA* 34 (June 1933). The latter article was from the *China Weekly Review* (Shanghai), 17 June 1933.

Initially, the distribution of imports from Japan did not attract Europeans in Singapore, because Japanese goods gave no business to the merchant's office in Britain, and, moreover, because of the notoriously low profit margins. Nevertheless, by early 1934 a number of European merchant houses had made arrangements to import Japanese piece goods, but in this were cut short by the introduction of the quota system which replaced Imperial Preference, and applied to the Straits Settlements as well as the Malay Peninsula (see chapter 3). Not having previously imported from Japan, Singapore's European houses received only a small share of quota rights.[32]

In the old trades, two important changes occurred in Singapore's mercantile structure. One was the growth of a large Japanese mercantile community and associated changes in the distribution of imports in Singapore. The goods Japanese merchants imported were almost entirely from Japan.[33] During World War I an upsurge in imports from Japan had given 'Japanese merchants their opportunity'.[34] From 1918 manufacturers in Japan were represented in Singapore by the Japanese Commercial Museum. It had a standing exhibition of goods and collection of samples, and the staff arranged business contacts in Japan and took orders. By 1932 the Japanese commercial community in Singapore had grown sufficiently in strength and self-awareness to form the Singapore Japanese Chamber of Commerce, which consisted of approximately 50 firms and downtown shops but excluded banks and shipping companies. Some Japanese importers such as Mitsui Bussan Kaisha and Senda & Company were general merchants and conducted import, export and shipping business. However, many firms concentrated on the import trade. For example, Shimota Company dealt chiefly in piece goods; Nanyo Shokai had a general goods trade; and Santei Shokai imported bicycles.[35]

Japanese, like European, merchants relied very largely on Asian dealers for distribution,[36] but often not the same ones most prominently associated with European merchant houses. The cotton piece goods trade was the most striking example of a shift in the relative importance of competing groups of Asian dealers in Singapore.[37] The Circular Road dealers

[32] *SSTC 1933–34* I, p.59, III, pp.73, 349; Hartland, *Economic conditions, 1937*, pp.8, 11.
[33] Boulter, *Economic conditions, 1931*, p.15; Hartland, *Economic conditions, 1934*, p.6.
[34] *1921 census*, p.90.
[35] *SSTC 1933–34* I, p.59, II, pp.777–78, 781, V, p.46; 'Japanese trade', *MRCA* (Feb. 1933), p.41; *Directory 1927, 1939*; *1931 census*, pp.87, 200.
[36] *SSTC 1933–34* I, pp.60–61.
[37] Analysis of the distribution of piece goods is based on ibid. I, pp.19–22, 54, 60, 61, II, pp.332, 343, 402, 509–11, 781–83; Beale, *Review of trade, 1928*, pp.63–64; August Brauer, *The cotton-goods market of British Malaya* (Washington, DC: US Department of Commerce, 1931), pp.7–10; *Chinese commercial directory* (1932), section v; Mills, *British rule*, p.141.

remained loyal to British piece goods, and, mainly because of this, dwindled in number from the about 30 firms in 1929 to 15 in 1933. Singapore Chinese who distributed Japanese piece goods were predominantly the so-called High Street dealers. They were mostly Cantonese and concentrated along North Bridge Road, South Bridge Road and in Arab Street. However, because of Singapore Chinese boycotts of Japanese products in 1928 and from October 1931 to mid-1932, Chinese dealers in the city were hesitant to distribute piece goods known to be from Japan. Their reluctance created a major opening for Indian dealers. By 1933 Indian along with some Arab dealers were chiefly responsible for the distribution of Japanese piece goods in Singapore.

Japanese importers sold for cash in competing for business in the bazaar trade through price. This was advantageous for Japanese merchants because, as recent arrivals, they were less able than European houses to assess Asian creditworthiness. It was also advantageous in avoiding default risk which was at its greatest in the early 1930s when Japanese merchants' businesses were expanding. Asian dealers were able to deal in Japanese goods partly because they used their own money or borrowed from banks or moneylenders; partly because an emphasis on rapid turnover reduced the need for finance; and partly because merchandise bought from Europeans on credit could be promptly re-sold, even at a loss, and cash from the sale spent on Japanese goods.[38]

The other change in mercantile structure was that local Chinese, and also Indian, firms became sufficiently important as importers to constitute, in addition to European and Japanese merchants, a third principal channel through which imports reached Singapore. For local Asian firms, Japanese manufactures offered the main opportunity to enter the import trade, and the prominence of local importers increased as these goods took a growing share of the Singapore market. There were two reasons why it was much easier for Asian firms to import Japanese than British, Continental or American manufactures. One was that, unlike the entry barrier to the import trade from Europe arising from the lack of a London office, the absence of an office in Japan posed no problem in starting to import Japanese goods: contacts could easily be established through the Commercial Museum in Singapore.

The second, and more important, reason was that 'With a few exceptions business with Japan is conducted on an "open market" basis, as opposed to the system of agents and sub-agents upon which much of the Colony's trade in manufactured goods with other countries is conducted'.[39] The open market system – unlike the exclusive distribution arrangements

---

[38] *SSTC 1933–34* II, p.508.   [39] Ibid. I, p.60.

associated with the agency system – readily admitted the competition of local Asian firms as importers. Since many Singapore importers could obtain goods of the same nature from Japan, this competition led to 'considerable price-cutting between importers in Singapore'[40] and a consequent reduction in profit margins. Local Asian firms may still have been at a disadvantage in comparison to Japanese importers because the latter usually had greater capital resources and possibly some edge in negotiating directly with manufacturers in Japan.[41] But as importers they had one very distinct advantage over Japanese and European merchants: they could accept small profit margins because of the low overheads possible for an enterprise closely controlled and managed by its proprietor, and because of their forward integration as dealers, and possibly retailers, which reduced distribution costs.[42]

The development of Asian, especially Indian, firms as importers was illustrated by the piece goods trade.[43] In the 1920s a number of Indian firms trading in silk, cotton and rayon opened their own offices in Japan. The High Street Chinese also began to import more Japanese piece goods, and some Chinese firms, either individually or in groups, began to maintain buying offices in Japan. However, the Chinese boycott of Japan from October 1931 left Indian and Arab firms as the main local Asian importers able to respond to the boom in Japanese piece goods. By 1933 these firms were said to account for a large share of the import of Japanese cotton and silk goods.[44] For example, by then Maganlal Nagindas & Company did a sufficiently large business with Japan to justify opening a branch there; and although R. E. Mohamed Kasim & Co. were the agents for a big cotton mill in Glasgow, the firm kept this agency only 'for the name's sake'[45] and had almost entirely replaced imports from Britain with those from Japan.

In Singapore, local Asian importers were major beneficiaries of the British Malayan quota system. Indian firms in particular received a substantial share of quota rights, since government licences to import piece goods from Japan were based on imports between January 1933 and March 1934. Local Asian importers benefited from the quota system in two ways. First, since quotas were untaxed, those with licences to import from Japan either reaped windfall gains as importers or sold their quota rights, in which a lively trade developed. Second, countries in the British Empire were exempt from quotas, and Empire manufacturers of cheap cloth – the closest substitute for Japanese goods – gained most in increased

[40] Ibid.   [41] Ibid. III, pp.349–50, II, pp.681, 782, IV, p.410.
[42] Hartland, *Economic conditions, 1937*, pp.11, 8; Beale, *Review of trade, 1928*, p.63; 'Customs duties committee', *SSLCP 1932*, p.C158; *SSTC 1933–34* III, p.349.
[43] *SSTC 1933–34* I, pp.57, 59–61, II, pp.388, 402, 511, 680–82, 782, III, p.349, IV, p.430; Beale, *Review of trade, 1928*, pp.13, 19, 63–64; Odell, *Cotton goods*, p.22.
[44] *SSTC 1933–34* I, p.60.   [45] Ibid. III, p.349.

exports to Singapore. These piece goods came from Hong Kong and, especially, from India, and were handled largely by Chinese and Indian firms respectively.[46]

The role of local Asian importers should not be exaggerated: their activities were confined chiefly to goods for the bazaar trade and were by no means dominant there. Furthermore, by 1937/39 the Japanese share in Singapore's import trade had fallen to 16% (table 9.1); less than a third of British Malayan imports of cotton piece goods came from Japan. The various restrictive measures in Netherlands India and British Malaya partly explain the reduction in Singapore's imports from Japan, but more significant was a Chinese boycott in British Malaya of all Japanese goods, which by September 1937 was 'fairly complete'.[47]

Yet by 1937 greater imports of Japanese goods had already made an important contribution to the emergence of local Asian importers, and so helped to lay a basis for Singapore's further economic development. Trade with Japan afforded local Asian firms their main opportunity to realize profits from importing as well as from distribution. Moreover, it offered local firms their principal links with suppliers in developed countries and encouraged the practice of direct dealing with them. In both respects, the experience gained in importing from Japan strengthened the local Asian mercantile community and made it less reliant on international contacts established through Singapore's European merchant houses.

---

[46] Jumabhoy, *Multiracial Singapore*, pp.84–85, 58; 'Report on quotas', *SSAR 1935* I, pp.474, 476, *1937* I, p.640, *1938* I, p.337; Singapore Chamber of Commerce, *Report 1938*, p.18, *1939*, pp.12, 14.

[47] 'Report on the boycott of Japanese goods', *MRCA* 85 (Sept. 1937), and see *Straits Times*, 23 Aug. 1937.

Part Three

Staple port and rapid growth, 1947–1990

10   The staple port resurgent: development to 1959

'When the Union Jack was lowered on Fort Canning, in Singapore, on that Sunday morning it marked the sudden and dramatic end of an epoch in our Colonial Empire.'

Letter to *The Times*, 24 Feb. 1942

'When at school I was taught that Singapore is impregnable and I thought then as I think now, What in the heck is Great Britain doing in Singapore, anyway? All right, it's in a fine position to control the sea-lanes but I can't see that this off-shore European island (meaning ourselves) has any business there, Raffles or no Raffles.'

George Beardmore, *Civilians at war: journals, 1938–1946* (Oxford, 1986), p.125

By 1950 Singapore had largely recovered from the devastation of World War II, and again began to develop economically. The present chapter traces the course of this development to 1959. In assessing Singapore's pre-World War II economic growth and free trade inheritance, section I sums up the arguments of Part Two of this book, and puts them in the context of post-war development. The remainder of the chapter deals with the 1950s. Section II looks at Singapore's trade, which remained that of a staple port. In section III, the linkages arising from this trade through the expansion of infrastructure, manufacturing industry and financial development are examined. During the 1950s the decisive changes in Singapore were demographic and political, the subjects of sections IV and V respectively. Politics acquired a new importance in shaping the economy in the run-up to the independence Singapore gained in 1959, and this subject forms the chapter's concluding section.

I

The argument in Part Two is that before World War II Singapore grew as an integral part of a 'vent for surplus' region centred on Malaya and, even more, Netherlands India (Indonesia). Singapore as a port, market and financier provided the essential services component in the venting process which underlay rapid regional growth. As part of this growth – increasingly dependent on specialization in the production of three staples – Singapore developed as a staple port.

Trade had a dynamic role in growth, and made it a story of the enlargement of markets, transmission of knowledge, entrepreneurial response and successful creation of linkages, all largely achieved through the medium of Singapore. The city put regional traders and producers in contact with world markets, stimulated enterprise and capital accumulation and furnished the necessary 'inducement goods' of manufactures from the West and food from Southeast Asia. In the Malayan region, staple-led growth was not a dead end which left the periphery impoverished and the staple port economically stranded.

Singapore was different from other staple ports, in both its demographic growth and its free trade inheritance. In the Malay Peninsula, bringing surplus resources into use by opening up foreign markets required large-scale immigration. As a result, Singapore developed as a Chinese city – an anomaly in the region. By the end of the 1930s Singapore's staunchly free trade ideology also contrasted sharply with that of most staple ports as well as with other parts of Southeast Asia. Typically, the early 1930s was a turning point in attitudes towards intervention in the market. Often, as in Indonesia, the experience of the slump had a lasting influence: 'it was the regulated and not the free economy that the Indonesians inherited from the Dutch, and the tendency of governments of independent Indonesia has been to add new regulations without removing the old ones'.[1]

The same thing might have happened in Singapore, if, as elsewhere, important interest groups had favoured a regulated economy. But in the early 1930s free trade was the overriding interest of the dominant group in Singapore's European mercantile community which had been created by the shipping conference system and, subsequently, by the rubber industry. Their voice and representations to the Colonial Office and Straits Settlements government were fundamental in maintaining Singapore as a free port.[2]

The exporters and shippers were champions of free trade because Singapore required unhindered access to cheap imports to attract primary commodity exports to the port: 'Freedom for both exports and imports is necessary because of their reactions on each other ... What is now proposed

[1] Benjamin Higgins, *Economic development* revised edn (New York, 1968), p.693; see also Hla Myint, 'Inward and outward-looking countries revisited: the case of Indonesia', *BIES* 20, 2 (1984), p.45.

[2] For example, see PRO CO 717/84/82452 Edward Boustead & Co. to Oliver Marks, Secretary, Association of British Malaya, 20 Nov. 1931; *Straits Times*, 26 Feb. 1935; *SSTC 1933–34* III, p.73.

is to limit the importation of the cheap piece goods which the sellers of our produce require'.[3] To safeguard this produce trade, the exporters were 'ready to sacrifice their import interests', and in a 'free trade fight'[4] in 1933 and 1934 easily defeated Singapore's protectionist lobby of local Singapore manufacturers and European firms who had the distribution of imported manufactured goods as their main business.[5]

Yet by 1935 Singapore's exporters and shippers began to support some form of trade restriction, because Japanese competition, formerly confined mainly to the bazaar trade, had become severe in the export of rubber to New York and the provision of shipping services. Pressure to abandon free trade gained further strength by mid-1936,[6] but soon decreased because Japanese competition in exporting from British Malaya and providing shipping services from Singapore, as well as in the distribution of manufactured imports, lessened from the latter part of the year. At first this was because the Japanese directed their competitive efforts elsewhere, but from 1937 it was also because the Singapore Chinese boycott of Japanese merchants began. Subsequently, debate in Singapore over competition from Japan faded amidst preparations for World War II.

Singapore's post-World War II economic development must be interpreted in light of the successful 1930s' defence of free trade. Events could have taken a quite different course if a strategy of tariffs and trade restriction, with accompanying import-substitution policies and strong encouragement for British Malayan political unity, had been implemented in the 1930s. As it happened, Singapore began – and ended – the 1950s with an unbroken free trade tradition. That inheritance was an important element in the split with Malaysia; and it was fundamental to the post-1965 development of export-oriented manufacturing in Singapore.

L. G. Reynolds defines a turning point as when extensive growth (a rise in national income at the same rate as population increase) turns into intensive growth (a rise in income per capita), and for Malaya dates this point as starting from the second half of the nineteenth century.[7] His chronology would be consistent with the present study's view that by 1900 Singapore had become a modern city and acquired many of its prominent features. After 1900 regional economic growth continued to transform Singapore and the surrounding region, but at uneven rates both between

[3] Singapore Chamber of Commerce, *Report 1934*, pp.16–17.
[4] *Straits Times*, 26 Feb. 1935.
[5] Singapore Chamber of Commerce, *Report 1934*, pp.18–19; *Straits Budget*, 7 June 1934.
[6] *Straits Budget*, 25 April 1935 and 30 July 1936; Denis Soo Jin and Tenaka Kyoko, 'Japanese competition in the trade of Malaya in the 1930s', *Southeast Asian Studies* 21, 4 (1984), pp.391–92, 397.
[7] Lloyd G. Reynolds, 'The spread of economic growth to the third world', *Journal of Economic Literature* 21, 3 (1983), pp.943, 958–60.

city and hinterland and within the latter. Singapore developed the furthest. The contention that 'few, if any, European ... colonies experienced anything that could be described as sustained economic development'[8] certainly does not apply to Singapore or to the Colony of the Straits Settlements.

Between 1870 and 1900 and, somewhat unusually among staple ports, again from 1909 to 1929, Singapore's exports grew rapidly.[9] Overall economic growth in Singapore reflected this. The high per capita income Singaporeans enjoyed by the mid-1950s, discussed in chapter 1, indicates Singapore's achievement of substantial intensive growth prior to World War II.

There is also strong qualitative evidence of intensive growth. Between 1901 and 1939 Singapore's considerable economic progress, described in Part Two of this book, was apparent in physical infrastructure, the development of institutions including international commodity markets and Chinese banks, and a measure of industrialization. In the Malayan region, as in other developing areas, an elaborate infrastructure accompanied economic growth rather than being a pre-condition for it;[10] much of this infrastructure was concentrated in Singapore. Its experience bears out W. A. Lewis' observation that in tropical development 'the lion's share' of infrastructure went to urban areas.[11]

Those who gained substantially from pre-war economic growth in Singapore included, as well as owners of foreign enterprise, a significant proportion of the local, non-European population. They were men who were engaged in commerce and industry, as well as those who comprised a large part of the growing professional middle class. In Singapore, the value of a stable environment created by colonial government, said to be 'often only for the benefit of a small number of traders and investors from the colonizing nation',[12] extended much more widely through the social structure.

Both before and after 1900 Singapore's growth met most of the conditions identified by R. E. Caves as conducive to intensive economic growth. These included a lack of substantial economies of scale in production of the export staples, encouragement to social overhead capital construction, development of local processing industry and extensive

---

[8] Malcolm Gillis, et al. *Economics of development* 3rd edn (New York, 1991), p.26.

[9] See above, table 2.1. For export growth in Singapore's hinterland, see Angus Maddison, *Economic growth in Japan and the USSR* (London, 1969), pp.29, 36; Bart van Ark, 'The volume and price of Indonesian exports, 1823 to 1940: the long-term trend and its measurement', *BIES* 24, 3 (1988), pp.87–120.

[10] P. T. Bauer, 'Remembrance of studies past: retracing first steps' in Gerald M. Meier and Dudley Seers, eds. *Pioneers in development* (New York, 1984), p.30.

[11] Lewis, *Growth and fluctuations*, p.217.   [12] Gillis, *Economics of development*, p.26.

participation by local entrepreneurs.[13] After 1910 the fulfilment of these conditions was largely due to the rubber-pineapple complex and its effect on Singapore Chinese. The story of Singapore's inter-war economic development would probably have been very different if, instead of rubber, a staple of equal export value but higher capital intensity and with significant production economies of scale had emerged.

Unlimited immigration into Singapore until the 1930s checked the possibility of large gains in intensive growth. Impoverished rural populations from south China and southern India came to Singapore, and, in the absence of employment opportunities in the manufacturing sector or international services, were pushed into low-paid services. No figures exist for income distribution, but Singapore's many hawkers, rickshaw pullers and domestic servants, together with densely-packed Chinatowns, were indicative of a large gap between rich and poor.

Social indicators improved substantially after 1900, but nevertheless continued to suggest considerable poverty. The official records show that infant mortality, expressed as the number of deaths under one year of age per thousand births, fell by about a third between 1911 and 1931, and then by another third by 1939, to 130. This figure was high – equivalent to a low-income country in 1990 – although it may have been overstated, due to the inclusion of deaths of children over one year old; in 1947, when recording was corrected by matching it with birth registration documents of the ages of infants at death, the rate was 87.[14]

Furthermore, the general literacy rate per thousand of the population as a whole – 314 in 1931 and 374 in 1947 – was low. The figures partly reflected the large numbers of immigrants who had come to Singapore as uneducated young adults and the interruption of normal education due to the Japanese occupation.[15] However, before the War only about half of children aged 6–12 attended school; in 1947 the proportion still had not reached two-thirds.[16] These factors left a burden, if a diminishing one, of illiteracy through the 1980s.[17]

Despite the indicated pre-war progress in economic development, by Western standards Singapore was a less developed economy on the eve of World War II. Characteristics of less developed status included industrial and financial dualism, surplus labour, a segmented labour market and

---

[13] Caves, 'Export-led growth', pp.433–37.
[14] *1931 census*, p.110; Phillips, *Births and deaths, 1940–1947*, pp.4, 9.
[15] *1931 census*, p.94; *1947 census*, p.90; IBRD, *Economic development of Malaya*, p.364.
[16] IBRD, *Economic development of Malaya*, pp.120–21, 364; K. E. Mackenzie, *Economic and commercial conditions in the Federation of Malaya and Singapore, March 1951* (London, 1952), p.17.
[17] Prior to the 1970 census, literacy was defined as 'ability to read and write a simple letter in a language'. *1970 census*, I, p.100, and see *1947 census*, p.90; *1931 census*, p.94.

widespread poverty. It was largely the pre-World War II economy and society with which Singapore started the 1950s: World War II and the Japanese occupation had made surprisingly little difference in a strictly economic sense.

II

During the 1950s Singapore's exports continued to grow; resurgence of the staple port prevented a frequently predicted decline or stagnation in the 'entrepot' trade. Between 1937/39 and 1957/59 the export volume of primary commodities (appendix table A.2) increased almost two and a half times; excluding petroleum on the grounds of its limited impact on Singapore, the export volume of primary commodities rose from 894,000 tons to 1·2 million tons. But in per capita terms, the volume of Singapore's primary exports fell, from 1·37 tons in 1937/39 to 0·85 tons in 1957/59.[18] It was desirable to build a more diversified economy than could be achieved through reliance on the staple port alone; Singapore's economy needed to shift towards industry, and to the services which would be required by the region as it industrialized further.[19]

In 1957/59 staples continued to dominate Singapore's trade (appendix table A.4). Food and primary commodities, Standard International Trade Classification (SITC) sections 0–4, comprised almost three-quarters of total export value. Rubber (231) and petroleum (333 + 334 + 335) accounted for 70% of these five sections of non-manufactures, and for over half of all export value. Exports of smelted tin (687), included as manufactures, remained similar in volume to pre-war levels until after the mid-1950s (appendix table A.2). In 1959 all major smelting work in Singapore ceased when the Straits Trading Company transferred to enlarged smelters at Butterworth (Penang).[20] Nevertheless, Singapore's international tin market continued to operate for some time.[21]

Petroleum exports expanded substantially during the 1950s, and by mid-decade were four times greater in volume than in 1937/39 (appendix table A.2). The Royal Dutch Shell group maintained the Far Eastern head-quarters of its tanker fleet at Singapore, and Caltex began marketing

---

[18] Population figures are for 1937 and 1957 and from Phillips, *Births and deaths, 1940–1947*, p.12 and the *1957 census* and table 10.5.

[19] Cf. W. M. Corden, 'Prospects for Malayan exports' in T. H. Silcock and E. K. Fisk, eds. *The political economy of independent Malaya* (Canberra, 1963), pp.106–7; State of Singapore, *Development plan 1961–1964* (Singapore, 1961), p.13.

[20] Singapore, *Annual report of the Division of Commerce and Industry of the Ministry of Finance Singapore 1960* (Singapore, 1963), p.7 (hereafter *Commerce and industry*).

[21] *Commerce and industry 1964*, p.7.

operations there in 1959.[22] Singapore was already 'the biggest oil storage, blending, packing and bunkering base in South-East Asia', and among the largest in the world, when oil refining operations were inaugurated at the port in 1960.[23]

But above all, Singapore's trade (imports + exports) – and so its economy – still depended on rubber. Throughout the 1950s rubber normally accounted for two-fifths to over a half of Singapore's exports (appendix table A.1) and for a much higher percentage if export statistics had excluded re-exports of food and manufactures to the region. Singapore's trade, it was observed, 'reflects the prosperity of its neighbours, and this is governed largely by the price of rubber'.[24] Peaks in the value of Singapore's total trade corresponded, with a slight lag, to the three peaks in rubber prices: in 1950–1951 during the dramatic but brief Korean War boom, in 1955–1956, and again in 1959–1960.

During the 1950s rubber exports averaged 621,000 tons annually, almost twice the 1934 inter-war peak of 316,000 tons. Most of Singapore's rubber came from outside Malaya, the bulk of it from Indonesia. Indonesia's contribution was recognized by the authorities in Singapore: US dollars were provided to Indonesia by inter-government agreement according to rubber sent to the British port.[25] In 1957/59, when Singapore exported an annual average of 663,000 tons of rubber, officially recorded import figures showed that by value 53·2% of rubber came from non-Malayan sources – four-fifths from Indonesia and the rest mainly from Sarawak and North Borneo.[26] The contribution of non-Malayan imports was sufficient to make Singapore easily the world's biggest primary rubber market; sales in 1960 amounted to about 37% of world production.[27]

Poor statistics and under-reporting of output and trade in Indonesia during the 1950s, due to attempts to evade pervasive government controls, preclude an accurate picture of smallholder rubber production in the Outer Provinces. But over the decade, production was substantially greater than before World War II. And, in comparison to the inter-war period, a higher

---

[22] 'Shell in Singapore and Borneo', *Malaya* (Aug. 1955), p.30; 'Dr. Goh opens new Caltex oil plant', *Singapore Trade* (May 1964), pp.15–18.

[23] *Commerce and industry 1960*, p.12; 'Report of the commission of inquiry into the port of Singapore', *SLA* (sessional paper no.S10 of 1957), pp.6, 10, 12.

[24] Benham, *Economic survey*, p.27; see also Lim Chong Yah, *Economic development of modern Malaya* (Kuala Lumpur, 1967), pp.14–23, 89, 97.

[25] William C. Hollinger, 'The trade and payments agreement programme of Indonesia, 1950–1955', *EDCC* 4, 2 (1956), pp.189–90; United Nations, *Economic survey of Asia and the Far East 1955* (Bangkok, 1956), p.157.

[26] Singapore, *Singapore trade statistics*, 1957–1959.

[27] Singapore, *Annual report 1961*, p.117; 'Biggest rubber market in the world ... ', *Singapore Trade* (Jan. 1961), pp.8–14; Joan Wilson, *The Singapore rubber market* (Singapore, 1958), pp.4–5.

proportion of this output was almost certainly sent to Singapore rather than exported direct. Available statistics suggest that during the 1950s over a half, and probably nearer three-fifths, of Indonesian smallholder output went first to Singapore.[28]

In part, barter continued to explain Indonesia's heavy reliance on exporting through Singapore, although barter arrangements were probably less important in accounting for exports via the port than before World War II. For rubber and tropical produce, two kinds of barter trade – legal and illegal – existed in Singapore Chinese traders' dealings with Indonesia.[29] In legal barter trade, the interlinked nature of trade between Singapore Chinese and outport dealers was officially recognized by the Indonesian authorities and provided a rationale for sanctioning the commerce: in this trade, which was only between Singapore and nearby areas of Indonesia, it was argued that for Indonesians 'Barter is necessary ... as they do not have officially recognized banking facilities'.[30]

The illegal barter trade was larger than the legal. In a free, unregulated market, a proportion, possibly quite large, of this commerce might have been drawn to Singapore as before the War, due to the ability of traders in the city to exchange manufactured goods and food for primary exports and provide finance.[31] But the immediate reason for the trade was that because of government regulation in Indonesia, Singapore's free port status became a magnet even more powerful than it had been in the inter-war period. Indonesian exporters able to trade with Singapore, if only by smuggling, benefited substantially in comparison to dealing through legal channels, due to both considerable official Indonesian underpayment for exports and artificially high import prices. As a result, Indonesian traders could obtain more manufactured goods if rubber and produce were bartered in Singapore than marketed legally, and could sell these manufactures at a large profit in Indonesia. Thus, Indonesian regulation set up a 'virtuous'

[28] For statistics for the volume of Indonesian rubber exports and exports to Singapore before World War II and from 1950–1962, see table 6.2; W. L. Korthals Altes, *General trade statistics 1822–1940*, vol.12a *Changing economy in Indonesia* (The Hague, 1991), p.164; *Commerce and industry 1960*, p.5; Indonesia, Biro Pusat Statistik, *Statistik Konjunktur* (monthly survey), table 8a (Jakarta), Oct. 1957, p.49, Aug. 1963, p.47.

[29] The following draws on Mackenzie, *Economic and commercial conditions*, pp.97–99; Hollinger, 'Trade and payments', pp.190–91; W. M. Corden and J. A. C. Mackie, 'The development of the Indonesian exchange rate system', *MER* 7, 1 (1962), pp.53–55; C. G. F. Simkin, 'Indonesia's unrecorded trade', *BIES* 6,1 (1970), pp.17–44; Mark M. Pitt, 'Alternative trade strategies and employment in Indonesia' in Anne O. Krueger, et al., eds. *Trade and employment in developing countries* (Chicago, 1981), pp.186–203.

[30] Tan Guan Aik, 'Barter fulfils needs of trading', *Singapore Trade* (May 1962), p.14.

[31] Cf. H. V. Richter, 'Indonesia's share in the entrepot trade of the states of Malaya and Singapore prior to Confrontation', *MER* 11, 2 (1966), p.31; Tan Puay Yong, 'Where pepper is king', *Singapore Trade* (April 1962), p.25; G. F. Ray, 'The economy of Asian spices', *MER* 8, 1 (1963), p.56.

circle for both the Singapore economy and Indonesians in contact with the port: high 1950s world rubber prices stimulated Outer Province small-holder production; Singapore Chinese traders provided the means for Indonesians to realize these prices; and Singapore's trade in rubber and the reshipment of manufactures expanded accordingly, with further important benefits for the island's large remilling industry, discussed below.[32]

Through the 1950s Singapore was the largest single market for Indonesian products because of its importance as an outlet for Outer Province exports.[33] In addition to the large volume of Outer Province rubber and petroleum exported through Singapore, it handled a variety of tropical produce including copra, pepper, sago and coffee. Singapore gained in importance as a pepper market; by the 1960s, mainly reflecting Indonesian production, the city's traders dealt in half the world's pepper.[34]

Heavy reliance on trade with Singapore, Indonesia's severe economic problems and Javanese dislike of Singapore Chinese lay behind attempts by Jakarta to divert exports from Singapore and to set up free ports in competition with it. These threats to Singapore have characterized relations with Indonesia almost since the time of Raffles, but were particularly intense in the 1950s and early 1960s. However, talk of a rival free port was apparently not taken very seriously by the Singapore government which came to power in 1959: 'it believes Sukarno's government is incapable of creating anything which would be free from official incompetence, endless procrastination, and corruption'.[35] At the end of the 1950s the real danger to Singapore's trade was not the diversion of exports from Indonesia, but that economy's collapse and a consequent reduction in the volume of trade through Singapore.[36]

In the 1950s the destination of Singapore's primary exports (table 10.1) shifted from the United States to Europe, one of the few periods during the twentieth century when Singapore's export trade was not closely tied to America. The change was largely the result of more rubber being sent to Europe, including eastern Europe, due to greater automobile and tyre production there, and the growing use of synthetic rubber in the United States.

The United Kingdom remained the largest single source of manu-factured imports (table 10.1), at least in part reflecting the still-important agency house system, foreign exchange controls and colonial ties.

[32] Cf. Silcock, *Commonwealth economy*, pp.43–44.
[33] For statistics for Indonesian exports by direction in the 1950s, see Biro Pusat Statistik, *Statistik Konjunktur*, Aug. 1963, pp.26–31.
[34] Ray, 'Economy of Asian spices', p.57.
[35] Mills, *Southeast Asia*, p.266.
[36] Corden, 'Prospects', pp.106–7; Silcock, *Commonwealth economy*, pp.43–44.

Table 10.1 *Singapore trade by direction, 1957/59 and 1988/90 (annual averages)*

	1957/59				1988/90			
	Imports		Exports		Imports		Exports	
	$000	%	$000	%	$000	%	$000	%
Southeast Asia	**2,229,456**	**57.0**	**1,317,149**	**39.3**	**17,001,002**	**17.3**	**19,161,813**	**22.0**
Malaysia	742,144	19.0	694,688	20.7	13,558,703	13.8	11,694,565	13.4
Indonesia	1,066,791	27.3	244,642	7.3	not published			
Thailand	142,220	3.6	82,283	2.5	2,601,246	2.6	5,142,415	5.9
Vietnam	41,698	1.1	49,737	1.5	n.l.		n.l.	
Sarawak, North								
Borneo, Brunei	200,837	5.1	164,467	4.9	201,666	0.2	904,541	1.0
Burma	33,496	0.8	23,937	0.7	96,960	0.1	235,624	0.3
Philippines	2,269	0.1	57,395	1.7	542,427	0.6	1,184,668	1.4
Europe, North								
America and Japan	**1,045,944**	**26.7**	**1,381,892**	**41.2**	**52,606,712**	**53.5**	**42,268,754**	**48.5**
United Kingdom	390,957	10.0	278,808	8.3	2,884,251	2.9	2,753,219	3.2
Europe	270,696	6.9	594,735	17.7	12,281,443	12.5	11,432,996	13.1
United States	127,015	3.2	253,309	7.6	16,147,717	16.4	19,787,459	22.7
Canada	11,390	0.3	46,226	1.4	566,623	0.6	769,423	0.9
Japan	245,886	6.3	208,814	6.2	20,726,678	21.1	7,525,657	8.6

Rest of world							
Hong Kong	637,790	16.3	653,872	19.5	28,688,940	29.2	25,693,390	29.5
China	86,295	2.2	50,881	1.5	2,845,217	2.9	5,545,026	6.4
India	135,122	3.4	75,498	2.3	3,489,941	3.6	2,048,809	2.4
Taiwan	66,395	1.7	62,144	1.8	600,877	0.6	1,764,733	2.0
South Korea	104,518	2.7	12,685	0.4	4,348,976	4.4	2,759,483	3.2
Sri Lanka	1,131	0.0	16,576	0.5	2,886,155	2.9	1,781,615	2.0
Australia	2,430	0.1	12,147	0.4	63,999	0.1	443,634	0.5
Others	112,726	2.9	118,724	3.5	1,835,932	1.9	2,342,956	2.7
	129,172	3.3	305,216	9.1	12,617,843	12.8	9,007,134	10.3
Total	3,913,191	100.0	3,352,913	100.0	98,296,654	100.0	87,123,957	100.0

Notes:

1 For 1957/59 Malaysia refers to the Federation of Malaya and for 1988/90 Sarawak, North Borneo, Brunei refers to Brunei only.
2 For correct 1957 and 1959 import figures see the corrigenda published in *Singapore external trade statistics* in 1958 and 1960 respectively.
3 Figures for Vietnam include Cambodia and Laos.
4 Columns may not add to totals due to rounding.

Sources: Singapore, *Singapore trade statistics*, 1957–1960, 1988–1990.

Nevertheless, criticism, which could have been voiced at any time from the late nineteenth century about United Kingdom manufacturers, was commonplace. For example, in the distribution of radios, 'British makers persisted in trying to sell too expensive models which did not conform to highly specialised local tastes. Other frequent complaints about British goods concern high prices, protracted delivery periods and poor after-sale service'.[37]

These shortcomings were not associated with German and Japanese suppliers. Japan's recovery in Singapore's import market may have been hindered by memories of World War II, but was probably held back much more by restrictions on textile imports from Japan to conserve British Malayan dollar earnings from rubber for the benefit of the sterling area and so the United Kingdom.[38] The Japanese government-backed Japan External Trade Organization (JETRO) was established as the successor to the Commercial Museum to promote and display Japanese products, and during the later 1950s a number of Japanese firms, including importers and exporters, set up in Singapore.[39]

Thus, during the 1950s the basis for Japanese trade, which existed in the 1930s, was reconstructed. Although in 1957/59 imports from Japan were still relatively small, as table 10.1 shows, they were soon to become much larger. By 1963 television was the 'current craze'[40] in Singapore (Television Singapura began in February of that year) and many of the new receivers were from Japan. Indeed, 'long before the television service was started, Japanese sets were already being displayed lavishly at big departmental stores, while other brands were being, so to speak, unpacked'.[41]

In the 1950s Malaya constituted Singapore's main export market in the region (tables 10.1 and 10.2). Even so, in 1957/59, exports to the remainder of Southeast Asia were almost as large as to Malaya. However, Indonesia, as the tables also show, was much less important than Malaya as a market for Singapore's re-exports, although the published statistics may understate actual trade.[42]

---

[37] Geoffrey Borland, 'How to regain a market', *Singapore Trade* (May 1961), p.33.
[38] United Nations, *Economic survey 1954*, p.150, *1955*, p.157; 'Textile imports', *Economic Bulletin* 2, 4 (1952), p.2.
[39] Anthony Oei, 'Japan: going up … ', *Singapore Trade* (Dec. 1961), pp.22–24, and see Chalmers Johnson, *MITI and the Japanese miracle* (Stanford, 1982), pp.230–32.
[40] Antony Oei, 'Japanese trade', *Singapore Trade* (May 1963), p.10.   [41] Ibid, p.11.
[42] This comparatively small reliance on the import of goods via Singapore suggests that, as indicated above, barter trade was less important than before World War II as an explanation for Indonesian exports via Singapore. However, Singapore dealers probably would not have reported goods clandestinely sent to Indonesia in exchange for rubber and tropical produce, so that exports from Singapore may appear in the statistics as less than they were.

Table 10.2 *Singapore trade with Indonesia and Malaya, 1950–1962* (*$000*)

	Indonesia		Malaya	
	Imports	Exports	Imports	Exports
1950	630,817	229,249	1,129,000	543,000
1951	1,231,416	459,139	1,402,400	725,100
1952	796,422	401,503	880,500	651,400
1953	688,196	215,036	677,500	556,400
1954	795,197	135,647	693,800	509,200
1955	1,018,938	188,362	997,300	586,900
1956	1,020,227	220,214	831,061	696,155
1957	1,099,479	250,274	784,717	705,048
1958	965,164	352,268	639,511	659,261
1959	1,135,730	131,384	802,205	719,756
1960	999,309	121,121	852,896	842,978
1961	829,200	194,269	723,589	886,244
1962	804,239	292,491	727,655	941,554

Notes:
1 For 1950–55 figures for trade with Malaya are from Ow, *Singapore's trade with West Malaysia*, p.2. These figures agree closely with recorded trade statistics published by the Federation of Malaya which, beginning in 1950, include trade with Singapore. See Federation of Malaya, *Imports and exports (including trade with Singapore)* (quarterly series), 1950–1956.
2 For 1956–62 imports from Malaya are valued f.o.b. and exports to Malaya c.i.f.
Sources: Singapore, *Report of the department of commerce and industry 1955*, pp. 28, 32; Ow, *Singapore's trade with West Malaysia*, p.2; Singapore, *Singapore trade statistics*, 1957–1963.

In 1957/59 textiles were Singapore's single largest manufactured export at the two-digit level of disaggregation into broad types of goods (appendix table A.4). In this trade, many neighbouring countries aimed 'to by-pass Singapore if they can, but in practice they are successful only to a certain extent'.[43] Singapore's main advantage in the re-shipment of textiles was that it held stocks obtained when prices were low. This availability of stocks, together with Indonesia's sudden foreign exchange crises, was particularly important in explaining both exports to Indonesia and their somewhat erratic nature (table 10.2). When foreign exchange became available, Indonesian 'importers so fear that another exchange crisis will overtake them before their imports can be effected, that they order from the nearest sources of supply, to the great benefit of the growing industries of Hong Kong and Singapore and of the entrepot trade of the latter'.[44]

[43] Tan Swee Siang, 'Our merchants really know their stuff', *Singapore Trade* (Jan. 1962), p.27.   [44] King, *Money*, p.59, and see Tan, 'Our merchants', p.31.

Until 1954 Singapore's rice trade remained under the control of the government as the sole importer, but in the later 1950s earlier patterns quickly reasserted themselves. Singapore Chinese rice traders established both 'connections with rice-millers in Bangkok, in some cases extending to actual investment' and 'close connections' with the State Agricultural Marketing Board in Rangoon.[45] In 1957/59, when Singapore exported an annual average of 188,000 tons of rice, and retained imports were 94,700 tons (just half the level of exports),[46] it was the world's biggest rice trading centre outside the producing countries.[47]

III

Linkage effects unfold over time:[48] just as Parts One and Two of this book trace the impact of staple exports in the creation and strengthening of infrastructural and industrial linkages over the seven decades to World War II, so in the 1950s these linkages continued to develop as the rubber and petroleum trades expanded. The 1950–51 Korean War-inspired boom stimulated industrial activity,[49] and during the remainder of the decade, industrial progress, helped by further upturns in the rubber market, was rapid. Comprehensive industrial statistics are not available but, following on the high rubber prices of 1955, between 1956 and 1957 the aggregate output of Singapore's manufacturing industries rose by over 50%.[50] Annual surveys of manufacturing industry during the 1950s reveal an increasingly diversified industrial structure and the establishment of a number of new enterprises each year.[51] By the end of the decade, 'Singapore's manufacturing industries use[d] modern methods of production';[52] it was, however, often said that Singaporeans lacked technical know-how.[53]

In 1957 manufacturing accounted for 15·7% of employment in Singapore (appendix table A.10), and in 1960 for 16·6% of GDP. Most manufacturing employment was in firms with 30 or more workers.[54] Processing of primary exports constituted a significant part of industrial activity, of which, as before the War, the remilling of Indonesian rubber

---

[45] 'Rice: our main suppliers are Thailand, Burma; our best customers Malaya, Indonesia', *Singapore Trade* (Dec. 1960), p.41.

[46] Singapore, *Singapore trade statistics, 1957–1959.*

[47] 'Rice: our main suppliers', p.39.   [48] Hirschman, 'Linkages', p.211.

[49] *Commerce and industry 1954*, p.153.   [50] *Commerce and industry 1959*, p.18.

[51] See the annual series, *Commerce and industry*, 1954–1960. Some statistics for industrial production are available in Malayan statistics, *Digest of economic and social statistics*, 1954–1958, section 7 and Singapore, *Monthly digest of statistics* 1, 12 (Dec. 1962), pp.28–39.   [52] *Development plan 1961–1964*, p.16.

[53] *Master plan, study groups*, p.49; 'An industrial development programme' by F. J. Lyle, *SLA 1959*, pp.9, 29.   [54] *Development plan 1961–1964*, p.16.

was the mainstay. Between 1950 and 1954 Singapore imported from all sources an annual average of 117,000 tons of rubber for remilling, but this fell to an average of 49,000 tons in 1955/56, as mills were again established in Indonesia. From 1955 to 1960 annual average imports of rubber for smoking and remilling were 69,000 tons, about the 1955/56 level for the two activities combined.[55] Singapore's oil mills constituted another important processing industry, and depended for supplies of copra on the close commercial connections of the city's Chinese with Indonesia.[56]

Most industrial growth during the decade was underwritten by import substitution. There were some noteworthy additions to intermediate and capital goods sectors, as well as to the consumer goods industries of clothing and foodstuffs. Singapore's first steel and iron rolling mill began operating in 1956; and among Singapore's many general engineering works, some built bus and truck bodies. A United States-owned motor vehicle assembly plant employed 5,000 people, including a considerable number of fitters, mechanics, welders and machine operators.[57] However, between 1947 and 1957 employment in the manufacture of metals, machines, etc. grew at a slightly slower pace (2·6% annually) than employment as a whole in Singapore (2·8%).

There was also diversification due to the successful establishment of export-oriented industry. Singapore's first yarn spinning mill, established in 1953, had a capacity of 2·5 million lbs. per year, and exported the whole of its output to Asia, Australia and South Africa. Most rubber footwear, of which production reached a peak of four million pairs in 1956, was exported.[58]

Local Singapore Chinese banks continued to grow, and their expansion, as well as being a major institutional development. made a substantial contribution to financing local Asian industry. In 1949 the Overseas Union Bank (OUB), a predominantly Teochew undertaking,[59] began business. The OUB, together with the pre-war Oversea-Chinese Banking Corporation (OCBC) and United Overseas Bank (formerly the United Chinese Bank), became Singapore's three dominant private banks. The OUB repeated the earlier pattern of a heavy dependence on rubber entrepreneurs

---

[55] *Commerce and industry 1956*, p.14, *1960*, p.6. Statistics for the latter half of the decade combine data for rubber imported for remilling and/or smoking, rather than for remilling alone, as had previously been the case. The data for 1955 and 1956, the only two years when these two sets of statistics overlap, show that in 1955, 22,000 tons of rubber, remilled in Indonesia, were sent to Singapore for smoking alone, and in 1956, 34,800 tons.

[56] *Commerce and industry 1954*, p.155, *1955*, p.159.

[57] *Commerce and industry 1954*, p.157, *1955*, pp.158, 160, *1956*, p.159.

[58] United Nations, *Economic survey 1953*, p.96, *1954*, p.153; *Commerce and industry 1955*, p.159, *1956*, p.161, *1958*, p.16.

[59] Lee, *Monetary and banking development* (1990), p.40.

– including Tan Lark Sye – as founders and sponsors.[60] Similarly, Singapore's other main Chinese banks continued to rely on the backing of rubber entrepreneurs, notably Lee Kong Chian, and, in the case of the OCBC, the direct descendants of the original entrepreneurs.[61] One explanation for the continued association between rubber and Chinese banking was no doubt that, as a result of the Korean War boom, the rubber trade and remilling business of both Tan Lark Sye (Aik Hoe) and Lee Kong Chian profited and grew substantially – the latter firm made profits 'in terms of millions'.[62]

European banks accepted a wider range of business than before the War and were said to 'have been responsible for medium-term investment in local industry'.[63] Nevertheless, segmentation remained a feature of Singapore's organized financial markets, as evidenced by the contrasting balance sheet structure of Chinese ('local') and European ('overseas') banks:

four or five overseas banks account for about two-thirds of the total deposits and for over 80 per cent of the overseas assets, but for only about half of the local advances, etc.; their lending in Malaya tends to be restricted by the limited scope for business which they consider acceptable and within their legitimate field – chiefly the finance of overseas and internal trade and other working capital requirements of larger firms ... The typical local bank, on the other hand, although still concerned primarily with commodity finance, appears ... to take a somewhat wider view of what constitutes acceptable business.[64]

The lack of a central bank in Singapore, the regional status of Chinese banks which resulted in, at best, weak links to an external wholesale credit market and the region's specialized and strongly cyclical economy, exposed Singapore's Chinese banking system to considerable risk. This necessitated high reserve ratios, which constrained local lending. However, lending must have received a stimulus from the effect of the Korean War on the value of rubber exports and very sharp expansion of the money supply which followed, and then from further increases reflecting the high rubber prices of 1955 and 1959 (appendix table A.9).

[60] See Overseas Union Bank, *25th anniversary 1949–1974* (Singapore, 1974), which has biographies of its founder directors.
[61] Peter Absalom, 'Stability and fair dealing', *Singapore Trade* (Nov. 1964), p.25; United Overseas Bank, *Growing with Singapore* (Singapore, 1985), p.110; Lee Sheng-Yi, 'Ownership and control of local banks', *Singapore banking and finance 1980/81*, p.112.
[62] Oral History, *Pioneers*, interview with Lee Seng Gee, B000040/08, p.31, and see pp. 30, 32; Tan Eng Joo, B000018/14, p.10. On opportunities which 1950s booms in rubber created for Singapore Chinese entrepreneurs, paralleling the 1920s boom, see Yoshihara Kunio, *The rise of ersatz capitalism in South-East Asia* (Singapore, 1988), pp.214–21.
[63] King, *Money*, p.52.
[64] IBRD, *Economic development of Malaya*, pp.472–73. See also G. M. Watson and Sir Sydney Caine, *Report on the establishment of a central bank in Malaya* (Kuala Lumpur, 1956), pp.4–7; King, *Money*, pp.68–69.

In the 1950s Chinese and European banks remained more complementary than competitive, but together constituted what could be
regarded as a modern financial sector. However, financial dualism was a
marked feature of Singapore's economy, where a variety of moneylenders
– including Chettiars – chit funds, pawnbrokers and small shopkeepers
continued to meet a large demand for informal finance.[65] The Malayan
stock exchange, of which Singapore was the centre, did not really take off
until 1961. Even then, in its first boom of company flotations, which lasted
until 1964, 'Few local companies sought industrial capital, and the fact
that these did not receive as much response as the foreign firms will not give
much incentive to local industrialists'.[66] Often, however, local enterprises
probably did not wish to raise finance on the Singapore market, for fear of
dilution of ownership which could lead to a takeover by rivals, or even
another ethnic or racial group.

By 1959, despite considerable progress during the decade, industrial
development in Singapore could not be described as spectacular; nor could
the city be regarded as an industrial centre. Nevertheless, a solid foundation
for industrialization had been built. From this base, subsequent export-led
growth in manufacturing could develop, although it required the additional ingredients of lower Singapore wages (discussed in chapter 11) to
ensure competitiveness and foreign capital to bring technology.

During the 1950s the Singapore government could no doubt have done
more to promote industry, but it was not guilty of neglecting it, a charge
often levelled at colonial regimes. Singapore had always had a good
infrastructure, and government ensured its provision and upkeep. Pasir
Panjang became, with St. James', a second major power station, the Paya
Lebar airport opened in 1955, while the Queen's Dock, completed in 1956,
brought the total number of dry docks to six. Large new port works in the
East Lagoon scheme were begun to provide new wharfage, necessitated by
the increased tonnage and size of ships calling at Singapore (appendix table
A.6).[67] Industrial training facilities and apprenticeship schemes, despite
some exceptions like the Singapore Harbour Board, were inadequate in
Singapore, but in 1956 the government started to remedy this with the
establishment of the Singapore Polytechnic.[68] Government also acted, in
part through the Colonial Development Corporation, to establish indus-

[65] Charles Gamba, 'Poverty, and some socio-economic aspects of hoarding, saving and
   borrowing in Malaya', *MER* 3, 2 (1958), pp.33–66.
[66] P. J. Drake, 'The new-issue boom in Malaya and Singapore 1961–1964', *EDCC* 18, 1
   (1969), p.91, and see pp.75–77 and *Master plan, study groups*, p.58.
[67] *Commerce and industry 1958*, p.15; *Development plan 1961–1964*, p.16; 'Report of the
   commission of inquiry into the port of Singapore', *SLA 1957*, pp.7, 10, 21; Singapore,
   First development plan 1961–1964: review of progress, pp.18, 38.
[68] *Master plan, study groups*, p.57; *Commerce and industry 1956*, p.159.

trial estates.[69] In 1957 the Singapore Industrial Promotion Board was established, and at the end of 1958, two measures – the Pioneer Industries (Relief from Income Tax) Bill and the Industrial Expansion (Relief from Income Tax) Bill – were introduced to attract new enterprises to Singapore and encourage the expansion of existing firms.[70]

These were all policies which the PAP adopted, beginning in June 1959. The Party was 'committed to a programme of industrialisation'.[71] The new government quickly set up the Economic Development Board as a replacement for the Singapore Industrial Promotion Board, and made it both a financing institution for industry and an industrial corporation to establish new industries and open industrial estates. However, just as the PAP took power, an industrial development programme was initiated in the Federation of Malaya. New industries set up in Malaya could obtain 'pioneer status' and (in contrast to the inter-war decades) tariff protection.[72] For Singapore this was a potentially serious departure because of the substantial 'import substitution' market in Malaya, which was looked to as a basis for continued industrialization.

IV

Singapore's demography was altered fundamentally in the 1950s by the end of large-scale immigration (appendix table A.7). Despite the rubber boom at the beginning of the decade, the movement of people to and from China was a fraction of its pre-war level; and in 1953 (after which immigration statistics were no longer published), new immigration laws effectively ended the inflow of manual workers.[73] Equally, however, in post-war Singapore, adjustment to poor trade conditions was no longer possible through 'encouraging the return of surplus labourers to their own countries';[74] it was now necessary to provide employment for a stable population.

---

[69] United Nations, *Economic survey 1955*, p.156; *Commerce and industry 1956*, p.159; King, *Money*, p.81; Sir William Rendell, *The history of the Colonial Development Corporation 1948–1972* (London, 1976), pp.67–68, 130, 227.

[70] Singapore, Singapore Industrial Promotion Board, *First year report March 1957 – April 1958* (Singapore, 1958), pp.1–19; *Commerce and industry 1958*, p.15; 'The importance of pioneering', *Singapore Trade* (July 1961), pp.8–13.

[71] *Commerce and industry 1959*, p.19.

[72] 'Industrial development programme' by Lyle, *SLA 1959*, pp.8–11.

[73] Colony of Singapore, *Annual report of the immigration department 1953* (Singapore, 1954), pp.1–2; International Labour Office, *Report to the government of Singapore on social security measures* Cmd.56 of 1957 (Singapore, 1957), p.3.

[74] 'Report of the committee on minimum standards of livelihood', *SLA* (sessional paper no. Cmd. 5 of 1957), p.5.

Table 10.3 *Singapore unemployment rates, 1957–1990*

1957	4.9	1974	3.9
1966	8.9	1980	3.5
1968	7.3	1984	2.7
1970	6.0	1986	6.5
1972	4.7	1988	3.3
1973	4.5	1990	1.7

Notes:
1   Data for 1957, 1970, 1980 and 1990 are census figures.
2   Data to 1980 inclusive refer to the percentage of the labour force aged 15–64 years, and from 1984 to persons aged 15 years and over.
Sources: 1957 census, p.175; *Singapore parliamentary debates* 35, 1 (1 March 1976) (appendix to budget statement), col.117–18; *Singapore sample household survey, 1966,* p.87; *Economic and social statistics, 1960–1982,* p.32; *Yearbook of statistics 1988,* p.58; *1990 census: Statistical release 4, Economic characteristics,* pp.21, 37.

Open unemployment, some 5 % in 1957 (table 10.3), was not high.[75] But, as in its pre-war economy, Singapore had a substantial amount of 'surplus labour'. No doubt a proportion of casual workers, including much of dock labour and most of those in building and construction, were less than fully employed, but they were not generally regarded as surplus labour. The term applied instead to 'hawkers of food and other things [who] with the small traders and the trishaw riders and others form a numerous group of "self-employed" … many who seek a livelihood in such occupations can hardly be regarded as fully employed in them, while they equally cannot well be regarded as unemployed. Such conditions of "half-employment" apply also to many nominal employees of small shops, trading concerns and cafes'.[76]

Poverty in Singapore was mainly due to the classical explanations of irregular employment, illness or death of the chief family breadwinner or large family size, usually requiring the maintenance of elderly relatives or many young children.[77] In 1957, 19 % of Singapore households and 25 % of individuals were found to be in poverty, defined as a household income 'insufficient for minimum standards'. For a family of a man, wife and two children, this minimum standard required a monthly income of $102; the average wage of male workers in regular employment was about $150 a

[75]   It was observed that the claim of the Singapore Development Plan that in 1959 10% of Singapore's population was unemployed was an estimate, and open to question. Anthony Bottomley, 'The role of foreign branch plants in the industrialisation of Singapore', *MER* 7, 1 (1962), p.26. See also 'Minimum standards of livelihood', *SLA 1957,* p.51; *Report on social security,* pp.9, 47; Benham, *Economic survey,* p.28.
[76]   'Minimum standards of livelihood', *SLA 1957,* p.3; see also *Report on social security,* pp.9, 47.
[77]   This paragraph is based on 'Minimum standards of livelihood', *SLA 1957,* pp.13–26.

Table 10.4 *Singapore population growth, 1931–1980 (% average annual increase)*

	Total growth	Natural increase	Migrational surplus
1931–1947	3.3	1.7	1.6
1947–1957	4.4	3.6	0.8
1957–1970	2.8	2.7	0.1
1970–1980	1.5	1.4	0.1

Sources: 1980 census: Administrative report, p.89.

Table 10.5 *Singapore population by race, 1947–1990*

	Persons	Chinese %	Indians %	Malays %	Others %
1947	938,144	77.8	7.7	12.1	2.4
1957	1,445,929	75.4	9.0	13.6	2.0
1970	2,074,507	76.2	7.0	15.0	1.8
1980	2,413,945	76.9	6.4	14.6	2.1
1990	3,016,379	74.7	7.6	13.5	4.2

Sources: 1957 census, pp.43–44; 1970 census, pp.46, 53; 1980 census, pp. 89–91; 1990 census: Statistical release 1, Demographic characteristics, pp.xiii, 2.

month, but 'the commonest wage' was between $100 and $120 a month. It was estimated that a transfer of from 1·5% to 2·25% of national income would have eliminated this poverty.

Another main demographic change was a rapid rise in the birth rate with the ending of mass immigration, and so the emergence of a much more normal population structure. Between 1931 and 1947 population grew at 3·3% annually, primarily due to natural increase (table 10.4).[78] By 1947 Singapore Island had 938,000 inhabitants (table 10.5).

Table 10.4 shows that between 1947 and 1957 Singapore's population grew at 4·4% annually, 'a rate which is the highest known in the world'.[79] Natural increase accounted for almost all this growth; less than a fifth was due to net immigration and migration (table 10.4). The result was a rise in

[78] However, the population was also swelled by refugees who had come to the city in 1940 because of Japan's invasion of Malaya, and the failure of the Japanese rationing system during World War II to operate effectively outside the larger towns and villages, which encouraged the drift of people to Singapore. *Master plan, study groups*, p.20; *1947 census*, p.34.

[79] *Development plan 1961–1964*, p.1. However, this rate was already falling. The 1970 census identified 'the period 1956–1957 … [as] a critical turning point towards a declining fertility trend'. *1970 census* I, p.36.

Table 10.6 *Singapore labour force growth, 1947–1990*

	Persons	Male	Female
(a) *Number*			
1947	357,535	310,484	47,051
1957	480,267	393,797	86,470
1970	726,676	539,223	187,453
1980	1,115,958	730,606	385,352
1990	1,562,819	934,320	628,499
(b) *Average annual growth rate*			
1947–57	3.0	2.4	6.3
1957–70	3.2	2.4	6.1
1970–80	4.4	3.1	7.5
1980–90	3.4	2.5	5.0
1947–90	3.5	2.6	6.2

Notes:
1   Data for 1947–80 refer to persons aged 10 years and over and for 1990 to persons aged 15 years and over. The 1980 figure for persons aged 15 years and over was 1,112,079.
2   The 1947 figure refers to total gainfully employed and so is not strictly comparable with other data. In 1957 the numbers of gainfully employed were: total 471,918, males 387,708 and females 84,210.
Sources: 1957 census, pp.84, 220; *1970 census* I, p.161; *1980 census: Administrative report*, p.105, *Release no.4. Economic characteristics*, p.29; *1990 census: Statistical release 4, Economic characteristics*, pp.2, 37.

the dependency burden, in which the youngest age groups predominated.[80] However, Singapore had some breathing space before population increase began to translate into very rapid labour force growth.

Even so, between 1947 and 1957 the labour force grew at 3·0% annually, and its female component at 6·3% (table 10.6). Nevertheless, in 1957 the female participation rate, 21·6%, was still low in comparison to subsequent levels. Singapore's labour force growth provided an elastic supply of labour, but despite this, wages in Singapore remained high by Asian and by international standards.[81] In 1957 the average wage of male workers of $150 a month was equivalent to 79s a week, which was almost a third of average weekly earnings of men aged 21 and over working a 48·2-hour week as manual workers in manufacturing in the United Kingdom.[82]

[80] 'Minimum standards of livelihood', *SLA 1957*, pp.2, 5, 55; *Report on social security*, p.66.
[81] 'Industrial development programme' by Lyle, *SLA 1959*, p.7; 'Minimum standards of livelihood', *SLA 1957*, p.30.
[82] Mitchell and Jones, *Second abstract of British historical statistics*, p.148. By contrast, in 1975 hourly compensation costs for production workers in manufacturing in Singapore were one-quarter of those for United Kingdom workers. US Department of Labor, Bureau of Labor Statistics, *International comparisons of hourly compensation costs for*

Demographic factors helped to explain alterations in Singapore's housing stock and, accordingly, changes in the city's appearance. Before the War the great mass of Singaporeans, often single people intending to return to China, had crowded into the centre. Squatter settlements, although not entirely unknown, were unusual in Singapore: in 1931 there were perhaps 2,000 squatter dwellings.[83] By 1947, however, municipal Singapore had some 20,000 families of squatters and a total squatter population of at least 100,000. They 'live in huts made of attap [palm thatch], old boxes, rusty corrugated iron etc. with no sanitation, water, or any of elementary health requirements'.[84] In part, these squatter settlements, which by the early 1950s spread over the entire outer city, reflected the saturation of central Singapore. The centre was already heavily built up in 1947, and subject to serious overcrowding, both per acre and per dwelling; two-fifths of those in Singapore Municipality lived in houses of 21 inhabitants or more, and the average number of inhabitants in such houses was 34.[85] Other, equally important explanations for the squatter settlements may have been the unaffordability and unsuitability of space in central Singapore for many larger families: erection of an attap dwelling on the outskirts of the city was the only way to obtain accommodation.[86] Reflecting continued rapid population increase, squatter settlements remained a feature of Singapore until the 1970s, when widespread government rehousing eliminated most of them.

V

During the 1950s vigorous political debate broke out for the first time in Singapore. Uncertainty over the economic future, awareness of the need for industrialization and the expectation that this would require union with Malaya heightened debate. As in other countries with decolonization obviously on the agenda, politics engaged many of the most talented individuals, and tended to have a leftist bias. Goh Keng Swee, later Singapore's finance minister, recalled of being an LSE student in the 1950s that 'In those days I was mixed up with Marxists'.[87]

production workers in manufacturing 1991 Report 825 (Washington, DC: US Department of Labor, June 1992), p.6.
[83] *1931 census*, p.49; Colony of Singapore, *Report of the housing committee Singapore, 1947* (Singapore, 1947), pp.1–3.   [84] *Housing committee 1947*, p.1.
[85] *1947 census*, p.129. In British Malaya, the term 'house' was ambiguous. In general, the Singapore figures reflected the subdivision of dwellings with a common entrance to accommodate a large number of people. Ibid. p.125.
[86] *Housing committee 1947*, p.1; Goh, *Urban incomes*, pp.8, 14, 15, 62, 64, 65; Colony of Singapore, *Report of the land clearance and resettlement working party* (Singapore, 1956), pp.3–4.   [87] Goh Keng Swee, interview with the author, 17 Aug. 1989.

Table 10.7 *Singapore industrial stoppages, 1954–1990*

	Number	Workers involved	Man-days[a] lost		Number	Workers involved	Man-days[a] lost
1954	8	11,191	135,206	1973	5	1,312	2,295
1955	275	57,433	946,354	1974	10	1,901	5,380
1956[b]	29	12,373	454,455	1975	7	1,865	4,835
1957	27	8,233	109,349	1976	4	1,576	3,193
1958	22	2,679	78,166	1977	1	406	1,011
1959	40	1,939	26,588	1978	0	0	0
1960	45	5,939	152,005	1979	0	0	0
1961	116	43,584	410,889	1980	0	0	0
1962	88	6,647	165,124	1981	0	0	0
1963[c]	47	33,004	388,219	1982	0	0	0
1964	39	2,535	35,908	1983	0	0	0
1965	30	3,374	45,800	1984	0	0	0
1966	14	1,288	44,762	1985	0	0	0
1967	10	4,491	41,322	1986	1	61	122
1968	4	172	11,447	1987	0	0	0
1969	0	0	8,512	1988	0	0	0
1970	5	1,749	2,514	1989	0	0	0
1971	2	1,380	5,449	1990	1	98	196
1972	10	3,168	18,233				

Notes:
a   Figures relate to man–days lost within the year shown, irrespective of whether the stoppages began in that year or earlier.
b   Stoppages due to civil disturbances in October 1956 are excluded.
c   Figures include the two–day general strike in October involving approximately 19,700 workers and 34,300 man–days lost.
Sources: Malayan statistics, digest of economic and social statistics, Dec. 1961, p.15; *Economic and social statistics, 1960–1982*, p.42; *Yearbook of statistics 1990*, p.77.

Although often described as a decade of industrial unrest,[88] experience during the 1950s was much less uniform than this characterization suggests. In 1950 Singapore had only one strike and 'that was a matter of personal animosities rather than a genuine employment dispute';[89] similarly, during 1951 Singapore experienced just five strikes, while in 1954 only eight industrial stoppages occurred (table 10.7). Elections in 1955 as a result of the Rendel Constitutional Commission to establish a measure of self-government – the first elections to be held in Singapore – explain the particularly high figures for days lost that year.[90] The trade union

[88] E.g. Chia Siow Yue, 'The role of foreign trade and investment in the development of Singapore' in Walter Galenson, ed. *Foreign trade and investment: economic development in the newly industrializing Asian countries* (Madison, WI, 1985), p.287.
[89] Mackenzie, *Economic and commercial conditions*, p.23.
[90] Yeo Kim Wah, *Political development in Singapore 1945–55* (Singapore, 1973), pp.126–27, 266–67; King, *Money*, p.81.

movement, which had been encouraged by the colonial government,[91] was at that time gaining considerable strength. Union membership more than doubled between 1954 and 1957, when 35% of Singapore workers were said to belong to trade unions.[92] Yet workers involved and man-days lost in industrial stoppages declined sharply from 1956 until after the 1959 election. In the early 1960s the People's Action Party, formally allied with the Communists, encouraged strikes to promote itself, as did other political parties. Such politically expedient strikes help to account for the upsurge in work stoppages in 1963 and 1964.[93]

Three aspects of government and politics in Singapore promoted stability and set it apart from the experience of decolonization in many countries. First, after post-war destitution and neglect due to the Japanese occupation,[94] and the hiatus of the British military administration, or BMA (also known as the Black Market Administration), stable government had time to reassert itself. Decolonization and complete self-rule was an extended process; Singapore did not gain internal independence until 1959, the island became part of Malaysia in 1963 and achieved full independence only in 1965.

Second, beginning in the late 1940s, there was substantial and visible social as well as economic progress in Singapore. The fall in infant mortality of more than 50% between 1947 and 1957, and good social services available by the end of the 1950s, were described in chapter 1.[95] An improvement of overall literacy rates per thousand from the 374 in 1947 to 523 in 1957[96] reflected a new policy after World War II to provide free, universal primary education and the expansion of the education system during the 1950s.[97] In 1949 the University of Malaya in Singapore was established as the successor to Raffles College, begun in 1928. Table 10.8 shows Singapore's comparatively high educational provision by 1960 – still substantially less than in developed countries but considerably above

[91] Awbery and Dalley, *Labour and trade union organisation*, p.25; 'Singapore trade unions', *Economic Bulletin* 2, 4 (1952), p.1.

[92] Alex Josey, *Trade unionism in Malaya* (Singapore, 1958), p.17; Charles Gamba, 'Trade unionism in Malaya', *Far Eastern Survey* 23 (1954), p.28.

[93] Pang Eng Fong, 'Changing patterns of industrial relations in Singapore' in Peter S. J. Chen and Hans Dieter-Evers, eds. *Studies in ASEAN sociology* (Singapore, 1978), p.426.

[94] Mackenzie, *Economic and commercial conditions*, pp.1–2; 'Minimum standards of livelihood', *SLA 1957*, p.9.

[95] Between 1947 and 1959 the colonial administration 'developed one of the best medical services in South-East Asia'. Nalla Tan, 'Health and welfare' in Ernest C. T. Chew and Edwin Lee, eds. *A history of Singapore* (Singapore, 1991), p.346.

[96] *1947 census*, p.90; *1957 census*, p.76; *1970 census* I, p.100.

[97] Singapore, *Education policy in the Colony of Singapore: ten years' programme* (Singapore: Government Printing Office, 1948), p.5; *1957 census*, p.77.

Table 10.8 *Singapore and comparative educational enrolment levels, 1960* (*% of age group*)

	Primary	Secondary	Higher education
Middle-income countries			
Lower	66	10	3
Upper	88	20	4
Industrial countries	114	64	16
Singapore	111	32	6
South Korea	94	27	5

Source: World Bank, *World development report 1983*, pp.196–97.

South Korea's.[98] Singapore's 1961 development plan stressed 'The high level of education of the youthful population' which would create an adaptable labour force.[99]

The third aspect encouraging stability was that Singapore's local, non-European population, largely excluded by the colour bar from the civil service before World War II, gained much greater experience during the 1950s through election to office, employment in the civil service and serving on government-appointed committees.[100] T. H. Silcock drew attention to the long interlude between the outbreak of World War II and Singapore's independence a quarter of a century later, together with the particular experience its eventual leaders gained during this period, as an important reason for the high quality of leadership and government in Singapore: 'There is no way in which anyone could rely on reproducing the effects of the Japanese Occupation, the Singapore Social Survey, the Emergency, Lee Kuan Yew's strategy, and the impact of the creation and division of Malaysia, on some very able young people with a tradition created by the traumas of Raffles College'.[101]

---

[98] South Korea is often given as an example of an LDC beginning from a high educational base, and this is cited as a cause of its subsequent rapid economic development: Chris Manning and Pang Eng Fong, 'Labour market trends and structures in ASEAN and the East Asian NIEs', *Asian-Pacific Economic Literature* 4, 2 (1990), p.63; Dornbusch and Park, 'Korean growth', pp.397–99.   [99] *Development plan 1961–1964*, p.16.

[100] For example, Goh Keng Swee, working as a civil servant, gained an international reputation as the author of *Urban incomes and housing* (the Singapore social survey), and S. Rajaratnam served on the Committee on Minimum Standards of Livelihood.

[101] T. H. Silcock, *A history of economics teaching and graduates: Raffles College and the University of Malaya in Singapore 1934–1960* (Singapore, 1985), pp.293–94. The traumas at Raffles College referred to included 'coming to terms with the political situation [and] ... playing a leading role in bringing the University of Malaya into existence.' Ibid. p.93.

Of course, in 1959 Singapore's future was unclear, and any political outcome might have occurred, but that is close to asserting a truism. In light of Singapore's self-interest and economic history, by 1959, especially with the military defeat of the Malayan Communists by the British, a fairly conservative political solution was the probable future for Singapore. F. Benham, a close academic observer of Singapore at the time, made this point in 1957: 'there seem no good grounds for supposing that stable, political and economic conditions will not continue. It is most unlikely that any government which may come to power will follow policies adverse to industry and trade'.[102] His assessment was correct. Even so, it might have been difficult to envisage the vigour of the post-1959 PAP economic development initiative, made possible by decolonization. The success of that initiative itself promoted political stability, but first it brought about striking economic change in the 1960s and beyond.

[102] Frederic Benham, 'Western enterprise in Indonesia and Malaya', *MER* 2, 2 (1957), p.52.

11 Markets, government and growth, 1960–1990

Between 1960 and 1990 Singapore grew rapidly, and for almost all this period trade was again the engine of growth. But three changes set these decades apart from earlier twentieth-century development. First, economic development ceased to depend on staples as the economy diversified, initially through manufactures and then through financial and business services. By 1970 manufacturing had made sufficient impact on the economy to be regarded as a leading sector. Three years later, manufacturing ended the labour surplus condition, and with it the dual economy, analysed in earlier chapters, so that 1973 may be dated as a turning point in economic development.

The second change was that growth stemmed from a new set of entrepreneurs in the form of public (i.e. government) enterprises and, even more, multinational enterprises (MNEs). By 1990 agency houses, so fundamental to Singapore's pre-World War II economic development, had, with a few exceptions, disappeared; local Chinese entrepreneurs, although still found especially in primary commodity exports, took a back seat. Third, an activist government committed to development guided economic transformation. Planning, begun with the report of a United Nations team in 1961,[1] lay behind Singapore's growth.

After 1960 the look of Singapore altered fundamentally from a still largely coastal city made up of shophouses and fringed by squatter dwellings to an island-wide settlement of satellite new towns (19 by the 1990s), built as high-rise public housing. Although the old British government area on one side of the Singapore River changed little, the Central Business District (CBD) opposite boasted a growing cluster of skyscrapers in which Singapore Chinese banks were prominent, and one of their number the tallest. Retailing remained in central Singapore, but now in shopping centres, so numerous as to afford Singaporeans perhaps the world's highest per capita shopping centre square footage.

---

[1] United Nations, *A proposed industrialization programme for the State of Singapore* (New York: UN Commission for Technical Assistance, 1961).

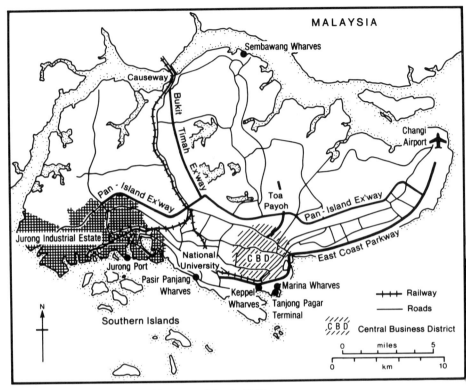

Figure 11.1   Singapore Island, 1990

Additions to infrastructure, typically planned by the government and
built under its direction, both contributed to change and accelerated it. As
figure 11.1 shows, expressways linked the centre and main industrial estate
of Jurong in the west – still swamp in 1959 – and Changi Airport, the
replacement for Paya Lebar, to the east. A bus service, placed under
government management in 1978, and, from the later 1980s, a world-class
mass rapid transit system provided efficient public transport. The port
spread over the island to five sites, including Pasir Panjang outside central
Singapore, where government planning relocated the trade of the Singapore River. Nearby, government planners also sited the large new National
University campus.

    The present chapter concentrates on the economic growth which made
possible these changes. Because the same government spanned the entire
31 years, and because infrastructure and institutions established in the
1960s were basic to the growth of the 1970s and 1980s, the three decades
may be considered as a whole. The chapter's first section reviews the

performance of the economy and its structural transformation. The next two sections concentrate on Singapore's external economic relationships and analyse respectively the structure of trade and manufactured exports.

A principal theme of the chapter is that Singapore's development relied on a combination of external free trade and strong internal economic control. This latter is the subject of section IV, which looks at savings and investment, and of section V, which focuses on economic planning. Section VI examines Singapore's natural comparative advantage as a financial centre and how government policies and planning augmented comparative advantage. In section VII, the relationship between macroeconomic policy, planning and economic development is considered. Sweeping social changes accompanied economic growth, and are indicated in section VIII. The chapter's last section assesses the Singapore government's ability successfully to implement its policies and the political/institutional conditions which made possible this implementation.

I

Figures 1.4 and 11.2 and tables 11.1 and 11.2 show the nature and outlines of Singapore's economic development from 1960 to 1990. Five main features can be discerned. One is sustained, exceptionally high growth rates of output. Over the period, real GDP increased elevenfold, doubling between 1960 and 1969, again between 1970 and 1979 and once more between 1980 and 1990 (appendix table A.12). From 1970 to 1990 real per capita GDP more than tripled.

GDP grew at 7% per annum or over in 23 of the 31 years. There were four periods of particularly rapid growth: the beginning of the 1960s; double-digit growth from 1966 to 1973; rates ranging from 6·9% to almost 10% during 1976 to 1984; and increases averaging close to 10% from 1987 to 1990. Singapore's growth, far above the long-term rate of developed countries, supports a convergence hypothesis: that rapid growth reflects a process of 'catching up', made possible by drawing on existing world knowledge and technology.[2]

Second, the structure of trade changed, and after 1970 grew decisively away from a staple port character to emphasize increasingly the export of Singapore-made manufactures. An indication of the export orientation of Singapore's manufacturing is that non-petroleum direct manufactured

---

[2] William J. Baumol, 'Productivity growth, convergence and welfare: what the long-run data show', *American Economic Review* 76, 5 (1986), pp.1072–85.

Table 11.1 *Singapore macroeconomic indicators, 1960–1990*

	1960-66	1966-69	1960-69	1970-79	1980-90
Annual real GDP growth rate	5.7	13.6	8.0	8.3	6.4
Annual inflation rate[a]	1.1	1.0	1.1	5.8	1.8
Savings ratio[b]	6.7	18.2	11.5	28.8	41.2
Investment ratio[b]	17.5	24.8	20.7	40.5	41.9

Notes:
a   GDP deflator.
b   The savings ratio and investment ratio are defined respectively as Gross National Savings and Gross Capital Formation divided by Gross Domestic Product. All variables are in real terms deflated by the GDP deflator.
Sources: Appendix tables A.12 and A.13.

exports (goods not simply re-exported) rose from 12.7 % of GDP in 1966 to almost half in 1979 and nearly two-thirds by 1990 (table 11.3). Singapore first industrialized when the volume of world manufactured exports was expanding rapidly.[3] But swift export growth continued, despite the slowdown in world trade after 1973, and showed how quickly MNEs may move 'footloose' production processes to an advantageous site like the Republic.

Third, economic growth was accompanied by fundamental structural transformation (table 11.2 and appendix table A.11). Two principal changes occurred. The share of manufacturing in total output increased rapidly, from 16·6 % in 1960 and 20·5 % in 1967 to 28·4 % by 1973. In 1990 manufacturing contributed 29 % of GDP and accounted for 29·1 % of employment. The other structural change was the altered composition of the tertiary sector. Services in Singapore were defined as the three categories of transport and communications; financial and business services; and public administration, community, social and personal services. Between 1960 and 1990 the third of these categories, which encompassed the 'soft' or predominantly labour supply-pushed components of the tertiary sector, fell continuously in both share of output and employment. By contrast, especially after 1973, as economic development gained pace, the tertiary sector's 'hard' or rest-of-the-economy pulled components expanded.[4]

Overall, the service sector's contribution to GDP fell until 1970, but then

---

[3] Between 1963 and 1973 the volume of world manufactured exports grew at an annual average rate of 11·5 %. GATT, *International trade 1984/85* (Geneva, 1985), p.4.
[4] The division is not exact, however. Public administration, community, social and personal services also included services like medicine, education and tourism, which are tradeable and contributed to Singapore's foreign exchange earnings.

Table 11.2 *Singapore GDP by industrial sector, 1960–1990 (1985 market prices, %)*

	1960	1967	1970	1973	1978	1980	1984	1990
Agriculture & fishing	3.6	2.8	2.2	1.7	1.3	1.1	0.8	0.3
Quarrying	0.2	0.2	0.2	0.2	0.2	0.2	0.3	0.1
Manufacturing	16.6	20.5	24.8	28.4	28.2	29.5	25.0	29.0
Electricity, gas, water	1.7	2.0	1.9	1.9	2.0	2.0	1.9	2.1
Construction	5.3	8.6	9.5	8.1	7.2	7.1	12.5	5.3
Commerce	24.6	23.6	22.0	20.9	19.8	18.9	17.0	17.6
Transport & communications	8.8	6.9	7.3	8.5	11.1	12.0	13.0	14.2
Financial & business services	14.0	15.5	16.9	17.6	18.6	20.5	23.6	26.2
Community, social and personal services	19.6	17.8	14.9	13.3	12.7	11.6	11.3	10.4
Total	(100.0)	(100.0)	(100.0)	(100.0)	(100.0)	(100.0)	(100.0)	(100.0)
GDP at 1985 market prices ($m)	5,058.5	8,283.1	12,172.4	17,273.6	24,046.0	28,832.5	39,572.5	57,049.4
Less: Imputed bank service charges	53.6	93.3	160.2	296.8	707.1	1,340.8	2,666.6	3,576.3
Add: import duties	235.8	276.4	356.1	405.6	420.3	496.0	511.5	526.6

Sources: Singapore national accounts 1987, pp.45–48; Economic survey, 1989, p.112, 1992, p.112.

$000,000

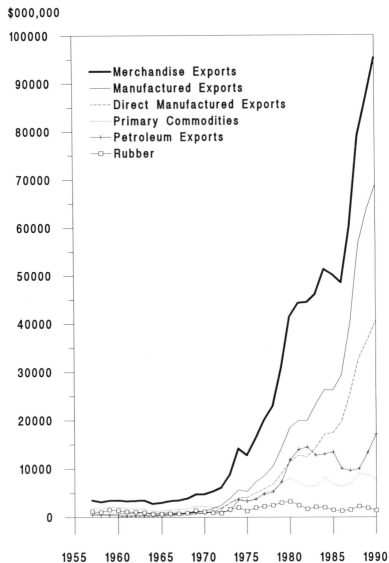

Figure 11.2   Singapore merchandise exports and main export
categories, 1957–1990

began to rise again; its share of output increased from less than two-fifths
in 1973 to over half by 1990. In Singapore, a high proportion of the 'hard'
services were internationally tradeable. The main diversification, and
greatest growth, in tradeable services came through the Republic's

Table 11.3 *Singapore direct manufactured exports, 1960–1990 (1985 market prices)*

	1960	1966	1967	1969	1979	1990
$m	542.5	933.3	1,127.5	1,827.4	12,368.0	35,891.4
% of GDP	10.7	12.7	13.6	17.0	47.1	62.9

Notes:
1 Data are deflated by the GDP deflator for manufacturing.
2 Statistics refer to firms with 10 or more workers, and exclude petroleum, rubber processing and granite quarrying.
Sources: Appendix tables A.3 and A.12; *Singapore national accounts 1987*, pp.50–51; *Economic survey, 1988*, p.102, *1989*, p.114, *1990*, p.115, *1991*, p.97.

development as an international financial centre. After 1978 financial and business services emerged as an engine of growth, and over the next 12 years were the fastest-growing sector, with annual average real growth of 10·6%, compared to 7·5% for the economy as a whole. By 1990 financial and business services provided 26·2% of GDP, or almost as much as manufacturing, but, reflecting the capital-intensive nature of many traded services, made up just 10·9% of employment, a third of that in manufacturing.

The successful expansion of financial and business services represented the most important part of development planning to establish Singapore as a centre for what government planners termed 'brain services' – activities with a high human capital content and typically dependent on substantial inputs of formal education.[5] Many of the brain services were ancillary to being a financial centre, and included in the GDP category of financial and business services – accounting and auditing, legal services, advertising, market research and computer and management consultancy. Other brain services like architecture, engineering and design services had linkages arising from Singapore's role as a financial centre to a consequent demand for construction and communications.

Between 1973 and 1990 transport and telecommunications services also expanded strongly, but these activities were, in contrast to the financial sector, often similar to functions Singapore had traditionally performed. Like the old Singapore Harbour Board, the Port of Singapore Authority offered efficient and competitive services for shipping. Shipping tonnage

---

[5] Hon Sui Sen, *Economic pattern in the 1970s* (budget speech, 1972) (Singapore, 1972), pp.19–23; Singapore, Ministry of Trade and Industry, *Highlights of Singapore's economic development plan for the eighties* (Singapore, n.d.), pp.9–13; Singapore, Economic Committee, *The Singapore economy: new directions* (Singapore, 1986), pp.139–43, 177–92.

clearing from Singapore more than doubled in the 1970s and almost doubled again during the 1980s (appendix table A.6). The large number of oil tankers calling at Singapore contributed substantially to this growth of tonnage, and so to making Singapore the world's busiest port. More shipping traffic also came to Singapore due to the international increase in the price of oil bunkers dating from the 1970s: ships began to call at fewer ports to conserve fuel, which concentrated more shipping on Singapore. In turn, the shipping drawn to the port expanded its role in the handling and warehousing of transhipment cargo and the transhipment of empty containers.[6] The production of bunker fuel, almost as a by-product of Singapore's oil refineries, kept the price of bunkers low, which had an important linkage for Singapore's port of call and transhipment business. By the end of the 1980s Singapore was the world's largest supplier of ships' bunkers and also, reflecting an increased role in the provision of transport services in the Asia-Pacific region, the world's largest container port.[7]

The network of Asia-Pacific air routes which focused on Singapore, and the rapid growth of Singapore Airlines to make the Republic the world's fifth largest international air carrier, promoted a range of air transport services analogous to those arising from international shipping.[8] At the end of the 1980s Singapore inaugurated a policy to serve as an air hubbing centre: non-Singapore carriers were allowed to base operations on Singapore (in the same way that Conference shipping lines traditionally had) and operate regional feeder services to and from the Changi hub to connect with international routes.[9] Spin-offs from the establishment of Changi as a major airport included aircraft servicing and repair, provision of fuel, cargo transhipment, aircraft meals and duty-free sales. Pilots and passengers alike looked to arrival in Singapore, in preference to other Southeast Asian capitals, as the location to place international telephone calls because of its instant telecommunications links. This was indicative of

---

[6] Wong Seng Chee, 'Development of Singapore into the world's third largest port', *NSC Statistical News* 2, 2 (1979), pp.1–2. Singapore was the world's busiest port in terms of shipping tonnage handled, but far from this in terms of the number of vessels. Tonnage figures reflected oil tankers calling at Singapore.

[7] 'PSA is world's no.1 port three times over, says Mah', *Straits Times Weekly*, 22 Feb. 1992; *Containerisation international yearbook 1992* (London, 1992), pp.6–7; 'S'pore is world's top bunkering port', *Singapore Bulletin* 16, 8 (June 1988).

[8] 'For so busy a hub, only an airtropolis would do', *New York Times*, 7 Dec. 1990; 'SIA makes it to ranks of world's top 5 airlines', *Straits Times Weekly*, 24 Oct. 1992. As an international carrier, in 1991 Singapore ranked behind the US, UK, Japan and Germany. By the 1990s Singapore's airport could accommodate 24 million passengers a year, the largest in the Asia-Pacific region.

[9] '10 airlines keen on hubbing operations here, says CAAS', *Straits Times Weekly*, 12. Oct. 1991.

an international telephone traffic fundamental to all internationally-traded services. By 1988 international calls from Singapore numbered one-third as many as made from the whole of Japan.[10]

Fourth, high savings and investment characterized Singapore's economic development. An urban economy and international services centre like Singapore required heavy infrastructural investment. Because of the need to finance this investment, in the 1950s 'one of the great open questions [was] whether the new democracy of Singapore can exercise the self-restraint necessary to emulate the capital creation of Victorian England, based on voluntary abstinence, or of Communist Russia, based on compulsory abstinence'.[11] The PAP enforced state-directed abstinence. As a result, the savings ratio, still under 10% in 1964, reached 27% in 1973, over 30% by 1976, and averaged over 40% from 1983 (appendix table A.13).

The investment ratio also increased sharply, and from 1970 was sustained at high levels, with gross capital formation usually over 40% of GDP (appendix table A.13). As in South Korea, the Singapore government used employee pension funds to finance planned government investment. In the 1970s Singapore saved enough to finance almost two-thirds, and by the 1980s virtually the whole, of its capital formation (table 11.1). However, the process of capital accumulation was more complex than suggested by this apparently increasing reliance on domestic savings. Throughout the post-1966 period, direct foreign investment made a growing contribution to capital formation, as discussed in section IV.

Fifth, Singapore's post-1959 development occurred with low inflation, remarkable for an economy already chronically short of labour by the late 1970s. For 18 of the 30 years from 1961 to 1990, the GDP deflator was 2·6% or less, and exceeded 5% in only seven years, despite high world inflation and Singapore's very open economy. The annual inflation rate averaged below 2% in every decade except the 1970s (table 11.1 and appendix table A.12).

II

In Singapore, the transition from reliance on traditional staple exports to non-traditional, domestically-produced manufactured exports spread over the 1960s. It involved a period of import substitution which, although

[10] GATT, *International trade 1989/90* (Geneva, 1990), I, p.39.
[11] Sydney Caine, 'The importance of capital', *MER* 1, 1 (1956), p.5.

Tons 000

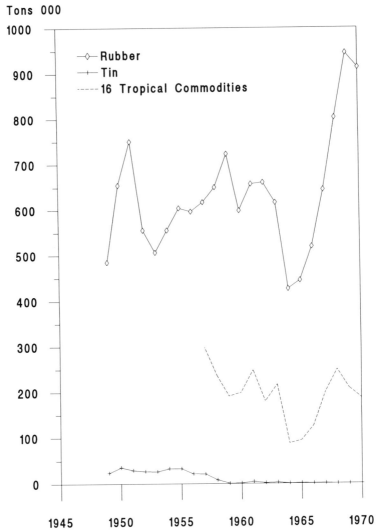

Figure 11.3   Singapore volume of exports of rubber, tin and 16
tropical commodities, 1949–1970

brief, was nevertheless significant in engendering economic growth and
establishing support institutions for subsequent export-oriented manufacturing. The years 1960 to 1965 were unusual in Singapore's economic
development, in that growth was not export-led. There was a downturn in
staple exports, accentuated by Indonesia's Confrontation (appendix tables
A.1, A.2 and figure 11.3). Singapore's rapid GDP growth to the mid-1960s

was chiefly due to expansion in the manufacturing and construction sectors. The former depended principally on import-substituting industries encouraged by the formation of Malaysia; increased construction reflected economic planning which concentrated on investment in infrastructure. The Economic Development Board (EDB), as the government's agent, was set up as 'the spearhead for industrialisation by direct participation in industry' and building necessary infrastructure.[12] Heavy developmental expenditure, most prominently on the Board's new industrial estate at Jurong, created a base for future export-oriented industrialization, but yielded little in either industrial production or exports until at least mid-decade.[13]

During the later 1960s, after the separation from Malaysia, industrialization gained new momentum, as Singapore turned outwards to manufacture for export; the manufacturing sector expanded swiftly from 1967 onwards (table 11.2). Co-ordination through the EDB was basic to the new export drive, and the success of the EDB spawned additional development-oriented institutions when, in 1968, the Board's largest industrial estate, at Jurong, came under the management of the Jurong Town Corporation, and the financial arm of the EDB became the Development Bank of Singapore.[14]

But through the second half of the 1960s Singapore's economy still depended heavily on staple exports, both rubber and petroleum. In 1966, with the end of Confrontation, the resumption of trade with Indonesia was 'the main impetus to economic growth', while 'the last two years of the decade were exceptionally good ... The principal thrust was an unparalleled expansion of our entrepot trade'.[15] Appendix tables A.1, A.2 and A.3 document the upsurge in primary commodity trade, also graphed in figure 11.3; the 1967/69 SITC sections 0–4, consisting of food and primary commodities, made up almost two-thirds of total exports (appendix table A.4). If petroleum products were included in the 1969 statistics for direct manufactured exports (as in the official statistics but not appendix table A.3), the value of these exports would be almost doubled,

---

[12] Singapore, *First development plan 1961–1964: review of progress*, p.37, and see *SLA Debates*, Economic Development Board bill (24 May 1961), cols. 1516–1545; 'The EDB', *Singapore Trade* (Sept. 1961), pp.18–21; M. O'Connor, 'EDB plays vital role in industrial finance', *Singapore Trade and Industry* (July 1966), pp.37–38, 40, 48, 62–63.

[13] Goh, *Decade* (budget speech, 1970), pp.6, 8; Singapore, *First development plan 1961–1964: review of progress*, p.37.

[14] Peter Lim, 'Singapore sets up her own industrial bank', *Singapore Trade and Industry* (Sept. 1968), pp.9–11.

[15] Goh, *Decade* (budget speech, 1970), pp.10, 11. In 1969, 'entrepot trade was still the mainstay of the Republic's economy'. *Commerce and industry 1969*, p.3; see also Goh Chok Tong, *Singapore: state of the economy 1968* (Singapore, Ministry of Finance, 1968), p.10.

Table 11.4 *Singapore primary commodity and food exports in world trade, 1971/74 and 1984/87 (annual averages)*

SITC number and description			US$000	% of world total	World ranking
231	Natural rubber	1971/74	528,750	17.9	2
		1984/87	756,391	19.1	3
4242	Palm oil	1971/74	75,901	6.2	6
		1984/87	228,570	11.2	2
334	Petroleum products, refined	1971/74	882,774	5.2	5
		1984/87	5,158,239	10.1	2
075	Spices	1971/74	49,074	13.5	2
		1984/87	160,084	12.3	3
071	Coffee and substitutes	1971/74	n.l.		
		1984/87	175,588	1.4	17
035	Fish, salted, dried, smoked	1971/74	1,848	0.3	27
		1984/87	14,506	1.2	–

Notes:
1   For 1971/74 Palm oil refers to 422 Fixed vegetable oil nonsoft and Dried fish to 03201 Fish prepared preserved.
Sources: UN, *International trade statistics yearbook 1975* II, pp.46, 50, 61, 89, 93, 207, *1976* II, p.89, *1988* II, pp.12, 29, 33, 45, 77, 396.

and the 1966–69 growth rate in manufactured exports would be two-thirds higher.

After 1970 Singapore remained a major world exporter of primary commodities, as shown by table 11.4; locally manufactured exports represented 'export addition' in the sense of building on this staple port base. The large petroleum trade and post-1959 growth as a refining centre caused Singapore to be dubbed 'the Houston of the East'.[16] As before World War II, Singapore's locational advantages and minimal regulation of the operation of international oil companies largely explained the petroleum trade, which was now based on Middle Eastern crude (accounting for the large share of 1988/90 imports from 'Others' in table 10.1) sent to Singapore for refining and distribution eastwards. Quick production adjustment to changed world market conditions by oil majors which operated on Singapore's offshore islands made the

[16] For example, see Tilak Doshi, *Houston of Asia: the Singapore petroleum industry* (Singapore, 1989); Shankar Sharma, *Role of the petroleum industry in Singapore's economy* (Singapore, 1989).

Table 11.5 *Indonesia, Malaysia and Thailand exports to Singapore,*
1971/73–1985/87 (annual averages)

	US$000	% of country's total exports	% of total Singapore imports
Indonesia			
1971/73	207,407	10.1	5.5
1981/83	2,808,690	12.8	10.0
1985/87	1,340,430	8.0	4.8
Malaysia			
1971/73	480,461	23.0	12.8
1981/83	2,950,135	23.4	10.5
1985/87	2,886,271	18.3	10.3
Thailand			
1971/73	89,900	7.8	2.4
1981/83	525,414	7.7	1.9
1985/87	799,378	8.7	2.8

Notes:
1 Exports are valued f.o.b. and imports c.i.f.
2 Singapore import figures do not show trade with Indonesia.
Sources: UN, *International trade statistics yearbook 1975* I, pp.482, 626, 936, *1985* I, p.870, *1986* I, pp.513, 623, 937, *1988* I, pp.430, 542, 791, 858.

Republic a 'swing' or balancing refining centre in the Asia-Pacific region.[17]

It is often not appreciated that Singapore also continued to conduct other large primary commodity trades (table 11.4). In 1984/87 the Republic handled almost a fifth of world rubber exports and was the main world rubber market.[18] Singapore ranked as the world's third largest exporter of spices, and one of the principal world markets for pepper.

[17] 'A sudden revival for East Asian oil', *New York Times*, 4 Feb. 1991; 'Republic the "swing" refining centre of Asia-Pacific: BG Lee', *Straits Times Weekly*, 19 May 1990; 'Singapore fills up the tank', *Time*, 23 July 1990.

[18] On Singapore's status as a leading world rubber market in the 1980s and reasons for this, see Huff, 'Development of the rubber market'. An important addition to location, communications infrastructure and the ready availability of finance as explanations for Singapore's importance as a rubber market was close regulation. In explaining why Singapore remained the region's rubber market between 1960 and 1990, considerable significance attached to the assurance of an 'honest market' in the Republic but often not elsewhere in Southeast Asia. In 1967 the Rubber Trade Association, representing both European and Chinese interests, which regulated the Singapore rubber market, was reconstituted as a statutory body and so came under government control. Oral History, *Pioneers*, Tan Eng Joo, B000018/14, pp.13, 36–37, 61.

These trades depended, as historically, mainly on Indonesia, which sent 12·8% in 1971/74, and 8% in 1985/87, of its exports to the Republic (table 11.5).

Singapore Chinese family-owned firms conducted the bulk of primary commodity trade. By the late 1980s Lee Rubber handled perhaps a quarter of all rubber exported from Indonesia and Malaya. The firm adapted several aspects of Western corporate structure; probably the outstanding Singapore multinational, it helped to make the descendants of Lee Kong Chian one of Singapore's two billionaire families. As rubber shippers, Lee Rubber gained sufficient market power largely to ignore the stipulations of the Far Eastern Freight Conference (successor to the Straits Homewards Conference), although between the late 1960s and 1980s the cartel's position also weakened considerably due to outside competition from Korean and Taiwanese shipping.[19]

Another instance of Chinese firms organizing Singapore's primary commodity trade was Ong Siong Kai, known as the 'pepper king', who ran Hiang Kie on behalf of members of his family. The Republic's modern communications allowed Ong, from his Singapore office, to keep in constant touch with his agents in Indonesia and buyers in London, Amsterdam, New York and Tokyo. At the beginning of the 1990s Chinese produce traders, including Ong, still met towards the end of each morning at the Chinese Produce Exchange, located on the upper floor of a shophouse in North Canal Road.[20]

In Singapore's trade, 1973 was the first year when direct manufactured exports – goods with some part of their value added through manufacture in Singapore – exceeded primary commodity exports excluding petroleum (figure 11.2 and appendix table A.3). During the 1970s and 1980s direct manufactured exports accounted for most of Singapore's export of manufactures, although there was also a large trade in the redistribution of manufactured goods entirely made elsewhere. This redistributive trade is approximately indicated by the difference between manufactured exports and direct manufactured exports given in appendix table A.3.

After 1971/73 the two main features of exports from Singapore (appendix table A.4) were the growing dominance of manufactures and the introduction of new products. Manufactures (SITC 5–8) increased from two-fifths of total exports in 1971/73 to almost three-quarters in 1988/90;

[19] Teo Kim Yam (Lee Rubber), interview with the author, 10 Aug. 1989; 'A wealth of billionaires', *Forbes*, 24 July 1989, pp.208–10; United Nations, *Transnational corporations in world development* (New York, 1988), p.385.

[20] Ong Siong Kai, interview with the author, 2 Aug. 1989. For a list of Chinese firms trading in rubber and tropical produce, see Singapore Chinese Chamber of Commerce and Industry, *Directory 88–89* (Singapore, 1988), pp.92–93, 211–21.

Table 11.6 *Singapore trade in integrated circuits and disk drives, 1980–1990*

	Imports		Exports	
	No.	$000	No.	$000
(a) *Integrated circuits*				
(SITC rev.3				
7764200)				
1980	10,230,682	592,807	16,076,761	1,523,883
1981	11,517,652	766,346	24,602,519	1,398,650
1982	13,562,249	927,024	26,739,235	1,494,122
1983	n.l.	1,160,764	n.l.	1,887,510
1984		1,555,494		2,437,373
1985		1,714,740		2,066,959
1986		2,084,390		2,112,365
1987		2,674,776		3,344,405
1988		3,859,782		4,384,440
1989		4,697,282		4,760,735
1990		5,504,310		5,092,958
(b) *Disk drives*				
(SITC rev.3				
7526100)				
1980	n.l.	n.l.	n.l.	n.l.
1981				
1982				
1983				
1984				
1985				
1986	432,843	136,463	3,940,714	1,939,005
1987	779,398	206,318	6,281,475	3,338,613
1988	1,625,346	501,380	8,898,932	5,052,704
1989	3,275,657	744,783	10,613,392	5,654,976
1990	7,450,780	1,128,910	17,575,116	7,599,376

Sources: Singapore, *Singapore trade statistics*, 1980–1990.

over this period exports of manufactures grew more than twelvefold in nominal value. By the 1980s the great bulk of manufactured exports consisted of machinery and transport equipment (SITC 7). Electrical and electronics goods within SITC divisions 75 and 76 – unknown in Singapore even in 1970 – comprised a large part of these exports. Singapore's trade in integrated circuits emerged between 1980 and 1984, disk drives between 1986 and 1990 (table 11.6). Shipment of electrical and electronics goods to the United States again made America Singapore's principal export market (table 10.1).

The frequently small value added to goods exported, even when subject to manufacturing in Singapore, continued to render the trade statistics an uncertain guide to activities actually undertaken on the island. One attempt to solve this problem was the publication of figures for so-called domestic exports from Singapore, shown by appendix table A.5 for the same SITC classifications as in appendix table A.4. Comparison of the two tables suggests the sometimes doubtful criteria used to identify 'domestic exports'. For example, refined petroleum exports were not as important to Singapore's economy, as appendix table A.5 suggests. The concept of net domestic exports – exports excluding their import content – was developed in an attempt to remedy the difficulty of interpreting Singapore's trade statistics, and to rank exports by the extent of their local manufacture. Use of this concept confirmed the increasing importance of manufacturing activity actually undertaken in Singapore.[21]

The swift appearance of MNE multi-plant operations to make electronics goods in the region during the 1980s added considerable relevance to the idea of net domestic exports. By 1988/90 MNEs' production decisions had created a new regional division of labour, based on skill differences, differential factor prices, especially for labour, and superior communications facilities in Singapore. Often Singapore had a services role in regional production; the Republic's exports of electronics goods might therefore have high import content and low domestic value added. For example, electronics components could be imported to Singapore for re-shipment to Malaysia for assembly, and after completion of work there imported again by Singapore, perhaps as a finished good like a television set, for checking and warehousing, before export to a final destination.[22]

MNE multi-plant operations, together with Malaysia's rapid economic development, which led to a growing demand for manufactures, largely accounted for Singapore's trade with Malaysia in 1988/90 (table 10.1), and for the heavy reliance of that country's trade on the Republic (table 11.5). Thus, Singapore's trade pattern with Malaysia changed fundamentally after 1957/59 (tables 11.7 and 11.8). Imports from Malaysia which, at the end of the 1950s, and even in 1978/80, consisted largely of raw materials and food, were by 1988/90 chiefly manufactures, principally machinery and transport equipment. Similarly, although manufactures accounted for less than half of Singapore's exports to Malaysia in 1957/59, in 1988/90 the proportion was over three-quarters.

---

[21] Peter J. Lloyd and Roger J. Sandilands, 'The trade sector in a very open re-export economy' in Lim Chong Yah and Peter J. Lloyd, eds. *Singapore: resources and growth* (Singapore, 1986), pp.183–219; Roger J. Sandilands, 'Savings, investment and housing in Singapore's growth', *Savings and Development* 16, 2 (1992), pp.121–22.

[22] Singapore, Ministry of Trade and Industry, *Economic survey of Singapore 1987* (Singapore, 1988), pp.35, 36, *1990*, pp.89–90, 96–97, *1991*, pp.79–80.

Table 11.7 *Singapore imports from Malaysia, 1957/59–1988/90 (annual averages)*

SITC	1957/59 $000	1957/59 %	1978/80 $000	1978/80 %	1988/90 $000	1988/90 %
0–4 Raw materials and food, of which	693,385	93.4	4,172,914	76.8	5,237,957	38.6
3 Mineral fuels	446	0.1	929,119	17.1	2,034,975	15.0
5–8 Manufactures, of which	38,523	5.2	1,241,982	22.9	8,278,210	61.1
7 Machinery and transport equip.	12,998	1.8	569,360	10.5	5,374,018	39.6
9 Unclassified	10,236	1.4	19,315	0.3	42,537	0.3
Total imports	742,144	100.0	5,434,215	100.0	13,558,703	100.0
% of total Singapore imports	19.0		13.7		13.8	

Notes:
1 Data for 1957/59 refer to the Federation of Malaya.
2 Columns may not add to total due to rounding and errors in the trade statistics.
Sources: Singapore, *Singapore trade statistics*, 1957–1959, 1978–1990.

Table 11.8 *Singapore exports to Malaysia, 1957/59–1988/90 (annual averages)*

SITC	1957/59		1978/80		1988/90	
	$000	%	$000	%	$000	%
0–4 Raw materials and food, of which	330,865	47.3	1,640,138	35.6	2,600,698	22.2
0 Food	183,504	26.4	508,160	11.0	444,312	3.8
3 Mineral fuels	66,325	9.5	941,600	20.4	1,715,979	14.7
5–8 Manufactures, of which	338,628	48.4	2,887,334	62.6	8,943,496	76.5
7 Machinery and transport equip.	100,744	14.5	1,499,529	32.5	5,121,896	43.8
9 Unclassified	30,196	4.3	85,506	1.8	150,704	1.3
Total exports	694,688	100.0	4,612,978	100.0	11,694,565	100.0
% of total Singapore exports	20.7		14.5		13.4	

Notes and sources: as for table 11.7.

Table 11.9 Singapore manufacturing statistics, 1960–1990 ($m)

	1960	1965	1967	1970	1973	1980	1984	1990
No. of establishments	548	1,000	1,200	1,747	2,079	3,355	3,648	3,703
No. of workers	27,416	47,334	58,347	120,509	198,574	285,250	274,391	351,674
Materials	302.8	693.3	1,160.9	2,668.4	5,065.0	21,415.2	27,474.4	45,396.4
Output	465.6	1,086.4	1,687.2	3,891.0	7,938.1	31,657.9	41,077.9	71,333.2
Value added	142.1	348.4	478.6	1,093.7	2,540.6	8,521.9	11,106.3	21,606.8
Sales:								
Total	457.0	1,075.5	1,666.4	3,846.2	7,961.3	30,946.7	40,910.7	71,647.8
Direct exports	164.3	349.2	508.2	1,523.0	4,269.8	19,172.9	25,057.8	46,999.5
Employees' remuneration	66.8	131.7	170.3	397.6	861.4	2,526.9	4,045.0	6,852.2
Capital expenditure	9.8	59.2	84.8	421.3	788.0	1,861.9	2,168.1	4,184.4

Notes:
1 Refers to firms of 10 or more workers and includes petroleum but excludes rubber processing and granite quarrying.
2 Materials refer to actual consumption in production of raw or basic materials, chemicals and packing materials.
3 Value added is defined as the difference between the value of gross output and the value of total input and work given out.
4 Employees' remuneration includes wages and salaries, employers' contribution to the Central Provident Fund and pension and other benefits such as food, lodging and medical care.
5 Capital expenditure covers expenditure on all capital assets including land, building and structures, transport equipment, machinery and office equipment.

Sources: Census of industrial production, 1990, p.1.

Table 11.10 *Singapore real annual average growth rates in manufacturing excluding petroleum, 1960–1990 (%)*

	1960–90	1960–67	1967–73	1973–90	1973–80	1980–90	1980–84	1986–90
Direct exports	16.2	10.4	31.8	10.8	12.8	11.4	5.5	16.5
Output	12.3	12.0	22.7	9.0	10.7	9.1	4.2	15.6
Value added	12.8	12.2	26.7	8.7	10.3	8.6	4.2	12.7

Notes:

1   Data are deflated by the GDP deflator for manufacturing (1985=100). Growth rates are calculated by fitting a least-squares linear regression trend line to the logarithmic annual values for the relevant period.

2   Statistics refer to firms with 10 or more workers and exclude rubber processing and granite quarrying.

3   For 1960–65, output and value added figures include petroleum, so that growth rates with 1960 as the initial year are somewhat understated. In 1960 the manufacture of chemicals, chemical products and products of petroleum and coal (industrial codes 31 + 32) accounted for 13.7% of total manufacturing output and 6.8% of value added.

4   For 1966–69, petroleum refers to industrial code 32, 'Manufacture of products of petroleum and coal', and for subsequent years to industry groups 353 + 354, 'Petroleum refineries and petroleum products'.

Sources: Appendix table A.3; *Census of industrial production 1960–61*, p.90, *1962*, p.15, *1963*, p.19, *1964*, p.14, *1965*, p.7, *1966*, p.17, *1968*, p.75, *1969*, p.10, *1978*, pp.24–27, *1988*, pp.18–23, *1990*, pp.18–23; *Singapore national accounts 1987*, pp.50–51; *Economic survey 1988*, p.102, *1989*, p.114, *1990*, p.115, *1991*, p.97.

Table 11.11 *Singapore manufacturing statistics by capital ownership, 1968–1990*

	Establishments No. and %	Workers No. and %	Output $m and %	Value-added $m and %	Direct exports $m and %	Capital expenditure $m and %
1968						
Total	**1,586**	**74,833**	**2,175.7**	**611.8**		**89.6**
Wholly local	80.5	58.7	41.1	40.8	n.a.	33.2
Majority local	7.8	15.1	12.8	15.2		24.3
Wholly or majority foreign	11.7	26.2	46.1	44.0		42.5
1975						
Total	**2,385**	**191,528**	**12,610.1**	**3,411.1**	**7,200.7**	**622.6**
Wholly local	66.9	32.8	18.0	24.3	8.9	20.7
Majority local	11.1	15.2	10.7	13.0	7.0	14.7
Wholly or majority foreign	22.0	52.0	71.3	62.7	84.1	64.6
1980						
Total	**3,355**	**285,250**	**31,657.9**	**8,521.9**	**19,172.9**	**1,861.9**
Wholly local	64.2	28.2	15.6	19.1	7.1	14.2
Majority local	11.0	13.4	10.7	13.5	8.2	11.2
Wholly or majority foreign	24.8	58.4	73.7	67.4	84.7	74.6
1990						
Total	**3,703**	**351,674**	**71,333.2**	**21,606.8**	**46,999.5**	**4,184.4**
Wholly local	67.7	29.0	15.1	16.4	7.8	17.8
Majority local	8.9	12.0	9.0	10.9	6.4	11.5
Wholly or majority foreign	23.4	59.0	75.9	72.7	85.8	70.7

Notes:
1 Figures include petroleum but exclude rubber processing and granite quarrying.
2 Columns may not add to totals due to rounding.
Sources: Census of industrial production 1968, p.8, 1975, p.16, 1980, p.4, 1990, p.4.

III

The means by which Singapore achieved its rapid post-1966 manufacturing development are summed up in the explanation that 'we imported entrepreneurs in the form of multinational corporations and the government itself became an entrepreneur in a big way'.[23] Strong government intervention was required for this injection into Singapore's economy of multinationals and public enterprise. Together they afforded the two types of 'entrepreneurial substitute' possible, and obviated any need for the PAP government to look to the Chinese-educated and China-oriented Chinese who had traditionally made up Singapore's entrepreneurs.

Manufacturing production depended heavily – and increasingly – on exports. This export orientation is measured by direct exports of manufactures as a percentage of total sales of manufactures. The proportion rose from 31% in 1967 to 54% by 1973, and 66% in 1990 (calculated from table 11.9). Between 1960 and 1990 direct exports of manufactures excluding petroleum grew at a real rate of 16·2% per annum; growth during the six-year period from 1967 leading up to the 1973 turning point was exceptionally rapid, at 31·8% almost double the long-term rate (table 11.10). Beginning in 1967, the growth rate of direct exports of manufactures was always above that of manufactured output, but the gap between the two was greatest between 1967 and 1973.

Foreign firms were almost wholly responsible for manufactured exports and dominated the manufacturing sector as a whole by 1975 (table 11.11). Subsequently their prominence further increased: wholly- and majority-foreign-owned firms accounted for three-quarters of manufactured output and 86% of direct exports in 1990. The creation of linkages from foreign manufacturing firms to indigenous Singaporean suppliers has been identified.[24] But the importance of foreign firms in manufacturing (table 11.11) indicates that linkages created in this sector were largely to other foreign-owned firms. Since MNEs organized the marketing of the goods they made, Singapore avoided the otherwise considerable difficulty for an LDC of breaking into world markets.[25]

[23] Goh Keng Swee, interview with the author, 17 Aug. 1989.

[24] Linda Y. C. Lim and Pang Eng Fong, 'Vertical linkages and multinational enterprises in developing countries', *World Development* 10, 7 (1982), pp.585–95. Similarly, the rise of local Singaporean multinationals in manufacturing, like Singatronics, has been pointed out, but this was not an impressive feature of Singapore's economic development. Lim Mah Hui and Teoh Kit Fong, 'Singapore corporations go transnational', *JSEAS* 17, 2 (1986), pp.336–65; 'Singatronics sets the pace in Singapore's development', *Financial Times*, 6 Oct. 1987; *Economic survey 1987*, p.40.

[25] The Singapore government always recognized that a country's inability to market its products constituted a barrier to breaking into world markets. Goh Keng Swee, *Two years of economic progress* (budget speech, 1967), p.25; *Economic survey 1990*, p.94.

Table 11.12 *Singapore manufacturing by size of firm, 1963–1988 (%)*

	Total	Tiny (5–9 workers)	Small (10–49 workers)	Medium (50–99 workers)	Large (100 and over workers)
	No. firms				
1963	1,542	44.4	44.9	6.9	3.8
1983	5,752	37.1	45.7	8.4	8.8
1988	5,594	35.2	46.7	7.7	10.4
	No. workers				
1963	41,340	11.5	36.4	17.7	34.4
1983	285,742	5.1	18.4	11.7	64.8
1988	335,889	3.3	15.4	9.2	72.1
	Output ($ 000)				
1963	888,841	5.1	27.9	30.4	36.6
1983	37,804,526	1.5	11.4	9.0	78.1
1988	56,993,727	0.9	9.9	7.7	81.5
	Value-added ($ 000)				
1963	267,970	5.7	23.5	23.0	47.8
1983	10,035,366	2.1	13.1	11.4	73.4
1988	18,811,207	1.1	9.6	7.7	81.6

Sources: *Census of industrial production 1963*, pp.7, 83, *1983*, pp.2, 133, *1988*, pp.2, 185.

Singapore's experience does not support the argument that LDC industrialization can be achieved by means of small firms. Between 1967 and 1990 the number of establishments rose threefold, but employment sixfold (table 11.9). Large firms of 100 or more workers were even more important to industrialization than this suggests (table 11.12). By 1988 large firms, although making up just 10% of firms, employed 72% of workers, and accounted for 82% of both output and value added.[26]

A significant part of manufacturing employment (table 11.13) related to oil, not in refining but in the construction of drilling rigs and support vessels for exploration in the region, and in tanker repair and construction, which formed the basis for four major shipyards. For ship repair, Singapore progressed to rank as 'the most efficient and cheapest repair centre in the world'.[27] In Singapore's twentieth-century development,

---

[26] For elaboration of these arguments, see W. G. Huff, 'Entrepreneurship and economic development in less developed countries', *Business History* 31, 4 (1989), pp.86–97.
[27] 'Singapore winning hub role', *Lloyds List*, 5 Feb. 1990. See also 'Sunrise for Singapore shipyards', *Financial Times*, 29 Nov. 1989.

extensive manufacturing linkages arising from petroleum were slow in unfolding, but as they were formed their impact was substantial. A textile and garments industry also developed. It originated when the prospect of a Malaysian common market attracted Chinese industrialists to Singapore, notably from Hong Kong, who stayed to export after 1965, supported by a large quota under the Multi-Fibre Agreement.[28]

However, electronics and electrical goods became by far the largest single source of manufacturing employment and output. Production depended virtually entirely on foreign MNEs, especially from the United States. By the beginning of the 1970s Singapore had the lion's share of offshore assembly activities of the United States and European semi-conductor industries,[29] just as in the late 1980s it accounted for at least half of world production of disk drives.[30]

Export-oriented manufacturing provided a solution to Singapore's need for jobs which, with the upsurge in new entrants to the labour force due to the high 1950s birth rate, had become pressing by the later 1960s. Manufacturing employment stood at 58,000 in 1967, but expanded three and a half times by 1973 and fivefold by 1980 (table 11.9). Between 1967 and 1973 jobs in the production of electronics and electrical goods and in textiles and garments accounted for about half the rise in employment (table 11.13).

In inter-war Singapore high wage costs made manufacturing internationally uncompetitive, and this factor was fundamental in explaining the lack of greater export-oriented industrialization (chapter 7). Through the mid-1960s, despite under-employment and growing unemployment in Singapore, the historical problem of internationally uncompetitive wages persisted: Singapore was 'a high cost producer by Asian standards',[31] with wage costs '20–30% too high for world markets'.[32] If Singapore had remained part of Malaysia, high wages might have been accommodated within tariff- and quota-protected import-substituting industrialization. But after the 1965 split with Malaysia, high wage levels were a problem which had to be solved if Singapore was to embark on export-oriented industrialization.

---

[28] These points are discussed at greater length in W. G. Huff, 'Patterns in the economic development of Singapore', *Journal of Developing Areas* 21, 3 (1987), p.312.

[29] Y. S. Chang, *The transfer of technology: economics of offshore assembly – the semi-conductor industry* (New York: UNITAR, 1971), pp.40–44.

[30] Singapore, Economic Development Board, *Electronics manufacturers' directory 1990/91*, pp.25–26.   [31] 'Industrial development programme' by Lyle, *SLA 1959*, p.7.

[32] United Nations, *Proposed industrialization programme*, p.115. It is unclear why wages remained high. In addition to the weight of history, this may have reflected the ability to pay relatively high wages in a region where the economy was based on natural resources, the willingness of firms in the modern sector to pay wages well above the average to attract the best workers and the power of trade unions.

Table 11.13 *Singapore manufacturing employment and output, 1967–1990 (%)*

	1967	1973	1980	1984	1990
(a) *Employment*					
Textiles and garments	13.1	17.6	12.9	10.8	8.8
Printing and publishing	8.5	3.9	4.2	5.2	4.5
Petroleum refineries and products	1.1	1.6	1.2	1.3	0.9
Transport equip.	10.3	12.8	9.6	9.1	7.4
Machinery except electrical and electronic	3.5	3.9	7.1	7.8	6.9
Electrical machinery and apparatus	3.2)	22.4)	5.6	6.0	6.3
Electronic products and components	)	)	25.1	26.4	34.9
Instrumentional equip. and photographic and optical goods		3.3	3.7	1.9	2.2
Others	60.3	34.5	30.6	31.5	28.1
Total persons	**58,347**	**198,574**	**285,250**	**274,391**	**351,674**
(b) *Output*					
Textiles and garments	3.6	7.6	4.2	3.3	3.0
Printing and publishing	4.1	2.1	1.7	2.3	2.5
Petroleum refineries and products	21.6	24.8	36.4	30.3	15.9
Transport equip.	5.5	9.7	6.5	4.8	5.3
Machinery except electrical and electronic	1.8	2.6	5.3	4.7	4.7
Electrical machinery and apparatus	2.5)	15.8)	3.1	3.6	3.4
Electronic products and components	)	)	16.8	23.4	39.1
Instrumentional equip. and photographic and optical goods	n.a.	1.6	1.2	0.7	1.1
Others	60.9	35.8	24.8	26.9	25.0
Total $m	**1,687.2**	**7,938.1**	**31,657.9**	**41,077.9**	**71,333.2**

Notes:
1   Refers to firms with 10 or more workers and excludes rubber processing and granite quarrying.
2   For 1967 textiles and garments include footwear except for rubber footwear.
3   Figures for 1967 refer to petroleum products only.
Sources: *Census of industrial production 1967*, p.17, *1973*, pp.9–10, *1988*, pp.15–20, *1990*, pp.15–20.

The necessary adjustment in Singapore's labour market might eventually have come through market forces. Indeed, this may actually have begun after 1960: wages generally increased less than for Asian competitors, 'owing to labour surplus' and unemployment due to the British military withdrawal from Singapore beginning in 1967.[33] But it was government which stepped in decisively to effect adjustment and, moreover, then to enforce internationally competitive wages. Government control of the labour market was embodied in legislation: two measures, the Employment Act and the Industrial Relations (Amendment) Act of 1968, 'depoliticised the labour movement, established *de facto* government control over unions [and] transferred bargaining power from workers to employers'.[34] Few work stoppages occurred after 1967; they had been virtually eliminated by 1977. Singapore's total of two work stoppages involving 159 workers in the 13 years 1978–1990 cannot have reflected a free labour market (table 10.7).

By 1969, for comparable job classifications in key electrical and electronics assembly industries, hourly compensation costs in Singapore were less than one-eleventh of the United States' level, and below those in South Korea, Taiwan and Hong Kong (table 11.14). Productivity in Singapore was equal to that in these three countries, and at least as high as in the United States.[35]

Low-wage but productive, reliable labour secured through government intervention was fundamental in accounting for the decision of MNEs to locate in Singapore for component and assembly electronics work as part of vertically integrated international manufacturing. In addition to wage levels, distance costs and government influences help to explain MNEs' locational decisions;[36] on both counts, supply response effected through government made Singapore attractive to MNEs. Its geographical position helped to cut distance costs, while the government's provision of good communications infrastructure made an important contribution by minimizing the time and expense of shipment to and from the island.

---

[33] Leong Mun Keong, *Wage levels of selected countries* (Singapore, Ministry of Finance, 1971), p.25; see also Ng, *Comparative evaluation*, p.42.

[34] Linda Lim and Pang Eng Fong, *Trade, employment and industrialisation in Singapore* (Geneva: ILO, 1986), p.11.

[35] Leong, *Wage levels*, pp.2–7, 13–19, 25; United States Tariff Commission, *Economic factors affecting the use of items 807·00 and 806·30 of the tariff schedule of the United States* (Washington, DC: US Tariff Commission, 1970), pp.166–73.

[36] Helleiner, 'Manufactured exports', pp.35–41; Sharpston, 'International sub-contracting', pp.111–18. For a useful list of reasons why international business found Singapore attractive, see Singapore International Chamber of Commerce, *Investors guide to the economic climate of Singapore* (Singapore, 1989), pp.1–6; see also 'The incentives that Singapore offers', *Singapore Trade and Industry* (Oct. 1967), pp.27–29.

Table 11.14 *Singapore, competitor countries and United States: average hourly earnings for workers assembling United States materials (including supplementary compensation) for comparable United States job classifications in selected product groups, 1969*

	Local US$ per hour	United States US$ per hour	Ratio of United States to local earnings
Semiconductors			
Singapore	.29	3.22	11.1
South Korea	.33	3.32	10.1
Hong Kong	.28	2.84	10.1
Mexico	.61	2.56	4.2
Jamaica	.30	2.23	7.4
Office machines and parts (including elect- tronic memories)			
Singapore	.29	3.36	11.6
South Korea	.28	2.78	9.9
Hong Kong	.30	2.92	9.7
Taiwan	.38	3.67	9.7
Mexico	.48	2.97	6.2

Sources: US Tariff Commission, *Economic factors*, p.A–90.

Furthermore, the widespread and growing use of English reduced the language component of distance costs, particularly for American firms.

Government influences – political risk as perceived by MNEs, fiscal incentives offered by the host country and facility of business operation – also worked strongly in Singapore's favour. Political stability and social quiescence greatly reduced the danger of interruption to MNE production, especially important for component manufacture and intra-firm trade. Singapore offered generous fiscal incentives, including tax holidays and reductions, and 100 % foreign ownership of equity. Planning in Singapore which made available ready-to-move-into industrial sites attracted MNEs, as did the efficient and honest government bureaucracy. In 1973, 'Texas Instruments simply got browned off with red tape in Taiwan and revamped its investment plans to centre on Singapore – the company was in operation only 50 days after the investment decision was made'.[37]

From 1967 trade gave Singapore access to technology and (in contrast to

---

[37] 'Drive for foreign investment becomes increasingly selective', *Financial Times*, Singapore survey, 1 Oct. 1973. Singapore offered incentives through 'pioneer' status to a large number of firms. For development policies and statistics for pioneer establishments, see Singapore, Economic Development Board, *Annual report 1970* (Singapore, 1971), pp.22–28, 70–73.

its tiny domestic market) the world market. Rapid economic growth was thereby promoted in two ways. First, trade afforded a 'vent for surplus': Singapore could export, through making manufactured goods, labour which was surplus in being under-employed or which would otherwise have been unemployed. The latter included new labour force entrants, whose numbers were swelled by the high pre-1957 birth rate.[38] Second, trade made possible a reallocation of labour to more productive employment, and Singapore's domestic economy responded to this opportunity. It is illuminating, as H. Myint suggests, to think of 'vent for surplus' and 'productivity' gains as complementary. In Singapore, higher output was realized through an interplay between the forces introduced by international trade and the forces of domestic economic development.[39]

Job creation for unemployed and underemployed labour was facilitated by the labour-intensive and unskilled nature of many manufacturing jobs, especially in electronics and the textile and garment industries. As was observed, 'The electronic components we make in Singapore probably require less skill than that required by barbers or cooks, consisting mostly of repetitive manual operations'.[40] Unemployment fell from 8·9 % in 1966 to 4·5 % in 1973 (table 10.3), the latter effectively constituting full employment.

The 1973 turning point from labour surplus to labour scarcity signified the end of the dual economy in Singapore. Manufacturing's labour-intensive character and still-fast growth in employment opportunities after 1973 enabled Singaporeans easily to find jobs, even in the context of rapid expansion in the labour supply (table 10.6). In contrast to the lack of female employment in inter-war Singapore or even the 1950s,[41] women joined the labour force in large numbers after 1970 (table 11.15). The subsequent still-rapid growth in manufacturing employment opportunities encouraged both a further increase in female participation rates to 44 % by 1980 and almost certainly a continuing process of labour reallocation. The proportion of own-account, and unpaid family, workers in Singapore's labour force fell from 20·7 % in 1970 to 13·3 % in 1980, by which time 5·8 % of Singapore's employed population were hawkers and domestic servants, compared to 12·9 % in 1957. In 1990 the share of own-account and unpaid family workers had declined further to 7·8 %.[42]

---

[38] Cf. Goh, *Two years* (budget speech, 1967), pp.8–13; Lee Soo Ann, *Singapore goes transnational* (Singapore, 1977), p.31.

[39] Hla Myint, 'Adam Smith's theory of international trade in the perspective of economic development', *Economica* 44 (1977), p.245.

[40] Goh, *Decade* (budget speech, 1970), p.27.   [41] *1970 census* I, p.147.

[42] Saw Swee-Hock, *The labour force of Singapore* (1980 census monograph no.3) (Singapore, 1984), p.40; Khoo Chian Kim, *Census of population 1980 Singapore: Release no.4. Economic characteristics* (Singapore, 1981), p.131; appendix table A.10; Lau Kak En,

Table 11.15 *Singapore labour force participation rates by age and sex, 1957–1990 (%)*

Age Group	Male				Female			
	1957	1970	1980	1990	1957	1970	1980	1990
15–19	59.4	55.7	47.5	30.0	23.4	43.0	50.7	31.8
20–24	92.3	92.9	93.4	82.8	22.9	53.6	78.4	82.2
25–29	98.0	98.0	97.2	94.8	96.5	30.8	58.7	77.9
30–34	98.6	98.3	97.9	95.4	17.3	22.7	44.2	65.4
35–39	98.5	98.4	98.0	96.4	20.8	19.3	37.1	57.9
40–44	98.0	98.1	97.6	96.7	26.3	17.8	33.2	54.2
45–49	97.0	96.2	95.7	94.7	30.1	17.5	26.5	45.9
50–54	93.5	88.1	89.6	88.2	28.8	17.5	20.4	35.6
55–59	85.1	73.9	70.7	69.0	24.7	16.2	14.5	22.4
60–64	66.9	55.6	52.5	49.5	17.1	13.4	11.3	13.8
65–69	49.8	41.2	38.6	35.2	10.5	9.8	9.5	9.8
70–74	31.0	25.8	25.1	16.9 }	4.7	5.7	6.2	4.3 }
75 and over	17.4	14.4	13.3		2.1	2.1	2.5	
Overall	87.7	82.3	81.5	79.0	21.6	29.5	44.3	53.0

Notes:
1   The 1990 figures for age group 70-74 refer to 70 and over.
Sources: 1970 census I, pp.138 140, 161; Economic survey 1990, p.135; 1990 census: Statistical release 4, Economic characteristics, pp.4, 37.

Table 11.16 *Singapore real average monthly earnings for all workers and selected industries, 1978–1990 ($)*

	Index all workers (1988=100)	All workers	Manufactur-ing	Commerce	Financing, insurance, real estate & business services	Com-munity, social and personal services
1978	57.9					
1979	60.5					
1980	63.0	813	676	792	1,089	926
1981	66.5	858	728	866	1,111	918
1982	73.7	951	773	916	1,216	1,139
1983	79.4	1,024	848	977	1,325	1,227
1984	84.6	1,091	913	1,024	1,432	1,346
1985	92.5	1,193	982	1,057	1,421	1,425
1986	95.3	1,230	1,005	1,089	1,444	1,493
1987	96.5	1,245	1,036	1,069	1,474	1,499
1988	100.0	1,290	1,091	1,120	1,545	1,545
1989	107.6	1,388	1,192	1,205	1,690	1,632
1990	113.6	1,465	1,278	1,294	1,785	1,675

Notes:
1   Real earnings are nominal earnings deflated by the corresponding year's consumer price index (Sept. 1987 – Aug. 1988 = 100). Nominal earnings include basic wage/salary, overtime payments, commissions, shift/food/housing/transport allowances, service point payments and other regular cash payments. They exclude employers' Central Provident Fund contributions, annual wage supplement, variable payments/bonuses, skills development fund levy, and payments in kind.
2   The average for the year is calculated in August.
Sources: Singapore, *Yearbook of labour statistics 1988*, p.23, *1989*, p.23, *1990*, p.23.

Full employment would almost certainly have set up strong inflationary wage pressure and internationally uncompetitive pay rises, driving MNEs elsewhere, had not the government in 1972 inaugurated the National Wages Council, a tripartite body which published guidelines for pay increases. Although not mandatory, these guidelines were closely observed. The government controlled unions; more than this, a measure of its power was that, in the absence of a statutory or other overt enforcement mechanism to limit wage payments by foreign MNEs, the latter did not bid up wages, despite incentives to do so as a result of labour scarcity and Singapore's attractiveness as a location. Increases in real wages averaged

Singapore census of population 1990: Statistical release 4, Economic characteristics (Singapore, 1993), pp.8–9. In 1980, 12·5% of females worked as electrical and electronics component assemblers, and this was the largest single source of female employment. Saw, *Labour force*, pp.47–48. For a discussion of unemployment and surplus labour up to 1970, see *1970 census* I, pp.143–96.

Table 11.17 *Singapore, United States, Japan and Asian NICs hourly compensation costs for production workers in manufacturing, 1975–1990 (current US$ and index, United States = 100)*

	1975 $	1975 Index	1980 $	1980 Index	1987 $	1987 Index	1990 $	1990 Index
United States	6.36	100	9.87	100	13.52	100	14.88	100
Japan	3.05	48	5.61	57	10.83	80	12.64	85
Singapore	0.84	13	1.49	15	2.31	17	3.78	25
South Korea	0.33	5	0.97	10	1.65	12	3.82	26
Taiwan	0.40	6	1.00	10	2.26	17	3.95	27
Hong Kong	0.76	12	1.51	15	2.09	15	3.20	22
Asian NICs	0.50	8	1.15	12	2.06	15	3.75	25

Notes:
1 Hourly compensation includes all direct payments to workers before any payroll deductions and employer expenditures for legally required insurance programmes and contractual and private benefit plans. It may also be adjusted upwards to include taxes on payrolls or employment or downwards to reflect subsidies and so reflect labour costs.
2 Asian NICs refers to a United States trade–weighted average level for Singapore, South Korea, Taiwan and Hong Kong.
Sources: US Department of Labor, *International comparisons 1991*, pp.5, 6, 12–14.

just 1·7% from 1973 to 1978.[43] Then, boosted initially by a three-year wage correction policy decreed by Singapore planners, real wages doubled by 1990 (table 11.16). Between 1975 and 1990, however, Singapore wages converged on the average of the Asian NICs (table 11.17), against which the government measured its success in containing labour costs.

During the later 1970s and 1980s, planning in Singapore which emphasized technical education and industrial training for workers[44] attracted MNEs. Electronics multinationals tended to move to Singapore at earlier stages of product development or for specialized, niche work. By the 1980s virtually every international electronics producer was represented in Singapore,[45] and workers were more likely to make a finished product than only components. During this 1980s phase of development, semi-conductor production declined in relative importance, and computer

[43] 'An interim report of the deliberations of the Economic Committee', *Economic survey of Singapore 1985* (second quarter) (Singapore, 1985), p.20.
[44] *Parliamentary Debates* 35, 1 (1 March 1976) (budget speech), cols.27–28. For a list of facilities established for manpower development, see Singapore, Ministry of Labour, *Yearbook of labour statistics 1991* (Singapore, 1992), pp.105–32. Beginning in 1969, the school system was restructured towards vocational and technical education. Goh Keng Swee, *The practice of economic growth* (Singapore, 1977), p.101.
[45] For a list of firms in the electronics industry, see Singapore, Economic Development Board, *Electronics manufacturers' directory 1990/91.*

peripherals, especially disk drives, and computers became the more important part of the island's electronics industry (table 11.6 and appendix table A.4).[46] Higher skills and the use of more capital contributed to raising value added per manufacturing worker in Singapore and allowed the rise in real wages.[47]

Real wages in manufacturing, however, lagged behind other sectors of the economy (table 11.16). Average weekly hours worked in manufacturing were above most sectors and increased slightly during the 1980s to 48·6.[48] In 1990, 72 % of those in electronics production were female, compared to 43 % in the rest of manufacturing.[49]

Singapore did not achieve any gains between 1973 and 1990 in the value-added share of gross output, a measure of technical development in manufacturing (table 11.18). In electronics, this ratio actually fell. At the end of the 1980s manufacturing still depended on MNEs for technology; as pointed out in chapter 1, little research and development was undertaken in Singapore. Studies indicated that larger inputs of capital and labour – not, as usual in industrial countries, technical progress, or so-called total factor productivity growth – almost entirely accounted for Singapore's expansion of manufacturing output.[50]

Thus it appeared questionable whether the legislation and policy instruments like the National Wages Council, which successfully regulated wage costs, were appropriate also to effect industrial restructuring towards higher value-added activities and the increased productivity which is at the heart of the economic development process.[51] That the Republic's leaders recognized the need for more indigenous technology as well as training programmes and education to effect restructuring was indicated by a

[46] Linda Lim and Pang Eng Fong, *Foreign direct investment and industrialisation in Malaysia, Singapore, Taiwan and Thailand* (Paris, 1991), pp.123–28.
[47] For discussion of the growing use of skilled labour, see Roger J. Sandilands and Tan Ling-Hui, 'Comparative advantage in a re-export economy: the case of Singapore', *Singapore Economic Review* 31, 2 (1986), pp.34–56; Lim Chong Yah, 'Trade in manufactures: a Singapore perspective', *Southeast Asian Studies* 25, 3 (1987), pp.321–22.
[48] Singapore, Ministry of Labour, *Yearbook of labour statistics 1990* (Singapore, 1991), p.32.
[49] Singapore, Economic Development Board, *Report on the census of industrial production 1990* (Singapore, 1992), pp.102–16.
[50] Y. Tsao, 'Growth without productivity: Singapore manufacturing in the 1970s', *Journal of Development Economics* 18, 1/2 (1985), pp.25–38; Lawrence B. Krause, et al. *The Singapore economy reconsidered* (Singapore, 1987), pp.14–17; Alwyn Young, 'A tale of two cities: factor accumulation and technical change in Hong Kong and Singapore', *NBER Macroeconomics Annual* 7 (1992), pp.36–38, 45. Broadly, it is possible to define the growth of GDP as depending on an increase in labour, an increase in capital, and an increase in the productivity of these factors of production. This last is termed total factor productivity growth.
[51] Richard Disney and Ho Soo Kiang, 'Do real wages matter in an open economy? The case of Singapore 1966–1987', *Oxford Economic Papers* 42 (1990), pp.637–39, 654–55; Lim, *Policy options*, pp.35–36.

Table 11.18 *Singapore manufacturing value added as a percentage of output, 1973–1990*

	1973	1978	1984	1990	% of total 1990 value added
All industries	32.0	26.3	27.0	30.3	100.0
Textiles	38.8	32.7	32.8	32.9	0.6
Garments	28.5	32.6	33.6	30.8	2.4
Printing and publishing	55.1	50.8	56.6	53.5	4.3
Industrial chemicals and gases	51.9[a]	35.6	23.9	33.6	4.9
Petroleum refineries and products	18.4	10.5	7.7	14.6	7.7
Fabricated metal products	36.8	34.5	38.7	34.8	6.1
Machinery except electrical and electronic	39.9	49.1	45.7	37.5	5.9
Electrical machinery and apparatus	39.0[b]	33.7	37.6	36.1	4.1
Electronic products and components		32.2	29.9	27.7	35.7
Transport equip.	46.8	47.4	51.7	42.6	7.5
Instrumentation equip. photographic and optical goods	37.7	52.0	54.4	46.4	1.7
Others	26.6	24.9	33.1	37.9	19.1

Notes:
[a] Refers to industrial chemicals
[b] Includes electronic products
Sources: *Census of industrial production 1973*, pp.35–41, *1987*, pp.18–22, *1990*, pp.18–23.

planning departure in the 1990s to achieve productivity gains through technical progress: the state was to spearhead research and development and take the lead in raising this spending in Singapore.[52]

The second 'entrepreneurial substitute', public or state-owned enterprises (SOEs),[53] was less a break with the past than might at first appear, since in part it grew out of a colonial inheritance of statutory boards – like the Singapore Harbour Board, typically efficiently run. It also stemmed from the takeover of British military facilities. The former Royal Naval

[52] Singapore, National Science and Technology Board, *Window of opportunities: national technology plan 1991* (Singapore, 1991), pp.5, 29–30; 'PM: get ready for the super league contest', *Straits Times Weekly*, 22 Aug. 1992.
[53] SOE is defined as a productive entity owned or controlled, via a public equity holding of more than 10%, by a public authority, and producing a marketable output. Mason, *Economic and social modernization of Korea*, p.272.

Dockyard became Sembawang Shipyard in 1968 and, along with a government stake in Keppel and Jurong Shipyards, constituted substantial state participation in the shipbuilding and repairing industry. Similarly, former Royal Air Force operations gave rise to a number of state aviation-related companies.

However, the Singapore government also began, as non-statutory undertakings, a range of enterprises that the colonial administration would have considered outside the scope of government, including Singapore Airlines (SIA), Neptune Orient Lines (an international shipping line) and International Trading Company (Intraco). The main non-statutory public enterprises, often themselves with subsidiaries and associated companies, were owned through three government holding companies. Government companies were estimated to number 490 in 1983, including the subsidiaries of statutory boards. Singapore's state-owned enterprises remained notable for efficient and effective management, and the vast majority of SOEs appear to have run at a profit or at least broken even.[54] But reflecting a philosophy that private enterprise would provide the main force for growth, the SOE sector was never large by LDC standards, and in 1985 probably accounted for no more than 10% of GDP.[55]

The prominence of MNEs and, in the domestic economy, SOEs, led to widespread complaints about the 'crowding out' of local entrepreneurs. Partly in response, a privatization policy announced in March 1985 began to reduce the importance of the SOE sector. In Singapore, arguments for privatization to promote efficiency lacked force, but this programme, which distributed equity in SOEs, helped to allay criticism of the limited presence of domestic entrepreneurship in the economy.

IV

The driving force in Singapore's savings process was public sector savings – the current surplus in the consolidated accounts of the public sector. These savings increased from less than a quarter of national savings in 1974 to three-fifths by 1984 (table 11.19).[56] Public sector savings consisted of the

[54] Linda Low, 'Public enterprises in Singapore' in You Poh Seng and Lim Chong Yah, eds. *Singapore: twenty-five years of development* (Singapore, 1984), pp.253–87; Krause, 'Hong Kong and Singapore', pp.s62–s64.

[55] In 1971 industrial establishments in the public sector accounted for 3·8% of manufacturing employment, 3·6% of output and 8·8% of value added. Subsequent growth came primarily through private enterprise. Singapore, Department of Statistics, *Report on the census of industrial production 1971* (Singapore, 1972), pp.9, 11.

[56] For discussion of public sector savings, see Lim, *Policy options*, pp.215–31; Linda Low, 'The financing process in the public sector in Singapore', *Bulletin for International Fiscal Documentation* 39, 4 (1985), pp.159–65.

Table 11.19 *Singapore sources of gross national savings, 1974–1985*

| | Gross national savings | Public sector savings | | Private sector savings | | | |
| | | | | Central Provident Fund | | Other (corporate + personal) | |
	$m	$m	% GNS	$m	% GNS	$m	% GNS
1974	3,220	736	22.8	643	20.0	1,841	57.2
1975	3,985	1,362	34.2	821	20.6	1,802	45.2
1976	4,580	1,470	32.1	831	18.1	2,279	49.8
1977	5,079	2,021	39.8	888	17.5	2,170	42.7
1978	5,928	2,230	37.6	1,027	17.3	2,671	45.1
1979	7,300	2,801	38.4	1,534	21.0	2,965	40.6
1980	8,282	3,407	41.1	2,036	24.6	2,839	34.3
1981	10,483	4,261	40.6	2,599	24.8	3,623	34.6
1982	12,885	5,936	46.1	3,506	27.2	3,443	26.7
1983	16,306	8,649	53.0	3,849	23.6	3,808	23.4
1984	18,596	11,291	60.7	3,166	17.0	4,139	22.3
1985	16,543	11,052	66.8	4,159	25.1	1,332	8.1

Notes:
1   Gross national savings equal public sector savings plus private sector savings. Public sector savings are the current surplus in the consolidated accounts of the public sector, which consists of government plus seven major statutory boards, namely the Housing and Development Board, Jurong Town Corporation, Public Utilities Board, Port of Singapore Authority, Telecommunication Authority of Singapore, Urban Redevelopment Authority and Sentosa Development Corporation. Central Provident Fund savings are the net addition that year to the accumulated fund due to members' withdrawals of funds. This figure was normally less than members' contributions. Other private sector savings are gross national savings minus public sector and Central Provident Fund savings. Figures which divide other private sector savings into corporate and personal savings are not available.
2   The 1985 figure for public sector savings is provisional. Comparable figures for public sector savings are not available after 1985, due to changes in the official statistics.
Sources: Appendix table A.13; *Parliamentary Debates* vol.36, no.10 (28 Feb. 1977), cols. 607–8, vol.37, no.7 (27 February 1978), cols. 485–86, vol.38, no.7 (5 March 1979), cols. 417–18; *Economic Survey 1979*, p.30, *1980*, p.36, *1981*, p.40, *1982*, p.45, *1983*, p.49, *1984*, p.43, *1985*, p.34, *1986*, p.38, *1987*, p.46; *Yearbook of statistics 1982/83*, p.194, *1985/86*, p.216.

government's budget surplus, together with the surpluses realized by statutory boards. Statutory boards were, as in pre-1959 Singapore, used to organize infrastructural provision, and, like a number of other colonial institutional arrangements, were harnessed by the PAP government for economic development to much greater effect after independence. The boards often had 'substantial commercial operations'[57] and their monopoly power, either legislated or natural, enabled the government to realize large profits to create public sector savings so long as reasonable commercial efficiency was maintained.[58] Seven main boards – the Housing and Development Board, Jurong Town Corporation, Public Utilities Board, Port of Singapore Authority, Urban Redevelopment Authority, Telecommunication Authority of Singapore and Sentosa Development Corporation – were central in determining public sector savings.

The private sector's contribution to Singapore's high savings rate (table 11.19) was largely due to savings forced by the government through a social security scheme taken over from the colonial government – the Central Provident Fund (CPF). The CPF increased the domestic savings rate because (unusually among developing countries) it operated on the provident fund principle: on retirement, individuals were paid benefits determined by total past contributions from themselves and their employers plus interest, rather than payments being made to retirees from the contributions of those still working. Collection was effected through withholding at source employers' and employees' contributions to the CPF, typically in equal shares and based on an employee's wages.[59]

The CPF grew rapidly, and, helped by full employment and growing wage employment, 'widened' to encompass the large majority of Singapore workers by 1973 (table 11.20). Subsequently, the higher female labour force participation rates added substantially to the number of workers in the scheme. Simultaneously, there was a 'deepening' of the CPF as total contributions were put up to 50% of employees' wages by 1984, and as real wages rose. After 1974 public-sector and CPF savings progressively reduced the importance of voluntary private sector savings. The contribution of voluntary private savings fell from almost three-fifths of national savings in 1974 to less than one-quarter by 1983.

W. A. Lewis emphasized an economy's conversion to a higher savings ratio as central to the economic development process, and argued that achievement of this savings rate required growing inequality of income distribution away from workers and in favour of domestic capitalists. Singapore's economic development differed from Lewis' formal two-sector construct in adding government as a crucial third agent.[60] The government organized the arrival in Singapore of foreign private capitalists – MNEs – through giving them a strong bargaining position in a way similar to that

---

[57] Singapore, Public Sector Divestment Committee, *Report of the public sector divestment committee* (Singapore, 1987), p.61, and see pp.43–49.   [58] Ibid, pp.19–20.

[59] A Singapore citizen taking out citizenship of another country forfeited accumulated CPF savings.

[60] Lewis, 'Economic development with unlimited supplies of labour', pp.139–91. Outside his formal model, however, Lewis drew attention to the importance of government.

Table 11.20 *Singapore Central Provident Fund, 1955–1990*

	Contributors		Rates of contribution (employee + employer)	Annual addition to national savings		Accumulated Fund due to members	
	persons 000	% of labour force	%	$m	% of gross national savings	$m	% of GDP
1955	180.0	40.0	10.0	9.1	n.a.	9.1	n.a.
1959	n.a.		10.0	28.6	n.a.	119.6	n.a.
1965	278.4	49.7	10.0	52.7	15.5	359.0	12.1
1969	367.7	50.8	13.0	92.5	9.5	632.2	12.6
1973	609.3	74.5	26.0	454.7	16.4	1,770.7	17.3
1978	779.4	79.9	33.0	1,027.4	17.3	5,981.4	33.5
1980	863.6	79.0	38.5	2,035.7	24.6	9,551.2	38.1
1984	943.0	79.4	50.0	3,165.7	17.0	22,670.4	56.6
1990	1,021.7	67.4	39.5	4,594.8	16.2	40,646.4	64.1

Notes:

1 The labour force includes persons aged 15–64 except for 1990, when persons aged 15 years and over are included. In 1984, 72.3% of the labour force aged 15 years and over contributed. For 1955 the labour force was estimated to be 450,000 persons. The 1957 census recorded 471,918 persons as gainfully employed, and in 1957 215,000 persons (45.6%) of the labour force contributed to the Central Provident Fund. The increase over 1955 was mainly due to the inclusion of domestic servants in the scheme from 1956.

2 The percentages contributed by employees were 5% (1955, 1959, 1965), 6.5% ((1969), 11% ((1973), 16.5% (1978), 18% (1980), 25% (1984), 23% (1990). In 1990, contribution rates varied according to the employees' ages. The rates given are for employees below age 55. Rates of contribution were subject to a maximum monthly contribution.

3 The annual addition to national savings is measured as the change that year in the accumulated fund owed to members.

Sources: Central Provident Fund, *Chairman's statement and accounts 1956* (SLA sessional paper no. S.6 of 1957), p.1; *Chairman's statement and accounts 1957* (SLA sessional paper no. S.3 of 1958), p.2; *Chairman's statement and accounts 1965* (Parliamentary Paper S.6 of 1967), p.2; *Chairman's statement and accounts 1970* (Parliamentary paper S.20 of 1971), pp.2–3; Central Provident Fund, *Annual report 1983*, p.34, 1987, p.24, 1990, p.31; *Economic and social statistics 1960–1982*, pp.32, 44, 184; *Singapore sample household survey, 1966*, p.87; *Yearbook of statistics 1983–86*, p.52, *1991*, pp.55, 70, 239; table A.13.

required by Lewis. But job creation by these firms reduced unemployment, which probably avoided any worsening of income distribution and, moreover, increased the domestic savings potential.[61] Singapore's government, doubting workers' capacity for abstinence, realized this potential through the CPF. Since foreign capitalists, unlike the domestic capitalists depicted by Lewis, could not be expected to have any Singapore loyalty in the local re-investment of profits, firms were compelled to add to workers' savings through contributions to the CPF.

Through borrowing from the CPF at below-market interest rates, the government obtained a cheap, non-inflationary source of finance and relied extensively on it to provide infrastructure and public goods. At the same time, in its public sector mobilization of finance by the extraction of savings through monopoly power, Singapore operated a state-directed capitalism which, in J. G. Gurley and E. S. Shaw's terminology, was a technology of finance resembling socialist central planning more than private free market capitalism. Public sector savings, like those of the CPF, were put at the government's disposal.[62]

In addition to government control of savings through the CPF, there was also a large indirect transfer of savings from the private sector to the government as a result of voluntary deposits with the Post Office Savings Bank. The Bank was required to use most of the money deposited with it to buy government securities, or as deposits with the Monetary Authority of Singapore.[63] Deposits with the Post Office Savings Bank had the advantage of being tax-exempt, and two years after becoming a statutory board in 1972, the Bank began to offer a higher interest rate than commercial banks.[64] By the mid-1980s purely savings deposits with the Post Office Savings Bank exceeded those of all Singapore's commercial banks put together.[65]

Domestic capital resources were mobilized for economic development when the government used its control over savings for investment in projects such as housing and infrastructure. The government also required a compulsory contribution from employers to a Skills Development Fund

---

[61] However, measures of income distribution in Singapore, discussed in section VIII below, do not take account of MNEs. Therefore, any judgement on income distribution must be made with reservations.

[62] Cf. John G. Gurley and E. S. Shaw, 'Financial structure in economic development', *EDCC* 15, 3 (1967), p.262.

[63] Colin Simkin, 'Does money matter in Singapore?', *Singapore Economic Review* 29, 1 (1974), p.12; Lim, *Policy options*, p.380; Monetary Authority of Singapore, *Annual report 1990/91*, p.49.

[64] Wong Kum-Poh, 'Saving, capital inflow and capital formation' in Lim and Lloyd, eds. *Singapore: resources and growth*, pp.57–58; Lim, *Policy options*, pp.340–43; Monetary Authority of Singapore, *Annual report 1991/92* (Singapore, 1992), p.59.

[65] Lim, *Policy options*, p.226.

Table 11.21 *Singapore gross fixed capital formation by public and private sectors, 1960–1990 (1985 market prices, annual averages)*

	Gross fixed capital formation	Public sector		Private sector	
	$m	$m	%	$m	%
1960/66	1,093.0	423.3	38.2	684.3	61.8
1967/69	2,382.2	716.4	30.2	1,652.2	69.8
1960/69	1,479.8	511.2	34.4	974.7	65.6
1970/79	6,648.6	1,800.3	27.4	4,782.1	72.6
1980/90	16,297.1	4,692.6	28.8	11,604.5	71.2

Sources: Appendix table A.14.

which was used as part of a programme to train workers for higher technology jobs and develop human capital.[66] Infrastructure provided under government auspices was the most modern and efficient possible, including port, airport, telecommunications, roads and a mass rapid transit system. For business in Singapore, the effect was to provide a subsidy which reduced expenses of operating within the Republic as well as of reaching world markets.

The rapid accumulation of physical capital which characterized the Singapore model came principally from the private sector (table 11.21 and appendix table A.14). Even from 1960 to 1966, when planning in Singapore stressed government provision of infrastructure, the public sector accounted for no more than 38% of all gross fixed capital formation in Singapore. During the 1970s and from 1980 to 1990, nearly three-quarters of this capital formation came from the private sector.

Singapore's high investment could increasingly have been domestically financed, as evidenced by the ratio of gross national savings to gross capital formation (GNS/GCF in the last column of appendix table A.13). Indeed, by the late 1980s national savings exceeded gross capital formation, reflected in a current account surplus on the balance of payments. But it was generally accepted that the government invested a high proportion of Singapore's public savings abroad in equities and bonds, real estate and short-term assets.[67] In effect, through this government investment abroad,

[66] Lim Chong Yah, 'The NWC as I see it' in S. Jayakumar, ed. *Our heritage and beyond: a collection of essays on Singapore, its past, present and future* (Singapore, 1982), p.53; Richard Hu Tsu Tau, *Budget statement 1988* (Singapore, 1988), p.6.

[67] The Government of Singapore Investment Corporation was set up at the end of 1981 to manage these investments. The investment created an inflow of dividends, interest and profits to set against the outflow arising from direct foreign investment, avoiding a potential strain on the current account of the balance of payments. For criticism of the

Table 11.22 *Singapore measures of the contribution of direct foreign investment to capital accumulation, 1967–1990* (*1985 market prices, annual averages*)

	Gross fixed capital formation (GFCF)	Foreign investment in manufacturing sector gross fixed assets		IMF figures for direct foreign investment in Singapore	
	$m	$m	% of GFCF	$m	% of GFCF
1967/69	2,382.2	261.4	11.0	219.0	9.2
1970/79	6,648.6	896.7	13.5	1,471.3	22.1
1980/90	16,297.1	2,110.8	13.0	4,012.5	24.6

Sources: Appendix tables A.14 and A.16; International Monetary Fund, *Balance of payments statistics yearbook*, vol.27, *1967–74*, p.1 of Singapore section, vol.29, *1978*, p.532 and part 1 of the following years: *1985*, p.559, *1986*, p.581, *1987*, p.597, *1992*, p.576; International Monetary Fund, *International financial statistics yearbook 1990*, pp.634–35.

Singapore exchanged an outflow of national savings for an inflow into the domestic economy of private foreign capital, which brought with it technology and assured access to markets. The exchange explains a part of what might otherwise seem a paradox: that high savings largely relied on the public sector but high investment came chiefly from the private sector.

Appendix table A.15 makes apparent the small role of domestic investment in manufacturing and suggests substantial direct foreign investment in Singapore, dominated by the United States and Japan. Capital inflows in the form of direct foreign investment are shown in table 11.22. These figures substantiate the growing contribution of direct foreign investment to Singapore's capital formation and suggest that the proportion rose from perhaps a tenth in 1967/69 to as much as a quarter by the 1980s.

Government injections in the form of infrastructure, investment incentives and an increasingly educated workforce were fundamental in explaining large private sector investment. Every $1 increase over the previous decade in public sector capital formation was associated with an increase in private sector capital formation of $3 during the 1970s, and $2·5 in the 1980s (table 11.21). The relationship does not indicate causation, but is at least suggestive of the possibility of long-term 'crowding in', rather than 'crowding out', due to government expenditure. A crowding in effect might also be expected because government injections

government policy of investing abroad rather than in Singapore, see Koh Ai Tee, 'Savings, investment and entrepreneurship' in Krause, et al. *Singapore economy*, p.81.

were strongly complementary to the private sector and increased the economy's absorptive capacity.[68] Crowding in would help to explain the paradox indicated above of high public sector savings and yet reliance on private sector capital formation: public sector savings which financed infrastructure brought even higher private sector investment. A possible drawback, however, was that the private industry crowded in was largely foreign. Even though Singapore had long been used to a high foreign presence, there arose a 'morning after feeling' of wishing it had provided more entrepreneurship, technology and venture capital for itself.

V

The leaders of independent Singapore began with a general belief in the effectiveness of planning but no definite idea of the course it should follow. A coherent, clearly-defined development strategy, essential to any shade of planning, emerged from the later 1960s as political leaders and planners increasingly perceived the strength of the world economy's new flows of trade and foreign investment. As part of the same process, Singapore's leaders found control over strategic domestic markets and institutions the most effective way to respond to these opportunities in the world economy in order to meet the main planning objectives of providing jobs, absorbing surplus labour and achieving rapid economic growth.[69] There was no ideological commitment to free enterprise as such: 'The government has to be the planner and the mobilizer of the economic effort' but 'the free enterprise system, correctly nurtured and adroitly handled, can serve as a powerful and versatile instrument of economic growth'.[70]

Interventionism in Singapore's post-1959 development was organized around government directives, and so had considerably more force than indicative planning. Evaluation of development plans and planning objectives is complicated by the fact that, like most government matters in Singapore, described even in the 1990s as a 'corporate state that is mainly run by PAP technocrats',[71] key documents were kept secret.[72] Only

---

[68] David Alan Aschauer, 'Does public capital crowd out private capital?', *Journal of Monetary Economics* 24 (1989), pp.171–88.

[69] Goh Keng Swee, interview with the author, 17 Aug. 1989.

[70] Goh Keng Swee, *The Asian*, 20 Aug. 1972.

[71] Shee Poon Kim, 'Singapore in 1991', *Asian Survey* 32, 2 (1992), p.119.

[72] The main published planning documents in Singapore were Singapore, *Development plan 1961–1964* (1961); United Nations, *Proposed industrialization programme* (1961); Singapore, *First development plan 1961–1964: review of progress* (1964); Hon, *Economic pattern* (budget speech) (1972); Singapore, *Economic development plan for the eighties* (c.1981); Economic Committee, *Singapore economy: new directions* (1986); Singapore, Economic Planning Committee, Ministry of Trade and Industry, *The strategic economic plan* (Singapore, 1991); Singapore, National Science and Technology Board, *Window of*

'highlights' of the *Economic development plan for the eighties* were published, although subsequent plans were discussed more fully. It is clear, however, that planning for manufacturing development in Singapore never involved detailed blueprints, because of the priority accorded to reaction to the international market, impossibility of predicting its course and need for flexibility to ensure a quick and competitive response. Yet there were requirements common to all industries – good infrastructure and a cheap, disciplined and trained labour force – and these were made prime objectives which were then systematically met.

More than this, however, Singapore planners, helped by intelligence from EDB overseas offices, closely monitored the world market, and initiatives were undertaken to attract desirable industries. For example, the potential of electronics was spotted on a 1966 ministerial visit to Taiwan.[73] The EDB targeted manufacturing activities, in that the Board looked for industries beneficial to Singapore – on criteria like value added, skill content and capital intensity – which were likely to be attracted to the Republic, enquired as to the necessary incentives including tax concessions and then provided them.[74] But in manufacturing, the aims remained general; Singapore planners' approach to the international economy contrasted with the targeted protectionism and idea of 'picking winners' practised in Japan, South Korea and Taiwan. Rather, in keeping with a tiny domestic economy, Singapore adhered to free trade and tried to be attractive to a range of activities through supply-oriented policies, an approach later likened to backing all the horses in a race.[75] In the public sector, largely responsible for infrastructural development, rolling five-year plans operated. The Ministry of Finance was responsible for the broad orchestration of policies until the formation of the Ministry of Trade and Industry in 1979; institutions such as the EDB and Jurong Town Corporation organized planning in their specialized areas.

Singapore planning featured the concentration of decision making in a few hands, also observed elsewhere in East Asia.[76] In Singapore's 'top-down' approach, at the summit the planning system was described as 'a high degree of good and eclectic steersmanship'.[77] Typically, the same

opportunities (1991); Singapore, SEP Working Group (Ministry of Trade and Industry), *Implementation of the strategic economic plan* (Singapore, 1993).

[73] C. C. Wee, 'Export – Singapore's new road to prosperity', *Singapore Trade and Industry* (Aug. 1966), p.54; Goh Keng Swee, 'MNCs brought jobs and sparked change', *Straits Times Weekly*, 29 Aug. 1992.

[74] Singapore, Economic Development Board, *Yearbook 1991/92* (Singapore, 1992), pp.26–27.   [75] Goh, 'MNCs brought jobs'. See also *Strategic economic plan*, p.68.

[76] Mason, *Economic and social modernization of Korea*, pp.257, 493; Robert Wade, *Governing the market* (Princeton, 1990), pp.195–227, particularly p.217.

[77] Linda Low, 'The Singapore economy in 1987', *Southeast Asian Affairs* 15 (Singapore, 1988), p.259.

men, for example Hon Sui Sen and Joseph Pillay, served as directors for a host of public enterprises and government development initiatives, which economized on entrepreneurial talent.[78] Moreover, the policy helped to ensure loyalty to the government and to further its tight control. The PAP leadership achieved effective implementation of plans and policies through the lower levels of bureaucracy by a willingness to pay government officials as much or more than the private sector and by an emphasis on individual accountability.[79] By the 1990s plan review procedures were given a public fascia.[80]

VI

In the development of financial and business services, a more precise planning strategy prevailed than for manufacturing. It was set out in the 1972 budget speech, strengthened in the *Economic development plan for the eighties* (1981) and further elaborated later that decade in *The Singapore economy: new directions* (1986). Significantly, this more targeted approach to planning reflected Singapore's greater market power in attracting financial services based on 'natural' comparative advantage – that is, when a free, competitive market prevails. Location on the world's main east–west communications network and the existing presence in the Republic of a critical mass of international financial institutions, ancillary services and infrastructure gave Singapore more freedom to 'pick winners' in financial services than in manufacturing. Starting in the later 1960s, the rapid expansion of international financial intermediation emphasized and widened Singapore's locational advantages. For specifically offshore dealings, the island linked the Atlantic, Middle East and Pacific regions, which in the 1970s enabled Singapore to become a funding centre, acting as an entrepot between deposit centres like Bahrain in a region of surplus funds and arranging centres like Hong Kong near ultimate borrowers.[81] Because Singapore bridged the time zone gap between the New York/ London and Hong Kong/Tokyo markets, it could emerge as a leading foreign exchange dealing centre with the initiation of 24-hour international

---

[78] Alex Josey, 'Public servant with a talent for the bold plan, wide sweep', *Singapore Trade and Industry* (April 1969), pp.8–14; 'Hon Sui Sen: key man for new era of industrial development', *Singapore Trade and Industry* (Jan. 1969), p.44; Jay Lee, 'How M[onetary] A[uthority] [of] S[ingapore] directs Singapore Inc.', *Euromoney* (Sept. 1984), p.105; 'Pillay to retire from civil service at the end of year', *Straits Times Weekly*, 24 July 1993.

[79] Chew Soon Beng, *Small firms in Singapore* (Singapore, 1988), pp.222–23.

[80] SEP Working Group, *Implementation of the plan.*

[81] Claudio Dematte, 'International financial intermediation: implications for banking and regulators', *Banca Nazionale del Lavoro Quarterly Review* 136 (1981), p.101; John B. Caoutte, 'Time zones and the arranging centres', *Euromoney* (July 1978), pp.48–54.

trading. By the 1990s Singapore was the fourth-largest foreign exchange market after London, New York and Tokyo.[82]

Financial services would not have become an engine of growth in Singapore's economy in the absence of an activist government. One aspect of the government's contribution to the development of financial and business services was the provision of frequently overlooked public goods – the maintenance of honest markets, an environment conducive to easy operation and the stability of the Singapore dollar. In a sense, these public goods were no more than the British colonial government had supplied. But that would be to understate the real achievement of the PAP government, since such public goods were dissipated in other parts of Asia.

The separation from Malaysia (and in 1973 the full split between the Singapore and Malaysian currencies) allowed the Singapore government freedom of action to initiate policies promoting financial development and, in contrast to most developing countries, obviated possible conflicts among national economic development objectives.[83] In 1968 the Singapore government, in consultation with international banks, spotted the possibility of an Asian dollar market similar to that for Eurodollars. The government immediately reacted by abolishing for deposits made by Asian Currency Units (ACUs) – any banking unit operating in the Singapore Asian Dollar Market – a withholding tax of 45 % on interest paid to non-residents, quickly followed by a variety of other measures targeted at establishing the market.[84] This activist government policy 'stole the march on Hong Kong', where the authorities lacked a similar development commitment. Although Hong Kong subsequently moved to establish a dollar market, by then the advantage lay decisively with Singapore, and a successful challenge to the Republic proved impossible.[85]

In the 1970s the Singapore government aggressively built on Singapore's comparative advantage in financial and business services through the introduction of financial innovations. Together, the Development Bank of Singapore and the Monetary Authority of Singapore, established in 1971 as a quasi-central bank, became strong and responsive institutions which the government could use in its strategy to develop Singapore as the 'Zurich of the East'.[86] The growth of the Asian Dollar Market showed

[82] Singapore, *Economic survey 1992*, p.66.
[83] Monetary Authority of Singapore, *Annual report 1971* (Singapore, 1972), pp.23–28.
[84] Zoran Hodjera, 'The Asian currency market: Singapore as a regional financial centre', *IMF Staff Papers* 25, 2 (1978), pp.224–25.
[85] Y. C. Jao, 'Hong Kong's future as a financial centre', *Three Banks Review* 145 (1985), pp.44–45 and 'The rise of Hong Kong as a financial center', *Asian Survey* 19, 7 (1979), pp.692–93.
[86] 'Singapore dollar shows its strength' and 'Growing sophistication in the financial community', *Financial Times*, Singapore survey, 1 Oct. 1973.

how the government, in pursuit of a target, characteristically moved, initially through 'permissive' legislation, to attract a new financial activity by reducing transaction costs through measures to lower taxes and facilitate the ease of setting up and operation for foreign firms.[87] But when the market proved unresponsive, the government was willing to take the lead: the government-owned Development Bank of Singapore, and then the Singapore government itself, started the Asian Dollar Bond Market by floating US dollar-denominated bonds. As the private sector, after initial hesitation, embarked on similar initiatives, the Asian Dollar and Bond Markets – with their respectively short and longer-term maturities – introduced significant market specialization and complementarity in Singapore's offshore banking system.[88]   The Asian Dollar Market remained the more important of the two, and after reaching US$54·4 billion by 1980, grew to US$390·4 billion in 1990, annual average growth of 21·8%.[89]

Along with the Development Bank of Singapore, local Singaporean banks were strong enough to take advantage of and contribute to Singapore's development as a financial centre. The important non-government banks were the Chinese banks discussed in chapters 7 and 10: the Oversea-Chinese Banking Corporation, United Overseas Bank and Overseas Union Bank. After 1968 they took control of a number of other Chinese banks founded before and after World War II. These acquisitions were generally allowed to maintain their traditional identity, which gave retail banking in Singapore an apparently diverse face, but in reality the OCBC, UOB and OUB formed three large, private banking groups. These three banking groups and the Development Bank of Singapore came to be known as the Singapore 'Big Four'.[90]

The establishment of Singapore as a '"financial supermarket", offering the widest range of financial services'[91] was central to the *Economic development plan for the eighties*; during that decade, every budget statement contained new measures aimed at financial innovation. A

---

[87] For example, see *Parliamentary Debates* 39, 10 (5 March 1980) (budget speech), cols.628–31.

[88] Hon, *Economic pattern* (budget speech, 1972), p.16; Singapore, *Parliamentary Debates* 32, 10 (26 Feb. 1973) (budget speech), col.460; Lee Sheng-Yi, 'Developing Asian financial centres' in Augustine H. H. Tan and Basant Kapur, eds. *Pacific growth and financial interdependence* (Sydney, 1986), pp.212–15.

[89] Monetary Authority of Singapore, *Annual report 1990/91*, p.92.

[90] These and other institutional developments in Singapore's financial sector are traced in Lee, *Monetary and banking development* (1990), pp.73–104, 238–60; 'Keppel Corp. takes control of ACB', *Straits Times Weekly*, 14 April 1990. By 1990 the Tat Lee Bank was the only independent domestic bank outside the four, and actively pursued a policy of international expansion to try to meet competition from them.

[91] *Economic development plan for the eighties*, pp.10–11.

complementary thrust of government policy which aimed at attracting international financial institutions to Singapore was demonstrably successful. From 1981 to 1990, while there remained 13 Singapore local banks offering a full range of banking services, the number of foreign banks rose from 86 to 128, and merchant banks from 39 to 68. By 1990 there were 199 ACUs, since virtually all banks and merchant banks dealt in Asian dollars.[92]

Singapore's ever-growing cluster of financial institutions created opportunities for specialization and scale economies for these institutions, and so reinforced government efforts towards broadening and deepening financial services in the Republic. In association with the Monetary Authority of Singapore, the government targeted specific financial instruments and institutions and strongly encouraged them with fiscal incentives. These were instrumental in establishing a new futures and options market, organized through the Singapore International Monetary Exchange (SIMEX). It offered a variety of contracts – with Eurodollar futures the most popular – and operated on a 24-hour mutual-offset basis with the Chicago Mercantile Exchange. By the later 1980s, as the government had planned, merchant banking appeared to have taken off in Singapore, and it was increasingly a centre for fund management.[93]

However, despite Singapore's position as a financial centre with links to regional demand,[94] local Singapore firms often encountered difficulty in raising capital from foreign institutions located in the Republic. Furthermore, firms which did not qualify for a listing on the Stock Exchange of Singapore (SES) found it difficult to raise capital. Recognizing the need for Singapore firms to have better access to capital, government promoted the 1986 Stock Exchange of Singapore Dealing and Automated Quotation to provide a second tier market for smaller- and medium-sized local firms. However, the SES could not contribute fully to financial centre development due to its small capitalization. A purpose of the Singapore government's privatization programme was to increase the SES's capitalization, since more quoted Singapore equities were required to draw to the Republic a critical mass of foreign institutions and fund managers. They would in turn attract listings from neighbouring countries needed to establish Singapore as the principal Association of South East Asian Nations stock market.[95] Towards the same end, Singapore liberalized restrictions to allow majority foreign ownership of brokerage houses.

---

[92] Monetary Authority of Singapore, *Annual report 1990/91*, p.81.
[93] For example, see *Economic survey 1990*, pp.8, 69–70; Monetary Authority of Singapore, *Annual report 1990/91*, pp.29, 33, *1991/92*, p.40.
[94] *Economic survey 1986*, pp.12–13.
[95] Public Sector Divestment Committee, *Report*, p.43; 'Pressing ahead with privatisation', *Financial Times*, Singapore survey, 9 Aug. 1990.

By 1990 Singaporeans had benefited considerably from the city's growth as a financial centre and consequent expansion of employment in financial and business services (appendix table A.11 and table 11.16). As the main component of brain services targeted by the government, financial and business services provided high-quality jobs, reflected in wages considerably above the average in Singapore. Brain services, as had been the planning intention, helped Singapore to move away from a dependence on cheap labour and towards higher value added, human capital-intensive jobs.[96]

Services-based development had important implications for Singapore's educational system. By 1967 the government had determined that 'We will cease making the mistakes which nearly all developing countries are now making – over-producing unemployable numbers of educated white-collar workers and not turning out the skilled artisans and technicians we need for industrial growth'.[97] By contrast, brain services, as well as fitting in with the PAP's emphasis on English education, required a strong expansion of tertiary education; enrolment in higher education grew at 3·7% per annum between 1967 and 1979 but at over twice that rate during the 1980s.[98]

VII

Although macroeconomic policy is often regarded as only a short-term, even minor adjunct of structural and institutional planning, temporary macroeconomic instability can destroy attempts at longer-term planning. Macro-policy instruments evolved in Singapore were therefore essential to the overall planning effort and, like it, were made effective through a high degree of government control in selected areas.

Singapore's exceptionally low inflation was a principal achievement of macroeconomic policy and became a cornerstone of it. Macroeconomic management was unconventional, in that a government's ability to attain international competitiveness in labour costs through limiting wage rises to productivity gains is not typically among the range of policy instruments available. In Singapore, the substitution of institutional arrangements centred on the National Wages Council for a conventional macro-policy

---

[96] Statistics Division, Ministry of Labour, 'Wages and earnings in the financial sector, 1979–1982', *Singapore Statistical News* 6, 2 (1983), pp.1–6; *Economic survey 1985*, p.12; Economic Committee, *Singapore economy: new directions*, pp.32, 171, 181, 219–21; *1990 census: Statistical release 4, Economic characteristics*, pp.13–15, 20–21; Singapore, Ministry of Labour, *Report on wages in Singapore 1991* (Singapore, 1992), pp.132–39.

[97] Singapore, Ministry of Labour, *Annual report 1967* (Cmd. 7 of 1969), quote on the front cover extracted from a speech by the Minister for Finance, Goh Keng Swee.

[98] Singapore, *Yearbook of statistics 1976*, p.198, *1985/86*, p.268, *1991*, p.304.

instrument – the exchange rate – freed the latter to become an instrument targeted specifically on inflation.[99] Because in a heavily re-export economy like Singapore's, with a large, internationally-traded goods sector, import and export prices tended to rise about equally, domestic inflation was kept low by allowing the exchange rate to appreciate in line with foreign inflation. The expectation of a rise in value of the Singapore dollar consequent on increased world inflation would have led to a rush of foreign funds into the Singapore currency, unduly pushing up its value, and making impossible control by the Monetary Authority of Singapore, had the Singapore authorities not prevented the internationalization of the Singapore dollar. Singapore imposed a withholding tax on interest earned by non-residents on Singapore dollar holdings, and issued directives to the banking system.[100]

To some extent, there was truth in the argument that Singapore's high, government-forced savings contributed to dampening inflationary pressures by mopping up private-sector purchasing power which would otherwise have gone into non-internationally-traded goods – personal services, food distribution and, above all, building and construction – and pushed up their prices. Changes in CPF employee contributions were used to control private-sector purchasing power, and, in conjunction with National Wages Council 'recommendations', to fine tune Singapore's international wage competitiveness.[101] High savings also helped to counterbalance the expansionary effect of large inflows of foreign capital.[102] However, the more important role of the high level of savings in macroeconomic management was to provide a non-inflationary way to finance the three government-defined priorities of infrastructure, housing and the accumulation of foreign reserves.

Insofar as the government 'released' CPF savings back into the domestic economy, purchasing power was directed towards the first two of these objectives. Because the government could borrow from the CPF at below-market interest rates and had access to a ready source of savings, it was

[99] For example, see Monetary Authority of Singapore, *Annual report 1983/84* (Singapore, 1984), p.4, *1989/90*, p.7.

[100] For discussion of these economic policies, see Lim, *Policy options*, pp.301–89; W. M. Corden, 'Macroeconomic targets and instruments for a small open economy', *Singapore Economic Review* 29, 2 (1984), pp.27–37; Lee Sheng-Yi, 'Some aspects of foreign exchange management in Singapore', *Asia Pacific Journal of Management* 1 (1984), p.209.

[101] Lim, 'The NWC as I see it', pp.52–59; Wong Kum Poh, 'The financing of trade and development in the ADCs: the experience of Singapore' in Wontack Hong and Lawrence B. Krause, eds. *Trade and growth of the advanced developing countries in the Pacific basin* (Seoul, 1981), pp.133, 137.

[102] Wong, 'Saving, capital inflow and capital formation', pp.56, 62; Sandilands, 'Savings, investment and housing', pp.129–30.

able to avoid financing infrastructure development through high taxes or, more important, through money creation. The refusal of the Singapore government to incur government deficits financed by borrowing from a central bank made possible continued adherence to a currency board system (another colonial legacy) which itself promoted low inflation by restricting the money supply.[103]

From 1968 CPF beneficiaries were permitted to withdraw savings to spend on housing, and, in conjunction with a subsidized public housing programme, this ensured that almost all Singapore households became home-owners. Housing ownership was a government priority because of the social stability thereby promoted. In addition to housing, subsequent further liberalizations of restrictions on the use of CPF funds allowed withdrawals against spending on medical care, approved shares and some educational expenses. Most of these expenditures are, in a broad sense, investment, not consumption.

By the late 1980s Singapore's foreign reserves were even bigger than in some advanced industrial countries,[104] and growing rapidly, due to the emergence of persistent surpluses on the current account of the balance of payments and continued large net inflows of foreign capital. This foreign reserve accumulation contained the largest normative element of the three government priorities indicated. There was some rationale for savings, which enabled Singapore to build up high foreign exchange reserves in a part of the world like Southeast Asia, where political instability has a habit of appearing suddenly. More important, however, the use of savings both from the public sector and CPF to accumulate large foreign reserves reflected the opinion of the government that it acted as the people's agent and knew best – an attitude summed up by the government as its fiduciary duty: 'to earn the best and safest returns on the assets under its care'.[105]

Public compliance in saving through the CPF was strengthened by the expectation of low inflation, which would protect the real value of savings. At the same time, the rapid gains in real wages (table 11.16) and spread of home ownership to almost all Singaporean households induced acceptance of government wage control, and thereby completed a 'virtuous circle' of macroeconomic policy: low inflation, with consequent real exchange rate competitiveness, and extensive infrastructure helped to ensure continued foreign capital inflows giving access to MNE technology and marketing

---

[103] Commitment to a currency board system was made immediately after the split with Malaysia. See Singapore, *Parliamentary Debates* 24 (13 Dec. 1965), col.54 (budget speech). For a statement citing the importance of high savings as a means to create physical infrastructure and promote economic growth, see *Strategic economic plan*, p.64.

[104] Lim, *Policy options*, p.17.

[105] B. G. Lee Hsien Loong, 'Keynote address at the Enterprise '92 Conference', (Singapore), 25 Aug. 1992, pp.9–10.

which made real wage gains possible. Furthermore, these gains were largely guaranteed, since Singapore citizens wishing to work were almost assured of a job. The job security of Singapore nationals was, in part, underwritten through hosting up to 200,000 guest workers by the mid-1970s who could be sent home, and so bore much of the risk of unemployment in an economic downturn. In 1985 there was a net reduction of 96,000 jobs, but over three-fifths of those affected were foreign workers.[106] These workers thus came to fulfil a function similar to that of recently-arrived immigrants from south China before World War II.

It has been stressed that Singapore had important similarities to a state socialist economy in the government's control over savings and promotion of a high rate of investment. Under state socialism, the determination of an optimal share of savings in national income is a policy choice and, equally, the possibility of wasteful overinvestment is a danger. Although in Singapore reliance on foreign investment limited the state's scope to determine an optimal investment share, whether government enforced 'oversaving' was an important macroeconomic issue by the mid-1980s. Singaporean critics of the government[107] maintained that the savings level decreed was inefficient because it led to a misallocation of resources. Related to this was the criticism that high savings did not maximize the utility of the nation because of the unnecessary sacrifice of current consumption – a critique increasingly heard by the late 1980s as the savings ratio began to exceed the investment ratio (appendix table A.13). Additionally, a number of influential Singaporeans and non-Singaporeans felt that Singapore planners were guilty of promoting overinvestment – again causing the unwarranted sacrifice of utility by Singapore citizens.[108] For socialist economies, such overinvestment was warned against by M. Kalecki.[109]

Although not making reference to debates over optimal investment in socialist economies, A. Young found that as a result of overinvestment, Singapore's before-subsidy rate of return on capital had been pushed to one of the lowest in the world: government policies of high forced savings and targeting to attract industries were mistakes.[110] Young's calculations

[106] *Economic survey 1985*, p.4. For an indication of the large expansion of foreign workers and their impact on Singapore's demographic mix, see *1980 census: Release 4, economic characteristics*, pp.4–5.

[107] Lim, *Policy options*, pp.37, 234–35; Koh, 'Savings, investment and entrepreneurship', pp.85–86.

[108] Armartya Sen, 'On optimising the rate of savings', *Economic Journal* 71 (1961), pp.484–86; Otto Eckstein, 'Capital theory and some theoretical problems in development planning', *American Economic Review* 51, 2 (1961), pp.92–95.

[109] M. Kalecki, 'Outline of a method of constructing a prospective plan' in A. Nove and D. M. Nuti, *Socialist economics* (London, 1972), pp.214–15, 221.

[110] Young, 'Tale of two cities', pp.37–38, and see 'Comment' by Robert J. Barro, p.59.

showed a real rate of return on capital which averaged 10·3% for 1980–1989; this compared to an average real prime lending rate of 5%.[111]

No entirely satisfactory answer is possible to the questions of oversaving and of overinvestment in Singapore. As indicated, the high level of savings may be justified in part on the positive grounds of making some contribution to low inflation and partly in the normative terms of promoting both internal stability through the spread of home ownership and external security through foreign reserve accumulation. Whether or not the savings rate was optimal in the sense of maximizing the present value of Singaporeans' total expected utility over some given time horizon cannot be known because of the practical impossibility of discovering and aggregating individual utilities to arrive at any meaningful social utility function. If this function could be discovered but did not correspond to government priorities achieved through forced savings, this would amount to saying that the preference of Singapore citizens differed from what could be described as a revealed state preference function built around the priorities of infrastructure, housing and foreign reserve accumulation.[112]

Because Singapore was in effect exchanging through investment abroad part of its domestic savings for foreign capital inflows in the form of direct foreign investment, high investment in Singapore could to some degree have been achieved without such high savings. To this extent savings and investment levels were separate issues. However, investment levels can be judged on a criterion other than utility maximization. Singapore's investment levels appear consistent with the approach developed to apply to socialist economies that optimal investment is that which maximizes economic growth. B. Horvat argued that the optimal investment ratio, determined by an economy's absorptive capacity or ability to make productive use of new investment, was around 35%.[113] Given the undoubtedly high absorptive capacity in Singapore, and since an urban economy requires considerably more capital than one with a rural sector,[114] investment ratios in the Republic seem unlikely to have been excessive, judged on the criterion of growth maximization. Evidence which shows that in Singapore the rate of return on capital (marginal efficiency of investment) was no more than about 5% above real interest rates, supports

---

[111] Singapore, *Yearbook of statistics 1990*, p.236. Calculation of this real rate of interest uses the GDP deflator in appendix table A.12.

[112] On the concept of a state preference function, see Jan Drewnowski, 'The economic theory of socialism: a suggestion for reconsideration', *Journal of Political Economy* 69, 4 (1961), pp.341–54; Evsey D. Domar, *Essays in the theory of economic growth* (New York, 1957), pp.253–54.

[113] Branko Horvat, 'The optimum rate of investment reconsidered', *Economic Journal* 75 (1965), pp.572–76.

[114] See, for example, W. Arthur Lewis, *Development planning* (London, 1966), p.160.

this conclusion, since such a rate would be close to the share of investment in national income which maximizes growth.

Almost certainly the Singapore government, in keeping with the stress which historically it placed on investment,[115] had as its maximand growth, not utility. Nevertheless, by the 1990s government felt the necessity publicly to respond to foreign critics of oversaving and overinvestment.[116] At the beginning of the 1990s government planners seemed to have determined that Singapore's margin of national savings over gross domestic capital formation, yielding the surplus on the Republic's balance of payments, was to be used to invest abroad, beginning Singapore's passage, like Taiwan and South Korea, towards becoming a creditor nation. In this Singapore effort, the previous reliance on SOEs as an entrepreneurial substitute required that these government enterprises lead Singapore Inc. abroad.[117] At the same time, however, efforts to promote local entrepreneurship abroad were designed to respond to Singapore citizens' complaints of oversaving and foster the continued rapid economic growth historically basic to the political acceptability of the PAP, discussed in section IX.

VIII

After 1959 the social and demographic transformation which accompanied economic growth was pushed, shaped and almost certainly hurried by the PAP government. The impact of its policies was soon evident: the 1970 census remarked that 'the main motivating factor of population movement in Singapore today is the planned programme of the Government'.[118] The PAP did not question the necessity to direct the lives of Singaporeans in matters such as choosing a marriage partner, number of children, and a host of petty aspects of social behaviour. Over the 1970s and 1980s, as state power increased, so did this interventionist propensity. By the end of the

---

[115] From the start, the PAP government decided on a higher investment ratio as 'the paramount need ... In an economy which wants to expand its basic wealth at a fast rate, a target like 20% or more should be aimed at'. *SLA Debates* 22, 2 (28 Nov. 1963), col.103 (budget speech, Goh Keng Swee). According to Goh, initially no attempt was made to raise the level of domestic savings because it was felt that personal income levels were too low. He recalled telling Lee Kuan Yew in 1968 that double-digit growth would be achieved as a result of increased savings. Goh, interview with the author, 17 Aug. 1989.

[116] See, for example, 'Too much savings? Not true – BG Lee', *Straits Times Weekly*, 29 Aug. 1992; Lee, 'Keynote address', 25 Aug. 1992.

[117] 'Singapore's external economy: trends and prospects', *Economic survey of Singapore 1993* (first quarter) (Singapore, 1993), pp.26–30; 'S[enior] M[inister] [Lee Kuan Yew]: way to take Singapore Inc. abroad', *Straits Times Weekly*, 9 Jan. 1993.

[118] *1970 census* I, p.246. See also Elizabeth Thompson and Henry Wardlaw, 'Growth and change in Singapore', *Royal Australian Planning Institute Journal* (April 1971), p.46.

1980s government could be judged 'on the whole very intrusive in both the economy and the society'.[119]

Between 1957 and 1970 Singapore's annual population growth slowed to 2·8%, and from 1970 to 1990, reflecting a combination of family planning and economic development, even further to under 2% (tables 10.4 and 10.5).[120] Slower population growth contributed to the rapid gains in a range of development indicators (table 11.23). Singaporeans enjoyed great improvements in health and medical facilities, as well as secondary education and literacy, although primary education enrolment remained at the level reached by 1960.

After 1957 the proportions of Singapore's population by race (table 10.5) changed relatively little; Chinese accounted for over three-quarters of the total. The Malays raised their share somewhat, but still lagged behind other groups in income,[121] in the proportion of students attending university[122] and, most important, in integration into Singaporean society. Although the Singapore government willingly engaged in 'social engineering', it strongly adhered to a policy of merit, judged on a competitive basis. The Malays' socio-economic position in Singapore under this policy was probably its most conspicuous failure.[123] The values of Singaporeans remained strongly materialistic, and after 1960 gained more than a tinge of puritanism, reminiscent of Victorian England, and encouraged by the PAP government.

Singapore's development strategy was to emphasize growth, to spend on long-term investment, not short-term consumption, and to leave to one side redistributional concerns.[124] Initially, the 1950s economic development and expanded education system and social services made this feasible; over the longer term, the policy's success was underwritten by much higher incomes and a virtual elimination of the absolute poverty revealed by the 1953–54 Social Survey.[125] Available evidence indicates that in the mid-1960s Singapore had a rather unequal personal income distribution, 0·50 as measured by the Gini coefficient. Although studies conflict, the coefficient

[119] Krause, 'Hong Kong and Singapore', p.s62.
[120] On family planning and for a list of government disincentives to large families, see Khoo Chian Kim, *Census of population 1980 Singapore: Administrative report* (Singapore, 1983), p.148.
[121] Lau Kak En, *Singapore census of population 1990: Statistical release 2, Households and housing* (Singapore, 1992), p.7; *1990 census: Statistical release 4, Economic characteristics*, p.16.
[122] Lau Kak En, *Singapore census of population 1990: Statistical release 3, Literacy, languages spoken and education* (Singapore, 1993), p.10.
[123] Cf. 'PM pledges to back plans to aid Malays', *Straits Times*, 21 July 1990.
[124] *Development plan 1961–64*, pp.6, 18; Singapore, *Parliamentary Debates* 24 (13 Dec. 1965), cols.52, 69 (budget speech); Lee, *Social revolution*, p.6.
[125] Lim, *Policy options*, p.393.

Table 11.23 *Singapore development indicators, 1960–1990*

	1960	1970	1980	1990
Population (m persons mid-year)	1.6	2.1	2.4	3.0
GNP per capita (current US$)	450[b]	920	4,420	11,160
GNP per capita world ranking[a]	33[b]	27	21	19
Real growth rate GNP per capita (US$)		5.2	6.7	5.7
		(1960–70)	(1970–80)	(1980–90)
Life expectancy at birth	65	68	72	74
Infant mortality (aged 0-1) per 000 live births	35	14[e]	12	7
Population per physician	2,360	1,400[d]	1,150	840
Population per nursing person	650	390[d]	320	314
Daily calorie supply (per capita)	2,286[b]	2,819[d]	3,158	3,198[g]
Percentage of age group enrolled in education:				
Primary	111	111[e]	107	110[g]
Secondary	32	53[e]	55	69[g]
Tertiary	6	8[e]	8	n.a.
Literary rate (aged 10 years and over)	52.3[c]	72.2	83.0[f]	90.1

Notes:
a   Excludes predominantly oil-exporting countries.
b   Refers to 1965.
c   1957 census figure.
d   Refers to 1974.
e   Refers to 1975.
f   Aged 15 years and over.
g   Refers to 1989.
Sources: World Bank, *World Bank atlas 1967*, p.3, *1972*, p.3, *1983*, p.18, *1991*, p.9;
World Bank, *World development report 1978*, p.109, *1979*, p.169, *1981*, pp.135, 175,
177, *1982*, p.151, *1983*, pp.193, 195, 197, *1984*, p.267, *1992*, pp.219, 273, 275;
Economic and social statistics, 1960–1982, p.7; *1970 census*, I, pp.100–1; *1990
census: Statistical release 3, Literacy, languages and education*, pp.xii, xiii; *Yearbook of
statistics 1990*, pp.15, 311.

may have improved to about 0·44 by 1975; if so, it then retrogressed to the
upper 40s by the mid-1980s.[126] However, the 1990 census showed a
household income distribution over all ethnic groups of 0·43.[127] The
tendency for more equal income distribution on a household than a

---

[126] V. V. Bhanoji Rao and M. K. Ramakrishnan, 'Economic growth, structural change and
income inequality, Singapore, 1966–1975', *MER* 21, 2 (1976), pp.92–122; Lee Sheng-Yi,
'Income distribution, taxation, and social benefits of Singapore', *Journal of Developing
Areas* 14, 1 (1979), pp.71–98; Lim, *Policy options*, pp.398–403. The Gini coefficient
measures inequality of income distribution on a scale between zero (perfect equality) and
one (perfect inequality). In practice, Gini coefficients range between about 0·3 and 0·7.
[127] *1990 census: Statistical release 2, Households and housing*, p.10.

personal basis suggested by some studies was consistent with Singapore's high female participation rates (table 11.15); by 1980, 55·1 % of households had more than one person working,[128] and in 1990, 40% of married couples had both husband and wife working.[129] Between 1980 and 1990 real household incomes doubled.[130]

Public expenditure on education, infrastructure and health often disproportionately benefits middle income groups, and instances of this redistributive tendency were evident in Singapore, for example in university education.[131] But any overall propensity to redistribution in favour of higher income groups may have been limited by the nature of taxation. Even in the mid-1980s only about half of Singaporeans paid direct income tax; consumption-based taxes declined from a third in 1970 to a quarter of government revenue by 1985. During the later 1980s 'non-tax revenue' contributed a third to a half of total government revenue and financed a similar proportion of expenditure (government policy traditionally avoided overall budget deficits). The Singapore government published little information on the sources of non-tax revenue; most appears to have come from dividend receipts from public enterprises, in part derived from the power to tax through monopoly pricing, and then increasingly from the investment abroad of surpluses which created an inflow of dividends.[132]

With the establishment of the Housing and Development Board (HDB) in 1960, the government began a vigorous public housing policy. It contained a substantial subsidy element and constituted probably Singapore's most important in-kind redistributive measure. Over the next three decades public housing reached down to virtually all Singaporeans. The government approach was to build small, basic units as fast as possible, and in 1970 nearly three-quarters of those in HDB flats lived in overcrowded or acutely overcrowded conditions.[133] By 1990, when the standard of publicly-built housing had substantially improved, almost 90% of Singaporeans were accommodated in it.[134]

---

[128] *1980 census: Administrative report*, pp.123, 130.
[129] *1990 census: Statistical release 2, Households and housing*, p.15.   [130] Ibid. p.7.
[131] The tendency is described by 'Director's law'. G. J. Stigler, 'Director's law of public income distribution', *Journal of Law and Economics* 13 (1970), pp.1–10. For a discussion of this issue in LDCs, see Richard Goode, *Government finance in developing countries* (Washington, DC, 1984), pp.282–99. For attempts to assess the issue in Singapore, see Lee, 'Income distribution', pp.91–97; 'State gives more than it gets from average Singapore family', *Straits Times Weekly*, 4 April 1992.
[132] Mukul G. Asher, 'Fiscal system and practices in Singapore' in Mukul G. Asher, ed. *Fiscal systems and practices in ASEAN* (Singapore, 1989), pp.131–83; Lim, *Policy options*, pp.373–75; Singapore, *Yearbook of statistics 1991*, p.256.
[133] *1970 census* I, pp.227–28. The census figures excluded single-person households; the average number of rooms per HDB household was 1·92. Ibid. p.219.
[134] *1990 census: Statistical release 2, Households and housing*, p.16.

The government housing programme and the CPF, after Singaporeans were allowed to withdraw savings to purchase HDB flats, transformed Singapore from a city of tenants to one of owners. By 1990, 88% of households owned the houses they occupied, compared with over half in 1980 and less than one-third in 1970.[135] Government upgrading of public housing estates, including privately-owned dwellings, involved a heavy subsidy; at the beginning of the 1990s the PAP announced its intention to upgrade first in constituencies which voted most heavily for the Party.[136]

Consequent on the near-universal public housing and a deliberate government resettlement programme, after 1960 the previously well-defined concentrations of Chinese ethnic groups, Malays and Indians disappeared. By 1970, too, there had begun 'a gradual shift from the traditional type of economic activities largely associated with specific ethnic groups'.[137] Subsequently this greatly speeded up under the pressure of full employment, as well as government education policy specifying English as the first language and a 'speak Mandarin' campaign. Labour market segmentation based on Chinese dialect groups lost its inter-war rationale.

Nevertheless, the use of Chinese dialects persisted. The 1980 census drew attention to the 'entrenched position' of dialects, particularly in poorer households. By 1990, however, Chinese dialects were the predominant language in only 48% of Chinese households, compared to 76% of households in 1980. The frequency with which English was used increased with the economic status of Chinese households, and in 1990, 21% of Chinese households communicated principally in English, compared to 30% in Mandarin.[138] Dialect-speaking Chinese cited as an important reason for emigration from Singapore the emphasis on Mandarin.[139] Of particular importance was the educational disadvantage at which it placed their children, due to an inability to pass examinations in this particular Chinese language. This translated into a severe career disadvantage in Singapore's fiercely merit-based society.

---

[135] *1980 census: Administrative report*, p.124; *1990 census: Statistical release 2, Households and housing*, p.17.

[136] 'Vote will decide upgrading priority', *Straits Times Weekly*, 18 April 1992.

[137] *1970 census* I, p.188, and see p.201.

[138] *1980 census: Administrative report*, p.143, and see pp.137–42; *1990 census: Statistical release 3, Literacy, languages spoken and education*, p.15.

[139] For example, see 'The emigrants: a special report', *Straits Times Weekly*, 6 April 1991. By the late 1980s emigration from Singapore to Western countries was considered a problem.

IX

Economic development in Singapore after 1959 depended very considerably on government interventionism, which successfully adapted the
domestic economy to changes in the international economy. Singapore's
experience showed that it may be necessary – not merely 'possible' – to use
'dictatorial' means to allow the 'free market' to work. Since LDC
governments are typically interventionist, but with often poor results, why
did interventionism succeed in Singapore?

Part of the answer will already be apparent: the substantial 'transformation capacity' of Singapore, as indicated by the economy's responsiveness to change, central to earlier twentieth-century development. That
capacity gave Singapore leaders more degrees of freedom in engineering
change when opportunities in the international economy appeared.[140]
'Great men', as held in chapter 1, do not alone explain a country's
economic development.

But the 'quality of intervention' matters. It rests on four, interrelated,
factors – government autonomy from interest groups; stability, both initial
and perpetuated by a favourable sequencing of events; material gains for
the bulk of the population which, together with a perceived likelihood of
stability, promotes government control without harsh repression; and the
ability, good economic judgement and policy choices of individuals in
charge of the government. Discussion of these four considerations
constitutes the rest of the answer to the success of government interventionism in Singapore.

The first of the four factors – the autonomy of government – allows an
all-out, systematic commitment to economic development, which is a
different, altogether rarer, thing than the proclaimed allegiance to the goal
of development usual in LDCs during the 1950s and 1960s. Government
identification with, and capture by, particular interest groups – a lack of
autonomy – was typically the rock on which a determined, sustained drive
to development foundered. Singapore had such interest groups in a local
entrepreneurial class deriving from its Chinese-educated, China-oriented
majority as well as a similarly oriented trade union movement.

The political achievement of Lee Kuan Yew's PAP in the 1959 colonial
government-sponsored elections and afterwards was to gain the backing of
the majority of the Chinese population. Chinese often still say that Lee

---

[140] Transformation capacity refers to the efficiency with which an economy can move
resources from one sector to another. For a discussion of the concept of transformation
capacity, see Henry J. Bruton, et al. *Sri Lanka and Malaysia* (New York, 1992), pp.308,
327–28, 336–37; Albert Fishlow, 'Review of Handbook of development economics',
Journal of Economic Literature 29, 4 (1991), p.1736.

won the support of the rickshaw pullers. But subsequently, Lee, in control of the levers of state power, split in 1961 with the leftist wing of the PAP. He was able to neutralize his political opponents with a carefully-judged combination of repression and achievement-oriented policies, which gained endorsement, if not a mass popular following.

The Lee Kuan Yew government saw its political future not as 'an outpost of Peking' but as an agent of rapid economic development. The English-educated, Chinese leadership, headed by Lee, feared the local Chinese business class which advocated China and Chinese-language rights, and once in power was determined not to be beholden to it. Among the leaders of the Chinese business community who strongly supported China and Chinese-language education, Tan Kah Kee had been the foremost inter-war figure. After the War he was 'the real Chinese leader with a mass following'.[141] When Tan went to China, his successor was Tan Lark Sye.

In 1956 Tan Lark Sye was instrumental in the establishment of the Chinese-language Nanyang University as a bastion of Chinese culture, with the support of a wide section of the Chinese business community and Chinatown. In 1963, in the first business session of the new Singapore Legislative Assembly, Lee Kuan Yew addressed head-on the issue of Nanyang University, and drew attention to its wider implications:

The Nanyang University Council has hitherto spurned every Government grant to help it raise its standards and put its organisation into shape, largely because the Communists have been able to manipulate some leaders of the Chinese merchant community who have pretensions to greatness, and perhaps to inherit the mantle of another Chinese patriot like the late Mr. Tan Kah Kee … a situation is developing which, if left unchecked within five years, will make it more a University of Yenan than of Nanyang with young pro-Communist graduates and student leaders manipulating the entire governing Council of Nanyang University.[142]

Tan Lark Sye had as trenchant views, expressed in his well-known observation that English education resulted in 'increasing taxes, laying traps, turning out fools and wasting public funds'. He warned that 'If we do not take steps to preserve our culture now … in 40 or 50 years perhaps

[141] Lee Khoon Choy, *On the beat to the hustings* (Singapore, 1988), p.25. At the end of the 1980s in Singapore, Tan Kah Kee postgraduate scholarships were awarded under the auspices of the Singapore Chinese Chamber of Commerce. *Straits Times*, 24 July 1989.
[142] *SLA Debates* vol. 22, first session of the Legislative Council, Part I (9 December 1963), col.147. In that debate (col.255), Koo Young called Lee's remarks 'a great insult to the members of the Chinese Chamber of Commerce. Mr. Tan Kah Kee is a real patriot … The Prime Minister said that he is a Chinese. But to me patriotism and anti-colonialism transcend all national boundaries.' For Lee's later reflections on the education issue and Nanyang University, see Stern, 'Geoffrey Stern interview: Lee Kuan Yew', p.24.

we shall no longer call ourselves Chinese'.[143] His views did not prevail: at the beginning of the 1980s, Nanyang University was subsumed under government direction into the English-language Singapore National University.[144]

The PAP's decision to rely for economic development on MNEs and SOEs allowed Singapore's local business elite largely to be excluded from the decision-making process. Businessmen could not decide policy, 'nor can they exert pressure on the government'.[145] The PAP appears never seriously to have considered some adaptation, frequently suggested in the mid-1960s, of a Hong Kong development model reliant on small Chinese manufacturing enterprise and so local entrepreneurs.[146] Nor was backing derived from the Chinese trade union movement which had flourished in Singapore. Rather, new unions, which did not have roots in the older Chinese radicalism, were created as part of the PAP's overall economic strategy.

Interventionism invites the danger of 'government failure' – a lapse into inept economic policies. In Singapore, the fundamental check against this was the PAP's need for rapid economic development to protect the Party's own interest in gaining re-election, and that of a predominantly English-educated Chinese middle class, which formed the PAP's most basic constituency. Reliance on MNEs to deliver growth, and the fact that most directly productive activity in the economy was left to them, furnished an additional check against government failure.

The second and third factors – a sequencing to produce stability and material gains – which account for the quality of intervention can be considered together. Historical evolution produced in Singapore a sequencing which gave rise to stable government, competent administration and strong, efficient institutions, variables with great explanatory power in accounting for economic growth, as development economics stresses.[147] First, in 1959 Singapore inherited a successful economy and, as Lee Kuan

---

[143] 'Focus: Singapore '80', *Far Eastern Economic Review*, 1 Aug. 1980, p.73; see also Yeo, *Political development*, p.161.
[144] In 1991 the government moved to transfer the Nanyang University alumni rolls to the new Nanyang Technological University. 'Nantah grads against plans to transfer alumni rolls', *Straits Times Weekly*, 29 June 1991; see also 'The future of Nantah's past', *Straits Times Weekly*, 27 July 1991.
[145] Lee Sheng-Yi, 'Business elites in Singapore' in Chen and Evers, *Studies in ASEAN sociology*, p.50.
[146] *SLA Debates*, First session of the legislative assembly, Part II (18 Nov. 1964), col.702; *Parliamentary Debates*, First session of the first parliament, vol.24 (14 Dec. 1965), col.121.
[147] Reynolds, 'Spread of economic growth', p.976; Roundtable Discussion, 'Development strategies: the roles of the state and the private sector', *Proceedings of the World Bank Annual Conference on Development Economics 1990* (1991), comment by N. Stern, p.435.

Yew emphasized, a stable and efficiently functioning administration.[148] Acceptance of the past prevented any break in government.

During a second stage from 1959 to 1966, including the period of Singapore's brief experience of policies of import-substituting industrialization as part of Malaysia, the Singapore government laid the basis, through the EDB, for development-oriented institutions. After 1966 these institutions – the EDB, Development Bank of Singapore and Jurong Town Corporation – could be harnessed to export-oriented industrialization. Reliance on the same, small group of men to serve as directors for these and other state undertakings gave continuity and flexibility to Singapore's development effort.[149]

In the third and final stage, as the government extended and consolidated its control – notably over the trade unions – management of the mass media was a key part of the overall effort. A leading Singapore economist emphasized how this was seen as contributing to economic development: 'The mass media can be made to play a crucial role in an all-out and all-round development effort ... The deliberate omission of such a use by a government in a poor country is unforgivable irresponsibility, whatever is the view in some unrealistic circles in already affluent societies about press freedom'.[150] A former government minister elaborated the last point: 'How many Singaporeans really want free speech anyway? They want orderliness, a decent living'.[151] Both of these were achieved. Corruption, endemic in many LDCs, was absent in Singapore. The Republic was – and remained in 1990 – among the few Asian exceptions to G. Myrdal's 'soft state', characterized by a lack of social discipline, unwillingness of the people to accept obligations and weak (or no) enforcement of policies by the government.[152]

The Singapore government acted systematically to break up potential political or special interests based on racial or ethnic (Chinese dialect) groups. This policy could be extended to virtually all Singaporeans

[148] See above, chapter 1.
[149] The same was true in South Korea: Mason, *Economic and social modernization of Korea*, p.493.
[150] Lim Chong Yah, 'Development economics by R. M. Sundrum: a review article', *MER* 28, 1 (1983), p.96. For a discussion of Singapore and Malaysian newspapers closed down or banned, see Chen Ai Yen, 'The mass media, 1819–1980' in Chew and Lee, *History*, p.307. In 1993 foreign publications which had their circulation banned or restricted included *Time, Asian Wall Street Journal, Far Eastern Economic Review, Asia Week* and the *Economist*. 'Two faces of Singapore: lofty aims, press curbs', *New York Times*, 5 Aug. 1993.
[151] S. Rajaratnam, former Foreign Minister, quoted in Ian Buruma, *God's dust: a modern Asian journey* (London, 1989), p.143.
[152] Gunnar Myrdal, *Asian drama* (Harmondsworth, Mddx., 1968), pp.66–67, 891–900 and 'Need for reforms in underdeveloped countries' in Sven Grassman and Erik Lundberg, eds. *The world economic order* (London, 1981), p.519.

through an educational approach which made English the first language in all schools, and the rehousing programme.[153]

The obvious economic progress – in the appearance of Singapore, housing and gains in real wages – contributed to the PAP's acceptance by voters and Singapore's one-party elected parliament. But the government took no chances: 'opponents of the government have been relentlessly harried and it takes courage for a professional person to stand openly against the PAP'.[154] No more than mild criticism of the government was tolerated. A law lecturer at the National University observed of the Singapore judiciary: 'It is absolutely futile for people to talk about challenging Executive decisions in court. If it is not legal, the Government will make it legal, and it will make it legal retrospectively'.[155]

Fourth, the calibre of Singapore's post-1959 political leadership cannot be doubted. An elite very much in the British, rather than the populist American, tradition, the same, small group of leaders dominated politics between independence in 1959 and Lee Kuan Yew's 1990 retirement, by then as the world's longest-serving Prime Minister. The observation of Thomas Silcock is telling: 'The number of those who made the difference and enabled Singapore to make so much of a not very obvious opportunity was probably not above fifty. They have meant far more to Singapore than any spreading of economic doctrine among the population in general or even among the educated parts of the population'.[156]

Distinguishing features of these men were their personal integrity and a high level of formal education with, more specifically, often extensive training in economics. This last did not extend to Lee Kuan Yew. But his approach to economics was 'that of a person recognising that he has some training in the subject [who] uses it to appraise the judgement of fully professional economists and use their advice to check some of his own ideas'.[157] By contrast, almost everywhere else in post-colonial Asia, leaders had political skills associated with their role in independence movements, but little regard for economic considerations.[158]

Milton Friedman looked at Singapore, remarked that Lee Kuan Yew was a 'benevolent dictator', and drew the lesson that 'it is possible to combine a free private market economic system with a dictatorial political

---

[153] There was, as Lee Kuan Yew acknowledged of the rehousing programme, a price to pay in dislocation and loss of traditional kinship ties. 'New scheme to keep the people together', *Straits Times Weekly*, 29 Feb. 1992.
[154] 'A fresh style in Singapore' (editorial), *Financial Times*, 28 Aug. 1991.
[155] 'Stand up and be quoted', *Straits Times Weekly*, 13 July 1991.
[156] Silcock, *History of economics teaching*, p.293.   [157] Ibid. p.315.
[158] Scalapino, *Politics of development*, p.45; Bruce Glassburner, 'An Indonesian memoir', *BIES* 27, 1 (1991), p.51.

system'.[159] But the lesson is more subtle: that Singapore successfully combined authoritarian interventionism at home and *international* free trade. Above all, the genius of Singapore's interventionist government – and so ultimately its quality – was to recognize the importance of vigorous policies to take advantage of free international trade but avoid interference with it. The strong internal policy measures effected to achieve an export-oriented development strategy render it inaccurate to call Singapore a free, private market economic system. The Singapore development strategy had important elements of a command system that directed and encouraged private enterprise towards market opportunities arising in the international economy – itself increasingly shaped by multinational enterprise. After 1965 free trade was consistent with the requirements of Singapore's economy, which depended on the three export sectors of primary commodities, manufactures and services. Through free trade, Singapore maximized its geographical advantage of location, as it had historically.

[159] Milton Friedman, 'A welfare state syllogism', speech to the Commonwealth Club, San Francisco, 1 June 1990, pp.12–13.

12 Conclusion

As indicated in the Introduction, the two purposes of this study have been to trace the course of Singapore's twentieth-century economic growth and, in light of it, to indicate how the experience of Singapore fits into a broader framework of development theory. The first of these objectives was addressed in earlier chapters, and many of the appropriate conclusions were drawn there. Since chapter 1 provided a summary of Singapore's growth, that will not be repeated here. This conclusion is confined to observations on the implications of Singapore's economic growth for development theory and brief comment on Singapore's future development which the vantage point of historical perspective allows.

Development economics, probably more than any branch of economics, experiences a constant tension between interpretations which emphasize the theoretically generalizable and others which favour the 'special case'. The analysis of all less developed areas is amenable to both, but Singapore, because of its several peculiarities explored in the course of this book, is perhaps particularly open to argument for the special case.

Nevertheless, the present study made the point that for the seven decades between 1870 and 1939, Singapore was largely similar in its economic development to a number of major port cities in Asian, African and Latin American 'vent for surplus' regions. Just as the venting of surplus and specialization in natural resource-intensive products, or staples, led to growth in the producing regions as a whole, so staple exports were the engine of economic development of these regions' major port cities. While the main economic activities of such cities – which I call staple ports – became bound up with hinterland production, in serving the staple exporting regions staple ports developed economically as distinctly specialized components of the overall growth process and experienced rapid urbanization.

'There is very little', J. G. Williamson argues, 'that is unique about Third World migration and city growth'. It replicates the pattern of 'Britain during the First Industrial Revolution and, I suspect, most of the other nineteenth-century industrial revolutions which followed'. Consequently, Williamson considers that the observations of 'urbanization without industrialization' by B. F. Hoselitz and W. A. Lewis lack validity.[1] But this is to ignore the late nineteenth- and twentieth-century growth of staple ports, which shows that city growth, even when quite rapid, need not be driven by industrialization.

Singapore's growth could not be seen as substantially the result of industrialization, except in a remote sense that its urbanization was the product of the industrialization of (as much as anywhere) Detroit, supplemented by large reservoirs of labour in south China and India. Relatively high proportions of the labour force in manufacturing, like the 16% in inter-war Singapore, cannot be accepted as a proof that urbanization followed from industrialization. Rather, urbanization and the industrialization based on the processing of staples were both driven by the *export* of these commodities. The growing populations attracted to staple ports by trade in staples created a domestic market which led to most of the additional ensuing industrialization, chiefly in primary import-substituting industry.

In terms of development theory, the growth of staple ports suggests a theoretical approach which draws on three more general ideas. One is 'vent for surplus' theory, originated by Adam Smith and elaborated in the work of H. Myint to apply to less developed regions.[2] The second is the staple theory of H. Innis, R. E. Caves and others, and the third the concept of linkages.[3] These three approaches are interrelated. Staple exports were often the result of surpluses vented, while staple theory and linkages have 'much in common'. At the forefront of staple theory are the economic linkages created. The concept of linkages focuses on how, given the nature and technological requirements of economic activities engendered by the staple, 'one thing leads (or fails to lead) to another'.[4] The study of Singapore as a staple port showed how one staple led to another, the role of Singapore in promoting this growth and so hinterland development, and the linkages which a succession of staples created for the port, in turn resulting in its own economic growth.

The presence of linkages gives a dynamic necessary to the economic development process, since the venting of a surplus is merely analogous to

[1] Jeffrey G. Williamson, 'Migration and urbanization' in Chenery and Srinivasan, eds. *Handbook of development economics* I, pp.440, 461; see also W. Arthur Lewis, 'Reflections on development' and 'Comments' by Jeffrey G. Williamson in Ranis and Shultz, eds. *State of development*, pp.13–30; Bert F. Hoselitz, 'Urbanization and economic growth in Asia', *EDCC* 5 (1957), pp.42–54.
[2] Myint, '"Classical theory" of international trade' and 'Adam Smith's theory of international trade'.
[3] Watkins, 'Staple theory of economic growth'; Caves, 'Export-led growth' and '"Vent for surplus" models'.   [4] Hirschman, 'Linkages', pp.217, 220.

the realization of economic rents or quasi-rents on underutilized natural resources.[5] Without this dynamic, the gains from staple exports would soon be exhausted and trade fail to fulfil an engine of growth role. In Singapore's development, many of the linkages created involved service activities. Staple port development gives 'vent for surplus' and staple theories a particular, services-based application.

Services, as P. T. Bauer has urged,[6] require more explicit consideration in a theory of economic development than they have hitherto received. A necessary element in the analysis of staple ports is a theory of comparative advantage in services. The latter has just begun in the study of international trade, but Singapore's experience strongly suggests that although comparative advantage may have initially derived largely from location, increasingly it also depended on accumulated physical and human capital. The latter came from British agency houses and, as much, if not more, from a critical mass of Chinese traders with close links to the hinterland. The activities of merchants and traders, together with Singapore's locational advantages of high nodality for regional and international shipping, afforded important economies of scale in handling and marketing commodities. Such opportunities for scale economies are basic to any theory of comparative advantage in services. The city's provision of these services has been essential to the dynamic supply response needed to make regional export expansion viable over the long run.

Other staple ports' economic development, if not always as spectacular as Singapore's, may be explained in similar terms. Generally, staple port development produced large, modern cities with infrastructure dispro-portionate to their surrounding hinterlands and, it was often thought, a sufficient basis for subsequent economic growth in newly-independent developing countries. In fact, however, as post-World War II experience showed, the port and hinterland were part of the same, interlinked development problem. This relationship tended to be overlooked in theories which, like many of the 1950s and early 1960s, concentrated on industrialization but took agriculture largely for granted.

Typically, the later twentieth-century economic development difficulties of staple ports featured rapid population growth but a levelling off, or even decline, in the staples themselves, and perhaps powerful interest groups closely allied to staple production. Under these conditions, the economics of transition for port and hinterland, joined like Siamese twins, did not prove easy. To be sure, the port was a natural centre for industrialization through import substitution. But after the easy, primary import-

[5] Caves, 'Export-led growth', pp.408, 435.
[6] Bauer, 'Remembrance of studies past' in Meier and Seers, Pioneers, p.36.

substitution phase of non-durable consumer goods – often already substantially accomplished during development as a staple port – a secondary
phase of import substitution, involving the replacement of imports of
capital goods and durable consumer goods, usually ran into problems.
With an end to surplus land and in the absence of an agricultural
revolution, the hinterland generally did not offer a substantial market for
goods produced as part of the secondary phase of import substitution.
Furthermore, import-substitution regimes which turned the internal terms
of trade against agriculture and encouraged capital-intensive and import-
intensive technologies, with the resulting industry centred in the staple
port, further depressed hinterland development. A result was large inflows
of rural labour which were attracted by higher wages in the urban area and
its modern manufacturing sector but often went into unemployment or
underemployment. The disproportionate provision of social amenities in
the city to which the prevailing 'urban bias' gave rise, built naturally
enough on the industry, infrastructure and political power already centred
in the staple port, and often completed the picture.

In all these respects, Singapore's uniqueness among staple ports – as
always a free port, demographically distinct and politically separate from
the most important parts of its hinterland – was evident before World War
II. These features of Singapore gained heightened relevance from the 1960s
onwards. During this period of Singapore's economic development, the
argument for the special case needs to be accorded greater weight.

Singapore's twentieth-century experience of trade as an engine of
growth was not uniform. For the first six decades of the century, and even
briefly in the late 1960s, the trade acting as an engine of growth depended
on exports from the surrounding region, principally Indonesia, which
required services and gave rise to manufacturing activities in Singapore. It
has been observed that the fact 'that some LDCs began growing more than
a century ago, and that primary exports were an effective engine of growth,
may ... appear odd. This is not the way growth occurs in post-1945 growth
models'.[7] Odder still, and even less considered in the growth literature, is
the fundamental role that staple ports have played in economic development. In the mechanism of trade as an engine of growth, Singapore
was the drive shaft.

From the later 1960s, the role of trade in Singapore's economic
development altered as the island began manufacturing for export on a
large scale. Initially, exports of manufactures, like trade's earlier 'vent for
surplus' role for the region, also had a venting function for unemployed or

[7] Lloyd G. Reynolds, 'Inter-country diffusion of economic growth, 1870–1914' in Mark
Gersovitz, et al., eds. *The theory and experience of economic development* (London, 1982),
p.330.

under-employed labour available in Singapore as a result of its earlier economic development and rapid post-World War II population growth. Export of this surplus labour, in the sense of being embodied in the manufactured goods which the island sent abroad, replaced the pre-World War II 'solution' to unemployment in Singapore of mass immigration to China. When Singapore reached full employment in 1973, trade acted as an engine of growth chiefly by providing the means for still further specialization; and, consistent with the classical theory of comparative costs dating from Ricardo, it led to beneficial resource reallocation within Singapore, especially of labour. Trade's vent for labour surplus and gains from factor reallocation explained much of Singapore's high post-1966 manufacturing growth rates; significant technical change, measured as improvement in total factor productivity, was absent in Singapore. In manufacturing for export, Singapore's small size and production for the world market allowed the Republic fully to obtain gains from trade specialization and realize available economies of scale.

The broad pre- and post-1965 divisions should not be taken to imply a static relationship between trade and economic activity in Singapore. On the contrary, both periods were marked by frequent change and developmental linkages with the rest of the world. Nearly every page of this book indicates the dynamic gains – J. S. Mill's 'indirect benefits' – of trade for Singapore through making available new skills, technology, management and entrepreneurship, inflows of labour as well as capital, and the import of manufactured materials and capital goods which combined to push the production possibilities frontier outwards.[8] Singapore's own responsiveness to opportunity was fundamental to the process.

In this analysis of trade and growth, which emphasizes internal supply factors,[9] important distinctions in Singapore's economic development are evident. Before World War II, and through the 1950s, the extreme responsiveness of supply in Singapore which allowed trade to become so important to economic development typically reflected individual decision-making under competitive conditions – the unconscious co-operation of the market. The economy functioned, in R. H. Coase's phrase, not as 'an organisation but an organism'.[10] The predominant assumption was laissez-faire: it was expected that government would not intervene

---

[8] For a classic restatement of these classical ideas of the dynamic gains of trade, see Gottfried Haberler, *International trade and economic development* (Cairo, 1959), pp.5–15; see also Ragnar Nurkse, 'International trade theory and development policy' in Ellis, ed. *Economic development for Latin America*, pp.238, 252; N. F. R. Crafts, 'Trade as a handmaiden of growth: an alternative view', *Economic Journal* 83 (1973), pp.875–77.

[9] Irving B. Kravis, 'Trade as a handmaiden of growth: similarities between the nineteenth and twentieth centuries', *Economic Journal* 80 (1970), pp.850–72.

[10] R. H. Coase, 'The nature of the firm', *Economica* 4 (1937), p.387.

economically. Government was clearly subordinate to the forces of the market, and was designed to give them free play. This was not inconsistent with a strong administrative tradition, which underwrote the stable, ordered state everywhere basic to economic development.

Beginning in 1959, however, Singapore increasingly became a government-directed society, popularly known as Singapore Inc. Few places better fit the description of the pursuit of economic development as 'an effort at deliberate control of the course of human affairs',[11] made possible in part because a small island like Singapore is easily managed. After 1965 the fundamental departure in Singapore was not, as often argued, the adoption of free trade, which continued to have a strong local lobby, but the decisions to intervene decisively in the labour market and whenever necessary to take active steps to ensure the presence of the conditions for economic growth. The role of government therefore found little space in the discussion of Singapore's economic development before World War II, but occupied a much more prominent place afterwards. Consequently, a large part of Singapore's twentieth-century development experience could be cited in favour of a neo-classical counter-revolution in development economics, which has at its core 'the rejection of intervention. Government was the problem rather than the solution'.[12] But post-1959 development in Singapore ran directly counter to this new thinking.

Since in LDCs tightly-controlled and interventionist one-party states are nothing out of the ordinary, chapter 11 considered why in Singapore this proved so compatible with economic development. Part of the answer lies in a theme stressed in Singapore's economic development: that its history, geography and human resource endowment pointed to a capacity to transform which, given favourable world demand conditions, made possible government orchestration of development. But government policy choices were also important, and fundamental to these was the quality of, and the drive to achieve economic development on the part of, an elite, English-educated, Western-oriented political leadership. A prominent feature in the post-1965 Singapore government reordering of society was the use and study of English as the main language: it is among the ironies of history that Singapore – the world's greatest assemblage of overseas Chinese – flourished through the twentieth century by becoming culturally less and less Chinese.

Post-1959 economic development in Singapore is relevant to many of the major issues in development economics. Economic development in Singapore supports L. G. Reynolds' 'head start' hypothesis that previous

---

[11] Francis X. Sutton, 'Introduction' to the issue 'A world to make: development in perspective', *Daedalus* 118, 1 (1989), p.xiii.

[12] Fishlow, 'Review of Handbook of development economics', p.1730.

experience is important in explaining economic development: countries which grew rapidly after World War II were usually those where growth acceleration began much earlier.[13] Consideration of twentieth-century development in Singapore points to a 'habit of growth' and high levels of income which made easier the subsequent achievement of rapid growth, as was also true of Taiwan, South Korea and Hong Kong.[14] 'Take-off' for Singapore was not concentrated in a span of ten or twenty years as specified by W. W. Rostow, but, as S. Kuznets argued, was part of a build-up of momentum and a long transition.[15]

The idea of dualism remains among the most important organizing concepts in development economics, partly because the development process itself so frequently gives rise to a dual economy. Before World War II rapid economic development produced within Singapore an economic dualism, not in an urban–rural sense but in the division of the tertiary sector between modern and traditional services. The latter accommodated much of the large and persistent inflows of immigrant labour which Singapore's prosperity attracted from rural areas situated some 1,500 miles to the north-east in south China and almost as far westwards in southern India. The size of these reservoirs of labour and the poverty of their people compared to Singapore's prevented in the island's economy the contraction of the traditional sector, central to economic development as described in the Lewis and Fei–Ranis dual economy models under assumptions of a closed economy and zero population growth.[16]

By the 1960s Singapore faced a potential problem of net population inflow from its hinterland as migration from Malaya gained strength. The 1961 Development Plan argued that because industrialization in Singapore would attract large numbers of Malayan migrants, 'a paradoxical situation would most probably arise. Increasing levels of employment would not decrease unemployment but increase it',[17] an observation subsequently formalized in the Harris–Todaro model.[18] Almost certainly per capita GNP in Singapore, which by 1990 was some five to 20 times above that in

[13] Lloyd G. Reynolds, 'Economic development in historical perspective', *American Economic Review* 70, 2 (1980), p.95.

[14] Samuel Pao-San Ho, 'Colonialism and development: Korea, Taiwan and Kwangtung' in Ramon H. Myers and Mark R. Peattie, eds. *The Japanese colonial empire, 1895–1945* (Princeton, 1984), pp.364–69; Mason, *Economic and social modernization of Korea*, pp.448–50; Frank Leeming, 'The earlier industrialization of Hong Kong', *Modern Asian Studies* 9, 3 (1975), pp.337–42.

[15] W. W. Rostow, 'Leading sectors and the take-off' and S. Kuznets, 'Notes on the take-off' in W. W. Rostow, ed. *The economics of take-off into sustained growth* (London, 1963), pp.8–9, 35–40.

[16] Lewis, 'Economic development with unlimited supplies of labour'; J. C. H. Fei and G. Ranis, *Development of the labor surplus economy* (Homewood, IL, 1964).

[17] Singapore, *Development plan 1961–1964*, p.10.

[18] Harris and Todaro, 'Migration, unemployment', pp.146–52.

the surrounding region, would have led to large labour inflows had Singapore not split with Malaysia in 1965 to become a city state, and so gained the ability to close its borders. It would otherwise have been difficult to end the unskilled labour surplus condition which Singapore inherited from earlier economic growth, and during the 1970s to move decisively towards being a developed country.

Singapore's ability to regulate labour flows allowed it fully to capture the benefits of earlier staple port development. Nor, as a city state with a fully open trade sector, did its economy have the problem of 'unbalanced' growth in a dual economy context, where a failure to raise agricultural productivity would have led to sharply rising food prices and halted the development process. Rather, helped by location on world transport routes, Singapore had a perfectly elastic supply curve for food: all that was required could be obtained at a constant price, paid for by exports of manufactures and services. It seems likely that Singapore would have grown fast, as has Malaysia, if the two countries had remained together, but not so fast or spectacularly.

Singapore's development emphasizes the importance of industrialization, savings, capital accumulation, labour mobilization and state activism. All these, which together A. K. Sen labels the themes of 'traditional development economics',[19] became contentious in the literature on economic development just as they took on relevance in Singapore. The Singapore model's systematic enforcement of mass thrift through a provident fund as a means to raise the savings ratio deserves the wider attention of development economists. So too does the role of the National Wages Council in curbing inflationary pressures and avoiding real exchange rate overvaluation, although perhaps in few countries will enforceability be as achievable.

From the 1970s much work in development economics stressed – not least in light of Singapore's success – the necessity to rely on markets and 'get prices right' as opposed to state intervention, which carried with it the danger of 'government failure'. It is less than obvious to the present writer, however, why these two views often seem to be treated as irreconcilable opposites. The administrative capability of a government is fundamental to economic development. As Singapore shows, when this capability exists the government can play an important developmental role. The Singapore government constantly monitored international competitiveness and intervened to set the right prices to clear labour markets, which enabled the island's economy to take advantage of opportunities for trade and industrialization.

[19] Armartya Sen, 'Development: which way now?' *Economic Journal* 93 (1983), pp.745–53.

Access to international markets was essential to Singapore, and its government treated market signals with respect. But there were few areas of the economy or society in which it was not willing to intervene to ensure what it regarded as the appropriate response. Government, though judging projects on commercial criteria, did not hesitate to step in to provide what the market might not, or to become involved in the economy. Infrastructure of all descriptions, provision of training programmes, the accentuation of education, an emphasis on it and housing as merit goods and control of the media were obvious instances. Public enterprises, as Singapore's example confirms, can be run efficiently, and a sort of political entrepreneurship can effectively organize multinational enterprise as a substitute for local entrepreneurship.

Clear policy lessons from Singapore's achievement of economic development were adaptability to world conditions, pragmatism and a relative absence of ideology – the test of what worked, regardless of whether this came through the market or required economic planning. An author has, perhaps, a vested interest in revealing complex secrets. But in considering Singapore, it is hard not to agree with W. A. Lewis that 'The Economics of development is not very complicated; the secret of successful planning lies more in sensible politics and good public administration'.[20]

The most general lessons from Singapore's development are variants of some well-known remarks in development theory: R. Nurkse's that 'a country is poor because it is poor' and G. M. Meier's later amendment that 'a country is poor because of poor policies'.[21] Recalling the sustained twentieth-century performance of the Singapore economy, the conclusion to be drawn from post-1959 development is that Singapore became rich because it was already relatively rich, and because it had good policies. The Singapore government itself made much the same observation as early as 1963: 'Geography and history have conspired to make this island an oasis of progress and plenty in a turbulent and chaotic region of Asia ... human resources [and] an honest administration can turn this into a metropolis that Malaysia can be proud of'.[22]

In terms of traditional trade theory, a Heckscher–Ohlin model, which uses two factors of production, does not adequately capture Singapore's twentieth-century economic development. There are many factors of production, and even a stylized analysis of Singapore's economic

---

[20] Lewis, *Development planning*, preface.
[21] Meier, *Leading issues*, preface to fifth edition.
[22] *SLA Debates* vol.22 no.3 (29 Nov. 1963), col.134, 'New chapter in our history', speech by Yang Di-Pertuan Negara for the Singapore government.

development requires a broader factor proportions model.[23] Development can be seen as involving four main factors: the natural resource of location, physical capital and two kinds of labour. Singapore began life with location as its only natural resource, and has been fortunate that this has been not a wasting, but a growing asset. The value of Singapore's location was continuously enhanced through changes in communication methods – the opening of Suez, the introduction of the telegraph, and the development of regional shipping, rail and road networks. In the 1950s and early 1960s population growth outpaced the (then) developmental possibilities associated with the island's location and, in the absence of other, more conventionally-interpreted, natural resources like mineral deposits, pushed the Republic towards the rapid development of manufacturing. Its successful establishment helped Singapore to accumulate capital and alter the workforce composition from unskilled to skilled labour. Subsequently, changes in shipping patterns and the development of air transport and satellite communication created fresh nodal properties and again enhanced Singapore's locational advantages. Development in Singapore may be expected to exploit these, and increasingly to emphasize sectors intensive in their use of the growing supplies of capital and skilled labour.

The Rybczynski theorem, building on two-factor Heckscher–Ohlin analysis, predicts that an increasing endowment of one factor will reduce the production of goods intensive in the other factor. Thus, in Singapore the accumulation of capital or a greater nodality should lead to the contraction of labour-intensive industries.[24] Singapore's slowing population growth and high labour force participation rates also point in this direction. It seems doubtful that Singapore's attempt to offset labour scarcity and organize workers in Johore and the Indonesian island of Batam as part of a 'triangle of growth' will reverse the trend to more location-, capital- and skill-intensive activities.

For Singapore, the importance of geographical considerations in its most recent, services-based development emphasizes the continuity that has run through the island's history. Because future services-based development is likely to depend heavily on the region, this raises the question always asked about Singapore's future: can it survive as a city state? The answer is that so long as governments in the region continue to favour essentially market, as opposed to centrally-planned, economies, Singapore can thrive as a city state. The recent growth of skilled service

[23] W. M. Corden and Ronald E. Findlay, 'Concluding remarks' in Bertil Ohlin, et al., eds. *The international allocation of economic activity* (London, 1977), pp.539–40; John Williamson, *The open economy and the world economy* (New York, 1983), pp.46–47.

[24] Williamson, *Open economy*, p.52.

activities in Singapore will help ensure this success. Neighbouring countries rely on Singapore for many of these newer brain services. The provision of such services is less subject to nationalistic restriction than physical flows of goods and gives rise to interdependencies that are more difficult to untangle. What Singapore requires for continued development is an open world trading system, regional peace and internal stability: capitalism, international interdependence and efficient administration are the conditions under which the city has traditionally flourished.

Two things which could decisively reverse Singapore's progress are the interruption of peace in the immediate Malayan region, and, even more, the establishment of centrally-planned economic systems in one or more of the neighbouring states. In the latter event, economic relationships with Singapore would become, not a matter of market considerations, but of policy, and no-one could say what the outcome of this policy formulation would be. But Singapore's substantial human capital, accumulated physical infrastructure and, not least, geographical advantages, are too great to be lightly ignored. As has been observed, 'Great cities do not arise by accident, and they are not destroyed by whim.'[25] That observation surely fits Singapore.

[25] Rhoads Murphey, *Shanghai: key to modern China* (Cambridge, MA, 1953), p.205.

Appendix tables

Table A.1 *Singapore value of total merchandise imports and exports and of major exports, 1870–1970 ($000)*

	Merch-andise imports	Merch-andise exports	Tin	Rubber	Petrol-eum
1870	38,659	25,851	2,229	n.l.	n.l.
1871	33,826	27,712	2,877		
1872	39,764	34,275	4,153		6
1873	42,477	34,306	2,374		2
1874	41,710	33,715	1,875		16
1875	39,586	34,439	2,031		40
1876	41,379	33,661	1,461		66
1877	44,310	35,208	1,740		78
1878	42,717	32,712	1,477		149
1879	48,665	41,219	1,962		284
1880	54,162	46,175	3,211		286
1881	65,273	53,638	3,921		403
1882	67,203	52,934	4,230		322
1883	71,443	60,546	4,685		400
1884	73,885	57,835	3,849		366
1885	69,269	51,839	3,551		345
1886	69,427	53,186	4,735		399
1887	79,434	65,930	9,403		393
1888	94,866	88,683	11,174		477
1889	102,471	94,132	10,910		554
1890	99,457	79,049	10,812		607
1891	92,122	78,102	11,305		547
1892	96,597	84,354	13,389		680
1893	108,244	92,880	15,841		620
1894	133,465	114,088	19,254		1,150
1895	137,386	114,734	19,417		1,386
1896	137,220	114,631	17,739		953
1897	153,151	127,915	18,514		753
1898	170,733	141,209	22,390		668
1899	194,518	165,072	31,464		875
1900	225,774	185,788	34,505		2,282
1901	231,674	194,810	36,896		2,238
1902	246,078	209,278	38,592		1,543
1903	255,385	211,524	41,782		3,422
1904	245,079	199,956	41,796	26	5,818
1905	238,347	197,619	38,980	528	1,068
1906	234,702	202,211	46,333	1,648	833
1907	239,723	201,830	43,929	2,895	835
1908	212,237	181,050	33,478	2,940	922
1909	219,332	185,627	32,038	5,438	925

Table A.1 (*Cont.*)

	Sixteen important tropical commod- ities	Canned pine- apples	Palm oil	Rice	Dried and salted fish	Sugar
1870	7,658	n.l.	n.l.	1,006	191	138
1871	7,313			1,026	235	272
1872	9,722			1,687	409	288
1873	10,795			2,254	527	258
1874	9,502			1,666	551	218
1875	10,721			2,357	500	215
1876	9,518			2,869	732	184
1877	11,809			2,073	955	148
1878	10,983			2,788	806	233
1879	13,402			4,301	929	449
1880	14,042			4,698	1,195	369
1881	16,147			5,181	1,785	434
1882	16,670			4,950	1,684	381
1883	20,175			5,448	1,956	258
1884	19,040			5,233	1,910	377
1885	17,381			4,010	1,532	937
1886	18,633			5,274	1,418	1,250
1887	21,856			5,281	1,447	955
1888	23,322			5,378	2,283	585
1889	28,783			7,060	2,778	764
1890	28,954			7,374	2,428	1,347
1891	28,291			7,034	3,367	682
1892	27,959			9,671	2,921	973
1893	26,599			11,060	4,098	1,307
1894	33,714			13,043	4,569	1,947
1895	34,423			12,284	4,746	1,363
1896	35,017			15,073	3,936	890
1897	34,500			21,534	4,750	1,595
1898	41,031			19,152	5,035	1,758
1899	48,729			16,248	5,853	1,881
1900	55,316			17,937	6,376	2,682
1901	55,971			23,346	6,093	3,322
1902	62,893			27,050	6,489	2,641
1903	57,599			27,353	5,213	3,286
1904	48,154	2,471		22,911	6,047	3,133
1905	49,388	2,788		22,303	7,763	4,570
1906	49,952	3,246		22,087	6,980	3,939
1907	50,564	3,272		23,727	6,573	3,546
1908	43,507	2,656		28,787	7,088	3,343
1909	46,447	2,152		28,043	8,190	3,428

Table A.1 (*Cont.*)

	Merch-andise imports	Merch-andise exports	Tin	Rubber	Petrol-eum
1910	257,441	219,520	34,669	9,838	854
1911	271,265	226,768	41,373	12,435	473
1912	302,486	241,814	47,879	10,270	724
1913	328,267	256,154	55,875	13,961	621
1914	277,120	228,330	40,905	21,328	663
1915	338,173	303,860	55,000	54,642	1,206
1916	430,767	377,950	51,410	103,254	3,213
1917	527,980	491,849	60,828	171,637	841
1918	576,165	496,637	73,454	139,136	696
1919	727,008	720,347	72,427	260,934	1,259
1920	890,079	724,271	70,491	232,510	1,956
1921	484,802	415,808	41,713	83,918	1,890
1922	456,540	414,959	44,721	104,132	10,762
1923	580,321	512,781	46,727	158,185	34,833
1924	636,942	551,010	75,168	151,856	30,768
1925	1,001,526	899,853	72,556	405,844	71,127
1926	997,075	874,758	76,338	342,328	78,658
1927	930,577	791,614	91,929	271,354	73,659
1928	776,449 [b]	652,825 [b]	82,565	162,407	n.a.
1929	809,988	658,964	76,560	183,592	49,494
1930	625,921	526,016	47,257	100,461	n.a.
1931	393,313	326,419	29,800	49,934	65,101
1932	335,851	269,487	24,565	28,536	58,145
1933	315,332	289,624	51,208	45,451	42,285
1934	382,420 [b]	331,880 [b]	45,333	124,045	44,649
1935	380,782	345,552	52,725	112,379	50,911
1936	416,202	365,742	63,457	131,428	42,416
1937	553,207	492,141	77,692	206,172	54,047
1938	402,027	339,475	39,082	120,511	54,924
1939	480,908	435,886	69,527	178,765	52,561
1949	n.a.	n.a.	120,591	381,691	121,621
1950	3,273,497	3,025,750	207,190	1,405,274	160,677
1951	5,027,204	4,745,242	261,457	2,518,844	201,701
1952	3,750,056	3,199,610	217,429	915,895	307,796
1953	3,020,706	2,654,114	172,292	750,764	341,584
1954	3,024,853	2,685,518	195,912	785,088	350,556
1955	3,862,736	3,368,699	202,192	1,399,635	371,097
1956	3,929,349	3,428,975	138,657	1,216,551	446,236
1957	4,091,837	3,478,133	133,562	1,171,094	444,964
1958	3,740,065	3,140,343	48,337	1,045,556	370,308

Table A.1 (*Cont.*)

	Sixteen important tropical commod- ities	Canned pine- apples	Palm oil	Rice	Dried and salted fish	Sugar
1910	61,258	1,804		27,610	7,792	3,517
1911	51,386	2,478		29,618	8,496	3,926
1912	53,988	3,135		34,711	8,452	7,689
1913	55,577	3,115		35,881	8,669	6,865
1914	49,336	2,619		34,776	7,842	5,550
1915	48,994	3,133		42,330	8,332	5,789
1916	48,646	4,414		48,835	9,710	8,625
1917	53,831	1,567		55,242	10,126	24,203
1918	55,713	837		58,530	10,363	23,194
1919	103,601	3,287		54,384	13,638	24,041
1920	105,095	7,178		29,186	20,452	21,065
1921	60,850	6,211		42,811	19,919	11,793
1922	67,692	6,694		36,864	16,253	5,895
1923	70,229	5,547		32,884	13,515	9,167
1924	78,094	8,153		35,451	15,128	8,660
1925	81,345	7,415		45,217	15,343	7,260
1926	83,970	7,006		53,034	16,620	7,187
1927	71,695	7,494		50,664	15,769	6,749
1928	n.a.	7,761		n.a.	n.a.	n.a.
1929		8,735				
1930		7,297				
1931		6,545		10,231		
1932		7,002		9,599		
1933	30,108	5,382	1,031	7,047	7,059	526
1934	31,270	5,971	1,034	5,927	6,991	568
1935	39,888	6,644	2,528	8,492	6,244	701
1936	35,314	7,099	3,066	8,772	6,750	727
1937	43,654	6,988	4,834	7,965	6,670	982
1938	30,519	6,372	4,063	10,541	7,191	742
1939	33,189	8,869	3,472	8,504	7,191	1,035
1949	n.a.	5,551	24,407	4,650	3,723	4,367
1950		11,049	22,243	7,925	9,665	3,101
1951		15,714	26,434	34,522	29,381	9,622
1952		11,625	30,302	60,682	36,749	5,277
1953		17,797	17,710	28,210	23,746	2,788
1954		23,461	15,822	23,139	9,510	5,045
1955		27,172	17,810	20,410	3,643	7,592
1956		29,048	20,737	29,422	4,740	9,962
1957	270,005	31,229	16,516	79,146	13,143	30,564
1958	239,650	31,145	17,730	100,277	9,696	20,344

Table A.1 (*Cont.*)

	Merch- andise imports	Merch- andise exports	Tin	Rubber	Petrol- eum
1959	3,907,670	3,440,263	4,448	1,533,074	371,657
1960	4,077,686	3,477,053	5,161	1,426,513	379,209
1961	3,963,265	3,308,532	29,035	1,134,494	334,065
1962	4,035,804	3,416,760	10,601	1,092,309	354,981
1963	4,279,056	3,474,539	17,191	972,527	376,613
1964	3,478,666	2,771,946	6,006	644,823	361,624
1965	3,807,191	3,004,088	8,312	668,818	429,695
1966	4,065,670	3,373,602	7,210	760,906	591,606
1967	4,406,545	3,490,611	5,290	755,059	675,472
1968	5,083,834	3,890,681	272	868,583	806,717
1969	6,243,592	4,740,682	765	1,403,487	927,529
1970	7,533,843	4,755,763	692	1,162,413	818,055

Table A.1 (*Cont.*)

	Sixteen important tropical commod-ities	Canned pine-apples	Palm oil	Rice	Dried and salted fish	Sugar
1959	215,164	26,586	19,078	52,097	9,340	15,625
1960	244,073	25,243	23,811	62,214	9,316	17,794
1961	235,209	31,017	20,107	57,107	9,410	17,761
1962	191,067	34,324	19,532	79,478	10,264	11,469
1963	232,287	35,541	22,616	87,746	6,477	40,930
1964	122,089	37,127	24,924	44,274	4,075	31,157
1965	140,183	46,839	35,814	39,974	3,222	12,426
1966	177,192	48,714	36,335	44,090	3,738	6,183
1967	258,204	45,256	38,952	41,754	3,069	7,346
1968	292,556	47,565	39,607	42,904	3,268	6,764
1969	265,470	48,781	49,354	25,652	3,806	5,235
1970	290,388	50,774	86,683	18,940	4,350	8,935

[a] For 1928-33 estimated by the addition of inter-port trade, see notes and sources, pp.383-85.

[b] For 1934-39 excludes trade with the UMS and SS, see notes and sources, pp.383-85.

Table A.2 *Singapore volume of major exports, 1870–1970 (tons)*

	Tin	Rubber	Petroleum	Sixteen important tropical commodities	Canned pine-apples
1870	4,427	n.l.	n.l.	76,074	n.l.
1871	5,262			77,547	
1872	6,280		n.a.	78,481	
1873	3,989			78,230	
1874	4,538			76,386	
1875	5,887			90,796	
1876	4,042			91,266	
1877	5,087		595	113,598	
1878	5,351		1,293	105,726	
1879	5,366		3,647	117,226	
1880	7,058		4,081	126,845	
1881	8,018		4,712	133,834	
1882	7,589		4,319	121,292	
1883	9,368		5,790	141,906	
1884	8,938		5,125	151,066	
1885	7,564		5,098	138,312	
1886	8,098		6,007	142,505	
1887	13,678		5,944	144,675	
1888	15,126		5,175	167,710	
1889	19,473		6,743	175,033	
1890	19,295		8,876	187,894	
1891	20,783		8,923	226,919	
1892	21,118		11,087	226,166	
1893	24,770		10,161	225,743	
1894	30,190		20,067	252,329	
1895	32,921		18,781	243,901	
1896	32,713		12,401	261,805	
1897	30,814		10,144	244,454	
1898	31,545		8,859	243,413	
1899	25,651		21,279	271,089	
1900	27,416		40,808	258,122	
1901	32,137		44,396	245,404	
1902	28,920		29,371	257,861	
1903	29,411		44,360	266,398	
1904	31,800	5	90,231	255,065	14,450
1905	28,798	83	16,770	272,602	17,688
1906	30,678	328	11,799	274,292	22,837
1907	30,002	646	14,758	295,822	27,296
1908	29,719	914	12,533	315,355	23,146
1909	27,859	1,077	14,241	325,445	20,716

Table A.2 (*Cont.*)

	Palm oil	Rice	Dried and salted fish	Sugar	Total
1870	n.l.	30,588	1,832	1,292	114,213
1871		28,772	2,008	2,597	116,186
1872		43,544	4,072	3,276	135,653
1873		63,940	8,286	2,540	156,985
1874		43,295	4,704	2,605	131,528
1875		65,870	4,148	2,417	169,118
1876		74,061	6,189	1,962	177,520
1877		45,097	5,918	1,431	171,726
1878		51,654	5,983	1,403	171,410
1879		86,900	5,689	3,454	222,282
1880		100,303	7,582	2,694	248,563
1881		120,244	13,029	3,063	282,900
1882		124,503	14,402	2,707	274,812
1883		134,374	19,327	1,938	312,703
1884		128,298	17,374	3,287	314,088
1885		103,288	13,379	10,069	277,710
1886		123,932	13,100	13,771	307,413
1887		129,400	12,712	11,868	318,277
1888		124,429	17,839	5,915	336,194
1889		198,273	22,047	6,742	428,311
1890		148,552	19,691	13,903	398,211
1891		148,960	28,238	6,566	440,389
1892		182,834	25,735	9,677	476,617
1893		231,228	39,270	11,664	542,836
1894		262,114	43,211	16,356	624,267
1895		240,927	39,616	13,321	589,467
1896		273,627	35,085	7,591	623,222
1897		332,431	36,657	13,958	668,458
1898		276,789	34,702	15,443	610,751
1899		244,925	41,032	15,156	619,132
1900		256,414	43,621	21,637	648,018
1901		344,273	39,022	26,588	731,820
1902		362,330	38,295	23,370	740,147
1903		302,084	26,586	26,474	695,313
1904		312,365	31,830	26,903	762,649
1905		298,452	45,522	34,974	714,889
1906		306,631	45,249	39,748	731,562
1907		301,509	39,817	37,474	747,324
1908		374,012	41,880	32,628	830,187
1909		393,138	45,824	33,939	862,239

Table A.2 (*Cont.*)

	Tin	Rubber	Petroleum	Sixteen important tropical commod-ities	Canned pine-apples
1910	26,724	1,487	17,630	346,237	15,764
1911	26,186	2,812	11,614	300,558	16,813
1912	27,686	2,524	16,492	306,294	18,780
1913	32,481	5,921	9,919	291,494	24,149
1914	32,053	12,436	14,860	290,204	22,443
1915	41,605	27,046	20,742	302,785	26,141
1916	34,686	44,986	65,828	256,765	25,268
1917	33,880	79,444	10,186	259,880	7,959
1918	28,948	100,515	4,833	229,733	3,534
1919	33,748	157,317	6,444	321,829	8,256
1920	27,516	134,616	8,572	276,816	14,417
1921	30,233	133,385	9,552	260,514	21,367
1922	33,490	160,498	56,451	314,977	22,924
1923	27,176	144,452	187,952	302,178	27,195
1924	35,777	151,259	189,671	301,364	35,329
1925	32,755	179,343	351,035	278,759	38,301
1926	31,461	192,463	414,791	283,295	36,894
1927	37,634	200,307	466,257	247,741	36,259
1928	42,756	201,263	n.a.	277,847	42,739
1929	43,352	253,875	368,629	290,114	55,352
1930	37,468	233,799	n.a.	264,657	53,515
1931	29,784	220,545	442,603	257,199	54,620
1932	20,840	184,296	420,106	274,011	58,139
1933	30,913	230,352	394,082	298,441	51,769
1934	23,550	315,990	453,958	280,322	57,166
1935	27,999	258,579	511,457	311,878	60,481
1936	37,511	218,697	480,939	311,790	64,243
1937	38,150	285,933	627,518	322,155	65,197
1938	24,784	225,751	742,949	283,372	64,382
1939	36,044	259,238	681,242	303,199	74,050
1949	23,935	484,848	1,522,957	n.a.	7,115
1950	35,855	655,025	1,906,991		13,173
1951	29,399	750,221	1,880,855		15,761
1952	27,013	555,343	2,358,420		10,913
1953	26,853	506,480	2,613,622		16,264
1954	33,263	555,297	2,732,430		19,890
1955	33,322	604,152	3,115,858		25,898
1956	21,330	596,600	2,936,508		28,333
1957	20,843	617,198	3,005,649	298,167	34,837
1958	7,884	650,204	2,459,169	236,986	38,754

Table A.2 (*Cont.*)

	Palm oil	Rice	Dried and salted fish	Sugar	Total
1910		387,344	46,787	32,302	874,275
1911		354,599	51,142	36,415	800,139
1912		338,968	46,182	70,265	827,191
1913		419,968	46,314	66,427	896,673
1914		451,271	41,552	50,540	915,359
1915		565,713	47,611	37,347	1,068,990
1916		617,569	54,009	49,272	1,148,383
1917		647,194	50,351	142,454	1,231,348
1918		506,128	46,616	159,940	1,080,247
1919		259,342	56,314	71,089	914,339
1920		99,011	55,473	35,200	651,621
1921		317,188	61,032	50,090	883,361
1922		309,047	52,933	33,627	983,947
1923		287,068	46,620	42,304	1,064,945
1924		269,962	56,369	42,312	1,082,043
1925		348,007	62,206	50,351	1,340,757
1926		391,987	63,719	48,646	1,463,256
1927		398,535	60,787	47,228	1,494,748
1928		n.a.	n.a.	n.a.	n.a.
1929					
1930					
1931		128,890			
1932		136,356			
1933	9,202	115,291	45,592	7,511	1,183,153
1934	12,603	113,308	49,020	8,961	1,314,878
1935	18,045	140,562	45,114	11,806	1,385,921
1936	21,478	147,808	48,067	12,514	1,343,047
1937	28,344	114,555	48,053	14,765	1,544,670
1938	33,111	159,756	50,606	10,802	1,595,513
1939	36,061	137,622	53,434	11,588	1,592,478
1949	35,004	11,615	5,829	8,034	
1950	34,475	19,112	14,775	6,345	
1951	31,192	71,780	30,563	16,441	
1952	31,865	92,387	40,406	9,055	
1953	26,174	43,367	27,605	5,977	
1954	23,645	48,537	10,434	14,056	
1955	27,153	54,739	3,694	22,235	
1956	28,996	71,610	6,067	27,988	
1957	22,094	197,401	11,636	59,880	4,267,705
1958	27,867	241,613	9,264	51,119	3,722,860

Table A.2 (*Cont.*)

	Tin	Rubber	Petroleum	Sixteen important tropical commod- ities	Canned pine- apples
1959	677	722,580	2,494,965	191,225	36,599
1960	775	598,378	2,687,573	198,970	35,937
1961	4,141	657,032	3,206,767	247,882	42,307
1962	1,409	660,618	3,747,152	179,770	45,569
1963	2,268	616,192	3,994,567	216,800	48,485
1964	608	425,957	4,302,193	87,377	50,389
1965	721	444,214	5,464,218	93,888	63,572
1966	661	518,919	7,074,025	125,506	66,866
1967	522	644,425	8,253,626	199,993	62,436
1968	35	802,264	10,214,137	249,491	69,277
1969	71	944,932	11,495,273	208,796	68,212
1970	61	912,748	11,977,239	186,828	67,788

Table A.2 (*Cont.*)

	Palm oil	Rice	Dried and salted fish	Sugar	Total
1959	26,026	125,084	10,419	39,104	3,646,679
1960	33,767	154,837	9,887	46,264	3,766,388
1961	29,015	140,334	9,453	51,997	4,388,928
1962	30,402	184,841	8,160	42,304	4,900,225
1963	36,593	219,951	5,537	75,487	5,215,880
1964	36,962	107,005	3,570	53,327	5,067,388
1965	46,925	97,561	2,860	43,234	6,257,193
1966	55,063	104,857	3,846	26,735	7,976,478
1967	61,547	78,144	3,133	32,174	9,336,000
1968	89,990	71,810	3,126	26,495	11,526,625
1969	111,384	47,542	3,686	17,802	12,897,698
1970	131,160	45,059	3,732	26,770	13,351,385

Tables A.1 and A.2. Notes:
1   Merchandise imports and exports exclude trade in treasure of bullion and specie as well as parcel post for the years this was recorded. Until 1934 merchandise imports and exports are comparable series. For 1928–33 available statistics exclude trade with the other Straits Settlements, but this was estimated. On the basis of the share of Inter-Port merchandise trade in total merchandise trade in 1924/27, for each of the years 1928–33 2.1% was added to imports and 3.4% to exports. For 1934–39 trade with the Unfederated Malay States and the Straits Settlements is excluded. Using the above estimates for trade with the Straits Settlements and recorded trade figures for the Unfederated Malay States, in 1931/33 Singapore's trade with the SS and UMS accounted for 9.0% of the port's imports and 9.9% of its exports. The figures for 1934–39 are understated by roughly these percentages. From 1934 figures for Singapore's trade with the FMS are from the latter's customs reports.
2   For 1904–32 rubber is para rubber, and for 1933–39 it includes rubber, dry (smoked sheet and crepe); rubber, wet (sheet, scrap, lump and bark); and latex, concentrated, revertex, etc. Previous to 1912 rubber transhipped at Singapore from Malaya was included in the trade returns. Petroleum comprises kerosene, liquid fuel (first in the trade returns in 1898 as petroleum residue) and motor spirit (first in the trade returns in 1904 as benzine). The sixteen tropical commodities are: arecanuts, Borneo rubber, coffee, copra, coconut oil, gambier, groundnuts, gums (benjamin, copal, dammar), gutta percha and gutta inferior (jelutong), illipnuts, nutmegs, pepper (black, white, long), rattans, sago (flour, pearl), tapioca (flake, flour, pearl) and tobacco. For 1870–1927 rice was returned as a single category. The figures for 1931–32 exclude cargo rice which in 1933 constituted 5.2% of imports and 0.4% of exports. For 1933–39 rice includes cargo, parboiled, cleaned (white) and broken, clean.
3   Volume figures not published in tons were converted as follows: 16.8 piculs equal one ton; 280 gallons of motor spirit equal one ton; 35 cases of kerosene equal one ton; 31 cases of pineapples equal one ton.
4   For 1928–32 figures for the value of individual commodities were obtained by multiplying recorded volume figures and average declared export values at Singapore taken from 'Foreign trade of Malaya', *SSAR 1932*, p.608. Use of this

method for 1921–27 and 1933 showed very close agreement with the recorded trade
values. For the sixteen tropical commodities, however, the method could not be
used, because for 1928–32 average declared export values are not available for all
commodities.

5   For 1928–39 figures for individual commodities exclude exports to Malaya. The
omission is particularly important in the case of rice, sugar and petroleum. In
1925/27 36.5% of the volume of Singapore's rice exports and 64.2% of its sugar
exports went to Malaya. Therefore, available figures for rice and sugar are not
comparable with earlier years. In 1925/27 24.6% of the volume of Singapore's
petroleum exports went to Malaya. But this percentage is not necessarily a good
guide to the subsequent understatement of petroleum exports which may have varied
because of the considerable growth of the petroleum trade. Exports of dried and
salted fish are understated by about 7.9% – in 1925/27 the proportion by volume
sent to Malaya. Exports of tin, rubber, pineapples and palm oil to Malaya were
negligible. So too were those of the sixteen tropical commodities except for coffee,
coconut oil, groundnuts and tobacco. In 1925/27 exports of the sixteen tropical
commodities to Malaya were 8,345 tons, or 3.1% of the total. That percentage
may be taken as approximately the understatement for 1928–39 of exports of the
sixteen tropical commodities owing to the exclusion of trade with Malaya.

6   For 1928–32 coconut oil and tobacco are excluded from the sixteen tropical
commodities. In 1925/27 coconut oil and tobacco accounted for 3.5% of the export
volume of the sixteen commodities. However, in 1925/27 almost a third of coconut
oil and tobacco exports, equal to 1.1% of total exports of the 16 tropical
commodities, went to Malaya. For 1928–32 the understatement in exports of the 16
tropical commodities is therefore about 5.5%, consisting of the 3.1% of these
exports to Malaya (note 5) and 2.4% (3.5% less 1.1%) of coconut oil and tobacco
exported elsewhere than to Malaya.

7   From 1950 imports are valued c.i.f. except imports from Malaya, which are valued
f.o.b. Exports are valued f.o.b. except exports to Malaya, which are valued c.i.f.

8   For 1950–56 merchandise imports and exports were obtained by adding figures
from the official trade returns, which exclude trade with the Federation of Malaya,
to figures for Singapore's trade with the Federation, given in Ow, *Singapore's trade
with West Malaysia*. From 1950 figures include parcel post under exports but not
imports; and under exports began to include bunkers and stores for ships and
aircraft. From 1956 the official trade returns exclude consignments of less than
$100 in trade with Malaya. These consisted largely of petroleum products. For
most of the individual commodities shown, the effect of excluding exports to the
Federation is negligible but, as in earlier periods, important for petroleum, rice,
dried fish and sugar. Comparison of the years 1956 and 1957 gives an indication of
the understatement before 1957.

9   For 1957–70 all figures are from the official trade returns. Rubber includes items
231011 to 231019, 231021 and 231029, and for 1962–70 group 231; tin, 687011 or
687101; petroleum value includes all of group 313 or 332, but volume for 1957–61
includes all of 313 oil, petroleum processed except 313041 lubricating oil and
313042 grease, lubricating, and for 1962–70 all of 332 excluding 332511 and
332521 lubricating oil, 332512 and 332522 lubricating grease and 332911 hydraulic
brake fluid; palm oil, 412060 or 422200; canned pineapples, 053011 or 053901;
rice, 042; dried and salted fish, 031023 and 031024 or 031203 and 031204; sugar,
061020 or 061200 or 061101. The sixteen tropical commodities include the same
items as in earlier periods with the exceptions that Borneo rubber was not listed in
the trade returns and illipnuts are omitted since they were not listed separately but
included as part of 221099 oilseeds, oilnuts and oil kernels n.e.s.

10 For 1964–70 figures for rice, dried fish and sugar are not comparable with earlier
periods because of the exclusion from the official statistics of exports to Indonesia.

Tables A.1 and A.2. Sources: SS, *Blue books*, 1870–1899; SS, *Return of imports and exports*, 1900–1927 (for 1900, 1905, 1911 and 1921–1923 quarterly returns; for 1924–1927 half-yearly returns); *Statistical tables relating to British self-governing dominions, crown colonies and protectorates, 1911*; *SSTC 1933–34* IV, pp.465–82, 499; 'Foreign trade of Malaya', *SSAR 1928*, p.622, *1932*, p.608; Malaya, *Foreign imports and exports*, 1933–1937; Malaya, *Foreign trade of Malaya*, 1934–1939; FMS, *Report on the trade and customs department for the year 1931* (Supplement to the 'FMS government gazette', May 20, 1932); FMS, *Report on the customs and excise department*, 1934–1939; Registrar of Malayan Statistics, Singapore (or Department of Statistics, Singapore), *External trade of Malaya* (monthly series) 1950–1964; Singapore, *Report of the department of commerce and industry*, 1954–1956; Ow, *Singapore's trade with West Malaysia*, p.2; SLA, 'The external trade and balance of payments of Singapore, 1956', Sessional Paper no. Cmd 3, 1958, p.1; Singapore, *Singapore trade statistics*, 1957–1970.

Table A.3 *Singapore total exports and main export categories, 1957–1990 ($000)*

	Merchandise exports	Direct manufactured exports	Manufactured exports	Primary commodities excl. petroleum	Petroleum exports	Rubber
1957	3,478,133	n.a.	763,677	1,960,585	506,172	1,176,681
1958	3,140,343		702,953	1,785,956	433,113	1,050,613
1959	3,440,263		637,697	2,202,377	387,754	1,537,042
1960	3,477,053	157,871	734,759	2,141,024	391,766	1,431,843
1961	3,308,532	172,462	848,684	1,842,636	372,287	1,140,477
1962	3,416,760	205,556	928,977	1,809,210	415,249	1,092,309
1963	3,474,539	193,300	993,565	1,787,197	432,044	972,527
1964	2,771,946	222,123	881,373	1,289,307	361,713	644,823
1965	3,004,088	294,651	934,371	1,362,672	429,889	668,818
1966	3,373,602	321,998	970,447	1,517,156	592,063	760,906
1967	3,490,611	410,407	906,202	1,569,839	675,472	755,059
1968	3,890,681	520,540	937,751	1,761,263	807,191	868,583
1969	4,740,682	687,104	1,117,545	2,341,052	927,550	1,403,487
1970	4,755,763	942,960	1,320,718	2,195,855	818,383	1,162,413
1971	5,371,255	1,194,539	1,803,137	2,016,659	1,138,239	942,797
1972	6,149,386	1,823,636	2,532,225	1,911,483	1,159,909	842,541
1973	8,906,779	3,025,449	3,977,297	2,990,013	1,356,333	1,626,880
1974	14,154,607	4,006,515	5,713,139	3,755,762	3,654,123	2,031,375
1975	12,757,908	4,098,039	5,337,278	2,939,920	3,407,632	1,302,637
1976	16,265,863	5,084,453	7,277,775	3,950,751	3,743,746	1,980,025
1977	20,090,317	5,888,072	8,637,616	5,128,780	4,834,615	2,236,699
1978	22,985,450	6,872,096	10,570,251	5,634,475	5,279,068	2,460,241
1979	30,940,086	9,127,572	14,304,368	7,154,351	7,337,219	3,069,270
1980	41,452,314	11,554,103	18,521,967	8,098,638	11,827,968	3,292,115
1981	44,290,787	12,762,261	19,924,558	6,979,425	13,980,571	2,453,959

1982	44,472,789	12,450,976	19,938,813	6,345,598	14,437,326	1,742,819
1983	46,154,891	14,353,767	23,400,997	6,459,344	12,761,948	2,105,757
1984	51,340,021	17,129,382	26,361,322	8,248,861	12,992,266	2,019,296
1985	50,178,848	17,452,877	26,260,322	6,806,888	13,456,085	1,491,456
1986	48,495,486	19,848,663	29,415,383	6,404,981	13,456,085	1,335,204
1987	60,265,732	25,598,759	40,114,254	7,000,241	9,649,930	1,535,091
1988	79,051,262	32,842,508	56,777,499	8,908,399	10,008,532	2,274,105
1989	87,116,455	36,688,003	63,777,668	8,770,751	13,333,118	1,884,654
1990	95,204,154	40,664,962	68,851,749	7,936,241	17,156,489	1,405,338

Notes:

1 Petroleum includes the following SITC groups: for 1957–61, 312 petroleum, crude and partly refined and 313 petroleum products; for 1962–78, 331 petroleum, crude and 332 petroleum products; for 1979–90 333 petroleum oils, crude, 334 petroleum products, refined, and 335 petroleum products n.e.s. Between 1957 and 1990 almost all exports consisted of petroleum products (313, 332 or 334).

2 Direct manufactured export figures exclude petroleum, rubber processing and granite quarrying. They refer to firms with 10 or more workers, so that the true figure for these exports (as recorded in the trade statistics) is somewhat understated. However, tiny firms, of less than 10 workers, accounted for only a small proportion of manufactured exports. Figures for direct manufactured exports given in the *Census of industrial production* were adjusted to exclude petroleum as follows. For 1960–65, the figures exclude sales of 'Other manufactures of chemicals, chemical products and products of petroleum and coal' (industrial code 3191) to all destinations outside Singapore, and for 1966–69 these sales of 'Manufactures of petroleum and coal' (industrial code 32). From 1970, the figures in the table exclude direct exports of petroleum refineries and petroleum products (industry groups 353 and 354).

3 The figures for manufactured exports are SITC sections 5 through 8 from the trade statistics. The difference between manufactured exports and direct manufactured exports approximately corresponds to Singapore's re-export trade in manufactures as distinct from goods manufactured there. Additionally, however, this difference includes manufactured production of firms with less than 10 workers. Most of this output was not exported.

4 Primary commodities and food include SITC sections 0 through 4, except petroleum, as indicated in note 1 above.

5 Rubber includes the following SITC groups: for 1957–78, 231 crude rubber; for 1979–88, 232 natural rubber; for 1989–90, 231 crude rubber, natural gums.

Sources: Singapore, *Singapore trade statistics*, 1956–1990; *Census of industrial production*, 1960–61 – 1990.

Table A.4 *Singapore commodity composition of imports and exports, 1957/59–1988/90 [annual averages, $000 and (% of total)]*

SITC Rev 3	Commodity	1957/59		1961/63		1967/69	
		Imports	Exports	Imports	Exports	Imports	Exports
0	*Food and live animals*	**675,322** (17.3)	**477,655** (14.2)	**767,041** (18.7)	**513,156** (15.1)	**869,287** (16.6)	**515,638** (12.8)
07	Coffee and spices	142,323	167,311	131,840	176,191	119,289	212,852
1	*Beverages and tobacco*	**80,862** (2.1)	**69,091** (2.1)	**75,379** (1.8)	**60,255** (1.8)	**99,464** (1.9)	**53,504** (1.3)
2	*Crude materials exc. fuels*	**1,322,311** (33.9)	**1,386,832** (41.4)	**1,070,389** (26.2)	**1,196,922** (35.2)	**707,221** (13.5)	**1,236,913** (30.6)
231	Natural rubber	1,115,759	1,254,778	922,883	1,068,437	500,988	1,009,043
24	Cork and wood	28,751	14,960	35,008	25,213	88,101	81,926
3	*Mineral fuels*	**684,178** (17.5)	**442,582** (13.2)	**586,779** (14.3)	**407,120** (12.0)	**865,885** (16.5)	**805,878** (20.0)
333	Petroleum, crude	47,563	46,703	121,841	51,307	329,951	274
334 + 335	Petroleum, refined and products	634,657	395,643	463,982	355,220	533,482	803,239
4	*Animal and veg. oils and fats*	**31,332** (0.8)	**49,159** (1.5)	**36,829** (0.9)	**42,089** (1.2)	**62,275** (1.2)	**82,188** (2.0)
4222 + 4224	Palm oil, crude, refined and kernel	19,485	17,775	22,031	20,906	38,057	42,973

SITC Rev 3	Commodity	1971/73		1982/84		1988/90	
		Imports	Exports	Imports	Exports	Imports	Exports
0	*Food and live animals*	**1,091,513** (10.7)	**571,026** (8.4)	**3,754,460** (6.2)	**2,436,193** (5.1)	**4,481,667** (4.6)	**3,018,791** (3.5)
07	Coffee and spices	179,729	191,002	687,107	808,835	688,716	1,012,593
1	*Beverages and tobacco*	**126,081** (1.2)	**57,450** (0.9)	**405,416** (0.7)	**212,272** (0.4)	**1,056,308** (1.1)	**942,315** (1.1)
2	*Crude materials exc. fuels*	**1,021,628** (10.0)	**1,491,750** (21.9)	**2,480,385** (4.1)	**3,193,320** (6.7)	**2,677,632** (2.7)	**3,560,893** (4.1)
231	Natural rubber	640,133	1,137,406	1,669,232	1,955,957	1,272,752	1,854,699
24	Cork and wood	150,170	180,900	336,534	380,702	335,341	586,523
3	*Mineral fuels*	**1,414,720** (13.8)	**1,227,213** (18.0)	**18,684,234** (31.0)	**13,590,335** (28.7)	**14,409,537** (14.7)	**13,628,402** (15.6)
333	Petroleum, crude	922,188	3,037	14,888,023	165,534	9,953,973	123,128
334 + 335	Petroleum, refined and products	489,228	1,215,124	3,786,011	13,231,646	4,442,786	13,376,252
4	*Animal and veg. oils and fats*	**177,429** (1.7)	**176,774** (2.6)	**913,170** (1.5)	**982,993** (2.1)	**872,699** (0.9)	**887,442** (1.0)
4222 + 4224	Palm oil, crude, refined and kernel	133,417	124,528	95,349	498,667	200,532	168,961

Table A.4 (*Cont.*)

SITC Rev 3	Commodity	1957/59 Imports	1957/59 Exports	1961/63 Imports	1961/63 Exports	1967/69 Imports	1967/69 Exports
5	*Chemicals*	**114,411** (2.9)	**73,656** (2.2)	**159,354** (3.9)	**99,801** (2.9)	**265,502** (5.1)	**124,201** (3.1)
51 + 52	Chemicals, organic and inorganic	22,302	14,884	30,693	20,402	51,617	18,542
541	Medicinal products	23,463	12,560	27,299	14,734	44,666	18,763
57 + 58	Plastic materials	n.l.		11,772	4,597	35,534	10,949
6	*Basic manufactures*	**472,142** (12.1)	**359,804** (10.7)	**596,604** (14.6)	**388,201** (11.4)	**1,056,528** (20.1)	**388,990** (9.6)
63	Cork and wood mfs. exc. furniture	9,086	6,690	7,399	5,053	21,701	37,536
64	Paper and paperboard mfs.	35,459	12,091	50,081	19,289	77,597	22,466
65	Textile yarn, fabrics etc.	230,805	149,043	272,377	155,098	572,037	146,187
66	Non-metallic mineral mfs.	38,512	25,331	51,486	47,300	73,950	34,608
67	Iron and steel	71,487	29,335	91,852	45,958	152,730	46,816
68	Non-ferrous metals	10,776	64,973	18,106	28,733	37,909	19,255
687	Tin	3,156	62,234	6,495	19,347	4,439	2,972
69	Metal mfs. n.e.s.	43,775	39,879	98,092	52,096	94,677	63,803
7	*Machinery and transport equip.*	**253,851** (6.5)	**174,919** (5.2)	**448,933** (11.0)	**313,812** (9.2)	**805,112** (15.4)	**291,163** (7.2)
75	Office mach. and data processing equip.	n.l.		n.l.		n.l.	
751	Office mach.	8,084	4,271	12,232	8,835	15,819	5,618
752	Data processing equip.	n.l.		n.l.		n.l.	
75261	Disk drives	n.l.		n.l.		n.l.	

SITC Rev 3	Commodity	1971/73		1982/84		1988/90	
		Imports	Exports	Imports	Exports	Imports	Exports
5	*Chemicals*	**554,134** (5.4)	**265,682** (3.9)	**2,956,178** (4.9)	**2,047,465** (4.3)	**7,220,301** (7.3)	**5,635,166** (6.5)
51 + 52	Chemicals, organic and inorganic	105,622	39,016	801,277	603,351	1,636,322	1,899,948
541	Medicinal products	77,396	48,903	213,278	310,785	370,686	362,498
57 + 58	Plastic materials	110,524	33,791	774,783	330,945	2,029,757	1,738,895
6	*Basic manufactures*	**2,096,662** (20.5)	**683,445** (10.0)	**8,180,716** (13.6)	**3,715,463** (7.9)	**13,648,769** (13.9)	**6,754,658** (7.7)
63	Cork and wood mfs. exc. furniture	50,856	143,842	256,545	504,437	385,461	611,350
64	Paper and paperboard mfs.	148,567	33,379	568,590	188,708	1,179,878	526,789
65	Textile yarn, fabrics etc.	906,805	271,918	1,998,142	778,936	3,095,700	1,524,063
66	Non-metallic mineral mfs.	174,634	33,741	1,168,196	345,814	1,347,760	463,397
67	Iron and steel	429,771	71,385	2,072,219	526,711	2,922,161	790,809
68	Non-ferrous metals	94,009	21,467	521,462	727,828	2,071,087	1,479,622
687	Tin	9,607	4,170	44,378	544,494	61,700	390,915
69	Metal mfs. n.e.s.	239,972	83,202	1,289,263	518,920	1,902,340	1,032,832
7	*Machinery and transport equip.*	**2,785,284** (27.2)	**1,309,631** (19.2)	**18,228,323** (30.2)	**14,363,018** (30.4)	**43,400,513** (44.1)	**42,937,807** (49.3)
75	Office mach. and data processing equip.	n.l.	216,580	1,276,172	1,656,318	6,213,807	13,582,271
751	Office mach.	69,161		206,697	299,751	315,074	555,977
752	Data processing equip.	n.l.		469,236	718,378	2,725,271	9,767,202
75261	Disk drives	n.l.		n.l.		791,691	6,102,352

Table A.4 (*Cont.*)

SITC Rev 3	Commodity	1957/59		1961/63		1967/69	
		Imports	Exports	Imports	Exports	Imports	Exports
76	Telecommunications and sound equip.	n.l.		49,647	16,477	63,207	11,851
761	Television receivers	n.l.		n.l.		n.l.	
762	Radio-broadcast receivers	n.l.		n.l.		n.l.	
763	Video and sound recorders	n.l.		n.l.		n.l.	
764	Telecommunications equip. n.e.s.	n.l.		n.l.		n.l.	
77	Electrical mach. and apparatus n.e.s.	n.l.		n.l.		n.l.	
772	Electrical circuit apparatus	n.l.		n.l.		n.l.	
773	Electry distributing equip.	n.l.		n.l.		n.l.	
775	Household goods	n.l.		n.l.		n.l.	
776	Electronic valves	n.l.		n.l.		n.l.	
7764990	Integrated circuits	n.l.		n.l.		n.l.	
778	Electrical mach. and apparatus n.e.s.	n.l.		n.l.		n.l.	
781+782+783+785	Road motor vehicles	73,754	63,689	165,283	127,371	157,615	94,986
792	Aircraft	448	357	1,076	646	36,986	1,336
793	Ships and boats	7,691	2,541	4,255	4,198	35,574	7,484
8	*Misc. manufactures*	**185,134** (4.7)	**93,063** (2.8)	**268,891** (6.6)	**121,929** (3.6)	**405,919** (7.7)	**182,812** (4.5)
84	Clothing	38,546	24,647	69,493	30,530	83,698	66,027
87	Scientific instruments	56,103	11,255	69,345	18,269	125,903	28,660
88	Photographic equip.	n.l.		n.l.		n.l.	

SITC Rev 3	Commodity	1971/73 Imports	1971/73 Exports	1982/84 Imports	1982/84 Exports	1988/90 Imports	1988/90 Exports
76	Telecommunications and sound equip.	194,882	165,757	2,141,346	2,786,675	6,863,443	10,190,353
761	Television receivers	n.l.		246,481	597,469	845,124	2,042,221
762	Radio-broadcast receivers	n.l.		396,965	1,017,874	1,071,650	2,754,055
763	Video and sound recorders	n.l.		610,684	351,176	1,424,005	1,688,558
764	Telecommunications equip. n.e.s.	n.l.		887,215	820,156	3,522,664	3,705,518
77	Electrical mach. and apparatus n.e.s.	n.l.		5,577,127	5,062,751	13,890,475	10,513,066
772	Electrical circuit apparatus	n.l.		881,998	1,065,803	2,422,412	1,537,548
773	Electry distributing equip.	n.l.		379,731	69,188	684,257	282,496
775	Household goods	n.l.		193,348	357,968	349,742	613,437
776	Electronic valves	n.l.		3,233,244	2,958,589	7,890,733	6,487,899
7764990	Integrated circuits	n.l.		1,214,427	1,939,668	1,582,457	4,746,044
778	Electrical mach. and apparatus n.e.s.	n.l.		581,391	444,298	4,687,125	1,014,767
781+782+783+785	Road motor vehicles	347,939	154,745	800,062	235,889	1,247,398	423,480
792	Aircraft	175,653	39,767	1,185,783	400,798	1,729,705	721,955
793	Ships and boats	152,653	64,894	1,185,921	1,073,141	1,468,401	935,414
8	*Misc. manufactures*	**776,728** (7.6)	**512,127** (7.5)	**3,998,723** (6.6)	**3,107,765** (6.6)	**9,085,529** (9.2)	**7,808,007** (9.0)
84	Clothing	83,452	227,099	593,953	1,050,880	1,401,669	2,691,228
87	Scientific instruments	295,182	97,837	659,668	360,603	1,508,344	1,023,306
88	Photographic equip.	n.l.		895,890	382,087	2,074,915	1,132,762

Table A.4 (*Cont.*)

SITC Rev 3	Commodity	1957/59		1961/63		1967/69	
		Imports	Exports	Imports	Exports	Imports	Exports
9	*Unclassified*	**83,746** (2.2)	**226,152** (6.7)	**82,509** (2.0)	**256,660** (7.6)	**107,463** (2.0)	**359,370** (8.9)
932	Ship and aircraft bunkers and stores	0	165,256	0	167,322	0	246,924
Total	*All commodities*	**3,903,501** (100.0)	**3,352,913** (100.0)	**4,092,708** (100.0)	**3,399,944** (100.0)	**5,244,657** (100.0)	**4,040,658** (100.0)

SITC Rev 3	Commodity	1971/73		1982/84		1988/90	
		Imports	Exports	Imports	Exports	Imports	Exports
9	*Unclassified*	**191,106** (1.9)	**514,041** (7.6)	**692,532** (1.2)	**3,673,742** (7.8)	**1,443,700** (1.5)	**1,950,475** (2.2)
932	Ship and aircraft bunkers and stores	126	345,554	0	3,156,907	0	2,272,157
Total	*All commodities*	**10,235,285** (100.0)	**6,809,140** (100.0)	**60,294,137** (100.0)	**47,322,567** (100.0)	**98,296,654** (100.0)	**87,123,957** (100.0)

Notes:

1   From 1956 Singapore's trade statistics follow the United Nations Standard International Trade Classification (SITC). Trade is divided into sections (one digit), divisions (two digit), groups (three digit) and items (seven digit). Here, when the last digits are zero, they are dropped, and the number becomes a four or five digit one.

   For Singapore, published data are consistent within the following periods: 1956–59, 1960–74, 1975–78, 1979–88, 1989–90. From 1989 Singapore data accord with SITC (revision 3) which is used as the basis for the above table. Some attempt, explained below, has been made to achieve comparability by the reclassification both of 1956–1988 data for divisions in groups according to SITC (rev. 3) or to combine data to give consistency with earlier groups. Because of this latter, groups sometimes appear in combined form, for example 334 + 335 in the case of petroleum. On the whole, however, this has not been attempted within section 7, machinery and transport equipment, where classification after 1974 differs considerably from that before 1974 due to the introduction of new products, especially electrical and electronic goods.

2   Until 1979, 333 petroleum, crude refers to 312 or 331 petroleum, crude and partly refined and so is not strictly comparable with data for 1982–90.

3   For 1961–73, 76 telecommunications and sound equipment refers to 724 telecommunications apparatus. The figure for 1961/63 refers to the average for 1962 and 1963 only.

4   For plastic materials figures for 1961/63 are the average for 1962 and 1963 only.

5   For 1957–73, 751 office machines refers to 714 office machines; 792 aircraft and 793 ships and boats to groups 734 and 735 respectively of the same descriptions.

6   For 1957–73 road motor vehicles refers to group 732 and for 1982–90 to group 781, 782, 783 and 785. Since 785 includes non-motorized cycles, the two periods are not strictly comparable.

7   Until 1980, 88 photographic equipment was included in 87, professional and scientific instruments, and no attempt was made to separate this division.

8   For 1988/90, 932 ship and aircraft bunkers and stores refers to 1988 only, since from 1989 group 932 excludes bunkers and so is not comparable with earlier periods.

Sources: Singapore, *Singapore trade statistics*, 1956–1973, 1982–1990.

Table A.5 *Singapore commodity composition of domestic exports,*
1982/84–1988/90 [annual averages, $000 and (% of total)]

SITC Rev 3	Commodity	1982/84	1988/90
0	*Food and live animals*	**502,313**	**965,800**
		(1.6)	(1.7)
07	Coffee and spices	152,937	280,136
1	*Beverages and tobacco*	**117,242**	**318,328**
		(0.4)	(0.6)
2	*Crude materials exc. fuels*	**407,889**	**481,588**
		(1.3)	(0.9)
231	Natural rubber	112,140	39
24	Cork and wood	48,229	50,438
3	*Mineral fuels*	**12,929,584**	**13,165,238**
		(41.4)	(23.6)
333	Petroleum, crude	0	0
334 + 335	Petroleum, refined and products	12,741,407	13,041,952
4	*Animal and veg. oils and fats*	**520,669**	**655,388**
		(1.7)	(1.2)
4222 + 4224	Palm oil, crude, refined and kernel	202,649	108,924
5	*Chemicals*	**984,036**	**3,360,817**
		(3.2)	(6.0)
51 + 52	Chemicals, organic and inorganic	302,021	1,195,457
541	Medicinal products	224,765	144,495
57 + 58	Plastic materials	180,359	1,165,574
6	*Basic manufactures*	**1,214,019**	**1,917,693**
		(3.9)	(3.4)
63	Cork and wood mfs. exc. furniture	275,967	214,958
64	Paper and paperboard mfs.	95,443	323,951
65	Textile yarn, fabrics etc.	172,457	222,098
66	Non-metallic mineral mfs.	153,068	123,030
67	Iron and steel	99,502	189,279
68	Non-ferrous metals	109,070	132,727
687	Tin	59,234	19,871
69	Metal mfs. n.e.s.	264,285	640,218

Table A.5 (*Cont.*)

SITC Rev 3	Commodity	1982/84	1988/90
7	*Machinery and transport equip.*	**9,215,305** (29.5)	**29,233,432** (52.3)
75	Office mach. and data processing equip.	1,346,038	12,012,486
751	Office mach.	245,969	417,009
752	Data processing equip.	621,649	8,820,428
75261	Disk drives	n.l.	5,846,216
76	Telecommunications and sound equip.	2,050,559	6,739,245
761	Television receivers	455,335	1,305,916
762	Radio-broadcast receivers	817,427	1,991,968
763	Video and sound recorders	154,842	719,611
764	Telecommunications equip. n.e.s.	622,954	2,721,750
77	Electrical mach. and apparatus n.e.s.	4,037,499	7,531,478
772	Electrical circuit apparatus	850,278	1,149,033
773	Electry distributing equip.	33,994	179,045
775	Household goods	317,751	508,892
776	Electronic valves	2,411,842	4,720,828
7764990	Integrated circuits	1,818,593	3,688,719
778	Electrical mach. and apparatus n.e.s.	326,038	675,792
781+782+783+785	Road motor vehicles	15,665	124,776
792	Aircraft	50,452	61,687
793	Ships and boats	793,653	303,215
8	*Misc. manufactures*	**2,099,014** (6.7)	**4,749,997** (8.5)
84	Clothing	803,105	1,796,803
87	Scientific instruments	160,147	576,245
88	Photographic equip.	201,190	293,679
9	*Unclassified*	**3,222,931** (10.3)	**1,005,361** (1.8)
932	Ships and aircraft bunkers and stores	3,116,633	2,205,881
Total	*All commodities*	**31,213,001** (100.0)	**55,853,640** (100.0)

Notes:
1   For 1988/90, 932 ship and aircraft bunkers and stores is for 1988 only, since from 1989 group 932 excludes bunkers and so is not comparable with earlier periods.
Sources: Singapore, *Singapore trade statistics*, 1982–1990.

Table A.6 Merchant vessels clearing from Singapore, 1900–1990

Year	All vessels 000 NRT	Vessels of 50 NRT and over, 1900-1930, and 75 NRT and over, 1931-1990		Year	All vessels 000 NRT	Vessels of 50 NRT and over, 1900-1930, and 75 NRT and over, 1931-1990	
		No.	000 NRT			No.	000 NRT
1900	5,392	4,649	4,834	1952	21,150	7,995	20,312
1901	6,008	4,924	5,454	1953	23,020	8,708	22,267
1902	6,264	5,086	5,693	1954	24,566	9,444	24,012
1903	6,607	5,290	5,994	1955	26,541	9,979	26,025
1904	6,743	5,429	6,156	1956	30,035	10,702	29,556
1905	6,984	5,268	6,402	1957	n.a.		
1906	7,215	5,281	6,662	1958	32,505	10,755	32,065
1907	7,324	5,161	6,784	1959	33,291	10,712	32,879
1908	7,461	5,161	6,948	1960	34,923	10,842	34,449
1909	7,503	5,320	7,069	1961	38,395	10,883	37,919
1910	7,897	5,341	7,419	1962	41,912	11,104	41,405
1911	8,258	5,761	7,718	1963	41,485	11,597	41,085
1912	8,738	5,957	8,221	1964	40,854	10,296	40,670
1913	9,205	6,084	8,618	1965	44,523	10,934	44,325
1914	8,690	5,962	7,994	1966	50,892	12,188	50,676
1915	7,768	5,821	6,964	1967	57,823	13,718	57,535
1916	7,401	5,774	6,612	1968	63,338	15,524	63,037
1917	6,173	5,326	5,362	1969	64,884	16,978	64,535
1918	5,509	4,752	4,696	1970	74,690	19,019	74,277
1919	7,922	5,615	7,024	1971	78,317	19,681	77,648
1920	9,443	5,772	8,562	1972	89,675	18,628	88,739
1921	9,793	5,699	8,972	1973	93,994	18,884	92,518

1922	9,875	5,868	9,142
1923	11,040	6,243	10,258
1924	11,798	6,488	10,946
1925	12,828	7,136	11,990
1926	13,671	7,996	12,852
1927	14,483	8,982	13,634
1928	15,563	9,705	14,697
1929	16,460	9,768	15,579
1930	16,606	9,112	15,920
1931	15,291	7,020	14,599
1932	15,013	6,725	14,375
1933	14,800	6,428	14,214
1934	15,522	6,814	14,897
1935	15,754	6,796	15,116
1936	15,849	6,534	15,187
1937	17,096	6,761	16,397
1938	16,330	6,474	15,631
1939	16,494	6,455	15,809

1974	104,586	19,617	103,028
1975	104,332	20,201	102,608
1976	114,313	19,995	111,710
1977	129,890	20,616	127,355
1978	138,405	21,829	135,588
1979	153,424	23,721	149,655
1980	158,688	24,820	155,369
1981	176,073	26,097	171,951
1982	186,607	27,892	181,723
1983	188,868	27,909	183,441
1984	175,011	26,429	169,613
1985	170,507	27,566	165,593
1986	204,392	30,717	199,863
1987	211,691	30,260	208,205
1988	245,852	32,569	236,833
1989	267,757	34,884	259,412
1990	297,600	39,010	287,858

Notes:
1   Net registered tonnage (NRT) is the close-in space for cargo and passenger accommodation.
2   For 1960–72 statistics may differ slightly from those in *Economic and social statistics, 1960–1982*, the collection of which were somewhat erratic.

Sources: 'Marine Department', SSAR, 1900–1915, 1917–1930; SS, Blue books, 1916–1917, 1931–1939; Malayan Statistics, *Digest of statistics*, 1949–1952; *Report of the Marine Department, 1952–1972*; *Economic and social statistics, 1960–1982*, p.142; *Yearbook of statistics 1988*, p.200; Port of Singapore Authority, personal communication.

Table A.7 *Chinese immigrants examined at Singapore and Chinese deck passengers leaving for China, 1900–1952*

	Immigrants examined	Deck passengers leaving Singapore	Deck passengers leaving British Malayan ports	Difference between Chinese examined and deck passengers leaving
1900	200,947			
1901	178,778			
1902	207,156			
1903	220,321			
1904	204,796			
1905	173,131			
1906	176,587			
1907	227,342			
1908	153,452			
1909	151,752			
1910	216,321			
1911	269,854			
1912	251,644			
1913	240,979			
1914	147,150			
1915	95,735			
1916	183,399	61,630		121,769
1917	155,167	41,282		113,885
1918	58,421	35,585		22,836
1919	70,912	37,590		33,322
1920	126,077	68,383		57,694
1921	191,043	98,986		92,057
1922	132,886	96,869		36,017
1923	159,019	78,121		80,898
1924	181,430	87,749		93,681
1925	214,692	77,920		136,772
1926	348,593	120,308		228,285
1927	359,262	155,198		204,064
1928	295,700	149,354		146,346
1929	293,167	139,967		153,200
1930	242,149	167,903		74,246
1931	79,025	150,720	213,992	-134,967
1932	33,534		282,779	-249,245
1933	27,796		86,555	-58,759
1934	98,864		68,129	30,735
1935	141,892		69,025	72,867
1936	149,517		80,578	68,939
1937	246,371		66,502	179,869

Table A.7 *(Cont.)*

	Immigrants examined	Deck passengers leaving Singapore	Deck passengers leaving British Malayan ports	Difference between Chinese examined and deck passengers leaving
1938	98,863		54,603	44,260
1949	41,460	48,667		-7,207
1950	24,288	16,793		7,495
1951	15,945	29,880		-13,935
1952	7,393	11,980		-4,587

Notes:
1 For 1930–38 figures for immigrants vary somewhat according to which year of the *SSAR* is used. For the above figures the years used were 1932, 1936 and 1938.
2 Figures for Chinese deck passengers leaving British Malayan ports are first available in 1931; after that date figures for deck passengers leaving Singapore are not available. It was estimated that from 1911–15 400,000 Chinese deck passengers left Singapore for China.
3 From 1949–52 figures refer to Chinese deck passengers to and from China and Hong Kong.

Sources: *1921 census*, p.21; *1931 census*, p.113; 'Secretary for Chinese affairs', *SSAR*, 1930–1938; 'Progress of the people of the Straits Settlements', *SSAR*, 1934–1938; Malayan Statistics, *Digest of statistics*, 1949–1953.

Table A.8 *Chinese immigration of men, women and children at Singapore, 1900–1952*

	Chinese immigrants examined at Singapore	Men	Women	Children	Chinese deck passengers leaving Singapore for China
1900	200,947	180,477	11,982	8,488	
1901	178,778	158,809	11,822	8,147	
1902	207,156	184,198	13,151	9,807	
1903	220,321	193,339	14,539	12,443	
1904	204,796	179,650	14,395	10,751	
1905	173,131	148,869	13,714	10,548	
1906	176,587	153,624	12,478	10,485	
1907	227,342	197,284	16,265	13,793	
1908	153,452	129,913	12,909	10,630	
1909	151,752	128,878	12,126	10,748	
1910	216,321	184,856	16,395	15,070	
1911	269,854	226,126	22,738	20,990	
1912	251,644	206,018	23,327	22,299	
1913	240,979	197,872	22,847	20,260	
1914	147,150	121,355	13,017	12,778	
1915	95,735	76,545	10,632	8,558	
1916	183,399	145,314	20,344	17,741	61,630
1917	155,167	122,748	16,571	15,848	41,282
1918	58,421	39,787	8,594	10,040	35,585
1919	70,912	44,276	13,883	12,753	37,590
1920	126,077	83,940	22,382	19,755	68,383
1921	191,043	138,785	28,723	23,535	98,986
1922	132,886	98,364	18,213	16,309	96,869
1923	159,019	115,100	22,296	21,623	78,121
1924	181,430	126,710	27,753	26,967	87,749
1925	214,692	152,406	30,003	32,283	77,920
1926	348,593	252,878	49,897	45,818	120,308
1927	359,262	252,504	58,777	47,981	155,198
1928	295,700	192,809	55,526	47,365	149,354
1929	293,167	205,139	46,325	41,703	139,967
1930	242,149	161,029	42,896	38,224	167,903
1931	79,025	49,723	17,149	12,153	150,720
(1931)					(213,992)
1932	33,534	18,741	8,652	6,141	(282,779)
1933	27,796	13,535	8,199	6,062	(86,555)
1934	98,864	52,023	29,678	17,163	(68,129)
1935	141,892	81,775	38,621	21,496	(69,025)
1936	149,517	69,558	54,233	25,726	(80,578)
1937	246,371	99,698	100,166	46,507	(66,502)
1938	98,863	31,152	42,748	24,963	(54,603)

Table A.8 (*Cont.*)

	Chinese immigrants examined at Singapore	Men	Women	Children	Chinese deck passengers leaving Singapore for China
1949	41,460	25,821	8,466	7,173	48,667
1950	24,288	13,953	4,753	5,582	16,793
1951	15,945	10,332	3,095	2,518	29,880
1952	7,393	3,223	2,343	1,827	11,980

Notes:
1 Children were defined as under 12 English years of age.
2 For 1916–18 figures for men and children are approximate.
3 For 1931–38 the figures in brackets are for Chinese deck passengers leaving British Malayan ports.
4 See also notes for table A.7.
Sources: as for table A.7.

Table A.9 *Malayan currency area monetary base, 1910–1966 ($)*

	30 June	31 Dec.
1910	32,339,160	34,583,460
1911	35,648,960	36,859,310
1912	39,466,207	39,572,134
1913	44,223,518	43,222,548
1914	43,827,548	48,487,648
1915	48,623,648	57,702,348
1916	64,082,317	63,394,140
1917	83,074,040	87,068,993
1918	87,007,740	86,408,740
1919	87,281,836	174,631,974
	(4 March 1920)	
	(183,212,222)	
1920	135,170,353	101,587,187
1921	85,016,688	84,596,807
1922	71,981,983	72,944,005
1923	78,682,061	81,123,025
1924	83,741,142	85,491,478
1925	103,572,298	161,432,313
1926	163,393,463	163,279,713

	30 June	31 Dec.
1927	130,856,923	117,805,414
1928	115,713,145	115,636,274
1929	107,967,787	104,159,136
1930	91,064,645	82,423,391
1931	74,425,876	67,414,796
1932	68,366,250	68,496,575
1933	66,908,386	66,964,286
1934	68,776,090	75,786,490
1935	77,061,390	77,122,486
1936	78,004,886	83,984,121
1937	97,561,521	104,975,512
1938	105,253,927	105,300,470
1939	105,260,209	126,215,109
1940	157,817,899	164,578,897
1946		405,885,090
1947		412,103,847
1948		400,938,886
1949		402,943,640

	31 Dec.
1950	633,487,211
1951	764,109,203
1952	786,797,439
1953	740,923,669
1954	778,958,620
1955	915,420,660
1956	942,840,095
1957	943,100,508
1958	948,530,912
1959	1,077,726,238
1960	1,133,337,328
1961	1,131,579,796
1962	1,188,592,193
1963	1,231,623,122
1964	1,307,117,580
1965	1,409,819,293
1966	1,510,040,872

Notes:

1   Official statistics give gross, net and active circulation of currency notes. The above figures are for gross currency notes in circulation and correspond to the currency note component of the monetary base, M0. Net circulation was officially defined as gross circulation less the amount held by Government Treasuries in the SS and FMS. Since treasuries in British Malaya had no monetary functions any cash which they held was part of the money supply (King, *Money*, pp.64–65). Treasury holdings were negligible, normally less than 1% of gross circulation. Active circulation was net circulation less the amount held by commercial banks. After 1947 net circulation figures were not published. (King, *Money*, p.64.) Active circulation, usually 70% to 80% of the gross figure

before World War II and 80% to 90% afterwards, was the currency note component of M1, currency in the hands of the non-bank public. Figures for sight deposits which would allow construction of a series for M1 are not available until 1947.

2 Before World War II figures are for the currency of the Colony of the Straits Settlements, FMS and UMS. The currency also circulated freely in parts of British Borneo. From 1952 figures are for a Malayan Currency Area which included Singapore, the Federation of Malaya, Sarawak, North Borneo (Sabah) and Brunei.

3 Currency note issue was first introduced in 1899 followed by the introduction of a silver dollar by the Straits Settlements government in October 1903. Before then the Straits Settlements had no standard coin of their own, and at the beginning of 1903 the currency of the Colony 'consisted mainly of British and Mexican dollars, subsidiary coin and government notes' ('Working of the Malayan Currency Commission', *SSAR 1938* II, p.597 and see Anthonisz, *Currency reform*, p.1). After the introduction of the Straits dollar, the importation of British and Mexican dollars was prohibited and in August 1904 these were demonetized (King, *Money*, p.11). In 1906 under a gold exchange standard currency notes began to be issued at the rate of Straits Settlements $60 = £7 (one dollar = 2s 4d). The arrangement was subsequently altered to a sterling exchange standard. It effectively operated from World War I when Britain went off the gold standard and was officially enacted in 1923. Currency notes were issued and backed solely by the Colony of the Straits Settlements until 1938 when a Malayan Currency Commission comprising the SS, FMS and UMS was constituted. From 1952 a Board of Commissioners of Currency was established for the Malayan Currency Area (King, *Money*, pp.25–26). In all parts of the Area after 1952, the Malayan dollar became the sole legal tender (King, *Money*, pp.24–26). The Board of Commissioners continued in existence until June 1967 when it was replaced by Bank Negra Malaysia, the Board of Commissioners of Currency, Singapore, and the Brunei Currency Board. The exchange rate remained $60 = £7 until the Singapore and Malaysian currency split in 1967.

4 Before World War II total currency nominally in circulation consisted of currency notes, Straits silver dollars and half-dollars, banknotes, subsidiary silver coin, copper coin and nickel five-cent pieces. However, currency notes accounted for the great and increasing bulk of currency. Straits silver dollars and half-dollars were the other main form of currency before World War II, but are not shown in the above figures. This somewhat understates the monetary base before World War I, but would probably overstate it during the inter-war period, as by 1933 'silver dollars had practically gone out of circulation' ('Working of the Malayan Currency Commission', *SSAR 1938* II, p.599). In 1910 the figure recorded for the gross circulation of Straits silver dollars and half-dollars was $7,969,814, in 1913, $6,604,013, and in 1933 it was $3,400,734. For figures for 1909 to 1913, see 'Working of the Currency Department', *SSAR 1913*, p.245 and for 1913 to 1938, see 'Working of the Malayan Currency Commission', *SSAR 1938* II, p.606. The Chartered Bank stopped issuing banknotes by 1904 and the Hongkong and Shanghai Bank by 1908, after which banknotes became a negligible component of the monetary base (Lim, *Economic development of modern Malaya*, pp.222–23). For figures and estimates of banknotes in circulation for 1906–1940, see Lee, *Monetary and banking development* (1974), p.364. Nominally, between 1906 and 1939 a substantial value of subsidiary silver coin and copper coin circulated. Before World War I the monetary base is probably somewhat understated because of the exclusion of these coins, but by the inter-war period most subsidiary silver

Table A.9 (*Cont.*)

coin and copper coin had been exported or melted down by the public. The value of nickel coin consisting of the five-cent pieces was negligible ('Working of the Currency Department', *SSAR 1928*, pp.163–64). From 31 December 1952 the silver coins formerly issued by the Straits Settlements government or the Board of Currency Commissioners, Malaya, were no longer legal tender. Legal tender coins now consisted of nickel, cupro–nickel and bronze coins of denominations under one dollar (King, *Money*, pp.28, 37, 153).

5   The figure for 4 March 1920 was the pre-World War II high.

6   For 1948-66, figures refer to post-Liberation notes only.

Sources: 'Financial report and statements' appx. A, *SSAR* 1910–1911; 'Working of the Currency Department', *SSAR*, 1912–1937; 'Working of the Malayan Currency Commission', *SSAR 1938*; Malaya, *Malayan Currency Commission, 1941 to 1946*; Short, 'Indigenous banking', p.75; Lee, *Monetary and banking development* (1974 and 1990); Anthonisz, *Currency reform*; King, *Money*, pp.11, 26–28, 37, 64–65, 153; Lim, *Economic development of modern Malaya*, pp.221–30; Malaysia, *Commissioners of currency 1968*, pp.3, 11.

Table A.10 *Singapore employment by industry, 1921–1957*

	1931 Singapore Municipality		1921 Singapore Island		1931 Singapore Island		1947 Singapore Island		1957 Singapore Island	
	persons	%	persons	%	persons	%	persons	%	persons	%
1. *Agriculture, fishing and mining*	**9,587**	**4.9**	33,933	15.9	32,299	**13.5**	30,277	**8.8**	**34,269**	**7.3**
2. *Manufacture and work in material substances*	**33,825**	**17.4**	**33,293**	**15.6**	**38,217**	**16.0**	**60,426**	**17.5**	**78,275**	**16.7**
a. Woodworking; furniture and basketware manufacture	11,349	5.8	10,805	5.0	12,463	5.3	9,334	2.7	10,248	2.2
b. Food, drink and tobacco manufacture	2,234	1.2	2,947	1.4	2,704	1.1	7,092	2.1	9,204	2.0
c. Clothing manufacture	3,906	2.0	4,428	2.1	4,148	1.7	5,980	1.7	9,674	2.1
d. Footware manufacture	1,888	1.0	1,652	0.8	1,933	0.8	2,684	0.8	3,208	0.7
e. Rubber goods manufacture	1,640	0.8	n.l.		2,455	1.0	1,990	0.6	312	0.0
f. Manufacture of metals, machines, implements, conveyances, jewellery and watches	10,059	5.2	10,118	4.7	11,363	4.8	19,441	5.6	26,231	5.6
g. Other	2,749	1.4	3,343	1.6	3,151	1.3	13,905	4.0	19,398	4.1
3. *Construction*	**5,026**	**2.6**	**4,305**	**2.0**	**5,654**	**2.4**	**7,648**	**2.2**	**24,628**	**5.2**

Table A.10 (*Cont.*)

4. *Transport and communications*	**42,444**	**21.9**	**49,436**	**23.1**	**47,192**	**19.8**	**51,861**	**15.0**	**50,347**	**10.7**
a. Water including wharves and warehouses	20,851	10.7	19,792	9.2	22,727	9.5	29,713	8.6	24,516	5.2
b. Rickshaw and hand cart	10,386	5.4	18,380	8.6	10,537	4.4	7,246	2.1	3,382	0.7
c. Other road transport	7,911	4.1	7,657	3.6	9,902	4.2	10,432	3.0	15,541	3.3
d. Other	3,296	1.7	3,607	1.7	4,026	1.7	4,470	1.3	6,908	1.5
5. *Commerce and finance*	**57,845**	**29.8**	**50,788**	**23.8**	**63,841**	**26.8**	**83,049**	**24.0**	**121,533**	**25.9**
a. Wholesale and retail dealing including agency houses	35,921	18.5	34,734	16.3	39,642	16.6	45,904	13.3	85,436	18.2
b. Hawking and street selling	20,499	10.6	15,042	7.1	22,725	9.5	29,541	8.5	28,873	6.2
c. Banking, money-lending, pawn-broking and money-changing	1,080	0.5	486	0.2	1,110	0.5	2,243	0.6	4,878	1.0
d. Other	345	0.2	526	0.2	364	0.2	5,361	1.6	2,346	0.5
6. *Public administration and defence*	**5,321**	**2.7**	**8,907**	**4.2**	**6,864**	**2.9**	**54,310**	**15.7**	**52,823**	**11.3**
7. *Professions*	**10,564**	**5.5**	**3,546**	**1.7**	**11,840**	**5.0**	**7,558**	**2.2**	**25,570**	**5.4**
a. Medicine, dentistry and veterinary	5,123	2.6	1,460	0.7	5,554	2.3	2,079	0.6	10,381	2.2
b. Education	3,223	1.7	984	0.5	3,769	1.6	2,928	0.9	12,060	2.6

c. Other	2,218	1.2	1,102	0.5	2,517	1.1	2,551	0.7	3,129	0.6
8. *Personal service*	**29,427**	**15.2**	**29,278**	**13.7**	**32,441**	**13.6**	**50,438**	**14.6**	**82,377**	**17.5**
a. Domestic service	21,847	11.3	19,369	9.1	24,134	10.1	28,132	8.1	31,291	6.7
b. Hotels, lodging houses, restaurants and clubs	1,724	0.9	3,258	1.5	1,953	0.8	12,744	3.7	15,707	3.3
c. Entertainment and sport	1,567	0.8	1,417	0.7	1,680	0.7	4,179	1.2	6,261	1.3
d. Other	4,289	2.2	5,234	2.4	4,674	2.0	5,383	1.6	29,118	6.2
9. *Total (1 – 8)*	**194,039**	**100.0**	**213,486**	**100.0**	**238,348**	**100.0**	**345,567**	**100.0**	**469,822**	**100.0**
10. *Other or indeterminate*	27,991		25,124		52,281		11,968		2,096	

Notes:

1 Figures are from the industry tables of the censuses, except the 1931 figure for rickshaw and hand cart pullers, and the 1957 figures for hawkers, which are from the occupational table.

2 For 1957, Agriculture excludes 7,483 persons engaged in the processing and treatment of rubber, oil palm and coconut products off estates (*1957 census*, p.82). These persons are included in Manufacture and work in material substances (other).

3 For 1947, Manufacture and work in material substances (other) includes 5,240 persons in rubber milling, packing, etc.

4 Manufacture and work in material substances includes electricity, gas and water supply (as other) from the 1957 census classifications 60, 61 and 62. Classification 63, sanitary services, is included above under Personal service, other. A negligible number were recorded as employed in electricity, gas and water in the census returns until 1957. The 1921 census returned 273 persons in electricity, gas and water supply, and the 1931 census seven persons.

5 Construction refers to the category building, decorating and contracting used in the censuses prior to 1957.

6 For 1957, Rickshaw and hand cart refers to trishaw pedallers.

7 For 1957, Professions includes the census classifications 921, 923, 924, 925, 928, 931, 933, 935.

8 For 1931, Other or indeterminate are those which the census classified by occupation but not by industry.

Sources: 1921 census pp.236–39; *1931 census*, pp.246–47, 252–79; *1947 census*, pp.473–76; *1957 census*, pp.202–15, 223, 226; *1970 census* I, p.179.

Table A.11 *Singapore employment by industrial sector, 1947–1990*

	1947	1957	1970	1980	1990
(a) Persons					
Agriculture	29,086	32,668	22,458	16,962	5,128
Quarrying	1,247	1,601	2,168	1,139	766
Manufacturing	58,922	74,237	143,100	324,121	447,436
Electricity, gas, water	750	4,038	7,615	8,464	6,710
Construction	9,375	24,628	43,126	72,346	122,135
Commerce	75,445	114,309	152,910	229,759	337,519
Transport and communications	52,976	50,347	79,041	119,917	146,553
Financial and business services	7,604	21,720	23,071	79,412	167,222
Public administration, community, social and personal services	110,374	146,274	177,022	224,554	303,542
Unclassified	11,756	2,096	381	416	0
Total	**357,535**	**471,918**	**650,892**	**1,077,090**	**1,537,011**
(b) Percentage					
Agriculture	8.1	6.9	3.5	1.6	0.3
Quarrying	0.4	0.3	0.3	0.1	0.1
Manufacturing	16.5	15.7	22.0	30.1	29.1
Electricity, gas, water	0.2	1.0	1.2	0.8	0.4
Construction	2.6	5.2	6.6	6.7	7.9
Commerce	21.1	24.2	23.5	21.3	22.0
Transport and communications	14.8	10.7	12.1	11.1	9.5
Financial and business services	2.1	4.6	3.5	7.4	10.9
Public administration, community, social and personal services	30.9	31.0	27.2	20.9	19.8
Unclassified	3.3	0.4	0.1	0.0	0.0
Total	**100.0**	**100.0**	**100.0**	**100.0**	**100.0**

Notes:

1   For 1947, the above classification largely follows the 1957 reclassification of 1947 data. However, the 1947 census included persons 15 years of age and over, and the 1957 census, persons aged 10 years and over. The author of the 1957 census report pointed out that it was not possible to reconcile this and other discrepancies between the two censuses.

2   For 1947, Financial and business services includes items 104, 105, 106, 108, 109 and 110 from the 1947 classification. In 1957, Financial and business services includes industrial classifications 72, 73, 74 and 93. The result of these classifications for 1947 and 1957 may be somewhat to understate the importance of Financial and business services in the earlier year. This possibility is increased by item 107 in the 1947 data, General trading and agency (not classifiable above), amounting to 6,030 persons, which is likely to have included some business services.

3   For 1957, Manufacturing includes industrial classifications 3 and 4 and 7,483 persons engaged in the processing of rubber, oil palm and coconut oil products off estates (*1957 census*, p.82). Accordingly, this figure has been deducted from Agriculture. The resulting figure for Manufacturing is less than the figure given in the *1957 census*, p.84, but greater than that in the *1970 census*, I, p.179, which excluded rubber, palm oil and coconut oil processing from both Manufacturing and Agriculture. In 1957, Electricity, gas and water comprise classifications 60, 61 and 62. Classification 63, Sanitary services, is included in Public administration etc. The census classification Activities not adequately defined, is deducted from the 1957 industrial classification 9, Services, and put in the category Unclassified. For 1957, Commerce includes Import, export, wholesale and retail trade (*1957 census*, p.84 and p.218, classifications 71, 75 and 76).

Sources: 1947 census, pp.473–76; *1957 census*, pp.82–84, 216–18; *1970 census* I, p.179; *1980 census: Administrative report*, p.110; *1990 census: Statistical release 4, Economic characteristics*, p.94.

Table A.12 *Singapore GDP and GDP deflator, 1960–1990 ($m)*

	GDP current prices	annual % change	GDP 1985 market prices	annual % change	GDP deflator 1985 market prices	annual % change
1960	2,149.6		5,058.5		42.5	
1961	2,329.1	8.4	5,490.4	8.5	42.4	-0.2
1962	2,513.7	7.9	5,878.1	7.1	42.8	0.9
1963	2,789.9	11.0	6,493.3	10.5	43.0	0.5
1964	2,714.6	-2.7	6,213.7	-4.3	43.7	1.6
1965	2,956.2	8.9	6,626.8	6.6	44.6	2.1
1966	3,322.7	12.4	7,328.3	10.6	45.3	1.6
1967	3,748.5	12.8	8,283.1	13.0	45.3	0.0
1968	4,315.0	15.0	9,464.3	14.3	45.6	0.7
1969	5,019.9	16.3	10,730.0	13.4	46.8	2.6
1970	5,804.9	15.6	12,172.4	13.4	47.7	1.9
1971	6,840.5	17.8	13,698.8	12.5	49.9	4.6
1972	8,195.0	19.8	15,526.2	13.3	52.8	5.8
1973	10,256.9	25.2	17,273.6	11.3	59.4	12.5
1974	12,610.1	22.9	18,441.2	6.8	68.4	15.2
1975	13,443.0	6.6	19,171.4	4.0	70.1	2.5
1976	14,650.9	9.0	20,548.5	7.2	71.3	1.7
1977	16,039.0	9.5	22,143.3	7.8	72.4	1.5
1978	17,830.4	11.2	24,046.0	8.6	74.2	2.5
1979	20,523.0	15.1	26,284.7	9.3	78.1	5.3
1980	25,090.7	22.3	28,832.5	9.7	87.0	11.4
1981	29,339.4	16.9	31,603.1	9.6	92.8	6.7
1982	32,669.9	11.4	33,772.3	6.9	96.7	4.2
1983	36,732.8	12.4	36,537.2	8.2	100.5	3.9
1984	40,047.9	9.0	39,572.5	8.3	101.2	0.7
1985	38,923.5	-2.8	38,923.5	-1.6	100.0	-1.2
1986	38,663.5	-0.7	39,641.4	1.8	97.5	-2.5
1987	42,635.8	10.3	43,387.5	9.4	98.3	0.8
1988	49,998.0	17.3	48,221.6	11.1	103.7	5.5
1989	56,844.2	13.7	52,678.0	9.2	107.9	4.1
1990	63,438.9	11.6	57,049.4	8.3	111.2	3.1

Sources: Singapore national accounts 1987, pp.45–50, 63–64; Yearbook of statistics 1991, pp.85, 86; Economic survey 1992, pp.111–13.

Table A.13 Singapore indicators of savings, investment and capital formation, 1960–1990 (current market prices $m)

	Gross national savings	Gross domestic savings	Gross capital formation	Gross domestic product	Savings ratio GNS/GDP	Investment ratio GCF/GDP	GNS/GCF
1960	-52.3	-56.4	244.5	2,149.6	-2.4	11.4	-21.4
1961	-54.7	-81.2	269.8	2,329.1	-2.3	11.6	-20.3
1962	148.2	114.3	391.2	2,513.7	5.9	15.6	37.9
1963	106.7	60.2	487.1	2,789.9	3.8	17.5	21.9
1964	249.3	223.5	542.2	2,714.6	9.2	20.0	46.0
1965	341.0	291.4	647.7	2,956.2	11.5	21.9	52.6
1966	540.0	455.7	729.4	3,322.7	16.3	22.0	74.0
1967	611.3	515.3	831.2	3,748.5	16.3	22.2	73.5
1968	865.3	791.6	1,075.2	4,315.0	20.0	24.9	80.5
1969	972.9	905.0	1,437.4	5,019.9	19.4	28.6	67.7
1970	1,129.7	1,065.4	2,244.5	5,804.9	19.5	38.7	50.3
1971	1,286.7	1,293.9	2,778.1	6,840.5	18.8	40.6	46.3
1972	2,000.3	2,014.5	3,392.7	8,195.0	24.4	41.4	59.0
1973	2,770.2	3,004.2	4,045.2	10,256.9	27.0	39.4	68.5
1974	3,220.2	3,665.9	5,709.8	12,610.1	25.5	45.3	56.4
1975	3,985.2	3,954.0	5,370.4	13,443.0	29.6	39.9	74.2
1976	4,579.9	4,782.3	5,981.7	14,650.9	31.3	40.8	76.6
1977	5,079.3	5,374.9	5,799.1	16,039.0	31.7	36.2	87.6
1978	5,928.4	6,059.8	6,957.4	17,830.4	33.2	39.0	85.2
1979	7,299.8	7,454.8	8,899.9	20,523.0	35.6	43.4	82.0
1980	8,282.0	9,411.8	11,627.6	25,090.7	33.0	46.3	71.2
1981	10,482.5	11,953.5	13,587.0	29,339.4	35.7	46.3	77.2
1982	12,885.2	14,218.2	15,658.8	32,669.9	39.4	47.9	82.3
1983	16,306.1	16,932.0	17,595.8	36,732.8	44.4	47.9	92.7
1984	18,596.4	18,304.3	19,417.3	40,047.9	46.4	48.5	95.8
1985	16,543.4	15,605.5	16,551.2	38,923.5	42.5	42.5	100.0
1986	15,588.5	15,037.9	14,894.8	38,663.5	40.3	38.5	104.7
1987	16,304.8	17,225.7	16,636.6	42,635.8	38.2	39.0	98.0
1988	20,224.0	20,962.2	18,435.0	49,998.0	40.4	36.9	109.7
1989	24,518.3	24,824.6	19,782.1	56,844.2	43.1	34.8	123.9
1990	28,361.5	28,580.2	25,202.3	63,438.9	44.7	39.7	112.5

Sources: Singapore national accounts 1987, pp.56–58; Yearbook of statistics 1991, pp.84, 85; Economic survey 1992, p.120.

Table A.14 *Singapore gross fixed capital formation by public and private sectors, 1960–1990 (1985 market prices)*

	Gross fixed capital formation	Public sector		Private sector	
	$m	$m	%	$m	%
1960	518.1	183.8	35.3	337.3	64.7
1961	747.1	268.6	35.7	483.9	64.3
1962	891.2	333.5	37.0	567.0	63.0
1963	1,101.6	448.9	40.0	672.3	60.0
1964	1,335.4	544.5	40.0	815.0	60.0
1965	1,506.2	556.9	36.6	963.8	63.4
1966	1,551.4	627.0	39.7	951.1	60.3
1967	1,769.8	586.3	33.1	1,185.3	66.9
1968	2,347.8	771.1	32.8	1,577.8	67.2
1969	3,028.9	791.8	26.5	2,193.5	73.5
1970	4,032.6	920.8	23.3	3,024.2	76.7
1971	5,022.1	958.7	19.7	3,912.6	80.3
1972	5,759.4	1,447.7	25.6	4,216.3	74.4
1973	6,246.7	1,274.0	21.0	4,803.7	79.0
1974	6,994.6	1,523.7	22.3	5,302.7	77.7
1975	6,729.9	1,918.4	28.8	4,749.5	71.2
1976	7,055.4	2,391.7	33.8	4,683.0	66.2
1977	7,187.3	2,582.9	35.7	4,656.6	64.3
1978	8,199.9	2,678.3	32.7	5,521.6	67.3
1979	9,257.7	2,307.0	24.9	6,950.7	75.1
1980	11,126.6	2,772.7	24.9	8,353.9	75.1
1981	12,810.3	3,133.6	24.5	9,676.7	75.5
1982	15,405.7	4,463.1	29.0	10,942.6	71.0
1983	17,067.7	5,806.7	34.0	11,261.0	66.0
1984	18,677.4	6,295.1	33.7	12,382.3	66.3
1985	16,424.8	5,939.5	36.2	10,485.3	63.8
1986	14,614.5	6,188.8	42.3	8,425.7	57.7
1987	15,065.1	5,470.6	36.3	9,594.5	63.7
1988	17,311.6	4,095.5	23.7	13,216.1	76.3
1989	19,138.9	3,563.9	18.6	15,575.0	81.4
1990	21,625.4	3,888.8	18.0	17,736.6	82.0

Notes:
1   Public sector and private sector fixed capital formation may not add to available figures for gross fixed capital formation. The percentages for public and private sector are based on the total of these two figures added together.
Sources:*Singapore national accounts 1987*, pp.73–74, 77–78, 81–82; *Economic survey 1988*, p.108, *1989*, p.120, *1990*, p.121, *1991*, p.103.

Table A.15 *Singapore investment commitments in manufacturing, 1972–1990 ($m)*

	Total	Local	Foreign	United States	Japan	United Kingdom	Nether-lands	Other Europe	Others
1972	194.5	38.2	156.3	24.7	79.3	0.0	0.0	21.6	30.7
1973	295.9	71.8	224.1	8.8	151.4	1.9	0.6	41.4	20.0
1974	291.9	123.1	168.8	64.5	44.6	25.8	0.0	2.3	31.6
1975	306.3	59.5	246.8	45.6	23.6	56.2	81.4	29.8	10.2
1976	303.2	42.8	260.4	92.9	76.1	14.8	20.0	15.3	41.3
1977	396.4	33.8	362.6	153.5	129.4	21.4	0.0	26.3	32.0
1978	812.4	46.6	765.8	146.9	158.4	156.2	200.0	62.4	41.9
1979	943.6	120.2	823.4	259.9	319.4	91.9	4.5	64.9	82.8
1980	1,413.5	224.4	1,189.1	505.7	135.3	129.5	1.0	229.9	187.7
1981	1,862.9	641.6	1,221.4	674.3	212.1	83.1	1.2	144.4	106.3
1982	1,704.5	542.0	1,162.5	533.0	73.7	283.1	62.8	75.9	133.9
1983	1,775.8	506.0	1,269.8	571.7	166.6	207.5	99.2	87.4	137.4
1984	1,828.4	493.7	1,334.7	805.9	166.6	186.6	70.3	68.2	37.1
1985	1,120.4	232.4	888.0	427.3	244.1	69.4	75.2	56.4	15.6
1986	1,450.0	259.4	1,190.6	443.4	493.8	93.4	57.1	68.3	34.6
1987	1,743.0	295.0	1,448.0	543.5	601.1	42.4	70.9	172.5	17.6
1988	2,007.3	349.6	1,657.8	586.6	691.3	56.6	82.9	218.6	21.7
1989	1,958.7	333.3	1,625.4	520.2	541.2	174.6	174.0	195.6	19.8
1990	2,484.3	266.8	2,217.5	1,054.8	708.2	89.9	72.6	272.8	19.2

Notes:

1 Excludes petrochemicals.
2 In 1987, after the formation of the Research and Statistics Unit, Economic Development Board, investment figures were re-classified to show more accurately the ultimate source of capital/funds. For example, the source of capital for a locally registered company, if in fact a United States company, would now invariably appear as the United States and not perhaps as Singapore. As a result of re-classification, for 1980–87 but not for earlier years, figures for investment commitments are somewhat inconsistent between the periods 1972–79 and 1980–90.
3 Rows may not add to totals due to rounding.

Sources: Singapore Economic Development Board, *Annual report 1982/83*, p.12; *Yearbook 1988/89*, p.12, *1990/91*, p.16.

Table A.16 *Direct foreign investment in Singapore's manufacturing sector, 1966–1990*

	Anual change in foreign investment in gross fixed assets, $m	% of gross fixed capital formation		Annual change in foreign investment in gross fixed assets, $m	% of gross fixed capital formation
1966	82	12.5	1979	1,107	14.7
1967	64	8.7	1980	1,171	11.5
1968	151	15.1	1981	1,882	14.7
1969	146	11.0	1982	2,085	13.4
1970	395	20.9	1983	1,895	10.9
1971	580	23.9	1984	3,027	15.8
1972	708	22.9	1985	809	4.9
1973	376	10.4	1986	665	4.6
1974	395	8.2	1987	1,858	12.3
1975	326	6.7	1988	3,003	17.3
1976	359	6.8	1989	3,728	18.0
1977	406	7.4	1990	3,302	13.9
1978	1,097	17.2			

Notes:
1   Figures for 1966–80 are not strictly comparable with those for 1981–90, due to a re-classification of data beginning in 1987.

Sources: Singapore Economic Development, *Annual report 1971–74*, p.68, *1982/83*, p.11; *Yearbook 1986/87*, p.17, *1990/91*, p.17, *1991/92*, p.11; *Singapore national accounts 1987*, pp.73–74; *Economic survey 1988*, p.108, *1989*, p.120, *1990*, p.121, *1991*, p.103.

Bibliography

UNPUBLISHED OFFICIAL RECORDS

Federated Malay States, original correspondence, PRO CO 717.

Straits Settlements, original correspondence, PRO CO 273, and register of correspondence, CO 426.

Monthly Review of Chinese Affairs, beginning Sept. 1930 in CO 273 series.

ANNUAL SERIES AND STATISTICS – MALAYA, MALAYSIA AND SINGAPORE

Federated Malay States, *Manual of statistics relating to the Federated Malay States* (Kuala Lumpur), annual series, 1904–1929.

Federated Malay States, *Proceedings of the Federal Council of the Federated Malay States* (Kuala Lumpur), annual series, 1909–1940.

Federated Malay States, *Report on the administration of the Mines Department and on the mining industry*, annual series, 1904–1939 (published in Kuala Lumpur and for 1910–1933 as a supplement to *FMS government gazette*).

Federated Malay States, *Report on the Customs and Excise Department* (Kuala Lumpur), annual series, 1934–1939.

Federated Malay States Railways, *Annual report* (for 1930 and 1931 published as a supplement to *FMS government gazette*; from 1932 continued as *Railways report*. Published in Kuala Lumpur).

Federation of Malaya, *Imports and exports* (Kuala Lumpur or Johore Baharu), quarterly series, 1948–1958.

Malaya, *Average prices, declared trade values, exchange, currency and cost of living* (Singapore), annual series, 1922–1939.

Malaya, *Foreign imports and exports* (Singapore), annual series, 1921–1937.

Malaya, *The foreign trade of Malaya* (Singapore), annual series, 1929–1939.

Malaya, *Rubber statistics handbook* (Singapore), annual series, 1930–1940.

Malayan agricultural statistics by D. H. Grist (Kuala Lumpur), annual series, 1931–1939.

Port of Singapore Authority, *Annual report* (Singapore), 1964–1990.

Registrar of Malayan Statistics, Singapore (or Chief Statistician, Singapore), *Malayan statistics, digest of economic and social statistics* (variously titled) (Singapore), quarterly or monthly series, 1946–1961.

Registrar of Malayan Statistics, Singapore (or Singapore, Department of Statistics), *External trade of Malaya* (Singapore), monthly series, 1950–1964.

Singapore annual report, 1946–1990, variously titled *Annual report on Singapore* (1946–1947); *Colony of Singapore annual report* (1948–1958); *State of Singapore annual report* (1959–1963); *Singapore yearbook* (1964–1970); *Singapore* (1971–1990).

Singapore, Chief Statistician (or Department of Statistics), *Monthly digest of statistics* (Singapore), 1962–1990.

Singapore, Department of Statistics, *Singapore external trade statistics* (from 1975 *Singapore trade statistics*) (Singapore), annual, quarterly or monthly series, 1956–1990. From 1989 published by the Trade Development Board.

Singapore, Department of Statistics (or Economic Development Board), *Report on the census of industrial production* (Singapore), annual series, 1959–1990.

Singapore, Department of Statistics, *Shipping and cargo statistics* (Singapore), quarterly or monthly series, 1977–1990. From July 1986 published by the Port of Singapore Authority.

Singapore, Department of Statistics, *Yearbook of statistics* (Singapore), annual series, 1967–1992.

Singapore, Economic Development Board, *Annual report* (or *Yearbook*) (Singapore), 1961–1991/92.

Singapore, Economic Development Board, *Leading international companies in manufacturing and technical services* (Singapore), annual series, 1985–1988.

Singapore Harbour Board, *Report and accounts* (Singapore), annual series, 1914–1964.

Singapore Improvement Trust, *Annual report* (Singapore), 1927–1947 (one vol.), annual series, 1948–1959.

Singapore Legislative Assembly, *Debates* and sessional papers (Singapore), annual series, 1957–1964.

Singapore, Marine Department (issued by various Departments), *Annual report* (Singapore), 1952–1972.

Singapore, Ministry of Labour, *Report on the labour force survey of Singapore* (Singapore), annual series, 1973–1991.

Singapore, Ministry of Labour, *Yearbook of labour statistics* (Singapore), annual series, 1976–1991.

Singapore, Ministry of Labour, *Report on wages in Singapore* (Singapore), annual series, 1986–1991.

Singapore, Ministry of Trade and Industry, *Economic survey of Singapore* (Singapore), annual and quarterly series, 1974–1992.

Singapore, Monetary Authority of Singapore, *Annual report* (Singapore), 1971–1991/92.

Singapore, *Parliamentary Debates* (Singapore), annual series, 1965–1990.

Singapore, *Proceedings of the Legislative Council of the Colony of Singapore* (Singapore), annual series, 1948–1955.

Singapore, *Report of the Department of Commerce and Industry* (from 1955 Ministry of Commerce and Industry; from 1959 Division of Commerce and Industry [or Trade Division], Ministry of Finance) (Singapore), annual series, 1954–1970.

Singapore, Singapore Industrial Promotion Board, *First year report March 1957– April 1958* (Singapore, 1958).

Straits Settlements, *Annual departmental reports of the Straits Settlements* (Singapore), 1888–1938.

Straits Settlements, *Blue book* (Singapore), annual series, 1870–1939.

Straits Settlements, *Proceedings of the Legislative Council of the Straits Settlements* (Singapore), annual series, 1872–1939.

Straits Settlements, *Return of imports and exports* (Singapore), annual series, 1900–1927.

GOVERNMENT PUBLICATIONS AND STATISTICS – NETHERLANDS INDIA AND INDONESIA

Netherlands India, *Statistiek van den Handel en de In-en Uitvoerrechten in Nederlandsch-Indie* (Batavia), annual series, 1900–1923 and 1924–1938 continued under the title, 'Jaaroverzicht van den In-en Uitvoer van Nederlandsch-Indie' (imports and exports, Netherlands India), *Mededeelingen van het Centraal Kantoor voor de Statistiek* (Batavia).

Netherlands India, Centraal Kantoor voor de Statistiek, *Statistisch Jaaroverzicht van Nederlandsch-Indie* (statistical abstract, Netherlands India) (Batavia), annual series, 1922–1931, continued as *Indisch Verlag* (Netherlands Indian report), part II.

Netherlands India, Central Bureau of Statistics, *Rubber in the Netherlands East Indies* (Weltevreden, 1925).

Netherlands Indies, Department of Agriculture, Industry and Commerce, *1930 handbook of the Netherlands East-Indies* (Buitenzorg, Java, 1930).

Netherlands India, *Volkstelling 1930* (1930 census). Eight vols. (Batavia, 1933–36).

Netherlands India, Central Bureau of Statistics, Concept Publicatie C. K. S. (Mededeeling no. 162), 'Het Handelsverkeer met Singapore, 1825–1937' (unpublished typescript, 1938).

Netherlands India, Central Bureau of Statistics, Concept Publicatie C. K. S. (Mededeeling no. 163), 'Handelsbetrekkingen met Nederland, 1825–1937' (unpublished typescript, 1938).

Netherlands India, Central Bureau of Statistics, *Statistical pocket book of Indonesia 1941* (Batavia, 1941).

Indonesia, Kantor Pusat Statistik (later Biro Pusat Statistik), *Statistik Konjunktur* (Jakarta), monthly series, 1955–1963.

OTHER TRADE STATISTICS

Annual statement of the sea-borne trade and navigation of Burma (Rangoon), annual series, 1900/01–1939/40.

Statistics on the import and export trade of Siam, 1901. Port of Bangkok (Bangkok, 1901), continued under various titles and from 1923–24, *The foreign trade and navigation of the Kingdom of Siam* (Bangkok).

Annual statement of the trade of the United Kingdom with foreign countries and British possessions (in PP), 1897–1920.

Statistical tables relating to British self-governing dominions, crown colonies, possessions, and protectorates (in PP), 1870–1912.

GOVERNMENT REPORTS AND PUBLICATIONS – MALAYA, MALAYSIA AND SINGAPORE.

Report of the commissioners appointed enquire into the state of labour in the Straits Settlements and protected native states, 1890 (Singapore, 1891).

Report of the commission on the Eastern Shipping or Straits Homeward Conference as affecting the trade of the Colony (Straits Settlements Legislative Council Paper no. 40 of 1902) (Singapore, 1902).

Report by Messrs. Coode, Son & Matthews on proposed harbour improvements at Singapore (1904).

Tanjong Pagar Dock Company, Singapore, *Report on proposed re-construction of wharves, and extension of dock accommodation* by Coode, Son & Matthews and Mr. J. R. Nicholson, 15 Oct. 1904.

Simpson, W. J., *Report on the sanitary condition of Singapore* (Singapore, 1907).

Report of the commission to enquire into the conditions of indentured labour in the Federated Malay States by C. W. C. Parr (Federal Council Paper no. 11 of 1910).

Proceedings and report of the commission appointed to inquire into the cause of the present housing difficulties in Singapore, and the steps which should be taken to remedy such difficulties. Two vols. (Singapore, 1918).

Report of the commissions appointed by the Governor of the Straits Settlements and High Commissioner of the Federated Malay States to enquire into certain matters relating to the public service. Two vols. (Singapore, 1919).

'Committee to enquire into preferential tariffs and protective duties in the SS and FMS', *Proceedings of the Federal Council, FMS*, 1921.

Report of the commissions appointed by the Governor of the Straits Settlements and High Commissioner of the Federated Malay States to report on the present state of trade depression and the extension of credit facilities (Singapore, 1921).

Singapore Harbour Board, *A short history of the port of Singapore with particular reference to the undertakings of the Singapore Harbour Board* (Singapore, 1922).

Report of the Harbour Boards' Committee appointed by the government of the Straits Settlements (Singapore, 1926).

Singapore Harbour Board, *Report by G. W. A. Trimmer, chairman, on his proposal to extend the facilities of the wharf department* (Singapore, 1927).

Grist, D. H., *Nationality of ownership and nature of constitution of rubber estates in Malaya* (Kuala Lumpur, 1933).

Report of the committee appointed by the Governor of the Straits Settlements and High Commissioner for the Malay States to report on the practicability and desirability of a customs union of all the Malay states (Singapore, 1933).

Report of the commission appointed by the Governor of the Straits Settlements to enquire into and report on the trade of the Colony, 1933–1934. Five vols. (Singapore, 1934).

Federated Malay States Railways, *Fifty years of railways in Malaya, 1885–1935* (Kuala Lumpur, 1935).

Blythe, W. L., *Methods and conditions of employment of Chinese labour in the Federated Malay States* (Kuala Lumpur, 1938).

Fermor, Lewis Leigh, *Report upon the mining industry of Malaya* (Kuala Lumpur, 1939).

Straits Settlements, *Annual report of the Marine Department 1939* (Singapore, 1940).

Report on the working of rubber regulation in Malaya during 1939 (Federal Council Paper no. 19 of 1940) (Kuala Lumpur, 1940).

British Military Administration, Singapore, *The entrepot trade of Singapore* (Singapore, 1945).

Bingham, R. P., *Report of the Labour Department 1946* (Singapore, 1947).

Colony of Singapore, *Report of the housing committee Singapore, 1947* (Singapore, 1947).

Colony of Singapore, *Annual report on the registration of births and deaths for the years 1940–47* by E. J. Phillips (Singapore, 1948).

Malaya, *Report of the working of the Malayan Currency Commission for the period 1st January 1941 to 31st December 1946* by W. D. Godsall (Singapore, 1948).

Singapore Department of Social Welfare, *A social survey of Singapore: a preliminary study of some aspects of social conditions in the municipal area of Singapore, December 1947* (Singapore, 1948).

Singapore Harbour Board, *The port of Singapore* (Singapore, 1949).

'The resuscitation of the Malayan canned pineapple industry', *Minutes of the Legislative Council of the Federation of Malaya with council papers for the period* (*second session*) *March 1949 to January 1950*, paper no. 14.

Colony of Singapore, *Report of the hawkers inquiry commission, 1950* (Singapore, 1950).

Allen, D. F., *Report on the major ports of Malaya* (Kuala Lumpur, 1951).

Benham, Frederic, *The national income of Malaya, 1947–49* (Singapore, 1951).

Federation of Malaya, *Report of the mission of enquiry into the rubber industry of Malaya* (Kuala Lumpur, 1954).

Colony of Singapore, *Master plan, written statement* (Singapore, 1955).

Colony of Singapore, *Master plan, report of survey* (Singapore, 1955).

Colony of Singapore, *Master plan, reports of study groups and working parties* (Singapore, 1955).

Colony of Singapore, *Report of the commission of inquiry into the public passenger transport system of Singapore* (Singapore, 1956).

Colony of Singapore, *Report of the land clearance and resettlement working party* (Singapore, 1956).

Goh Keng Swee, *Urban incomes and housing: a report on the social survey of Singapore, 1953–54* (Singapore, 1956).

Watson, G. M. and Caine, Sir Sidney, *Report on the establishment of a central bank in Malaya* (Kuala Lumpur, 1956).

Benham, Frederic, *Economic survey of Singapore 1957* (Singapore, 1957).

Howlett, R. A., *A report on the tourist industry of Singapore* (Singapore, 1957).

State of Singapore, *Development plan 1961–1964* (Singapore, 1961).

Singapore, Economic Planning Unit, Prime Minister's Office, *First development plan 1961–1964: review of progress for the three years ending 31st December 1963* (Singapore, 1964).

Singapore, Ministry of National Development and Economic Research Centre,

University of Singapore, *Singapore sample household survey, 1966* (Singapore, 1967).

Goh Chok Tong, *Singapore: state of the economy, 1968* (Singapore, Ministry of Finance, 1969).

Ow Chwee Huay, *Singapore's trade with West Malaysia* (Singapore, Ministry of Finance, 1969).

Chan Wah Yoke, *A study of Singapore's domestic exports of manufactures 1960–1968* (Singapore, Ministry of Finance, 1970).

Chan Wah Yoke, *A study of Singapore's exports and re-exports of petroleum to Japan* (Singapore, Ministry of Finance, 1970).

Koh Cher Siang, *Port costs and port efficiency: Singapore, Yokohama, Hong Kong* (Singapore, Ministry of Finance, 1970).

Malaysia, *Report of the Board of Commissioners of Currency Malaya and British Borneo* by Tan Siew Sin (Kuala Lumpur, 1970).

Ng Kiat Chong, *A comparative evaluation of industrialisation of Hong Kong, Taiwan, South Korea and Singapore* (Singapore, Ministry of Finance, 1970).

Leong Mun Keong, *Wage levels of selected countries* (Singapore, Ministry of Finance, 1971).

Singapore, Department of Statistics, *Singapore national accounts 1960–1973* (Singapore, 1975).

Singapore, Ministry of Trade and Industry, *Highlights of Singapore's economic development plan for the eighties* (Singapore, n.d.).

Singapore, Department of Statistics, *Economic and social statistics, Singapore 1960–1982* (Singapore, 1983).

Singapore, Economic Committee, *The Singapore economy: new directions* (Singapore, 1986).

Singapore, National Wages Council Subcommittee, *Wage reform* (Singapore, 1986).

Singapore, Public Sector Divestment Committee, *Report of the public sector divestment committee* (Singapore, 1987).

Singapore, Department of Statistics, *Singapore national accounts 1987* (Singapore, 1988).

Singapore, SME Committee, *Report on enterprise development: SME master plan* (Singapore, 1989).

Monetary Authority of Singapore, *The financial structure of Singapore* 3rd edn (Singapore, 1989).

Singapore, National Science and Technology Board, *Window of opportunities: national technology plan 1991* (Singapore, 1991).

Singapore, Economic Planning Committee, Ministry of Trade and Industry, *The strategic economic plan* (Singapore, 1991).

Singapore, SEP Working Group (Ministry of Trade and Industry), *Implementation of the strategic economic plan* (Singapore, 1993).

SS AND SINGAPORE LEGISLATIVE PAPERS

'Report of the commissioners to enquire into the state of traffic on the Singapore River', *SSLCP 1899*.

'The shipping commission', *SSLCP 1899*.

'Proposed harbour improvements', *SSLCP 1902*.

'Singapore harbour improvements', *SSLCP 1902*.

'Correspondence regarding the position and requirements of the Tanjong Pagar Dock Company, Limited', *SSLCP 1905*.

Stuart, A, 'Report on shipping freight conferences operating in the Straits Settlements', *SSLCP 1908*.

'Two appendices to the proceedings of the Royal Commission on Shipping Conferences', *SSLCP 1908*.

'Petition of merchants, etc. of Singapore, to the unofficial members of Council regarding shipping conferences', *SSLCP 1910*.

'Minutes of a meeting held at the Colonial Office on the 25th May, 1911, between Sir John Anderson, GCMG, Governor of the Straits Settlements, and representatives of the Homeward Java and Straits Conference and the New York Steamer Conference', *SSLCP 1911*.

'The registration of imports and exports ordinance 1886', *SSLCP 1915*.

'Singapore River improvement scheme', *SSLCP 1919*.

'Commission on profiteering, Straits Settlements', *SSLCP 1920*.

'Report of the committee to inquire into the present system of the registration of imports and exports in the Straits Settlements and Federated Malay States', *SSLCP 1921*.

'Report of the select committee to consider the constitution of the Legislative Council of the Straits Settlements', *SSLCP 1921*.

'Singapore Kallang Basin and reclamation', *SSLCP 1921*.

'Report of the committee to consider the problem of destitution among various sections of the community', *SSLCP 1923*.

'Report of the committee to consider what amendments, if any, should be made to the existing rules and by-laws under Ordinance no. 109 (Petroleum)', *SSLCP 1926*.

'Report of the trade statistics committee', *SSLCP 1927*.

'Report on the pineapple conference', *SSLCP 1931*.

'Report of the committee to investigate the hawker question in Singapore', *SSLCP 1932*.

'Report of the customs duties committee, 1932', *SSLCP 1932*.

'Review of the affairs of the Colony of the SS', *SSLCP 1932*.

'Report of the commission of inquiry into the port of Singapore', *SLA 1957*.

'Report of the committee on minimum standards of livelihood', *SLA 1957*.

'Report of the Singapore constitutional conference held in London in March and April 1957', *SLA 1957*.

'External trade and balance of payments of Singapore', *SLA 1958*.

'An industrial development programme' by F. J. Lyle, *SLA 1959*.

CENSUSES

Merewether, E. M., *Report on the census of the Straits Settlements, 1891* (Singapore, 1892).

Innes, J. R., *Report on the census of the Straits Settlements taken on the 1st March, 1901* (Singapore, 1901).

Hare, George Thompson, *Federated Malay States, census of population, 1901* (Kuala Lumpur, 1902).

Marriott, H., *Census report of the Straits Settlements, 1911* (Singapore, 1911).

Pountney, A. M., *Federated Malay States: review of census operations and results, 1911* (London, 1911).

Nathan, J. E., *The census of British Malaya, 1921* (London, 1921).

Vlieland, C. A., *British Malaya, a report on the 1931 census* (London, 1932).

Del Tufo, M. V., *Malaya, a report on the 1947 census of population* (London, 1949).

Chua, S. C., *State of Singapore, report on the census of population, 1957* (Singapore, 1964).

Arumainathan, P., *Report on the census of population 1970 Singapore*. Two vols. (Singapore, 1973).

Khoo Chian Kim, *Census of population 1980 Singapore* (Singapore: *Administrative report*, 1983; and nine separate volumes, released 1980 and 1981, and five census monographs published 1982 to 1985).

Lau Kak En, *Singapore census of population 1990* (Singapore: *Advance data release*, 1991; *Demographic characteristics* [statistical release 1], 1992; *Households and housing* [statistical release 2], 1992; *Literacy, languages spoken and education* [statistical release 3], 1993; *Economic characteristics* [statistical release 4], 1993).

BRITISH PARLIAMENTARY PAPERS

Further papers relating to the Malay States. Reports for 1890 (PP 1892, LVI).

Trade of the British empire and foreign competition. Despatch from Mr. Chamberlain to the governors of colonies and the High Commissioner of Cyprus and the replies thereto (PP 1897, LX).

Trade and shipping of South-East Asia (PP 1900, LXXXVII).

Reports on the Federated Malay States for 1901 (PP 1902, LXVI).

Reports on the Federated Malay States for 1903 (PP 1905, LIV).

Commission to enquire into the use of opium in the Straits Settlements and the Federated Malay States. Three vols. (PP 1909, LXI).

Report of the Royal Commission on shipping rings, with minutes of evidence and appendices. Five vols. (PP 1909, XLVII and XLVIII).

Reports on British trade in British West Africa, Straits Settlements, British Guiana and Bermuda (PP 1913, LXVIII).

Report on the commercial situation in Siam at the close of the year 1919 (PP 1920, XLIII).

ISC, *Report on Prai River railway wharves (Penang Harbour)* (PP 1926, XII).

ISC, *Report on the harbour of Singapore* (PP 1928–29, VII).

Report by the Right Honourable W. G. A. Ormsby Gore, M.P. (Parliamentary Under-Secretary of State for the Colonies) on his visit to Malaya, Ceylon and Java during the year 1928 (PP 1928–29, V).

ISC, *Report on Port Swettenham, Federated Malay States* (PP 1930–31, XIV).

Report of Brigadier-General, Sir Samuel Wilson, Permanent Under-Secretary of State for the Colonies on his visit to Malaya, 1932 (PP 1932–33, X).

Labour conditions in Ceylon, Mauritius and Malaya. Report by Major G. St. Orde Browne (PP 1943, IX).

Malayan Union and Singapore, statement of policy on future constitution (PP 1945–46, XIX).

Federation of Malaya, summary of revised constitutional proposals (PP 1946–47, XIX).

GOVERNMENT REPORTS – UNITED KINGDOM

1. Department of Overseas Trade

Beale, L. B., *A review of the trade of British Malaya in 1928* (London, 1929).

Boulter, R., *Economic conditions in British Malaya to 28th February 1931* (London, 1931).

Hartland, A., *Economic conditions in British Malaya to 20th December 1934* (London, 1935).

Hartland, A., *Report on economic and commercial conditions in Malaya to 5th March 1937* (London, 1937).

Willmot, R. B., *Report on economic and commercial conditions in Malaya, March 1939* (London, 1939).

Awbery, S. S. and Dalley, F. W., *Labour and trade union organisation in the Federation of Malaya and Singapore* (London, 1948).

Mackenzie, K. E., *Economic and commercial conditions in the Federation of Malaya and Singapore, March 1951* (London, 1952).

2. Other

ISC, *British shipping in the orient* (London, 1939).

Macmichael, Sir Harold, *Report on a mission to Malaya* (London, 1946).

Greaves, Ida, *Colonial monetary conditions* (London, Colonial Office, research studies no.10, 1953).

King, Frank H. H., *Money in British East Asia* (London, Colonial Office, research studies no.19, 1957).

Freedman, Maurice, *Chinese family and marriage in Singapore* (London, Colonial Office, research studies no. 20, 1957).

GOVERNMENT REPORTS – UNITED STATES

Shriver, J. Alexis, *Pineapple-canning industry of the world* (Washington, DC: US Department of Commerce, 1915).

Odell, Ralph, M., *Cotton goods in the Straits Settlements* (Washington, DC: US Department of Commerce, 1916).

Figart, David M., *The plantation rubber industry in the middle east* (Washington, DC: US Department of Commerce, 1925).

Holt, E. G., *The marketing of crude rubber* (Washington, DC: US Department of Commerce, 1927).

Brauer, August, *The cotton-goods market of British Malaya* (Washington, DC: US Department of Commerce, 1931).

Barker, P. W., *Rubber statistics, 1900–1937: production, absorption, stocks and prices* (Washington, DC: US Department of Commerce, 1938).

US Tariff Commission, *Economic factors affecting the use of items 807·00 and 806·30 of the tariff schedules of the United States* (Washington, DC: US Tariff Commission, 1970).

US Department of Labor, Bureau of Labor Statistics, *International comparisons of hourly compensation costs for production workers in manufacturing 1991* Report 825 (Washington, DC: US Department of Labor, June 1992).

INTERNATIONAL ORGANIZATIONS – REPORTS AND STATISTICS

United Nations, Economic Commission for Asia and the Far East, *Economic survey of Asia and the Far East* (Bangkok), annual series, 1953–1965.

International Bank for Reconstruction and Development, *The economic development of Malaya* (Singapore, 1955).

International Labour Office, *Report to the government of Singapore on social security measures* (published as Cmd. 56 of 1957, Singapore, 1957).

United Nations, *International trade statistics yearbook* (New York), annual series, 1959–1988.

United Nations, *A proposed industrialization programme for the State of Singapore* (New York: UN Commission for Technical Assistance, 1961).

International Bank for Reconstruction and Development, *Report on the economic aspects of Malaysia* (Kuala Lumpur, 1963).

International Monetary Fund, *Balance of payments statistics yearbook* (Washington, DC), annual series, 1967–1992.

World Bank, *World Bank atlas* (Washington, DC), annual series, 1967–1991.

World Bank, *World development report* (Washington, DC and later Oxford), annual series, 1978–1992.

GATT, *International trade* (Geneva), annual series, 1981/82–1990/91.

United Nations, Economic and Social Commission for Asia and the Pacific, *A study on liner shipping services and freight rates for ASEAN major export trade routes* (Bangkok, 1985).

International Monetary Fund, *International financial statistics yearbook 1990* (Washington, DC, 1990).

DIRECTORIES, HANDBOOKS AND VOLUNTARY ASSOCIATIONS

British Malaya: Malayan trade facts and figures (Malayan Information Agency, London, 1929).

British Malaya: trade and commerce (Malay States Information Agency, London, 1924).

Bunting, B., Georgi, C. D. V. and Milsum, J. N., *The oil palm in Malaya* (Malayan Planting Manual no. 1) (Kuala Lumpur, 1934).

Chinese Commercial Directory of Singapore, Penang, Malacca, Kuala Lumpur, Batupahat, Muar (Singapore, 1932).

Chinese year book, annual publication (Shanghai, 1935–1937).

Grist, D. H., *An outline of Malayan agriculture* (Malayan Planting Manual no. 2) (Kuala Lumpur, 1935).

Indian Chamber of Commerce, Singapore, *Memorandum and articles of association* (Singapore, Sept. 1937).

Manchester Association of Importers and Exporters, *Annual report 1911.*

Planters' Association of Malaya, General Labour Committee (British Malaya), *Report of special committee on Chinese labour* (Kuala Lumpur, 1922).

Ridley, Henry N., *The story of the rubber industry in Malaya* (Malay States Development Agency, London, 1912).

Rotary Club of Singapore, *Singapore as an industrial centre* (Singapore, 1931).

Singapore: a handbook of information presented by the Rotary Club and Municipal Commissioners of the town of Singapore (Singapore, 1933).

Singapore Chamber of Commerce, *Annual report* (Singapore, 1895–1940).

Singapore Chinese Chamber of Commerce, *Fifty-eight years of enterprise* (Singapore, 1964).

Singapore Chinese Chamber of Commerce and Industry, *80th anniversary souvenir magazine* (Singapore, 1986).

The Singapore directory for the Straits Settlements, 1877, continued annually from 1879 as *The Singapore and Straits directory*; from 1922 as *The Singapore and Malayan directory*; from 1949 as *The Straits Times directory of Singapore and Malaya* (or Malaysia); and from 1984 as *Times business directory of Singapore* (Singapore).

Singapore dollar directory, annual publication (Singapore, 1918–?).

Singapore Indian Chamber of Commerce, *Report*, (Singapore), annual series, 1936–1990.

Singapore manufacturers' exhibition, 2–9 Jan. 1932 (Singapore, 1932).

Straits Chinese British Association, *Golden jubilee souvenir* (Singapore,1950).

Rubber Trade Association of Penang, *Souvenir number in commemoration of the thirty-second anniversary of the Rubber Trade Association of Penang and the official opening of the new premises, 1951* (Penang, 1951).

BUDGET SPEECHES (Minister for Finance)

Goh Keng Swee, *Two years of economic progress* (Singapore, 1967).

Goh Keng Swee, *Decade of achievement* (Singapore, 1970).

Hon Sui Sen, *Economic pattern in the 1970s* (Singapore, 1972).

Goh Chok Tong, *Towards higher achievement* (Singapore, 1981).

Hu, Richard Tsu Tau, *Budget statement* (Singapore), 1986–1992.

SPEECHES (Government Ministers)

Lee Kuan Yew, *Social revolution in Singapore* (speech to the British Labour Party Conference, 1967) (Singapore, 1967).

Lee Kuan Yew, 'A promising start for the 1970s', 1970 National Day Message (Singapore, 1970).

S. Rajaratnam, 'Singapore: global city', address to the Singapore Press Club, 6 Feb. 1972 (Singapore 1972).

Hon Sui Sen, 'The new phase of industrial development in Singapore', address to the Singapore Press Club, 23 March 1973 (Singapore, 1973).

Lee Kuan Yew, 'Extrapolating from the Singapore experience', speech at the 26th world congress of the International Chamber of Commerce, Orlando, Florida, 5 Oct. 1978 (Singapore, 1978).

'Singapore's economic policy: vision for the 1990s', speech by B. G. (Res) Lee
    Hsien Loong at the Commonwealth Institute, London, 30 Jan. 1986.
'Managing transition in political leadership', speech by B. G. (Res) Lee Hsien
    Loong at the International Herald centennial conference, 11 Nov. 1987.
'Singapore and the Asian NICs: similarities and contrasts', speech by Richard Hu,
    Minister for Finance to the Insead Club, Harvard Club and Oxford &
    Cambridge Society (Singapore), 10 Dec. 1987.
B. G. Lee Hsien Loong, 'Keynote address at the Enterprise '92 Conference'
    (Singapore), 25 Aug. 1992.

NEWSPAPERS AND MAGAZINES

1. Daily, weekly and monthly.
Far Eastern Economic Review (Hong Kong).
Financial Times (London).
Malay Mail (Kuala Lumpur).
Malaya Tribune (Singapore).
Mirror (Singapore).
Singapore Bulletin (Singapore).
Singapore Free Press (Singapore).
Singapore Investment News (published by the Singapore Economic Development
    Board).
Singapore Trade (from 1965 *Singapore Trade and Industry*), 1960–1976 (published
    by or in cooperation with the Ministry of Finance).
Straits Budget (Singapore).
Straits Times (Singapore).
Sunday Times (Singapore).
The Times (London).
Wall Street Journal (New York).

2. Special or commemorative issues.
Straits Times, Singapore Centenary Supplement, 7 Feb. 1919.
Manchester Guardian Commercial, special section on British Malaya, 19 Feb. 1925.
Malaya Tribune memento, Singapore manufacturers' exhibition, 2–9 Jan. 1932.
Straits Times, Singapore manufacturers' exhibition supplement, 2–9 Jan. 1932.
One hundred years of progress, centenary number of the Singapore Free Press, 8 Oct.
    1935.
The global port, Straits Times supplement commemorating PSA's silver jubilee, 3
    April 1989.
Lloyd's List, Singaport '90 special report, 5 Feb. 1990.

THESES AND UNPUBLISHED TYPESCRIPTS

Benis, R. H., 'Reminiscences of the old firm' (Barker & Co.) (unpublished
    typescript, 10 Nov. 1953).
Friedman, Milton, 'A welfare state syllogism' (speech to the Commonwealth Club,
    San Francisco, 1 June 1990).
Ong Theng Hong, 'The Straits Trading Company, 1887–1937' (unpublished B.A.
    honours academic exercise, University of Malaya, Singapore, 1958).

Ritchie, F. G., 'The early days of ship surveying and of Ritchie & Bisset, 1866–1928' (unpublished typescript, 1952).

Ungphakorn, Puey, 'The economics of tin control' (unpublished Ph.D. thesis, University of London, 1949).

ARTICLES

Abrahamsson, B. J., 'Recent developments in international shipping with reference to Singapore', *MER* 14, 2 (1969).

'An old hand', 'Tin mining in Malaya, II: the eighties and nineties', *British Malaya* (June 1926).

Arasaratnam, Sinnippah, 'Indian associations and the growth of leadership among Malayan Indians', *Journal of the Historical Society, University of Malaya* 3 (1969–70).

van Ark, Bart, 'The volume and price of Indonesian exports, 1823 to 1940: the long-term trend and its measurement', *BIES* 24, 3 (1988).

Arndt, H. W., 'Comparative advantage in trade in financial services', *Banca Nazionale del Lavoro Quarterly Review* 164 (1988).

Aschauer, David Alan, 'Does public capital crowd out private capital?', *Journal of Monetary Economics* 24 (1989).

Baldwin, R. E., 'Patterns of development in newly settled regions', *Manchester School of Economic and Social Studies* 24, 2 (1956).

Baldwin, R. E., 'Export technology and development from a subsistence level', *Economic Journal* 73 (1963).

Bardhan, Pranab K., 'Interlocking factor markets and agrarian development: a review of issues', *Oxford Economic Papers* 32, 1 (1980).

Bauer, P. T., 'Remembrance of studies past: retracing first steps' in Gerald M. Meier and Dudley Seers, eds. *Pioneers in development* (New York, 1984).

Baumol, William J., 'Productivity growth, convergence and welfare: what the long-run data show', *American Economic Review* 76, 5 (1986).

Bell, Clive, 'Credit markets and inter-linked transactions' in H. Chenery and T. N. Srinivasan, eds. *Handbook of development economics* I (Amsterdam, 1988).

Bellows, Thomas J., 'Singapore in 1988', *Asian Survey* 29, 2 (1989).

Benham, Frederic, 'Western enterprise in Indonesia and Malaya', *MER* 2, 2 (1957).

Blythe, W. L., 'Historical sketch of Chinese labour in Malaya', *JMBRAS* 20, 1 (1947).

Bottomley, Anthony, 'The role of foreign branch plants in the industrialisation of Singapore', *MER* 7, 1 (1962).

Bottomley, Anthony, 'Some economic implications of the proposed Malaysian federation from the point of view of Singapore', *MER* 7, 2 (1962).

Braddell, Roland, 'Reconstruction of Malaya', *British Malaya* (Aug. 1944).

van den Broek, J., 'The Netherlands Indies as a producer of tin ', *Bulletin of the Colonial Institute of Amsterdam* 3, 1 (1939).

Caves, Richard E., '"Vent for surplus" models of trade and growth' in Robert E. Baldwin, et al., *Trade, growth and the balance of payments* (Chicago, 1965).

Caves, Richard E., 'Export-led growth and the new economic history' in Jagdish N. Bhagwati, et al., eds. *Trade, balance of payments and growth* (Amsterdam, 1971).

Cheah Hock Beng, 'Export-oriented industrialisation and dependent development: the experience of Singapore', *Institute of Development Studies Bulletin* 12, 1 (1980).

Chen Chun-Po, 'Chinese overseas', *Chinese Year Book, 1935–36* (Shanghai, 1936).

Chen Chun-Po, 'Chinese overseas', *Chinese Year Book, 1936–37* (Shanghai,1937).

Cheng, Homer, 'The network of Singapore societies', *Journal of the South Seas Society* 6, 2 (1950).

Cheng Lim-Keak, 'Changing patterns of spatial organization in Singapore', *Journal of the South Seas Society* 35, 1 and 2 (1980).

Chiang Hai Ding, 'The statistics of the Straits Settlements foreign trade, 1870–1915', *MER* 10, 1 (1965).

Chua Joon Eng and Morgan, Theodore, 'The accuracy and external consistency of Singapore's trade statistics', *MER* 17, 1 (1972).

Chow, S. C. and Papanek, G. F., 'Laissez-faire, growth and equity – Hong Kong', *Economic Journal* 91 (1981).

Chowdhury, A. and Kirkpatrick, Colin, 'Industrial restructuring in a newly industrializing country: the identification of priority industries in Singapore', *Applied Economics* 19, 7 (1987).

Coase, R. H., 'The nature of the firm', *Economica* 4 (1937).

Cole, William E. and Sanders, Richard D., 'Internal migration and urban employment in the third world', *American Economic Review* 75, 3 (1985).

Cole, William E. and Sanders, Richard D., 'Reply', *American Economic Review* 76, 3 (1986).

Coope, A. E., 'The kangchu system in Johore', *JMBRAS* 14, 3 (1936).

Corden, W. M. 'Macroeconomic targets and instruments for a small open economy', *Singapore Economic Review* 29, 2 (1984).

Corden, W. M. and Findlay, Ronald E., 'Concluding remarks' in Bertil Ohlin, et al., eds. *The international allocation of economic activity* (London, 1977).

Courtenay, C. E., 'Malayan pineapples: part I. Pre-war and post-war conditions', *British Malaya* (July 1952).

Crafts, N. F. R., 'Trade as a handmaiden of growth: an alternative view', *Economic Journal* 83 (1973).

Department of Agriculture, Industry and Commerce, Netherlands Indies, 'Native rubber cultivation in the Netherlands East Indies', *BRGA* 13, 2 (1931).

Department of Agriculture, SS and FMS, 'Packing and transport of palm oil', *MAJ* 21, 4 (1933).

Devitt, Hugh M., 'The Singapore rubber market', *BRGA* 1, 1 (1919).

Dicken, Peter and Kirkpatrick, Colin, 'Services-led development in ASEAN: transnational regional headquarters in Singapore', *Pacific Review* 4, 2 (1991).

Disney, Richard and Ho Soo Kiang, 'Do real wages matter in an open economy? The case of Singapore 1966–1987', *Oxford Economic Papers* 42 (1990).

Dobby, E. H. G., 'Singapore: town and country', *Geographical Review* 30, 1 (1940).

Dornbusch, Rudiger and Park, Yung Chul, 'Korean growth policy', *Brookings Papers on Economic Activity* no. 2 (1987).

Drabble, J. H., 'Investment in the rubber industry in Malaya c.1900–1922', *JSEAS* 3, 2 (1972).

Drabble, J. H., 'Some thoughts on the economic development of Malaya under British administration', *JSEAS* 5, 2 (1974).

Drabble, J. H. and Drake, P. J., 'More on the financing of Malayan rubber, 1905–1923', *Economic History Review* 2nd ser. 27, 1 (1974).

Drabble, J. H. and Drake, P. J., 'The British agency houses in Malaysia: survival in a changing world', *JSEAS* 12, 2 (1981).

Drake, P. J., 'The new-issue boom in Malaya and Singapore 1961–1964', *EDCC* 18, 1 (1969).

Drake, P. J. 'Natural resources versus foreign borrowing in economic development', *Economic Journal* 82 (1972).

Drake, P. J., 'Southeast Asian monies and the problem of a common measure, with particular reference to the nineteenth century', *Australian Economic History Review* 31, 1 (1991).

Eastham, J. K., 'Rationalisation in the tin industry', *Review of Economic Studies* 4, 1 (1937).

'Edward Boustead and Company', *BRGA* 13, 4 (1931).

Elliott, T. H., 'Multinationals in developing countries', *Spectrum* (published by SEATO) 2, 1 (1973).

Ellis, Thomas Flower, 'A brief account of the Malay tin industry', *Proceedings of the Chemical and Metallurgical Society of South Africa* 2 (1897).

Fang Fu-an, 'Shanghai labour', *Chinese Economic Journal* 7, 2 (1930).

Farrer, R. J., 'The Municipality in my time', *One hundred years of progress, centenary number of the Singapore Free Press*, 8 Oct. 1935.

Fergusson, Sir Ewen, 'Singapore and tin: a unique system of purchasing ore', *Malaya* (March 1955).

Fisher, C. A., 'The railway geography of British Malaya', *Scottish Geographical Magazine* 64, 3 (1948).

Fishlow, Albert, 'Review of Handbook of development economics', *Journal of Economic Literature* 29, 4 (1991).

Fletcher, Max E., 'The Suez Canal and world shipping, 1869–1914', *Journal of Economic History* 18, 4 (1958).

Freedman, Maurice, 'Immigrants and associations: Chinese in nineteenth century Singapore', *Comparative Studies in Society and History* 3, 1 (1960).

Gamba, Charles, 'Poverty, and some socio-economic aspects of hoarding, saving and borrowing in Malaya', *MER* 3, 2 (1958).

Gamba, Charles, 'Chinese associations in Singapore', *JMBRAS* 39, 2 (1966).

Georgi, C. D. V., 'The Selangor bulk oil installation plant', *MAJ* 21, 11 (1933).

Goh Keng Swee, 'Entrepreneurship in a plural economy', *MER* 3, 1 (1958).

Goh Keng Swee, 'Management in the developing society', *MER* 8, 1 (1963).

Goh Keng Swee, 'Social, political and institutional aspects of development planning', *MER* 10, 1 (1965).

Greenberg, Michael, 'Malaya – Britain's dollar arsenal', *Amerasia* 5, 4 (1941).

Grist, D. H., 'The Malayan pineapple industry', *MAJ* 18, 4 (1930).

Grist, D. H., 'Cultivation of pineapples', *MAJ* 18, 5 (1930).

Gurley, John G. and Shaw, E. S., 'Financial structure in economic development', *EDCC* 15, 3 (1967).

'Guthrie & Company, Limited', *BRGA* 13, 1 (1931).

Harris, John R. and Todaro, Michael P., 'Migration, unemployment and development: a two-sector analysis', *American Economic Review* 60, 1 (1970).

Helleiner, G. K., 'Manufactured exports from less-developed countries and multinational firms', *Economic Journal* 83 (1973).

Hicks, Ursula K., 'The finance of the city state', *MER* 5, 2 (1960).

Hill, Hal and Pang Eng Fong, 'Technology exports from a small, very open NIC: the case of Singapore', *World Development* 19, 5 (1991).

Hirschman, Albert O., 'A generalized linkage approach to development, with special reference to staples', *EDCC* 25 supplement (1977).

Hirschman, Albert O., 'Linkages' in John Eatwell, Murray Milgate and Peter Newman, eds. *The new Palgrave: economic development* (London, 1989).

Ho, Samuel P. S., 'South Korea and Taiwan: development prospects and problems in the 1980s', *Asian Survey* 21, 12 (1981).

Hodder, B. W., 'Racial groupings in Singapore', *Malayan Journal of Tropical Geography* 1 (1953).

Hodjera, Zoran, 'The Asian currency market: Singapore as a regional financial centre', *IMF Staff Papers* 25, 2 (1978).

Horvat, Branko, 'The optimum rate of investment reconsidered', *Economic Journal* 75 (1965).

Hoselitz, Bert F., 'Urbanization and economic growth in Asia', *EDCC* 5 (1957).

Huff, W. G., 'Patterns in the economic development of Singapore', *Journal of Developing Areas* 21, 3 (1987).

Huff, W. G., 'Barter, money, credit and Singapore's international rice trade, 1870–1939', *Explorations in Economic History* 26, 2 (1989) and 'Editor's note' 27, 3 (1990).

Huff, W. G., 'Entrepreneurship and economic development in less developed countries', *Business History* 31, 4 (1989).

Huff, W. G., 'Sharecroppers, risk, management, and Chinese estate rubber development in inter-war British Malaya', *EDCC* 40, 4 (1992).

Huff, W. G., 'Capital markets, sharecropping and contestability: Singapore Chinese in the inter-war British Malayan estate rubber and pineapple industries' in Gareth Austin and Kaoru Sugihara, eds. *Local suppliers of credit in the third world* (London, 1993).

Huff, W. G., 'The development of the rubber market in pre-World War II Singapore', *JSEAS* 24, 2 (1993).

Hughes, Helen, 'Catching up: the Asian newly industrializing economies in the 1990s', *Asian Development Review* 7, 2 (1990).

Hughes, T. W. H., 'Notes on tin smelting in the Malay peninsula', *Records of the Geological Survey of India* 22, 4 (1899).

Islam, Iyanatul and Kirkpatrick, Colin, 'Export-led development, labour-market conditions and the distribution of income: the case of Singapore', *Cambridge Journal of Economics* 10 (1986).

Jao, Y. C., 'The rise of Hong Kong as a financial center', *Asian Survey* 19, 7 (1979).

Jao, Y. C., 'Hong Kong's future as a financial centre', *Three Banks Review* 145 (1985).

Kelley, Allen C., 'Economic consequences of population change in the third world', *Journal of Economic Literature* 26, 4 (1988).

King, A. W., 'Plantation and agriculture in Malaya, with notes on the trade of Singapore', *Geographical Journal* 93, 2 (1939).

Kirby, Captain S. W., 'Johore in 1926', *Geographical Journal* 71, 3 (1928).

Krause, Lawrence B., 'Hong Kong and Singapore: twins or kissing cousins?', *EDCC* 36, 3 supplement (1988).

Kravis, Irving B., 'Trade as a handmaiden of growth: similarities between the nineteenth and twentieth centuries', *Economic Journal* 80 (1970).

Krugman, Paul R., 'Developing countries in the world economy', *Daedalus* 118, 1 (1989).

Kuznets, S., 'Notes on the take-off' in W. W. Rostow, ed. *The economics of take-off into sustained growth* (London, 1963).

Lake, Harry, 'Johore', *Geographical Journal* 3, 3 (1894).

Lee, Jay, 'How MAS directs Singapore Inc.', *Euromoney* (Sept. 1984).

Lee Sheng-Yi, 'The development of commercial banking in Singapore and the states of Malaya', *MER* 11, 1 (1966).

Lee Sheng-Yi, 'The balance of payments of the states of Malaya and Singapore, 1947–1964', *Kajin Ekonomi Malaysia* 3, 2 (1966) and 4, 1 (1967).

Lee Sheng-Yi, 'Money, quasi-money and income velocity of circulation in Malaya and Singapore, 1947–1965', *EDCC* 19, 2 (1971).

Lee Sheng-Yi, 'Some basic problems of industrialisation in Singapore', *Journal of Developing Areas* 7, 2 (1973).

Lee Sheng-Yi, 'Public enterprise and economic development in Singapore', *MER* 21, 2 (1976).

Lee Sheng-Yi, 'Ownership and control of local banks', *Singapore Banking and Finance* (1980/81).

Lee Sheng-Yi, 'Some aspects of foreign exchange management in Singapore', *Asian Pacific Journal of Management* 1 (1984).

Lewis, W. Arthur, 'Economic development with unlimited supplies of labour', *Manchester School of Economic and Social Studies* 22, 2 (1954).

Lewis, W. Arthur, 'The dual economy revisited', *Manchester School of Economic and Social Studies* 47, 3 (1979).

Lewis, W. Arthur, 'The slowing down of the engine of growth', *American Economic Review* 70, 4 (1980).

Lewis, W. Arthur, 'The state of development theory', *American Economic Review* 74, 1 (1984).

Lewis, W. Arthur, 'Reflections on development' in Gustav Ranis and T. Paul Schultz, eds. *The state of development economics* (Oxford, 1988).

Lie Siao Sing and Hia Hwee Yong, Robert, 'Singapore trade statistics', *Singapore Statistical Bulletin* 4, 1 (1975).

Lim Chong Yah, 'Development economics by R. M. Sundrum: a review article', *MER* 28, 1 (1983).

Lim Chong Yah, 'Trade in manufactures: a Singapore perspective', *Southeast Asian Studies* 25, 3 (1987).

Lim, Linda, 'Singapore's success: the myth of the free market economy', *Asian Survey* 23, 6 (1983).

Lim, Linda, 'Singapore in Southeast Asia', *Journal of Southeast Asian Business* 6, 4 (1990).

Lim Mah Hui and Teoh Kit Fong, 'Singapore corporations go transnational', *JSEAS* 17, 2 (1986).

Louis, Henry, 'The production of tin', *Mining Journal, Railway and Commercial Gazette* 69 (10 June 1899).

Low, Linda, 'The financing process in the public sector in Singapore', *Bulletin for International Fiscal Documentation* 39, 4 (1985).

Macfadyen, Sir Eric, 'Managing agents in the eastern plantation industry', *Tropical Agriculture* 31 (1954).

McHale, T. R., 'Changing technology and shifts in supply and demand for rubber: an analytical history', *MER* 9, 2 (1964).

Mackie, J. A. C., 'The Indonesian economy: 1950–1963', *Schriften des Instituts für Asienkunde Frankfurt* 16 (1964).

McKillop, John and Ellis, Thomas Flower, 'Tin smelting at Pulau Brani, Singapore', *Proceedings of the Institution of Civil Engineers* 125, 3 (1896).

Milsum, J. N., 'Pepper in Malaya', *MAJ* 18, 6 (1930).

Murphey, Rhoads, 'New capitals of Asia', *EDCC* 5, 3 (1957).

Murphey, Rhoads, 'Colonialism in Asia and the role of port cities', *East Lakes Geographer* 5 (1969).

Myint, Hla, 'The "classical theory" of international trade and the underdeveloped countries', *Economic Journal* 68 (1958).

Myint, Hla, 'Adam Smith's theory of international trade in the perspective of economic development', *Economica* 44 (1977).

Myint, Hla, 'Inward and outward-looking countries revisited: the case of Indonesia', *BIES* 20, 2 (1984).

Nathan, J. E., 'Changes in the flow of trade', *Manchester Guardian Commercial*, special section on British Malaya, 19 Feb. 1925.

Naw Mee-Kau and Chan Chan-leong, 'Structure and development strategies of the manufacturing industries in Singapore and Hong Kong', *Asian Survey* 22, 5 (1982).

North, Douglass C., 'Location theory and regional economic growth', *Journal of Political Economy* 63, 3 (1955).

Nurkse, Ragnar, 'International investment to-day in the light of nineteenth-century experience', *Economic Journal* 64 (1954).

Nurkse, Ragnar, 'International trade theory and development policy' in Howard S. Ellis, ed. *Economic development for Latin America* (London, 1961).

'Overseas Chinese remittances to China', *Far Eastern Economic Review*, 17 March 1948.

Owen, Norman G., 'The rice industry of mainland Southeast Asia, 1850–1914', *Journal of the Siam Society* 59 (1971).

Pasqual, J. C., 'Chinese tin mining in Selangor', *Selangor Journal* 4 (1895).

Pang Eng Fong, 'Economic development and the labor market in a newly industrializing country: the experience of Singapore', *Developing Economies* 19, 1 (1981).

Pang Eng Fong and Lim, Linda, 'Foreign labour and economic development in Singapore', *International Migration Review* 16, 3 (1982).

Platteau, Jean-Philippe and Abraham, Anita, 'An inquiry into quasi-credit contracts: the role of reciprocal credit and interlinked deals in small-scale fishing communities', *Journal of Development Studies* 23, 4 (1987).

Pugh, Cedric, 'Housing and development in Singapore', *Contemporary Southeast Asia* 6, 4 (1985).

Raffles, Sir T. S., 'The founding of Singapore', *JMBRAS* 42, 1 (1969).

Ranis, Gustav, 'Industrial sector labour absorption', *EDCC* 21, 3 (1973).

Ranis, Gustav, 'Analytics of development: dualism' in H. Chenery and T. N. Srinivasan, *Handbook of development economics* I (Amsterdam, 1988).

Ranis, Gustav, 'Labour surplus economies' in John Eatwell, Murray Milgate and Peter Newman, eds. *The new Palgrave: economic development* (London, 1989).

Ranis, Gustav, 'The role of institutions in transitional growth: the East Asian newly industrializing countries', *World Development* 17, 9 (1989).

Ranis, Gustav and Fei, John C. H., 'A theory of economic development', *American Economic Review* 51, 4 (1961).

Ray, G. F., 'The economy of Asian spices', *MER* 8, 1 (1963).

Reynolds, Lloyd G., 'Economic development in historical perspective', *American Economic Review* 70, 2 (1980).

Reynolds, Lloyd G., 'Inter-country diffusion of economic growth, 1870–1914' in Mark Gersovitz, et al., eds. *The theory and experience of economic development* (London, 1982).

Reynolds, Lloyd G., 'The spread of economic growth to the third world', *Journal of Economic Literature* 21, 3 (1983).

Richter, H. V., 'Indonesia's share in the entrepot trade of the states of Malaya and Singapore prior to Confrontation', *MER* 11, 2 (1966).

Richter, H. V., 'Problems of assessing unrecorded trade', *BIES* 6, 1 (1970).

Riedel, James, 'Trade as the engine of growth in developing countries, revisited', *Economic Journal* 94 (1984).

Roemer, Michael, 'Resource-based industrialization in the developing countries', *Journal of Development Economics* 6 (1979).

Rosenstein-Rodan, P. N., 'Problems of industrialisation of eastern and south-eastern Europe', *Economic Journal* 53 (1943).

Rostow, W. W., 'Leading sectors and the take-off' in W. W. Rostow, ed. *The economics of take-off into sustained growth* (London, 1963).

'S', 'A planting pioneer', *BRGA* 10, 9 (1928).

Sanders, J. O., 'The Malayan railway', *Malaya* (Sept. 1952).

Sandilands, Roger J., 'Savings, investment and housing in Singapore's growth, 1965–90', *Savings and Development* 16, 2 (1992).

Sandilands, Roger J. and Tan Ling-Hui, 'Comparative advantage in a re-export economy', *Singapore Economic Review* 31, 2 (1986).

Saul, S. B., 'The economic significance of "constructive imperialism"', *Journal of Economic History* 18, 2 (1957).

Scitovsky, Tibor, 'Economic development in Taiwan and South Korea: 1965–81', *Food Research Institute Studies* 19, 3 (1985).

Seow, Greg F. H., 'The service sector in Singapore's economy: performance and structure', *MER* 24, 2 (1979).

Sen, Armartya, 'On optimising the rate of savings', *Economic Journal* 71 (1961).

Sen, Armartya, 'Development: which way now?' *Economic Journal* 93 (1983).

Sharpston, Michael, 'International sub-contracting', *Oxford Economic Papers* 27, 1 (1975).

Shell Co. Ltd., 'Shell in Singapore and Borneo', *Malaya* (Aug. 1955).

Short, Brock K., 'Indigenous banking in an early period of development: the Straits Settlements, 1914–1940', *MER* 16, 1 (1971).

Silcock, Thomas H., 'Some problems of economic growth in the British territories in Southeast Asia', *Weltwirtschaftliches Archiv* 80, 2 (1958).

Simkin, C. G. F., 'Indonesia's unrecorded trade', *BIES* 6, 1 (1970).

Simkin, Colin, 'Does money matter in Singapore?', *Singapore Economic Review* 29, 1 (1984).

'Singapore harbour and dock works', *Engineering*, issues of 29 Nov., 13 Dec. and 20 Dec. 1918.

Singh, Bhupinder, 'Post-war Japanese competition in Malaya', *MER* 1, 1 (1956).

Stern, Geoffrey, 'The Geoffrey Stern interview: Lee Kuan Yew', *LSE Magazine* 2, 4 (Winter 1990/91).

Stern, N., 'The economics of development: a survey', *Economic Journal* 99 (1989).

Stifel, Laurence, D., 'The growth of the rubber economy of southern Thailand', *JSEAS* 4, 1 (1973).

Stillson, Richard T., 'The financing of Malayan rubber, 1905–1923', *Economic History Review* 2nd ser. 24, 4 (1971).

'The story of the Straits Steamship Co.', *British Malaya* (May 1927).

Summers, Robert and Heston, Alan, 'The Penn world table (mark 5): an expanded set of international comparisons, 1950–1988', *Quarterly Journal of Economics* 106, 2 (1991).

Tan Ee Leong, 'Dr Lee Kong Chian (1893–1967)', *Annual of the China Society of Singapore* (1964–1967).

Tan Guan Aik, 'Barter fulfils needs of trading', *Singapore Trade* (May 1962).

Tan Tek Soon, 'Chinese local trade', *Straits Chinese Magazine* 6, 23 (1902).

Todaro, Michael P., 'Internal migration and urban unemployment: comment', *American Economic Review* 76, 3 (1986).

Tregonning, K. G., 'Tan Cheng Lock: a Malayan nationalist', *JSEAS* 10, 1 (1979).

Trimmer, G. W. A., 'Singapore port problems', *Straits Budget*, 17 Oct. 1929.

Tsao, Y., 'Growth without productivity: Singapore manufacturing in the 1970s', *Journal of Development Economics* 18, 1/2 (1985).

Turnbull, C. M., 'The Johore gambier and pepper trade in the mid-nineteenth century', *Journal of the South Seas Society* 15, 1 (1959).

Turnbull, C. M., 'British planning for post-war Malaya', *JSEAS* 5, 2 (1974).

Turnbull, C. M., 'The post-war decade in Malaya: the settling dust of political controversy' *JMBRAS* 60 (1987).

Vlieland, C. A., 'The population of the Malay peninsula: a study in human migration', *Geographical Review* 24, 1 (1934).

Vlieland, C. A., 'The 1947 census of Malaya', *Pacific Affairs* 22, 1 (1949).

Vredenbregt, Jacob, 'The Haddj', *Bijdragen Tot de Taal-, Land-, en Volkenkunde* 118, 1 (1962).

Vredenbregt, Jacob, 'Bawean migrations', *Bijdragen Tot de Taal-, Land-, en Volkenkunde* 120, 1 (1964).

Wade, Robert, 'Dirigisme Taiwan-style', *Institute of Development Studies Bulletin* 15, 2 (1984).

Walters, Alan, 'Currency boards' in John Eatwell, Murray Milgate and Peter Newman, eds., *The new Palgrave: money* (London, 1989).

Wardlaw, Henry, 'Planning in Singapore', *Royal Australian Planning Institute Journal* (April 1971).

Warren, Jim, 'The Singapore rickshaw pullers: the social organization of a coolie occupation, 1880–1940', *JSEAS* 16, 1 (1985).

Watkins, Melville H., 'A staple theory of economic growth', *Canadian Journal of Economics and Political Science* 29, 2 (1963).

Westphal, Larry E., 'Industrial policy in an export-propelled economy: lessons from South Korean experience', *Journal of Economic Perspectives* 4, 3 (1990).

White, Lawrence, 'Indonesia's unrecorded trade – a comment', *BIES* 6, 2 (1970).

Wilkinson, Barry and Legett, Chris, 'The management of compliance', *Euro-Asia Business Review* 4, 3 (1985).

Williamson, Jeffrey G., 'Comments on "Reflections on development"' in Gustav Ranis and T. Paul Schultz, eds. *The state of development economics* (Oxford, 1988).

Williamson, Jeffrey G., 'Migration and urbanization' in H. Chenery and T. N. Srinivasan, eds. *Handbook of development economics* I (1988).

Wong Lin Ken, 'The trade of Singapore, 1819–1869', *JMBRAS* 33, 4 (1960).

Wong Lin Ken, 'Singapore: its growth as an entrepot port, 1819–1941', *JSEAS* 9, 1 (1978).

Woodruff, William, 'Growth of the rubber industry of Great Britain and the United States', *Journal of Economic History* 15, 4 (1955).

Wurtzburg, C. E., 'Singapore Straits Steamship Company Ltd.', *British Malaya* (Nov. 1946).

Yen Ching-Hwang, 'The overseas Chinese and late Ch'ing economic modernization', *Modern Asian Studies* 16, 2 (1982).

Yong, C. F., 'A preliminary study of Chinese leadership in Singapore, 1900–1941', *JSEAH* 9, 2 (1968).

Yong, C. F., 'Emergence of Chinese community leaders in Singapore, 1890–1941', *Journal of the South Seas Society* 30, 1 and 2 (1975).

Yong, C. F., 'Leadership and power in the Chinese community of Singapore during the 1930s', *JSEAS* 8, 2 (1977).

Yong, C. F., 'British attitudes toward the Chinese community leaders in Singapore, 1819–1941', *Journal of the South Seas Society* 40, 1 and 2 (1985).

Yotopoulos, Pan A. and Floro, Sagrario L., 'Income distribution, transaction costs and market fragmentation in informal credit markets', *Cambridge Journal of Economics* 16, 3 (1992).

Yuen Choy Leng, 'The Japanese community in Malaya before the Pacific war: its genesis and growth', *JSEAS* 9, 2 (1978).

You Poh Seng, 'The housing survey of Singapore 1955', *MER* 2, 1 (1957).

You Poh Seng and Yeh, Stephen H. K., 'The sample household survey of Singapore, 1966', *MER* 12, 1 (1967).

Young, Alwyn, 'A tale of two cities: factor accumulation and technical change in Hong Kong and Singapore', *NBER Macroeconomics Annual 1992* 7 (1992).

BOOKS

Allen, G. C. and Donnithorne, Audrey G., *Western enterprise in Indonesia and Malaya* (London, 1954).

Amjad, Rashid, *The development of labour-intensive industry in ASEAN countries* (Geneva: ILO, 1981).

Amsden, Alice H., *Asia's next giant: South Korea and late industrialization* (New York, 1989).

Andrews, James M., *Siam, second rural economic survey* (Bangkok, 1935).

Anthonisz, J. O., *Currency reform in the Straits Settlements* (London, c.1915).

Arasaratnam, Sinnappah, *Indians in Malaysia and Singapore* (Bombay, 1970).

Arasaratnam, Sinnappah, *Pre-modern commerce and society in southern Asia* (Kuala Lumpur, 1972).

Archives & Oral History Department, Singapore, *Pioneers of Singapore: a catalogue of oral history interviews* (Singapore, 1984).

Arndt, H. W., *Economic development: the history of an idea* (Chicago, 1987).

Asher, Mukul G., *Forced savings to finance merit goods: an economic analysis of the Central Provident Fund scheme of Singapore* (Canberra: Australian National University Centre for Research on Federal Financial Relations, occasional paper 36, 1985).

Asher, Mukul G., ed. *Fiscal systems and practices in ASEAN* (Singapore, 1989).

Asher, Mukul G. and Osborne, Susan, eds. *Issues in public finance in Singapore* (Singapore, 1980).

Babcock, Glen D., *History of the United States Rubber Company* (Muncie, IN, 1966).

Barlow, Colin, *The natural rubber industry* (Kuala Lumpur, 1978).

Basu, Kaushik, *The less developed economy* (Oxford, 1984).

Bauer, P. T., *The rubber industry* (London, 1948).

Bauer, P. T., *West African trade* (London, 1954).

Bellow, Walden and Rosenfeld, Stephanie, *Dragons in distress: Asia's miracle economies in crisis* (San Francisco, 1990).

Bellows, Thomas J., *The People's Action Party of Singapore: emergence of a dominant party system* (New Haven, 1970).

Benham, Frederic, *The national income of Singapore 1956* (London, 1959).

Bird, Isabella L., *The golden chersonese and the way thither* (Kuala Lumpur, 1967).

Birnberg, Thomas B. and Resnick, Stephen A., *Colonial development: an econometric study* (New Haven, 1975).

Boeke, J. H., *The structure of the Netherlands Indian economy* (New York, 1942).

Boeke, J. H., *Economics and economic policy of dual societies* (Haarlem, 1953).

de Boer, M. G. and Westermann, J. C., *Een Halve Eeuw Paketvaart, 1891–1941* (Amsterdam, 1941).

Bogaars, George, *The Tanjong Pagar Dock Company, 1864–1905* (Singapore, 1956).

Booth, Anne, O'Malley, W. J. and Weidmann, Anna, eds. *Indonesian economic history in the Dutch colonial era* (New Haven, 1990).

Braddell, Roland, *The lights of Singapore* (London, 1934).

Bradford, Colin I. and Branson, William H., eds. *Trade and structural change in Pacific Asia* (Chicago, 1987).

Broek, Jan O. M., *Economic development of the Netherlands Indies* (New York, 1942).

Bruton, Henry J., et al., *Sri Lanka and Malaysia* (New York, 1992).

Buchanan, Iain, *Singapore in Southeast Asia* (London, 1972).

Butcher, John G., *The British in Malaya, 1880–1941* (Kuala Lumpur, 1979).

Cameron, John, *Our tropical possessions in Malayan India* (Kuala Lumpur, 1965).

Cator, W. J., *The economic position of the Chinese in the Netherlands Indies* (Oxford, 1936).

Caves, Richard E. and Jones, Ronald W., *World trade and payments* 4th edn (Boston, 1985).

Central Provident Fund Study Group, report in a special issue of the *Singapore Economic Review* 31, 1 (1986).

Chan Heng Chee, *A sensation of independence: a political biography of David Marshall* (Singapore, 1984).

Ch'en, Jerome and Tarling, Nicholas, eds. *Studies in the social history of China and South-East Asia* (London, 1970).

Chen, Peter S. J., ed. *Singapore development policies and trends* (Singapore, 1983).

Chen, Peter S. J. and Evers, Hans-Dieter, *Studies in ASEAN sociology* (Singapore, 1978).

Chen Ta, *Emigrant communities in south China: a study of overseas migration and its influence on standards of living and social change* (London, 1939).

Chen Yu-Kwei, *Foreign trade and industrial development in China* (Washington, DC, 1956).

Cheng Siok-Hwa, *The rice industry of Burma, 1852–1940* (Kuala Lumpur, 1968).

Chew, Ernest C. T. and Lee, Edwin, eds. *A history of Singapore* (Singapore, 1991).

Chiang Hai Ding, *A history of Straits Settlements foreign trade, 1870–1915* (Singapore, 1978).

Chin Kee Onn, *Malaya upside down* (Singapore, 1946).

The China Navigation Company, 1872–1957 (a short history reprinted from the *Blue Funnel Bulletin* of Jan. 1958).

Chng Meng Kng, Low, Linda and Toh Mun Heng, *Industrial restructuring in Singapore* (Singapore, 1988).

Christian, John L., *Burma* (London, 1945).

Clarke, Roger and McGuinness, Tony, eds. *The economics of the firm* (Oxford, 1987).

Coble, Parks M., *The Shanghai capitalists and the nationalist government, 1927–1937* (Cambridge, MA, 1980).

Collis, Maurice, *Wayfoong: the Hong Kong and Shanghai Banking Corporation* (London, 1965).

Cook, Paul and Kirkpatrick, Colin, eds. *Privatisation in less developed countries* (Brighton, 1988).

Corbo, Vittorio, et al., *Export-oriented development strategies* (Boulder, CO, 1985).

Cowan, C. D., ed. *The economic development of South-East Asia* (London, 1964).

Cunyngham-Brown, Sjovald, *The traders* (London, 1971).

Dharmasena, K., *The port of Colombo, 1860–1939* (Colombo, 1980).

Djamour, Judith, *Malay kinship and marriage in Singapore* (London, 1959).

Dobby, E. H. G., *Monsoon Asia* (London, 1961).

Doshi, Tilak, *Houston of Asia: the Singapore petroleum industry* (Singapore, 1989).

Doyle, Patrick, *Tin mining in Larut* (London, 1879).

Drabble, J. H., *Rubber in Malaya, 1876–1922* (Kuala Lumpur, 1973).

Drabble, J. H., *Malayan rubber: the interwar years* (London, 1991).

Elliott, Alan J. A., *Chinese spirit-medium cults in Singapore* (London, 1955).

Emerson, Rupert, *From empire to nation* (Boston, 1962).

Emerson, Rupert, *Malaysia: a study in direct and indirect rule* (Kuala Lumpur, 1964).

Ferris, George M., *A study of the securities market in Singapore and Malaysia* (Singapore, 1970).

Furnivall, J. S., *Netherlands India: a study of plural economy* (Cambridge, 1939).

Furnivall, J. S., et al., *Netherlands East Indies* II (London: Naval Intelligence Division, Geographical Handbook Series, 1944).

Galbraith, John Kenneth, *The nature of mass poverty* (Cambridge, MA, 1979).

Galenson, Walter, ed. *Foreign trade and investment: economic development in the newly industrializing Asian countries* (Madison, WI, 1985).

van Gelderen, J., *The recent development of economic foreign policy in the Netherlands East Indies* (London, 1939).

George, F. J., *The Singapore saga* (Singapore, 1985).

Gilmour, Andrew, *My role in the rehabilitation of Singapore: 1946–1953* (Singapore, 1973).

Godley, Michael R., *The mandarin-capitalists from Nanyang: overseas Chinese enterprise in the modernization of China, 1893–1911* (Cambridge, 1981).

Goh Keng Swee, *The economics of modernization* (Singapore, 1972).

Goh Keng Swee, *The practice of economic growth* (Singapore, 1977).

Gopalakrishnan, V. and Perera, Ananda, eds. *Singapore changing landscapes* (Singapore, 1983).

Guillemard, Sir Laurence, *Trivial fond records* (London, 1937).

Gullick, John, *Malaysia: economic expansion and national unity* (London, 1981).

Haberler, Gottfried, *International trade and economic development* (Cairo, 1959).

Haberler, Gottfried, *A survey of international trade theory* (Princeton, 1961).

Harrisons & Crossfield, *One hundred years as East India merchants, 1844–1943* (London, 1944).

Helfferich, Emil, *Behn, Meyer & Co. – Arnold Otto Meyer*. Two vols. (Hamburg, 1983).

Hicks, John, *A theory of economic history* (London, 1969).

Highlands and Lowlands Para Rubber Company Ltd., 50th anniversary history of the company, 1906–1956 (London, 1956).

Hilgerdt, Folke, *Industrialization and foreign trade* (Geneva: League of Nations, 1945).

Hirschman, Albert O., *The strategy of economic development* (New Haven, 1958).

Ho, Samuel P. S., *Economic development of Taiwan, 1860–1970* (New Haven, 1978).

Hoffman, Ross J. S., *Great Britain and the German trade rivalry, 1875–1914* (Philadelphia, 1933).

Holland, W. L., ed. *Commodity control in the Pacific area* (London, 1935).

Hong, Wontack and Krause, Lawrence B., eds. *Trade and growth of the advanced developing countries in the Pacific basin* (Seoul, 1981).

Honig, Pieter and Verdoorn, Frans, eds. *Science and scientists in the Netherlands Indies* (New York, 1945).

Hoover, Calvin B., *Economic systems of the Commonwealth* (Durham, NC, 1962).

Hughes, Helen and You Poh-Seng, eds. *Foreign investment and industrialisation in Singapore* (Canberra, 1969).

Hughes, Helen, ed. *Achieving industrialization in East Asia* (New York, 1988).

Hyde, Francis, E., *Blue funnel: a history of Alfred Holt and Company of Liverpool from 1865 to 1914* (Liverpool, 1956).

Hyde, Francis E., *Far Eastern trade, 1860–1914* (London, 1973).

Ingram, James C., *Economic change in Thailand, 1850–1970* 2nd edn (Stanford, 1971).

Jackson, A. and Wurtzburg, C. E., *The history of Mansfield & Company, part I, 1868–1924* (Singapore, 1952).

Jackson, James C., *Planters and speculators: Chinese and European agricultural enterprise in Malaya, 1786–1921* (Kuala Lumpur, 1968).

Jackson, R. N., *Immigrant labour and the development of Malaya, 1786–1920* (Kuala Lumpur, 1961).

Jamaluddin, Mon bin, *A history of Port Swettenham* (Singapore, 1963).

Jayakumar, S., ed. *Our heritage and beyond: a collection of essays on Singapore, its past, present and future* (Singapore, 1982).

Jennings, Eric, *Wheels of progress: 75 years of Cycle and Carriage* (Singapore, 1975).

Jones, Leroy P. and SaKong, Il, *Government, business, and entrepreneurship in economic development: the Korean case* (Cambridge, MA, 1980).

Josey, Alex, *Trade unionism in Malaya* (Singapore, 1958).

Jumabhoy, R., *Multiracial Singapore* (Singapore, 1970).

Khoo Kay Kim, *The western Malay states, 1850–1873* (Kuala Lumpur, 1972).

van Klaveren, J. J., *The Dutch colonial system in the East Indies* (Rotterdam, 1953).

Knowles, L. C. A., *The economic development of the British overseas empire* (London, 1924).

Korthals Altes, W. L., *General trade statistics 1822–1940*, published as vol.12a *Changing economy in Indonesia* (The Hague, 1991).

Krause, Lawrence B., Koh Ai Tee and Lee (Tsao) Yuan, *The Singapore economy reconsidered* (Singapore, 1987).

Krishnan, R. B., *Indians in Malaya* (Singapore, 1936).

van Laanen, J. T. M., *Money and banking, 1816–1940*, published as vol. 6 *Changing economy in Indonesia* (The Hague, 1980).

Landon, Kenneth P., *The Chinese in Thailand* (New York, 1941).

League of Nations, *Economic stability in the post-war world: the conditions of prosperity after the transition from war to peace* (Geneva, 1945).

Lee, Eddy, ed. *Export-led industrialisation and development* (Geneva: ILO, 1981).

Lee Khoon Choy, *On the beat to the hustings: an autobiography* (Singapore, 1988).

Lee Poh Ping, *Chinese society in nineteenth century Singapore* (Kuala Lumpur, 1978).

Lee Sheng-Yi, *Monetary and banking development of Malaysia and Singapore* (Singapore, 1st edn 1974; 3rd edn 1990).

Lee Soo Ann, *Industrialization in Singapore* (Melbourne, 1973).

Lee Soo Ann, *Economic growth and the public sector in Malaya and Singapore, 1948–1960* (Singapore, 1974).

Lee Soo Ann, *Singapore goes transnational* (Singapore, 1977).

Leinbach, Thomas R. and Chia Lin Sien, *South-East Asian transport* (Singapore, 1989).

Lewis, W. Arthur, *Economic survey 1919–1939* (London, 1949).

Lewis, W. Arthur, *Development planning* (London, 1966).

Lewis, W. Arthur, *The evolution of the international economic order* (Princeton, 1978).

Lewis, W. Arthur, *Growth and fluctuations 1870–1913* (London, 1978).

Lewis, W. Arthur, ed. *Tropical development 1880–1913* (London, 1970).

Lim Chong Yah, *Economic development of modern Malaya* (Kuala Lumpur, 1967).

Lim Chong Yah, *Economic development in Singapore* (Singapore, 1980).

Lim Chong Yah and Lloyd, Peter J., eds. *Singapore: resources and growth* (Singapore, 1986).

Lim Chong Yah and associates, *Policy options for the Singapore economy* (Singapore, 1988).

Lim, Linda and Gosling, Peter L. A., *The Chinese in Southeast Asia*. Two vols. (Singapore, 1983).

Lim, Linda and Pang Eng Fong, *Trade, employment and industrialisation in Singapore* (Geneva: ILO, 1986).

Lim, Linda and Pang Eng Fong, *Foreign direct investment and industrialisation in Malaysia, Singapore, Taiwan and Thailand* (Paris: OECD, 1991).

Lister, Martin, *Mining laws and customs in the Malay peninsula* (Singapore, 1899).

Little, Ian M. D., *Economic development* (New York, 1982).

Lock, C. G. Wardford, *Economic mining* (London, 1895).

Lock, C. G. Wardford, *Mining in Malaya for gold and tin* (London, 1907).

Lockhart, R. H. Bruce, *Return to Malaya* (London, 1936).

Louis, Henry, *Metallurgy of tin* (New York, 1911).

Low, N. I., *Chinese jetsam on a tropic shore* (Singapore, 1974).

McFadyean, Sir Andrew, *The history of rubber regulation, 1934–1943* (London, 1944).

McGee, T. G., *The Southeast Asian city* (London, 1976).

McIntyre, W. David, *The rise and fall of the Singapore naval base, 1919–1942* (London, 1979).

Mackenzie, Compton, *Realms of silver: one hundred years of banking in the East* (London, 1954).

McKern, Bruce and Koomsup, Praipol, eds. *Minerals processing in the industrialisation of ASEAN and Australia* (Sydney, 1988).

McLellan, A., *The history of Mansfield & Company, part II, 1920–1953* (Singapore, 1953).

Macmillan, Allister, *Seaports of the Far East* 2nd edn (London, 1925).

Makepeace, Walter, Brooke, Gilbert E. and Braddell, Roland St. J., eds. *One hundred years of Singapore*. Two vols. (London, 1921).

Mansvelt, W. M. F., *Rice prices* (re-edited and continued by P.Creutzberg as vol. 4 *Changing economy in Indonesia*) (The Hague, 1978).

Marriner, Sheila and Hyde, Francis, *The senior John Samuel Swire, 1825–98: management in Far Eastern shipping trades* (Liverpool, 1967).

Mason, E. S., et al., *The economic and social modernization of the Republic of Korea* (Cambridge, MA, 1980).

Meek, John Paul, *Malaya: a study of governmental response to the Korean boom* (Ithaca: Cornell Southeast Asia Program data paper 17, 1955).

Meier, Gerald M., *Leading issues in economic development* 5th edn (New York, 1989).

Meier, Gerald M. and Seers, Dudley, eds. *Pioneers in development* (New York, 1984).

Mills, Lennox A., *British rule in eastern Asia* (London, 1942).

Mills, Lennox A., *Southeast Asia: illusion and reality in politics and economics* (Minneapolis, MN, 1964).

Minchinton, W. E., *The British tinplate industry* (London, 1957).

Mitchell, B. R. and Deane, Phyllis, *Abstract of British historical statistics* (Cambridge, 1971).

Mitchell, B. R. and Jones, H. G., *Second abstract of British historical statistics* (Cambridge, 1971).

Mitsubishi Economic Research Bureau, *Japanese trade and industry* (London, 1936).

Monetary Authority of Singapore, ed. *Papers on monetary economics* (Singapore, 1981).

Morgan, Theodore and Spoelstra, Nyle, eds. *Economic interdependence in Southeast Asia* (Madison, WI, 1969).

Myrdal, Gunnar, *The challenge of world poverty* (Harmondsworth, Mddx., 1971).

Nurkse, Ragnar, *Patterns of trade and development* (Stockholm, 1959).

Ooi Jin-Bee, *Land, people and economy in Malaya* (London, 1963).

Oshima, Harry T., *Economic growth in monsoon Asia* (Tokyo, 1987).

Overseas Union Bank, *25th anniversary, 1949–1974* (Singapore, 1974).

Pahang Consolidated Company, *Sixty years of tin mining: a history of the Pahang Consolidated Company, 1906–1966* (London, 1966).

Pang Eng Fong, *Education, manpower and economic development in Singapore* (Singapore, 1983).

Pang Eng Fong and Lim, Linda, *The electronics industry in Singapore* (Singapore, 1977).

Parmer, J. N., *Colonial labor policy and administration* (Locust Valley, NY, 1960).

Peet, G. L., *Political questions of Malaya* (Cambridge, 1949).

People's Action Party, *The tasks ahead: PAP's five year plan 1959–1964.* Two parts. (Singapore, 1959).

People's Action Party, *People's Action Party, 1954–1979* (Singapore, 1979).

Perkins, Dwight H., *China: Asia's next economic giant?* (Seattle, 1986).

Pillai, P. P., ed. *Labour in South East Asia* (New Delhi, 1947).

Port of Singapore Authority, *Anticipation of future needs* (Singapore, 1965).

Port of Singapore Authority, *A review of the past and a look into the future: 1961–1970 and 1970–1980* (Singapore, 1970).

Port of Singapore Authority, *The port of Singapore* (Singapore, c.1974).

Port of Singapore Authority, *Singapore: portrait of a port* (Singapore, 1984).

Port of Singapore Authority, *25th anniversary, 1964–1989* (Singapore, 1989).

Purcell, Victor, *Malaya: communist or free?* (London, 1954).

Purcell, Victor, *The memoirs of a Malayan official* (London, 1965).

Purcell, Victor, *The Chinese in Malaya* (Kuala Lumpur, 1967).

Puthucheary, J. J., *Ownership and control in the Malayan economy* (Singapore, 1960).

Quah, Jon S. T., Chan Heng Chee and Seah Chee Meow, eds. *Government and politics of Singapore* revised edn (Singapore, 1987).

Radius, Walter A., *United States shipping in transpacific trade, 1922–1938* (Stanford, 1944).

Raffles, Lady, *Memoir of the life and public services of Sir Thomas Stamford Raffles* (London, 1830).

Rees, Graham L., *Britain's commodity markets* (London, 1972).

Regnier, Philippe, *Singapore: city state in South-East Asia* (Honolulu, 1991).

Reith, G. M., *Handbook to Singapore* 2nd edn (Singapore, 1907).

Remer, C. F., *Foreign investments in China* (New York, 1933).

Robequain, Charles, *The economic development of French Indo-China* (London, 1944).

Rodan, Garry, *The political economy of Singapore's industrialization* (London, 1989).

Roff, W. R., *The origins of Malay nationalism* (Kuala Lumpur, 1967).

Rowe, J. W. F., *Studies in the artificial control of raw material supplies no.2* (London: London and Cambridge Economic Service, 1931).

Royal Dutch Petroleum Company, *Diamond jubilee book, 1890–1950* (The Hague, 1950).

Rubber Association of Singapore Seminar, *The marketing of natural rubber* (Singapore, 1974).

Sampson, Anthony, *The seven sisters* (London, 1976).

Sandhu, K. M., *Indians in Malaya: some aspects of their immigration and settlement, 1786–1957* (London, 1969).

Saravanamutu, Manicasothy, *The sara saga* (Penang, 1970).

Sayers, R. S., ed. *Banking in the British Commonwealth* (London, 1952).

Scalapino, Robert A., *The politics of development: perspectives on twentieth-century Asia* (Cambridge, MA, 1989).

Scherer, F. M. and Ross, David, *Industrial market structure and economic performance* 3rd edn (Boston, 1990).

Sharma, Shankar, *Role of the petroleum industry in Singapore's economy* (Singapore, 1989).

Shome, Parthasarathi, *Fiscal issues in South-East Asia* (Singapore, 1986).

Silcock, T. H., *The Commonwealth economy in Southeast Asia* (Durham, NC, 1959).

Silcock, T. H., *The economy of Malaya* (Singapore, 1966).

Silcock, T. H., *A history of economics teaching and graduates: Raffles College and the University of Malaya in Singapore 1934–1960* (Singapore, 1985).

Silcock, T. H., ed. *Readings in Malayan economics* (Singapore, 1961).

Silcock, T. H. and Fisk, E. K., eds. *The political economy of independent Malaya* (Canberra, 1963).

Sim, Victor, *Biographies of prominent Chinese in Singapore* (Singapore, 1950).

Singam, S. Durai Raja, *A hundred years of Ceylonese in Malaysia and Singapore (1867–1967)* (Petaling Jaya, Malaysia, 1967).

Singapore port and shipping handbook 1989 (Victoria, Australia: Charter Publications, 1988).

Skinner, G. William, *Chinese society in Thailand: an analytical history* (Ithaca, 1957).

Soliva, R., *An economic view of rubber planting* (Singapore, 1931).

Song Ong Siang, *One hundred years' history of the Chinese in Singapore* (London, 1923).

Stahl, Kathleen M., *The metropolitan organization of British colonial trade* (London, 1951).

Stockwell, A. J., *British policy and Malay politics during the Malayan Union experiment, 1942–1948* (Kuala Lumpur, 1979).

Straits Trading Company, *Straits refined tin* (Singapore, 1924).

Szezepanik, E., *The economic growth of Hong Kong* (London, 1957).

Tan, Augustine H. H. and Kapur, Basant, eds. *Pacific growth and financial interdependence* (Sydney, 1986).

Tan Chwee Huat, *Financial markets and institutions in Singapore* 6th edn (Singapore 1989).

Tan Kah Kee, *My autobiography* (text in Chinese) (Singapore, 1946).

Tregonning, K. G., *The Singapore Cold Storage, 1903–1966* (Singapore, n.d.).

Tregonning, K. G., *Home port Singapore: a history of the Straits Steamship Company Limited, 1890–1965* (Singapore, 1967).

Tregonning, K. G., ed. *Papers on Malayan history* (Singapore, 1962).

Tun Wai, U, *Burma's currency and credit* (Bombay, 1962).

Turnbull, C. M., *The Straits Settlements 1826–67: Indian presidency to crown colony* (London, 1972).

Turnbull, C. M., *A history of Singapore, 1819–1975* (Kuala Lumpur, 1977), and 2nd edn *A history of Singapore, 1819–1988* (Singapore, 1989).

United Engineers, *Progress* (n.d.).

United Overseas Bank, *Growing with Singapore: 50 years 1935–1985* (Singapore, 1985).

Vaughan, J. D., *The manners and customs of the Chinese of the Straits Settlements* (Singapore, 1879).

Vogel, Ezra F., *The four little dragons: the spread of industrialization in East Asia* (Cambridge, MA, 1991).

Wade, Robert, *Governing the market: economic theory and the role of government in East Asian industrialization* (Princeton, 1990).

Walling, R. N., *Singapura sorrows* (Singapore, 1931).

Warren, James Francis, *Rickshaw coolie: a people's history of Singapore (1880–1940)* (Singapore, 1986).

Wickizer, V. D. and Bennett, M. K., *The rice economy of monsoon Asia* (Stanford, 1941).

Wijeyewardene, Gehan, ed. *Leadership and authority: a symposium* (Singapore, 1968).

Williamson, John, *The open economy and the world economy* (New York, 1983).

Wilson, Dick, *Solid as a rock: the first forty years of the Oversea-Chinese Banking Corporation* (Singapore, 1972).

Winstedt, Richard, *Malaya and its history* 7th edn (London, 1966).

Winstedt, Sir Richard, *Start from alif: count from one: an autobiographical memoire* (Kuala Lumpur, 1969).

Wong, C. S., *A gallery of Chinese kapitans* (Singapore, 1963).

Wong Lin Ken, *The Malayan tin industry to 1914* (Tucson, 1965).

Wright, Arnold and Cartwright, H. A., *Twentieth century impressions of British Malaya* (London, 1908).

Wright, Arnold and Reid, Thomas H., *The Malay Peninsula* (London, 1912).

Wright, Clifton, *Cameos of the old Federated Malay States and Straits Settlements* (Ilfracombe, Devon, 1972).

Yap Pheng Geck, *Scholar, banker, gentleman soldier: the reminiscences of Dr. Yap Pheng Geck* (Singapore, 1982).

Yeo Kim Wah, *Political development in Singapore, 1945–1955* (Singapore, 1973).

Yip Yat Hoong, *The development of the tin mining industry of Malaya* (Kuala Lumpur, 1969).

Yong, C. F., *Tan Kah-Kee: the making of an overseas Chinese legend* (Singapore, 1987).

Yoshihara, Kunio, *Foreign investment and domestic response: a study of Singapore's industrialization* (Singapore, 1976).

Yoshihara, Kunio, *The rise of ersatz capitalism in South-East Asia* (Singapore, 1988).

You Poh Seng and Lim Chong Yah, eds. *Singapore: twenty-five years of development* (Singapore, 1984).

Youngson, A. J., *Hong Kong: economic growth and policy* (Hong Kong, 1982).

Yusuf, Shahid and Peters, R. Kyle, *Capital accumulation and economic growth: the Korean paradigm* (Washington, DC: World Bank, 1985).

Zimmerman, Carle C., *Siam rural economic survey, 1930–31* (Bangkok, 1931).

Index

Page numbers followed by *t* indicates that the reference is to be found in a table; page numbers followed by *n* indicates that the reference is to be found in a footnote; page numbers followed by *f* indicates that the reference is to be found in a figure.

Accra, 34

Adamson, Gilfillan & Co., 128, 133, 184, 187, 193

agency houses
 branches of, 185: up-country buying of Malayan rubber, 200–1
 end of, 299
 in export trade, 90, 118, 130–31, 133
 in import trade, 259–61: challenges to, in inter-war period, 262–64
 and investment in Singapore industry, 222–23
 in palm oil trade, 188–89
 in petroleum trade, 238–39
 in rubber trade, 186, 203: capital resources and buying power of, 182–88, 200; development of, 181–88; and direct marketing of Malayan rubber, 198, 200; secretarial functions of, 183–84, 186
 in tin industry, 253, 255

agriculture
 Brazilian, middlemen in, 20
 and development, 37
 in Malayan hinterland, 18
 See also estate agriculture

Aik Hoe & Co., 221

air traffic, in Singapore, 38
 1960–1990, 306–7

Aitken & Ong Siang, 235

Albert Dock, 245–46, 247*t*

Alexandra Brickworks, 222

Alfred Holt & Company's Ocean Steamship Co. (Blue Funnel Line), 66–67, 145–48

Amoy, 224

Amoy University, 234–35

Anglo-French & Bendixsens, 203

Anglo-Saxon Petroleum Company, 239

Anglo-Siam Corporation, 187

animal trade, in Singapore, 1957–1990, 388–89*t*, 396*t*

apparel
 exports from Singapore, 1925/27, 116*t*
 imports to Singapore, 1900–1937, 112–13*t*
 industry, in Singapore, 1960–1990, 322, 323*t*
 See also clothing manufacture; garment industry

Arab dealers, in import trade, 268–69

Archipelago Brewery Co., 222

architecture, in Singapore, 47, 299

arecanut trade, in Singapore, 96
 1900–1939, 73*t*, 74*t*
 in early 20th c., 84
 in inter-war years, 86

artisans, 178

Asian currency market, Singapore's role in, 342

Asian Currency Units, 342

Asian dealers, in import trade, 260–61, 264, 267–68

Asian Dollar Bond Market, 343

Asian Dollar Market, 342–43

Asian importers, of manufactured goods, 268–70

Asian races, in Singapore, 25
 See also Chinese; Indian; Malay

Asiatic Petroleum Company, 238–41, 243–44, 248–50

assembly industries, in Singapore, 214
 wages in, in 1960s, 324, 325*t*

Atlas Ice Company, 234

Australia
 as petroleum market, 241, 242*t*

447

British India. *See* India
British Malaya, 10*f*, 11, 26, 28–29
  economic development of, pattern of, in
    late 19th c., 67–68
  geographical definition of, xx–xxi
  immigration to, 150–57
  imports, of manufactured goods, 106,
    107*t*, 108, 109*t*
  money supply in, pre-World War II, 88,
    404–6*t*
  petroleum exports, 1937/39, 241, 242*t*
  petroleum imports, 1937/39, 240*t*,
    240–41
  railway development in, 148–49
  road development in, 148–49
  as rubber market, 201–2
  shipbuilding in, 249
  shipping traffic and tonnage between
    Singapore and, 124, 126*t*
  urban areas, racial composition of, 159
British military administration (BMA), 296
Britons, in Singapore, 167
Bruce Petrie Ltd., 203
Brunei, trade with Singapore
  in 1950s, 282*t*
  in 1988/90, 282*t*
Buenos Aires
  population of, growth of, 23
  as staple port, 22, 34
Bun Hin (Green Funnel) of Khoo Tiong
    Poh, 65
Burma
  export expansion, in late 19th c., 51
  immigration to, 151
  industrialization of, 22
  rice industry of, 17, 22: exports to
    Singapore, 103
  shipping traffic and tonnage between
    Singapore and, 123*t*, 125*t*. *See also*
    shipping, local
  trade with Singapore, 96: in late 19th c.,
    50*t*, 52*t*, 55, 55*t*, 56*t*; 1900–1939, 81*t*,
    82*t*; in 1950s, 282*t*; in 1988/90, 282*t*
business services, in Singapore, 38–40, 305
  development of, 341–45
bus system, of Singapore, 169, 300

Caltex, 278–79
Canada
  exports to Singapore, 1900/02–1937/39,
    258*t*
  trade with Singapore: in late 19th c., 50*t*,
    52*t*; 1900–1939, 81*t*, 82*t*; in 1950s,
    282*t*; in 1988/90, 282*t*
cane. *See* rattans

capital
  accumulation, and direct foreign
    investment in Singapore, 338, 338*t*,
    416*t*
  circulating: in tin industry, in late 19th
    c., 57–58; vs. fixed, 58*n*
  immigrant labour's need for, 173–74
  private, crowding in, due to government
    expenditure, 338–39
  rate of return on, and investment ratio in
    Singapore, 348–50
capital formation, in Singapore, 33, 37
  1960–1990, 307, 337, 337*t*, 413*t*, 414*t*
  contribution from direct foreign
    investment, 338, 338*t*, 416*t*
capitalism, state-directed, 336
capital market, Singapore's, pre-World
    War II, 87–88
cargo, general, handled at Singapore, 141*t*,
    143
carpenter shops, in Singapore, 211*t*, 213
cartels, in local shipping, 145, 148
catch crop, pineapples as, on rubber
    estates, 190
Caves, R. E., 276, 362
cement
  exports from Singapore, 1925/27, 116*t*
  imports to Singapore, 1900–1937, 112*t*,
    115
Central Business District, 299
Central Provident Fund, 334–36, 335*t*,
    346–47
Ceylon
  rice imports, from Singapore, 1900–1939,
    99*t*
  trade with Singapore: in late 19th c., 50*t*,
    52*t*; 1900–1939, 81*t*, 82*t*
Chamber of Commerce
  (European) Singapore, 44, 198
  Indian, 165
  Produce sub-Committee of European,
    133
  Singapore Chinese, 45, 164–65
  Singapore Japanese, 267
Chan & Eber, 235
Change Alley Rubber Communication
    Office, 202
Changi Airport, 38, 300, 300*f*, 306
Chartered Bank of India, Australia and
    China, 86, 88
chartering, shipping conference system and,
    132, 135
Chee Swee Cheng, 234
chemicals trade, in Singapore, 1957–1990,
    390–91*t*, 396*t*

    shipping, local
  tin smelting in, 250
People's Action Party, 29, 33, 38, 42
  achievements of, political/institutional
    factors in, 355–60
  industrial development policies, 290, 298
  interventionism. *See also* government
    intervention: in society, 350–54
pepper
  exports from Singapore, 1900–1939, 72,
    73*t*, 74*t*
  trade, in Singapore: in late 19th c.,
    51–52, 53*t*, finance, 64; in inter-war
    years, 86; in 1950s, 281; 1960–1990,
    311
pepper king, 312
Perak, 26
Perlis, 26
petrol
  production, 237
  See also motor spirit
petroleum
  effects on Singapore's economic
    development, 236
  exports: from British Malaya, 1937/39,
    241, 242*t*; from Netherlands India, 14,
    240*t*, 240–41; from Singapore:
    1870–1939, 45*f*, 46*f*, 1900–1939, 45*f*,
    46*f*, 72, 75, 77, 78*t*, 80, 1949–1970,
    309, 310*t*, 1957–1990, 386–87*t*, in
    1950s, 278–79, markets for, 241, 242*t*,
    value of, 1870–1970, 372–76*t*, volume
    of, 1870–1970, 378–85*t*; from Straits
    Settlements, 1925/27, 241, 242*t*
  imports to Singapore: in early 20th c.,
    84, 85*t*; 1925–39, 240*t*, 240–41
  industry: effects on shipping, 121; in
    inter-war period, 236; in Singapore,
    1960–1990, 310–11
  linkage effects, 236: in manufacturing,
    322. *See also* dry dock facilities
  production: European role in, 89;
    Singapore as centre of, 31, 236
  shipping, 241
  storage depots for, 238–40
  trade: in 1950s, 278; European role in,
    90; freedom from regulation, in
    Singapore, 240; growth in Singapore,
    236; locational advantages of
    Singapore for, 239–40; in Singapore:
    1957–1990, 386–87*t*, 388–95*t*, 396–70*t*,
    international distribution of, 241,
    242*t*; Singapore's functions in, 236–44.
    See also dry dock facilities

world demand for, in early 20th c., 75
petroleum products, 237
  See also fuel oil; kerosene; petrol
Philippine Islands
  shipping traffic and tonnage between
    Singapore and, 123*t*, 125*t*. *See also*
    shipping, local trade with Singapore:
    in late 19th c., 50*t*, 52*t*; 1900–1939,
    81*t*, 82*t*; in 1988/90, 282*t*
Philippines, trade with Singapore, in 1950s,
    282*t*
piece goods
  quota system for, in 1930s, 108–9
  silk, imports to Singapore, 1900–1937,
    114
  trade, in inter-war years, 264–65, 267–70
  See also cotton piece goods
Pillay, Joseph, 341
Pineapple King. *See* Lim Nee Soon
pineapples, canned
  canning, in Singapore, 211*t*, 212
  exports from Singapore, 193: in early
    20th c., 76–77; value of, 1870–1970,
    373–77*t*; volume of, 1870–1970,
    378–85*t*
  production: Chinese in, 192–93; and
    rubber production, 76–77, 88, 190–93,
    218–21
  shipping of, 122
Pioneer Industries (Relief from Income
    Tax) Bill, 290
pioneer status, for firms in investment in
    Singapore, 325*n*
Pirelli, local sales branch in Singapore, 262
police force, employment in, 177
political stability
  in Singapore, 296–98
  and success of interventionism, 355,
    357–59
political structure, in Singapore, 26–28, 32
  in 1950s, 294–98
politics, of development, 40–42
population, of Singapore, 1
  composition of, 3, 158, 351: in late 19th
    c., 57; 1947–1990, 292, 292*t*
  growth of, 23, 150, 157–59: 1931–1980,
    292*t*, 292–93; 1957–1990, 351
porcelain. *See* crockery and porcelain
port(s)
  basis, 134
  British Malaya's, 11
  and economic development, 3
  See also entrepot(s); staple port(s)
port dues, 134, 139
Port of Singapore, 138*f*

18; linkage to pineapple production, 76–77, 88, 190–93, 218–21
remilling/smoking, in Singapore, in 1950s, 286–87
scrap, handling in Singapore, 202–3
shipping, 186–87
smallholdings, 182*t*, 194–95: Asian, 180; Chinese, 194; Indonesian, 194–95; in Netherlands India, 194–95; Netherlands Indian native, 180; output from, in 1950s, 279–81; ownership of, 194
specialized buyers, 201
standard qualities for, 198
trade: in 1950s, 278–79; European role in, 90; in Singapore, 31: in early 20th c., 118, 1957–1990, 388–89*t*, 396*t*
traders (brokers), 197, 201–2
transhipment, through Singapore, 195
wet: imports to Singapore, 203–4; milling in Singapore, 205–7
world demand for, in early 20th c., 75, 82–83
Rubber Association, 195
rubber footwear, manufacture, in Singapore, 287
Rubber King. *See* Lim Nee Soon
Rybczynski theorem, 370

Sabah, 29.
  See also North Borneo
sago
  exports from Singapore, 1900–1939, 73*t*, 74*t*
  production, in Singapore, 211*t*, 212
St. James' Power Station, 210, 289
M. Samuel & Company, 238–39
Sandilands, Buttery & Co., 184, 187
Santei Shokai, 267
Saõ Paulo, 15–16, 34*n*
  population of, growth of, 23
Sarawak, 29
  petroleum exports from, 240*t*, 240–41
  trade with Singapore: in 1950s, 282*t*; in 1988/90, 282*t*
savings
  Chinese, 231
  in Singapore: 1960–1990, 37, 202*t*, 307, 368, indicators of, 413*t*, private sector, 333*t*, 334–36, public sector, 332–34, 333*t*; gross national, 1974–1985, 332–33, 333*t*; rate of, criticism of, in 1980s, 348–50; role in macroeconomic management, 346–47
sawmills, Singapore, 211*t*, 212

and pineapple production, 193
SCBA. *See* Straits Chinese British Association
SCCC. *See* Singapore Chinese Chamber of Commerce
seamen, Chinese as, 178–79, 244*n*
See Boh Ih, 233
Selangor, 26, 202, 252
Sembawang Shipyard, 332
semiconductor industry, Singapore's role in, 322, 329
Sen, A. K., 368
Senda & Company, 267
Sentosa Development Corporation, 334
servants, domestic, 173–75, 178, 326
service employment, in Singapore, 169, 305
  See also brain services; tertiary sector
services/service sector
  comparative advantage in, 363
  and economic development, 363, 370–71
  tradeable, in Singapore, 302*n*, 304–5
  See also brain services; tertiary sector
Shanghai Banking Corporation, 86
sharecropping, in rubber estate development, 191–92
Shaw, E. S., 336
Shell Transport and Trading Co., 239
Shimota Company, 267
shipbuilding
  in British Malaya, 249
  in Hong Kong, 249
  in Singapore, 249–50: state participation in, 332
shipping
  effects of World War I on, 122, 145
  freight: commission on, 131–32, 193; deferred rebate on, 128–29, 131*n*, 148; rate parity, shipping conference system and, 134, 136; secret rebate on, 128–31, 135, 184–85
  immigrant transport and, 154–55
  local, 124: British involvement in, 145–46; cartels in, 145, 148; definition of, 121; growth between 1912/13 and 1928/29, 144, 145*t*; use of port facilities, 137
  ocean-going: patterns of, 120–27; shipping conference system and, 136; use of port facilities, 137
  of palm oil, 189
  of petroleum, 241
  in produce exchange trade, 93, 129–33, 136
  of rubber, 186–87